Lecture Notes in Con
Founding Editors

Gerhard Goos
Juris Hartmanis

Editorial Board Members

Elisa Bertino, *Purdue University, West Lafayette, IN, USA*
Wen Gao, *Peking University, Beijing, China*
Bernhard Steffen, *TU Dortmund University, Dortmund, Germany*
Moti Yung, *Columbia University, New York, NY, USA*

The series Lecture Notes in Computer Science (LNCS), including its subseries Lecture Notes in Artificial Intelligence (LNAI) and Lecture Notes in Bioinformatics (LNBI), has established itself as a medium for the publication of new developments in computer science and information technology research, teaching, and education.

LNCS enjoys close cooperation with the computer science R & D community, the series counts many renowned academics among its volume editors and paper authors, and collaborates with prestigious societies. Its mission is to serve this international community by providing an invaluable service, mainly focused on the publication of conference and workshop proceedings and postproceedings. LNCS commenced publication in 1973.

Vishwas T. Patil · Ram Krishnan ·
Rudrapatna K. Shyamasundar
Editors

Information Systems Security

20th International Conference, ICISS 2024
Jaipur, India, December 16–20, 2024
Proceedings

Springer

Editors
Vishwas T. Patil
Indian Institute of Technology Bombay
Mumbai, Maharashtra, India

Ram Krishnan
The University of Texas at San Antonio
San Antonio, TX, USA

Rudrapatna K. Shyamasundar
Indian Institute of Technology Bombay
Mumbai, Maharashtra, India

ISSN 0302-9743　　　　　　　ISSN 1611-3349 (electronic)
Lecture Notes in Computer Science
ISBN 978-3-031-80019-1　　　ISBN 978-3-031-80020-7 (eBook)
https://doi.org/10.1007/978-3-031-80020-7

© The Editor(s) (if applicable) and The Author(s), under exclusive license to Springer Nature Switzerland AG 2025

This work is subject to copyright. All rights are solely and exclusively licensed by the Publisher, whether the whole or part of the material is concerned, specifically the rights of translation, reprinting, reuse of illustrations, recitation, broadcasting, reproduction on microfilms or in any other physical way, and transmission or information storage and retrieval, electronic adaptation, computer software, or by similar or dissimilar methodology now known or hereafter developed.
The use of general descriptive names, registered names, trademarks, service marks, etc. in this publication does not imply, even in the absence of a specific statement, that such names are exempt from the relevant protective laws and regulations and therefore free for general use.
The publisher, the authors and the editors are safe to assume that the advice and information in this book are believed to be true and accurate at the date of publication. Neither the publisher nor the authors or the editors give a warranty, expressed or implied, with respect to the material contained herein or for any errors or omissions that may have been made. The publisher remains neutral with regard to jurisdictional claims in published maps and institutional affiliations.

This Springer imprint is published by the registered company Springer Nature Switzerland AG
The registered company address is: Gewerbestrasse 11, 6330 Cham, Switzerland

If disposing of this product, please recycle the paper.

Preface

This book contains the proceedings of the 20th International Conference on Information Systems Security (ICISS 2024), held at The LNM Institute of Information Technology, Jaipur, India, from December 16 to 20, 2024. ICISS 2024 received 93 submissions, which underwent a rigorous double-blind review process. Each submission was reviewed by at least three members of the Technical Program Committee (TPC), which comprised 28 distinguished international researchers specializing in various areas of information security. The TPC was supported by six external sub-reviewers.

Following an evaluation and discussion of the reviews by the TPC members, 18 full papers and 6 short papers were accepted for the Regular Papers Track with an acceptance rate of 25.8%. Additionally, three papers were selected for the Industry/Demo Track.

The following sessions comprised the program: (i) System Security, (ii) Network Security, (iii) Attacks, (iv) Malware and Vulnerability Detection, (v) Privacy & Usability, (vi) AI Security, and (vii) Industry Demo/Practice.

The following Keynotes were integral parts of the program:

1. Scams in the Cryptocurrency Market, Alessandro Mei, Sapienza University of Rome
2. Security Tai Chi: The Art of Building & Attacking Secure Computing Systems, *Ahmad-Reza Sadeghi, Technical University of Darmstadt*
3. Data Security and Privacy in Emerging Scenarios, *Pierangela Samarati, University of Milan*
4. Biometrics and AI: Challenges and Opportunities, *Vincenzo Piuri, University of Milan*

Furthermore, the following Invited Talks were presented:

1. Large Language Models: Are Guarded Models Safe? *Atul Prakash, University of Michigan*
2. From Security to Scalability: The Multifaceted Role of Cryptographic Primitives in XRPL R&D, *Aanchal Malhotra, Ripple*
3. Towards Regulated, Private and Robust Central Bank Digital Currency, *Kari Kostiainen, ETH Zurich*
4. Modeling and Security Analysis of Attacks on Machine Learning Systems, *Anoop Singhal, NIST*

Additionally, the following pre-conference hands-on tutorials/workshops were conducted:

1. Deep Learning for Cybersecurity, *Rakesh Verma, University of Houston*
2. Android Security, *Vivek Balachandran, Singapore Institute of Technology*
3. Malware Hunt – Demystifying the Invisible Threats, *Saurabh Sharma, Kaspersky Labs*
4. A Workshop on Post-Quantum Cryptography, *Indivar Gupta (DRDO), R. Kabaleeshwaran (IIITDM Kurnool), Jitendra Kumar (C-DAC), Arpita Maitra (tcg crest), Raghavendra Patil (C-DAC), Balaji Rajendran (C-DAC), Prasanna Ravi (NTU Singapore), SD Sudarshan (C-DAC)*

We sincerely thank all the researchers who contributed their expertise to the conference audience. Our gratitude also extends to the authors who submitted their work for review, the session chairs, attendees, the local organizing team, and our host, LNMIIT. A special acknowledgment goes to the PhD Forum participants, where research scholars presented their work summaries.

We would like to extend our heartfelt thanks to the Steering Committee, our Patron, the Organizing Chair, the PhD Forum Chairs, the dedicated Publicity Chairs, and our outstanding Program Committee members. Their tireless efforts and support were instrumental in shaping this compelling program.

It is our pleasure to extend our gratitude to our publisher, Springer Nature, for their invaluable support in compiling this proceeding. We also wish to express our heartfelt gratitude to our sponsors: TCS Research, the Gold Sponsor; DRDO (Defence Research and Development Organisation), the Silver Sponsor; and C-DAC (Centre for Development of Advanced Computing), the Knowledge Partner. The generous support from these sponsors has allowed us to provide travel-grants to the research scholars. We are confident that these proceedings will be both stimulating and inspiring for your future research endeavours.

December 2024

Ram Krishnan
Vishwas T. Patil
Rudrapatna K. Shyamasundar

Organization

General Chair

R. K. Shyamasundar   IIT Bombay, India

Program Committee Chairs

Ram Krishnan   University of Texas at San Antonio, USA
Vishwas Patil   IIT Bombay, India

Patron

Rahul Banerjee   LNMIIT Jaipur, India

Organizing Chair

Jayaprakash Kar   LNMIIT Jaipur, India

Publicity Chairs

Enrico Bassetti   TU Delft, The Netherlands
Maurantonio Caprolu   KAUST, Saudi Arabia
Preetam Mukherjee   Digital University Kerala, India

Web Chair

Vishwas Patil   IIT Bombay, India

PhD Forum Chairs

Radhika BS NITK Surathkal, India
Preetam Mukherjee Digital University Kerala, India

Local Organising Committee

Abhijit Adhikari LNMIIT, India
Imran Alam LNMIIT, India
Vikas Bajpai LNMIIT, India
Ritesh Bhardwaj LNMIIT, India
Subrat Dash LNMIIT, India
Kanjalochan Jena LNMIIT, India
Sachin Kadam LNMIIT, India
Jayaprakash Kar LNMIIT, India
Harshvardhan Kumar LNMIIT, India
Kusum Lata LNMIIT, India
Nitesh Pradhan LNMIIT, India
Sandeep Saini LNMIIT, India
Santosh Shah LNMIIT, India
Preeti Singh LNMIIT, India

Advisory Steering Committee

Venu Govindaraju University at Buffalo, SUNY, USA
Sushil Jajodia George Mason University, USA
Somesh Jha University of Wisconsin, USA
Atul Prakash University of Michigan, USA
Pierangela Samarati University of Milan, Italy
RK Shyamasundar IIT Bombay, India

Organising Executive Committee

Venkata Badarla IIT Tirupati, India
Neminath Hubballi IIT Indore, India
Chandrashekar Jatoth NIT Raipur, India
Jayaprakash Kar LNMIIT, India
Vishwas Patil IIT Bombay, India
Somnath Tripathy IIT Patna, India

Program Committee

Shubham Agarwal	CISPA, Germany
Claudio Ardagna	University of Milan, Italy
Vijay Atluri	Rutgers Business School, USA
Enrico Bassetti	TU Delft, The Netherlands
Abhishek Bichhawat	IIT Gandhinagar, India
Maurantonio Caprolu	KAUST, Saudi Arabia
Sanjit Chatterjee	IISc, India
Pradeep Kumar D S	ZOHO Corporation, India
Rinku Dewri	University of Denver, USA
Aolin Ding	Accenture Labs, USA
Chethan Kamath	IIT Bombay, India
Hyoungshick Kim	Sungkyunkwan University, South Korea
NV Narendra Kumar	TCS Research, India
Zheng Li	CISPA, Germany
Luigi V. Mancini	Sapienza University of Rome, Italy
Mainack Mondal	IIT Kharagpur, India
Preetam Mukherjee	Digital University Kerala, India
Adwait Nadkarni	William & Mary, USA
Balaji Palanisamy	University of Pittsburgh, USA
Phu Phung	University of Dayton, USA
Silvio Ranise	Fondazione Bruno Kessler, Italy
Basavesh Shivakumar	Virginia Tech, USA
Sandeep Shukla	IIT Kanpur, India
Rajat Subhra	IIT Kharagpur, India
Vaishnavi Sundararajan	IIT Delhi, India
Shamik Sural	IIT Kharagpur, India
Laszlo Szekeres	Google, USA
Mahesh Tripunitara	University of Waterloo, Canada

External Reviewers invited by the PC

Radhika B. S.	NITK Surathkal, India
Sarath Babu	IIT Bombay, India
Sangita Roy	Thapar University, India
Mandru Suma Sri	IIT Bombay, India
Saurabh Sharma	Kaspersky Labs, India

tcs Research

Gold Sponsor

Silver Sponsor

Knowledge Partner

Abstracts of the Keynote Talks

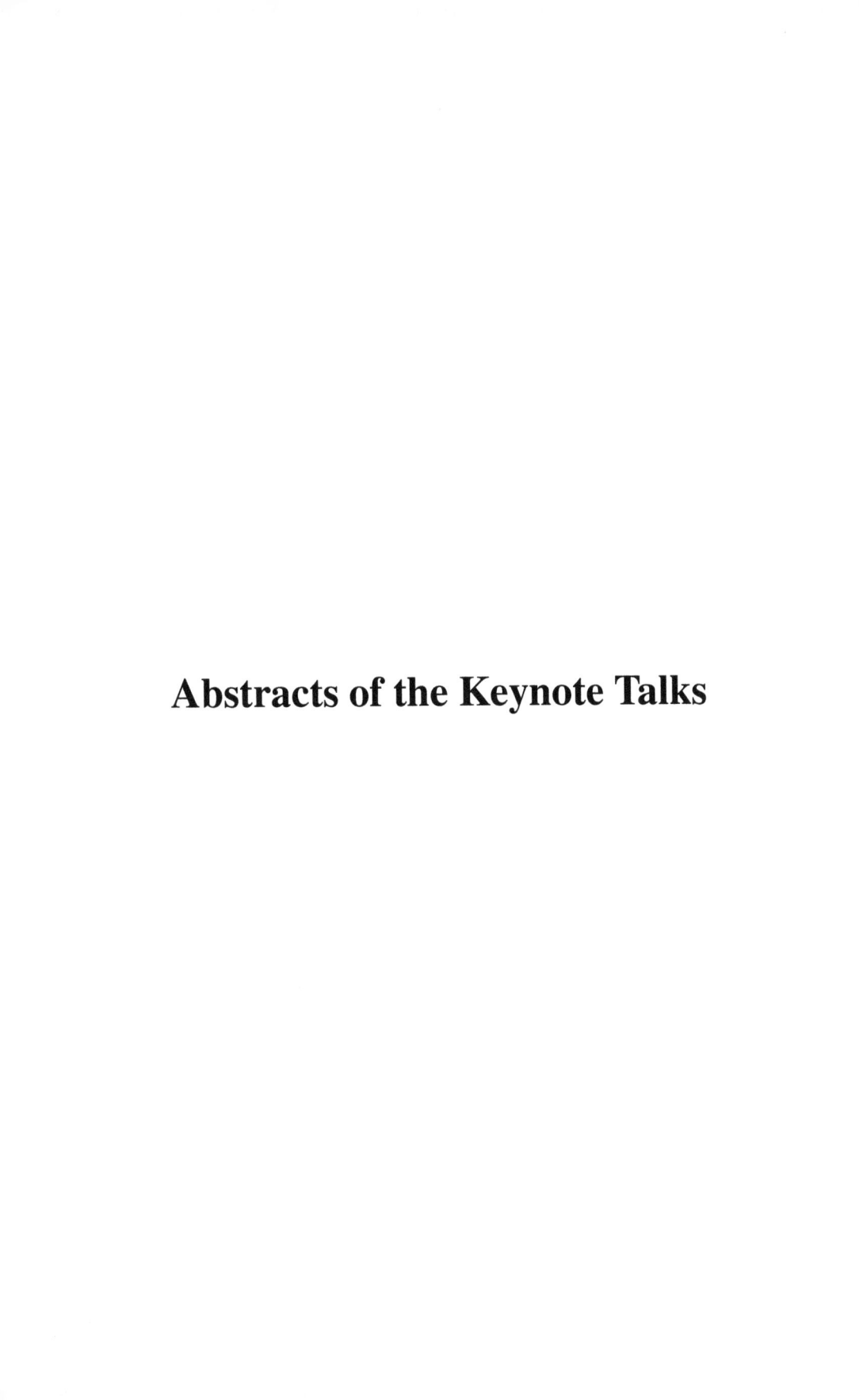

Scams in the Cryptocurrency Market

Alessandro Mei

Sapienza University of Rome
http://wwwusers.di.uniroma1.it/~mei/

Abstract. The cryptocurrency market is currently subject to minimal regulation. Although policymakers are working to increase safety for cryptocurrency investors, this is a complex task. Meanwhile, blockchain-related technologies are rapidly evolving, making investors vulnerable to numerous scams and market manipulations. In this talk, we will describe some of the most common fraudulent activities, demonstrate methods to measure these phenomena, and discuss potential countermeasures to help establish a safer cryptocurrency market.

Security Tai Chi: The Art of Building and Attacking Secure Computing Systems

Ahmad-Reza Sadeghi

Technical University of Darmstadt
https://www.informatik.tu-darmstadt.de/systemsecurity/people_sys/people_det ails_sys_45184.en.jsp

Abstract. The ever-increasing complexity of computing systems, coupled with emerging technologies like IoT and AI, poses many novel challenges in designing and implementing security concepts, methods, and mechanisms in hardware and software. This talk overviews our journey through the system security universe, highlighting the lessons learned in advancing state-of-the-art software and hardware-assisted security in academic research and industry collaborations. We discuss the severe threat posed by recent software-exploitable hardware vulnerabilities, which can jeopardize critical systems. Our experience organizing the world's largest hardware security competition alongside partners Intel and Synopsys since 2018 provides invaluable lessons in vulnerability discovery and mitigation strategies. Addressing the critical importance of hardware security and resilience, we explore emerging trends in pre-fabrication vulnerability detection methods such as hardware fuzzing. The talk concludes by outlining future directions for secure hardware design and addressing associated challenges.

Data Security and Privacy in Emerging Scenarios

Pierangela Samarati

University of Milan
https://samarati.di.unimi.it

Abstract. The rapid advancements in Information and Communication Technologies (ICTs) have been greatly changing our society, with clear societal and economic benefits. Cloud, Big Data, Internet of things, services and technologies that are becoming more and more pervasive and conveniently accessible, towards the realization of a 'smart' society'. At the heart of this evolution is the ability to collect, analyze, process, and share an ever-increasing amount of data to extract knowledge for offering personalized and advanced services. This typically also involves external parties for data management and computation that may be either not authorized to access data or not fully trusted. The complexity of this scenario introduces several security and privacy challenges. In this talk,I will illustrate some challenges related to guaranteeing confidentiality and integrity of data stored or processed by external providers.

Biometrics and AI: Challenges and Opportunities

Vincenzo Piuri

University of Milan
https://piuri.di.unimi.it

Abstract. Biometric technologies and applications are pervasively permeating our everyday life. Once typically used for authentication and for restricting access to critical (physical or digital) environments, biometrics are increasingly and seamlessly at the basis of many of the services and applications of today's smart society, from governmental and business services to leisure. The widespread adoption of biometrics, the enormous amount of biometrics data gathered, shared, and processed, as well as advancements in artificial intelligence open new challenges and opportunities in the field of biometrics and biometric data processing. These advancements in applications call for novel biometric solutions, able to operate in new and emerging scenarios seamlessly and balancing the need of catering advanced services based on biometrics while complying with the rightful desire for an ethical, secure, and privacy-respectful use of biometrics. In this talk, I will illustrate the main biometrics techniques discussing their characteristics, strengths, limitations, and applications. I will also discuss challenges and research directions, with particular focus on opportunities from the application of AI.

Abstracts of the Invited Talks

Large Language Models: Are Guarded Models Safe?

Atul Prakash

University of Michigan
https://web.eecs.umich.edu/aprakash/

Abstract. Large language models (LLMs) are typically aligned to be harmless to humans. Unfortunately, recent work has shown that such models are susceptible to automated jailbreak attacks that induce them to generate harmful content. As a result, more recent LLMs often incorporate an additional layer of defense, a Guard Model, which is a second LLM that is designed to check and moderate the output response of the primary LLM. We first review the strategy behind prior automated jailbreak attacks. Then, we discuss some of the recent work that shows that even guarded models are susceptible to jail-breaking. Finally, we discuss some future directions for research on more robust large language models.

From Security to Scalability: The Multifaceted Role of Cryptographic Primitives in XRPL R&D

Aanchal Malhotra

Ripple
https://www.linkedin.com/in/aanchal-malhotra-91005319/

Abstract. In this talk, we delve into the critical role of cryptographic primitives in driving research and development (R&D) on the XRPL blockchain. We explore how these primitives, such as hash functions, elliptic curve cryptography, and zero-knowledge proofs, contribute to the security, scalability, and privacy of XRPL. By understanding the fundamental building blocks of XRPL, researchers and developers can unlock new possibilities and create innovative solutions. We discuss specific use cases and challenges associated with cryptographic primitives in XRPL R&D, offering insights for future advancements.

Towards Regulated, Private and Robust Central Bank Digital Currency (CBDC)

Kari Kostiainen

ETH Zurich
https://syssec.ethz.ch/people/kkari.html

Abstract. Central Bank Digital Currencies (CBDCs) have gained significant attention recently. In this talk, we explain what is a CBDC and how it differs from digital payments and cryptocurrencies. We discuss desirable functionality and necessary security properties for CBDCs based on recent central bank documents and regulations. We consider CBDC systems that should work both in online and offline settings, and discuss their design challenges. In particular, we observe that achieving strong privacy protection and support for regulatory features such as holding limits and spending limits is difficult. We also note that double spending protection in the offline setting combined with strong privacy protections brings up new technical challenges. Finally, we present two novel designs for CBDCs, one for online scenarios and another for offline payments.

Modeling and Security Analysis of Attacks on Machine Learning Systems

Anoop Singhal

NIST

https://www.nist.gov/people/anoop-singhal

Abstract. Last several years have witnessed rapidly increasing use of machine learning (ML) systems in multiple industry sectors. Auto driving cars are using ML to process the images/videos from the cameras to understand the traffic signals and real time traffic around them. ML has been used to translate text from one language to another in several systems. Deep Learning has been used in products such as Google and Mozilla to understand speech.

However, it is widely recognized that the existing security analysis frameworks and techniques, which were developed to analyze enterprise (software) systems and networks, are not very suitable for analyzing ML systems. ML systems have new kinds of causality relationships which cannot be handled by current approaches for security analysis. For example, attack graphs are fundamental tools for enterprise security analysis but mainly focus on relationships between security vulnerabilities (such as CVEs – Common Vulnerabilities and Exposures) and exploits (which mainly focus on newly gained permissions/accesses). In contrast, a good foundation for analyzing security issues in ML systems must also capture the causality relationships involved in data poisoning and evasion attacks using adversarial examples. It is clear that such causality relationships are not really relevant to traditional attacks that involve exploitation of CVEs. Evasion attacks and data poisoning attacks can make ML systems misbehave. Evasion attacks refer to crafting adversarial examples after the training phase, so that models produce incorrect outputs. Data poisoning attacks refer to modifying the training data, so that the trained model will be maliciously altered. We take data poisoning attack against the word-to-word translation Machine Learning system as a motivating example to explain the concept of Causality Graphs.

We will present new techniques for modeling of Attacks on ML systems using Causality Graphs. These graphs are used to capture the data, model and library dependencies in a specific ML system: i) Data dependencies, ii) Model dependencies iii) Library Dependencies.

We will illustrate our methodology using a case study. We will present some of the challenges for designing mitigation strategies against attacks on ML Systems. Here is a list of some of the questions that the causality graph can be used to answer: 1) Which part of the ML system gets tainted due to the attack? 2) How far into the ML system the attack penetrate? 3) Will the proposed defense system be effective in preventing the attack? In summary, we will present a new methodology for modeling of attacks and security analysis of Machine Learning Systems.

Outlines of the Tutorials and Workshop

Deep Learning for Cybersecurity

Rakesh Verma[1] and Dainis Boumber[2]

[1] University of Houston
https://www2.cs.uh.edu/~rmverma/
[2] Aon IPS
https://dainis-boumber.github.io

Prerequisites

Mathematical maturity; Basics of Security including security goals, mechanisms, threat analysis and attacks such as malware, intrusion and phishing; Basics of Machine Learning including linear regression, supervised learning including basic loss functions especially categorical cross entropy, classification methods especially multi-layer perceptron model, and unsupervised learning especially clustering; Familiarity with basic text processing, natural language processing and understanding concepts; python programming.

Outline

Module 1: Introduction to Deep Leaning (2 h 30 mins lecture, 45 mins of exercises)

- Feedforward Networks (FFN)
- Convolutional Neural Networks (CNN)
- Long Short-term Memory (LSTM) model
- Attention, Transformers, LLMs
- Autoencoders
- Generative Models
- Parameter-efficient machine learning
- Adversarial Machine Learning including attacks and defenses
- Examples and exercises will include: Python notebooks for FFN, CNN, Transformers, BERT, and an open source LLM

Module 2: Applications to cybersecurity challenges (2 h lecture, 40 mins of exercises)

- Deceptive attacks including social engineering attacks, business email compromise, fake news, and romance/job scams
- Intrusion detection
- Malware detection
- Adversarial robustness of deep learning models for cybersecurity
- Techniques for explainable ML

- Key takeaways and directions for future research
- Examples and exercise will include deep learning models for deceptive attacks and adversarial robustness, explainability techniques

References

1. Goodfellow, I., et al.: Deep Learning (2017)
2. Verma, R., Marchette, D.: Cybersecurity Analytics. CRC Press, Boca Raton (2019)
3. Parisi, A.: AI for Cyber Security. Packt Press, Birmingham (2019)
4. Rao, M.: AI/ML in Cybersecurity (2023)

Android Security

Vivek Balachandran

Singapore Institute of Technology
https://www.vivekb.info/

This hands-on workshop focuses on static and dynamic analysis techniques to assess Android app security. Participants will learn how to use tools like Androwarn, Drozer, Frida, and BurpSuite to analyze apps, bypass security mechanisms, and intercept network traffic. By the end, attendees will be able to identify vulnerabilities in Android apps and understand techniques for securing them. Participants will have hands-on experience with tools for both static and dynamic analysis of Android apps. They will be able to assess app security, identify vulnerabilities, bypass SSL pinning, and manipulate app behaviors through Frida, gaining practical skills for Android security testing.

Prerequisites

Laptop with at least 8 GB RAM, VMware Workstation Pro/Player (for running the virtual machine), BurpSuite Community Edition, Genymotion, basic familiarity with command-line tools and Python

Outline

Module 1: Introduction to Android Security (30 mins)

- Overview of Android architecture
- Security model of Android OS
- Common vulnerabilities in Android apps
- Outcome: Understanding the basic architecture and security challenges in Android applications.

Module 2: Static Analysis with Androwarn (1 h)

- Overview of static analysis and Androwarn
- Analyzing APKs with Androwarn
- Interpreting Androwarn reports to identify permissions, activities, and potential vulnerabilities
- Hands-on: Analyze a sample APK and generate a report with Androwarn

- Hands-on: Identify permissions and investigate potential security risks
- Outcome: Ability to perform static analysis on an APK using Androwarn and understand its report.

Module 3: Dynamic Analysis Setup with Drozer (1.5 h)

- Introduction to Drozer and its functionalities
- Setting up Drozer on Linux and connecting to an Android emulator
- Using Drozer to enumerate app components (activities, services, broadcast receivers)
- Command examples for analyzing app attack surfaces and sending intents
- Hands-on: Install Drozer and analyze the FourGoats app to discover its attack surface
- Hands-on: Investigate vulnerable components and experiment with sending intents
- Outcome: Ability to use Drozer to conduct dynamic analysis, explore app components, and find exposed interfaces.

Module 4: Intercepting TraKic with BurpSuite (1 h)

- Setting up BurpSuite for Android traBic interception
- Configuring the Android emulator to route traffic through BurpSuite
- Configuring proxy settings on an emulator or physical device
- Intercepting HTTP/S traffic from the app
- Hands-on: Configure BurpSuite on the workstation and set up the Android emulator to forward traffic
- Hands-on: Capture and inspect traffic generated by a vulnerable app
- Outcome: Ability to configure BurpSuite as a proxy and capture HTTP/S traffic from an Android app.

Module 5: SSL Pinning Bypass with Frida (1 h)

- Overview of SSL pinning and its role in secure network communication
- Introduction to Frida for dynamic instrumentation
- Using Frida scripts to bypass SSL pinning in Android apps
- Hands-on: Load an APK that implements SSL pinning
- Hands-on: Run a Frida script to bypass SSL pinning and intercept HTTPS traffic in BurpSuite
- Outcome: Understanding of SSL pinning and ability to bypass it using Frida for deeper traffic analysis.

Module 6: Dynamic Instrumentation with Frida (1.5 h)

- Setting up Frida for dynamic analysis on an Android device
- Injecting JavaScript code to hook functions and alter app behavior
- Examples of function hooking (e.g., bypassing app security checks, altering function return values)
- Hands-on: Use Frida to hook a method in a sample app and modify its behavior
- Hands-on: Explore how to dynamically alter the app logic by injecting code
- Outcome: Ability to use Frida to hook into app functions and manipulate them for security testing.

Module 7: APK Decompilation and Source Code Analysis (45 mins)

- Introduction to dex2jar and JD-GUI for APK de-compilation

- Analyzing de-compiled code to identify sensitive information and logic
- Hands-on: De-compile a sample APK and locate critical functions in the source code
- Hands-on: Identify hard-coded secrets or vulnerable code paths
- Outcome: Ability to de-compile an APK and analyze the Java source code for security weaknesses.

Module 8: Wrap-Up and Q&A (15–30 mins)

- Review of key takeaways and best practices
- Resources for further learning and practice
- Open Q&A session for participants to ask questions
- Outcome: Reinforced understanding of Android security principles and tools.

Malware Hunt – Demystifying the Invisible Threats

Saurabh Sharma

Kaspersky Labs
https://www.linkedin.com/in/saurabh-sharma-813a6154

Prerequisites

VirtualBox, Windows 10 VM, C/C++ familiarity, Assembly basics

Outline

Module 1: Dynamic Analysis - Demystifying the Behavior of Malware
Understanding how malware operates and how to detect it is crucial in today's cyber-security landscape. In this module, we will be covering an end-to-end attack chain, which is a common method used by cyber-criminals to infect systems.

- Phishing Email: The attack begins with a phishing email, where an attacker sends a fraudulent email to a user, typically pretending to be a trusted entity. The email may contain malicious attachments, links, or instructions to trick the user into taking specific actions, such as clicking on a link.
- Silent Malware Deployment: When the user falls for the phishing email and clicks on the provided link or opens the malicious attachment, the malware is silently deployed in the background without the user's knowledge. This step is crucial for the attacker, as they gain access to the user's system without raising suspicion.
- Identifying Suspicious Network Connections: After the malware is deployed, it may attempt to communicate with the attacker's command-and-control (C2) server or other malicious entities over the network. Detecting these suspicious network connections can be a vital clue for identifying a potential malware infection.
- Suspicious Processes: Next, you'll be exploring the system's processes to find any suspicious ones that might be associated with the malware. Malware often runs as a hidden process, evading the user's attention. Host-Based Indicators: You'll then search for host-based indicators of the malware's presence. These indicators include persistence mechanisms, which are techniques used by malware to survive system reboots and maintain their foothold on the infected system. Additionally, you'll analyze disk activity performed by the malware to better understand its behavior. Malware's Motive: Lastly, you'll try to identify the motive behind the malware. This involves understanding the malware's purpose, whether it's ransomware seeking financial gain, spyware collecting sensitive information, or any other malicious intent.

- Outcome: By following these steps, users can gain a better understanding of how to detect and respond to potential malware infections on their systems. It's essential to stay vigilant and continuously update cybersecurity practices to protect against evolving threats.

Module 2: Static Analysis - Demystifying the Code of Malware In the first module, we used a dynamic analysis approach which involves observing the behaviour of a malware sample in a controlled environment, commonly referred to as a sandbox or virtual machine. During dynamic analysis, the malware is executed, and its actions are monitored and recorded. This approach allows one to observe the malware's behaviour in real-time and gather valuable information about its capabilities, such as process disguising, persistence mechanisms, communication with command and control servers, and downloading additional modules.

- Limitations of Dynamic Analysis: Some malware can detect that it's being analysed and may behave differently or not execute at all. The analysis environment might not perfectly replicate a real user's system, leading to potential differences in behaviour.
- Static Analysis (Code Analysis): Static analysis involves examining the malware's code and characteristics without executing it. This typically involves reverse engineering the code, disassembling it, and studying its structure to understand its functionality and inner workings. Static (code) Analysis helps us to uncover the below details:

- Hidden behaviour discovery: Static analysis can reveal hidden or encrypted parts of the malware that might not be evident during dynamic analysis.
- In-depth understanding: By examining the code, we can gain a deeper understanding of the malware's inner workings, for example;

- Process Injection: Techniques used to run malware inside a process
- Network Protocol Analysis: Understanding and decoding Command and Control packets format.

Module 3: Exploring Signature-Based Intrusion Detection: YARA and Snort

As you have learned how to demystify the behaviour of the malware in the first two modules of this course, you may want to write signatures to hunt similar malware on other hosts or want to detect/block malware command-and-control traffic at the firewall level. This module of the course will cover popular tools used for signature-based intrusion detection, but they have slightly different purposes and approaches:

- Yara – Allows you to create and define custom rules (signatures) to identify patterns within files or processes. These signatures are written in a human-readable and straightforward syntax. Yara is particularly effective for detecting specific characteristics, behaviour, or patterns of known malware or other targeted files.

- Identifying known malware: Yara is effective in detecting the presence of known malware families by matching their unique patterns.
- Hunting for specific behaviour: You can create Yara rules to identify specific behaviour, such as suspicious file names or registry keys.
- Indicator of Compromise (IOC) scanning: Yara can be used to scan systems for known IOCs related to recent security breaches or threat intelligence.

- Snort – It is an open-source network intrusion detection and prevention system. Unlike Yara, which primarily focuses on file-based analysis, Snort is designed to monitor network traffic and detect malicious activity in real-time. It uses a combination of predefined rules (known as Snort rules) and customizable rules to identify specific patterns or characteristics of known network-based attacks.
- Network intrusion detection: Snort can be deployed on network devices, such as firewalls or routers, to monitor traffic and detect attempts at unauthorized access or attacks.
- Network traffic analysis: It helps in identifying unusual patterns in network traffic, which may indicate malicious behavior like port scans or brute-force attacks.
- Prevention and response: Snort can be integrated with other security systems to block malicious traffic and facilitate incident response.

A Workshop on Post-Quantum Cryptography

Indivar Gupta[1], R. Kabaleeshwaran[2], Jitendra Kumar[3], Arpita Maitra[4], Raghavendra Patil[3], Balaji Rajendran[3], Prasanna Ravi[5], and SD Sudarsan[3]

[1] Defense Research & Development Organisation (DRDO)
https://drdo.gov.in/
[2] IIITDM Kurnool
https://iiitk.ac.in/
[3] Centre for Development of Advanced Computing (C-DAC)
https://cdac.in/
[4] tcg crest
https://www.tcgcrest.org/
[5] NTU Singapore
https://www.ntu.edu.sg/

Abstract. The emergence of quantum computers poses a significant risk to the security of commonly used public key cryptography, as they are likely to be vulnerable to quantum-based attacks. Post-Quantum Cryptography (PQC) is designed to rely on the computational hardness of specific problems in both quantum and classical contexts. Recently, the National Institute of Standards and Technology (NIST) has standardized quantum-resistant digital signatures and key establishment algorithms as part of PQC.

This workshop will explore various facets of Post-Quantum Cryptography, including challenges related to implementation and migration from existing cryptographic systems.

Prerequisites

Elementary knowledge of cryptography.

Module 1: Theory of PQC
Module 2: Development of PQC
Module 3: Hands-on exercise
Module 4: Demonstration

Acknowledgments.
R&D in IT Division, Ministry of Electronics & Information Technology (MeitY), Government of India.

Contents

System Security

Microarchitectural Security of Firecracker VMM for Serverless Cloud Platforms 3
   Zane Weissman, Thore Tiemann, Thomas Eisenbarth, and Berk Sunar

An OS Support for Tamper-Resistant Software Execution Using Empty Interruptions 25
   Soma Kato, Yui Koyanagi, and Tomoaki Ukezono

S-RFUP: Secure Remote Firmware Update Protocol 42
   Rakesh Podder, Tyler Rios, Indrajit Ray, Presanna Raman, and Stefano Righi

Securing Virtual Reality Apps Inter-process Communication 63
   Oluwatosin Falebita, Mahmoud Abdelgawad, Evan Anspach, and Indrakshi Ray

Network Security

Securing the Web: Analysis of HTTP Security Headers in Popular Global Websites 87
   Urvashi Kishnani and Sanchari Das

Countering Subscription Concealed Identifier (SUCI)-Catchers in Cellular Communications 107
   Julian Parkin and Mahesh Tripunitara

BP-MAP: A Secure and Convenient Mutual Authentication Protocol 127
   Harika Narumanchi, Lakshmi Padmaja Maddali, and N. Narendra Kumar

Effects of Soft-Domain Transfer and Named Entity Information on Deception Detection 146
   Steven Triplett, Simon Minami, and Rakesh M. Verma

Attack

Paving the Way: Advancing V2X Safety Through Innovative Attack Generation and Analysis Framework (V2X-SAF) 159
   Shubham Tomar and Meenakshi Tripathi

From Traits to Threats: Learning Risk Indicators of Malicious Insider
Using Psychometric Data 180
   *N'Famoussa Kounon Nanamou, Christopher Neal,
   Nora Boulahia-Cuppens, Frédéric Cuppens, and Anis Bkakria*

Identifying Insecure Network Configurations Through Attack Modeling
and Explainable AI 201
   Blessy Thomas, Sabu M. Thampi, and Preetam Mukherjee

QIris: Quantum Implementation of Rainbow Table Attacks 213
   Lee Jun Quan, Tan Jia Ye, Goh Geok Ling, and Vivek Balachandran

Malware and Vulnerability Detection

Insights from Running 24 Static Analysis Tools on Open Source Software
Repositories 225
   *Fabiha Hashmat, Zeyad Alwaleed Aljaali, Mingjie Shen,
   and Aravind Machiry*

REMEDII: Robust Malware Detection with Iterative and Intelligent
Adversarial Training 246
   Sanchit Gupta and Vireshwar Kumar

Semantics-Based Static Vulnerability Detection in Solidity Using Abstract
Interpretation 265
   Maitri Kushwaha, Arnab Mukherjee, Aishwarya Pandey, and Raju Halder

Privacy and Usability

Web Privacy Perceptions Amongst Indian Users 289
   *Gayatri Priyadarsini, Anshika Saxena, Aditi Dey, Prakriti,
   and Abhishek Bichhawat*

Enabling Privacy in IT Service Operations 310
   *Rohit Gupta, Rishabh Kumar, Sutapa Mondal, Mangesh Gharote,
   and Sachin Lodha*

Privacy-Preserving Photo Sharing: An SSI Use Case 320
   *Ashley Fraser, Abubakar-Sadiq Shehu, Nick Frymann, Paul Haynes,
   and Steve Schneider*

Zone Recovery Attack on a Secure Privacy-Preserving Ride-Matching
Protocol 330
   Shyam Murthy, Santosh Kumar Upadhyaya, and Srinivas Vivek

Making EULA Great Again: A Novel Nudge Mechanism to Improve
Readability, User Attention and Awareness 338
   Shamim Bin Zahid, Aishwarya Ghosh Bristy, Md. Musfikur Hasan Oli,
   Md. Fahim, Sarker Tanveer Ahmed Rumee, and Moinul Islam Zaber

A Decoupling Mechanism for Transaction Privacy 359
   Vishwas Patil and R. K. Shyamasundar

AI Security

Protecting Ownership of Trained DNN Models with Zero-Knowledge
Proofs 383
   Shungo Sato and Hidema Tanaka

MALAI: ML-Based Attack on Learning with Error Problem 404
   Mandru Suma Sri, Chakka Srikanth Yadav, Tikaram Sanyashi,
   and Virendra Singh

Patch Based Backdoor Attack on Deep Neural Networks 422
   Debasmita Manna and Somanath Tripathy

Industry Demo/Practice

Integrating Crypto-Based Payment Systems for Data Marketplaces:
Enhancing Efficiency, Security, and User Autonomy 443
   Vipul Walunj, Vasanth Rajaraman, Jyotirmoy Dutta, and Abhay Sharma

IntelliSOAR: Intelligent Alert Enrichment Using Security Orchestration
Automation and Response (SOAR) 453
   Surabhi Dwivedi, Balaji Rajendran, P. V. Akshay, Akshaya Acha,
   Praveen Ampatt, and Sithu D. Sudarsan

InTrust: An Asset Monitoring, Analysis and Vulnerability Assessment
System for Zero Trust Network 463
   N. Muraleedharan, Hrishikesh Rajendra Neve, Samar Sarkar,
   and Balaji Rajendran

Author Index 473

System Security

Microarchitectural Security of Firecracker VMM for Serverless Cloud Platforms

Zane Weissman[1], Thore Tiemann[2(✉)], Thomas Eisenbarth[2], and Berk Sunar[1]

[1] Worcester Polytechnic Institute, Worcester, MA, USA
{zweissman,sunar}@wpi.edu
[2] University of Lübeck, S-H, Lübeck, Germany
{t.tiemann,thomas.eisenbarth}@uni-luebeck.de

Abstract. Firecracker is a virtual machine manager (VMM) purpose-built by AWS for serverless cloud platforms—services that run code for thousands of end users on a per-task basis, automatically managing server infrastructure. In addition to architectural attacks, AWS states that microarchitectural attacks are included in their threat model. But this class of attacks relies on shared hardware, just as the scalability of serverless computing does, which opens a conflict of interest.

In this work, we investigate just how secure Firecracker is against microarchitectural attacks. We review Firecracker's stated isolation model and recommended best practices for deployment, identify potential threat models for serverless platforms, and analyze potential weak points. Then, we use microarchitectural attack PoCs to test the isolation provided by Firecracker and find that it offers little protection against Spectre or MDS attacks. We discover two particularly concerning cases: **(1)** a Medusa variant that threatens Firecracker VMs but *not* processes running outside of them, and is not mitigated by defenses recommended by AWS, and **(2)** a Spectre-PHT variant that remains exploitable even if recommended countermeasures–including disabled SMT–are in place.

Keywords: system security · microarchitectural security · virtual machines · hypervisor · serverless · cloud systems

1 Introduction

Serverless computing is an emerging trend in cloud computing where cloud service providers (CSPs) serve runtime environments to their customers. This way, customers can focus on maintaining their function code while leaving the administrative work related to hardware, operating system (OS), and sometimes runtime to the CSPs. Since individual functions are typically small, CSPs aim for fitting as many functions on a single server as possible to minimize idle times and, in turn, maximize profit. This must be achieved while preserving security for both the provider and clients. Containers offer some isolation at the operating system level with relatively little performance overhead, but they are unable to take advantage of some of the powerful virtualization features of modern CPUs and OSs that provide deeper isolation at an architectural level. To use these features with performance suitable for serverless computing, developers slimmed down the virtual machines (VMs) used for heavier cloud computing, creating what are now called MicroVMs.

Firecracker [1] is a virtual machine monitorVMM designed to run microVMs with memory overhead and start times comparable to those of common container systems. Firecracker is actively developed by Amazon Web ServicesAWS and has been used in production for serverless compute services since 2018 [1]. AWS's design paper [1] describes the features of Firecracker, how it diverges from more traditional virtual machines, and the intended isolation model that it provides: safety for *"multiple functions run[ning] on the same hardware, protected against privilege escalation, information disclosure, covert channels, and other risks"* [1]. Furthermore, AWS provides production host setup recommendations [5] for securing parts of the CPU and kernel that a Firecracker VM interacts with. *In this paper, we challenge the claim that Firecracker protects functions from covert and side-channels across microVMs. We show that Firecracker does not add to the microarchitectural attack countermeasures but fully relies on the host and guest Linux kernels and CPU microcode updates.*

Microarchitectural attacks like the various Spectre [10,17,26,27,30,44] and microarchitectural data sampling (MDS) [9,32,39,40] variants pose a threat to multi-tenant systems as they are often able to bypass both software and architectural isolation boundaries, including those of VMs, when CPU core resources are shared. In serverless environments, resources are expected to be overcommitted, which leads to multiple functions competing for and sharing compute resources on the same hardware. This directly leads to an increased microarchitectural attack surface for serverless environments. The attack surface is the greatest if simultaneous multi-threading (SMT) is enabled—as is the compute power of a CPU, as SMT increases performance by up to 30 % [31]. But even with SMT disabled, functions sharing compute resources in a time-sliced way remain vulnerable to some microarchitectural attacks [51].

AWS claims that Firecracker running on a system with up-to-date microarchitectural defenses will provide sufficient hardening against microarchitectural attacks [1]. The Firecracker documentation also contains specific recommendations for microarchitectural security measures that should be enabled. *In this work, we examine Firecracker's securityfontawesome5fontawesome5and reveal oversights in its guidance as well as wholly unmitigated threats.* After reviewing a pre-print of this paper, AWS has updated the Firecracker production host setup recommendations [6] (cf. Sect. 1.1).

In summary, our main contributions are:

– We provide a comprehensive security analysis of the cross-tenant and tenant-hypervisor isolation of serverless compute when based on Firecracker VM.
– We test Firecracker's defense capabilities against microarchitectural attack proof-of-concepts (PoCs), employing available hardware and kernel protections. We show that the virtual machine itself provides *negligible protection* against major classes of microarchitectural attacks.

– We identify a variant of the Medusa MDS attack that becomes exploitable from within Firecracker VMs *even though it is not present on the host*. The mitigation that protects against this exploit is not mentioned by AWS's Firecracker host setup recommendations. Additionally, we show that disabling SMT provides insufficient protection against the identified Medusa variant which urges the need of this mitigation.
 – We identify Spectre-PHT and Spectre-BTB variants which leak data with recommended countermeasures in place. The Spectre-PHT variants even remain a problem when SMT is disabled if the attacker and victim share a CPU core in a time-sliced fashion.

1.1 Responsible Disclosure

We informed the AWS security team about our findings and discussed technical details. The AWS security team claims that the AWS services are not affected by our findings due to additional security measures. AWS agreed that Firecracker does not provide micro-architectural security on its own but only in combination with microcode updates and secure host and guest operating systems. As such, the Firecracker developers have updated the microarchitectural attack section of the production host setup recommendations to make this very clear [6]. Updates to this section also include direct referral to OS and CPU vendor documentation on microarchitectural vulnerabilities and mitigations.

2 Background

2.1 Serverless Cloud Computing and MicroVMs

An increasingly popular model for cloud computing is serverless computing, in which the CSP manages scalability and availability of the servers that run the cloud user's code. The CSP can manage its users' workloads however it pleases, optimize for minimal operating cost, and implement flexible pricing where users pay for the execution time and memory that they use. The user does not need to worry about server infrastructure design or management, and so reduces the costs of development and maintenance work.

Serverless providers use a variety of systems to manage running functions and containers. Container systems like Docker, Podman, and LXD provide a convenient and lightweight way to package and run sandboxed applications in any environment. However, compared to the virtual machines used for many more traditional forms of cloud computing, containers offer less isolation and therefore less security. In recent years, major CSPs have introduced microVMs that back traditional containers with lightweight virtualization for extra security [1,49]. The efficiency of hardware virtualization with kernel-based virtual machine (KVM) and lightweight design of microVMs means that code in virtualized, containerized or container-like systems can run nearly as fast as unvirtualized code and with comparable overhead to a traditional container.

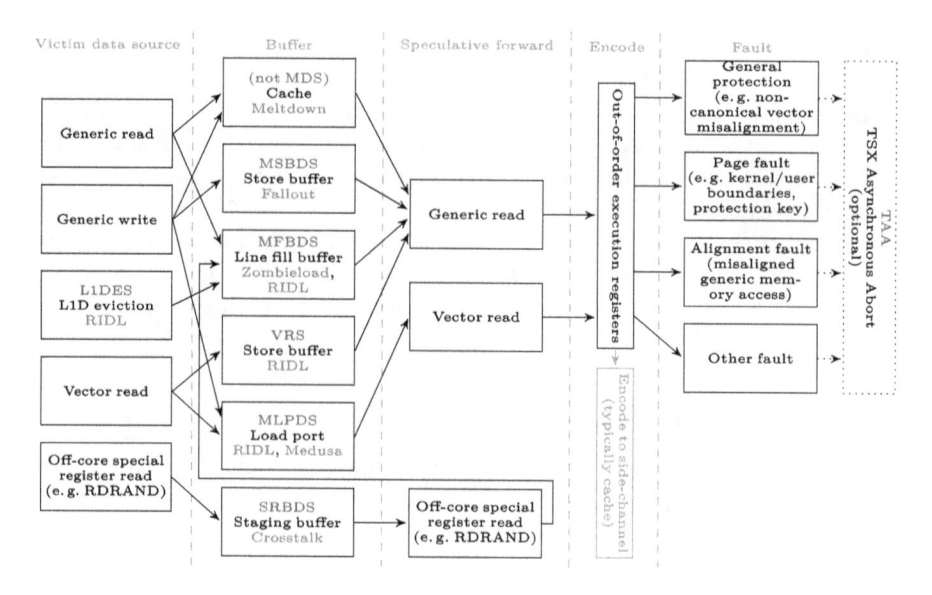

Fig. 1. Major MDS attack pathways and variant names on Intel CPUs. The blue names at the top are names of vulnerabilities given by Intel; the red names at the bottom are names given by researchers or the names of the papers in which the vulnerabilities were reported. Not all fault types work with all vulnerabilities on all systems—cataloging every known combination would be beyond the scope of this paper. (Color figure online)

2.2 Meltdown and MDS

In 2018, the Meltdown [29] attack showed that speculative execution could access data across security boundaries and encode it into a cache side-channel. This soon led to a whole class of similar attacks, known as microarchitectural data sampling (MDS), including Fallout [9], Rogue In-flight Data Load (RIDL)RIDL [39], TSX Asynchronous Abort (TAA) [39], and Zombieload [40]. These attacks all follow the same general pattern to exploit speculative execution:

1. The victim handles secret data that passes through a cache or CPU buffer.
2. The attacker executes a specifically chosen instruction that causes the CPU to speculatively forward the secret to the attacker's instruction.
3. The attacker preserves the transiently learned secret by sending it through a covert channel.

The original Meltdown vulnerability targeted cache forwarding and allowed data extraction in this manner from *any* memory address that was present in the cache. Newer MDS attacks target specific buffers in the on-core microarchitecture and work under more specific timing and co-location conditions.

2.3 Basic MDS Variants

Figure 1 charts the major known MDS attack pathways on Intel CPUs and the names given to different variants by Intel and by the researchers who reported them. Intel tends to categorize MDS vulnerabilities in their CPUs by the specific buffer from which data is speculatively forwarded, since these buffers tend to be used for a number of different operations. Intel names in this style include Microarchitectural Load Port Data Sampling (MLPDS), Microarchitectural Fill Buffer Data Sampling (MFBDS), Microarchitectural Store Buffer Data Sampling (MSBDS), Special Register Buffer Data Sampling (SRBDS), and Vector Register Sampling (VRS). L1 Data Eviction Sampling (L1DES) and TSX Asynchronous Abort (TAA) describe closely related vulnerabilities. L1DES is a method by which the attacker forces the victim's data from the cache into the buffer from which it is eventually leaked. TAA, described in detail in Sect. 2.4, is an alternate method for triggering speculative execution.

2.4 Medusa

Medusa [32] is a category of MDS attacks classified by Intel as MLPDS variants [20]. The Medusa vulnerabilities exploit the pattern-matching algorithms used to *speculatively* combine stores in the write-combine (WC) buffer (part of the load port) of Intel processors. There are three known Medusa variants, each exploiting a different feature of the WC buffer to cause a speculative leakage:

Cache Indexing: a faulting load is speculatively combined with an earlier load with a matching cache line offset.

Unaligned Store-to-Load Forwarding: a valid store followed by a dependent load that triggers a misaligned memory fault causes random data from the WC buffer to be forwarded.

Shadow REP MOV*:* a faulting REP MOV instruction followed by a dependent load leaks the data of a different REP MOV.

TSX Asynchronous Abort. The hardware vulnerability TSX Asynchronous Abort (TAA) [19] is a speculation mechanism for carrying out an MDS attack. While standard MDS attacks access restricted data with a standard speculated execution, TAA uses an atomic memory transaction as implemented by TSX. When an atomic memory transaction encounters an asynchronous abort due to a fault, the architectural state is "rolled back" to its state before the transaction started. During this rollback, instructions that have started speculatively executing can continue to do so, as in steps (2) and (3) of other MDS attacks. TAA impacts all Intel processors that support TSX, and the case of newer processors that are not affected by other MDS attacks, MDS mitigations or TAA-specific mitigations (such as disabling TSX) are required for protection against TAA [19].

Mitigations. Though Meltdown and MDS-class vulnerabilities exploit low level microarchitectural operations, they can be mitigated with microcode firmware patches on most vulnerable CPUs.

Page Table Isolation. Historically, kernel page tables have been included in user-level process page tables so that a user-level process can make a system call to the kernel with minimal overhead. Page table isolation (first proposed by Gruss et al. as KAISER [13]) maps only the bare minimum necessary kernel memory into the user page table and introduces a second page table only accessible by the kernel. With the user process unable to access the kernel page table, accesses to the rest of kernel memory are stopped before they reach the lower level caches where a Meltdown attack begins. Page table isolation works best when layered on top of kernel Adress Space Layout Randomization (ASLR), which randomizes the layout of kernel memory on each boot.

Buffer Overwrite. MDS attacks that target on-core CPU buffers require a lower-level and more targeted defense. Intel introduced a microcode update that overwrites vulnerable buffers when the first-level data (L1d) cache is flushed or the VERW instruction is run [20]. The kernel can then protect against MDS attacks by triggering a buffer overwrite when switching to an untrusted process.

The buffer overwrite mitigation targets MDS attacks at their source, but is imperfect. Processes remain vulnerable to attacks from concurrently running threads on the same core when SMT is enabled (since both threads share vulnerable buffers without the active process actually changing on either thread). On some Skylake CPUs, buffers are overwritten with stale data [39], and remain vulnerable even with mitigations enabled and SMT disabled. Still other processors are vulnerable to TAA but not non-TAA MDS attacks, and did not receive a buffer overwrite microcode update. On these CPUs, TSX must be disabled to prevent MDS attacks [14,19].

2.5 Spectre

In 2018, Jan Horn and Paul Kocher [26] independently reported the first Spectre variants. Since then, many Spectre (sub-)variants [10,17,25–27,30,44] have been discovered. Spectre attacks make the CPU speculatively access memory that would not be accessed architecturally and leak the data into the architectural state. Therefore, all Spectre variants consist of three components [22]:

The first component is the Spectre gadget that the CPU executes speculatively. Spectre variants are commonly distinguished by the source of the misprediction they exploit. Spectre-PHT–which allows for speculative bounds check bypass–results from the prediction outcome by the pattern history table (PHT) for conditional branches [10,25,26]. The branch target buffer (BTB) predictions of branch targets for indirect jumps allows for speculative return-oriented programming attacks through Spectre-BTB [10,26], Spectre-RSB exploits the return address prediction by the return stack buffer (RSB) [10,27,30]. Spectre-STL [17] exploits store-to-load (STL) dependency prediction to read stale data or provoke transient buffer overflows.

The second component is the attacker's control over the gadgets. Control may be possible through user input, file contents, or other architectural mechanisms. Additionally, transient mechanisms like LVI [42] or floating point value injection [36] may allow an attacker the necessary control over accessed data or executed instructions.

The third component is the covert channel that transfers the transient microarchitectural state into an architectural state to exfiltrate data. Cache covert channels [34,47] are the most prominent candidates but Spectre attacks using MDS [9,39,40] or port contention [12,37,38] are also known in the literature.

Mitigations. Many countermeasures are discussed in the literature. Early countermeasures target the availability or accuracy of covert channels [23,24,46], though, such countermeasures tend to be incomplete due to the numerous covert channels that may be used. Countermeasures that focus on removing the attacker's control over the prediction outcome are more promising and used today. Spectre-BTB is mitigated by Retpoline [41] or microcode updates like IBRS, STIBP, and IBPB [18]. Spectre-RSB can be mitigated through RSB filling or the IBRS microcode update and the SSBD [18] microcode update protects against Spectre-STL. Disabling SMT partitions branch prediction hardware between concurrent tenants but implies a significant performance penalty and still allows sequential tenants to share the branch prediction unit.

2.6 AWS Firecracker

Firecracker [1] is a microVM developed by AWS to isolate workloads on its serverless platforms. As a microVM, Firecracker sacrifices hardware, OS, and I/O flexibility to be very light-weight in the size of its code base and in-memory overhead, as well as very quick to boot or shut down. In their paper, AWS itemizes the design requirements for the isolation system that eventually became Firecracker as follows [1]:

> *Isolation:* It must be safe for multiple functions to run on the same hardware, protected against privilege escalation, information disclosure, covert channels, and other risks.
> *Overhead and Density:* It must be possible to run thousands of functions on a single machine, with minimal waste.
> *Performance:* Functions must perform similarly to running natively. Performance must also be consistent, and isolated from the behavior of neighbors on the same hardware.
> *Compatibility:* AWS Lambda [3] allows functions to contain arbitrary Linux binaries and libraries. These must be supported without code changes or recompilation.
> *Fast Switching:* It must be possible to start new functions and clean up old functions quickly.
> *Soft Allocation:* It must be possible to over commit CPU, memory and other resources, with each function consuming only the resources it needs, not the resources it is entitled to.

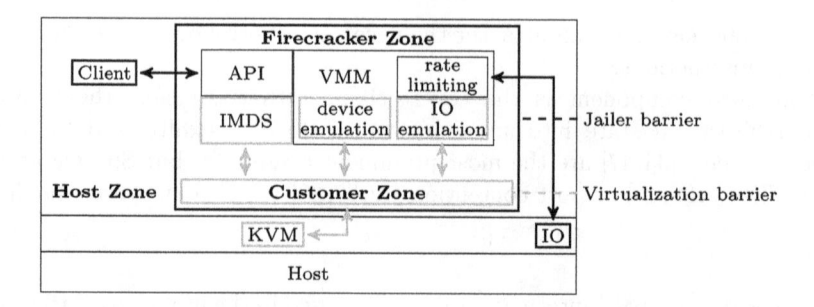

Fig. 2. Firecracker threat containment diagram—adapted from [4]. The jailer provides container-like protections for components running in the host user space. The customer workload runs inside a virtual machine.

We are particularly interested in the *isolation* requirement and stress that microarchitectural attacks are declared *in-scope* for the Firecracker threat model. The "design" page in AWS's Firecracker Git repository elaborates on the isolation model and provides a useful diagram which we reproduce in Fig. 2. The outermost layer of protection is the jailer, which uses container isolation techniques to limit interactions between the Firecracker process and the host kernel. Within the Firecracker process, there are threads for the VMM, management components, and guest workload inside the VM. Since the VM is isolated via hardware virtualization techniques, the user's code, the guest kernel, and the VMM operate in separate address spaces and cannot architecturally or transiently access each other's memory. However, many microarchitectural attacks including MDS and Spectre variants ignore address space boundaries and leak data or manipulate execution through internal CPU buffers.

Firecracker Security Recommendations. Prior to our disclosure to AWS, the Firecracker documentation recommended the following precautions for protecting against microarchitectural side-channels [5]: (1) disable SMT, (2) enable kernel page-table isolation, (3) disable kernel same-page merging, (4) use a kernel compiled with Spectre-BTB mitigation (e.g., IBRS and IBPB on x86), (5) verify Spectre-PHT mitigation, (6) enable L1TF mitigation, (7) enable Spectre-STL mitigation, (8) use memory with Rowhammer mitigation, and (9) disable swap or use secure swap. As a result of this work, the current version of this documentation [6] includes many of the same recommendations but emphasizes the incompleteness of the list and strongly recommends the use of security documentation from the Linux kernel and CPU vendors for the most up-to-date firmware patches and configuration recommendations.

3 Threat Models

We propose two threat models applicable to Firecracker-based serverless cloud systems:

1. The *user-to-user* model: a malicious user runs arbitrary code sandboxed within a Firecracker VM and attempts to leak data, inject data, or otherwise gain information about or control over another user's sandboxed application. In this model, we consider
   (a) the time-sliced sharing of hardware, where the instances of the two users execute in turns on the CPU core, and
   (b) physical co-location, where the two users' code runs concurrently on hardware that is shared in one way or another (for example, two cores on the same CPU or two threads in the same core if SMT is enabled).
2. The *user-to-host* model: a malicious user targets some component of the host system, e.g., the Firecracker VMM, KVM, or another part of the host system kernel. For this scenario, we only consider time-sliced sharing of hardware resources because the host only executes code if the VM exits, e. g. due to a page fault that has to be handled by the host kernel or VMM.

For both models, we assume that a malicious user is able to control the runtime environment of its application. In our models, malicious users do *not* possess guest kernel privileges. Therefore, both models grant the attacker slightly fewer privileges than the model assumed by [1] where the guest kernel is chosen and configured by the VMM but assumed to be compromised at runtime. Rather, the attacker's capabilities in our models match the capabilities granted to users in deployments of Firecracker in sAWS platforms.

4 Analysis of Firecracker's Containment Systems

Figure 2 shows the containment offered by Firecracker, as presented by AWS. In this section, we analyze each depicted component and their defenses against and vulnerabilities to microarchitectural attacks.

Kernel-based virtual machine (KVM) is the hypervisor implemented in modern Linux kernels that manages hardware virtualization of supervisor and user mode execution and context switches between VMs. Crucially, KVM's hardware virtualization includes address spaces for the guest kernel and guest user code that are separate from those of the host and of other guests—a significant barrier to both user-to-user and user-to-host attacks. Besides these architectural isolation mechanisms, KVM also implements mitigations against Spectre attacks on a VM-exit to protect the host OS or hypervisor from malicious guests. While ASLR is enabled for the guest userspace, Firecracker guest kernels lack kernel ASLR support, making them especially vulnerable to microarchitectural attacks that ignore address space boundaries [16]. Since KVM is part of the Linux kernel, we define KVM to not be a part of Firecracker. Therefore, countermeasures against microarchitectural attacks that are implemented in KVM cannot be attributed to Firecracker's containment system.

The *metadata, device, and I/O services* are the parts of the Firecracker VMM that interact directly with a VM. AWS touts the simplicity of these interfaces (for a reduced attack surface) and that they are written from scratch for Firecracker in Rust, a language known for its security features [7]. However, Rust most

Table 1. Overview of discovered microarchitectural vulnerabilities not fully prevented by the recommended production host settings for Firecracker prior to our disclosure.

Exploit Description	💧 only?	💧↔💧?	Mitigations
Medusa (CI[a] + block write secret)	✓	✓	mds (host)
Medusa (UStL[b])	✗	✓	mds (host) + nosmt
RIDL/MFBDS (alignment fault)	✗	✓	mds (host)
RIDL/MFBDS (in-process)	✗	✗	mds (host or VM)
Spectre-PHT	✗	✓	currently not available
Spectre-BTB	✗	✓	currently not available
Spectre-STL	✗	N/A	currently not available

[a] Cache Indexing variant, [b] Unaligned Store-to-Load variant

notably provides in-process protection against invalid and out-of-bounds memory accesses, but microarchitectural attacks can leak information between processes without directly hijacking a victim's process.

Another notable difference between Firecracker and many other VMMs is that all of these services are run within the same host process as the VM itself, albeit in another thread. While the virtualization of memory addresses within the VM provides some obfuscation between the guest's code and the I/O services, some Spectre attacks work specifically within a single process. However, Firecracker assumes that two guests run in separate VMs and therefore processes. So intra-process attacks pose less of a threat to real world systems.

The *jailer* provides an additional barrier of defense around a Firecracker instance in the event that the API or VMM are compromised. It protects the host system's files and resources with namespaces and control groups (cgroups), respectively [2]. Microarchitectural attacks do not threaten files, which are by definition outside the microarchitectural state. Cgroups allow a system administrator to assign processes to groups and then allocate and monitor system resource usage on a per-group basis [11]. It is plausible that limitations applied with cgroups could impede an attacker's ability to carry out certain microarchitectural attacks which rely on the ability to allocate large amounts of memory or precisely measure the timing of CPU operations. In practice, Firecracker is not distributed with any particular cgroup rules [2]; in fact, it is specifically designed so that the default Linux resource allocation can run many VMs efficiently [4].

None of Firecracker's isolation and containment systems seem to directly protect against user-to-user or user-to-host attacks. Thus, we proceeded to test various microarchitectural attack PoCs inside and outside of Firecracker VMs.

5 Analysis of Microarchitectural Attacks and Defenses in Firecracker MicroVMs

In this section we present our analysis of a number of microarchitectural side-channel and speculative attack PoCs on Firecracker microVMs. We test these

PoCs on the host and in Firecracker VMs, and test relevant microcode defenses in the various scenarios. We run our tests on a server with an Intel Skylake 4114 CPU which has virtualization hardware extensions and SMT enabled. The CPU runs on microcode version 0x2006b06[1]. The host OS is Ubuntu 20.04 with a Linux 5.10 kernel. We used Firecracker v1.0.0, v1.4.0, and v1.5.0–the latest version as of Oct. 2023–to run an Ubuntu 18.04 guest with Linux kernel 5.4 which is provided by Amazon when following the quick-start guide[2].

We find that the recommended production host setup provided with AWS Firecracker is insufficient when it comes to protecting tenants from malicious neighbors as is summarized in Table 1. Firecracker therefore fails in providing its claimed isolation guarantees. This is because

1. we identify a Medusa variant that only becomes exploitable when it is run across microVMs. In addition, the recommended countermeasures at the time of the research did not contain the necessary steps to mitigate the side-channel, or most other Medusa variants.
2. we show that tenants are not properly protected from information leaks induced through Spectre-PHT or Spectre-BTB when applying the recommended countermeasures. The Spectre-PHT variants remain a problem even when disabling SMT.
3. we observed no differences in PoC performance between the tested Firecracker versions.

We conclude that the virtualization layer provided by Firecracker has little effect on microarchitectural attacks, and Firecracker's system security recommendations were incomplete prior to revisions prompted by this work.

5.1 Medusa

We evaluated Moghimi's PoCs for the Medusa [32] side-channels (classified by Intel as MLPDS variants of MDS [20]) on the host system and in Firecracker VMs. There is one leaking PoC for each of the three known variants described in Sect. 2.4. We used two victim programs from the PoC library: the "Block Write" program writes a large amount of consecutive data in a loop (so that the processor will identify repeated stores and combine them). The "REP MOV" program performs a similar operation, but with the REP MOV instruction instead of many instructions moving smaller blocks of data in a loop.

Results. Table 2 shows the cases in which data is successfully leaked with all microarcitectural protections in the kernel disabled. The left two columns show the possible combinations of the three Medusa PoCs and the two included victim

---

[1] Updating the microcode to a newer version would disable TSX on our system which would make tests with TSX-based MDS variants impossible.
[2] https://github.com/firecracker-microvm/firecracker/blob/dbd9a84b11a63b5e5bf201e244fe83f0bc76792a/docs/getting-started.md.

Table 2. Presence of Medusa side-channels with all microarchitectural defense kernel options disabled. Note that the combination of cache indexing leak and block write secret (highlighted) works in Firecracker VMs but not on the host.

Leak	Secret	Host	Firecracker
Cache Indexing	Block Write	$\not\Rightarrow$	$\Rightarrow$
	REP MOV	$\Rightarrow$	$\Rightarrow$
Unaligned Store-to-Load	Block Write	$\Rightarrow$	$\Rightarrow$
	REP MOV	$\Rightarrow$	$\Rightarrow$
Shadow REP MOV	Block Write	$\not\Rightarrow$	$\not\Rightarrow$
	REP MOV	$\not\Rightarrow$	$\not\Rightarrow$

For some side-channels we observe leakage ($\Rightarrow$) on our system and for others we do not ($\not\Rightarrow$).

Table 3. Mitigations necessary to protect the host vs. Firecracker victims from Medusa attacks. Note that AWS's recommended mitigation–`nosmt`–does not prevent the highlighted cache indexing/block write variant that is enabled by Firecracker (cf. Table 2), or any other variants. All results were reproduced with Firecracker versions 1.0.0, 1.4.0, and 1.5.0.

		Bare metal		Firecracker		
Leak	Secret	mds	nosmt	mds(VM)	mds(H)	nosmt
Cache Indexing	Block Write	N/A	N/A	✗	✓	✗
	REP MOV	✓	✓	✓	✓	✓
Unaligned Store	Block Write	✓	✗	✗	✓	✗
	REP MOV	✦	✦	✗	✦	✦

Mitigations either prevent (✓) leakage, have no effect (✗), or must be combined (✦) to be effective.

programs. The right columns indicate which configurations work on the host and with the secret and leaking program running in parallel Firecracker instances. Most notably, with the Cache Indexing variant, the Block Write secret only works with Firecracker. This is likely because of the memory address virtualization that the virtual machine provides: the guest only sees virtual memory regions mapped by KVM, and KVM traps memory access instructions and handles the transactions on behalf of the guest. We found that the Shadow REP MOV variant did not work inside or outside of Firecracker.

We tested the effectiveness of `mds` and `nosmt` defenses against each combination of attacker and victim PoC on the host and in Firecracker VMs. Table 3 lists the protections necessary to prevent Medusa attacks in the host and Firecracker scenarios. Across the four vulnerabilities in Firecracker, only one is mitigated by

Table 4. Required mitigations to protect the host vs. Firecracker victims from MDS attacks. The recommended `nosmt` mitigation protects against most but not all MDS variants. Experiments on Firecracker v1.0.0, v1.4.0, and v1.5.0 yielded identical results.

	Exploit details		Host		Firecracker		
Name	Target buffer	Fault	nosmt	mds	nosmt (H)	mds (H)	mds (VM)
RIDL	Fill buffer	Alignment	✧	✧	✧	✧	✗
	Fill buffer	Page	✗[b]	✓	✗[b]	✓	✓
	Fill buffer	Page	✓	✗	N/A[c]	N/A[c]	N/A[c]
L1DES	Fill buffer	TSX abort	✓	✗	✓	✗	✗
RIDL	Load Port	Page	✓	✗	✓	✗	✗
RIDL/VRS	Store buffer	Page	✓	✗	✓	✗	✗
Crosstalk	Fill buffer	Page	✓	✗	N/A[a]	N/A[a]	N/A[a]

Mitigations either prevent (✓) leakage, have no effect (✗), or must be combined (✧) to be effective.
[a] `CPUID` instruction used in this PoC is emulated by the VM and has no microarchitectural effect.
[b] This attack leaks information about pages used in its own thread.
[c] PoCs had to be modified to run in two processes before they could be tested in the virtual machine. These PoCs did not work on bare metal or in virtual machines when split into two processes.

`nosmt` alone, and AWS does *not explicitly recommend* enabling the `mds` protection, though most Linux distributions ship with it enabled by default. That is to say, a multi-tenant cloud platform could be using Firecracker in a way that is compliant with AWS's recommended security measures and still be vulnerable to the majority of Medusa variants, including one where the Firecracker VMM itself leaks the user's data that would not otherwise be leaked.

5.2 RIDL and More

In this section, we present an evaluation of the RIDL PoC programs provided alongside van Schaik et al.'s 2019 paper [39]. RIDL is a class of MDS attacks that exploits speculative loads from buffers inside the CPU (not from cache or memory). The RIDL PoC repository also includes examples of attacks released in later addenda to the paper as well as one variant of the Fallout MDS attack.

Results. Table 4 shows some basic information about the RIDL PoCs that we tested and the efficacy of relevant countermeasures at preventing the attacks. More details are given in the appendix. We compared attacks on the host and in Firecracker to evaluate Amazon's claims of the heightened hardware security of the Firecracker microVM system. For tests on the Firecracker system, we

```
1  Vulnerability Spec store bypass: Mitigation; Speculative Store Bypass disabled via prctl and seccomp
2  Vulnerability Spectre v1:        Mitigation; usercopy/swapgs barriers and __user pointer sanitization
3  Vulnerability Spectre v2:        Mitigation; Full generic retpoline, IBPB conditional, IBRS_FW, STIBP conditional
                , RSB filling
```

Fig. 3. Spectre mitigations enabled in the host and guest kernel during the Spectre tests. This setup is recommended by AWS for host production systems [5].

distinguish between countermeasure flags enabled on the host system (H) and the Firecracker guest kernel (VM). Besides the nosmt and mds kernel flags, we tested other relevant flags (cf. Sect. 2.4, [15]), including kaslr, pti, and l1tf, but did not find that they had an effect on any of these programs. We excluded the tsx_async_abort mitigation since the CPU we tested on includes mds mitigation which makes the tsx_async_abort kernel flag redundant [14].

In general, we found that the mds protection does not adequately protect against the majority of RIDL attacks. However, disabling SMT does mitigate the majority of these exploits. This is consistent with Intel's [20] and the Linux developers' [15] statements that SMT must be disabled to prevent MDS attacks across hyperthreads. The two outliers among these PoCs are alignment_write, which requires both nosmt and mds on the host, and pgtable_leak_notsx, which is mitigated only by mds countermeasures. The leak relying on alignment_write uses an alignment fault rather than a page table fault leak to trigger speculation [39]. The RIDL paper [39] and Intel's documentation of the related VRS exploit [21] are unclear about what exactly differentiates this attack from the page-fault-based MFBDS attacks found in other PoCs, but our experimental findings indicate that the microarchitectural mechanism of the leakage is distinct. There is a simple and reasonable explanation for the behavior of pgtable_leak_notsx, which is unique among these PoCs for one key reason: it is the only exploit that crosses security boundaries (leaking page table values from the kernel) within a single thread rather than leaking from another thread. It is self-evident that disabling multi-threading would have little effect on this single-threaded exploit. However, the mds countermeasure flushes microarchitectural buffers before switching from kernel-privilege execution to user-privilege execution within the same thread, wiping the page table data accessed by kernel code from the line-fill buffer (LFB) before the attacking user code can leak it.

In contrast to Medusa, most of these PoCs are mitigated by AWS's recommendation of disabling smt. However, as with Medusa, the Firecracker VMM itself provides no microarchitectural protection against these attacks.

5.3 Spectre

While there have been many countermeasures developed since Spectre was first discovered, many of them either come with a (significant) performance penalty or only partially mitigate the attack. Therefore, system operators often have to decide for a performance vs. security trade-off. To evaluate the wide range of Spectre attacks, we rely on the PoCs provided by [10]. For Spectre-PHT,

Spectre-BTB, and Spectre-RSB, the repository contains four PoCs each. They differ in the way the attacker mistrains the BPU. The four possibilities are (1) *same-process*: the attacker has control over the victim process or its inputs to mistrain the BPU, (2) *cross-process*: the attacker runs its own code in a separate process to influence the branch predictions of the victim process, (a) *in-place*: the attacker mistrains the BPU with a branch instruction that resides at the same virtual address as the target branch, and (b) *out-of-place*: the attacker mistrains the BPU with a branch instruction at an address that is congruent to the target branch in the victim process. The first two and latter two options are orthogonal, so each PoC combines two of them. For Spectre-STL, only same-process variants are known, which is why the repository only provides two PoCs in this case. For cross-VM experiments, we disabled ASLR for the host and guest user space as well as for the host kernel[3] to ease finding congruent addresses that are used for mistraining.

Results. With *AWS recommended countermeasures* [5]–the default for the Linux kernels in use–enabled on the host system and inside Firecracker VMs, we see that Spectre-RSB is successfully mitigated on the host as well as inside and across VMs (cf. Table 5). On the other hand, *Spectre-STL, Spectre-BTB, and Spectre-PHT enabled information leakage* in particular situations.

The PoCs for Spectre-STL show leakage. However, the leakage only occurs within the same process and the same privilege level. As no cross-process variants are known, we did not test the cross-VM scenario for Spectre-STL. In our user-to-user threat model, Spectre-STL is not a possible attack vector, as no cross-process variants are known. If two tenant workloads would be isolated by in-process isolation within the same VM, Spectre-STL could still be a viable attack vector. In the user-to-host model, Spectre-STL is mitigated by countermeasures that are included in current Linux kernels and enabled by default.

For Spectre-PHT, the kernel countermeasures include the sanitization of user-pointers and the utilization of barriers (`lfence`) on privilege level switches. We therefore conclude that Spectre-PHT poses little to no threat to the host system. However, these mitigations do not protect two hyperthreads from each other if they execute on the same physical core in parallel. This is why all four Spectre-PHT mistraining variants are fully functional on the host system as well as inside Firecracker VMs. As can be seen in Table 5, VMs remain vulnerable *even if SMT is disabled*[4]. This makes Spectre-PHT a significant threat for user-to-user.

Spectre-BTB PoCs are partially functional when AWS recommended countermeasures are enabled. The original variant (1a) is fully functional while (1b) is successfully mitigated. Also, all attempts to leak information (2b) did not show any leakage. With (2a), however, we observed leakage. On the host system, the leakage occurred independent of SMT. Inside a VM, the leakage only occurred if all virtual CPU cores were assigned to a separate physical thread. Across VMs, disabling SMT removes the leakage.

---

[3] Kernel ASLR is not available in Firecracker guests [16].
[4] Simulated by making attacker and victim share the same physical core (◐ and ◑).

Table 5. Spectre PoCs run with Firecracker recommended countermeasures (cf. Fig. 3 and [5]). Experiments with Firecracker v1.0.0, v1.4.0, and v1.5.0 yielded identical results.

Variant	Platform	Configuration	Same process in-place	Same process out-of-place	Cross process in-place	Cross process out-of-place
PHT	🖥, 🔥	any	✗	✗	✗	✗
	🔥↔🔥	any	N/A	N/A	✗	✗
BTB	🖥	any	✗	✓	✗	✓
	🔥	◐	✗	✓	✗	✓
		◍	✗	✓	✓	✓
		❙❙	✗	✓	✗	✓
	🔥↔🔥	◍	N/A	N/A	✓	✓
		❙❙	N/A	N/A	✗	✓
RSB	🖥, 🔥	any	✓	✓	✓	✓
	🔥↔🔥	any	N/A	N/A	✓	✓
STL	🖥, 🔥	any	✗	N/A	N/A	N/A

Experiments were run on the host system (🖥), inside a single VM (🔥), or across two VMs (🔥↔🔥). Victim and attacker share the same virtual and physical thread (◐), the same physical thread in separate virtual cores (◍), or two neighboring physical threads in separate virtual cores (❙❙). Mitigations either prevent (✓) leakage or have no effect (✗).

Besides the countermeasures listed in Fig. 3, the host kernel has Spectre countermeasures compiled into the VM entry and exit point[5] to disable malicious guests from attacking the host kernel while the kernel handles a VM exit.

In summary, we can say that the Linux default countermeasures–which are recommended by the Firecracker developers–only partially mitigate Spectre.

Precisely, we show:

- Spectre-PHT and Spectre-BTB can still leak information between tenants in the guest-to-guest scenario with the AWS recommended countermeasures– which includes disabling SMT–in place.
- The host kernel is likely sufficiently protected by the additional precautions that are compiled into the Linux kernel to shield VM entries and exits. This, however, is orthogonal to security measures provided by Firecracker.

All leakage observed was independent of the Firecracker version in use.

---

[5] https://elixir.bootlin.com/linux/v5.10/source/arch/x86/kvm/vmx/vmenter.S#L191.

Evaluation. We find that Firecracker does not add to the mitigations against Spectre but solely relies on general protection recommendations, which include mitigations provided by the host and guest kernels and optional microcode updates. Even worse, the recommended countermeasures insufficiently protect serverless applications from leaking information to other tenants. We therefore claim that Firecracker does *not* achieve its isolation goal on a microarchitectural level, even though microarchitectural attacks are considered in-scope of the Firecracker threat model.

The alert reader might wonder why Spectre-BTB remains an issue with the STIBP countermeasure in place (cf. Fig. 3) as this microcode patch was designed to stop the branch prediction from using prediction information that originates from another thread. This also puzzled us for a while until recently Google published a security advisory[6] that identifies a flaw in Linux 6.2 that kept disabling the STIBP mitigation when IBRS is enabled. We verified that the code section that was identified as being responsible for the issue is also present in the Linux 5.10 source code. Our assumption therefore is that the same problem identified by Google also occurs on our system.

6 Impact

This work highlights the need for low-level defenses against microarchitectural attacks even when sophisticated virtualization and containerization isolation measures are in place. At the time of publishing, most of the vulnerabilities we evaluate in this paper are a few years old, and most have some countermeasures available or are even no longer present in the latest hardware; however, we consider wide selections of attack classes that have remained relevant for the better part of a decade since their initial discoveries. Meltdown and MDS-class attacks exploit a fundamental problem with the dependent speculative execution model that all modern CPU architectures employ for its powerful performance advantages. Buffer-clearing mitigations are only capable of plugging holes in this leaky ship one at a time, and there is no reason to believe that every hole has been found or that new designs won't introduce new holes. Similarly, Spectre attacks were introduced by sophisticated branch prediction techniques which are a source of significant performance gains in modern pipelined out-of-order processors. In particular, Spectre-PHT remains an open attack vector that is not mitigated in newer CPUs by either changes in the prediction units or microcode updates; the OS, VMM, or other software must provide protections. Therefore, it is likely that Spectre will remain an issue for software developers in future CPU generations.

7 Related Works

To our knowledge, this work is the first that evaluates a class of attacks in and out of a particular virtual machine platform. Other works have investigated software

---

[6] https://github.com/google/security-research/security/advisories/GHSA-mj4w-6495-6crx.

vulnerabilities in microVMs. Xiao et al. showed that even with the minimal attack surface between a microVM and the host kernel, an attacker from within the VM can trigger host kernel functions and system calls to perform a wide range of attacks, including privilege escalation, performance degradation, and crashing the host [45].

A number of works have focused on efficiently integrating trusted execution environments into MicroVMs or serverless platforms, with implementation methods including Intel SGX [8], Trusted Platform Modules (TPMs) [35], and pure software enclaves [50]. While these environments can harden and verify high-priority code, they can still be vulnerable to microarchitectural attacks. In some cases, the additional microcode and hardware in SGX and TPMs intended to provide isolation even introduce new exploits that strengthen existing attacks [33,43].

8 Conclusions

Cloud technologies constantly shift to meet the needs of their customers. At the same time, CSPs aim to maximize efficiency and profit, which incentivizes serverless CSPs to over-commit available compute resources. This behavior can be disastrous in the context of microarchitectural attacks that exploit shared hardware. In the past few years, the microarchitectural threat landscape changed frequently and rapidly, which makes attack mitigation a challenge, especially because some countermeasures at one system level may open new vulnerabilities at another. Therefore, each system must be considered as a whole.

We showed that the previously recommended countermeasures for the Firecracker VMM were incomplete and insufficient to meet its isolation goals and, with our disclosure to AWS, prompted a revision to the recommendations. Furthermore, many of the tested attack vectors showed leakage while countermeasures where in place. We identified the Medusa cache indexing/block write variant as an attack vector that only works across VMs, i. e. with additional isolation mechanisms in place. Additionally, we showed that disabling SMT–an expensive mitigation technique recommended and performed by AWS–does not fully protect against Medusa variants and Spectre-PHT if the attacker and target threads keep competing for hardware resources of the same physical CPU core. Unfortunately this is inevitably the case in high-density serverless environments. The short lifecycle of serverless functions raises the bar for successful micro-architectural attacks. But first results [51] show that microarchitectural attacks remain an existing threat. Furthermore, processor designs continue to evolve and speculative and out-of-order execution remain important factors in improving performance from generation to generation. So, it is unlikely that we have seen the last of new microarchitectural vulnerabilities, as the recent wave of newly discovered attacks [28,48,51] shows.

Acknowledgments. We thank Amazon Web Services for the discussions and provided feedback. This work was supported by the German Research Foundation (DFG) under Grants No. 439797619 and 456967092, by the German Federal Ministry for Education and Research (BMBF) under Grants SASVI and SILGENTAS, by the National Science Foundation (NSF) under Grant CNS-2026913, and in part by a grant from the Qatar National Research Fund.

Appendix

Required mitigations to protect the host vs. Firecracker victims from MDS attacks. The recommended nosmt mitigation protects against most but not all MDS variants. Experiments on Firecracker v1.0.0, v1.4.0, and v1.5.0 yielded identical results.

Exploit	Details			Bare metal		Firecracker		
	Name	Target buffer	Fault type	nosmt	mds	nosmt(H)	mds(H)	mds(VM)
alignment_write		Fill buffer	Alignment	⊕	⊕	⊕	⊕	✗
pgtable_leak_notsx	RIDL	Fill buffer	Page	✗[b]	✓	✗[b]	✓	✓
ridl_basic		Fill buffer	Page	✓	✗	N/A[c]	N/A[c]	N/A[c]
ridl_invalidpage		Fill buffer	Page	✓	✗	N/A[c]	N/A[c]	N/A[c]
pgtable_leak		Fill buffer	TSX abort*	✓	✗	✓	✗	✗
taa_read	RIDL/TAA	Fill buffer	TSX abort*	✓	✗	✓	✗	✗
taa_basic		Fill buffer	TSX abort*	✓	✗	N/A[c]	N/A[c]	N/A[c]
verw_bypass_l1des	RIDL/TAA	Fill buffer	TSX abort*	✓	✗	✓	✗	✗
loadport	RIDL	Load port	Page	✓	✗	✓	✗	✗
vrs	RIDL/VRS	Store buffer	Page	✓	✗	✓	✗	✗
cpuid_leak	Crosstalk	Fill buffer	Page	✓	✗	N/A[a]	N/A[a]	N/A[a]

Mitigations either prevent (✓) leakage, have no effect (✗), or must be combined (⊕) to be effective.
* Requires TSX.
[a] CPUID instruction is emulated by the VMM and has no microarchitectural effect.
[b] This attack leaks information about pages used in its own thread.
[c] PoCs were modified to run in two processes before they could be tested in the virtual machine. These PoCs did not work on bare metal or in virtual machines when split into two processes.

References

1. Agache, A., et al.: Firecracker: lightweight virtualization for serverless applications. In: NSDI, pp. 419–434. USENIX Association (2020)
2. Amazon Web Services: The Firecracker jailer (2021). f7886197. Accessed 05 July 2024
3. Amazon Web Services: AWS Lambda features (2023). https://aws.amazon.com/lambda/features/. Accessed 05 July 2024
4. Amazon Web Services: Firecracker design (2023). 9c51dc68. Accessed 05 July 2024
5. Amazon Web Services: Production host setup recommendations (2023). 9ddeaf32. accessed 05 July 2024
6. Amazon Web Services: Production host setup recommendations (2024). 8a1719fe. Accessed 05 July 2024
7. Balasubramanian, A., Baranowski, M.S., Burtsev, A., Panda, A., Rakamaric, Z., Ryzhyk, L.: System programming in rust: beyond safety. In: HotOS, pp. 156–161. ACM (2017)

8. Brenner, S., Kapitza, R.: Trust more, serverless. In: SYSTOR, pp. 33–43. ACM (2019)
9. Canella, C., et al.: Fallout: leaking data on meltdown-resistant CPUs. In: CCS, pp. 769–784. ACM (2019)
10. Canella, C., et al.: A systematic evaluation of transient execution attacks and defenses. In: USENIX Security Symposium, pp. 249–266. USENIX Association (2019)
11. Doleželová, M., et al.: Red hat enterprise linux 7 resource management guide–using cgroups to manage system resources on RHEL. Red Hat, Inc (2020). Accessed 05 July 2024
12. Fustos, J., Bechtel, M.G., Yun, H.: SpectreRewind: leaking secrets to past instructions. In: ASHES@CCS, pp. 117–126. ACM (2020)
13. Gruss, D., Lipp, M., Schwarz, M., Fellner, R., Maurice, C., Mangard, S.: KASLR is dead: long live KASLR. In: Bodden, E., Payer, M., Athanasopoulos, E. (eds.) ESSoS 2017. LNCS, vol. 10379, pp. 161–176. Springer, Cham (2017). https://doi.org/10.1007/978-3-319-62105-0_11
14. Gupta, P.: TAA - TSX Asynchronous Abort. The Linux Kernel Organization (2020). https://www.kernel.org/doc/html/latest/admin-guide/hw-vuln/tsx_async_abort.html. Accessed 05 July 2024
15. Hicks, T.: MDS - Microarchitectural Data Sampling. The Linux Kernel Organization (2019). https://www.kernel.org/doc/html/latest/admin-guide/hw-vuln/mds.html. Accessed 05 July 2024
16. Holmes, B., Waterman, J., Williams, D.: KASLR in the age of MicroVMs. In: EuroSys, pp. 149–165. ACM (2022)
17. Horn, J.: Speculative execution, variant 4: speculative store bypass (2018). https://bugs.chromium.org/p/project-zero/issues/detail?id=1528. Accessed 05 July 2024
18. Intel: Speculative Execution Side Channel Mitigations (2018). rev. 3.0
19. Intel: Intel transactional synchronization extensions (Intel TSX) asynchronous abort. Technical report (2019). doc. ID: 758370. Accessed 05 July 2024
20. Intel: Microarchitectural data sampling. Technical report (2019). doc. ID: 758366, ver. 3.0. Accessed 05 July 2024
21. Intel: Vector register sampling. Technical report (2020). doc. ID: 660231. Accessed 05 July 2024
22. Johannesmeyer, B., Koschel, J., Razavi, K., Bos, H., Giuffrida, C.: Kasper: scanning for generalized transient execution gadgets in the linux kernel. In: NDSS. The Internet Society (2022)
23. Khasawneh, K.N., Koruyeh, E.M., Song, C., Evtyushkin, D., Ponomarev, D., Abu-Ghazaleh, N.B.: SafeSpec: banishing the Spectre of a Meltdown with leakage-free speculation. In: DAC, p. 60. ACM (2019)
24. Kiriansky, V., Lebedev, I.A., Amarasinghe, S.P., Devadas, S., Emer, J.S.: DAWG: a defense against cache timing attacks in speculative execution processors. In: MICRO, pp. 974–987. IEEE Computer Society (2018)
25. Kiriansky, V., Waldspurger, C.A.: Speculative buffer overflows: attacks and defenses. CoRR arxiv:1807.03757 (2018)
26. Kocher, P., et al.: Spectre attacks: exploiting speculative execution. In: IEEE Symposium on Security and Privacy, pp. 1–19. IEEE (2019)
27. Koruyeh, E.M., Khasawneh, K.N., Song, C., Abu-Ghazaleh, N.B.: Spectre Returns! speculation attacks using the return stack buffer. In: WOOT @ USENIX Security Symposium. USENIX Association (2018)

28. Li, L., Yavarzadeh, H., Tullsen, D.: Indirector: high-precision branch target injection attacks exploiting the indirect branch predictor. In: USENIX Security Symposium (to appear). USENIX Association (2024)
29. Lipp, M., et al.: Meltdown: reading kernel memory from user space. In: USENIX Security Symposium, pp. 973–990. USENIX Association (2018)
30. Maisuradze, G., Rossow, C.: ret2spec: speculative execution using return stack buffers. In: CCS, pp. 2109–2122. ACM (2018)
31. Marr, D.T., et al.: Hyper-threading technology architecture and microarchitecture. Intel Technol. J. **6**(1), 4–15 (2002)
32. Moghimi, D., Lipp, M., Sunar, B., Schwarz, M.: Medusa: microarchitectural data leakage via automated attack synthesis. In: USENIX Security Symposium, pp. 1427–1444. USENIX Association (2020)
33. Moghimi, D., Sunar, B., Eisenbarth, T., Heninger, N.: TPM-FAIL: TPM meets timing and lattice attacks. In: USENIX Security Symposium, pp. 2057–2073. USENIX Association (2020)
34. Osvik, D.A., Shamir, A., Tromer, E.: Cache attacks and countermeasures: the case of AES. In: Pointcheval, D. (ed.) CT-RSA 2006. LNCS, vol. 3860, pp. 1–20. Springer, Heidelberg (2006). https://doi.org/10.1007/11605805_1
35. Parkegren, A., Veltman, M.: Trust in lightweight virtual machines: integrating TPMs into Firecracker. Chalmers University of Technology, University of Gothenburg, master thesis (2023)
36. Ragab, H., Barberis, E., Bos, H., Giuffrida, C.: Rage against the machine clear: a systematic analysis of machine clears and their implications for transient execution attacks. In: USENIX Security Symposium, pp. 1451–1468. USENIX Association (2021)
37. Rokicki, T., Maurice, C., Botvinnik, M., Oren, Y.: Port contention goes portable: port contention side channels in web browsers. In: AsiaCCS, pp. 1182–1194. ACM (2022)
38. Rokicki, T., Maurice, C., Schwarz, M.: CPU port contention without SMT. In: ESORICS (3). LNCS, vol. 13556, pp. 209–228. Springer, Heidelberg (2022)
39. van Schaik, S., et al.: RIDL: rogue in-flight data load. In: IEEE Symposium on Security and Privacy, pp. 88–105. IEEE (2019)
40. Schwarz, M., et al.: ZombieLoad: cross-privilege-boundary data sampling. In: CCS, pp. 753–768. ACM (2019)
41. Turner, P.: Retpoline: a software construct for preventing branch-target-injection (2018). https://support.google.com/faqs/answer/7625886. Accessed 05 July 2024
42. Van Bulck, J., et al.: LVI: hijacking transient execution through microarchitectural load value injection. In: IEEE Symposium on Security and Privacy, pp. 54–72. IEEE (2020)
43. Van Bulck, J., Piessens, F., Strackx, R.: SGX-step: a practical attack framework for precise enclave execution control. In: SysTEX@SOSP, pp. 4:1–4:6. ACM (2017)
44. Wikner, J., Razavi, K.: RETBLEED: arbitrary speculative code execution with return instructions. In: USENIX Security Symposium, pp. 3825–3842. USENIX Association (2022)
45. Xiao, J., et al.: Attacks are forwarded: breaking the isolation of microVM-based containers through operation forwarding. In: USENIX Security Symposium, pp. 7517–7534. USENIX Association (2023)
46. Yan, M., Choi, J., Skarlatos, D., Morrison, A., Fletcher, C.W., Torrellas, J.: InvisiSpec: making speculative execution invisible in the cache hierarchy. In: MICRO, pp. 428–441. IEEE Computer Society (2018)

47. Yarom, Y., Falkner, K.: FLUSH+RELOAD: a high resolution, low noise, L3 cache side-channel attack. In: USENIX Security Symposium, pp. 719–732. USENIX Association (2014)
48. Yavarzadeh, H., et al.: Pathfinder: high-resolution control-flow attacks exploiting the conditional branch predictor. In: ASPLOS (3), pp. 770–784. ACM (2024)
49. Young, E.G., Zhu, P., Caraza-Harter, T., Arpaci-Dusseau, A.C., Arpaci-Dusseau, R.H.: The true cost of containing: a gVisor case study. In: HotCloud. USENIX Association (2019)
50. Zhao, S., Xu, P., Chen, G., Zhang, M., Zhang, Y., Lin, Z.: Reusable enclaves for confidential serverless computing. In: USENIX Security Symposium, pp. 4015–4032. USENIX Association (2023)
51. Zhao, Z.N., Morrison, A., Fletcher, C.W., Torrellas, J.: Last-level cache side-channel attacks are feasible in the modern public cloud. In: ASPLOS (2), pp. 582–600. ACM (2024)

An OS Support for Tamper-Resistant Software Execution Using Empty Interruptions

Soma Kato[1], Yui Koyanagi[2], and Tomoaki Ukezono[1](✉)

[1] EECS, Fukuoka University, 8-19-1, Nanakuma, Jhonan-ku, Fukuoka-City, Fukuoka, Japan
{tl211246,tukezo}@cis.fukuoka-u.ac.jp
[2] Graduate School of Engineering, Fukuoka University, 8-19-1, Nanakuma, Jhonan-ku, Fukuoka-City, Fukuoka, Japan
td232006@cis.fukuoka-u.ac.jp

Abstract. Side-channel attacks are persistent vulnerabilities that exploit physical information surrounding a computer system, such as electromagnetic radiation, power consumption, and response time, to leak confidential information from within the system. The observed physical information is input into statistical analysis programs, or characteristics are discovered from processing steps within the computer system, allowing for the extraction of confidential information We propose a mechanism within the operating system to disrupt the power consumption waveforms, preventing the statistical analysis programs of power analysis attacks from functioning effectively. By implementing an API in the operating system to trigger empty interrupt processing solely for transforming the power consumption waveforms used in program sections handling confidential data, we aim to enhance tamper-resistance. In our evaluation, we demonstrated that the empty interrupt processing can effectively prevent the leakage of a 128-bit AES secret key, even with the analysis of one million power consumption waveforms, nearly entirely.

Keywords: Side-Channel Attack · Power Analysis Attack · OS · Interruption

1 Introduction

A side channel refers to hints in modern cryptography, indicating electromagnetic waves, information of power consumption, or processor response times emitted during cryptographic processing, as shown in Fig. 1. Attacks on encryption using side channels, known as side-channel attack (SCA), can easily render the security based on robust mathematical foundations ineffective [1].

In the Society 5.0 era, it is easy to imagine that attackers could steal one of a huge number of communicating terminal devices, such as IoT edge devices,

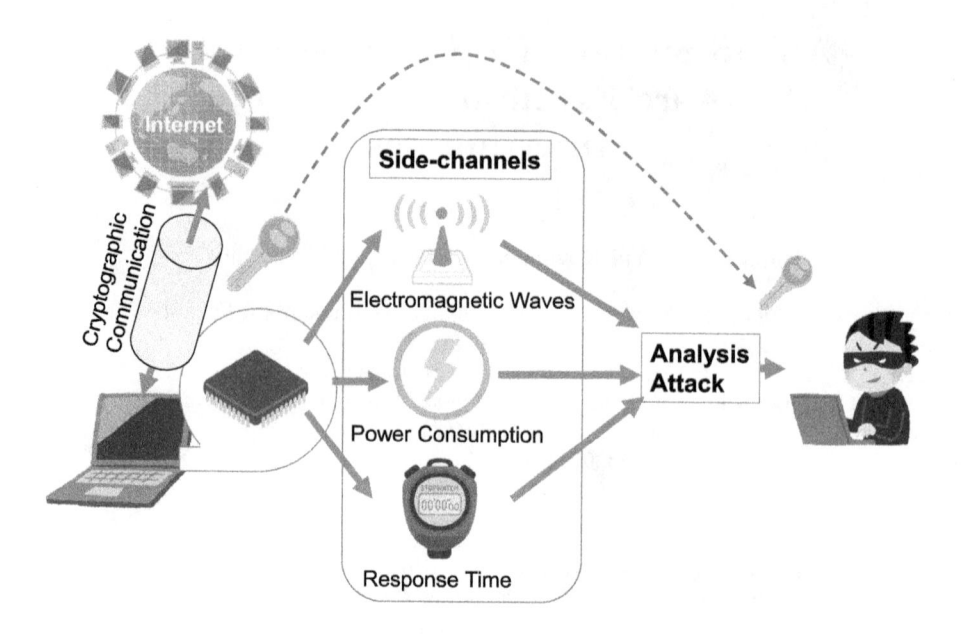

Fig. 1. Side-channel Attacks.

involved in Internet communications, enabling them to acquire information of side channels. Moreover, even if attackers cannot directly and physically observe side channels from devices, SCAs are still possible remotely through the Internet by peeking information form sensors. For instance, there have been reports of successful SCAs remotely targeting Amazon EC2 F1 instance that is provided as high-performance cloud computing resources by observing the voltage drops of a power supply unit as a side channel of power consumption [2,3]. The aforementioned researches successfully leaked the AES secret key within a remote computational host using a type of power analysis attack known as correlation power analysis (CPA [4]) configuring the tenant FPGAs as sensors. Thus, since the threat of SCAs against cryptographic systems was first proposed over 20 years ago, concerns about their vulnerability have been increasing day by day. However, a definitive solution has not yet been demonstrated, leaving Internet communication constantly exposed to danger.

Various countermeasures against side-channel attacks have been proposed at different layers of cryptographic implementations. Particularly, there are numerous proposals to mitigate the threat posed by side-channel attacks exploiting power consumption, which is considered a realistic threat. A prominent measure is the design of tamper-resistant circuits. This approach has been widely proposed as a countermeasure because integrated circuit chips can estimate the input values of circuits through the dynamic power consumption of transistors associated with changes in input values, which serves as a side channel [5–9]. However, these techniques are countermeasures permitted only to hardware designers who can design cryptographic systems as dedicated circuits. Additionally, it has been reported that these measures require an overhead of circuit implementation area ranging from two to ten times the original area, making them not easily adoptable [10].

At the software level, there are countermeasures to power analysis attacks on AES. These countermeasures are categorized into two types: masking [13,14] and hiding [11,12]. Masking in software masks the side channel of confidential data such as secret keys or round keys by executing random value operations when processing the intermediate values. This can be achieved by incorporating random operations into the algorithm that are not essential for the original cryptographic processing, thereby trading off execution speed for security. Such algorithmic modifications achieve countermeasures by influencing the amplitude domain of power consumption waveforms used in SCAs. Hiding reduces the correlation of targeted values at specific points in time by dispersing the occurrence of critical operations and intermediate values, thereby thwarting power analysis attacks. Dummy operation insertion and operation shuffling are effective techniques for implementing this countermeasure algorithmically. For example, it has been confirmed that simply inserting a random number of no-operation instructions into the algorithm enhances tamper-resistance. While these methods offer the advantage of relatively straightforward modification of the algorithm and ease of implementation, similar to masking, they come with the trade-off of decreased execution performance.

We propose a runtime hiding technique by the operating system (OS), rather than algorithmic modifications. Our approach applies countermeasures focusing on the time domain to existing binary code, eliminating or minimizing the need for program modifications for countermeasures of side-channel attack. We automate the hiding through the OS, activating it during process creation or system call API invocation, allowing cryptographic processing programs to obtain the effect of hiding automatically or semi-automatically. Our proposal leverages interrupts managed and controlled by the operating system, particularly by inducing frequent occurrences of non-significant interrupts when processing critical confidential data, achieving time-domain side-channel countermeasures. This paper evaluates the tamper-resistance of countermeasures using OS-generated interrupts and confirms their effectiveness. The contribution of this paper is to demonstrate that with the combination of a general-purpose microcomputer and operating systems, sufficiently fine-grained interrupt handling can disrupt the channel within the main cryptographic processing, thereby confirming that even AES programs without any specific countermeasures can be endowed with sufficiently high tamper-resistance.

2 Power Analysis Attacks

As one of the SCAs, there exists a power analysis attack. The power analysis attack infers secret keys of the cryptographic system from the dynamic power consumption required by the transistor switches. SCAs on power consumption are relatively potent as they have less noise compared to the electromagnetic side channels. This paper aims to enhance the tamper-resistance by the OS. We employ power analysis attacks to evaluate our proposed function, assessing how effectively it mitigates such attacks. In this section, we demonstrate the acquisition method of power consumption waveforms for power analysis attacks and the analysis of acquired waveforms, focusing on correlation power analysis, in our attack evaluation.

2.1 Correcting Power Traces

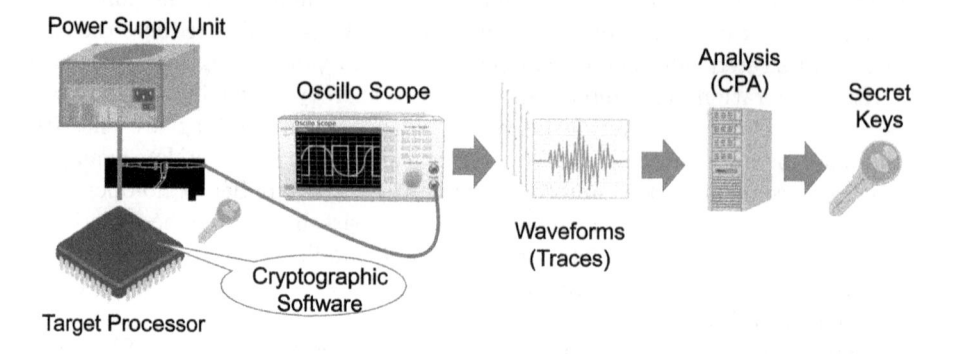

Fig. 2. Power Analysis Attacks.

Figure 2 illustrates an overview of the power analysis attack. While there are attack methods to remotely acquire power consumption waveforms as in previous studies, in our evaluation, we acquire the power consumption waveform using an oscilloscope. To examine power consumption, it is necessary to examine the current sent from the power supply unit. Therefore, in this study, by acquiring the voltage of the shunt resistor on the board where the target processor is installed with an oscilloscope, we examine the change in current and use it as the power consumption waveform. In power analysis attacks, the focus is on the change in power consumption rather than the absolute value of power consumption, making this measurement method sufficient. The waveform obtained from this measurement is commonly referred to as a trace. Traces are captured multiple times and serve as input for statistical analysis by computers. This statistical analysis is explained in the following subsection. Finally, this analysis can infer the secret key.

2.2 Correcting Power Traces

The 'analysis' depicted in Fig. 2 is carried out by computer programs, resulting in the output of the predicted cryptographic system key. There are generally two types of analysis: waveform-based analysis and statistical analysis. Waveform-based analysis focuses on the shape of the waveform and includes methods such as Simple Power Analysis (SPA) [1] and techniques utilizing deep learning. As for statistical analysis, a representative attack is correlation power analysis (CPA) [4]. SPA requires visual inspection and deep knowledge of the individual cryptographic algorithms for analysis. Deep learning can achieve high-accuracy attacks; however, it requires preparing training data for each subtle difference in boards or chips [15,16], posing computational challenges during actual attacks. Therefore, the most accessible method for power analysis attacks is CPA. CPA can accommodate subtle differences in board and chip implementations, enabling attacks with a single analysis algorithm. CPA uses Pearson's correlation coefficient to guess the encryption key. Pearson's correlation coefficient is determined by two sets of data. One is the value of power consumption W_i measured by an oscilloscope. The other is the value of Hamming distance $H_{i,K}$ which is calculated by 8-bit plaintext P_i and 8-bit estimated partial round key K. It is given by the following formula:

$$H_{i,K} = h(P_i \oplus K) \tag{1}$$

$h(P_i \oplus K)$ represents the Hamming weight of $(P_i \oplus K)$, the XORed value of P and K. The Hamming weight is the number of 1 s in a binary number. The value range is from 0 to 8, since $(P \oplus K)$ is 8-bit. The Pearson's correlation coefficient calculated from W_i and $H_{i,K}$ is given by the following formula:

$$\rho_{WH_K} = \frac{\frac{\sum_{i=0}^{N-1} W_i H_{i,K}}{N} - \frac{\sum_{i=0}^{N-1} W_i \sum_{i=0}^{N-1} H_{i,K}}{N^2}}{\sqrt{\frac{\sum_{i=0}^{N-1} W_i^2}{N} - (\frac{\sum_{i=0}^{N-1} W_i}{N})^2} \sqrt{\frac{\sum_{i=0}^{N-1} H_{i,K}^2}{N} - (\frac{\sum_{i=0}^{N-1} H_{i,K}}{N})^2}} \tag{2}$$

N represents the number of traces, W_i the power consumptions at i-th trace, and $H_{i,K}$ the value of Hamming weight at the i-th trace. $Cov(W, H_K)$ represents the covariances of W and H_K, σ_W and σ_{H_K} their respective standard deviations, and ρ_{WH_K} the correlation coefficients of W and H_K. The closest ρ_{WH_K} to the absolute value 1 represents the correlation coefficient when partial round key K is used. This operation to find the highest correlation coefficient is performed 256 times for each estimated partial round key. Then, the operation to find the partial round key is performed 16 more times to guess all partial round keys.

3 Tamper-Resistant Software Execution by OSs

In this paper, we propose countermeasures against CPA supported by OSs. Previous research has focused on improving tamper-resistance by modifying the circuits of cryptographic systems or algorithms to transform traces. However, circuit modifications for countermeasures entail high introduction costs, and algorithm modifications, in addition to the human cost of reprogramming, are challenging to apply to systems already operated as legacy program binaries. The effort to protect cryptographic system secret keys through an OS functionality for tamper-resistance is unprecedented, making our proposal and efforts novel in this research. By introducing an OS with our proposed technique into the system, it becomes possible to safely execute circuits and program binaries without countermeasures and operate the system.

We have identified a method to disrupt the statistical analysis of CPA by focusing on Formula 2. Formula 2 represents the method for calculating the correlation coefficient, where a value close to 1 indicates a high correlation with the predicted key, and a value close to 0 indicates a low correlation. Wi is used in this calculation, where i represents the sampling time of the waveforms (traces). In other words, by stretching or compressing the traces containing features and shifting the time points of i through some method, if we can intentionally approach the correlation coefficient of Formula 2 to near 0, we can enhance the tamper-resistance during software execution.

Based on the above considerations, we adopt interrupt handling managed by OSs to introduce elongation into the traces. While traces are being collected, the OS intentionally extends the time of cryptographic processing by executing interrupt handling, thereby elongating the traces. During this interruption handling, the handler does not perform any meaningful operation but remains idle. However, processes related to interrupt acceptance, such as interrupt permission control and register saving, are still carried out. We refer to such meaningless interrupt handling as empty interruption.

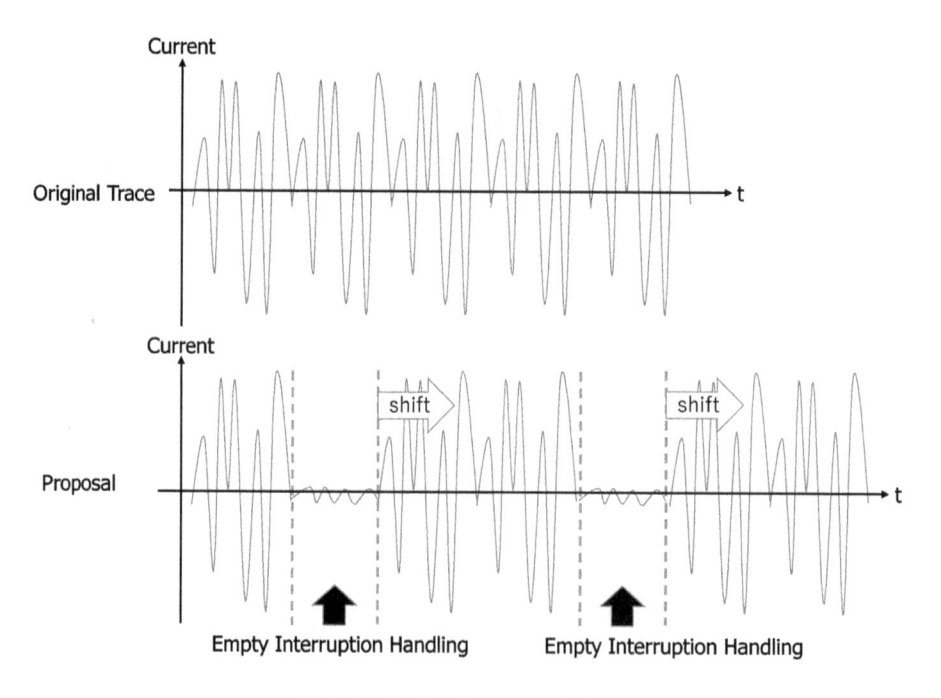

Fig. 3. Desired trace variation.

Figure 3 illustrates the desired trace variation targeted by our proposal. Power consumption traces, observable with the time axis as changes in supply current, are obtained by measuring the voltage across the shunt resistor of the power supply using an oscilloscope in an actual computer. According to Ohm's law, dividing the voltage across the shunt resistor by its resistance yields the current value. Power analysis attacks infer values within digital circuits by analyzing characteristics of these current variations. Our method disrupts this analysis by shifting these traces in the time domain. Interruptions occur during idle times, inserting consumption currents (shown in the figure) between cryptographic processing, effectively shifting the timeline of the traces. These interruptions, occurring at intervals different from the start cycle of repeated cryptographic operations, do not align consistently, varying each time cryptographic processing repeats. This shifting due to interruptions occurs evenly across a large number of traces, efficiently disrupting CPA.

An important aspect when using empty interrupts for the OS to elongate traces is the timing of interrupt occurrences. If interrupts occur at the same time consistently during cryptographic processing, it does not interfere with CPA. Rather, the handling of empty interrupts inserted into the traces should be evenly distributed at various timings within each trace. Therefore, we propose a method of generating empty interruptions using timer interrupts, where empty interruptions are triggered by periodic interrupts. With this proposal, if the interrupt period is smaller than the period of repeatedly executed cryptographic processing, interrupts will occur without necessarily coinciding with the same timing during cryptographic processing. Instead, interrupt occurrences will gradually shift during cryptographic processing. In our experiments, we gradually shortened the period of timer interrupts, starting from the point where improvements in tamper-resistance were observed, in order to evaluate to what extent tamper-resistance enhancement could be achieved at maximum.

Naturally, our proposed technique introduces idle computations into cryptographic processing, thus having the drawback of reducing the throughput of encryption and decryption operations. This drawback creates a trade-off relationship with the improvement of tamper-resistance. However, such trade-off relationships also exist in tamper-resistance improvement methods other than our proposed method. For example, WDDL [6], a tamper-resistance improvement method through hardware modifications, halves execution efficiency by adding precharge cycles, and algorithm modification methods similarly result in unnecessary increases in the number of execution instructions, as with our method. In our evaluation, in order to confirm whether the execution time overhead of our proposed method falls within a realistic range, we evaluate not only tamper-resistance but also the execution time overhead according to the interrupt period.

Additionally, if programmers are allowed to modify the program, there is no need to continuously generate empty interrupts during process execution. Instead, they can be generated only in the processing portion handling confidential information of cryptographic processing through ON/OFF control via system calls that are provided by the OS.

Although this is somewhat tangential to the essence of this paper, a cunning attacker may attempt to detect shifts in traces caused by interruptions. In other words, if a shift caused by an interrupt can be clearly detected within the traces, advanced attacking methods may be considered where the attacker removes the shifted portions from the traces in advance and inputs them into the analysis attack. However, the primary goal of our evaluation in this paper is to understand how shifts caused by interrupts affect the resistance against side-channel attacks, and we do not consider whether the attacker has any attacking methods to circumvent this. Furthermore, this issue can be easily resolved by using interrupt handlers that change power consumption with each interruption, rather than using empty interruption. Such handlers can use random numbers to execute power-intensive arithmetic operations (such as division emulation), thereby affecting the amplitude domain and making it difficult to detect the shifts within the traces.

4 Evaluation

4.1 Experimental Setup

We selected the ATxmega128D4 [17] as the target CPU for our attack evaluation. The Atmel ATxmega128D4 is an 8-bit microcontroller equipped with timer interrupts. Choosing a microcontroller as the evaluation target allows us to maintain consistent conditions when collecting traces repeatedly, as features like branch predictors and cache memory in more advanced CPUs can induce variations in the execution time of cryptographic processing based on the pre-execution state of the CPU. This ensures that only the effects of our proposed method are demonstrated.

In our evaluation, 128-bit AES is executed on the ATxmega128D4. Additionally, we implemented the empty interruption handler explained in Sect. 3 to evaluate our proposed method. The empty interrupt handler was implemented as a function of the operating system without any relation to the AES source code. In this experiment, we did not write a fully implemented operating system code that manages all computational resources. Instead, we limited ourselves to implementing the trap vector and a few handlers necessary to run a single program (AES). Among these handlers, in addition to the empty interruptions proposed in this paper, there is also a I/O (UART) driver for sending and receiving plaintext and ciphertext. The ATxmega128D4 features fine-grained timer interrupt functionality, allowing interrupts to be set as frequently as every clock cycle. Timer interrupts are driven using a counter per clock cycle, generating an interrupt when the counter reaches a value specified by the programmer. In our evaluation, we start with interrupt settings every 240 clock cycles, where the effect of tamper-resistance enhancement begins, and gradually decrease by 16 clock cycles until conducting attack evaluations at the practical limit of 144 clock cycles, as determined by actual measurements. This is because the settings timer interrupts below 144 clock cycles in AES encryption processing makes it practically impossible to measure due to the realistic overhead.

One might think that periodic interruptions could become a vulnerability in the countermeasure if the attacker becomes aware of their period. However, this concern can be considered unfounded. First, if the attacker observes from outside the chip, they cannot know the exact times at which interruptions that complete processing internally occur. Even if the countermeasure involves periodic processing, the attacker cannot accurately determine when the first interruption is triggered. Naturally, if the attacker cannot know the timing at which all interruptions occur, they cannot refine their analysis methods for attacking. This becomes even more difficult due to the variations in the amplitude domain implemented for each interrupt, as mentioned in the previous section, making it harder to observe from the shapes of traces.

For the comparative evaluation of proposed methods, two implementations of 128-bit AES were evaluated: one with no countermeasures, and another with tamper-resistant modifications known as dummy operations [18]. Both the proposed and comparison methods used the original AES source code as released by ChipWhisperer project [19].The dummy operation was evaluated in the referenced paper [18], adopting the Combined Function Argument approach with the lowest distinguishment success rate, and applied to the AES source code.

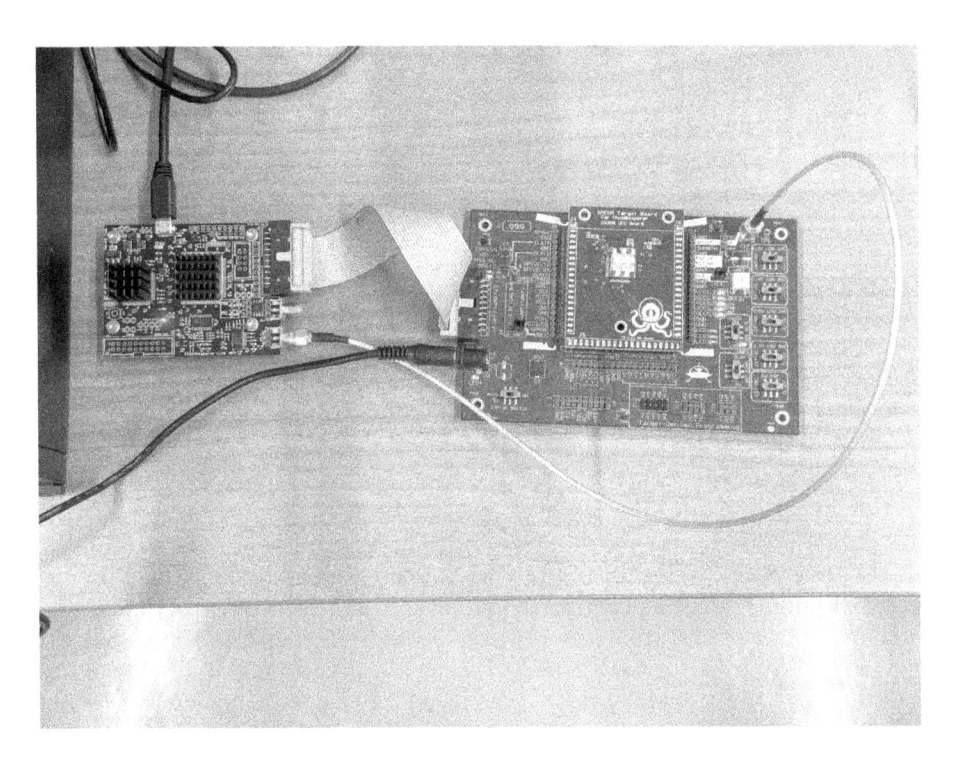

Fig. 4. Experimental Environment.

Figure 4 shows the experimental environment. The red board represents the power supplying board, from which the power consumption waveform (trace) is obtained by measuring the power current from the probe point of the shunt resistor in the upper right corner. The blue board installed in the center of the power board is the target board equipped with the ATxmega128D4 chip. The black board on the left side of the figure is a USB oscilloscope. Through this oscilloscope, plaintext is transmitted to the ATxmega128D4 from the flat cable and traces are collected until receiving the ciphertext. In our evaluation, we collected 1 million traces for each CPA. Including the execution time of CPA with 1 million traces, it takes approximately 2 days for one attack. The CPA program used in this paper was sourced from C. O'Flynn and is publicly available as open-source [19]. This CPA program can be executed for analysis in Python-executable environment.

4.2 Attack Results

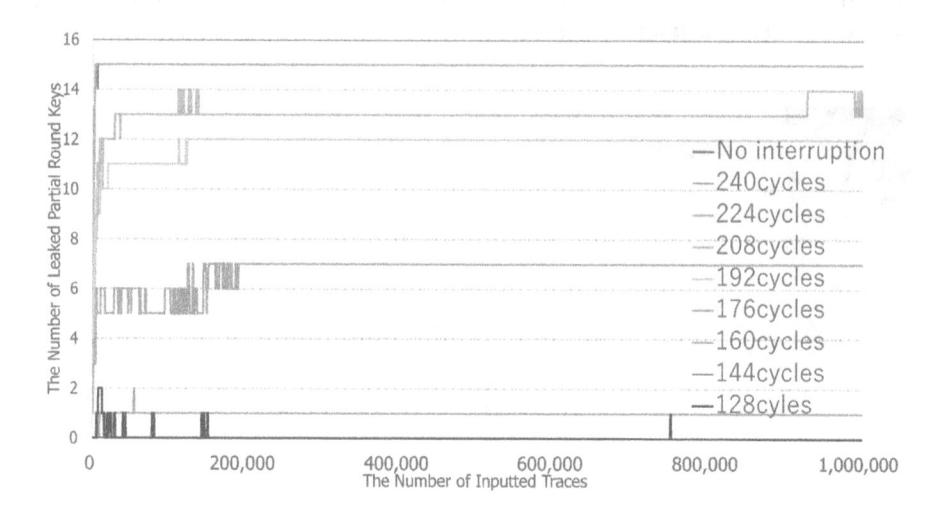

Fig. 5. Attack Results.

Figure 5 illustrates the results of the attack. The vertical axis of the figure represents the number of leaked partial round keys. In 128-bit AES, each round uses a round key of 128 bits (16 bytes). CPA predicts these round keys byte by byte. A portion of this 1-byte key is referred to as a partial round key. When all 16 bytes of the round key are obtained, the secret key can be uniquely determined through the inverse calculation of the key generation algorithm. The horizontal axis of Fig. 5 represents the number of traces input to CPA. Generally, the more input traces CPA has, the higher the probability of correctly predicting the key. Therefore, this graph should essentially show an upward trend. From the results of the attack, it is evident that while the 'No interruption' approach, which lacks countermeasures, quickly leaked all partial round keys, the number of leaked partial round keys decreased with all proposed methods set at or below 240 clock cycles, indicating an improvement in tamper-resistance. Furthermore, with 144 clock cycles, it was confirmed that hardly any keys leaked out of the attack with 1 million traces. This represents a remarkable level of security enhancement in environments without side-channel attack countermeasures at both the circuit and algorithm levels. Therefore, the effectiveness of tamper-resistance enhancement through empty interrupts has been confirmed.

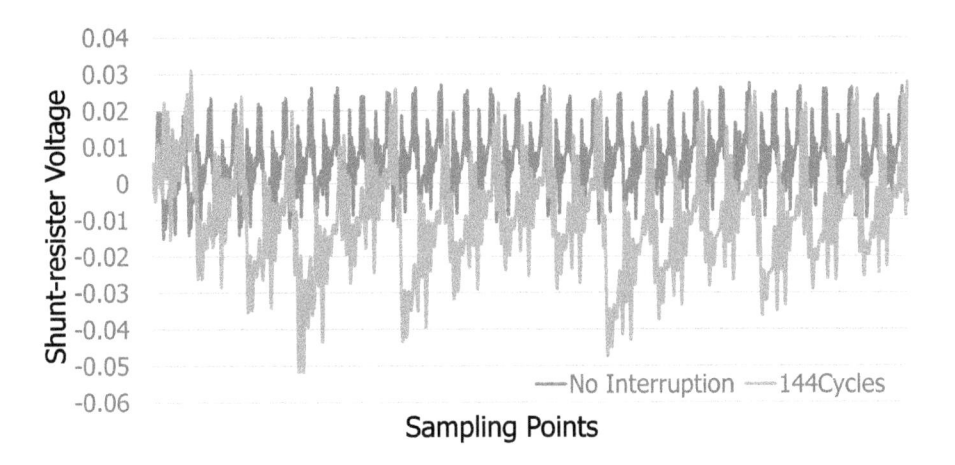

Fig. 6. Comparison of Shapes of Traces.

Figure 6 illustrates the shape of the traces actually measured. The vertical axis represents the voltage value of the shunt resistor, which is the power consumption. The horizontal axis represents the sampling points, indicating the passage of time. A clear change in shape can be observed when comparing 'No interruption' with 144 Cycles. Notably, it is not the amplitude but the period of the waveform that stands out. It is evident that the peaks of the power consumption waveform are significantly shifted in time, and this temporal shift is a factor disrupting the analysis of CPA.

Figure 7 shows a comparison of averages per sampling point using 5,000 traces collected in the measurement of CPA attack. As evident from the figure, the proposed method at 144 cycles shows smaller absolute average values and reduced amplitude. This is because the distinctive undulations observed in the graph in Fig. 5 were influenced by the oscillations inherent to the proposed method. These temporal fluctuations in trace alignment are the most significant contributing factor in disrupting CPA analysis.

4.3 Comparing and Analyzing Tamper-Resistance

From Fig. 5, it became apparent that our proposed method exhibits sufficient tamper-resistance even with analysis inputs of 1 million traces at 128 cycles

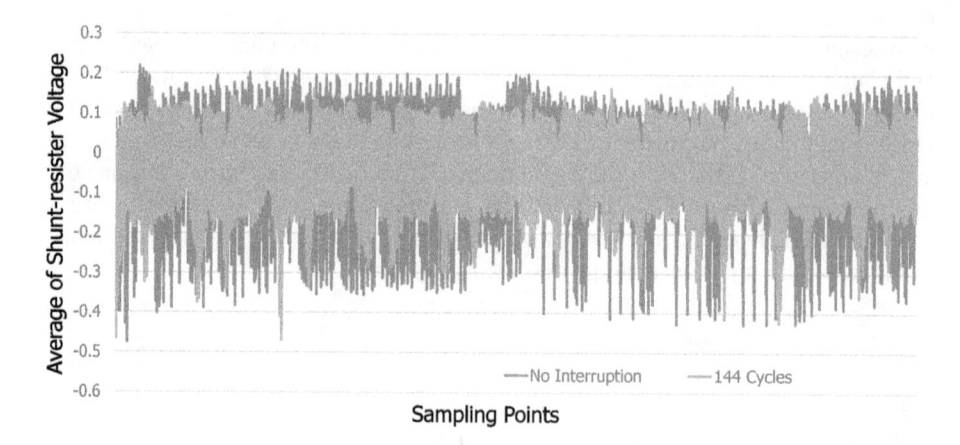

Fig. 7. Comparison of Average of Traces.

and 144 cycles. However, to adequately assess its tamper-resistance compared to other software-based methods [18], we must make comparisons. Therefore, we chose the dummy operation method as a comparative benchmark, which is a software-based tamper-resistance enhancement technique. Dummy operation involves modifying the AES program by adding unnecessary calls to the S-box function. It should be noted that our method does not require modification of the AES program. Thus, while not directly comparable due to differing approaches, we compare them as software-based methods involving execution time variations. According to the attack evaluation results, similar to our method at 144 cycles with 1 million traces, the dummy operation method did not leak any partial round keys. For comparison and analysis, we present the PGE (Partial Guessing Entorpy) showing the differences in security performance other than key leakage in Figs. 8, 9, and 10.

The PGE in Figs. 8, 9, and 10 indicates the ranking of correct partial round keys from 0 to 15 based on their recognition as important keys by CPA. Therefore, higher legends for each partial round key imply higher tamper-resistance. Our proposed method shows significant fluctuation in the predicted importance of each correct partial round key. Comparing Figs. 8 and 9, it is evident that as the cycle count decreases, the amplitude of fluctuations increases. On the other hand, the dummy operation used for comparison shows legends with extremely low PGE and almost no noticeable fluctuations. This is because the analysis results converge without being misled by predictions of dummy partial round key inputs. From these analysis results, it is evident that both our method and the comparison method exhibit sufficient tamper-resistance, despite their approaches being entirely different.

Since the proposed method and the comparison method represent different approaches to enhancing tamper-resistance, they can be combined to reinforce security measures. Figure 11 illustrates the PGE for the hybrid approach, where the proposed method configures at 144 cycles. As evident from the figure, the

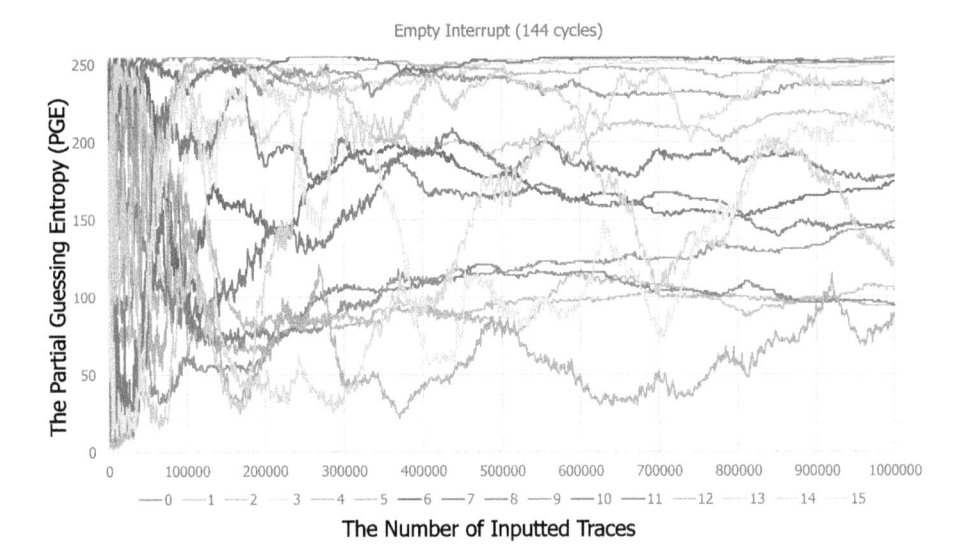

Fig. 8. PGE of 144 cycles of Empty Interrupt.

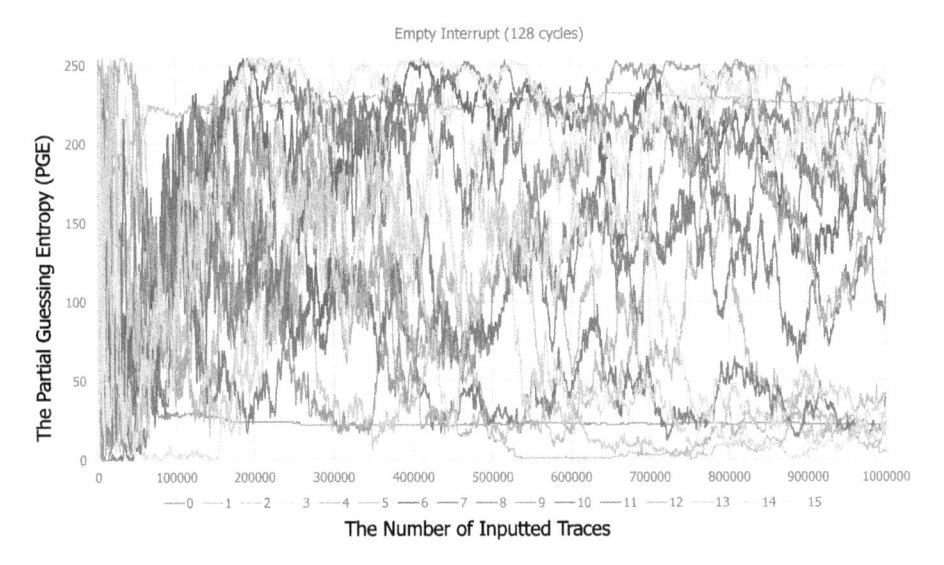

Fig. 9. PGE of 128 cycles of Empty Interrupt.

hybrid approach combines characteristics from both methods simultaneously. One advantageous aspect of this hybrid approach is that even if misleading dummy partial round keys induced by dummy operations were leaked to attackers, our method consistently varies predictions, thereby complicating analysis for potential attacks.

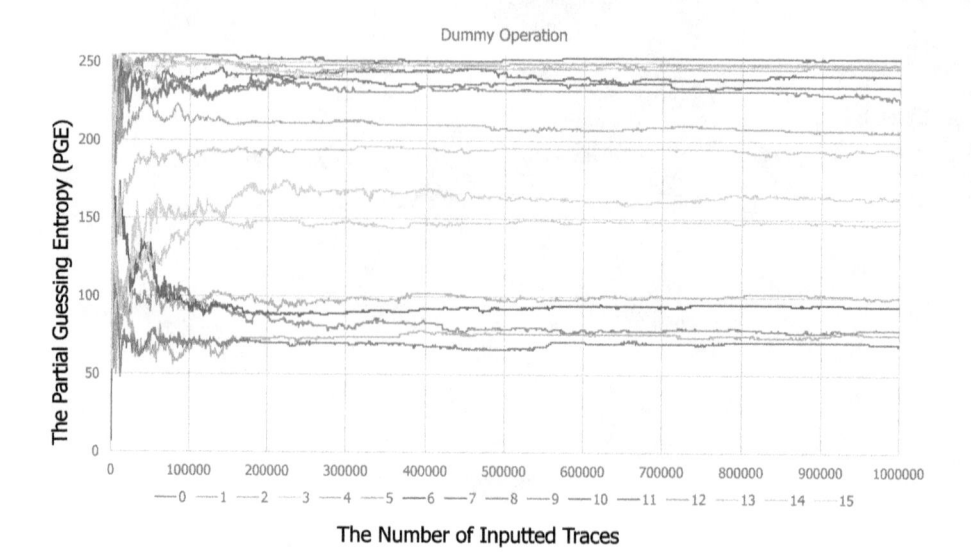

Fig. 10. PGE of Dummy Operation.

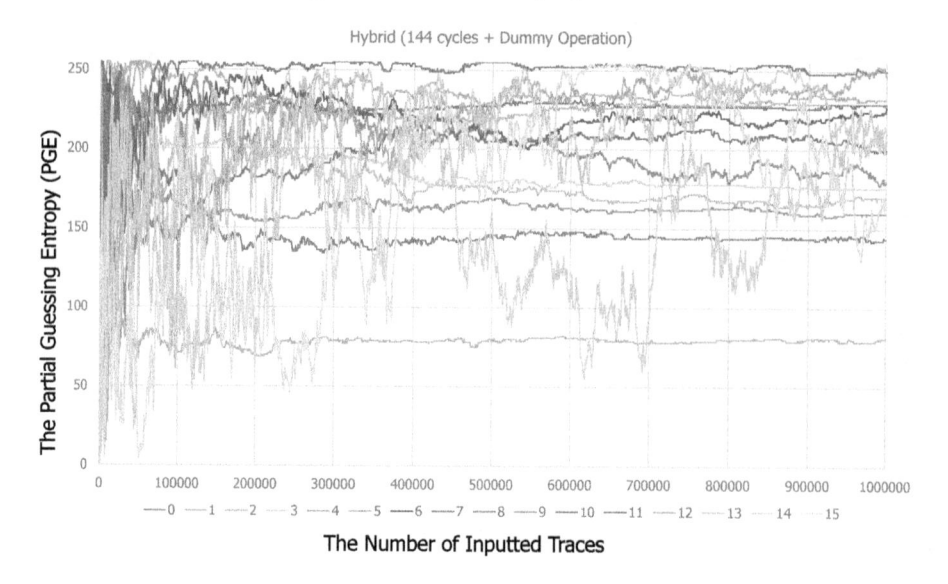

Fig. 11. Hybrid method of Empty Interrupt (144 cycles) and Dummy Operation.

4.4 Evaluation of Execution Time Overhead

Figure 12 illustrates the increase in the average execution time of AES due to empty interruptions, dummy operation, and hybrid method. This is the average time from the start to the end of trace collection for 1 million traces. It was confirmed that the execution time increased as the interrupt period decreased

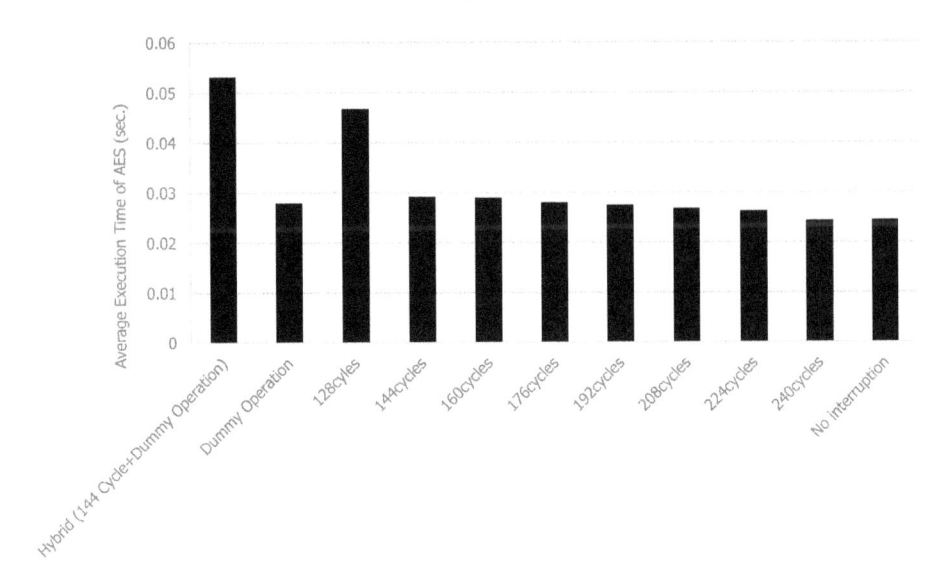

Fig. 12. Overheads of Software Execution.

from 'No interruption'. This is attributed to the increase in the number of execution instructions resulting from the insertion of empty interruption handling in the execution of the AES program. It was observed that 'No Interruption' took 0.02437 s, while 144 cycles, which showed the highest tamper-resistance in the attack evaluation in Fig. 5, took 0.02907 s. This indicates an approximately 19% increase in execution time. On the other hand, reducing the clock cycle period by one step to 128 cycles showed an 85% increase in execution time. This rapid increase in execution time continues even with further reduction in the clock cycle period. Therefore, it can be concluded that up to 144 cycles is reasonable in the evaluation environment of this paper. Considering that the countermeasure of WDDL [6], which involves the most labor-intensive hardware redesign, requires twice the execution time, it can be concluded that the trade-off in execution time increase of our proposed method is reasonable.

On the other hand, the overhead of the dummy operation method used as a comparative measure of tamper-resistance equaled that of 176 cycles. Based solely on this result, it may appear that the tamper-resistance performance against overhead favors the dummy operation method. However, it is important to recall that despite both being software-based methods for enhancing tamper-resistance, the proposed method employs a different approach. Therefore, combining dummy operation with the proposed method could achieve stronger security. However, as shown in evaluation of Fig. 12, the hybrid approach resulted in an average execution time that doubled compared to no countermeasures. This overhead is not negligible, so the applicability of the hybrid method depends on how much system designers are willing to tolerate AES communication speed reductions to enhance tamper-resistance. This consideration can influence the feasibility of implementing the hybrid method.

5 Conclusion

In this paper, we propose a side-channel protection method using empty interrupts provided by the OSs to enhance tamper-resistance, utilizing both unprotected circuitry and cryptographic program binaries. Our proposed method allows for easy enhancement of tamper-resistance without the need for circuit or algorithm modifications. In our evaluation using the ATxmega128D4 CPU and AES, our approach has been shown to effectively mitigate secret key leakage from power analysis attacks such as CPA. Furthermore, the increase in execution time, which is the trade-off, was found to be approximately 19%, demonstrating a realistically acceptable overhead.

Acknowledgments. This work was supported by JSPS KAKENHI Grant Number 24K14958, and by funding from Fukuoka University (Grant No. GR2410).

References

1. Kocher, P., Jaffe, J., Jun, B.: Differential power analysis. In: Wiener, M. (ed.) CRYPTO 1999. LNCS, vol. 1666, pp. 388–397. Springer, Heidelberg (1999). https://doi.org/10.1007/3-540-48405-1_25
2. Glamocanin, O., Coulon, L., Regazzoni, F., Stojilovic, M.: Are cloud FPGAs really vulnerable to power analysis attacks? In: Proceedings of of 2020 Design, Automation and Test in Europe Conference and Exhibition (DATE 2020), pp. 1007–1010 (2020)
3. Ramesh, C., et al.: FPGA side channel attacks without physical access. In: Proceedings of of IEEE 26th Annual International Symposium on Field-Programmable Custom Computing Machines, pp.45–52 (2018)
4. Brier, E., Clavier, C., Olivier, F.: Correlation power analysis with a leakage model. In: Joye, M., Quisquater, J.-J. (eds.) CHES 2004. LNCS, vol. 3156, pp. 16–29. Springer, Heidelberg (2004). https://doi.org/10.1007/978-3-540-28632-5_2
5. Tiri, K., Verbauwhede, I.: A logic level design methodology for a secure DPA resistant ASIC or FPGA implementation. In: Proceedings of Design, Automation and Test in Europe Conference and Exhibition (DATE2004), pp. 246–251 (2004)
6. Tiri, K., et al.: Prototype IC with WDDL and differential routing – DPA resistance assessment. In: Rao, J.R., Sunar, B. (eds.) CHES 2005. LNCS, vol. 3659, pp. 354–365. Springer, Heidelberg (2005). https://doi.org/10.1007/11545262_26
7. Popp, T., Mangard, S.: Masked dual-rail pre-charge logic: DPA-resistance without routing constraints. In: Rao, J.R., Sunar, B. (eds.) CHES 2005. LNCS, vol. 3659, pp. 172–186. Springer, Heidelberg (2005). https://doi.org/10.1007/11545262_13
8. Trichina, E.: Combinational Logic Design for AES SubByte Transformation on Masked Data. Cryptology ePrint Archive, 2003/236 (2003)
9. Nikova, S., Rechberger, C., Rijmen, V.: Threshold implementations against side-channel attacks and glitches. In: Ning, P., Qing, S., Li, N. (eds.) ICICS 2006. LNCS, vol. 4307, pp. 529–545. Springer, Heidelberg (2006). https://doi.org/10.1007/11935308_38

10. Koyanagi, Y., Ukezono, T.: A cost-sensitive and simple masking design for side-channels. In: Proceedings of 2023 IEEE Region 10 Technical Conference (TENCON 2023), pp. 731–736 (2023)
11. Herbst, C., Oswald, E., Mangard, S.: An AES smart card implementation resistant to power analysis attacks. In: Zhou, J., Yung, M., Bao, F. (eds.) ACNS 2006. LNCS, vol. 3989, pp. 239–252. Springer, Heidelberg (2006). https://doi.org/10.1007/11767480_16
12. Itoh, K., Takenaka, M., Torii, N.: DPA countermeasure based on the "masking method". In: Kim, K. (ed.) ICISC 2001. LNCS, vol. 2288, pp. 440–456. Springer, Heidelberg (2002). https://doi.org/10.1007/3-540-45861-1_33
13. Chari, S., Jutla, C.S., Rao, J.R., Rohatgi, P.: Towards sound approaches to counteract power-analysis attacks. In: Wiener, M. (ed.) CRYPTO 1999. LNCS, vol. 1666, pp. 398–412. Springer, Heidelberg (1999). https://doi.org/10.1007/3-540-48405-1_26
14. Clavier, C., Coron, J.-S., Dabbous, N.: Differential power analysis in the presence of hardware countermeasures. In: Koç, Ç.K., Paar, C. (eds.) CHES 2000. LNCS, vol. 1965, pp. 252–263. Springer, Heidelberg (2000). https://doi.org/10.1007/3-540-44499-8_20
15. Das, D., et al.: X-deepsca: cross-device deep learning side channel attack. In: Proceedings of 56th Annual Design Automation Conference (DAC 2019) (2019)
16. Wang, H., Brisfors, M., Forsmark, S., Dubrova, E.: How diversity affects deep-learning side-channel attacks. In: Proceedings of 2019 IEEE Nordic Circuits and Systems Conference (NORCAS 2019) (2019)
17. ATMEL Corporation, "8/16-bit AVR XMEGA D4 Microcontroller." https://pdf1.alldatasheet.jp/datasheet-pdf/download/391513/ATMEL/ATXMEGA128D4.html. Accessed 25 July 2024
18. Lee, J.H., Han, D.-G.: Security analysis on dummy based side-channel countermeasures -Case study: AES with dummy and shuffling. J. Appl. Soft Comput. **93**, 1–9 (2020)
19. O'Flynn, C., Chen, Z.D.: ChipWhisperer: an open-source platform for hardware embedded security research. In: Prouff, E. (ed.) COSADE 2014. LNCS, vol. 8622, pp. 243–260. Springer, Cham (2014). https://doi.org/10.1007/978-3-319-10175-0_17

S-RFUP: Secure Remote Firmware Update Protocol

Rakesh Podder[1](✉), Tyler Rios[1], Indrajit Ray[1], Presanna Raman[2], and Stefano Righi[2]

[1] Colorado State University, Fort Collins, CO, USA
{rakesh.podder,tyler.rios,indrajit.ray}@colostate.edu
[2] AMI US Holdings Inc., Duluth, GA, USA
{presannar,stefanor}@ami.com

Abstract. Traditional over-the-air (OTA) update mechanisms lack security features. As a result, OTA firmware updates expose a device to several threats including unauthorized update, introduction of malware in the firmware code and rollback of firmware to an vulnerable older version. A handful of domain specific OTA firmware update protocols, especially in the automotive sector, have started incorporating rudimentary security features; however, these are not always enough. Moreover, a lack of standardization can lead to compatibility issues. In this work, we introduce the Secure Remote Firmware Update Protocol (S-RFUP) for platform (We use the term "platform" to mean any computer or hardware device and/or associated operating system, or a virtual environment on which software can be installed and run. Source NISTIR 7698, https://nvlpubs.nist.gov/nistpubs/Legacy/IR/nistir7698.pdf) firmware updates that enhances security and operational integrity across firmware devices during the update procedure. We build upon the hardware root of trust functionality provided by the Project Cerberus to perform secure attestation. With a goal of providing uniformity across a multitude of platforms, we leverage industry standards such as Platform Level Data Model (PLDM), Management Component Transport Protocol (MCTP), and well established cryptographic algorithms. Incorporating PLDM and MCTP reduces the management complexity and ensure interoperability between different hardware and software components in platform. We provide a security analysis of the proposed S-RFUP framework and discuss its implementation, testing and validation results.

Keywords: PLDM · MCTP · Project Cerberus · Firmware Update · Hardware Root of Trust (HRoT)

1 Introduction

Firmware is a critical piece of software in all computing devices, serving as the intermediary between the hardware functionality and the software operations of these devices. Like any other software, firmware needs periodic updates to address vulnerabilities, enhance performance, and introduce new features. Traditionally, firmware updates had been conducted locally. However as devices grow in complexity (think, cloud servers) and scale (think Internet of Things (IoT)) significant challenges arise for local firmware updates, such as physical access requirements, operational downtime, and logistical complexities.

Remote Firmware Update (RFU) is emerging as a viable solution, enabling updates to be deployed over-the-air (OTA) [38], minimizing disruptions and eliminating the need for physical proximity. However, over-the-air (OTA) update mechanisms, while convenient, are often targeted by attackers such as replay attack [39], denial of services [23], legacy firmware update [41], tampering [42], fake and malicious updates [2], and eavesdropping [20]; these attacks allow adversaries to tamper with the firmware, execute arbitrary code or roll back the firmware version to expose prior vulnerabilities [8,37]. Recent vulnerabilities in the update mechanisms of Jeep Cherokee [26], Samsung SmartThings Hub[1], and Asus Router[2] highlight these concerns. Ensuring the security of RFU protects the integrity of the firmware, maintains device functionality, and safeguards sensitive information contained within these devices. This is particularly crucial in industries where compromised firmware could lead to severe operational disruptions.

In this paper, we describe our efforts to achieve high-level security and standardization in firmware updates across platforms. The proposed Secure Remote Firmware Update Protocol (S-RFUP) systematizes the update process and provides needed security features to protect against tampering, unauthorized firmware rollback and intellectual property (IP) theft. S-RFUP ensures compatibility across a diversity of devices, and reduces complexity, which, in turn, also enhances the overall security posture by minimizing the inconsistencies that can be exploited in an attack. S-RFUP leverages Project Cerberus' paradigm of hardware root of trust [21] to enable secure attestation, ensuring that all firmware and software boot processes are verified and secure and making it an ideal foundation for secure RFU. We integrate industry standards such as Platform Level Data Model (PLDM), Management Component Transport Protocol (MCTP) with Project Cerberus for standardizing remote management and monitoring of firmware updates. The proposed S-RFUP framework leverages strong cryptographic such as AES-256 and ECDH Key Exchange techniques to encrypt and decrypt messages during communication between Update Agent and Firmware Device.

The main contributions of this work are:

1. We present a novel framework (S-RFUP) that integrates industry standard protocols (PLDM, MCTP) with a hardware root of trust (HRoT) to ensure interoperable and secure RFU across multiple device platforms.
2. We extend Project Cerberus by introducing new libraries to handle PLDM message construction, PLDM over MCTP binding, and encryption for an end-to-end secure pipeline and standrization of RFU.

---

[1] CVE-2018-3926: https://nvd.nist.gov/vuln/detail/CVE-2018-3926.
[2] CVE-2021-3166: https://nvd.nist.gov/vuln/detail/CVE-2021-3166.

3. We perform empirical evaluations and security analyses to validate the functionality and effectiveness of the proposed protocol and demonstrate robustness against known vulnerabilities, ensuring a secure firmware update process respectively.

2 Related Works

Security researchers have demonstrated several concerns with conventional remote BIOS and EFI/UEFI firmware updates [1,2,4,20,23,37,39,41,42]. In the following, we discuss some of these works and limitations of proposed solutions.

The integrity of the system BIOS is essential for the security and operational reliability of computer systems, especially for critical systems such as cloud servers, healthcare devices etc. Unauthorized firmware modifications, including malicious firmware updates and alterations, present serious risks [35]. These unauthorized modifications can occur when attackers exploit vulnerabilities or insufficient security practices during a remote firmware update process to manipulate the BIOS, potentially introducing malware or Trojans that compromise data security, disrupt device functionality, or enable system hijacking [3]. The threat landscape is further complicated by man-in-the-middle attacks (MITM) [5] and supply chain attacks [27], which may intercept or tamper with firmware updates or embed malware. Such attacks leverage the foundational level operations of firmware, challenging both detection and mitigation efforts, and pose ongoing security concerns [6,16]. Cui et al. [8] present a proof-of-concept for printer malware that can perform network reconnaissance, extract data, and spread to additional devices. The research points out the inadequacies in the security of firmware update processes and the existence of vulnerabilities within third-party libraries used in firmware.

The widespread adoption of non-secure protocols like HTTP further exposes firmware update processes to potential MITM and backdoor exploits [4,34]. PsycoB0t [24] is a well known example of a worm infection during firmware update of a router. Additionally, there have been cases where vulnerabilities in update procedures are exploited to carry out firmware modification attacks [37]. Jack using "jackpotting" [18] demonstrated that unauthorized firmware modification can be done in ATM machines. Costin showcases the susceptibility of certain Lexmark printers to memory inspection and arbitrary firmware modifications by employing PostScript [7].

Both the academic community and the Internet Engineering Task Force (IETF) are working on creating software update mechanisms for Class 1 and Class 2 devices (Upkit [22,28]) and developing hot-patching techniques such as RapidPatch [17], and Hera [30] that can be potentially used. However, the emphasis in these protocols is on patching low capability devices and not necessarily on the security of the same. There are some works by researchers on designing secure firmware updates [9,19,20,29,36,40]. Falas et al. proposed a Public PUF model [14] for secure firmware updates, but its dependency on high computational resources and complex key management, limits its feasibility for low-power IoT devices and present scalability and standardization challenges in large-scale deployments. The OTA firmware update mechanism proposed by Frisch et al. [15], requires manual intervention to update the framework version and rebuild the firmware, potentially leading to higher latency in updates when API changes occur. Also, the method is unable to verify the cryptographic signature before writing the firmware to flash, potentially allowing corrupted or malicious updates to be partially written before being detected. Similarly, the proposed Narrowband IoT (NB-IoT) as the wireless communication standard for firmware updates by Mahfoudhi et al. [25], does not implement any support for firmware authenticity and confidentiality, and thus can be susceptible to legacy firmware update and MITM attacks. The current state-of-art protocols fails to provide a high-level security with standardization in firmware updates across diverse device ecosystem. Our proposed S-RFUP can provide firmware integrity, and a streamlined and standardized operational functionality to secure sensitive information during remote firmware update.

3 Background

3.1 Firmware Base Specifications

PLDM Base Specification [11] is a standardized protocol designed to facilitate efficient communication and management within platform management subsystems. The primary purpose of the *PLDM Base Specification* is to establish a common protocol for monitoring and controlling various platform components, such as sensors, firmware, and hardware subsystems. This includes inventory management, event notifications, control functions, and data transfer operations.

MCTP Base Specification [10] is a comprehensive communication model designed to facilitate interactions between management controllers and management devices within a platform. MCTP establishes a standardized protocol that can be implemented across various physical transport mediums, enabling flexible and robust platform management solutions. This protocol operates independently of the underlying bus properties and data-link layer messaging. This abstraction allows MCTP to be implemented over different transport bindings such as PCIe, SMBus/I2C, and potentially other mediums like USB and RMII in the future.

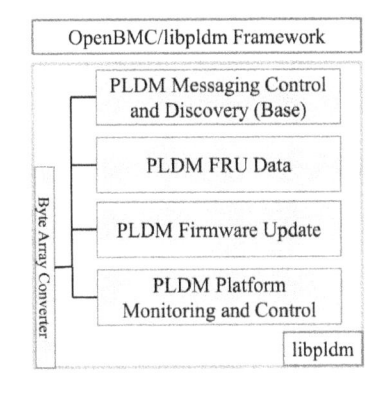

Fig. 1. OpenBMC/libpldm library Framework.

PLDM over MCTP Binding Specification [12] outlines how PLDM messages are transported over MCTP, establishing a common format and ensuring interoperability between different hardware and software components within a platform management subsystem. The main objective of the *PLDM over MCTP Binding Specification* is to establish the message format and protocol requirements for transmitting PLDM messages via the MCTP transport protocol.

We are using this specifications in our proposed S-RFUP framework to standardized and streamline the firmware update process.

3.2 PIT-Cerberus

Project Cerberus [21] is developed by Microsoft as a hardware root of trust (HRoT) specifically for server platforms. It enables secure boot functionality for device firmware, whether or not the devices inherently support secure boot. Additionally, it offers a secure method to verify and attest to the firmware state of the devices. We are using Project-Cerberus as a server-platform for Update Agent (UA) and as a HRoT for Firmware Device (FD).

3.3 OpenBMC/libpldm

This library is part of the OpenBMC project, aimed at providing an open-source firmware solution for baseboard management controllers (BMCs). The '*libpldm*' deals with the encoding and decoding of PLDM messages. Figure 1 shows various core module to facilitate tasks such as firmware updates, monitoring, and control of hardware devices across different hardware platforms.

4 Threat Model

In this section, we delineate the threat model pertinent to the secure remote firmware update protocol (S-RFUP).

4.1 Assumptions

For this work we made a number of assumptions. First, we assume the HRoT processor is considered tamper-proof and trusted. The company is deemed trustworthy, with no insider threats, and securely programs the HRoT processor with the PIT-Cerberus and related libraries and data. The Update Agent (UA) is honest and not curious, ensuring the protection of any stored confidential information against breaches of confidentiality and integrity. The company server used by UA is considered a trusted zone, protected by Intrusion Detection Systems (IDS) and Intrusion Prevention Systems (IPS), alongside strict security policies and personnel and not a target for intrusion and denial-of-service attacks. Protocols and cryptographic methods, the key size of Advanced Encryption Standard (AES), prime modulus of Elliptic-curve cryptography (ECC), curve selection for ECC, and the Digital Signature Algorithm (DSA), are carefully selected and implemented in a secure environment (SCIF[3]) to resist physical tampering and

---

[3] Sensitive Compartmented Information Facility.

side-channel attacks. The initial key establishment is completed before deployment and is not regarded as an issue. Encryption keys are generated with strong randomness and installed in the firmware devices during the manufacturing process.

4.2 Attacker Model

The primary target of the attacker is the communication channel between UA, and FD during firmware updates. We adopt the Dolev-Yao attacker model [13], where the attacker can eavesdrop, intercept, modify, or inject messages into the communication channel. Replay attacks involve attackers delaying or re-sending packets to mislead the FD or UA. Attackers might also inject false information to disrupt ongoing services. An attacker impersonating (MITM attacks) the UA or a legitimate FD could compromise firmware integrity or gain unauthorized access. The FD is vulnerable to physical tampering during transit, such as replacing the HRoT with a malicious microcontroller or embedding a hardware Trojan. To mitigate this, tamper-proof seals are assumed to protect the device during shipment, alerting the Recipient if breached. This paper does not consider scenarios involving physical tampering with the Firmware Device.

4.3 Desired Security Properties

The essential security properties required for network traffic within a secure remote firmware update protocol include data integrity, data authentication, data confidentiality, and data freshness.

- **Data Integrity**: Ensures that the firmware updates received by the Firmware Device (FD) have not been tampered with.
- **Data Authentication**: Verifies the source and integrity of the firmware update to ensure that the updates come from legitimate sources and prevent unauthorized modifications.
- **Data Confidentiality**: Maintains the secrecy of firmware data by protecting sensitive proprietary information from unauthorized access.
- **Data Freshness**: Guarantees that the firmware updates are recent.

By addressing these security properties, the protocol (S-RFUP) aims to provide a robust, secure, and reliable process for remote firmware updates.

5 Description of S-RFUP

The S-RFUP operates as a client-server model, as depicted in Fig. 2. The key entities within this protocol include the Hardware Root of Trust (HRoT), Firmware Devices (FD), Update Agent (UA), Sender, and Recipient. UA is a function within S-RFUP framework, designed to identify firmware devices, capable of executing a PLDM firmware update and to facilitate the transfer of component images to these devices. HRoT is the tamper-proof micro-controller

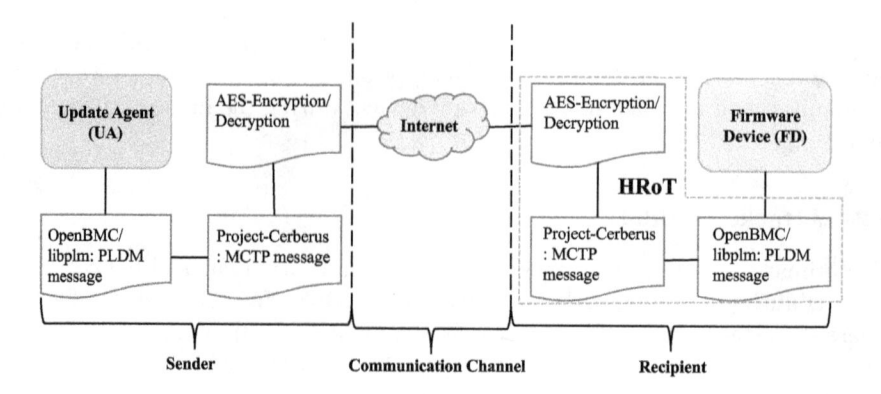

Fig. 2. High-level representation of S-RFUP framework.

that acts as the hardware root of trust. It is a critical component leveraging the Project Cerberus embedded framework for Firmware Device. FD is a PLDM endpoint (terminus) that comprises one or more processor elements that execute firmware. The Sender is the manufacturer or company responsible for maintaining the firmware and initiating firmware updates, while the Recipient is the end user utilizing the firmware device with HRoT capabilities.

5.1 Proposed Approach

The proposed S-RFUP framework is divided into two main segments; 1) the establishment of a secure channel, 2) the initiation of remote firmware update process. Initially, UA and FD establish a connection and compute public and private key pairs using Elliptic-curve Diffie-Hellman (ECDH) key agreement protocol [31,33]. UA generates an ECC (Elliptic Curve Cryptography) private key (d_U) - public key (q_U) pair, where, $q_U = d_U \times G$. G is the base point of the chosen elliptic curve. Then UA sends the public key (q_U) to the FD. FD generates a private key d_F, computes a public key $q_F = d_F \times G$ and an AES secret key $S = d_F \times q_U$. FD transmits its public key to the UA, which then computes the same AES secret key S as $S = d_U \times q_F = d_U \times \{d_F \times G\} = d_F \times \{d_U \times G\} = d_F \times q_U$.

In the second segment, as illustrated in Fig. 3, UA initiates the firmware updates, converting the firmware image into a Platform Level Data Model payload (*pldm* message) using '*OpenBMC/libplm*' library. The *pldm* message is then transformed to a *mctp* message by the Project-Cerberus using Management Component Transport Protocol (MCTP) & S-RFUP. After that, the *mctp* message is encrypted with AES encryption [32] schema ($encData = AESEncryption(mctp, S)$) using a shared key (S) generated previously by UA, before sending it to HRoT. HRoT, containing the Project Cerberus framework (MCTP Protocol) with S-RFUP functionalities, decrypts it using AES ($mctp = AESEncryption(encData, S)$) and converts the *mctp* to *pldm* message, before sending it to FD. Based on the request data (*pldm* message) FD generates an response data using '*libpldm*' and sends it back to UA.

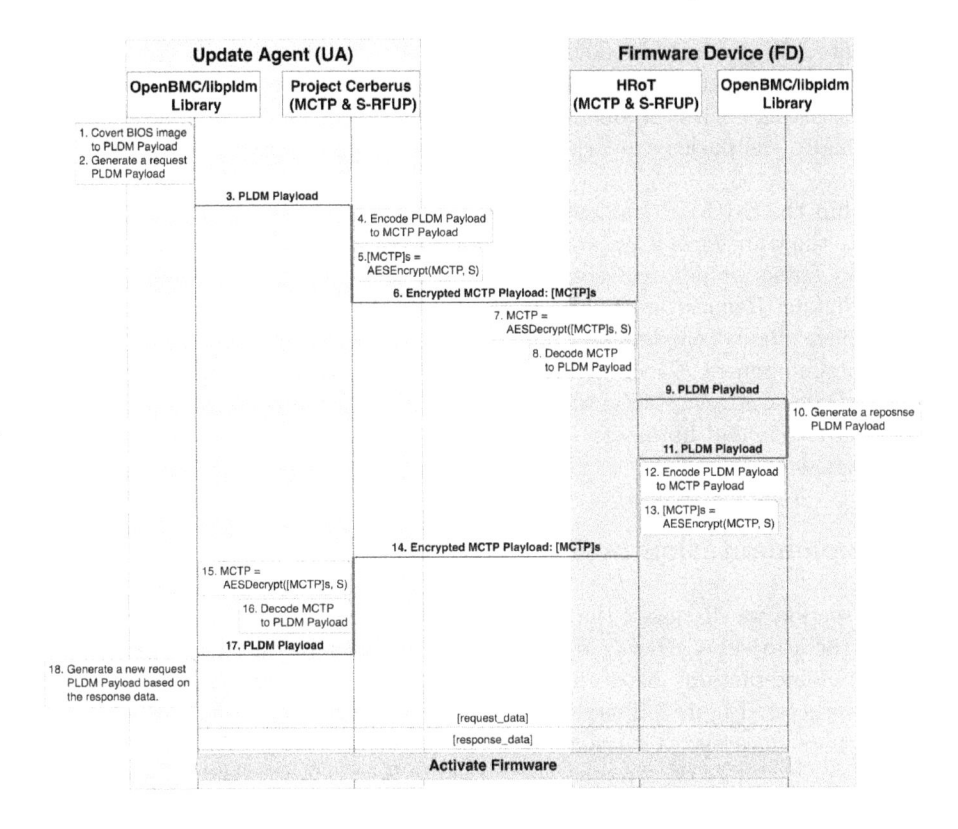

S-RFUP: Secure Remote Firmware Update Protocol   49

Fig. 3. Sequence diagram of S-RFUP firmware update process.

Similarly, if FD has request data, it follows the same encoding, encrypting, transferring, decrypting, and decoding steps, ultimately returning the response data to UA. This process will continue till all the firmware components (including firmware package header and payload) transfer to FD and FD activates the firmware updates.

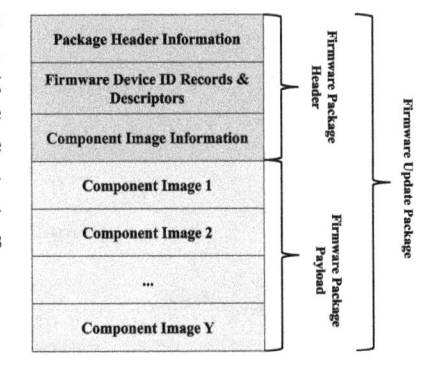

5.2 PLDM Firmware Update Package

Fig. 4. PLDM firmware update package.

The firmware update package is designed to work in conjunction with PLDM Firmware Update commands and contains several essential elements. These elements include a firmware package header that outlines the update package's contents as illustrated in Fig. 4. Specifically, the header provides a description of the overall packaging version and the date it was created. It also includes device identifier records, which specify the firmware devices (FDs) targeted for the update. Further, the header details the package contents, listing each component image's classification, offset, size, and version. Additionally, the package incorporates a checksum to ensure the integrity of the data.

Within the S-RFUP framework, three primary types of PLDM commands facilitate the transfer of firmware package headers and component images during updates. These include: {Inventory: QueryDeviceIdentifiers, GetFirmwareParameters},{Update: RequestUpdate, PassComponentTable, UpdateComponent, TransferComplete, VerifyComplete, ApplyComplete, ActivateFirmware, GetStatus, CancelUpdateComponent, CancelUpdate}, and {Transfer: RequestFirmwareData, GetPackageData, GetDeviceMetaData, GetMetaData}. These commands utilize the '*OpenBMC/libpldm*' library for efficient serialization and de-serialization of the PLDM messages.

6 Implementation of S-RFUP

In this section we discussed the implementation and execution flow of S-RFUP within the Project Cerberus framework. It outlines the libraries, procedural steps, and interactions between various components involved in the firmware update process. Figure 5 illustrates a generic *mctp* message that has encapsulated a *pldm* message. This *pldm* message is generated by UA using '*libpldm*' library. For each PLDM command described in Sect. 5.2, the fields of *pldm* message will be populated with different values. Once the *pldm* message is generated it will be encoded to *mctp* message shown in Fig. 5 before encrypting or decrypting. For this purpose, we developed the following core libraries that could handle the firmware update process (Table 1).

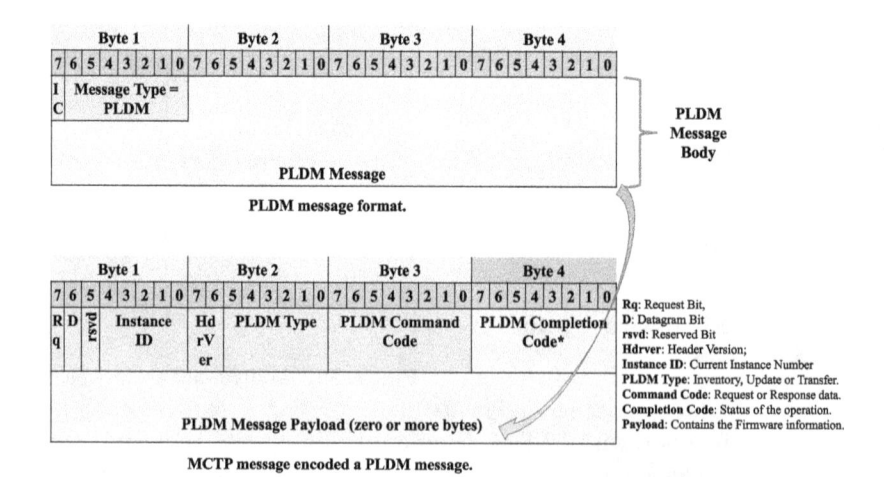

Fig. 5. Generic MCTP message encoded a generic PLDM message.

6.1 S-RFUP Core Libraries

Table 1. Description of S-RFUP core libraries.

Source	Function/API
New S-RFUP Libraries	
pldm_fwup_crypto	keyGeneration(), keyExachange(), secretKey() AESEncryption(), AESDecryption(), generateDSA()
cmd_interface_pldm	cmd_interface_pldm_process_request() ,cmd_interface_pldm_process_response()
pldm_fwup_handler	pldm_fwup_handler_run_update_ua(), pldm_fwup_handler_start_update_fd()
pldm_fwup_manager	pldm_fwup_manager_init(), pldm_fwup_manager_deinit().
pldm_fwup_protocol_commands	pldm_fwup_process_query_device_identifiers_request(), pldm_fwup_prcocess_get_firmware_parameters_request(), pldm_fwup_process_request_update_request(), pldm_fwup_process_request_update_response(), ..., pldm_fwup_generate_activate_firmware_request(), pldm_fwup_generate_activate_firmware_response()
pldm_fwup_protocol	struct pldm_fwup_protocol_version_string, struct pldm_fwup_fup_component_image_entry, struct pldm_fwup_protocol_component_parameter_entry
Modified Project Cerberus Libraries	
core/mctp	mctp_interface_process_packet()
core/projects/linux	platform_config()
core/tools/testing	setup_fwup_flash_virtual_disk()

The S-RFUP architecture employs a modular approach to firmware updates. The core modules of S-RFUP and their interaction with various external framework such as Project Cerberus and '*OpenBMC/libplm*', is illustrated in Fig. 6.

PLDM FWUP Crypto. The '*pldm_fwup_crypto*' supports the encryption and decryption of messages, securing communications across the network. It utilised the `aes.h` & `ecc.h` to generate ECDH key pair and AES encryption from Project Cerberus. A *Lamport* timestamp is incorporated within `AESEncryption()` & `AESDecryption()` before encrypting/decrypting the *mctp* message. We are also using ECC curve to generate a digital signature (DSA) to sign each encrypted *mctp* message for UA and FD. The `signature_verification_ecc.h` file helps to verify the figital signatures of UA/FD during update process.

PLDM Command Interface. Project Cerberus (or Cerberus) defines a generic command interface called '*cmd_interface*' for processing requests and responses in a command protocol. The '*cmd_interface_pldm*' extends '*cmd_interface*' to handle PLDM specific commands as shown in Table 1. It inherits the properties and function pointers from '*cmd_interface*' which are then defined during its initialization. Currently '*cmd_interface_ pldm*' only processes PLDM firmware update command types, but can be further extended to process others such as PLDM for FRU commands.

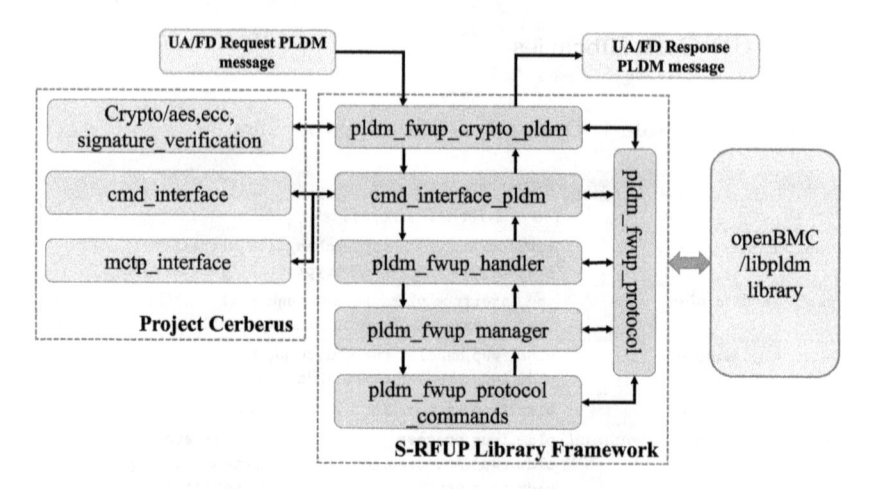

Fig. 6. S-RFUP library framework and interaction with Project Cerberus & *libpldm*.

Command Interfaces and MCTP: Cerberus uses MCTP as the protocol for which messages are exchanged throughout a Cerberus managed subsystem. MCTP is a flexible standard that can encapsulate other protocols such as Cerberus's own command protocol, SPDM. We modified the `mctp_interface_process_packet()` function to handle PLDM command. During the processing of MCTP packets Cerberus will interpret the MCTP header and extract the message type field which descries the type of payload that packet is carrying. The payload is then passed along to its respective command interface for further processing.

PLDM FWUP Manager. The '*pldm_fwup_manager*' is a library for managing the state of a PLDM-based firmware update and allowing other parts of the S-RFUP framework to modify or view the information present in the firmware update commands. An instance of it is passed along to the '*cmd_interface_pldm*' so that during the processing of firmware update commands the information needed to populate or save the fields of the commands can be accomplished.

PLDM FWUP Protocol Commands. The '*pldm_fwup_protocol_commands*' contains functions which perform the actual decoding and encoding of PLDM commands saving information to or populating message fields with information from the PLDM FWUP manager. For example, '`pldm_fwup_process_request_update_request()`' function is used to process incoming RequestUpdate PLDM commands saving information in the request data to the manager and extracting the manager's context to generate a RequestUpdate response.

PLDM FWUP Handler. The '*pldm_fwup_handler*' is the main driver code of S-RFUP. The handler mainly calls the API of the PLDM FWUP protocol commands and the MCTP interface API to generate, send, receive, process, and respond to PLDM firmware update commands. The most important fact is that at any time S-RFUP can be operating as either UA, performing firmware update on another device it manages or as the actual FD being updated. As such the '*pldm_fwup_handler*' interface contains two function pointers: `pldm_fwup_handler _run_update_ua()` for updating a firmware device in the subsystem as an UA and `pldm_fwup_handler_run_update_fd()` for updating S-RFUP's own firmware (FD) as directed by another UA.

Apart form this core libraries, S-RFUP also has '*pldm_fwup_protocol*' library header containing various structures, macros, and enumerations used by the above mentioned libraries. Table 1 shows the main libraries and some of API that we have designed, modified or used in the protocol. To convert the BIOS/BMC firmware images to a PLDM message we are mainly using `firmware_update.h` of '*libpldm*' library as external.

As explained in Sect. 5.2, the firmware component images reside in the Firmware Update Package where they are retrieved as needed using Cerberus's flash module. Since we are compiling and evaluating on Linux, a virtual flash module was created to simulate that functionality using disk I/O. We have developed a python script `setup_fwup _flash_virtual_disk()`, that located in the '*core/tools*' directory, generates a 4GB binary file divided into sections to simulate different flash regions: one for package data, one for meta data, and one for each two firmware components. These regions are populated with random bytes.

6.2 State Transitions

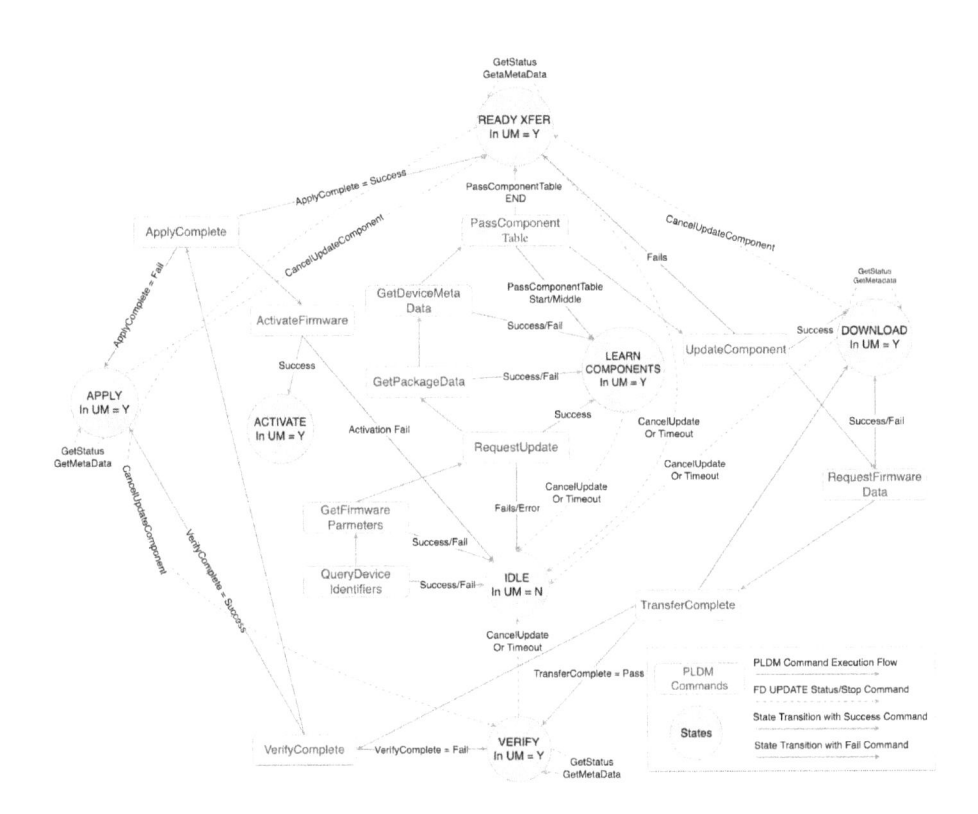

Fig. 7. State Transition Diagram with PLDM Commands.

Figure 7 outlines the various PLDM command and states that the Firmware Device (FD) can be during update process. Each circle in the diagram represents a distinct state the FD might be in and, each rectangular boxes represents a PLDM command. Whenever the FD is initialized, or when it undergoes a system reboot or device reset, it starts in the IDLE state. The execution starts from QueryDeviceIdentifiers and ends at ActivateFirmware. Every PLDM command on a successful execution transits to next PLDM command and the associated states also change. For example, if S-RFUP executes RequestUpdate command, on success it will move to GetPackageData and state of FD will change from IDLE to LEARN COMPONENTS. Similarly, if the execution fails or FD throws a compilation code error, the state of FD remains on IDLE. This design helps us to understand the FD's state with each PLDM command, so that a prompt diagnosis can be launched if any error occurs and it also helps to standardise the update process.

6.3 S-RFUP Update Flow in Project-Cerberus

The firmware update is performed in a sequential manner. Implementation for parallel operation and message exchange is not addressed in the paper. Additionally, the '*pldm_fwup_manager*' must be initialized and the PLDM command interface must obtain a reference to the manager prior to the start of the firmware update process.

Before UA initiates the update process, keyGeneration() function of '*pldm_fwup _crypto*' library is responsible for generating the ECC key pair for UA and FD. It loads the length of the key in *key_length*, initializes private key in *privkey*, public key in *pubkey*. keyExchange(): function exchanges the public key of UA and FD. On success, keyExchange() will initialize *pubkey_cli* with the UA's public key and load the *pubkey_serv* variable with a public key received from the FD. The secretKey() takes ECC private key from UA and FD, computes the secret key and loads in *secret* parameter.

S-RFUP Operating as UA Flow

1. First, S-RFUP checks the need to send QueryDeviceIdentifiers and GetFirmwareParameters based on the control boolean in pldm_fwup_handler_run_update_ua().
2. It then sends these inventory commands followed by the RequestUpdate command, passing information such as maximum transfer size and number of allowed outstanding requests, configurable in platform_config().
3. If package data is required, the device notifies S-RFUP, which then sends the necessary data via GetPackageData. Subsequently, S-RFUP may also send the GetDeviceMetaData command depending on the device's feedback.
4. Next, S-RFUP sends the PassComponentTable command, transferring component details to the device, which responds with compatibility codes.
5. Upon confirming compatibility, S-RFUP issues the UpdateComponent command for each component sequentially.

6. As the device requests firmware data using the RequestFirmwareData command, S-RFUP responds with the specified firmware portions.
7. After the firmware transfer, the device sends a TransferComplete command. If there is an error, S-RFUP might send a CancelUpdateComponent command.
8. S-RFUP waits for the VerifyComplete command within a preset timeout period, monitoring the status with potential GetStatus commands.
9. Once verification is complete, the device is expected to apply the update, followed by an ApplyComplete command.
10. These steps are repeated for each component until all are updated.
11. Finally, S-RFUP sends ActivateFirmware to activate the firmware, indicating with a boolean flag whether self-contained components should be activated immediately.

Please note that before sending the mctp message AESEncryption() encrypts the message using a secret key gnerated by secretKey(). This function takes secret key, message plus a timestamp, and use AES-GCM-256 method to encrypt the message and loads into *ciphertext* parameter. Each message then signed with a digital signature generate by generateDSA() function. Once the FD receives the message it verifies the signature. AESDecryption() function takes encrypted message (*ciphertext*), secret key (*secret*) as input, decrypts it and loads the message to the provided *plaintext* buffer. In the current implementation this metadata is written to a region in flash although depending on the metadat, it could be written to a structure or any other volatile memory.

S-RFUP Operating as FD Flow

1. S-RFUP waits for initial commands from the Update Agent (UA). If an inventory command is received, it anticipates a second inventory command.
2. Upon receiving inventory commands, S-RFUP processes the RequestUpdate command. It determines whether to send the GetPackageData command based on the UA's instructions and specifies the length of metadata to retain.
3. Following the RequestUpdate, S-RFUP issues the GetPackageData and handles any GetDeviceMetaData commands as required.
4. S-RFUP waits to receive the PassComponentTable command from the UA, which specifies which firmware components are to be updated.
5. Upon receiving the UpdateComponent command, S-RFUP verifies component compatibility and proceeds to request the necessary firmware data using the RequestFirmwareData command, specifying the needed data offset and length.
6. After receiving and writing firmware data to flash memory, S-RFUP issues a TransferComplete command, assuming successful transfer unless indicated otherwise.
7. S-RFUP verifies the firmware image by issuing a GetMetaData command, and comparing the received digital signature against its own.
8. Once verification is complete, S-RFUP directly applies the firmware image, and sends an ApplyComplete command to the UA.

9. Steps 5 to 8 are repeated for each firmware component requiring an update.
10. Finally, upon completing all updates, S-RFUP awaits the ActivateFirmware command to activate the updated firmware, with specifics such as timing handled according to settings in `platform_config()`.

The verification mechanism is left up to the user to implement and subsequently the assignment of the result field in the VerifyComplete command (by default set to success). In our case, S-RFUP issues the GetMetaData command with the UA responding with signatures[4] of the firmware image. S-RFUP would then take these and compare them to the DSA signature it generated with the received component image. Additionally, how the firmware is activated depends on the system specifications and user preferences.

6.4 Results and Discussions

We developed various experimental test scenarios to evaluate our framework for correctness, consistency and performance. We run our experiments on 2 virtual Linux servers. The client side (assumed as FD) has a 5000 MHz 12th Gen Intel(R) Core(TM) i7-12700K processor, x86_64 architecture, 20 cpus and UA (as server) in Intel(R) Xeon(R) CPU E5-1650 v4 @ 3.60 GHz, x86_64 architecture, 12 CPU(s).

All the S-FRUP PLDM firmware update libraries are available on GitHub[5]. All user guidelines, API descriptions, test results, and setup manuals are publicly available on GitHub.

In order to validate that the our protocol is working as it is supposed to, we used Project Cerberus with S-RFUP libraries (server platform) and '*OpenBMC/libpldm*' library as an Update Agent (UA) or server and a HRoT that is a micro-controller containing Project Cerberus with S-RFUP libraries and '*OpenBMC/libpldm*' library as a Firmware Device or client. We introduce '*cmd_chanel_tcp*' that uses a TCP socket for communication between UA and FD. It has `initialize_global_server_socket()` function that works with '*pldm_fwup_crypto*' & '*cmd_interface_pldm*' library to send the encrypted *mctp* packets to UA/FD. As designed and expected, our protocol delivers the anticipated results, with successful operations observed across both UA and FD.

---

[4] DSA with keys derived from ECC curve25519 has been used to generate signatures.
[5] https://github.com/AMIProject0/Project-Cerberus-PLDM/tree/master.

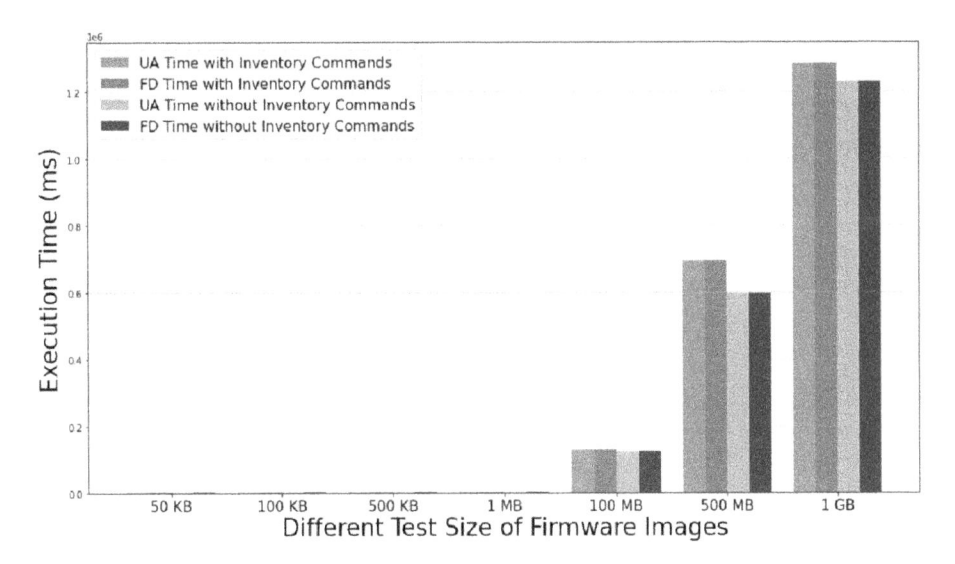

S-RFUP: Secure Remote Firmware Update Protocol 57

Fig. 8. UA Time vs FD Time for Firmware Update Tests (with and without Inventory Commands).

We have tested our framework with various firmware image sizes:{ 50 KB, 100 KB, ... , 500 MB, 1 GB }. Figure 8 illustrates a bar chart comparing the execution times for different firmware image sizes, both with and without inventory commands (as it is not always required for inventory commands). For 50 KB to 1 MB, the percentage increases in times are 55.68% (for UA) and 55.56% (for FD). If we compare the 50 KB to 1 GB sizes, the percentage increases in times are 60194.30% (UA) and 60190.13% (FD). The growth rate is exponential. But it is reasonable as, for 1 GB file it's takes only 128 s which is acceptable compare to state-of-art firmware update methods.

6.5 Exception and Error Handling

We have done an extensive software testing for the proposed protocol (S-RFUP). Throughout the development we have introduced several methods to handle errors of the compilation code, time-out exception for each PLDM command and tested the software in various test scenarios that shows the capability of the proposed framework.

Error Completion Codes. For each command, we have designed a specific structure to handle the response based on the compilation codes returned by a *pldm* message from UA/FD. Table 2 shows some of the PLDM commands and various scenarios of compilation code and they to handle the error. Let's say if UA send a RequestUpdate *pldm* message to FD and FD is currently on another firmware update process, the response *pldm* would contain a compilation_code =

ALREADY_IN_UPDATE_MODE and a return value of 0 × 81. If the FD can not do a firmware update right now it will send a response with compilation_code = *RETRY_REQUEST_UPDATE*. Similarly, we have designed error handling capabilities of each command for all possible states of FD.

Table 2. Command Responses and Descriptions for Firmware Updates. PBC: PLDM_BASE_CODES; AIUM: ALREADY_IN_UPDATE_MODE; UTIU: UNABLE_TO_INITIATE_UPDATE; RRU: RETRY_REQUEST_UPDATE; ITL: INVALID_TRANSFER_LENGTH; CNE: COMMAND_NOT_EXPECTED; DOFR: DATA_OUT_OF_RANGE; RRFD: RETRY_REQUEST_FW_DATA; CP: CANCEL_PENDING;

Command Name	Completion Codes	Return Value	Return By	Descriptions
QDI	PBC	0x00	FD	Executed successfully.
RU	PBC	0x00	FD	Executed successfully.
	AIUM	0x81		Already in update mode.
	UTIU	0x8A		Unable to enter update mode.
	RRU	0x8E		Requests a retry of the RequestUpdate command, needing more time to prepare.
RFD	PBC	0x00	UA	Executed successfully
	ITL	0x83		Image portion > MaxTransferSize.
	CNE	0x88		Command is not expected in the sequence.
	DOFR	0x89		Image portion offset exceeds the range.
	RRFD	0x91		Component image portion is not available.
	CP	0x87		When CancelUpdate initiated by FD previously.

Timing Specification A timing specification has been designed for every compilation codes and time-out exceptions. For RequestUpdate response message if compilation_code = *RETRY_REQUEST_UPDATE* sent by FD, it will assign an UA_T4[6] time specification for the process. It means the amount of time to wait before UA re-sends a RequestUpdate PLDM command after receiving the previous response. There are also, GetPackageData timeout ($1s \leq UA\_T5 \leq 5s$), Update mode IDLE timeout for FD ($60s \leq FD\_T1 \leq 120s$) and several others that we have specified. A detailed documentation about the timing specifications will be provided with the source code.

We have also designed several test scenarios to check various failure that can occur during firmware update process such as, if the UA/FD loses connections during update process then the program will wait until the timer specified time (UA_T7 or FD_T5) or if the connection is not back, it will revert back to the previous IDLE state and throws a timeout exception (GT_T1). The S-RFUP is thoroughly tested and validated to handle unexpected behaviours during firmware update process.

---

[6] For UA_T4 the $minTime = 1s$ and $MaxTime = 5s$.

7 Security Analysis

The proposed secure firmware update protocol (S-RFUP) effectively mitigates a range of security threats through a combination of robust encryption techniques, rigorous verification procedures, and systematic error handling mechanisms. The following analysis details how the identified threats are addressed using this approach and how the essential security properties are maintained. To prevent service unavailability (due to dos attack) and ensure continuous operation during the firmware update process, the protocol incorporates several exceptions and error handling mechanisms. These mechanisms are designed to catch and manage unexpected errors or attacks that could lead to server or service unavailability. By handling such scenarios promptly, the system avoids unwanted interruptions or crashes, maintaining service availability and reliability.

The communication between the UA and FD is protected using advanced encryption methods. Specifically, the Management Component Transport Protocol (MCTP) messages are encrypted using the S-RFUP 'crypto' library framework, which utilizes the Advanced Encryption Standard – Galois/Counter Mode – with a 256-bit key (AES-GCM 256). This encryption method is resistant to a variety of attacks, including *Known Plaintext Attack, (KPA), Chosen Plaintext Attack (CPA), Chosen Ciphertext Attack (CCA)*, and *Ciphertext-Only Attack (COA)*. By encrypting all communications, the protocol ensures that any intercepted data remains inaccessible to attackers, protecting sensitive information such as firmware/device information. Thus, data integrity is maintained by ensuring as data packets are delivered to the Recipient without any alterations. The protocol achieves this through the use of AES-GCM encryption, which includes built-in integrity checks to verify that the data has not been tampered with during transmission.

To mitigate replay attacks, the protocol employs unique session keys and *Lamport* timestamps. During each session, the UA and FD generate a new shared AES-GCM key using the ECDH key agreement protocol. This ensures that each session is encrypted with a unique key, preventing attackers from reusing intercepted messages in a different session. Thus, by employing *Lamport* timestamps we can verify the freshness of messages, ensuring that old messages cannot be replayed to disrupt the firmware update process, this gives the assurance of data freshness.

The protocol incorporates the Digital Signature Algorithm (DSA) with keys derived from ECC curve to authenticate legitimacy of the entities. This ensures that the recipient can verify the authenticity of the sender, protecting against impersonation attacks. By using digital signatures, the protocol ensures that only legitimate UA and FD entities can participate in the firmware update process, effectively preventing MITM attacks where an attacker could intercept and alter communications. This process confirms the authenticity of the data source and the integrity of the data itself. The use of ECDH for key exchange, combined with AES-GCM for encryption, provides robust protection against *Adaptive Chosen-Plaintext* and *Chosen-Ciphertext Attacks*. By generating a new secret key for each session, the protocol ensures that attackers cannot use previous encryption or decryption to infer the current encryption key. This dynamic key management system enhances security by preventing key reuse and complicating any attempts to compromise the communication through adaptive attacks.

This comprehensive security framework provides robust protection against eavesdropping, replay & MitM attacks, credential theft, and adaptive attacks, ensuring a secure and reliable remote firmware update mechanism. S-RFUP successfully maintains the essential security properties of data integrity, data authentication, data confidentiality, and data freshness, providing a secure, and reliable process for remote updates.

8 Conclusion

In this work, we propose S-RFUP as a uniform framework for secure remote firmware updates across mutitude of platforms. S-RFUP builds upon Project Cerberus hardware root of trust capabilities by integrating the industry-standard protocols PLDM & MCTP and conventional cryptographic protocols to ensure a secure, reliable, interoperable and easily manageable firmware update process. The implementation has been rigorously tested, validating its resilience against various security concerns and demonstrating its robustness in a controlled environment. We plan to open-source S-RFUP libraries. Future work involves enhancing the protocol's performance and security through implementing parallel firmware updates to increase efficiency, porting the hardware-agnostic S-RFUP to the microchip-specific I2C protocol, and validating the protocol across different firmware ecosystems to ensure robust performance and compatibility.

Acknowledgments. This work was partially supported by the U.S. National Science Foundation under Grant No. 1822118 and 2226232, the member partners of the NSF IUCRC Center for Cyber Security Analytics and Automation - AMI, NewPush, Cyber Risk Research, NIST and ARL - the State of Colorado (grant #SB 18-086) and the authors' institutions. Any opinions, findings, and conclusions or recommendations expressed in this material are those of the authors and do not necessarily reflect the views of the National Science Foundation, or other organizations.

References

1. Alrawi, O., Lever, C., Antonakakis, M., Monrose, F.: SOK: security evaluation of home-based iot deployments. In: 2019 IEEE Symposium on Security and Privacy (SP), pp. 1362–1380. IEEE (2019)
2. Basnight, Z., Butts, J., Lopez, J., Jr., Dube, T.: Firmware modification attacks on programmable logic controllers. Int. J. Crit. Infrastruct. Prot. **6**(2), 76–84 (2013)
3. Basnight, Z., Butts, J., Lopez, J., Jr., Dube, T.: Firmware modification attacks on programmable logic controllers. Int. J. Crit. Infrastruct. Prot. **6**(2), 76–84 (2013). https://doi.org/10.1016/j.ijcip.2013.04.004
4. Bellissimo, A., Burgess, J., Fu, K.: Secure software updates: disappointments and new challenges. In: HotSec (2006)
5. Conti, M., Dragoni, N., Lesyk, V.: A survey of man in the middle attacks. IEEE Commun. Surv. Tutorials **18**(3), 2027–2051 (2016)

6. Cooper, D., Polk, W., Regenscheid, A., Souppaya, M., et al.: Bios Protection Guidelines, vol. 800, p. 147. NIST Special Publication (2011)
7. Costin, A.: Hacking MFPS. In: The 28th Chaos Communication Congress (2011)
8. Cui, A., Costello, M., Stolfo, S.: When firmware modifications attack: a case study of embedded exploitation. In: NDSS (2013)
9. Dhakal, S., Jaafar, F., Zavarsky, P.: Private blockchain network for IoT device firmware integrity verification and update. In: 2019 IEEE 19th International Symposium on High Assurance Systems Engineering (HASE), pp. 164–170. IEEE (2019)
10. DMTF: Mctp base specification 1.2.0. DSP0236 (2009). http://dmtf.org/sites/default/files/standards/documents/DSP0236_1.2.0.pdf
11. DMTF: Platform level data model (pldm) base specification 1.0. DSP0240 (2009). http://dmtf.org/sites/default/files/standards/documents/DSP0240_1.0.0.pdf
12. DMTF: Platform level data model (pldm) for firmware update specification 1.0.1. DSP0267 (2009). https://dmtf.org/sites/default/files/standards/documents/DSP0267_1.0.1.pdf
13. Dolev, D., Yao, A.: On the security of public key protocols. IEEE Trans. Inf. Theory **29**(2), 198–208 (1983)
14. Falas, S., Konstantinou, C., Michael, M.K.: A modular end-to-end framework for secure firmware updates on embedded systems. ACM J. Emerg. Technol. Comput. Syst. (JETC) **18**(1), 1–19 (2021)
15. Frisch, D., Reißmann, S., Pape, C.: An over the air update mechanism for esp8266 microcontrollers. In: Proceedings of the ICSNC, the Twelfth International Conference on Systems and Networks Communications, Athens, Greece, pp. 8–12 (2017)
16. Fuchs, A., Krauß, C., Repp, J.: Advanced remote firmware upgrades using TPM 2.0. In: Hoepman, J.-H., Katzenbeisser, S. (eds.) SEC 2016. IAICT, vol. 471, pp. 276–289. Springer, Cham (2016). https://doi.org/10.1007/978-3-319-33630-5_19
17. He, Y., et al.: {RapidPatch}: firmware hotpatching for {Real-Time} embedded devices. In: 31st USENIX Security Symposium (USENIX Security 22), pp. 2225–2242 (2022)
18. Jack, B.: Jackpotting automated teller machines redux. Black Hat USA (2010)
19. Jain, N., Mali, S.G., Kulkarni, S.: Infield firmware update: challenges and solutions. In: 2016 International Conference on Communication and Signal Processing (ICCSP), pp. 1232–1236. IEEE (2016)
20. Keleman, L., Matić, D., Popović, M., Kaštelan, I.: Secure firmware update in embedded systems. In: 2019 IEEE 9th International Conference on Consumer Electronics (ICCE-Berlin), pp. 16–19. IEEE (2019)
21. Kelly, B.: Project cerberus security architecture overview specification. Open Compute Project (2017). https://learn.microsoft.com/en-us/azure/security/fundamentals/project-cerberus
22. Langiu, A., Boano, C.A., Schuß, M., Römer, K.: Upkit: an open-source, portable, and lightweight update framework for constrained IoT devices. In: 2019 IEEE 39th International Conference on Distributed Computing Systems (ICDCS), pp. 2101–2112. IEEE (2019)
23. Lau, P.T., Katzenbeisser, S.: Firmware-based dos attacks in wireless sensor network. In: Katsikas, S., et al. (eds.) ESORICS 2023. LNCS, vol. 14399, pp. 214–232. Springer, Cham (2023). https://doi.org/10.1007/978-3-031-54129-2_13
24. Maassen, A.: Network bluepill-stealth router-based botnet has been ddosing dronebl for the last couple of weeks (2009). https://www.dronebl.org/blog/8
25. Mahfoudhi, F., Sultania, A.K., Famaey, J.: Over-the-air firmware updates for constrained NB-IoT devices. Sensors **22**(19), 7572 (2022)

26. Miller, C., Valasek, C.: Remote exploitation of an unaltered passenger vehicle. Black Hat USA **2015**(S 91), 1–91 (2015)
27. Miller, J.F.: Supply chain attack framework and attack patterns. The MITRE Corporation, MacLean, VA (2013)
28. Moran, B., Tschofenig, H., Brown, D., Meriac, M.: A firmware update architecture for internet of things. Internet Requests for Comments, RFC Editor, RFC **9019** (2021)
29. Neves, B.P., Santos, V.D., Valente, A.: Innovative firmware update method to microcontrollers during runtime. Electronics **13**(7), 1328 (2024)
30. Niesler, C., Surminski, S., Davi, L.: Hera: Hotpatching of embedded real-time applications. In: NDSS (2021)
31. Podder, R., Abdelgawad, M., Ray, I., Ray, I., Santharam, M., Righi, S.: Correctness and security analysis of the protection in transit (pit) protocol. Available at SSRN 4980331 (2024)
32. Podder, R., Barai, R.K.: Hybrid encryption algorithm for the data security of esp32 based IoT-enabled robots. In: 2021 Innovations in Energy Management and Renewable Resources (52042), pp. 1–5. IEEE (2021)
33. Podder, R., Sovereign, J., Ray, I., Santharam, M.B., Righi, S.: The pit-cerberus framework: preventing device tampering during transit. In: 2024 IEEE 24th International Conference on Software Quality, Reliability and Security (QRS), pp. 584–595. IEEE (2024)
34. Samuel, J., Mathewson, N., Cappos, J., Dingledine, R.: Survivable key compromise in software update systems. In: Proceedings of the 17th ACM Conference on Computer and Communications Security, pp. 61–72 (2010)
35. Schmidt, S., Tausig, M., Hudler, M., Simhandl, G.: Secure firmware update over the air in the internet of things focusing on flexibility and feasibility. In: Internet of Things Software Update Workshop (IoTSU). Proceeding (2016)
36. Sun, S.: Design and implementation of partial firmware upgrade (2019)
37. Tsang, R., et al.: Fandemic: firmware attack construction and deployment on power management integrated circuit and impacts on IoT applications. In: NDSS (2022)
38. Vrachkov, D.G., Todorov, D.G.: Research of the systems for firmware over the air (fota) and wireless diagnostic in the new vehicles. In: 2020 XXIX International Scientific Conference Electronics (ET), pp. 1–4. IEEE (2020)
39. Wara, M.S., Yu, Q.: New replay attacks on zigbee devices for internet-of-things (IoT) applications. In: 2020 IEEE International Conference on Embedded Software and Systems (ICESS), pp. 1–6. IEEE (2020)
40. Wee, Y., Kim, T.: A new code compression method for FOTA. IEEE Trans. Consum. Electron. **56**(4), 2350–2354 (2010)
41. Wu, Y., et al.: Your firmware has arrived: a study of firmware update vulnerabilities. In: USENIX Security Symposium (2023)
42. Zhang, Y., Li, Y., Li, Z.: Aye: a trusted forensic method for firmware tampering attacks. Symmetry **15**(1), 145 (2023)

Securing Virtual Reality Apps Inter-process Communication

Oluwatosin Falebita[✉], Mahmoud Abdelgawad, Evan Anspach, and Indrakshi Ray

Department of Computer Science, Colorado State University, Fort Collins, CO 80523, USA
{oluwatosin.falebita,m.abdelgawad,pidge.anspach, indrakshi.ray}@colostate.edu

Abstract. As Virtual Reality (VR) technology continues to gain widespread adoption, concerns about cybersecurity threats in immersive environments are mounting. Inter-process communication (IPC) is prevalent in operating systems that power VR devices, allowing applications to interact. While facilitating interaction between apps, the IPC presents a significant risk, as malicious apps can exploit it to attack other apps. This vulnerability is rooted in the inherent security architecture and design implementations of these operating systems. This paper addresses IPC security by proposing a fine-grained security model that employs the NIST Next Generation Access Control (NGAC). It focuses on the Android environment to safeguard the IPC and secure the apps' interaction. This security model strengthens VR systems' defensive capabilities and ensures the safety of users' digital experiences. The security model is designed as an NGAC gateway that is adaptable at the kernel level and portable to various operating system architectures. This NGAC gateway fortifies Android-based VR devices and assures the consumer VR market. Such a security model is required for the VR security domain and will be transformative for the VR industry.

Keywords: Virtual Reality · Inter Process Communication · Next Generation Access Control (NGAC) · Virtual Reality Apps · Intent Attacks · Secure App Inter-Communication

1 Introduction

Virtual Reality (VR) has started to find its foothold in modern computing. However, they have yet to be fully secured against many cyberattacks targeting VR applications (apps) and devices. VR devices and apps are prone to various cyberattacks by compromising confidentiality, integrity, and availability properties in the form of eavesdropping [36], perception manipulation [35], and denial of service (DoS) [32] attacks. Moreover, the data captured by headset sensors, such as eye tracking, are sensitive. Such data must be protected during storage and transit. Security and privacy breaches have far-reaching and devastating consequences.

Researchers are now uncovering security concerns in VR environments such as Side Channel Spying/Eavesdropping [6,29,31], Perception Manipulation [11,12,35,39], and Man in the Middle attacks [36]. Many of these vulnerabilities are based on the insecure architecture of the device operating system (OS). They allow an adversary to gain access to protected data (*side channel spying/eavesdropping, man in the middle, headset tracking*) or to influence the perception of the headset user while using the VR device (*perception manipulation*).

VR apps require interaction with one another and request access to various system services. Many cyberattacks exploit weaknesses in the inter-process communication (IPC) prevalent in the operating system of these headsets, particularly devices powered by a custom Android operating system [11,36,40]. Previously found attacks, such as perception manipulation, rely on insecure IPC to manipulate virtual content by modifying configuration files and sensor settings using system calls.

The traditional access control mechanisms, such as discretionary access control (DAC) and mandatory access control (MAC), are enforced through the Security Enhanced Android (SEAndroid) [34], a customized version of SELinux used by the Binder IPC [34]. The Binder IPC mechanism allows components within a single process or across separate processes to communicate with one another in the Meta Horizon operating system [26], a custom version of VR operating system built on Android. Meta Quest VR devices are powered by Meta Horizon OS and relies primarily on Intent firewall and Intent filters to secure inter-process communication between apps. These mechanisms failed to identify malicious intent specifically when an implicit intent (a messaging object that allows an app to declare a general action to perform, which allows a component from another app to handle it) is utilized [2], resulting in intent spoofing or intent manipulation attacks on the device.

Meta Horizon OS utilizes DAC and MAC. DAC provides a user-centric model [23] where the user has the discretion to allow apps access to sensitive resources like the camera, microphone, or contacts through permission requests. However, this can lead to security risks if users are not careful about what permissions they grant. The OS implements MAC based on classifications and security labels through SEAndroid to enforce strict policies at the system level. However, these access control policies are determined by the lax firewall rules in the Intent firewall, which introduces vulnerabilities in the IPC. The current LSM hooks [34] Binder IPC is protected by context labels policies, which are matched with Intent Filters and the permission specified by the app developer. If none exist, such exported component remains vulnerable [2,4].

We therefore focus on NIST Next Generation Access Control (NGAC) to handle traditional access control's limitations. The NGAC has been standardized by the National Institute of Standards and Technology in alignment with the American National Standards Institute/International Committee for Information Technology Standards (ANSI/INCITS); refer to the standard "INCITS 565-2020" [21]. NGAC is a generic architecture that defines access control as a reusable set of data abstractions and attribute-based functions. It is suitable for expressing access control policies for a wide range of applications, including those spanning multiple distributed, interconnected processes and situational monitoring applications in which policies may be changed while they are deployed.

While several works [18,29,31] focus on applying new authentication schemes, encryption and other modular security on top of the existing operating system architecture [19], our work focuses on augmenting the existing framework by introducing NGAC, which is based on the attributes of the interacting apps. Adding NGAC as another authorization layer for IPC verification increases the efficiency of securing apps' interaction. This solution allows granular communication verification between apps to prevent malicious apps from performing malicious intent manipulation attacks on legitimate apps.

Key Contribution: This work has three contributions described as follows:

1. We identify the major access control attacks in a virtual reality environment.
2. We formulate access control policies, adhering to the NGAC model, to secure inter-process communication and illustrate how they can be enforced in virtual reality devices.
3. We develop a policy enforcement architecture suitable for Android-based virtual reality devices.

The rest of the paper is organized as follows. Section 2 discusses the background needed to understand this work. It covers details of the VR apps IPC and their security flaws. It also provides some details about the NIST NGAC. Section 3 describes the policy design for validating IPC in an Android environment. Section 4 provides a secure IPC architecture model using NGAC. Section 5 discusses attack mitigation through the NGAC security model. Section 6 explores the related work on VR security and Android IPC security. Finally, Sect. 7 summarizes our work and points to future plans.

2 Background

This section provides an overview of the VR app IPC structure, VR app IPC attacks, and NGAC model.

2.1 VR Apps Inter-process Communication

Meta Horizon OS is a modified version of Android [33]; it incorporates key Android features, notably the Binder, which is the primary IPC channel that allows apps and system resources to interact. Most Android-based VR operating systems utilize sandboxing to prohibit direct access to the resources of other apps and the Android system [20]. However, an app communicates with other apps and uses system services through the Binder using the following mechanisms.

Activity provides a user with an interface to interact with an app. An app can permit another app to launch its activities.

Broadcast services enable the system to transmit events to apps outside the typical user flow, allowing the apps to respond to system-wide broadcast announcements. A broadcast receiver operates in the background to manage incoming events.

Content providers are responsible for storing the app's data and facilitating the app's data sharing with other apps' components.

Services provides an entry point for keeping and running an app in the background without a user interface while performing various computational tasks.

VR app's inter-process communication utilizes the Binder driver and SELinux context labels to control access and determine which processes can communicate with other app components using the following essential components of the Binder:

Binder Driver: A kernel-level component that acts as the core of the Binder IPC mechanism. It manages the communication between processes and enforces security policies based on predefined SElinux context(label) consisting of user, role, type, and level [34]. The Binder driver oversees the creation of Binder objects, the passing of references, and the delivery of transactions. The Binder driver ensures that messages are securely and efficiently routed between processes.

Service Manager: It is the central registry for all Binder services in the system. When a service is created, it registers itself with the Service Manager, allowing other processes to discover and interact. The Service Manager acts as a lookup table for Binder services, enabling clients to find the Binder objects when they need to communicate.

Native Object: It defines an interface for the services a target process or an app provides. It serves as a concrete class that does the actual work of receiving calls from a client, processing those calls, and returning the results [8]; it creates a unique identifier called Binder token, which helps the Binder driver track and manage Binder references across different processes.

Proxy Object: A proxy object marshals method calls from the client process, sending them through the Binder framework to the actual service object in the service process.

A *Caller app* can interact with a *Target app* by specifying an *Intent*. An intent is a messaging object used to request an action from another app component. As shown in Fig. 1, the flow involves several steps and components.

Step 1 - Service Discovery: The caller app queries the service manager to check if any app offers the requested service. This requires the caller app to specify an intent for the operation it needs to be performed [1]. The service manager uses this intent to look up an appropriate service; if the result is null, then there are no apps on the device that can receive such an intent, and an app crash occurs with an error message, and the request will be terminated; if the result is not null, then at least one app can handle the request.

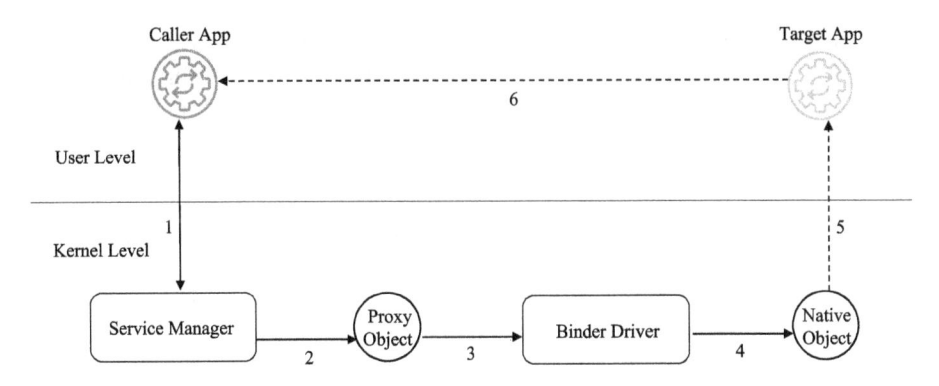

Fig. 1. VR Apps Binder Inter Process Communication

Step 2 - Proxy Object Creation: Upon receiving a not null result, the caller process creates a proxy object (node) that contains the intent to be performed on the target app.

Step 3 to 5 - Parcel copy: In steps 3 to 6, the binder driver copies data from the proxy object to the target app via the native object, preserving its structure and layout while performing the operation.

Step 6 - Receiving the Response: The target app returns the result of the request to the caller app.

2.2 VR Apps IPC Attacks

Once a VR app is installed, the operating system catalogs the app's declared services in the Service Manager to keep track of the intents that the app can handle. When a caller app initiates an activity using startActivity() or startActivityForResult() with an implicit intent, the system searches for compatible activities [3] that can perform such intent without checking for proper access control [15]. These inadvertently create potential pathways for unauthorized access such as immersive attacks [11] and immersive hijacking [39].

Immersive attacks [11] are defined as attacks that target the immersive nature of VR devices in order to exploit vulnerabilities in the perception of the immersed user. A successful immersive manipulation attack will result in a virtual environment modified to disrupt a user's task or cause physical or mental harm to the user. This work outlines four immersive attacks: the Chaperone Attack, the Disorientation Attack, the Human Joystick (Redirected walking) Attack, and the Overlay Attack. These attacks were performed on systems running OpenVR, for example, HTC Vive and Oculus Rift VR, by taking advantage of a weakness in the IPC framework's inability to determine whether the caller application is benign or malicious and whether it should be allowed to perform the requested operation(s) on the target application or system resources.

Immersive hijacking [39] presents a form of access control violation specifically targeting Meta VR platforms. This attack exploits weak access control in the operating system's IPC, which is crucial for facilitating various app interactions. These interactions range from launching other apps to sending and receiving data through intents. In a more specific instance, immersive hijacking targets the Meta Horizon Operating System (OS), a VR OS developed by Meta. This attack method cleverly exploits improper validation and access control in the IPC mechanism to create a deceptive layer of virtual reality within Meta OS, effectively generating a nested reality. The attack begins with side-loading a seemingly benign VR Home screen application onto a device and a spy script that runs in the background. When the user signals the system to exit the current application, expecting to return to the home environment, the spy script intercepts and destroys the signal, terminates the application, and initiates the malicious VR Home screen. This allows attackers to perform arbitrary operations, such as intercepting and modifying requests sent to other applications.

A significant area for security improvement in this setup is the device's operating system's insufficient IPC access control and validation process, which overly depends on permissions as determined by app developers. Often, these permissions are not strictly enforced, placing an undue security burden on the developers, with only minimal support from the operating system security framework.

2.3 NIST Next Generation Access Control (NGAC)

NGAC is a revolutionary approach to managing and implementing access control mechanisms [16]. It emphasizes more detailed, flexible, and context-aware policies compared to traditional models such as Discretionary Access Control (DAC), Mandatory Access Control (MAC), and Role-Based Access Control (RBAC). Each of the components of NGAC is specifically formulated to adapt to the changing security requirements of contemporary digital settings, encompassing Blockchain [27], Internet of Things (IoT) [10], and mobile devices.

NGAC utilizes the policy class, which can be conceptualized as a hierarchical graph consisting of a predetermined set of relations and access rights between policy components. It is used for making access control decisions using reference mediation and contains elements such as authorized users, access rights, objects, processes, and operations. The policy class defines several relationships among elements, including assignment, association, prohibition, and obligation relations [17].

- **Assignment** relation is used in expressing relationships between policy elements such as the relationship between users and user attributes, user attributes to other user attributes, resources to resource attributes, resource attributes to other resource attributes, user attributes to a policy class, and resource attributes to a policy class.
- **Association** relation establishes the authorization of access rights between policy elements such as user attributes and resource attributes. It determines which users can access specific resources and exercise specific access rights.
- **Prohibition** relations entail denying access rights between policy elements, such as user characteristics and resource attributes. It consists of two primary

prohibitions: user deny and process deny, which prohibits access to user and process respectively.
- **Obligation** can be employed to automatically adjust policies based on certain conditions related to access modes and patterns triggered by the execution of events. An obligation can be defined by two essential elements: an event pattern and a corresponding response. Our work considers controlling the IPC between apps. Thus, the obligation relations are omitted from the NGAC graph.

NGAC consists of five process points: Policy Decision Point, Policy Enforcement Point, Policy Administration Point, Event Processing Point, and Resource Access Point [9]. These policy points are briefly described as follows.

- **Policy Decision Point (PDP)** This is the core component responsible for making access control decisions based on predefined policies. The PDP evaluates access requests against the policies and determines whether to grant or deny the requests based on the applicable rules.
- **Policy Enforcement Point (PEP)** This component is responsible for enforcing the decisions made by the PDP. It acts at the point of access, ensuring that only authorized actions are allowed to proceed based on the decision provided by the PDP.
- **Policy Information Point (PIP)** The PIP stores attributes related to users, resources, and environmental conditions. The PDP uses these attributes to make informed access control decisions. The PIP can pull information from various sources, including directories, databases, and other external sources.
- **Policy Administration Point (PAP)** This component creates, manages, and deletes access control policies. The PAP provides an interface for administrators to define and modify the rules and policies that the PDP evaluates.
- **Event Processing Point (EPP)** serves as a critical functional component within a system. It operates by receiving event contexts and comparing them against predefined event patterns that are part of obligations. When a match is found, the EPP forwards the corresponding event responses to the Policy Decision Point (PDP).
- **Resource Access Point (RAP)** is a crucial functional entity designed to be the sole gateway for accessing designated protected resources. This exclusive access point ensures all interactions with these resources are centrally controlled and managed.

3 Policy Design for Securing VR Apps IPC Using NGAC

Virtual Reality Operating Systems (VROS) are complex environments that require robust access control mechanisms to ensure secure and authorized interactions within the virtual reality space. By leveraging the NGAC framework, we can design flexible and extensible policies that govern access to various components and functionalities of the VROS.

Using the NGAC approach, we aim to create a robust and scalable access control framework for VROS. This framework will enable precise control over resource access and virtual interactions while promoting security, compliance, and operational efficiency within the virtual reality space. The NGAC standard provides a logical, attribute-based approach to defining relationships between users (subjects), resources (objects), and the operations subjects can perform on objects. In the context of a VROS, subjects may represent virtual reality users, applications, or system processes, while objects can encompass virtual environments, system resources, or simulated resources.

Our current work focuses on controlling inter-processing communication. Consequently, in our model, caller apps are the subject, and target apps are the objects. The NGAC we propose will manage the access between caller apps and target apps, verifying their attributes and checking the privileges of the NGAC model to grant or deny access.

We identify the attributes of the caller apps and target apps within the VROS environment. Once the necessary attributes are defined, we build the NGAC model to fulfill the security policy requirements that dictate the conditions under which caller apps can access, manipulate, or interact with the target apps' virtual reality resources and functionalities. Throughout the security policy design process, we adhere to the NGAC standard's guidelines and best practices, ensuring that policy requirements are logically sound, unambiguous, and enforceable within the VROS environment. Additionally, we design security policies that are flexible and extensible, allowing for future modifications or additions as the VROS system's requirements evolve.

3.1 Identifying Policy Element of IPC

Policy elements are the fundamental components of the NGAC policy class, which include authorized subjects (S), processes (P), objects (O) operations (Op), and access rights (AR) [17]. The policy class comprises a finite set of relations between these elements used to grant or deny an access request. We determine operating system entities relevant to virtual reality and compile a list of the critical attributes required to define our policy class.

Subject: This is the caller app that requests a service from the target app. A caller app can be a user-installed application (third party) or a pre-installed application (native application). A caller app can request access to the components of another app through implicit intent and may require access to various system resources within the operating environment. We define a list of attributes CA as a set of finite attributes belonging to the caller app, described as:

For simplicity, we use the term "signed" to describe apps that have been signed by trusted entities such as Google Play, Oculus Store, or a device manufacturer's store. "unsigned" refers to apps not signed by these entities or those signed by untrusted sources. A "trusted source" refers to applications downloaded from a trusted entity. At the same time, "sideload" refers to apps installed on a device from other sources, such as the internet or external methods (e.g., ADB or file sharing).

1. CA_sig refers to caller app signature which is of the enumerated type [signed, unsigned].
2. CA_is is the caller app installation source, which is of the enumerated type [trusted source, sideload].

Object: The target app refers to the an application or system resource from which the caller app requests a service; the target app provides a finite set of services listed in the manifest file to the service manager. We define a list of attributes TA as a set of finite attributes belonging to the target app, described as:

1. TA_sig = target app signature which is of the enumerated type [signed, unsigned]
2. TA_is = target app installation source [trusted source, sideload]
3. TA_cat = target app type [non-native app, native app, system resources]

Access Rights: The caller app can specify an operation to perform on the target app based on the components provided. These operations are considered access rights in the context of access control. Examples of possible operations are listed below.

– Activity = startactivity, finish
– Services = bindservice, unbindservice
– Broadcast receivers = sendbroadcast, registerreceiver

3.2 NGAC IPC Policy Design

Virtual reality operating system includes various native apps (browser and photos) and system resources (camera, location, microphone, and haptic controller). It also includes non-native apps such as business, gaming, and entertainment. These apps need to be protected from malicious apps. The trusted apps are usually installed and signed by a trusted source (e.g., Meta Horizon store) or can be self-signed by the developer for development purpose and in such a case we consider the signature as unsigned; these trusted apps are allowed to perform operations such as *startActivity*, *bindService*, and *unbindService* on system resources and other apps. However, apps installed from untrusted sources (i.e., sideload) are suspicious. If the sideload apps are signed, we want to allow only specific operations to be executed on the system resources. Meanwhile, if the sideload apps are unsigned, there is a higher probability that they are malicious apps; in these cases, we want to stop or deny any operations on the system resources and other apps. Table 1 represents these restrictions of inter-process communication between VR apps in three security policies.

PC1 PC2, and PC4 show association relations between caller and target apps. However, PC2 grants only one operation, while PC1 and PC4 grants all operations. PC3 represents a prohibition relation, denying all operations on system resources and other target apps. These security policies are analyzed and

Table 1. IPC Policy

Policy ID	Policy Description
PC1	if caller app is from a trusted source and signed, it is granted permission to perform any operations on any signed target app.
PC2	if caller app is from a trusted source and unsigned then it can perform only *startActivity* operation on target app (system resources)
PC3	if caller app is sideload and unsigned, then deny all operations on any target app
PC4	if caller app is from a trusted source and signed, it is granted permission to perform any operations on unsigned target app.

transformed into the NGAC security model, an authorization graph shown in Fig. 2. Each policy represents one or many paths from caller apps through caller app attributes, associations or prohibition relations, and target app attributes to the target apps. These attributes have various values. The attributes, possible values, relations, and operations are described below.

- Activity = startActivity, finish
- Services = bindService, unbindService
- Broadcast receivers = sendBroadcast, registerReceiver
- **Basic elements:**
    - Caller app = {Custom App, Oculus Browser, Horizon Edge}
    - Caller app attributes = {CA_sig, CA_is}
    - Target app = {GoMeet, Photos }
    - Target app attributes = {TA_sig, TA_cat}
    - Access right = {startActivity, finish, bindService, unbindService, sendBroadcast, registerReceiver, query, insert, All}
    - Policy Class = {Intent Validation}
- **Relations:**
    - Assignment ={(Custom App, Side load), (Oculus Browser, Trusted Source), (Horizon Edge, Trusted Source), (GoMeet, Non-native app), (Photos, Native app) (Sideload, Unsigned), (Sideload, Signed), (Non-native app, Signed), (Native app, Signed) (System resources, Signed), (Unsigned, Intent Validation), (Signed, Intent Validation)}
    - Association = {(trusted, Grant[bindService], System resource), (Signed, Grant[All], Signed)}
    - Prohibitions = {(Unsigned, Deny[All], Signed)}

We use Depth-first search (DFS [25]) to derive the privilege list from the NGAC model. The privilege list states each caller app and its privileges (grant/deny) to perform operations on a target app. The privilege list is formatted as privilege list = [(caller App, [caller attributes], permission[access rights], [target attributes], target App)].

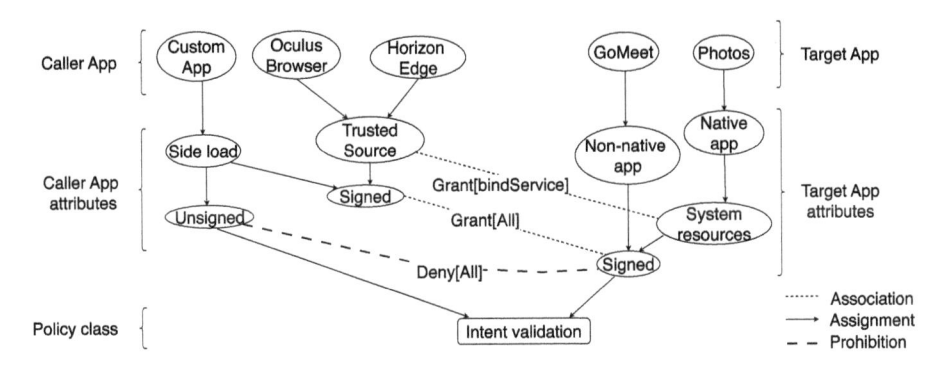

Fig. 2. NGAC Authorization Graph

Next, we formally define the *intent* as a set of NGAC basic elements (attributes) and design an algorithm that validates it against the privilege list to grant/deny inter-process communication between apps.

4 NGAC IPC Policy Architecture

The policy class for inter-process communication (IPC) with implicit intent is to guarantee that interactions between the caller app and the target app are validated before being executed on the target app. The validation process first intercepts an intent and then verifies the caller app signature and installation source. It also verifies the target app signature and type.

Definition 1 (Intent). *is defined as 6-tuple* $INTENT = \langle \mathcal{C}, \mathcal{T}, \mathcal{CA}, \mathcal{TA}, \mathcal{OP}, \mathcal{E} \rangle$, *where*

- $\mathcal{C}$ is a finite set of caller apps; $\mathcal{C} = \{c_1, c_2, \ldots, c_n\}$.
- $\mathcal{T}$ is a finite set of target apps; $\mathcal{T} = \{t_1, t_2, \ldots, t_n\}$.
- $\mathcal{CA}$ is a finite set of caller app's attributes;
  $\mathcal{CA} = \{ca_1, ca_2, \ldots, ca_n\}$.
- $\mathcal{TA}$ is a finite set of target app's attributes;
  $\mathcal{TA} = \{ta_1, ta_2, \ldots, ta_n\}$.
- $\mathcal{OP}$ is a finite set of access rights (operations) declared by the NGAC administrator; $\mathcal{OP} = \{op_1, op_2, \ldots, op_n\}$
- $\mathcal{E}$ is a function forms intents; $\mathcal{E} = \{(c, [ca], [op], [ta], t) \in c \times \mathcal{CA} \times \mathcal{OP} \times \mathcal{TA} \times t \mid c \in \mathcal{C}, ca \in \mathcal{CA}, op \in \mathcal{OP}, ta \in \mathcal{TA}, \text{ and } t \in \mathcal{T}\}$

For simplicity, we derive two lists: grant privilege and deny privilege list.

1. The grant privilege list generated from our model is as follows: (Horizon Edge, [trusted], Grant [bindService], [System resource, Native Apps], Photos), (Oculus Browser, [trusted, Signed], Grant[All], [Signed, Non-native Apps, System resource, Native Apps], GoMeet), (Oculus Browser, [trusted, Signed],

Algorithm 1: Intent Validation

Input : $Intent = \langle \mathcal{C}, \mathcal{T}, \mathcal{CA}, \mathcal{TA}, \mathcal{OP}, \mathcal{E} \rangle$
Input : $GrantPrivileges = [(callApp, [CallarAttrs], Grant[AR], [TargetAttrs], targetApp)]$
Input : $DenyPrivileges = [(callApp, [CallarAttrs], Deny[AR], [TargetAttrs], targetApp)]$
Output: $\{Grant, Deny\}$

/* validate intent against deny privilege list   */
1 **foreach** $privilge \in DenyPrivileges$ **do**
2   **if** $(privilge.callerApp = c \in Intent.C) \wedge (privilge.targetApp = t \in Intent.T) \wedge (match(privilge.CallarAttrs, CA) \wedge (match(privilge.TargetAttrs, TA) \wedge (match(privilge.AR, OP)$ **then**
3 | **return** $Deny$
4   **end**
5 **end**

/* validate intent against grant privilege list   */
6 **foreach** $privilge \in GrantPrivileges$ **do**
7   **if** $(privilge.callerApp = c \in Intent.C) \wedge (privilge.targetApp = t \in Intent.T) \wedge (match(privilge.CallarAttrs, CA) \wedge (match(privilge.TargetAttrs, TA) \wedge (match(privilge.AR, OP)$ **then**
8 | **return** $Grant$
9   **end**
10 **end**
11 **return** $Invalid$

Grant[All], [Signed, Non-native Apps, System resource, Native Apps], Photos), (Custom App, [Side load, Signed], Grant[All], [Signed, Non-native Apps, System resource, Native Apps], GoMeet), (Custom App, [Side load, Signed], Grant[All], [Signed, Non-native Apps, System resource, Native Apps], Photos)

2. The deny privilege list is: (Custom App, [Side load, Unsigned], Deny[All], [Signed, Non-native Apps, System resource, Native Apps], GoMeet), (Custom App, [Side load, Unsigned], Deny[All], [Signed, Non-native Apps, System resource, Native Apps], Photos).

The intent definition is used as input for Algorithm 1 along with the grant privilege and deny privilege lists generated from the NGAC model. Algorithm 1 iterates brute-forcibly over these privilege lists to find a match with intent parameters. From lines 1 to 5, it iterates over the deny privilege list. Each privilege instance is compared with the intent. If the caller apps attributes and target apps attributes matches the deny privilege list, and the operations required match the access rights, it returns "Deny". Otherwise, it iterates over the grant privilege list, lines 6 to 10, and does the same comparison; if it finds a match, it returns "Grant". If no match is found in both lists, line 11, it returns "Invalid". Algorithm 1 gives deny more precedence over the grant privileges; if the deny and grant occur at the same time (i.e., a conflict policy), it gives precedence to deny.

4.1 NGAC IPC Enforcement

NGAC IPC security module is designed as a library to secure IPC, and access control policies modification are restricted to the VR device manufacturers. Once an app is installed, the NGAC framework extracts the app attributes into the Policy Information Point.

Our fine-grained access control enforcement follows steps 1 to 13 to validate inter-process communication between apps, as shown in Fig. 3.

Supposing a caller app (Custom App) needs to launch the target app (GoMeet) by requesting an activity (e.g., startActivity) provided by the target app (GoMeet). We describe the access control steps as follows:

Step 1: Service Discovery
The caller app specifies an intent containing the intended action (android. intent. action.VIEW), category(android.intent.category.LAUNCHER), and the data (Uri. parse("package:com.gomeet.app")) required to perform the intended request. This intent is then forwarded to the service manager to identify the target app that can handle the caller app intent.

Step 2: Proxy Object creation
If the result is null, no apps on the device can handle such intent, and an app crash occurs with an error message, terminating the request. If the target app is found, as in our case, a node (proxy object) will be created.

Step 3: Entry to NGAC security model
The service manager conveys this proxy object, and the identified target app ID to the PEP for further verification and access control decision.

Step 4: Initiation of Access Request
PEP initiates an access request on behalf of the caller app attempting to access the target app. The PEP collects relevant information, such as the ID of the caller app, the target app ID, and the proxy object that contains the intent.

Step 5: Attributes query
The PDP queries the PAP for information about the caller and target apps to drive the access decision.

Step 6: Attributes retrieval
The PAP validates the query to fetch the caller app and target app attributes contained in the PIP.

Step 7: Policy evaluation
PAP returns the attributes to the PDP for policy evaluation.

Step 8: Policy decision process
The PDP retrieves the relevant policies from the policy class as contained in Table 1 and traverses the authorization graph, Fig. 2, to evaluate the request and decides whether to grant or deny the request made by the caller app and send its decision to the PEP.

Step 9: Decision communication and logging
If the response is granted, the PEP thoroughly resolves the proxy object to the RAP and logs the intent simultaneously to EPP; otherwise, it returns deny, ensuring a comprehensive validation.

Step 10: Exit from NGAC security model
The resource access point forwards the intent to the Binder Driver.

Step 11 to 12: Parcel Copy
The Binder Driver resolves the intent to the target app through the Target app native object to perform the operation on the target app.

Step 13: Receiving the Response
The target app returns the result of the request to the caller app.

This process occurs whenever an app attempts to access the services offered by another app or any other protected resource, ensuring a well-documented access history.

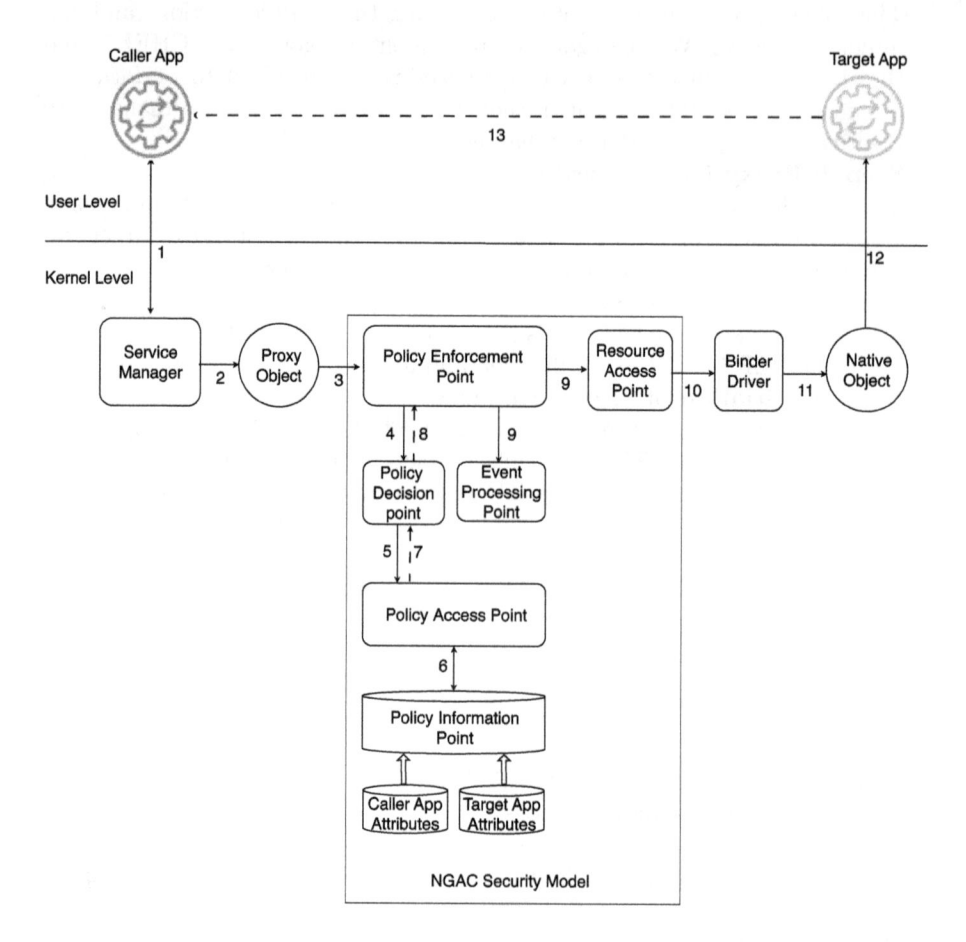

Fig. 3. NGAC IPC Enforcement Architecture

4.2 Portability to Meta Horizon Operating System

The IPC within the Meta Operating System occurs within the Android Generic Kernel Image (GKI). The IPC in the GKI utilize SEAndroid for access control which does not have enough validating mechanism to distinguish legitimate IPC requests. To provide validation, our model replaces the standard IPC in that kernel with an IPC model that is augmented with the NGAC-IPC process described in Fig. 4. This NGAC-IPC then operates at the kernel level of the meta device in the middle of the normal Android IPC process, managing how the different processes interact and access shared services. When a new app is registered, the NGAC IPC is given its shared resources and services to make decisions regarding requests.

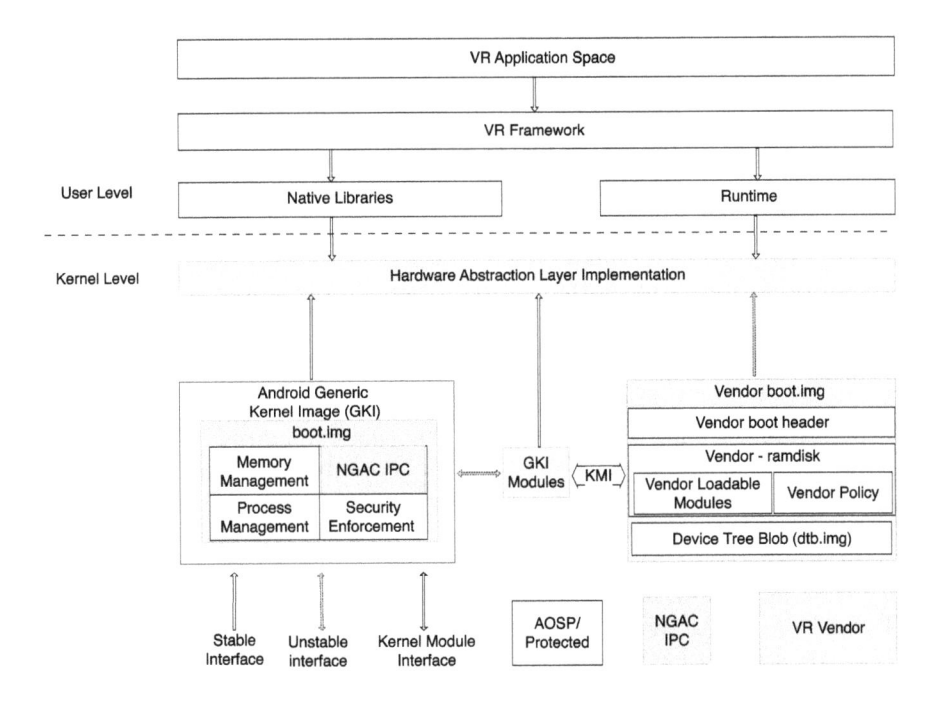

Fig. 4. NGAC IPC Portability with Meta Horizon OS

5 Discussion

We designed the policy class based on policy requirements (PC1, PC2, PC3, and PC4) to incorporate the caller app's attributes, including signature and installation source, and the target app's attributes, such as native apps, non-native apps, and system resources. These attributes are extracted from the app's manifest, and the intent is validated through policy processes to decide whether an operation should be allowed. The policy validation effectively serves as a shield against various attacks:

- Intent Hijacking: This attack occurs when an app intercepts an intent for another app and performs unauthorized operations. The policy PC3 prevents

intent hijacking attacks by ensuring intent communication is denied from caller apps that are side-loaded and unsigned or installed from a trusted source but unsigned (i.e., signed with a developer key) from accessing other apps or system resources.
- Intent Spoofing: In this attack, a malicious app generates a faked intent that looks to be from a legitimate app, leading the target app to do unwanted activities. The policy PC1 prevents such attacks by ensuring proper validation before forwarding intent to the binder.
- Intent Fuzzing: This attack sends malformed or random intents to an app to cause unexpected behavior or crashes. The policies PC1, PC2 and PC4 reduce the risk of intent fuzzing attacks by validating the operation and ensuring it has the relevant attributes to perform the operation.
- Privilege Escalation: Some intent attacks attempt to escalate privileges by exploiting flaws in how apps process intents. The policies PC1, PC2, PC4 ensure that caller apps can only communicate with specified target apps.
- Data Leakage: Malicious apps may attempt to access or extract sensitive data from other apps using intent-based attacks. The policy PC3 enforces tense validation to prevent unauthorized data access or leakage.

6 Related Work

The literature on VR security explores the vulnerabilities of VR platforms. It offers various solutions, operating system access restriction [39], Role-based Access Control (RBAC) [37]. However, these works are either limited to specific VR platforms [37] or lack the usability of the device's resources [39].

Our work addresses this research gap by safeguarding the inter-process communication in VR environments using the NIST Next-Generation Access Control (NGAC). NGAC IPC runs in the background to monitor system events. NGAC IPC's validation process, which intercepts intents and activates authorization processes, instills confidence in its effectiveness. NGAC's effectiveness in allowing the system administrator (VR device manufacturer) to add, modify, and remove policies invests a sense of security and control in safeguarding inter-process communication. This provides flexibility for securing VR apps in the Android environment. Our solution is also independent of any VR platform, providing a portable gateway that ensures VR app protection.

6.1 Related Work on VR Security

Android's Binder IPC uses a mandatory access control system named Intent Firewall (IFW) in version 4.4 [24] and relies heavily on firewall rules within the Intent Firewall [5]. It utilizes intent filters to resolve intents between interacting apps based on the permission levels set by app developers for each exported app component. When a developer fails to specify a permission level, the app component becomes exposed to intent-based attacks [24]. The operating system does not perform further validation to verify the origin of the calling app or the legitimacy of the requested action. This leads to unauthorized activity launches and the theft of arbitrary files through activity and intent redirection attacks. The adoption of Android Binder IPC in Virtual reality devices introduced a new form of attack vector. Several access control mechanisms have been applied to virtual reality devices in the past, with differing benefits and tradeoffs using different approaches.

Wei et al. [37] designed a content-oriented access control mechanism for the VR platform *OpenSim* that combines identity-based capabilities and RBAC to address the security issues that are faced by systems consisting of databases, servers, and one or more clients. However, this work was limited to the *OpenSim* platform and was not extended to the device to authorize processes or users running on the headset.

Casey et al. [11] exposed significant IPC vulnerabilities in the HTC Vive and Oculus Rift VR devices by exploiting the software interface level. They leverage vulnerabilities within OpenVR, a software library built on StreamVR, to create and execute malicious implicit intents that the IPC mechanism failed to prevent, leading to immersive attacks by modifying configuration files. The attack resulting from these malicious implicit intents was able to guide and control a VR user's actions and movements remotely without the user's knowledge, including built-in safety mechanisms such as the chaperone, which is a boundary that prevents the immersed user from venturing into unsafe physical locations specified by the user. To mitigate these attacks, they recommended implementing application signing as a security measure to prevent IPC attacks that result in unauthorized configuration file modifications. They also suggested using the Arya framework [28] to enhance security within existing VR systems by imposing policy on sensor inputs through input stream recognizers and visual output through virtual object abstraction. However, the offered solutions must address these vulnerabilities at the operating system level.

A further study by Yang et al. [39] recommended suggestions such as disabling app calls by non-system apps, app certificates, validating the authenticity of app calls, or preventing user access to the OS shell to prevent IPC attacks such as immersive hijacking and interception attacks. These recommendations limit the usability of the devices.

6.2 Related Work on Android IPC Security

Several works has been done in security Android IPC, Smalley et al. [34] protect the Binder by implementing new Linux Security Module (LSM) security hooks in the binder driver to enforce SELinux permission checks over inter-app communication and control operations, thereby restricting which processes can communicate and manage Binder references but could not protect against malicious intent.

IPC provenance was first introduced by Dietz et al. [14]. The author developed an approach (namely Quire) to providing provenance information on Android through explicit call-chain transmission, which introduces significant developer dependency, requiring them to modify and recompile their apps actively. This creates barriers to adoption, limits its ability to monitor existing apps, introduces potential performance issues, and exposes the system to trust and security risks based on developer compliance.

Backes et al. [7] proposed a system-centric solution (namely Scippa) for IPC provenance by tracking IPC calls at the system level, focusing on the Binder communication channels between apps. While this approach captures the sequence of IPC calls between apps it does validate the specific intent, data type, or action.

Kaladharan et al. [22] introduce the concept of a "Man-in-the-Binder" attack, which attack targets the Binder IPC mechanism as it intercepts data sent between Android applications and services, which are transmitted in plaintext, thus exposing sensitive application information. The authors propose an encryption scheme to secure the communications between them before passing the data through Binder. The encryption mechanism involves assigning a secret key between the kernel and each application or service. Although the author proposes lightweight cryptography to mitigate the performance, there may still be concerns about the impact on system performance, especially for applications that make frequent Binder calls.

Kraunelis et al. [26] modified the Binder library to detect and counter deceptive user interface attacks such as malicious activity launched on the Android via inspection and analysis of inter-process communication transactions in the operating system by recording application UIDs and timestamps whenever the *StartActivity* method is called. The recorded timestamp is then compared to the previously logged timestamp; if the time difference is less than a certain threshold, the UID of the previous caller is the launcher, and the current caller's UID does not own the package name. The activity is determined to be malicious, and action can be taken to mitigate the malware.

In a more recent work [30], Lyvas et al. explored encrypting transmitted intent data based on user-defined policies. Their approach generates a public/private key pair and a symmetric key via the Android Keystore for authentication and encryption. When an application starts an activity using an implicit intent, the system retrieves the source's keys, signs the intent with the private key, and encrypts it with the symmetric key. This allows users to control IPC by verifying the signature and decrypting the intent data. However, this system introduces overhead, with the highest measured cost being 190ms, depending on the data size.

Matteo De Giorgi [13] developed a tool called Ptracer to monitor system calls and inter-process communications in Android. Ptracer operates between the app and the kernel, intercepting and collecting data such as stack backtraces and system call parameters. It aims to detect debuggers, identify anomalies, and flag privacy concerns by analyzing how frequently an app requests sensitive data through kernel queries, focusing on dangerous behaviors related to privacy.

D. Wu et al. [38] introduce *SCLib*, a defense mechanism against component hijacking in Android applications. Operating at the app level, SCLib handles deployment without requiring system-level changes, making it adaptable across a fragmented Android ecosystem. It enforces MAC policies to verify incoming requests before execution, preventing unauthorized access to exported components, mitigating privilege escalation via permission hijacking, checking system-only broadcasts, and guarding against SQL injection attacks on content providers. However, it doesn't cover all attack vectors, such as unauthorized intent receipt by malicious apps.

7 Conclusion and Future Work

This paper addresses immersive attacks in Android-based Virtual Reality devices, namely immersive manipulation and hijacking attacks, due to improper process validation during VR app interactions. We designed an enforcement architecture, called Inter-Process Communication (IPC) enforcement, that unitizes NGAC access control to manage inter-process communication between apps and protect the Android environment from malicious apps attempting to access resources and other legitimate apps.

We formally defined the apps' attributes and relations required to build the NGAC model. We also designed an algorithm to validate these attributes and relations against apps' access requests to grant/deny inter-process communication. The implementation of the IPC enforcement is a work in progress, and efforts are ongoing to bring it to production. Future work will present the implementation of IPC enforcement and experiment with its effectiveness. We are confident that this work, including implementation, will be beneficial to the VR industry.

Currently, our approach focuses on compatibility with Android-based VR devices. It does not address the security concerns on the entire range of VR devices in the current commercial market or devices outside the VR space, such as AR devices or computers. Such devices may also be vulnerable to exploitation through IPC-related attacks and would benefit from extending this model into their domain space. This will be a part of our future works.

We plan to extend this model to provide more specific and secure IPC on Android devices and provide their implementation. We also would like to investigate applications of this model onto different IPC structures in different operating infrastructures, such as HTC Vive a Windows-based VR device to understand the differences in the application of NGAC on these devices' IPCs. This approach may also apply to other systems outside of VR with vulnerabilities in their IPCs; this work may be extended to Kubernetes in its node communications or to other Linux systems to provide a security layer surrounding process intents.

Acknowledgements. This work was supported in part by funding from NIST under Grant Number 60NANB23D152 NSF under Award Numbers CNS 1715458, DMS 2123761, CNS 1822118, NIST, ARL, Statnett, AMI, NewPush, and Cyber Risk Research.

References

1. Android, D.: Common intents (2024). https://developer.android.com/guide/components/intents-common
2. Android, D.: Intents and intent filters (2024). https://developer.android.com/guide/components/intents-filters
3. Android, D.: Let other apps start your activity (2024). https://developer.android.com/training/basics/intents/filters
4. Android, D.: Permissions (2024). https://developer.android.com/guide/topics/manifest/permission-element
5. Android Source, C.: Interact with other apps (2023). https://cs.android.com/android/platform/superproject/+/android14-qpr3-release:frameworks/base/services/core/java/com/android/server/firewall/IntentFirewall.java;l=58?q=intentFire&ss=android%2Fplatform%2Fsuperproject
6. Arafat, A.A., Guo, Z., Awad, A.: VR-spy: a side-channel attack on virtual keylogging in VR headsets. In: 2021 IEEE Virtual Reality and 3D User Interfaces (VR), pp. 564–572 (2021). https://doi.org/10.1109/VR50410.2021.00081
7. Backes, M., Bugiel, S., Gerling, S.: Scippa: System-centric IPC provenance on android. In: Proceedings of the 30th Annual Computer Security Applications Conference, pp. 36–45 (2014)
8. Baiqin, W.: Binder Architecture and Core Components (2021). https://medium.com/swlh/binder-architecture-and-core-components-38089933bba
9. Benigni, D., Francomacaro, S.: INCITS 499-201x (revision of INCITS 499-2013), information technology -next generation access control -functional architecture (NGAC-FA) due date: The public review is from (2016). https://standards.incits.org/higherlogic/ws/public/download/85867/eb-2016-00808-002-Public-review-register-INCITS-499-Comments-due-2-28-2017.zip
10. Bezawada, B., Haefner, K., Ray, I.: Securing home IoT environments with attribute-based access control. In: Proceedings of the Third ACM Workshop on Attribute-Based Access Control, pp. 43–53 (2018)
11. Casey, P., Baggili, I., Yarramreddy, A.: Immersive virtual reality attacks and the human joystick. IEEE Trans. Dependable Secure Comput. **18**(2), 550–562 (2019)
12. Cheng, K., Tian, J.F., Kohno, T., Roesner, F.: Exploring user reactions and mental models towards perceptual manipulation attacks in mixed reality. In: Proceedings of the 32nd USENIX Security Symposium (2023)
13. De Giorgi, M.: System calls monitoring in android: an approach to detect debuggers, anomalies and privacy issues (2023)
14. Dietz, M., Shekhar, S., Pisetsky, Y., Shu, A., Wallach, D.S.: Quire: lightweight provenance for smart phone operating systems. In: USENIX Security Symposium, vol. 31, p. 3. San Francisco, CA (2011)
15. Falebita, O.S.: Secure web-based student information management system. arXiv preprint arXiv:2211.00072 (2022)
16. Ferraiolo, D., Chandramouli, R., Kuhn, R., Hu, V.: Extensible access control markup language (XACML) and next generation access control (NGAC). In: Proceedings of the 2016 ACM International Workshop on Attribute Based Access Control, pp. 13–24 (2016)
17. Ferraiolo, D., Gavrila, S., Jansen, W.: Archived nist technical series publication archived publication series/number: Title: Publication date(s): Withdrawal date: Superseding publication(s) (2014). https://doi.org/10.6028/NIST.IR.7987r1

18. George, C., Khamis, M., Buschek, D., Hussmann, H.: Investigating the third dimension for authentication in immersive virtual reality and in the real world. In: 2019 IEEE Conference on Virtual Reality and 3D User Interfaces (VR), pp. 277–285. IEEE (2019)
19. George, C., et al.: Seamless and secure VR: adapting and evaluating established authentication systems for virtual reality. In: Proceedings of the CHI Conference on Human Factors in Computing Systems. NDSS (2017)
20. Google, D.: Application Sandbox (2024). https://source.android.com/docs/security/app-sandbox#:~:text=Because%20the%20Application%20Sandbox%20is,run%20within%20the%20Application%20Sandbox
21. Institute, A.N.S.: Information technology - next generation access control (NGAC). Information technology, ANSI, New York, NY (2020). Accessed 2023
22. Kaladharan, Y., Mateti, P., Jevitha, K.P.: An encryption technique to thwart android binder exploits. In: Berretti, S., Thampi, S.M., Dasgupta, S. (eds.) Intelligent Systems Technologies and Applications. AISC, vol. 385, pp. 13–21. Springer, Cham (2016). https://doi.org/10.1007/978-3-319-23258-4_2
23. Kashmar, N., Adda, M., Ibrahim, H.: Access control metamodels: review, critical analysis, and research issues. J. Ubiquitous Syst. Pervasive Netw. **16**(2), 93–102 (2022)
24. Klepp, T.: Cruel intentions: enhancing androids intent firewall. Ph.D. thesis, Technische Universität Wien (2020)
25. Kozen, D.C., Kozen, D.C.: Depth-first and breadth-first search. In: The Design and Analysis of Algorithms. Texts and Monographs in Computer Science, pp. 19–24. Springer, New York (1992). https://doi.org/10.1007/978-1-4612-4400-4_4
26. Kraunelis, J., Fu, X., Yu, W., Zhao, W.: A framework for detecting and countering android UI attacks via inspection of IPC traffic. In: 2018 IEEE International Conference on Communications (ICC), pp. 1–6. IEEE (2018)
27. Lawal, S., Krishnan, R.: Utilizing policy machine for attribute-based access control in permissioned blockchain. In: 2021 IEEE International Conference on Omni-Layer Intelligent Systems (COINS), pp. 1–6. IEEE (2021)
28. Lebeck, K., Ruth, K., Kohno, T., Roesner, F.: Securing augmented reality output. In: 2017 IEEE Symposium on Security and Privacy (SP), pp. 320–337. IEEE (2017)
29. Luo, S., Nguyen, A., Song, C., Lin, F., Xu, W., Yan, Z.: Oculock: exploring human visual system for authentication in virtual reality head-mounted display. In: 2020 Network and Distributed System Security Symposium (NDSS) (2020)
30. Lyvas, C., Lambrinoudakis, C., Geneiatakis, D.: Intentauth: securing android's intent-based inter-process communication. Int. J. Inf. Secur. **21**(5), 973–982 (2022)
31. Mathis, F., Williamson, J., Vaniea, K., Khamis, M.: Rubikauth: fast and secure authentication in virtual reality. In: Extended Abstracts of the 2020 CHI Conference on Human Factors in Computing Systems, pp. 1–9 (2020)
32. Odeleye, B., Loukas, G., Heartfield, R., Spyridonis, F.: Detecting framerate-oriented cyber attacks on user experience in virtual reality. In: VR4Sec: 1st International Workshop on Security for XR and XR for Security: Proceedings, pp. 1–5. Vancouver, B.C., Canada (virtual) (2021)
33. Raymer, E., MacDermott, Á., Akinbi, A.: Virtual reality forensics: Forensic analysis of meta quest 2. Forensic Sci. Int. Digital Invest. **47**, 301658 (2023)
34. Smalley, S., Craig, R.: Security enhanced (se) android: bringing flexible mac to android. In: Ndss, vol. 310, pp. 20–38 (2013)
35. Tseng, W.J., et al.: The dark side of perceptual manipulations in virtual reality. In: Proceedings of the 2022 CHI Conference on Human Factors in Computing Systems, pp. 1–15 (2022)

36. Vondráček, M., Baggili, I., Casey, P., Mekni, M.: Rise of the metaverse's immersive virtual reality malware and the man-in-the-room attack & defenses. Comput. Secur. **127**, 102923 (2023)
37. Wei, Y.G., Lu, Y., Hu, X.Y., Sun, B.: Research and application of access control technique in 3D virtual reality system opensim. In: 2013 Sixth International Symposium on Computational Intelligence and Design, vol. 2, pp. 65–68. IEEE (2013)
38. Wu, D., Cheng, Y., Gao, D., Li, Y., Deng, R.H.: Sclib: a practical and lightweight defense against component hijacking in android applications. In: Proceedings of the Eighth ACM Conference on Data and Application Security and Privacy (CODASPY 2018), pp. 299–306. ACM, Tempe, AZ, USA (2018). https://doi.org/10.1145/3176258.3176336
39. Yang, Z., Li, C.Y., Bhalla, A., Zhao, B.Y., Zheng, H.: Inception attacks: immersive hijacking in virtual reality systems. arXiv preprint arXiv:2403.05721 (2024)
40. Yarramreddy, A., Gromkowski, P., Baggili, I.: Forensic analysis of immersive virtual reality social applications. In: A Primary Accout, 2018 IEEE Security and Privacy Workshops, pp. 186–196. IEEE. San Francisco (2018)

Network Security

Securing the Web: Analysis of HTTP Security Headers in Popular Global Websites

Urvashi Kishnani[1] and Sanchari Das[1,2]

[1] University of Denver, Denver, CO 80208, USA
{Urvashi.Kishnani,Sanchari.Das}@du.edu
[2] George Mason University, Fairfax, VA, USA
sdas35@gmu.edu

Abstract. The surge in website attacks, including Denial of Service (DoS), Cross-Site Scripting (XSS), and Clickjacking, underscores the critical need for robust HTTPS implementation—a practice that, alarmingly, remains inadequately adopted. Regarding this, we analyzed HTTP security headers across $N = 3,195$ globally popular websites. Initially, we employed automated categorization using Google NLP to organize these websites into functional categories and validated this categorization through manual verification using Symantec Sitereview. Subsequently, we assessed HTTPS implementation across these websites by analyzing security factors, including compliance with HTTP Strict Transport Security (HSTS) policies, Certificate Pinning practices, and other security postures using the Mozilla Observatory. Our analysis revealed over half of the websites examined (55.66%) received a dismal security grade of 'F' and most websites scored low for various metrics, which is indicative of weak HTTP header implementation. These low scores expose multiple issues such as weak implementation of Content Security Policies (CSP), neglect of HSTS guidelines, and insufficient application of Subresource Integrity (SRI). Alarmingly, healthcare websites ($n = 59$) are particularly concerning; despite being entrusted with sensitive patient data and obligations to comply with data regulations, these sites recorded the lowest average score (18.14). We conclude by recommending that developers should prioritize secure redirection strategies and use implementation ease as a guide when deciding where to focus their development efforts.

Keywords: Website Security · HTTPS Implementation

1 Introduction

Websites are essential in the digital age, offering services across e-commerce, banking, healthcare, and more [27,28,40,84]. They, along with mobile apps, have seen a significant increase in traffic [23,29,50,64,88]. For example, in November 2022, YouTube and Facebook logged 74.8 billion and 10.7 billion monthly views, respectively [6,20,60]. The most popularly used secure protocol for data exchange between websites and clients is the HyperText Transfer

Protocol with the added Transport Layer Security (TLS) giving HTTPS [8,21]. The research community has long recognized the importance of securing websites and has developed various tools, techniques, and best practices to improve web security [19,22,66,68,79,82]. However, the implementation of these security practices remains inconsistent across different website categories and industries [34,49,59,89]. Moreover, research indicates that the complexity of the web ecosystem can magnify the impact of even a few exploitable HTTPS vulnerabilities [9,41,55,83,95]. The security of websites, including HTTP header implementation, is even more critical for websites involving financial transactions. This is particularly important for popular websites, as increased traffic correlates with more transactions. Thus, our study aims to answer the following research questions:

- **RQ1:** To what extent are the implementation and adherence to HTTP security headers, notably redirection protocols, the utilization of secure cookies, and Content Security Policy (CSP) directives, consistently observed as points of vulnerability or misconfiguration among widely-visited websites?
- **RQ2:** How does the implementation and compliance of multiple HTTP security headers vary across diverse website categories, including but not limited to Computers & Electronics, Finance, and Health? And how can these variations be ranked or categorized based on their robustness or potential vulnerabilities?

We collected a list of the 10,000 most popular websites and categorized them into 27 categories like Shopping, Games, etc. using Natural Language Processing (NLP). This categorization assists in linking these website categories to user-friendly functional groups. Next, we conducted a security evaluation of 3,195 categorized websites and analyzed their aggregated, category-wise, and individual security metric performance using Mozilla Observatory [62].

- Our study evaluates website security through the lens of popular website categories, an understudied area. This categorization helps us analyze differences in security measures among various types of websites correlated with their popularity and categorization, allowing us to identify specific vulnerabilities and tailor security improvements accordingly. Moreover, although security headers are typically among the initial aspects of security to be managed and tested in the web security community, the reality on a global scale appears to be concerning.
- Our results emphasizes the need for enhanced security measures on websites categorized as health, sports, and news, which have lower overall security rankings. Alarmingly, healthcare websites have the lowest security ratings, posing risks to users and potential non-compliance with global healthcare regulations. Furthermore, computer security websites scored poorly, with an average score of 31.89, which is concerning as well. In addition, 55.66% of the examined websites received a low security grade of 'F', indicating weak HTTP headers implementation that may leave these websites vulnerable various cyber threats, including XSS, man-in-the-middle (MiTM) attacks, clickjacking, and data breaches.

2 Related Works

2.1 Website Classification and Categorization

Prior studies have utilized URLs as the primary input for categorizing websites using the Naive Bayes approach [26,73]. URL analysis has also been used to filter malicious sites by examining lexical features with a Naive Bayes classifier [4]. Various works focus on detecting phishing websites through classification techniques [24,25,39,67,86,87,90]. Shabudin et al. proposed feature selection techniques to detect phishing sites [76]. Content-based website categorization faces challenges such as large data volumes, effective scraping, and robust algorithm training [7]. Bruni and Bianchi used web scraping and OCR for e-commerce website categorization, though their approach was limited [7]. Our research categorizes websites based on their function, analyzing homepage content rather than URLs to create functional groups, avoiding binary phishing detection.

2.2 Website Security

Effective website security evaluation tools should ensure compatibility, crawlability, vulnerability testing, detailed reporting, and usability with up-to-date databases and flexible interfaces (GUI or CLI) [47,79]. Mozilla Observatory meets these requirements and has been used to measure HTTPS protocol adoption [32] and analyze HTTPS headers on a large scale [53]. Fonseca et al. evaluated website security using SQL injection and XSS testing [35], while Johns et al. developed XSSDS for detecting XSS attacks [48]. Cernica et al. assessed website security via WordPress backup plugins [12], and Szydlowski et al. highlighted server-side solutions for mitigating client-side attacks like Trojan Horses [85]. Jammalamadaka et al. introduced "Delegate," a proxy-based architecture for secure web access [46]. Al et al. used w3af [94] and Skipfish [80] for a security evaluation of Saudi Arabian websites [3]. Our study adopts a similar approach to analyze HTTP security headers, with the added aspect of website categorization using NLP. Felt et al. [32] and Lavrenovs et al. [53] used Mozilla Observatory to track HTTPS header adoption. Gadient et al. found a lack of secure HTTP headers in mobile app URLs [37], and Mendoza et al. revealed inconsistencies in HTTP security across various web and mobile categories [59]. Stock et al. analyzed web security mechanisms in modern standards, suggesting areas for improvement [81], while Chen et al. identified gaps in developers' understanding of CORS [14]. Meiser et al. highlighted how domain relaxation via CORS adds security risks when subdomains are hosted by third parties [58].

3 Method

We developed a method to collect, categorize, and assess top websites' security, using Python for web scraping, Google NLP for categorization [18], and Mozilla Observatory for HTTPS header evaluation, across four main stages.

3.1 Resource Gathering

To form our initial data corpus, we first gathered the top websites using Tranco's list, which provides the most popular one million domains [70]. The data, collected on February 19, 2023[1], is based on aggregated rankings from various tools, such as Cisco Umbrella [77], Majestic [57], Quantcast [72], and Farsight [1]. By considering the website ranking over the last 30 days, the list minimizes the likelihood of manipulation. For our study, we selected the top 10,000 websites from the Tranco list as the basis for website categorization.

3.2 Preparation of Dataset

Website Scraping and Content Collection. To collect the text data from a website, we used the `cloudscraper 1.2.69` [93] Python module. This module is built to bypass Cloudflare's anti-bot page, which allows large scale crawling or scraping of websites without being blocked by Cloudflare. Websites not using Cloudflare will be handled as is. The module uses JavaScript to impersonate a regular web browser. The request is made to each website using the following `user-agent` header: `Mozilla/5.0 (Windows NT 10.0; Win64; x64) AppleWeb Kit/537.36 (KHTML, like Gecko) Chrome/110.0.0.0 Safari/537.36`. Once the content is scraped from the website, we used the Beautiful Soup Python module `beautifulsoup4 4.11.2` [54] to find HTML elements of interest using the appropriate tags: website's title using `title` tag, website's description `description` tag, website's content headers using `h1, h2, h3` tags, and website's content paragraph using `p` tag. This content was scraped from the landing page of the website, and not from any internally linked pages. The content from each tag was collected into one string which was then used for translation. We obtained content for 7,410 out of the 10,000 websites.

Translating Content. Using `deep-translator 1.10.1` [65] Python module, we translated the collected content into English. This module automates bulk translations and provides support for multi-language translation through various translation libraries, such as Google Translate, Microsoft Translate, and Libre Translator. We employed the Google Translate feature, which allows for only 1,000 characters to be translated in a single document. Websites are recommended to have the length of their title of about six to eight words and their description of no more than 250 characters [96]. Thus, we think using the first 1,000 characters of our scraped content is sufficient. Moreover, the website's description, part of the `meta` tag is part of Resource Description Framework (RDF) that can be used for cataloging [11]. Consequently, we truncated the website content to the first 1,000 characters and used that for translation. The translator was set up to automatically detect the source language and translate it into English. We successfully translated content from 7,399 websites.

---

[1] Available at https://tranco-list.eu/list/3VJNL.

Website Categorization. We performed the categorization using Google NLP API using the `google-cloud-language` 2.9.0 Python module [38]. Prior works have extensively used Google NLP for sentiment analysis [78]. We make use of the content classification feature of this API, as previously used to detect fake news [44] and create knowledge graphs [56]. Using this API requires a Google Cloud Developer account with the Natural Language API enabled for categorization. The response classifies websites into one to four levels of categories and sub-categories. For example, some websites only received one top-level category like Adult whereas some websites received up to four-levels of categories like "Business & Industrial → Shipping & Logistics → Freight Transport → Maritime Transport." Along with this, we also captured the confidence level as percentage of the NLP classifier for each website. At this stage, we obtained classification for a total of 6,914 websites. From these, we filtered websites using our inclusion criteria. We selected websites classified with at least 75% confidence level similar to prior work by Kumar et al. [52] obtaining 3,200 websites.

To verify the categorization method, we first determined the minimum number of websites required for manual verification. We calculated the z-score using a 95% confidence level and a 10% margin of error for our dataset of 3,200 websites, resulting in a sample size of 94. Consequently, we selected a subset of 100 websites, exceeding the minimum required size, by generating unique random numbers using the python `random` library. We sorted the websites by name and used these random numbers as indices to select 100 websites. To manually identify these websites' categories, we used a mix of understanding the website's category through researchers knowledge, checking the "about" page of the website, and using Symantec URL categorization tool[2]. For websites belonging to multiple categories, we used the primary category of the website and matched that with the Google NLP category with the highest confidence level. Through our manual verification process, we obtained a 91% accuracy score for categorization of websites with at least 75% confidence level.

3.3 Evaluation Using Mozilla Observatory

We utilized the Mozilla Observatory tool developed by Mozilla, which automatically analyzes and reports on different HTTP security headers based on Mozilla's web security guidelines [63] which in turn are based on OWASP compliance [36]. This tool performs a series of tests on the HTTP related headers of the websites, to determine the adoption of HTTPS for that website [32]. The tool reports various security measures for 12 different categories, with each category having an associated security benefit and implementation difficulty tagged with either Maximum, High, Medium, and Low. For example, for cookies category, it checks whether the cookies are secured with the HttpOnly attribute and whether any cookies were found in the first place. Each website begins with a score of 100 and then receives a final score based on the scores from each category. Depending on the analysis, each category receives either a positive score, a negative score,

---

[2] https://sitereview.bluecoat.com/.

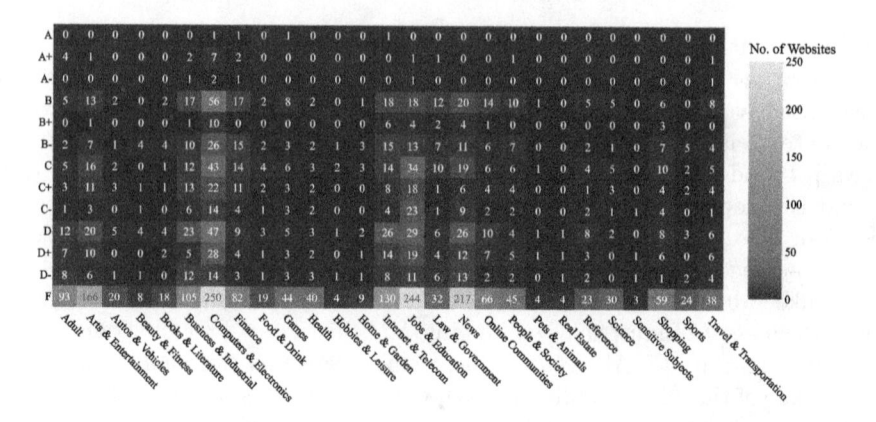

Fig. 1. Distribution of Websites Between Different Grades and Website Categories

or a base score of zero. This modifier is always a multiple of five, so the final score is always a multiple of five. A positive score indicates that the website has taken extra measures to strengthen the security for that header. A negative score indicates that the baseline implementation for the security header is not met, which may leave the website open to vulnerabilities [61].

Most categories give the websites either a score of zero or a negative score. If the website scores 90 or more, then it can receive extra credit from six possible categories: Cookies, Content Security Policy, HTTP Strict Transport Security, Subresource Integrity, and X-Frame-Options. The maximum possible score a website can receive is 135, and the minimum possible score is always zero. If a website's score aggregates to be less than zero, then it is capped at zero. The reported categories and their possible min-max score pairs are: Content Security Policy (+10, −25), Cookies (+5, −40), Cross-origin Resource Sharing (0, −50), Public Key Pinning (0, −5), Redirection from HTTP (0, −20), Referrer Policy (+5, −5), Strict Transport Security (+5, −20), Subresource Integrity (+5, −50), X-Content-Type-Options (0, −5), X-Frame-Options (+5, −20), X-XSS-Protection (0, −10), and configuration of Contribute JSON (0, −10).

Each score range has an associated letter grade given to the website. The possible grades along with their score ranges (in multiples of five) are: A+ (100–135), A (90–95), A− (85), B+ (80), B (70–75), B− (65), C+ (60), C (50–55), C− (45), D+ (40), D (30–35), D− (25), and F (0–20). The full report provides details of each category, the score modifier, and reason for the score. The tabular report offers an overview of the score in each category, the final score, and the letter grade. We note that the cookie analysis here does not give a count of how many cookies on the website were analyzed. We only obtain an indication of whether there were no cookies or at least one cookie. On a Linux virtual machine, we created a Bash script to automatically run all 3,200 websites through this tool. We collected reports successfully for 3,195 websites, which is sufficient for website analysis as illustrated by prior work using 1,000 websites [30]. Only five websites did not result in a successful run with the tool.

4 Results

4.1 Classification and Distribution of Categories

We classified the websites into various levels of categories and sub-categories chains. The classification yielded a total of 27 top-level categories (e.g., Shopping), 191 two-level category chains (e.g., Arts & Entertainment → Celebrities & Entertainment News), 433 three-level category chains (e.g., Autos & Vehicles → Vehicle Codes & Driving Laws → Vehicle Licensing & Registration), and 433 four-level category chains (e.g., Business & Industrial → Shipping & Logistics → Freight Transport → Maritime Transport). Only three categories had complete four-level category chains, with each leaf node being unique, resulting in the same number for both three-level and four-level category chains. Table 1 displays the top three sub-categories within each category.

4.2 Distribution of Security Grades and Scores

Mozilla Observatory assigns a letter-grade and a score to each website. More than half of the websites ($n = 1,777$, 55.62%) received an F grade, including 32.71% ($n = 1,045$) that scored zero, as shown in Fig. 1. We observed peaks at grades A+, B, C, and D, which encompass a broader range of scores. Figure 1 illustrates the distribution of website counts for both grades and website categories. The overall average score across all websites is 26.21. Upon examining the category-wise distribution of scores in Table 1, we find that the top five categories with the highest average scores are Law & Government, Finance, Computers & Electronics, Home & Garden, and Travel & Transportation. The bottom five categories with the lowest average scores are Health, Adult, Arts & Entertainment, Sports, and News. The highest score of 125 was achieved by only one website, www.gimp.org, a free and open-source image editor in the Computers & Electronics category. Further, we note that despite their purpose, websites in the Computer Security category ($n = 66$) scored only an average of 31.89, with min-max score pair (0,105).

4.3 Analysis of HTTP Security Headers

Mozilla Observatory provides a report on 12 security measures for each website, each having an associated security benefit: Maximum, High, Medium, and Low. We analyze the results based on the security benefit provided by each measure to offer guidance to researchers and developers prioritizing the most relevant measures. Figure 2 presents a heatmap of the scores obtained across each website category per security measure.

Maximum Benefit. When a user or browser connects to a website using the Hypertext Transfer Protocol (HTTP), the connection is typically served at port 80 of the website's server. The security standard requires websites to use Hypertext Transfer Protocol Secure (HTTPS) instead, typically served at port 443.

Table 1. Website Categories Along with their Top Three Sub-Categories List, Count of Websites (#), Average (Avg), and Maximum (Max) Scores (The Minimum Score for Each Category is Zero)

Category	Sub-Categories	#	Avg	Max
Computers & Electronics	Software, Enterprise Technology, Computer Security	520	31.97	125
Jobs & Education	Education, Jobs, Internships	415	23.78	115
News	Other, Technology News, Sports News	337	20.21	80
Arts & Entertainment	TV & Video, Music & Audio, Comics & Animation	254	19.94	100
Internet & Telecom	Web Services, Mobile & Wireless, Email & Messaging	244	27.87	95
Business & Industrial	Business Services, Advertising & Marketing, Business Operations	207	28.41	110
Finance	Banking, Investing, Insurance, Credit & Lending	163	32.30	115
Adult		140	18.75	105
Online Communities	File Sharing & Hosting, Social Networks, Photo & Video Sharing	118	26.02	80
Shopping	Shopping Portals, Classifieds, Consumer Resources	108	27.64	80
People & Society	Social Issues & Advocacy, Religion & Belief, Other	86	29.07	100
Law & Government	Government, Legal, Military	82	35.67	110
Games	Computer & Video Games, Roleplaying Games, Gambling	79	26.46	95
Travel & Transportation	Transportation, Hotels & Accommodations, Travel Guides & Travelogues	78	29.49	110
Health	Medical Facilities & Services, Health Conditions, Mental Health	59	18.14	75
Reference	General Reference, Language Resources, Geographic Reference	50	28.50	75
Science	Other, Computer Science, Mathematics	47	24.89	75
Sports	Team Sports, College Sports, Individual Sports	38	20.13	65
Food & Drink	Cooking & Recipes, Food & Grocery Delivery, Food & Grocery Retailers	35	27.14	75
Autos & Vehicles	Motor Vehicles (By Brand), Vehicle Shopping, Motor Vehicles (By Type)	34	24.12	75
Books & Literature	E-Books, Other, Audiobooks	32	26.41	75
Home & Garden	Home Improvement, Home & Interior Decor, Home Safety & Security	20	30.75	75
Beauty & Fitness	Fashion & Style, Face & Body Care, Fitness, Beauty Services & Spas	19	29.21	65
Hobbies & Leisure	Special Occasions, Crafts, Outdoors	9	26.67	65
Pets & Animals	Animal Products & Services, Wildlife	8	25.63	70
Real Estate	Real Estate Services, Real Estate Listings	7	21.43	40
Sensitive Subjects	Death & Tragedy, Recreational Drugs, War & Conflict	6	21.67	45

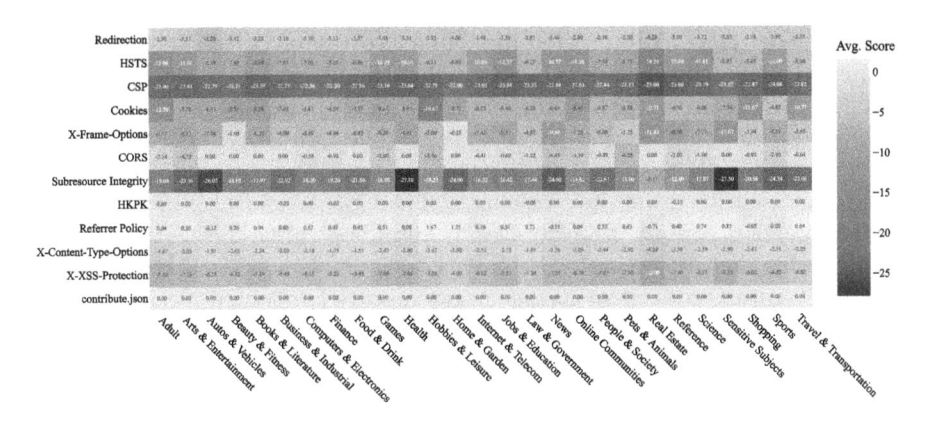

Fig. 2. Heatmap of the Distribution of Average HTTP Security Score between Different Security Headers and Website Categories

Since users often type website URLs starting with either `http://` or `https://`, website servers usually listen on both ports and must securely redirect HTTP traffic to HTTPS. This security measure is considered to have low implementation difficulty by Mozilla. All website categories received an average negative score for redirection. The top five categories with the highest average scores are: People & Society, Adult, Pets & Animals, Shopping, and Online Communities. In contrast, the bottom five categories with the lowest average scores are: Autos & Vehicles, Real Estate, Home & Garden, Sports, and Science.

High Benefit. Five of the categories by Mozilla Observatory were identified as a High security benefit and are discussed below. Addressing metrics with high security benefits can close significant HTTP implementation security gaps.

Strict Transport Security: Unlike redirection, where users visiting a site using the `http://` protocol are redirected to the website using `https://` by the website's server, HTTP Strict Transport Security (HSTS), an HTTP header, enables the browser to perform this action. After the server's first redirection, the browser may "remember" the protocol change and automatically upgrade all future requests by transparently changing the protocol in the URL. HSTS enhances website security by preventing users from bypassing any Transport Layer Security (TLS) and certificate-related errors. Weak HSTS implementation can make websites vulnerable to attacks such as SSLStrip [75]. Mozilla identifies this security measure as having low implementation difficulty. All website categories received an average negative score for Strict Transport Security. The top five categories with the highest average scores include Travel & Transportation, Shopping, Sensitive Subjects, Home & Garden, and Law & Government. In contrast, the bottom five categories with the lowest average scores are Real Estate, Adult, Jobs & Education, Science, and Online Communities.

Content Security Policy: Websites often use resources such as JavaScript libraries, Cascading Style Sheets (CSS), and media like images and videos, which can be loaded from external sources. In some cases, external sources may serve malicious scripts that lead to XSS attacks. The `Content-Security-Policy` (CSP) is an HTTP header that allows developers to control which external sources are used for a website's resources. The CSP header also provides additional protection against XSS attacks by disabling inline JavaScript. Mozilla identifies this security measure as having high implementation difficulty. All website categories received an average negative score for Content Security Policy. The top five categories with the highest average scores include Sensitive Subjects, Home & Garden, Beauty & Fitness, Finance, and Computers & Electronics. The bottom five categories with the lowest average scores are Real Estate, Sports, Jobs & Education, Reference, and Health.

Cross-Origin Resource Sharing: Cross-Origin Resource Sharing (CORS) helps website specify to the browser which external resources are permitted for loading resources from the website. The external resources can be identified either by the domain name, the protocol or scheme, or the port. For this, the HTTP header `Access-Control-Allow-Origin` can be used to specify the allowed external sources. This security measure is identified with low implementation difficulty by Mozilla. Nine website categories received an average score of zero whereas the remaining website categories received average negative score for CORS. The nine categories that received an average score of zero are: Home & Garden, Autos & Vehicles, Sensitive Subjects, Beauty & Fitness, Books & Literature, Real Estate, Business & Industrial, Food & Drink, and Health. The bottom five categories with the lowest average scores are: Pets & Animals, Hobbies & Leisure, Arts & Entertainment, News, and Games.

Cookies: Due to the stateless nature of the HTTP and HTTPS protocols, the connection between a client (web browser) and a website's server does not maintain any state-related data. Cookies, small blocks of data storing information on the browser, provide a means for maintaining state between the client and the server [69]. Since cookies may contain sensitive user account information and other identifying details, it is crucial to limit cookie access to the relevant websites or domains, thereby mitigating attacks such as session hijacking [17]. Mozilla identifies this security measure as having medium implementation difficulty. All website categories received an average negative score for Cookies. The top five categories with the highest average scores are: Sports, Computers & Electronics, People & Society, Science, and Reference. On the other hand, the bottom five categories with the lowest average scores are: Hobbies & Leisure, Adult, Shopping, Travel & Transportation, and Real Estate.

X-Frame-Options: Clickjacking is a common type of website-based attack, where a user is deceived into clicking a hidden or disguised element belonging to a different page, while assuming they are interacting with something else on their current page [43]. It is the developer's responsibility to ensure that their website cannot be used in clickjacking attacks originating from other websites.

The X-Frame-Options (XFO) HTTP header can be employed to control how a website is used within an Inline Frame or iFrame, an HTML element that can load an HTML page from within another HTML page. Effective implementation of both XFO and CSP can help protect against clickjacking [10]. Mozilla identifies this security measure as having low implementation difficulty. All website categories received an average negative score for X-Frame-Options. The top five categories with the highest average scores are: Home & Garden, Beauty & Fitness, Pets & Animals, Shopping, and Travel & Transportation. Conversely, the bottom five categories with the lowest average scores are: Sensitive Subjects, Real Estate, News, Reference, and Health.

Medium Benefit. Only one category reported by the Mozilla Observatory was identified as having a medium security benefit: Subresource Integrity.

Subresource Integrity: When websites load external JavaScript libraries from public content delivery networks (CDNs) like JQuery *jquery.org*, they become vulnerable to attacks if these external libraries get corrupted or modified due to an attack on the CDN itself. Such an attack on the CDN can lead to further attacks, such as denial of service (DoS) or credential theft, on all websites using the external library. To protect against these attacks, the World Wide Web Consortium (W3C) introduced the Subresource Integrity (SRI) standard. SRI allows external resources to be identified with their version, enabling the detection of modifications and preventing the loading of altered resources. Mozilla identifies this security measure as having medium implementation difficulty. All website categories received an average negative score for Subresource Integrity. The top five categories with the highest average scores are: Real Estate, Reference, Hobbies & Leisure, Online Communities, and Pets & Animals. The bottom five categories with the lowest average scores are: Health, Sensitive Subjects, Autos & Vehicles, News, and Sports.

Low Benefit. Mozilla Observatory identified five categories as providing low security benefits, which are discussed below.

Public Key Pinning: HTTP Public Key Pinning (HPKP) enables websites to associate their site with specific endpoint public keys, intermediate certificate authorities, or root certificate authorities. This prevents attackers from tricking certificate authorities into issuing unauthorized certificates for websites, reducing the risk of Man-in-the-Middle (MitM) attacks. Mozilla classifies this security measure as having maximum implementation difficulty. Four website categories received an average negative score for Public Key Pinning and the remaining received an average score of zero. The website categories that received an average negative scores (bottom four categories) are: Reference, Law & Government, Finance, and Business & Industrial.

Referrer Policy: The HTTP Referrer Policy enables developers to control how external requests are handled, minimizing the risk to user privacy. Mozilla identifies this security measure as having low implementation difficulty. Four website categories received an average negative score for Referrer Policy, one category received an average zero score, and the remaining categories received positive scores. The top five categories with the highest average scores are: Hobbies & Leisure, Home & Garden, Books & Literature, Sensitive Subjects, and Science, whereas, the bottom five categories with the lowest average scores are: Real Estate, News, Autos & Vehicles, Shopping, and Sports.

X-Content-Type-Options: X-Content-Type-Options HTML header specifies that browsers should only load external scripts and stylesheets if they are tagged with the correct Multipurpose Internet Mail Extensions (MIME) type. This prevents malicious content from being loaded onto websites, protecting against XSS attacks. Mozilla identifies this security measure as having low implementation difficulty. All website categories received an average negative score for X-Content-Type-Options. The top five categories with the highest average scores are: Home & Garden, Food & Drink, Hobbies & Leisure, Finance, and Autos & Vehicles, whereas, the bottom five categories with the lowest average scores are: Real Estate, Adult, Reference, News, and Online Communities.

X-XSS-Protection: The X-XSS-Protection HTTP header prevents XSS attacks in older browsers that do not support Content Security Policy (CSP). Mozilla identifies this security measure as having low implementation difficulty. All website categories received an average negative score for X-XSS-Protection. The top five categories with the highest average scores are: Home & Garden, Travel & Transportation, Finance, Law & Government, and Food & Drink, whereas, the bottom five categories with the lowest average scores are: Real Estate, Adult, Sensitive Subjects, People & Society, and Reference.

5 Discussion and Implications

The overall security of popular websites is alarmingly inadequate, prompting concerns about the potential risks to user data and the general online experience. A total of 1,777 (55.62%) websites received a grade 'F', with each category containing at least one website with a score of zero. In fact, 1,045 (32.71%) websites received a score of zero, and the average overall score was a meager 26.21 out of a possible 135. Given that these are some of the most popular websites, our findings emphasize the urgency for substantial improvements in their security practices. As browser security indicators such as the security padlock next to URL are not entirely trustworthy and may sometimes indicate about a website's HTTP implementation strength erroneously [33]. The adoption of Mixed Content policy[3] have ensured blocking non-secure content from being loaded in the browser, however, this measure still lacks in mobile device browsers [15]. This can arise due to inconsistencies in HTTP header implementation across desktop and mobile devices [59]. Furthermore, as seen in Fig. 2 metrics of CSP and SRI have received the lowest possible scores overall.

---

[3] https://w3c.github.io/webappsec-mixed-content/.

5.1 Critical Websites

Our category-wise analysis revealed that health-related websites had the lowest security scores. This is concerning because health information is sensitive and subject to strict regulations in many countries [5]. This could put patients' data at risk and may result in noncompliance with data protection laws such as Health Insurance Portability and Accountability Act (HIPAA) in the United States [2], Personal Data Protection Bill (PDPB) in India [71], Personal Information Protection Act (PIPA) in South Korea [51], and Personal Information Protection and Electronic Documents Act (PIPEDA) in Canada [45]. Further research is needed to understand the specific factors that contribute to the poor security performance of health websites, which may include inadequate technical expertise, resource constraints, or insufficient prioritization of security [42]. Another concerning category that received a low security score is adult websites. Poor security on adult websites can lead to significant risks, including the exposure of users' personal and sensitive data, and increased vulnerability to malware and phishing attacks [92]. Leakage of personal information through these attacks on adult websites can cause psychological distress for users and result in reputation damage for the websites involved [91].

5.2 Secure Redirection

Improper redirection can lead to Session Hijacking attacks [16]. Our analysis showed that all categories had an average negative score for the redirection metric. Only 53.02% of websites implemented redirection to HTTPS correctly, while the rest either lacked a secure redirection mechanism or had suboptimal implementations. Investigating the barriers to adoption of secure redirection, such as developer awareness or misconceptions about implementation complexity, could help identify strategies for encouraging more widespread implementation of this crucial security measure. For example, developers might underestimate the importance of secure redirection, assuming that other security measures are sufficient, or they might be unaware of the latest best practices and tools that facilitate secure implementation. The implementation of strict redirection policies, HST), and CSP in conjunction can achieve robust secure redirection [13].

5.3 Benefits with Implementation

Despite the high security benefits and low implementation difficulty of HSTS, X-Frame-Options, and CORS, websites continue to underperform in these categories. All website categories had negative average scores for HSTS and X-Frame-Options, while 18 of the 27 categories had negative average scores for CORS. These low scores resulted from bad implementation practices including short HSTS validity, not implementing X-Frame-Options, and having visible content via CORS headers or files. Prior work shows that bad practices and incorrect implementation of HSTS and HPKP can lead to further security vulnerabilities [74]. To improve the security of websites, developers should prioritize these metrics [31]. Research into the reasons behind this underperformance, such as a lack of awareness, technical challenges, or insufficient motivation, could help inform targeted interventions and resources to support developers in implementing these critical security measures.

6 Limitations and Future Work

We analyzed $N = 3,195$ websites selected from the top $M = 10,000$ websites on the Tranco list. In the future, we plan to scale up our analysis to encompass all $1M$ websites on Tranco's list. We also focused on the HTTP security headers of websites using Mozilla Observatory. Although Mozilla Observatory offers valuable insights into a website's implementation of 12 important HTTP headers, the tool could not successfully run on 5 out of the 3,200 categorized websites. Although this study was focused on analyzing HTTP security headers, in future, we aim to explore additional security and privacy aspects, including cookie variants, compliance with privacy regulations, data storage and handling protocols, and user authentication methodologies.

7 Conclusion

We conducted security evaluation of popular websites, focusing on HTTP security headers across 27 website categories—a largely understudied domain. We analyzed the top $M = 10,000$ globally popular websites, employing a three-step process of website content scraping, content translation, and NLP-based categorization to determine website categories. Subsequently, Mozilla Observatory was used to perform a detailed evaluation of HTTP security headers on $N = 3,195$ websites. The results revealed significant security deficiencies: 55.66% of the websites received a failing grade ('F'), and 32.71% scored zero out of a possible 135 points. Healthcare websites were particularly concerning, ranking lowest in security scores, highlighting risks to sensitive health-related data and potential non-compliance with stringent healthcare regulations. Secure redirection from HTTP to HTTPS, despite its critical importance and relatively low implementation complexity, was poorly handled across many sites. The study emphasizes the need for a systematic approach to implementing and auditing security headers to mitigate potential threats and secure the web infrastructure effectively.

Acknowledgement. We would like to acknowledge the Inclusive Security and Privacy-focused Innovative Research in Information Technology (InSPIRIT) Lab for supporting this work. Any opinions, findings, conclusions, or recommendations expressed in this material are solely those of the author.

References

1. Aaron Gee-Clough: Mirror, mirror, on the wall, who's the fairest (website) of them all? (2023). https://www.domaintools.com/resources/blog/mirror-mirror-on-the-wall-whos-the-fairest-website-of-them-all/. Accessed 15 Mar 2023

2. Act, A.: Health insurance portability and accountability act of 1996. Public Law **104**, 191 (1996)
3. Al-Sanea, M.S., Al-Daraiseh, A.A.: Security evaluation of Saudi Arabia's websites using open source tools. In: 2015 First International Conference on Anti-Cybercrime (ICACC), Riyadh, Saudi Arabia, pp. 1–5. IEEE (2015)
4. Aldwairi, M., Alsalman, R.: MALURLS: a lightweight malicious website classification based on URL features. J. Emerg. Technol. Web Intell. **4**(2), 128–133 (2012)
5. Baker, D.B.: Privacy and security in public health: maintaining the delicate balance between personal privacy and population safety. In: 2006 22nd Annual Computer Security Applications Conference (ACSAC 2006), pp. 3–22. IEEE (2006)
6. Bianchi, T.: Most popular websites worldwide as of November 2022, by total visits (2023). https://www.statista.com/statistics/1201880/most-visited-websites-worldwide/
7. Bruni, R., Bianchi, G.: Website categorization: a formal approach and robustness analysis in the case of e-commerce detection. Expert Syst. Appl. **142**, 113001 (2020)
8. Callegati, F., Cerroni, W., Ramilli, M.: Man-in-the-middle attack to the HTTPS protocol. IEEE Secur. Priv. **7**(1), 78–81 (2009)
9. Calzavara, S., Focardi, R., Nemec, M., Rabitti, A., Squarcina, M.: Postcards from the post-HTTP world: amplification of HTTPS vulnerabilities in the web ecosystem. In: 2019 IEEE Symposium on Security and Privacy (SP), pp. 281–298. IEEE (2019)
10. Calzavara, S., Roth, S., Rabitti, A., Backes, M., Stock, B.: A tale of two headers: a formal analysis of inconsistent Click-Jacking protection on the web. In: 29th USENIX Security Symposium (USENIX Security 2020), pp. 683–697 (2020)
11. Candan, K.S., Liu, H., Suvarna, R.: Resource description framework: metadata and its applications. ACM SIGKDD Explor. Newsl. **3**(1), 6–19 (2001)
12. Cernica, I., Popescu, N., et al.: Security evaluation of wordpress backup plugins. In: 2019 22nd International Conference on Control Systems and Computer Science (CSCS), New York, NY, USA, pp. 312–316. IEEE (2019)
13. Chang, L., Hsiao, H.C., Jeng, W., Kim, T.H.J., Lin, W.H.: Security implications of redirection trail in popular websites worldwide. In: Proceedings of the 26th International Conference on World Wide Web, Republic and Canton of Geneva, Switzerland, pp. 1491–1500. International World Wide Web Conferences Steering Committee (2017). https://doi.org/10.1145/3038912.3052698
14. Chen, J., et al.: We still don't have secure cross-domain requests: an empirical study of CORS. In: 27th USENIX Security Symposium (USENIX Security 2018), pp. 1079–1093 (2018)
15. Chen, P., Nikiforakis, N., Huygens, C., Desmet, L.: A dangerous mix: large-scale analysis of mixed-content websites. In: Information Security: 16th International Conference, ISC 2013, Dallas, Texas, 13–15 November 2013, Proceedings, pp. 354–363. Springer (2015)
16. Cheng, K., Gao, M., Guo, R.: Analysis and research on HTTPS hijacking attacks. In: 2010 Second International Conference on Networks Security, Wireless Communications and Trusted Computing, Piscataway, NJ, USA, vol. 2, pp. 223–226. IEEE (2010)
17. Dacosta, I., Chakradeo, S., Ahamad, M., Traynor, P.: One-time cookies: preventing session hijacking attacks with stateless authentication tokens. ACM Trans. Internet Technol. (TOIT) **12**(1), 1–24 (2012)
18. Heredia, D.: Website categorization with Python and Google NLP API (2023). https://www.danielherediamejias.com/website-categorization-python/. Accessed 15 Mar 2023

19. Das, S.: A risk-reduction-based incentivization model for human-centered multi-factor authentication. Indiana University (2020)
20. Das, S.: Design of secure, privacy-focused, and accessible e-payment applications for older adults. arXiv preprint arXiv:2410.08555 (2024)
21. Das, S., Abbott, J., Gopavaram, S., Blythe, J., Camp, L.J.: User-centered risk communication for safer browsing. In: Financial Cryptography and Data Security: FC 2020 International Workshops, AsiaUSEC, CoDeFi, VOTING, and WTSC, Kota Kinabalu, Malaysia, 14 February 2020, Revised Selected Papers 24, pp. 18–35. Springer (2020)
22. Das, S., Dev, J., Camp, L.J.: Privacy preserving policy framework: user-aware and user-driven. In: TPRC47: The 47th Research Conference on Communication, Information and Internet Policy (2019)
23. Das, S., Kim, A., Jelen, B., Streiff, J., Camp, L.J., Huber, L.: Towards implementing inclusive authentication technologies for older adults. Who are you (2019)
24. Das, S., Kim, A., Tingle, Z., Nippert-Eng, C.: All about phishing exploring user research through a systematic literature review. In: Proceedings of the Thirteenth International Symposium on Human Aspects of Information Security & Assurance (HAISA 2019) (2019)
25. Das, S., Nippert-Eng, C., Camp, L.J.: Evaluating user susceptibility to phishing attacks. Inf. Comput. Secur. **30**(1), 1–18 (2022)
26. Das, S., Salman, A.: A review of security threats from e-waste. In: Development in E-Waste Management: Sustainability and Circular Economy Aspects, p. 165 (2023)
27. Debnath, B., Das, A., Das, S., Das, A.: Studies on security threats in waste mobile phone recycling supply chain in India. In: 2020 IEEE Calcutta Conference (CALCON), pp. 431–434. IEEE (2020)
28. Debnath, B., Das, S., Das, A.: Study exploring security threats in waste phones a life cycle based approach. In: 2019 IEEE SmartWorld, Ubiquitous Intelligence & Computing, Advanced & Trusted Computed, Scalable Computing & Communications, Cloud & Big Data Computing, Internet of People and Smart City Innovation. IEEE (2019)
29. Dev, J., Das, S., Camp, L.J.: Privacy practices, preferences, and compunctions: WhatsApp users in India. In: HAISA, pp. 135–146 (2018)
30. Dewald, A., Holz, T., Freiling, F.C.: ADSandbox: sandboxing JavaScript to fight malicious websites. In: Proceedings of the 2010 ACM Symposium on Applied Computing, pp. 1859–1864 (2010)
31. Dolnák, I., Litvik, J.: Introduction to HTTP security headers and implementation of HTTP strict transport security (HSTS) header for HTTPS enforcing. In: 2017 15th International Conference on Emerging eLearning Technologies and Applications (ICETA), Piscataway, NJ, USA, pp. 1–4. IEEE (2017)
32. Felt, A.P., Barnes, R., King, A., Palmer, C., Bentzel, C., Tabriz, P.: Measuring HTTPS adoption on the web. Technical report, Google (2017)
33. Felt, A.P., et al.: Rethinking connection security indicators. In: Twelfth Symposium on Usable Privacy and Security (SOUPS 2016), Berkeley, CA, USA, pp. 1–14. USENIX Association (2016)
34. Fernandes, A.N., Markert, P., Das, S.: Where you're logged in: analyzing the usability of device activity pages (work-in-progress). In: Annual Computer Security Applications Conference, ser. ACSAC, vol. 22 (2023)
35. Fonseca, J., Vieira, M., Madeira, H.: Evaluation of web security mechanisms using vulnerability & attack injection. IEEE Trans. Dependable Secure Comput. **11**(5), 440–453 (2013)

36. The OWASP Foundation: Web security testing framework (2022). https://owasp.org/www-project-web-security-testing-guide/latest/3-The_OWASP_Testing_Framework/0-The_Web_Security_Testing_Framework. Accessed 28 May 2024
37. Gadient, P., Nierstrasz, O., Ghafari, M.: Security header fields in HTTP clients. In: 2021 IEEE 21st International Conference on Software Quality, Reliability and Security (QRS), New York, NY, USA, pp. 93–101. IEEE (2021)
38. Google: Google NLP (2023). https://cloud.google.com/natural-language. Accessed 15 Mar 2023
39. Gopavaram, S., Dev, J., Grobler, M., Kim, D., Das, S., Camp, L.J.: Cross-national study on phishing resilience. In: Proceedings of the Workshop on Usable Security and Privacy (USEC) (2021)
40. Gopavaram, S.R., Dev, J., Das, S., Camp, J.: IoTMarketplace: informing purchase decisions with risk communication. Technical report, Working Paper (2019). ftp://svn.soic.indiana.edu/pub/techreports/TR742.pdf
41. Hadan, H., Serrano, N., Das, S., Camp, L.J.: Making IoT worthy of human trust. In: TPRC47: The 47th Research Conference on Communication, Information and Internet Policy (2019)
42. Harvey, M.J., Harvey, M.G.: Privacy and security issues for mobile health platforms. J. Am. Soc. Inf. Sci. **65**(7), 1305–1318 (2014)
43. Huang, L.S., Moshchuk, A., Wang, H.J., Schecter, S., Jackson, C.: Clickjacking: attacks and defenses. In: USENIX Security Symposium, Berkeley, CA, USA, pp. 413–428. USENIX Association (2012)
44. Ibrishimova, M.D., Li, K.F.: A machine learning approach to fake news detection using knowledge verification and natural language processing. In: Advances in Intelligent Networking and Collaborative Systems: The 11th International Conference on Intelligent Networking and Collaborative Systems (INCoS-2019), pp. 223–234. Springer (2020)
45. Jaar, D., Zeller, P.E.: Canadian privacy law: the personal information protection and electronic documents act (PIPEDA). Int'l. In-House Counsel J. **2**, 1135 (2008)
46. Jammalamadaka, R.C., Van Der Horst, T.W., Mehrotra, S., Seamons, K.E., Venkasubramanian, N.: Delegate: a proxy based architecture for secure website access from an untrusted machine. In: 2006 22nd Annual Computer Security Applications Conference (ACSAC 2006), pp. 57–66. IEEE (2006)
47. Jiang, L., Chen, H., Deng, F., Zhong, Q.: A security evaluation method based on threat classification for web service. J. Softw. **6**(4), 595–603 (2011)
48. Johns, M., Engelmann, B., Posegga, J.: XSSDS: server-side detection of cross-site scripting attacks. In: 2008 Annual Computer Security Applications Conference (ACSAC), pp. 335–344. IEEE (2008)
49. Kishnani, U., Noah, N., Das, S., Dewri, R.: Privacy and security evaluation of mobile payment applications through user-generated reviews. In: Proceedings of the 21st Workshop on Privacy in the Electronic Society, pp. 159–173 (2022)
50. Kishnani, U., Noah, N., Das, S., Dewri, R.: Assessing security, privacy, user interaction, and accessibility features in popular e-payment applications. In: Proceedings of the 2023 European Symposium on Usable Security, pp. 143–157 (2023)
51. Ko, H., Leitner, J., Kim, E., Jeong, J.: Structure and enforcement of data privacy law in South Korea. Int. Data Priv. Law **7**(2), 100–114 (2017)
52. Kumar, A., Ghosal, T., Bhattacharjee, S., Ekbal, A.: Towards automated meta-review generation via an NLP/ML pipeline in different stages of the scholarly peer review process. Int. J. Digit. Libr. 1–12 (2023)

53. Lavrenovs, A., Melón, F.J.R.: HTTP security headers analysis of top one million websites. In: 2018 10th International Conference on Cyber Conflict (CyCon), New York, NY, USA, pp. 345–370. IEEE (2018)
54. Leonard Richardson: Beautiful soup (2021). https://pypi.org/project/beautifulsoup4/. Accessed 15 Mar 2023
55. Lichlyter, K., Kishnani, U., Hollenbach, K., Das, S.: Understanding professional needs to create privacy-preserving and secure emergent digital artworks. In: 9th Workshop on Inclusive Privacy and Security (WIPS) in Association with USENIX Symposium on Usable Privacy and Security (SOUPS) (2024)
56. Lukasik, M., Zens, R.: Content explorer: recommending novel entities for a document writer. In: Proceedings of the 2018 Conference on Empirical Methods in Natural Language Processing, pp. 3371–3380 (2018)
57. Majestic: Majestic (2023). https://majestic.com/. Accessed 15 Mar 2023
58. Meiser, G., Laperdrix, P., Stock, B.: Careful who you trust: studying the pitfalls of cross-origin communication. In: Proceedings of the 2021 ACM Asia Conference on Computer and Communications Security, pp. 110–122 (2021)
59. Mendoza, A., Chinprutthiwong, P., Gu, G.: Uncovering HTTP header inconsistencies and the impact on desktop/mobile websites. In: Proceedings of the 2018 World Wide Web Conference, Republic and Canton of Geneva, CHE, pp. 247–256. International World Wide Web Conferences Steering Committee (2018)
60. Momenzadeh, B., Gopavaram, S., Das, S., Camp, L.J.: Bayesian evaluation of user app choices in the presence of risk communication on Android devices. In: International Symposium on Human Aspects of Information Security and Assurance, pp. 211–223. Springer (2020)
61. Mozilla: Assessing security risk (2023). https://infosec.mozilla.org/guidelines/assessing_security_risk. Accessed 15 Mar 2023
62. Mozilla: Mozilla observatory (2023). https://observatory.mozilla.org/
63. Mozilla: Mozilla web security guidelines (2023). https://infosec.mozilla.org/guidelines/web_security. Accessed 15 Mar 2023
64. Neupane, S., et al.: On the data privacy, security, and risk postures of IoT mobile companion apps. In: IFIP Annual Conference on Data and Applications Security and Privacy, pp. 162–182. Springer (2022)
65. Nidhal Baccouri: Deep translator (2023). https://pypi.org/project/deep-translator/. Accessed 15 Mar 2023
66. Noah, N., Kishnani, U., Das, S., Dewri, R.: Privacy and security evaluation of mobile payment applications through user-generated reviews. In: Workshop on Privacy in the Electronic Society (WPES 2022) (2022)
67. Noah, N., Tayachew, A., Ryan, S., Das, S.: PhisherCop: developing an NLP-based automated tool for phishing detection. In: Proceedings of the Human Factors and Ergonomics Society Annual Meeting, vol. 66, pp. 2093–2097. SAGE Publications, Los Angeles (2022)
68. Noman, A.S.M., Das, S., Patil, S.: Techies against Facebook: understanding negative sentiment toward Facebook via user generated content. In: Proceedings of the 2019 CHI Conference on Human Factors in Computing Systems, pp. 1–15 (2019)
69. Park, J.S., Sandhu, R.: Secure cookies on the web. IEEE Internet Comput. **4**(4), 36–44 (2000)
70. Pochat, V.L., Van Goethem, T., Tajalizadehkhoob, S., Korczyński, M., Joosen, W.: Tranco: a research-oriented top sites ranking hardened against manipulation. In: Proceedings of the 2019 Network and Distributed System Security Symposium (NDSS), San Diego, CA, USA, pp. 1–15. Internet Society (2019)

71. Deva Prasad, M., Suchithra Menon, C.: The personal data protection bill, 2018: India's regulatory journey towards a comprehensive data protection law. Int. J. Law Inf. Technol. **28**(1), 1–19 (2020)
72. Quancast (2023). https://www.quantcast.com/. Accessed 15 Mar 2023
73. Rajalakshmi, R., Aravindan, C.: Naive bayes approach for website classification. In: Information Technology and Mobile Communication: International Conference, AIM 2011, Nagpur, Maharashtra, India, 21–22 April 2011, Proceedings, pp. 323–326. Springer, Heidelberg (2011)
74. de los Santos, S., Torrano, C., Rubio, Y., Brezo, F.: Implementation state of HSTS and HPKP in both browsers and servers. In: Cryptology and Network Security: 15th International Conference, CANS 2016, Milan, Italy, 14–16 November 2016, Proceedings 15, pp. 192–207. Springer, Cham (2016)
75. Selvi, J.: Bypassing HTTP strict transport security. In: Black Hat Europe, vol. 54, pp. 1–4. Black Hat, Amsterdam (2014)
76. Shabudin, S., Sani, N.S., Ariffin, K.A.Z., Aliff, M.: Feature selection for phishing website classification. Int. J. Adv. Comput. Sci. Appl. **11**(4), 311–317 (2020)
77. Shah, B.: Cisco umbrella: a cloud-based secure internet gateway (SIG) on and off network. Int. J. Adv. Res. Comput. Sci. **8**(2), 4–7 (2017)
78. Shalkarbayuli, A., Kairbekov, A., Amangeldi, Y.: Comparison of traditional machine learning methods and Google services in identifying tonality on Russian texts. In: Journal of Physics: Conference Series, vol. 1117, p. 012002. IOP Publishing (2018)
79. Shi, H.Z., Chen, B., Yu, L.: Analysis of web security comprehensive evaluation tools. In: 2010 Second International Conference on Networks Security, Wireless Communications and Trusted Computing, Wuhan, China, vol. 1, pp. 285–289. IEEE (2010)
80. Skipfish (2023). https://www.kali.org/tools/skipfish/. Accessed 15 Mar 2023
81. Stock, B., Mueller, M., Johns, M., Steffens, M.: The state of the art in client-side web security: standards, technologies, and shortcomings. Computing **96**(12), 1163–1190 (2014)
82. Surani, A., et al.: Security and privacy of digital mental health: an analysis of web services and mobile applications. In: IFIP Annual Conference on Data and Applications Security and Privacy, pp. 319–338. Springer (2023)
83. Surani, A., et al.: Security and privacy of digital mental health: an analysis of web services and mobile apps. In: Conference on Data and Applications Security and Privacy (2023)
84. Surani, A., Das, S.: Understanding privacy and security postures of healthcare chatbots. In: ACM CHI Conference on Human Factors in Computing Systems 2022 (2022)
85. Szydlowski, M., Kruegel, C., Kirda, E.: Secure input for web applications. In: Twenty-Third Annual Computer Security Applications Conference (ACSAC 2007), pp. 375–384. IEEE (2007)
86. Tally, A.C., Abbott, J., Bochner, A., Das, S., Nippert-Eng, C.: What mid-career professionals think, know, and feel about phishing: opportunities for university it departments to better empower employees in their anti-phishing decisions. Proc. ACM Hum.-Comput. Interact. **7**(CSCW1), 1–27 (2023)
87. Tally, A.C., Abbott, J., Bochner, A.M., Das, S., Nippert-Eng, C.: Tips, tricks, and training: supporting anti-phishing awareness among mid-career office workers based on employees' current practices. In: Proceedings of the 2023 CHI Conference on Human Factors in Computing Systems, pp. 1–13 (2023)

88. Tazi, F., et al.: Accessibility evaluation of IoT Android mobile companion apps. In: Extended Abstracts of the 2023 CHI Conference on Human Factors in Computing Systems, pp. 1–7 (2023)
89. Tazi, F., Shrestha, S., De La Cruz, J., Das, S.: SoK: an evaluation of the secure end user experience on the dark net through systematic literature review. J. Cybersecurity Priv. **2**(2), 329–357 (2022)
90. Unchit, P., Das, S., Kim, A., Camp, L.J.: Quantifying susceptibility to spear phishing in a high school environment using signal detection theory. In: Human Aspects of Information Security and Assurance: 14th IFIP WG 11.12 International Symposium, HAISA 2020, Mytilene, Lesbos, Greece, 8–10 July 2020, Proceedings 14, pp. 109–120. Springer (2020)
91. Vallina, P., Feal, Á., Gamba, J., Vallina-Rodriguez, N., Anta, A.F.: Tales from the porn: a comprehensive privacy analysis of the web porn ecosystem. In: Proceedings of the Internet Measurement Conference, pp. 245–258 (2019)
92. Vallina, P., Gamba, J., Feal, A., Vallina-Rodriguez, N., Fernández Anta, A., et al.: This is my private business! privacy risks on adult websites. In: IV Jornadas Nacionales de Investigación en Ciberseguridad (JNIC 2018) (2018)
93. VeNoMouS: cloudscraper (2021). https://pypi.org/project/cloudscraper/. Accessed 15 Mar 2023
94. w3af (2023). http://w3af.org/. Accessed 15 Mar 2023
95. Walsh, K., Tazi, F., Markert, P., Das, S.: My account is compromised-what do i do? Towards an intercultural analysis of account remediation for websites. In: Proceedings of the Sixth Workshop on Inclusive Privacy and Security (WIPS 2021): in Association with the Seventeenth Symposium on Usable Privacy and Security (SOUPS 2021) (2021)
96. Wilson, R.F., Pettijohn, J.B.: Search engine optimisation: a primer on keyword strategies. J. Direct Data Digit. Mark. Pract. **8**, 121–133 (2006)

Countering Subscription Concealed Identifier (SUCI)-Catchers in Cellular Communications

Julian Parkin and Mahesh Tripunitara[✉]

Department of Electrical and Computer Engineering, University of Waterloo, Waterloo, Canada
{jtparkin,tripunit}@uwaterloo.ca

Abstract. We address privacy in the context of cellular communications; in particular, a lingering problem that a subscriber can be tracked via use of a Subscription Concealed Identifier (SUCI) that is an encryption of their Subscription Permanent Identifier (SUPI). The attack leverages the 5G Authentication and Key Agreement (AKA) protocol. We address the problem via a change to the protocol, that is the use of an ephemeral identifier generated from the SUPI rather than the SUPI itself. We articulate a number of design constraints from our observations about prior proposed solutions, that our solution meets. We address also the fact that we need two such identifiers to be valid at any moment, practical considerations such as a particular backwards-compatibility that our solution has, a formal verification of our approach using a theorem prover that has previously been used for 5G-AKA, and limitations of our approach. As such, our work addresses an important gap in security in the context of cellular communications.

Keywords: Cellular communications · 5G · 5G-AKA

1 Introduction

Mobile communication over the cellular network is widespread: the number of *subscribers* is about 8 billion worldwide [19]. The security and privacy of subscribers is an important consideration for standards organizations such as the 3rd Generation Partnership Project (3GPP) [1], which standardizes the protocols and mechanisms that underlie the network. Our work pertains to the current, fifth generation (5G), and future, cellular standards. In Fig. 1, we show an abstraction of the communication model in 5G that follows the convention of prior work [12,13] and is appropriate for our work. The figure shows that there are three entities involved in an instance of communication: the subscriber's *User Equipment* (UE), a *Serving Network* (SN) and a *Home Network* (HN). The subscriber has a subscription with the HN, which they use to access the 5G network over-the-air via the SN's infrastructure.

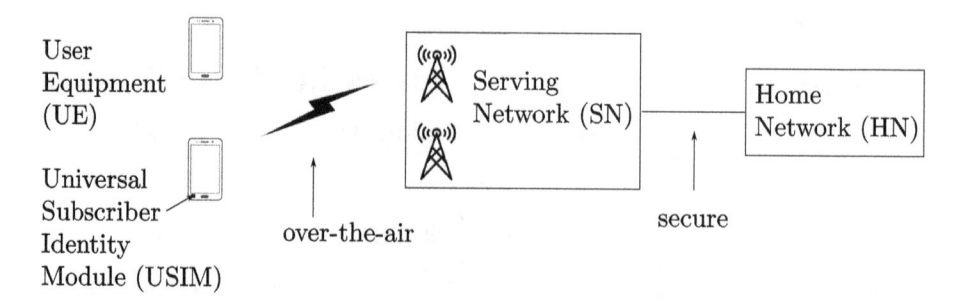

Fig. 1. An abstraction of 5G communications.

Over the years, the 3GPP standards, as they relate to security and privacy, have progressively improved from GSM, a second-generation (2G) mobile networks standard, through 5G, the most recent standard. A particular improvement that relates to our work is whether a subscriber can be tracked over multiple instances of their use of the cellular network. That is, suppose a subscriber S communicates over the cellular network at some location and time, and a subscriber T communicates at another location at a different time. Is $S = T$? A desirable privacy property is that it is difficult for an adversary who is able to listen into, and perhaps even actively participate in, over-the-air communications to answer this question.

5G improves with regards to this subscriber privacy property over prior standards by encrypting the subscriber's Subscription Permanent Identifier (SUPI) in over-the-air transmission. (The SUPI, as used in public mobile networks, is equivalent to the International Mobile Subscriber Identity, or IMSI [9].) The SUPI is a static string that is written into a tamper-resistant component, the Universal Subscriber Identity Module (USIM), in the subscriber's UE, and identifies the subscriber uniquely. Without such encryption, as was the case in earlier standards, it is easy for even a passive adversary, who could read over-the-air communications to track a subscriber based on the SUPI.

The Attack We Address. Notwithstanding the improvements towards security and privacy in 5G, recent work has shown that subscribers can be tracked via their use of the 5G Authentication and Key Agreement (AKA) and related protocols [15]. 5G-AKA is a challenge-response protocol that mutually authenticates the HN and the subscriber, while the SN acts as a transport. Such authentication is necessary to then authorize the subscriber to access the 5G network via the SN. The SN is assumed to have been authenticated by the HN, outside the context of 5G-AKA. A run of 5G-AKA is initiated by an Authentication Request message from the HN to which the subscriber must respond with a valid Authentication Response. We discuss 5G-AKA at a level of detail appropriate for this work in Sect. 2.1; in particular see Fig. 2 there.

Prior to a run of 5G-AKA with a subscriber, the HN must know the SUPI of the subscriber so it can then choose the correct secret key it shares with the subscriber. The HN discovers this by decrypting a Subscription Concealed Identifier (SUCI) that is an encryption of the SUPI. The HN is informed of the SUCI via one of two protocols that are separate from 5G-AKA: the subscriber may send a Registration Request that contains a SUCI (Fig. 2 prepends this to a run of 5G-AKA), or the subscriber may be issued an Identity Request by the SN to which it responds with an Identity Response which contains a SUCI. The HN may also be sent a SUPI by an SN who already knows the subscriber's identity, but this flow is not relevant to our work.

The class of attacks we address is called SUCI-catching [15]. It owes its name to an earlier class of attacks called IMSI-catching, in which a passive attacker listens over-the-air and observes plaintext SUPIs (or IMSIs) [25]. Figure 3 in Sect. 2.2 shows the attack. The attacker acquires a SUCI that corresponds to a SUPI of a subscriber, denote it S, that the attacker wants to track. It does so in one of two ways, which can be considered two variants of the attack: (1) by generating the SUCI itself, which requires it to know the SUPI of the subscriber it wants to track, or, (2) by listening over-the-air to a Registration Request or an Identity Response which contains a SUCI. Later, when the attacker wants to determine whether a subscriber T is the same as S, it causes the HN to send an Authentication Request to T, where that Authentication Request is in consequence to a Registration Request that was sent earlier by S that the attacker replays. The attacker then checks whether authentication succeeds for T. $S = T$ if it does. The attacker is able to tell whether the authentication succeeds in one of several ways: it can listen for whether an authentication response is sent by the subscriber or a particular kind of failure message, or even whether the subscriber appears to be able to send and receive application data (see Chlosta et al. [15] for more details).

Contributions. We devise a modification to 5G-AKA to mitigate the SUCI-catcher class of attacks. We adopt several design constraints in addressing the attack in the interest of sound design and practicality. Towards the former, we have proved that our modification both retains prior functionality and meets new security properties by augmenting a prior specification for 5G-AKA in the Tamarin theorem prover [12]. Towards the latter, our modified protocol requires no changes to message formats or protocol sequence, and thereby is backwards-compatible in that the SN is oblivious to the changes, and an HN can choose to adopt the modified protocol with only some of its subscribers and not others. Our design is to generate and use an ephemeral identifier that is derived from the SUPI, in place of the SUPI, and to update it following a similar ratcheting idea to that used in the Signal protocol [22], but with the different security goal of subscriber privacy. Our modification does come with trade-offs: it requires changes to the behaviour of both the HN and subscriber. However, we argue that our approach affords a strict improvement to subscriber-privacy and is practical, and is therefore appropriate for adoption in 5G and future cellular standards.

Organization. The remainder of the paper is organized as follows. In Sect. 2, we discuss 5G-AKA and the SUCI-catcher attack. In Sect. 3, we discuss design considerations for a solution, our solution and limitations. We address practicality in Sect. 3.3, and our work with Tamarin [11] on stating and proving desirable properties in Sect. 4. We discuss related work in Sect. 5, and conclude with Sect. 6, in which we discuss also future work.

2 5G-AKA and the Attack

In this section, we discuss 5G-AKA and the SUCI-catcher attack at a level of abstraction that is appropriate for our work. This provides sufficient background to then discuss our solution in Sect. 3.

2.1 5G AKA

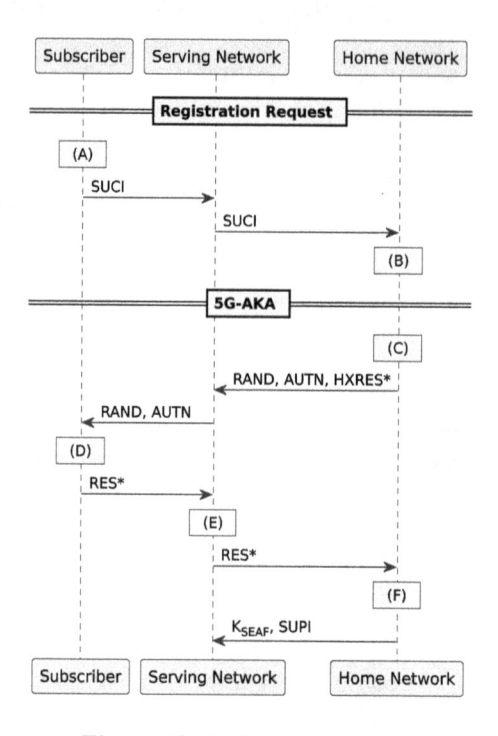

Fig. 2. 5G-AKA protocol flow.

Figure 2 shows the protocol flow of 5G-AKA. Computational steps (A) through (F) are abbreviated in the figure and detailed in this section. The Registration Request, which is not strictly part of 5G-AKA, is also included.

As we discuss in Sect. 1, the network architecture is abstracted into three components: a subscriber, an SN, and an HN. The subscriber and the HN are assumed to share a symmetric key K; the bootstrapping of this key is outside the scope of the protocol and is assumed to have been performed securely beforehand. For the subscriber, this key is stored in a USIM, which is part of the subscriber's UE. From our standpoint, the USIM is assumed to be tamper-proof, and thereby, the secrecy of the key K is preserved to only the subscriber and the HN.

The USIM also maintains a integer counter, called the Sequence Number (SQN), whose purpose is to provide replay protection. The SQN is updated to match the value received in each authentication request, and only authentication requests that increase it are accepted. The HN maintains its own copy of the SQN for each of its subscribers [5].

5G-AKA is a challenge-response protocol: the subscriber needs to provide a response RES* to a random challenge RAND. The steps performed by the parties are as follows.

(A) SUCI Encryption. The Subscriber encrypts its SUPI using the HN's public key, forming a SUCI:

$$\text{SUCI} \leftarrow \text{ECIES-ENC}(PK_{\text{HN}}, \text{SUPI})$$

The ECIES-ENC function represents the Elliptic-Curve Integrated Encryption Scheme [14]: the currently standardized method for encrypting SUPIs.

The SUCI additionally contains some plaintext elements identifying the HN for routing purposes [3].

(B) Subscriber Lookup. The HN decrypts the SUCI, allowing it to identify the subscriber and look up its corresponding K:

$$\text{SUPI} \leftarrow \text{ECIES-DEC}(SK_{\text{HN}}, \text{SUCI})$$
$$K \leftarrow \text{lookup-subscription}(\text{SUPI})$$

(C) Authentication Vector Generation. The HN then advances its copy of SQN and generates an authentication vector:

$$\begin{aligned}
\text{RAND} &\leftarrow \texttt{random}() \\
\text{MAC} &\leftarrow f_1(K, \text{SQN}_{\text{HN}} \| \text{RAND}) \\
\text{AK} &\leftarrow f_5(K, \text{RAND}) \\
\text{SQN}_{\text{ENC}} &\leftarrow \text{SQN}_{\text{HN}} \oplus \text{AK} \\
\text{AUTN} &\leftarrow \text{SQN}_{\text{ENC}} \| \text{MAC} \\
\text{XRES}^* &\leftarrow f_2(K, \text{RAND}) \\
\text{HXRES}^* &\leftarrow \text{SHA256}(\text{XRES}^* \| \text{RAND}) \\
K_{\text{SEAF}} &\leftarrow \text{KDF}(K, \text{RAND} \| \text{SQN}_{\text{ENC}} \| \text{SNname})
\end{aligned}$$

In these steps, f_1 and f_2 are Message Authentication Codes (MACs), and f_5 is a Key Derivation Function (KDF) [5]. The generation of the session key named K_{SEAF} has been abstracted into a single KDF for simplicity, while in the specification it is one of many keys in a key hierarchy derived from the authentication. (SEAF is an acronym for one of the components in the 5G architecture; from our standpoint, further details are unimportant.)

(D) Response Computation. The Subscriber computes an expected MAC value and an authentication response:

$$\begin{aligned}
AK &\leftarrow f_5(K, RAND) \\
SQN_{ENC} \| MAC &\leftarrow AUTN \\
SQN_{HN} &\leftarrow SQN_{ENC} \oplus AK \\
XMAC &\leftarrow f_1(K, SQN_{HN} \| RAND) \\
RES^* &\leftarrow f_2(K, RAND) \\
K_{SEAF} &\leftarrow KDF(K, RAND \| SQN_{ENC} \| SNname)
\end{aligned}$$

The Subscriber must check two requirements before accepting the authentication vector and sending the response.

1. XMAC matches the MAC received as part of AUTN.
2. The received SQN_{HN} is not older than the Subscribers current SQN.

If either requirement is not met, the Subscriber sends an message describing the failure. If the cause of the failure is the SQN check, the failure message includes an encrypted version of the Subscriber's SQN so that the HN may resynchronize [7]. These failure cases are not shown in Fig. 2.

(E) Response Check (SN). The SN checks RES* by hashing RES* ∥ RAND and comparing it to HXRES*. The SN then forwards RES* to the HN. Since the SN on its own only had access to HXRES*, the HN is assured that RES* originated from the Subscriber [7].

(F) Response Check (HN). The HN compares RES* to XRES* to check the response. If valid, it signals success to the SN with a message including the decrypted SUPI and K_{SEAF} [7].

2.2 The SUCI-Catcher Attack

As we mention in Sect. 1, if the SUPI were not encrypted in, for example, a Registration Request, as was the case prior to 5G, a passive attacker who listens to over-the-air messages, from a subscriber could easily track the subscriber, i.e., tells if two subscribers in two different places and/or at times correspond to the same subscriber. A device that is used has been called an IMSI catcher [25], which acts as a fake base station with which the subscriber establishes a radio link. The active nature of the IMSI catcher allows it to send an identity request, serving two purposes: (i) improving the efficiency of the attack by avoiding the need to wait for a naturally occuring registration request, and (ii) bypassing the use of temporary identifiers as an attack mitigation [10]. (3GPP standards have used temporary identifiers, such as the TMSI in 3G [10], or the 5G-GUTI in 5G [7], to reduce the use of permanent identifiers, but any SN must be able to issue an identity request as a fallback, so the temporary identifier is not relevant when considering an active attacker.) Use of the SUCI, instead, prevents this kind of attack. Two instances of a SUCI that correspond to the same SUPI are highly likely to be different, assuming that the encryption with the HN's public key is randomized, as best practice prescribes.

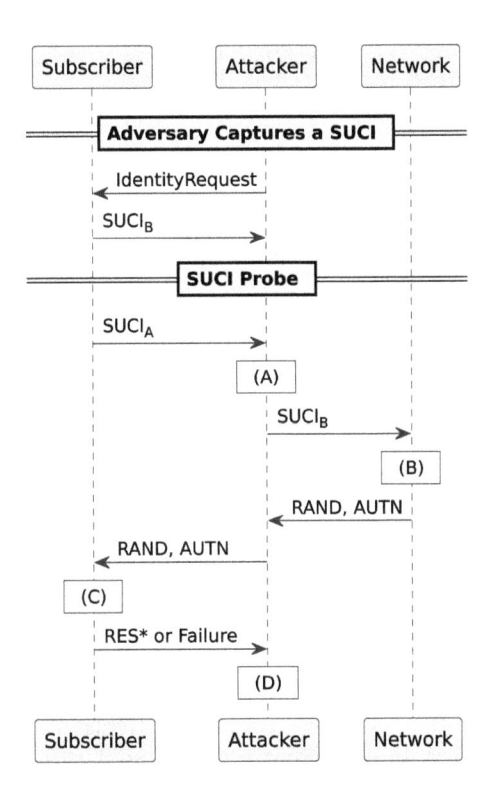

Fig. 3. 'SUCI-Catcher' attack on 5G-AKA subscriber anonymity

Recent prior work [15] presents a new attack that allows similar tracking of subscribers. Underlying the attack is that while the same SUPI will produce a different SUCI every time it is encrypted, the authentication process provides an oracle for the equivalence of SUCIs, i.e., whether they correspond to the same SUPI: if a registration request from a subscriber identified by $SUCI_A$ is forwarded to the SN with the SUCI replaced by $SUCI_B$, and the subscriber accepts the subsequent authentication challenge, then $SUCI_A$ and $SUCI_B$ must correspond to the same SUPI. The protocol flow for this attack is shown in Fig. 3, under the section labeled "SUCI probe." The Attacker is assumed to have man-in-the-middle capabilities over the radio link, by combining the fake base station of an IMSI Catcher with a method to send messages to a legitimate base station. In the figure, the SN and HN are grouped as one 'Network' entity since the internal details of 5G-AKA are not relevant to the attack.

The main steps in the attack, shown as (A) through (D) in the figure, are:

(A) The Attacker receives a Registration Request from an unknown subscriber identified by $SUCI_A$, and creates a Registration Request containing a known identity $SUCI_B$.
(B) The Registration Request triggers an Authentication Request as normal. The Authentication Vector is generated using the key for the Subscriber identified by $SUCI_B$.
(C) The subscriber attempts to validate the Authentication Vector sent by the network. It will only be accepted if it was generated using the same key as the Subscriber.
(D) The Attacker receives the response from the subscriber. If it is not a failure message, then $SUCI_B$ must identify this subscriber.

This new 'SUCI-Catcher' attack requires knowing a SUCI that corresponds to a particular subscriber (i.e. the one sent as $SUCI_B$). There are two ways to achieve this [15]:

1. Generating a SUCI by encrypting a known SUPI using the HN's public key.
2. Linking a subscriber to a captured SUCI using other surveillance mechanisms (e.g. security cameras).

These can be viewed as two variants of the same attack with differing difficulty of mitigation. In the second variant, the first section of Fig. 3 shows how the SUCI can be initially captured using an Identity Request, but it should be noted that an arbitrary amount of time may pass before the SUCI probe is performed.

Lowe's Taxonomy. The apparent problem in Fig. 3 is that the subscriber thinks it has initiated registration using $SUCI_A$, but the HN thinks the same subscriber has used $SUCI_B$. This is an agreement problem, so it is useful to consider how Lowe's taxonomy [21] could be applied to this situation. In particular, we reprise two properties from that work that are customarily desirable in an authentication protocol and have been leveraged in a prior analysis of 5G-AKA [12], *non-injective* and *injective agreement*. The former is a guarantee to an initiator A of a protocol with a responder B on a set of data items d that whenever A completes a run of the protocol with B, B has indeed been running the protocol previously, apparently with A, with B in the role of the responder, and both A and B agree on the data values of d. An important nuance here is that there has not necessarily been a one-to-one correspondence between the protocol runs of A and B. Injective agreement guarantees not only agreement on the data values of d, but also that each run of A corresponds to a unique run of B. The adjective *recent* may be added to either property, and is defined by Lowe as guaranteeing that B's run did not occur earlier than some (protocol-specific) bounded distance into past time.

Suppose we perceive the Registration Request combined with 5G-AKA as the protocol as it pertains to Lowe's taxonomy. Then we observe that non-injective agreement on a SUCI is neither necessary nor sufficient for variant (1) of the attack to be mitigated. To see why sufficiency does not hold, we observe that the definitions of Lowe [21] do not say anything about the case where the protocol does not complete. If SUCIs created by an adversary are rejected after the registration message, then the adversary may have learned something from the rejection—we are reliant on assumptions about how the protocol is implemented for this to not be the case. To see why necessity does not hold, we observe that Lowe [21] defines 'running the protocol' for the responding party as them having reached the most recent message observable by the initiator. In our case, this would be the RES* message. But then non-injective agreement is not achieved by preventing the adversary from generating their own SUCI: $SUCI_B$ may have been captured from a Registration Request that never proceeded to authentication, in which case the subscriber would not be defined as running the protocol while agreeing on $SUCI_B$.

Perhaps a better perspective would be to restrict the consideration of agreement on the SUCI to the Registration Request only, as a one-message protocol. Then, non-injective agreement means that if the HN accepts a registration request, the SUCI must have been sent by the subscriber, which rules out the attack variant (1). However, even injective agreement in this protocol does not suffice to claim that variant (2) of the attack is prevented. Injective agreement excludes the possibility of SUCI replay by providing that a Registration Request accepted by the HN corresponds to a unique request from the subscriber. However, it still allows a Registration Request that never reaches the HN to be stored by an adversary and sent later, which may still enable the attack.

Towards Mitigation. The above discussion as it relates to Lowe's taxonomy [21] provides a preview to the various existing mitigations we examine in the following section. Some mitigations focus on achieving a somewhat weak agreement by ensuring the SUCI cannot be generated by the adversary. Others use timestamps or other detection mechanisms to attempt to prevent replays, providing agreement when combined with mitigations of the first type. Yet, as just mentioned, agreement without recency still allows for a SUCI to be captured and used at an arbitrary later time.

We consider instead whether recent agreement can be achieved by using a sequence of ephemeral identifiers in place of the SUPI, so that previous Registration Requests become unusable for the reason that they decrypt to the wrong identifier. In the ideal case, the identifier changes for every session, providing a guarantee that the HN only accepts the most recent registration request; however, it is not possible to coordinate a synchronous update between two parties exchanging a finite number of messages over an asynchronous channel [20]. To resolve this, we provide an update procedure where the two parties advance their identifier sequence at different times, but where a successful authentication guarantees they have both advanced by one step.

Our protocol has parallels to the double-ratchet algorithm used in the Signal protocol [16,22], both in the application of a racheting mechanism suitable for asynchronous channels, and in the use of self-healing behavior to reduce the impact of attacks, but applied to the goal of subscriber privacy rather than authentication. The double-ratchet algorithm aims to achieve "post-compromise security" [16,17]: as the parties continuously update their keys using Diffie–Hellman shares included in the protocol messages, an adversary who has compromised the session may be prevented from reading future messages if they fail to capture all subsequent exchanges. Similarly, our protocol prevents the SUCI-catcher from linking the subscriber to a previous authentication if there has been a subsequent authentication in which the SUCI-catcher did not intervene.

3 Our Protocol

In this section we briefly outline prior approaches to mitigating the SUCI-Catcher and similar base-station impersonation attacks. We then introduce the goals of our protocol and explain how they represent an improvement over prior approaches. Based on this, we then describe our protocol.

Prior approaches fall broadly into one of the 7 categories. All of these are discussed by the 3GPP [6]. (i) Disallow attacker from computing SUCI; (ii) Include Timestamp in SUCI; (iii) Detect replay; (iv) Include MAC in SUCI; (v) Link Authentication Challenge to SUCI; (vi) Authenticate Base Station; (vii) adopt a new protocol. Space limitations preclude an elaborate discussion here; we address them in a longer version of this work [26]. Briefly, (i) is incompatible with the notion that the public portion of an HN's public-private key pair remains public; (ii) would cause a circular dependency given the manner in which current cellular devices synchronize time; (iii) does not provide provable security guarantees assuming that the HN is able to store only a finite number of prior SUCIs; (iv) does not address attack variant (2); (v) violates the 5G design that the registration and authentication protocols are not linked; (vi) requires a public-key infrastructure to distribute keys to entities approved by the HN; (vi) requires major changes.

3.1 Goals

Our primary goal is of course to prevent the SUCI-catcher attack. Specifically, variant (1) should be entirely prevented, while variant (2) should be defeated under a clear set of assumptions. Given also our discussion from the previous section, we adopt the following design constraints:

1. The HN's public key may be public.
2. The subscriber does not need a reliable time source.
3. There is no one-to-one relationship between registration and authentication.
4. The SN may participate in the protocol without any change to its software.

We call (4) above backwards-compatibility. This definition of backwards compatibility is useful because it ensures the possibility of gradual deployment: an HN may deploy the modified protocol without requiring that all their roaming partners, who may act as SN, support it. Under this definition of backwards compatibility, the authentication must still follow the basic sequence from Fig. 2 in Sect. 2 in that the SN does not need any new protocol logic.

Additionally, the message formats should be such that an existing SN would process them without error. While the packet format used for messages exchanged between the subscriber and SN includes a length field for RAND and RES*, it is not clear whether the SN would forward fields with abnormal length: the communications between the SN and HN use a defined HTTP API returning data in JSON format [4], so the SN is likely to validate individual fields when translating between JSON and the packet format used to exchange messages with the subscriber. The SN must also parse RES* since it will hash it when comparing to HXRES*, so it is clear the format of RES* cannot be changed. For these reasons, we assume the lengths of AUTN, RAND, and RES* cannot be changed, and that SHA256(RES*) must equal HXRES*.

3.2 Protocol Description

We propose the use of an ephemeral identifier in place of the SUPI in 5G-AKA. This impacts registration as well, because the SUCI in a Registration Request would now be computed from an ephemeral identifier rather than the SUPI directly. As a motivating example, consider a case where there is only one valid temporary identifier at a time, and both the subscriber and HN move to a new identifier after each authentication. In this case it is not possible for an adversary to compute a SUCI as the temporary identifier is not public. In addition, any captured SUCI becomes useless after an intervening authentication because it will no longer decrypt to the "current" identifier.

However, this hypothetical system is impractical as it is not possible for both the subscriber and HN to agree on when to move to the next identifier (this is the famous two generals' problem [20]). Consequently, we relax the requirement and have both entities maintain a window of two valid identifiers at a time: the "current" identifier and the "next" identifier. Even more specifically, only the subscriber may be ahead, not the HN. This allows for the subscriber to advance before the HN while still having valid identity. For concreteness, we consider the case where the each identifier, called an hSUPI for "hash SUPI," is the hash of the previous one—corresponding to the update rule $hSUPI_{n+1} = H(hSUPI_n)$. (See, however, 'On our use of repeated hashing' in the next section that addresses the specificity of this approach.)

Table 1 shows these proposed modifications in relation to the original 5G-AKA protocol. The HN includes the next hSUPI in its computation of the MAC tag so that the subscriber can use it to determine whether it is ahead of the HN and should update.

This modified protocol does not assume a directly preceding Registration Request: the 5G-AKA portion is still initiated by the network. If the subscriber

Table 1. Modified 5G-AKA protocol (ref. Fig. 2 for original steps)

Step	Change
(A)	Use hSUPI as the SUPI, $$\text{SUCI} \leftarrow \text{ECIES-ENC}(PK_{HN}, \text{hSUPI}_{UE,n})$$
(C)	Include hSUPI in the MAC, $$\text{MAC} \leftarrow f_1(K, \text{SQN}_{HN}, \text{RAND}, \text{hSUPI}_{HN,n+1})$$
(D)	1. Accept either of two possible MAC tags, $$\text{XMAC}_1 \leftarrow f_1(K, \text{SQN}_{HN}, \text{RAND}, \text{hSUPI}_{UE,n})$$ $$\text{XMAC}_2 \leftarrow f_1(K, \text{SQN}_{HN}, \text{RAND}, \text{hSUPI}_{UE,n+1})$$ 2. If the Authentication Vector is valid and MAC matched XMAC_2, advance hSUPI, $$\text{hSUPI}_{UE,n} \leftarrow \text{hSUPI}_{UE,n+1}$$
(F)	If RES* is accepted, advance hSUPI, $$\text{hSUPI}_{HN,n} \leftarrow \text{hSUPI}_{HN,n+1}$$

does need a SUCI for a registration request (or one is requested) then it should encrypt its current hSUPI as shown in the figure. The HN must look up the SUPI from either of the two possible hSUPIs (current and next).

We make two claims about this protocol that are proven using formal verification in Sect. 4. The first is that the update rule is correct in that, if the 5G-AKA key is secret, it is not possible to advance one party to a state where it is considered to have an invalid identifier by the other. In this way, it remains always possible to successfully authenticate. The second is that the agreement on the SUCI after the Registration Request is sufficiently strong that an adversary cannot generate SUCIs that are accepted by the HN. This mitigates variant (1) of the attack.

As to variant (2), after a successful authentication, the HN updates its hSUPI. In Sect. 4 we show this guarantees that the subscriber has previously updated to the same value, invalidating any captured previous SUCIs. It is still possible that a SUCI containing the new hSUPI was captured (e.g. if the authentication attempt does not complete on the first attempt, so the subscriber updates without the HN, and then uses the new hSUPI in a new registration request), but just one intervening authentication without a captured SUCI will prevent the subscriber from being linked to a previous interaction with the SUCI Catcher. We discuss the effectiveness of this mitigation further in the next section.

3.3 Practical Considerations

Before we discuss our formal verification in the next section, here, we briefly address the practicality of our proposal in a realistic network environment; more details are in our longer document [26].

Effectiveness. Do our changes and associated proof (in Sect. 4) provide a useful security guarantee in practice? We argue that they do: the nature of the SUCI-catcher attack is that it aims to correlate two authentication sessions separated in time. Thus, it is entirely reasonable to expect the subscriber to complete an intervening authentication with the network. This can be ensured by having the HN require authentication before accepting registration as a policy decision. The 5G-AKA specification already suggests this behavior for HNs wishing to ensure that Registration Requests it receives from an SN represent real subscribers [7].

Our Use of Repeated Hashing. Repeated hashing as a method for generating the sequence of hSUPI values may not be a particularly attractive method of pseudo-random number generation. We used this method for modelling within Tamarin (see the next section) as it is easy to describe and shows that unpredictability from previous outputs is not required for the proof.

Calculation and Storage of hSUPI. Our protocol requires both parties to store their hSUPI persistently, and ensure that the update process is atomic. This is similar to the requirements for the storage of the sequence number by both parties. Also, the 5G-AKA protocol provides an explicit mechanism to resynchronize the HN's sequence number to that of the subscriber [7]. Although it provides an "escape hatch" in the case of any unexpected logic error that desynchronizes the counter state, the resynchronization mechanism is a point of vulnerability for subscriber anonymity. As we mention in Sect. 5, some existing attacks exploit the resynchronization mechanism to defeat subscriber privacy [10,12,13]. Our protocol mitigates attacks that exploit the resynchronization mechanism [10,12,13] as they rely on replaying an authentication request to trigger resynchronization, but the replay would not have a valid MAC once the subscriber's hSUPI is advanced. To avoid similar attacks, we do not consider a resynchronization mechanism for the hSUPI sequence. As we discuss in Sect. 4, the Tamarin proof provides assurance that the subscriber and HN remain synchronized.

SUCI Format. Although in the Tamarin specification the SUCI is the straightforward asymmetric encryption of the SUPI, since this is sufficient to model its main features, an actual IMSI-based SUCI has a specific format requirement, specified by [2]. This format includes the mobile country code (MCC) and mobile network code (MNC) from the IMSI in plaintext, since they are needed to determine the country and HN respectively, to which the subscriber should be routed [3]. This can be retained in our modified protocol by continuing to copy these digits from the IMSI. A similar observation applies to the routing indicator digits used for intra-HN routing, although they are not part of the IMSI [3].

The part of the IMSI that is encrypted is the mobile subscription identification number (MSIN), which is used by the HN to look up the subscriber after decrypting the SUCI [7]. Since the MSIN consists of 9–10 decimal digits, one approach to recreate this would be to define a reduction function from the space of hSUPI values (e.g. 256 bits if using SHA256) to the space of MSIN values. However, this has the problem that even for 10-digit MSIN values, only a few hundred thousand subscribers can be supported before a collision is expected due to the birthday paradox (in fact it is even fewer since each subscriber has two valid hSUPIs as explained in the protocol description). This number can easily be exceeded by large network providers.

It would instead appear to be far easier to use the full hSUPI as an identifier since the HN will be the only one processing it. One concern with this is whether the argument against changing the authentication request—that there is no evidence the SN would process fields of non-standard length—applies here too. It turns out that it does not: the standard provides two encryption schemes, with different output size, and further reserves four protection scheme identifiers for proprietary schemes specific to each HN. The proprietary schemes are allowed to expand the input size by up to 3000 bytes (apparently to allow for post-quantum algorithms) [7]. For this reason, the SUCI is not expected to be a specific size, so it is reasonable to assume the SN will forward the slightly longer SUCI containing the hSUPI to the HN as normal.

Hardware Implementation. We expect our modified protocol to be easier to implement on the USIM than comparable modifications involving random nonces or public key cryptography. The original 3GPP USIM (for 4G and earlier) did not support random number generation, which is one reason that 5G-AKA, based on the original authentication primitives, only uses symmetric-key cryptography [12]. While our modification would require new logic to be implemented in the USIM, the pseudorandom sequence of ephemeral SUPIs, implemented through repeated hashing or otherwise, would only involve symmetric cryptographic primitives, which we expect are easier to implement on resource-constrained systems than asymmetric primitives. Our protocol also does not add any requirement for random number generation in the USIM, which would require specialized hardware that may not be present.

4 Formal Verification

We used the Tamarin theorem prover to formally verify the claimed properties of the hSUPI in Sect. 3. In this section, we explain the main details of our analysis. Some familiarity with Tamarin is assumed; we refer the reader to prior work [23,24,29] for an introduction.

We have made our full model, and associated utility scripts, available at [27] for free public download. Any `monotype` text in this section references a lemma from the model.

4.1 Modelling

As a starting point for our proof, we used the Tamarin model of 5G-AKA from [12]. To encode our modified protocol, the main operation that needed to be added was the computation of successive hSUPI values. The update rule chosen for our model is well-suited to implementation in Tamarin, as a hash function can be implemented as an arbitrary function symbol with no associated equations.

We also modelled the storage of the hSUPI by each party. A fact providing the current hSUPI for a given user is somewhere between a regular "linear" fact, which is consumed when used, and a persistent fact since while it can be modified, only one instance per user should exist. A natural way to implement this is using a linear fact, while ensuring that every rule that consumes it outputs a (potentially unchanged) replacement. Tamarin calls this an injective fact, and has special-case handling for some instances [28].

We implemented the protocol steps that had to accept two possible hSUPI values as two separate rules, using pattern matching (where legality is enforced by writing a rule's prerequisites to be of the desired form) to ensure the right rule is selected.

4.2 Analysis—Correctness

The first goal of our analysis was to show that it is always possible to successfully authenticate—that the hSUPI update rules ensure the two sides remain "in sync." To prove this aspect of correctness, we proved the two lemmas: `ue_hsupi_update` and `hn_hsupi_update`. They respectively assert two facts

1. When the subscriber updates its hSUPI to some value, the HN has previously updated to the subscriber's current hSUPI value.
2. When the HN updates its hSUPI to some value, the subscriber has previously updated to that new value.

Together, these two lemmas guarantee that the only two valid states of the hSUPI values are for both entities to have the same value, or for the subscriber to be one update ahead. This can be seen by considering an inductive argument on the sequence of updates, noting that both sides are initialized to the same value during subscriber registration as the base case.

Consistent with the experience of [12], we found that an oracle was required to prove our lemmas; the automated search was not effective for our protocol. In order to create an oracle, we considered what the "main argument" would be if the correctness of a lemma were to be presented manually. Using the graphical interface to Tamarin, it was possible to manually follow the argument for a few cases, and then use that experience to implement the same procedure in the oracle, so that it can be applied in automatic mode. In this respect, the theorem prover does not eliminate the need for intuition in developing an argument, but is effective at automating the analysis of a large number of cases.

Due to the stateful nature of the hSUPI updates, we used the inductive reasoning mode of Tamarin for the proofs of the update properties. Since the protocol does not guarantee a finite number of messages between updates, it was possible to search backwards infinitely without reaching the inductive hypothesis, so we developed two further lemmas that could be reused in the proofs: ue_hsupi_unchanged and hn_hsupi_unchanged. These lemmas provide that every hSUPI that is used originated from an update or initialization, which is a simple property provable on its own using induction. Their reuse allows other proofs to conclude the existence of a previous update in situations that would otherwise lead to the infinite search problem—where the backwards search does not reach the inductive hypothesis.

4.3 Analysis—Effectiveness

After the invariant preserved by the update lemmas, the second aspect of our protocol we sought to prove is the effectiveness of the mitigation against the SUCI-catcher attack. We expect that the ephemeral nature of the hSUPI provides non-injective agreement on the SUCI after the registration request. This property is expressed by the hn_suci_from_ue lemma.

Proving this lemma required two helper lemmas:

1. hn_ue_hsupi_unique, asserting that two subscribers do not have the same hSUPI.
2. hn_hsupi_secret, asserting that when the hSUPI is known to the adversary, either the initial hSUPI or the HN's private key was compromised.

When first implementing the hn_hsupi_secret lemma we encountered a limitation in Tamarin's ability to analyze the hSUPI sequence. Tamarin provides fact $K(x)$ for users asserting adversary knowledge, which normally should be used for lemmas about secrecy [30]. This fact is implemented as an action fact on the rule that enables the adversary to sent public messages—if the adversary can send something, then it must know it. The adversary knowledge is represented internally with two distinct types of fact: $K^{\downarrow}(x)$—knowing a term x that can be deconstructed (e.g. a tuple), and $K^{\uparrow}(x)$—knowing a term x that cannot be further deconstructed [23]. The problem with this is that $K(x)$ derives from $K^{\uparrow}(x)$, so a search for $K(\text{hSUPI}_n)$, will consider $K^{\uparrow}(\text{hSUPI}_n)$, leading to an infinite search sequence as $K^{\uparrow}(\text{hSUPI}_n)$ may be derived from $K^{\uparrow}(\text{hSUPI}_{n-1})$

(using the equation $\text{hSUPI}_n = \text{H}(\text{hSUPI}_{n-1})$), which in turn may be derived from $K^\uparrow(\text{hSUPI}_{n-2})$, and so on. Using induction fails to resolve this because the inductive hypothesis would be stated in terms of $K(x)$ rather than $K^\uparrow(x)$, and Tamarin does not currently model the implication $K(x) \Rightarrow K^\uparrow(x)$ [18]. To work around this limitation, we restated our lemma in terms of $K^\uparrow(x)$, using an undocumented feature where $K^\uparrow$ is available as KU. Doing so in a helper lemma is safe because it does not independently represent a required property and the conclusions of any lemmas proven using the helper lemma are unchanged.

One final change required to complete our proof was specifying exactly which parties may have particular secrets compromised in certain lemmas. This arose from an unexpected weakness in the generic style of property specification recommend by Tamarin, where each rule is tagged with assumptions on honest (i.e. uncompromised) parties [30]. When reusing a lemma with a compromise of a secret as a possible conclusion, the intention is for this compromise to be of a secret relevant to the security claim, a property expected to be provided by the explicit annotation of honest parties in the generic style of property specification. However, Tamarin is largely untyped (other that general distinctions such as fresh terms or constants). Avoiding strict typing has the advantage of preventing the accidental exclusion of attacks that may exist in a real implementation, but also allows conclusions that are not realistic. In the 5G-AKA model, the SN identities itself to the HN, technically allowing an adversary to provide the identity of an unrelated subscriber or HN as the SN's identity. Then, the annotation of the SN as honest in most protocol steps creates the assumption that this unrelated party is honest, preventing the conclusion that a compromised secret belongs to the HN or subscriber actually performing the protocol. This could be resolved by adding the assumption that the channel between the SN and HN is uncompromised, so the SN's identity could not be manipulated by the adversary, but this weakens the conclusion by relying on a security assumption not expected to be required in practice. Instead, the parties to whom a secret may actually belong were explicitly specified in each of our lemmas designed for reuse.

It is not expected that this weakness in the generic style of property specification affects existing work, since any counterexample accidentally excluded would have to be a result of the identity confusion, and the parties in 5G-AKA are not at all treated interchangeably. However, any divergence between a lemma and the formal property it is meant to represent is deserving of scrutiny, so future implementations may wish to avoid the issue. As well as the method used in our lemmas, which was easy to "retrofit" to an already annotated model, a possible approach could be to add explicit tagging to the identity in the annotations, as is already done for different secret items.

5 Related Work

We have cited several pieces of work throughout the prior sections in the context in which each is relevant to our work. In this section, we call out prior work that is most closely related.

Our work relates to 5G, and in particular, 5G-AKA, and consequently, 3GPP standards pertaining to 5G-AKA are relevant to our work. In particular, there is its security architecture [5] and security procedures [7], the latter of which specifies 5G-AKA. There has been prior work that points out linkability attacks in mobile networks; in particular, the kind of attack we address can be traced back to the work of Arapinis et al. [10]. More directly, the class of attacks we address are discussed in the more recent work of Chlosta et al. [15] who, in turn, credit the work of Basin et al. [12] with identifying the fundamental problem: that 5G-AKA when paired with Registrarion Requests suffers from SUCI-linkability, i.e., that it can be identified that two SUCIs correspond to the same SUPI. Chlosta et al. [15] explore, more fully, the practicality of the attack, and the scale at which it can be carried out. Our work relates to the work of Basin et al. [12] also with regards to the manner in which we carry out verification: we rely on that work's specifications for 5G-AKA in the Tamarin theorem prover as the starting point for our own specifications. In the course of that part of the work, we have pointed out challenges with carrying out such verification. Similar observations have been made by Borgaonkar et al. [13] for a different class of attacks that exploits the resynchorization mechanism in 5G-AKA for its sequence number. That work observes the difficulty of using a theorem prover such as Tamarin on account of the need to model partial information that is recovered by the XOR-ing of two values. Our work relates also to mitigations that have been proposed for various deficiencies in 5G-AKA, and the SUCI-catcher attack, in particular, studies from the 3GPP [6,8], all of which we address in Sect. 3.

6 Conclusion and Future Work

We have addressed an attack that prior work calls SUCI-catcher against 5G cellular networks. The attack is able to identify whether two SUCIs, which are encrypted forms of a subscriber's permanent identifier called a SUPI, correspond to the same SUPI, and thereby is able to link two sessions as belonging to the same subscriber. We have studied prior proposals for mitigation, and in light of their deficiencies, proposed our solution, in which, rather than using a SUPI directly to generate a SUCI, we generate a SUCI from an emphemeral identifier that is generated from the SUPI. We have explored a number of issues related to our solution and in particular, tout its practicality and security. Towards the former, we have proposed a notion of backwards-compatibility that our solution meets, which includes within it the property that packet and message formats require no change, and thereby, the SN is oblivious to the new protocol's use. Towards the latter, we have formally verified our protocol by building on prior work on the verification of 5G-AKA.

There is considerable scope for future work. An aspect is a deeper study on the practicality of our solution by, for example, actually implementing it in a 5G network and studying its functioning and performance. Another, which we mention in Sect. 3.3 is the resynchronization of the ephemeral identifier in case of software or hardware failure; this must be designed carefully so as not to introduce more security vulnerabilities. More broadly, the fact that we are able to use an identity other than the SUPI which is issued by the HN to authenticate leads one to think of our proposal as a limited kind of "bring your own identity" to authenticate oneself in a cellular network; a generalization of this notion is interesting topic for future work. There is the question also as to whether the oracles and intermediate lemmas we have developed to carry out our proofs in Tamarin can be generalized and incorporated into the theorem prover so they are useful for other work.

References

1. 3GPP: About 3GPP (2022). https://www.3gpp.org/about-us. Accessed 30 May 2023
2. 3rd Generation Partnership Project: Technical Specification Group Core Network and Terminals: Non-access-stratum (NAS) protocol for 5G system (5GS). 3GPP TS 24.501 v17.5.0 (2021)
3. 3rd Generation Partnership Project: Technical Specification Group Core Network and Terminals: Numbering, addressing and identification. 3GPP TS 23.003 v18.1.0 (2023)
4. 3rd Generation Partnership Project: Technical Specification Group Core Network and Terminals: Unified data management services. 3GPP TS 24.501 v18.1.0 (2023)
5. 3rd Generation Partnership Project: Technical Specification Group Services and System Aspects: Security architecture. 3GPP TS 33.102 v16.0.0 (2020)
6. 3rd Generation Partnership Project: Technical Specification Group Services and System Aspects: Study on authentication enhancements in the 5G system (5GS). 3GPP TR 33.846 v17.0.0 (2021)
7. 3rd Generation Partnership Project: Technical Specification Group Services and System Aspects: Security architecture and procedures for 5G system. 3GPP TS 33.501 v17.4.1 (2022)
8. 3rd Generation Partnership Project: Technical Specification Group Services and System Aspects: Study on 5G security enhancement against false base stations (FBS). 3GPP TR 33.809 v0.20.0 (2022)
9. 3rd Generation Partnership Project: Technical Specification Group Services and System Aspects: System architecture for the 5G system (5GS). 3GPP TS 23.501 v18.1.0 (2023)
10. Arapinis, M., et al.: New privacy issues in mobile telephony: fix and verification. In: Proceedings of the 2012 ACM Conference on Computer and Communications Security, CCS 2012, pp. 205–216. Association for Computing Machinery, New York (2012). https://doi.org/10.1145/2382196.2382221
11. Basin, D., Cremers, C., Dreier, J., Meier, S., Sasse, R., Schmidt, B.: Tamarin prover. https://tamarin-prover.github.io/. Accessed 28 Mar 2023
12. Basin, D., Dreier, J., Hirschi, L., Radomirovic, S., Sasse, R., Stettler, V.: A formal analysis of 5G authentication. In: Proceedings of the 2018 ACM SIGSAC Conference on Computer and Communications Security, CCS 2018, pp. 1383–1396. Association for Computing Machinery, New York (2018). https://doi.org/10.1145/3243734.3243846

13. Borgaonkar, R., Hirschi, L., Park, S., Shaik, A.: New privacy threat on 3G, 4G, and upcoming 5G AKA protocols. Proceedings on Privacy Enhancing Technologies **2019**(3), 108–127 (2019). https://doi.org/10.2478/popets-2019-0039
14. Certicom Research: Sec 1: Elliptic curve cryptography; version 2.0 (2009). http://www.secg.org/sec1-v2.pdf
15. Chlosta, M., Rupprecht, D., Pöpper, C., Holz, T.: 5G SUCI-catchers: still catching them all? In: Proceedings of the 14th ACM Conference on Security and Privacy in Wireless and Mobile Networks, WiSec 2021, pp. 359–364. Association for Computing Machinery, New York (2021). https://doi.org/10.1145/3448300.3467826
16. Cohn-Gordon, K., Cremers, C., Dowling, B., Garratt, L., Stebila, D.: A formal security analysis of the signal messaging protocol. In: 2017 IEEE European Symposium on Security and Privacy (EuroS&P), pp. 451–466 (2017). https://doi.org/10.1109/EuroSP.2017.27
17. Cohn-Gordon, K., Cremers, C., Garratt, L.: On post-compromise security. In: 2016 IEEE 29th Computer Security Foundations Symposium (CSF), pp. 164–178 (2016). https://doi.org/10.1109/CSF.2016.19
18. Cremers, C., Lukert, P.: K vs KU. Comments on GitHub issue (2021). https://github.com/tamarin-prover/tamarin-prover/issues/447. Accessed 25 May 2023
19. Ericsson: Ericsson mobility report (2022). https://www.ericsson.com/4ae28d/assets/local/reports-papers/mobility-report/documents/2022/ericsson-mobility-report-november-2022.pdf. Accessed 30 May 2023
20. Gray, J.N.: Notes on data base operating systems. In: Bayer, R., Graham, R.M., Seegmüller, G. (eds.) Operating Systems. LNCS, vol. 60, pp. 393–481. Springer, Heidelberg (1978). https://doi.org/10.1007/3-540-08755-9_9
21. Lowe, G.: A hierarchy of authentication specifications. In: Proceedings 10th Computer Security Foundations Workshop, pp. 31–43 (1997). https://doi.org/10.1109/CSFW.1997.596782
22. Marlinspike, M.: The double ratchet algorithm (2016). https://www.signal.org/docs/specifications/doubleratchet/. Accessed 25 May 2023
23. Meier, S.: Advancing automated security protocol verification. Ph.D. thesis, ETH Zurich (2013)
24. Meier, S., Schmidt, B., Cremers, C., Basin, D.: The TAMARIN prover for the symbolic analysis of security protocols. In: Sharygina, N., Veith, H. (eds.) Computer Aided Verification, pp. 696–701. Springer, Heidelberg (2013)
25. Park, S., Shaik, A., Borgaonkar, R., Seifert, J.P.: Anatomy of commercial IMSI catchers and detectors. In: Proceedings of the 18th ACM Workshop on Privacy in the Electronic Society, WPES 2019, pp. 74–86. Association for Computing Machinery, New York (2019). https://doi.org/10.1145/3338498.3358649
26. Parkin, J.: Identity and security in 5G authentication. Master's thesis, University of Waterloo (2024)
27. Parkin, J., Tripunitara, M.: Countering SUCI-catchers in cellular communications. https://github.com/Julian2n7000/countering-suci-catchers-model/
28. The Tamarin Team: Tamarin prover manual: advanced features (2016). https://tamarin-prover.com/manual/develop/book/011_advanced-features.html. Accessed 10 Apr 2023
29. The Tamarin Team: Tamarin prover manual: introduction (2016). https://tamarin-prover.github.io/manual/book/001_introduction.html. Accessed 10 Apr 2023
30. The Tamarin Team: Tamarin prover manual: property specification (2016). https://tamarin-prover.github.io/manual/book/007_property-specification.html. Accessed 10 Apr 2023

BP-MAP: A Secure and Convenient Mutual Authentication Protocol

Harika Narumanchi[✉], Lakshmi Padmaja Maddali, and N. Narendra Kumar

TCS Research, Hyderabad, India
`{h.narumanchi,lakshmipadmaja.maddali,naren.nelabhotla}@tcs.com`

Abstract. Authentication is a fundamental step in achieving security. Most often the authentication is asymmetric, in the sense that the server authenticates a client, while the client has no means to ascertain it is interacting with the legitimate server. Many attacks leverage this asymmetry. Consequently mutual authentication becomes a crucial aspect. There are only a few mutual authentication protocols mostly based on passwords or certificates. However, due to the emergent requirements of user privacy what is needed is a mutual authentication mechanism that preserves user privacy while providing strong security guarantees. Further, any practical mutual authentication scheme must support a versatile mechanism for user account recovery. Bilinear pairings is a mathematical tool that enables a party to prove the possession of a secret without having to reveal the secret, and is the basis for many modern cryptographic constructs such as Zero-Knowledge Proofs. In this paper, we propose a novel mutual authentication scheme, BP-MAP, that leverages bilinear pairings to provide a secure, efficient, and convenient mutual authentication system. BP-MAP scheme consists of protocols for client registration, mutual authentication, account recovery and reset. This is achieved by a non-trivial application of bilinear pairings to realize a fruitful combination of privacy, security and user-convenience. Security of BP-MAP scheme and its constituent protocols is established, and it is argued that BP-MAP is computationally efficient when compared to state-of-the-art protocols that provide similar functions.

Keywords: Mutual Authentication · Account Recovery · Bilinear Pairings · ElGamal Encryption · Passwordless authentication

1 Introduction

Authentication in machine to machine (M2M) communication is crucial to maintain security, confidentiality and integrity of a network. It ensures security by providing access to only the authorized devices to communicate with each other, thus preventing unauthorized access to systems, that steal or modify information. Confidentiality in M2M networks is enabled using data encryption mechanisms and make sure that no-one other than the intended recipient of information has intercepted the transmitted information. Integrity in M2M data transmission is ensured using digital signatures that guarantees trustworthiness and correctness of the data transmitted between machines and verified that data is not tampered. While authentication ensures that a device can verify the identity of the communication party, it does not guarantee that the communicating party verified the identity of requesting device. Mutual authentication involves two-way verification where both requesting party and communicating party verify each other's identities before exchanging data. Mutual authentication is particularly useful in applications such as financial applications, healthcare and so on that involve transmission of sensitive data. Overall, mutual authentication is vital for enhancing robustness, trustworthiness of M2M systems and ensure that requester is communicating with a legitimate server and vice versa.

The factors by which a user is authenticated are (1) Knowledge ("something user knows") - for example, a password, security question, a personal identification number (PIN) (2) Ownership ("something user has") - for example, Identity card, hardware token (3) Inherence ("something user is") - for example, fingerprint, retinal pattern or other biometric information. Authentication mechanisms that rely on multiple factors are more difficult to compromise than those mechanisms that use only single factor [10].

Password based authentication (based on factor "knowledge") is one of the common forms of authentication used in practice. However, when a user enrols with a server using password information, the registration and authentication processes expose the hash of password information to the server which is prone to various types of password guessing attacks such as dictionary attacks [2], credential stuffing [1], brute-force attacks [17], password spraying [3] and so on.

Further, password based authentication systems come with the following challenges: attacker can capture password while client and server communicate for authentication; users often select weak passwords, making them susceptible to guesswork or cracking; reusing passwords across multiple accounts increases the risk of security breaches. Cybercriminals can employ phishing emails or fake websites to trick users into revealing their passwords. This can lead to unauthorized usage of applications using the stolen password.

To make the attacks complex, password based authentication is usually combined with an additional factor such as an One Time Password - OTP ("based on factor Ownership") or a biometric ("based on factor Inherence"). However, users need to carry additional devices for positive authentication which can hinder usability. Multiple factors require additional hardware and can be expensive to implement. Moreover, OTPs can be intercepted through attacks such as SIM swapping [4]. Collecting biometric information also raises privacy concerns for the users about how their data is stored and processed.

With the advent of public key infrastructure (PKI), adoption of certificate based authentication has grown to enable enterprise and Internet security to secure access to network and Internet communications (for example SSL/TLS). Certificate based authentication also enables mutual authentication of client and server to authenticate each other ensuring secure and trusted interactions. The major challenge with certificate based authentication is the certificate management lifecycle from issuance to revocation which becomes an additional burden to organizations.

Modern systems are adopting passwordless authentication [9] to eliminate the need for passwords (static information) and managing certificates. Instead, it combines multiple factors such as possession of a trusted device ("something you have") and biometric features such as fingerprint, face and so on ("something you are") to authenticate a user. This approach is significantly complex to attack and more user friendly than the password based approach. Despite these advantages, implementing passwordless authentication may require additional investment in new hardware and users should maintain multiple copies of key at a trusted third-party for account recovery in case of device loss.

From user's perspective, existing authentication methods require users to remember multiple passwords, maintain additional copies of keys with the trusted third parties, carry additional devices and periodically update the revoked certificates for successful authentication. From system's perspective, current systems store database of password hashes, user biometric information and so on which can be an attractive target to the attackers. Moreover, certificate based authentication systems need to manage certificate lifecycle which can be cumbersome. To circumvent such challenges from bother user as well as system perspective, there is a need for an efficient authentication mechanism that reduces burden on both.

The key idea is to enable a party to demonstrate to another that it knows a secret without revealing it. We achieve this by leveraging an efficient mathematical tool - the bilinear pairings to define BP-MAP a secure, efficient and convenient mutual authentication scheme. BP-MAP scheme also allows mutual authentication in much more efficient way without additional cost of maintaining specialized infrastructure.

Important merits of BP-MAP in comparison to the existing techniques include: (1) Privacy: User authentication without revealing any password information. (2) Security: Mutual authentication between the client and the server at no additional cost (3) User-convenience: Ability to recover user account in case of forgetting any one of the parameters.

Our contributions include the following:

- BP-MAP can authenticate a user without revealing his/her password information to a third-party identity provider. This is done by using bilinear parings to authenticate user without sending password information to the server.
- BP-MAP solution eliminates the need for storing any keys on multiple devices or storing password information on server side. This addresses the problems with the password based authentication systems by eliminating the need for password transmission to the server during authentication phase; hence no scope of password theft/security vulnerabilities/replay attacks during transit. Username and public key (a function of password, but not the actual password) are only transmitted once during registration or setup phase. User does not need to remember the password.

- BP-MAP construction does not rely on physical device binding for authentication. Hence, more user-friendly even in case of loss/device theft. This does not necessitate specialized hardware or software, making it a cost-effective choice for businesses.

The paper is organized as follows: Sect. 2 presents the background needed for understanding our approach. This section includes an overview of the core cryptographic primitives used in our protocol, specifically bilinear pairing and ElGamal encryption. Section 3 details BP-MAP, the bilinear pairing based mutual authentication scheme, which is our contribution, including client registration and mutual authentication in Sect. 3.1, account recovery and reset mechanisms in Sect. 3.2, security analysis in Sect. 3.3, performance analysis in Sect. 3.4 and business use-cases in Sect. 3.5. Section 4 provides a comparison with the existing literature. Finally, Sect. 5 concludes with a summary of findings and future research directions.

2 Background

BP-MAP is based on two fundamental cryptographic primitives, namely Bilinear pairings [14] and ElGamal encryption [13]. To make the paper self-sufficient, this section include an explanation of these primitives.

2.1 Bilinear Pairings

Bilinear pairings is a special type of function that maps pairs of elements from two groups to a third group while preserving certain algebraic properties. These pairings are used to design several advanced cryptographic protocols such as Zero Knowledge Proofs (ZKP) [15], Identity-Based Encryption (IBE) [7] and Attribute-Based Encryption (ABE) [25]. The security of protocols using bilinear pairings relies on the computational hardness of Elliptic Curve Discrete Logarithm Problem (ECDLP) [18,22].

Let G_1 and G_2 be elliptic curve additive groups and G_T be a multiplicative group, all of prime order p. Let $P \in G_1$, $Q \in G_2$, be generators of G_1 and G_2 respectively. Here *group* is a set together with an operation, elements of the set satisfy certain properties when operated upon and *generator* is an element from a group that can result in every other element in the group when repeatedly operated upon.

A pairing is a map $e : G_1 \times G_2 \to G_T$ with the following properties:

- Bilinearity: $\forall a, b \in \mathbb{Z}$: $e(aP, bQ) = e(P, Q)^{ab}$
- Non-degeneracy: $e(P, Q) \neq 1$
- For practical purposes, e has to be computable in an efficient manner

For usage in cryptographic context, symmetric pairings are considered with $G_1 = G_2 = G$ and G is represented multiplicatively with generator g. In this case, bilinearity translates to:

$$\forall a, b \in \mathbb{Z} \; e(g^a, g^b) = e(g, g)^{ab}$$

2.2 ElGamal Encryption

ElGamal encryption is a public-key cryptosystem based on the Diffie-Hellman key exchange [11]. An ElGamal encryption scheme has parameters: a cyclic group G, q denotes the order of G, and g is a generator of G. ElGamal encryption system works as follows:

1. **Key Generation**
   - Generate a private key x chosen randomly from $\mathbb{Z}_q$, such that $0 < x < r_q$
   - Compute public key v as $v = g^x$
   - Publish public profile (G, q, g, v)
2. **Encryption**
   - Map the message M to be shared to an element m of the group G
   - Generate a random integer y
   - Compute the ciphertext $c_1 = g^y$ and $c_2 = m.v^y$
   - Send the ciphertext (c_1, c_2) to the recipient
3. **Decryption**
   - Receive the ciphertext (c_1, c_2)
   - Compute the shared secret $s = c_1^x$
   - Compute the original message $M = c_2.s^{-1}$

3 Bilinear Pairing Based Mutual Authentication Protocol

Mutual authentication is a process where both the client and server authenticate each other using cryptographic techniques. We achieve this by leveraging an efficient mathematical tool - the bilinear pairings. Bilinear pairing enables a party to prove the possession of a secret to the counter-party without revealing the underlying sensitive information. Further, ElGamal encryption scheme is leveraged to encrypt/decrypt messages between the client and server for ensuring secure communication between the parties. In this section, the construction of an efficient, secure and user-friendly mutual authentication scheme called BP-MAP, and the various protocols involved are described.

Bilinear pairing holds the following property: $e(g^a, g^b) = e(g, g)^{ab}$. This property is exploited in BP-MAP for achieving mutual authentication as described below. Let a and b be the private keys of the two parties involved in the communication, the corresponding public keys are derived as $v = g^a$ and $u = g^b$. Party 1 possesses its private and public keypair $(a$ and $g^a)$, and the public key of Party 2 (g^b). Similarly, Party 2 has their private and public keypair $(b$ and $g^b)$ along with Party 1's public key (g^a). Both parties can compute the left-hand side (LHS) of the equation $e(g^a, g^b)$, as they know g^a and g^b. Note that deriving the private key (a) from the knowledge of the corresponding public key (g^a) is as hard as solving the elliptic curve discrete logarithm problem (EC-DLP).

BP-MAP uses the same keys for the purposes of both pairing and encryption/decryption. Consequently, the server holds one public-private key pair per user instead of a single key pair. This minimizes the impact of key theft, even if attacker compromise one user's keys it does not compromise the entire system.

To prevent replay attacks, a freshness challenge z which is a randomly generated value is used in every session. The use of freshness challenge ensures that exchange of messages between parties, involved in the communication, is secure. Even if an attacker intercepts and tries to replay a previous session's messages they will fail because the freshness challenge will change (be random). We take advantage of the following property of bilinear pairings to mitigate replay attacks: Let z be the freshness challenge; party 1, computes $e(g^z, u^a)$ and sends the response to party 2. Similarly party 2 computes $e(g^z, v^b)$. Using bilinear property $e(g^a, g^b) = e(g, g)^{ab}$, the challenge response verification translates to:

$$e(g^z, u^a) = e(g^z, v^b) \implies e(g^z, (g^b)^a) = e(g^z, (g^a)^b)$$

System Setup. BP-MAP system parameters include two cyclic groups G, G_T of prime order r_p. G is a group of points on an elliptic curve, and G_T is a subgroup of a finite field, both having the same order r_p. The server selects a generator g for the group G and defines a bilinear pairing function $e : G \times G \to G_T$. Further, the server maintains a public-private key pair $(SPubK, SPriK)$ used exclusively for client registration only. The public profile of the scheme is $(G, G_T, e, g, r_p, SPubK)$. The notations used in our proposed solution are summarized in Table 1.

Table 1. Notation

Symbol	Description
G, G_T	cyclic groups of prime order r_p
g	generator of G
e	bilinear pairing function
r_p	order of group G
z	freshness challenge
$SPubK$	server public key
$SPriK$	server private key
x	client secret
$v = g^x$	client public key
y	server secret
$u = g^y$	shared secret

BP-MAP involves the following protocols: (1) Client Registration, (2) Mutual Authentication, (3) Forgot Username, (4) Forgot Shared Secret, and (5) Reset Private Key.

3.1 Registration and Authentication

In this section, the protocols in BP-MAP for user registration and mutual authentication are described.

Client Registration. *Client registration* is a process where each client registers their username and public key with the server. This information is validated and verified by the server to ensure authenticity of the client. The purpose of client registration is to establish a unique and secure identity within a system. This enables secure authentication and communication between the client and server by ensuring that only the verified clients can access services offered by the service provider. Figure 1 depicts a sequence diagram illustrating a user registration to the server via the client device.

The client registration process includes the following steps:

1. *Generate Keypair*: Client invokes key generation algorithm to randomly select a private key, $x \xleftarrow{R} \mathbb{Z}_p$, such that $0 < x < r_p$ and computes public key v as $v = g^x$.
2. *Generate Username*: Client selects a username.
3. *Send Request:* Client sends username and its public key v in an encrypted form $Enc_{SPubK}(username, v)$ to the server.
4. *Decrypt Request*: Server decrypts $Enc_{SPubK}(username, v)$ with its private key $SPriK$ to get $(username, v)$.
   If *username*, sent by the client, already exists, server prompts the client to choose a different *username*.
5. *Generate Server Secret, Shared Secret*: Server selects $y \xleftarrow{R} \mathbb{Z}_p$ (server secret), such that $0 < y < r_p$. Server computes a shared secret $u = g^y$ and checks if (u, v) is unique. Server repeats this process until (u, v) is unique. In BP-MAP scheme, u simultaneously acts as server public key (for encryption) and also as shared secret between server and the client. Thus, in BP-MAP server holds one public-private keypair per user instead of single keypair, thereby minimizing the damage due to key compromise. Uniqueness of (u, v) plays an important role with helping the user recover his *username* in case he forgets it.
6. *Send Shared Secret:* Server sends $Enc_v(u)$ to the client along with acknowledgement of successful registration.

Upon successful registration, the client and server store $g, username, v, u$. In addition, server keeps its private key y secret while the client keeps its private key x secret. Note that $u^x = v^y = g^{xy}$, enabling both the server and client to compute this quantity without knowing x and y simultaneously. Further note that the security of BP-MAP depends solely on keeping the triple $(username, u, v)$ secret.

Mutual Authentication. *Mutual authentication or two-way authentication* is a process where both the client and server verify each other's identities simultaneously. First, the client authenticates the server to confirm that it is communicating with the legitimate server and then the server verifies the client identity. This verification is crucial for establishing secure and trusted connection between client and server especially in the context of web browsing and networking applications. Figure 2 depicts a sequence diagram illustrating the mutual authentication process.

```
┌─────────────────────────────────────────────────────────────────────┐
│              Client                              Server             │
│                                                                     │
│ 1. Generate Keypair                                                 │
│    (sk, pk) = (x, gˣ)=(x, v)                                        │
│ 2. Generate Username                                                │
│    (username)           3. Send Request                             │
│                         (Enc_SPubK(username, v))                    │
│                        ────────────────────────▶                    │
│                                                 4. Decrypt Request  │
│                                                    to get           │
│                                                    (username, v)    │
│                         6. Send Shared Secret   5. Generate Server  │
│                         (Enc_v(u))                 Secret, Shared   │
│                        ◀────────────────────────   Secret = (y, gʸ) │
│                                                    = (y, u)         │
└─────────────────────────────────────────────────────────────────────┘
```

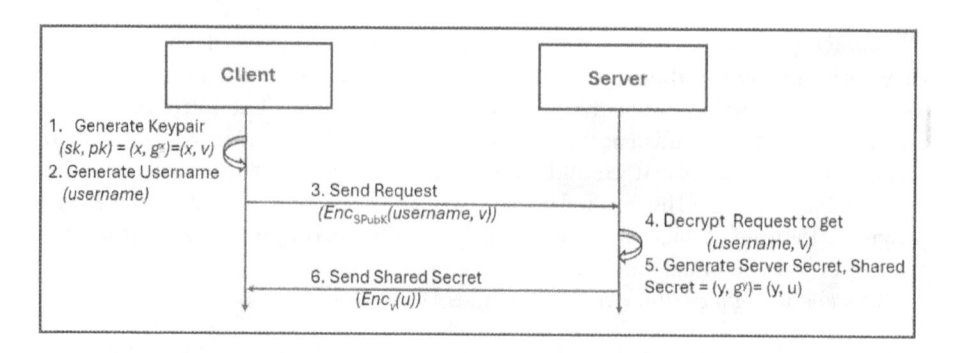

Fig. 1. Client Registration Protocol

1. *Generate Challenge*: Client generates a freshness challenge z_1 such that $z_1 \xleftarrow{R} \mathbb{Z}_p$ and $0 < z_1 < r_p$.
2. *Authentication Request with User Challenge*: Client challenges the server to authenticate itself by sending *username* and challenge z_1.
3. *Compute Response*: Server retrieves the public key v, corresponding to *username* and computes response $resp_{s1} = e(g^{z_1}, v^y)$. Server generates a freshness challenge z_2 such that $z_2 \xleftarrow{R} \mathbb{Z}_p$ and $0 < z_2 < r_p$.
4. *Server Response with Server Challenge*: Server sends $resp_{s1}$ and challenge z_2 to the client.
5. *Server Response Verification*: Client computes $resp_{c1} = e(g^{z_1}, u^x)$ and verifies whether $resp_{c1} == resp_{s1}$. If the response verification is successful, server is authenticated. The client also computes its verification response $resp_{c2} = e(g^{z_2}, u^x)$.
6. *User Response*: Client sends its verification response $resp_{c2}$ to the server for authentication.
7. *Client Response Verification*: Server computes $resp_{s2} = e(g^{z_2}, v^y)$ and verifies whether $resp_{c2} == resp_{s2}$. If the client response verification is successful, client is authenticated.

3.2 Account Recovery and Reset

In this section, the ability of BP-MAP to help a user recover and/or reset his account is illustrated.

Forgot Shared Secret. *Forgot Shared Secret* process is one of the crucial account recovery mechanisms, involving recovery of a forgotten shared secret. This step is important for maintaining secure access to the data and services and ensures that only authorised clients can regain access to their accounts. Figure 3 depicts a sequence diagram illustrating a method for transmitting a shared secret by the server to the client device, in case if shared secret is forgotten by the user. The *forgot shared secret* protocol involves the following steps:

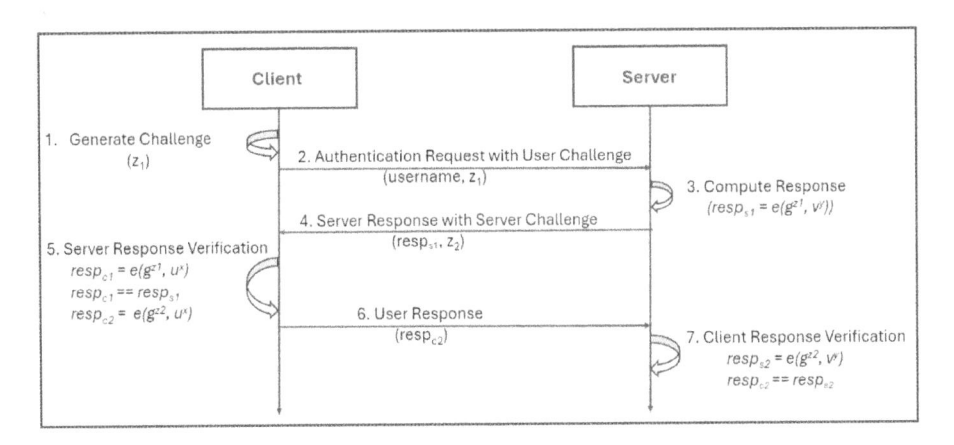

Fig. 2. Mutual Authentication Protocol

1. *Send Username*: Client sends *username* to the server with a request to retrieve shared secret.
2. *Generate Challenge*: Server generates random challenge z such that $z \xleftarrow{R} \mathbb{Z}_p$ and $0 < z < r_p$, and encrypts it using client's public key to get $Enc_v(z)$. Since user claims to have forgotten the shared secret, the only basis by which the client can be authenticated is by his knowledge of private key. And therefore the challenge has to be encrypted and sent. BP-MAP uses ElGamal encryption scheme.
3. *Send Encrypted Challenge*: Server sends encrypted challenge $Enc_v(z)$ to the client.
4. *Decrypt Challenge*: Client decrypts encrypted challenge using its private key x to get z.
5. *Compute Response*: Client computes response $resp = e(g^z, v)$.
6. *Send Response*: Client sends $resp$ to the server.
7. *Verify Response*: Server computes $result = e(g^z, v)$ and verifies $resp == result$

$$e(g^z, v) \stackrel{?}{=} e(g^z, v) \tag{1}$$

8. *Send Shared Secret*: If response verification is successful, server sends shared secret in encrypted form $Enc_v(u)$ to the client. In the client registration workflow, the public key associated with a username is publicly known. Therefore, it is important to protect the shared secret u, so that the association of u with the *username* remains a secret. This helps to maintain the security of BP-MAP scheme.

Forgot Username. The *forgot username* is a part of account recovery mechanism designed to help users to recover their forgotten username. The workflow ensures that clients can securely regain access to their accounts after verification and access their services. Figure 4 depicts a sequence diagram illustrating

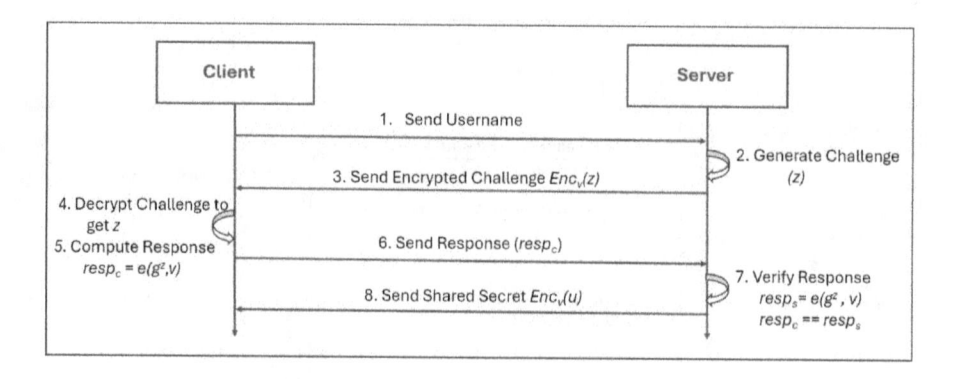

Fig. 3. Forgot Shared Secret Protocol

a method of transmitting the username associated with the user by the server to the client device, in case if the username is forgotten by the user/client. This workflow involves the following steps:

1. *Send Request*: Client sends shared secret u and its public key v in an encrypted form $Enc_u(u,v)$ to the server to retrieve its *username*.
2. *Decrypt Request*: Server decrypts $Enc_u(u,v)$ with its private key y to get (u,v).
3. *Verify User Authenticity*: Server looks for the tuple (u,v) in the authentication database to retrieve the corresponding *username*, if any.
4. *Send Username*: If tuple (u,v) is found, server sends *username* to the client.

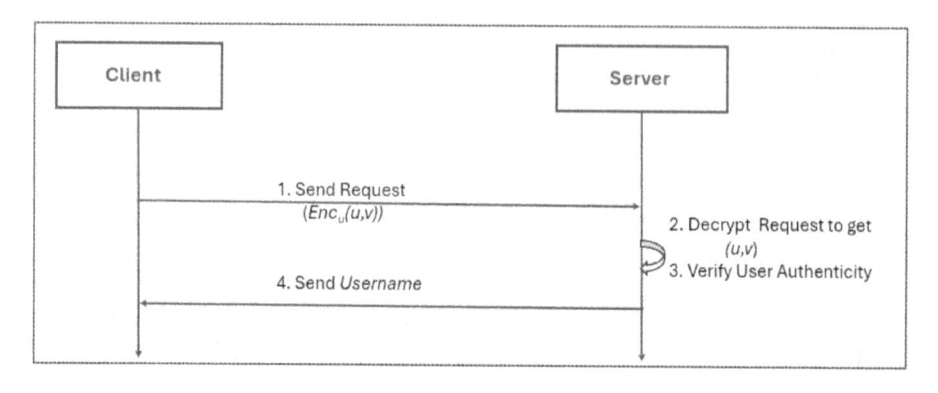

Fig. 4. Forgot Username Protocol

Reset Private Key. The *reset private key* process is part of the account recovery mechanism designed to help clients recover or replace their private key. This protocol addresses scenarios where a client either forgets their private key or wishes to reset it explicitly. In both the cases, the client generates a fresh keypair and initiates the reset process. Server verifies the client's identity through authentication and after successful verification the server updates the public key. This workflow ensures that clients can securely regain access to their accounts after verification and access their services. Figure 5 depicts a sequence diagram illustrating a method of resetting the private key by the user. The *reset private key* protocol involves the following steps:

1. *Create new Keypair*: Client invokes key generation algorithm to randomly select a new private key, $x' \xleftarrow{R} \mathbb{Z}_p$, such that $0 < x' < r_p$. Client computes the corresponding public key v' as $v' = g^{x'}$.
2. *Send Request*: Client sends $Enc_u(username, u, v')$ to the server to modify its secret key.
3. *Decrypt Request*: Server decrypts $Enc_u(username, u, v')$ using its private y to get $(username, u, v')$.
4. *Verify User Authenticity*: Server looks for the tuple $(username, u)$ in the authentication database to verify authenticity of the client. Due to the security conditions in BP-MAP scheme, only the genuine user can correctly provide the pair $(username, u)$. Upon successful verification, server updates the old public key v with new public key v' and checks the uniqueness of (u, v'). If (u, v') pair already exists, server generates new random shared secret u' until (u', v') is unique and updates u to u' in it's database.
5. *Send Shared Secret*: Upon successful updation of new keypair, server sends ACK to client. In case u is updated to u', server also sends $Enc_{v'}(u')$ to the client.

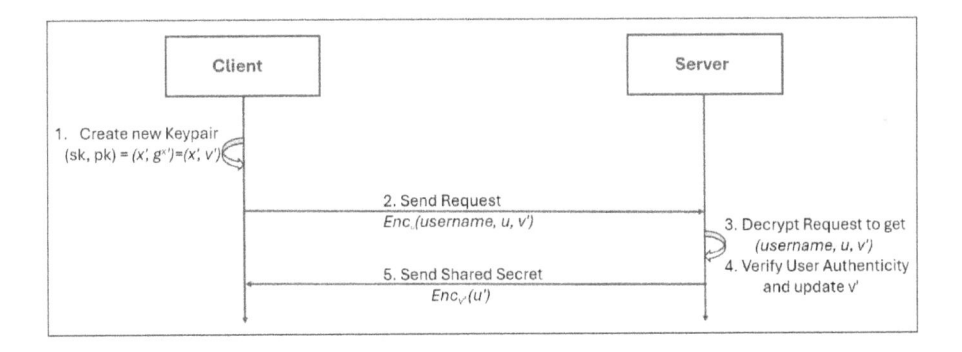

Fig. 5. Reset Private Key Protocol

3.3 Security Analysis

Adversarial/Threat Model: We assume a Dolev-Yao adversary [12] with the following key assumptions: (1) adversary has full control over the network i.e.

adversary can intercept, modify, delete and insert messages, (2) adversary is limited to polynomial time computations; can make only polynomial time queries to the oracles and cannot break cryptographic primitives like encryption, digital signatures or hash functions if they are assumed to be secure, (3) adversary knows the details of the cryptographic protocols being used, (4) adversary can compose and decompose messages i.e., adversary can extract certain components and construct new messages from these components, (5) adversary does not know the secret keys of honest parties unless they have been compromised, (6) adversary can impersonate a legitimate user, and (7) adversary can store messages and replay them at a later time for exploiting protocols. This model provides a strong basis for evaluating the security of cryptographic protocols against potential attacks.

Security of the BP-MAP scheme relies crucially on the fact that only the legitimate user and the server know the triple $(username, v, u)$. In this section, this is established through systematic reasoning under the assumption of the adversarial model above.

Security of Individual Protocols: In the following, the security of individual protocols is established under the assumption that unbounded concurrent instances of the same protocol are in progress. In other words, it is established that the attacker cannot learn anything nor successfully impersonate either a legitimate user or the server in a successful run of any of the protocols taken independently.

In the *client registration* protocol, user sends the chosen username and the generated public key encrypted with the public key of the server. Therefore, only the server can decrypt such messages. Note that the attacker cannot tamper the message to replace the public key of the user with his own public key to be able to decrypt the shared secret sent by the server. Further, the server response with the shared-secret is encrypted with the user's public key thereby ensuring its security. Thus, by the end of a successful run of the *client registration* protocol, the server and the legitimate user will have established the triple $(username, v, u)$ as shared data.

In the *mutual authentication* protocol, while the attacker can observe, know and store all the messages, as they are in plain text, he cannot make any future use of the associations between z_i and r_i for $i \in 1, 2$, because z_is are nonces which by definition will be used only once by the respective entities. Further, due to the underlying hardness assumptions of the bilinear pairings, and the attackers lack of knowledge of x, y, u and v, he will not be able to construct the r corresponding to a z. Thus, by the end of a successful run of the *mutual authentication* protocol, the server and the legitimate user will have successfully established the identity of the party they are communicating with.

In the *forgot username* protocol, since the first message is encrypted with u, only the server can decrypt the message. Note that the attacker does not gain anything by replaying such a message, because servers response of username is in plain. Thus, by the end of a successful run of the *forgot username* protocol, the attacker can only learn the username.

In the *forgot shared secret* protocol, while the attacker can tamper the first message and replace the username with any other username it knows/learnt (a particular case of interest could be using its own username), server sends the nonce encrypted with the public key corresponding to the username it receives in the first step. At this stage, the attacker cannot continue the protocol run successfully because he is not aware of the public key of the user who initiated the first message. So for a successful continuation of the protocol beyond step 1, the attacker should not tamper step 1. Because of this, attacker cannot learn anything from step 2, nor can successfully tamper it. Attacker cannot do much with step 3 either, due to the fact that he does not know z nor v, nor can replay this from an earlier session (due to the freshness of z). In summary, there is no way that the attacker can play an active role in a successful run of the *forgot shared secret* protocol.

In the *reset private key* protocol, since the attacker has no knowledge of the contents being encrypted nor the encryption keys, he cannot play an active role in a successful run of the protocol.

In summary, the protocols are secure when considered individually. The attacker cannot (i) play an active role in a successful run of any of the protocols, (ii) learn anything from the *client registration* and *reset private key* protocols, and (iii) learn anything other than the username of the user initiating the *mutual authentication, forgot username*, and *forgot shared secret* protocols.

Security of the BP-MAP Scheme: In the following, the security of the BP-MAP scheme is established under the assumption that unbounded concurrent instances of all the protocols are in progress. In other words, it is established that the attacker cannot learn anything nor successfully impersonate either a legitimate user or the server in a successful run of any of the protocols, even in case where he is allowed access to unbounded concurrent instances of all the protocols in the scheme.

Note that the first message in the *client registration* protocol is based on public key encryption, whereas in all other instances of the BP-MAP scheme, ElGamal encryption is used. *Client registration* protocol is insulated from impacting runs of other protocols and being impacted by information learnt from instances of other protocols in the scheme. Therefore, the security of the *client authentication* protocol immediately follows from the individual security of the protocol.

Note that the *mutual authentication* protocol is based solely on computing pairings involving nonces, and knowledge of x or y, rendering replay attacks useless. *Mutual authentication* protocol is insulated from impacting runs of other protocols and being impacted by information learnt from instances of other protocols in the scheme. Therefore, the security of the *mutual authentication* protocol immediately follows from the individual security of the protocol.

The first messages in the *forgot username* and *reset private key* protocols have a similar structure and are encrypted with the shared secret corresponding to the user. However, due to the difference in the number of components in these messages, combined with the fact that the attacker does not know the shared secret, means that the attacker can only leverage/replay the first messages learnt in these protocol instances in instances of the same protocol. The *forgot username* and *reset private key* protocols are insulated from impacting runs of other protocols and being impacted by information learnt from instances of other protocols in the scheme. Therefore, the security of the *forgot username* and *reset private key* protocols immediately follows from the individual security of the respective protocols.

Note that the attacker can learn several usernames by observing the first message in the instances of the *mutual authentication* protocol or the server response in the instances of the *forgot username* protocol. The attacker can successfully fool the server by initiating an instance of the *forgot shared secret* protocol, but will not be able to complete step 3 in the protocol by responding to the server challenge. On the other hand when a legitimate user initiates the *forgot shared secret* protocol, the attacker learns nothing about u or v other than u_v. Note that the attacker can successfully fool a legitimate user by impersonating the server. He does so in the following manner: by observing prior instances of the *forgot shared secret* protocol involving the same username, he learns the association between the username and u_v. During a new run of the protocol, the attacker sends u_v in step 2, ignores the user response in step 3, and sends u_v again in step 4. Of course, this attack succeeds only if the user had not reset his private key in the interim. Note that there is no way for the attacker to know which users have registered or reset their private keys due to the encrypted messages in these protocols.

In summary, while the attacker can carry out denial-of-service attacks on the BP-MAP scheme, he cannot learn any secrets. In particular, the secrecy of the triple ($username, u, v$) is preserved throughout.

3.4 Performance Analysis

In this section, computation costs are derived for each protocol in the BP-MAP scheme.

Table 2 summarizes the primitive operations used in the protocols of BP-MAP scheme, and provides a symbolic notation for the time taken for one computation of each of the primitives.

Table 3 provides the computation cost for the registration, mutual authentication protocols as well as the account recovery mechanisms.

3.5 Business Use-Cases

In this section, prominent industrial use-cases of BP-MAP are discussed where mutual authentication plays an important role in establishing trust and ensuring that both parties are legitimate and authorized.

Internet of Things (IoT): In IoT, devices often connect to a remote server or other devices for its functionality. In this scenario, unauthorized devices connecting to the server lead to security risks. Therefore, mutual authentication

Table 2. Notation for performance analysis

Notation	Time taken for
t_{bp}	bilinear pairing
t_{cmp}	comparing points on an elliptic curve
t_{dbq}	database query
t_{dbu}	database update
t_{dec}	decryption
t_{enc}	encryption
t_{exp}	modular exponentiation
t_{inv}	inverting an element
t_{mul}	multiplication

Table 3. Computation cost of protocols in the BP-MAP scheme

Workflow	Computation Cost
Client Registration	$t_{dbq} + t_{dbu} + t_{dec} + t_{enc} + 7t_{exp} + t_{inv} + 2t_{mul}$
Mutual Authentication	$4t_{bp} + 2t_{cmp} + t_{dbq} + 4t_{exp}$
Forgot Shared Secret	$2t_{bp} + t_{cmp} + t_{dbq} + 8t_{exp} + 2t_{inv} + 4t_{mul}$
Forgot Username	$t_{dbq} + 3t_{exp} + t_{inv} + 2t_{mul}$
Reset Secret Key	$2t_{dbq} + 2t_{dbu} + 7t_{exp} + 2t_{inv} + 4t_{mul}$

between IoT device and server ensures that device connects with the legitimate server and vice versa.

In the initial phases of device provisioning, each IoT device is assigned a public and private key pair during manufacturing. A certificate authority issues a digital certificate to the device, binding the public key to its identity. At first connection, the client device sends a message to the server that includes its digital certificate and a nonce. The server responds with its own message and a nonce. Further, IoT device and server mutually authenticate by exchanging challenges and computing responses using their private keys. Once mutual authentication is performed, a session key is derived, which is used to encrypt further information to be exchanged in the secure channel. The major challenge with the mutual authentication in IoT is the issuance and management of certificates in resource constrained devices, which imposes additional burden on the IoT server.

Virtual Private Networks (VPNs): VPNs provide secure connections to access corporate networks and its resources over public networks, such as the internet. In VPN, tunnel ensures that all data communication between client device and VPN server is encrypted securely using keys exchanged after mutual authentication. This process enhances security of the protocol by verifying identities of both the parties, thus preventing unauthorized access.

Initially, client sends a connection request to the VPN server. In response to the connection request, VPN server sends its digital certificate to the client. Similarly, the client sends its digital certificate to the VPN server. Both client and VPN server then authenticate each other's certificates against a trusted certificate authority. Once the certificates are mutually verified, handshake process begins to establish an SSL connection and generation of session key. Upon successful completion of the handshake, a secure VPN tunnel is established and all further communication is encrypted using the session key. The major challenge in this process lies in certificate management and the revocation process, which imposes an additional burden to the VPN server. Moreover, there is trust on the certificate authority, a third-party entity for issuance and validation of certificates.

BP-MAP scheme comes in very handy in both these scenarios because of its low computational requirements and easier maintenance compared to the traditional certificate based mechanisms.

4 Comparison with Literature

In the literature, various combinations of authentication and recovery mechanisms exist. These include: ZKP-based authentication, passwordless authentication, mutual authentication, and recovery mechanisms. In this section, these approaches are briefly discussed, and the benefits of BP-MAP in comparison to them are highlighted.

ZKP-Based Authentication: ZKP-based authentication methods proposed by Kara et al. [16] and Li Lu et al. [21] authenticate users without revealing passwords. [16] use zero knowledge proofs to mask the password using random numbers while [21] proposes pseudo-trust that generates verifiable pseudonym in peer-to-peer systems, using a one-way hash function to authenticate users without revealing original identity. ZKP-based schemes involve complex mathematical constructions and are computationally expensive. In comparison, BP-MAP is more practical, efficient as it simplifies the process by using bilinear pairings that are computationally much lighter for client-server mutual authentication without transmitting password information or any data from which the password can be easily derived.

Passwordless Authentication: Passwordless authentication methods use pass-keys as an alternative to traditional password-based systems. When a user chooses the passkey option, the website/app (server) sends a unique challenge to their device. The device then prompts the user to verify their identity, using methods like fingerprint or PIN. Upon successful verification, the device signs the challenge with its private key and sends it back to the server. The server then verifies the signature using the stored public key, granting access without a password. Kunke et al. [19] discuss password-less authentication systems like FIDO2. FIDO2 offers high security but it is device-dependent and incur additional overhead of maintaining multiple copies of key for resetting the passkey, thereby limiting usability. In contrast, BP-MAP is a device-independent authentication mechanism, which is more user-friendly. Unlike the passwordless mechanisms that involve hardware tokens and require an initial investment, BP-MAP does not require any specialized hardware, making it more cost-effective. Further, BP-MAP eliminates the need for storing keys on multiple devices/third party servers.

Mutual Authentication: Otway *et al.* [24] propose an efficient mutual authentication via a mutually trusted third-party. Li *et al.* [20] proposed a lightweight mutual authentication protocol based on a novel public key encryption scheme. Amin *et al.* [5] proposed a remote user authentication scheme using smart card using three factors. This scheme requires clients to share hash of the password to the server for verifying the user authenticity. Tseng *et al.* [26] proposed a mutual authentication protocol using bilinear pairings well suited for smart cards with limited computing capability. Nikravan *et.al.* [23] proposes a protocol for multi-factor authentication leveraging Identity based encryption using a trusted gateway and third-party private key generator which generates partial public-private keys using user's personal information. In this approach, managing partial and full public-private keys is complex. If the trusted gateway is compromised, the security of the protocol is compromised, and attackers will be able to impersonate the users. A part of multi-factor authentication process is delegated to the trusted gateway to make it suitable for resource constrained devices. Moreover, masked passwords are sent to the server during the user's registration phase. Also, account recovery mechanisms do not talk about username recovery. Amin *et al.* [6] propose bilinear pairings based mutual authentication and key agreement protocol for smart cards. In this protocol, the user needs to remember the password, and stores hash of the password on the smart card. In password recovery phase, password is directly displayed to the user. In contrast, BP-MAP does not require any trusted third-party for mutual authentication nor require password information to be shared to the server in any form. BP-MAP is application agnostic and can be used across various domains. Moreover, our account recovery mechanisms are more comprehensive and cover various aspects including username, shared secret and private key recovery, reset private key.

mTLS (mutual TLS) [8] uses certificates issued by trusted Certificate Authorities to authenticate both parties during the TLS handshake. This method involves the complexity of managing certificates and handling certificate revocation. In contrast, BP-MAP is based on bilinear pairing for secure authentication of parties without passwords. This method offers strong security based on mathematical hardness and eliminates password-related vulnerabilities. Additionally, it simplifies deployment process by removing the need for certificate issuance and management, potentially reducing overhead.

Recovery Mechanism: Kunke *et al.* [19] described twelve account recovery mechanisms from the literature which we categorized under three main approaches: (i) approaches where the user needs to remember auxiliary information, (ii) approaches that have a device dependency, and (iii) approaches where keys/passwords have to be stored with third parties. The account recovery feature in our solution is superior as it does not require users to remember additional information, nor does it depend on devices or third parties.

5 Conclusions and Future Work

In this paper, our main contribution is the design of BP-MAP a secure, efficient and convenient mutual authentication scheme to verify user authenticity without revealing password information to the server. More precisely, using our protocol a client and server can mutually authenticate each other without learning any secret information. This is achieved using two cryptographic primitives: (1) Bilinear Pairings (2) ElGamal Encryption. Our second main contribution is the design of efficient account recovery mechanisms to recover accounts in cases where the user forgets username/shared secret/private key. Our protocol is efficient when compared to the state-of-the-art passwordless authentication schemes. In summary, BP-MAP simultaneously provides the following features: (1) Privacy: User authentication without revealing any password information, (2) Security: Mutual authentication between the client and the server at no additional cost, (3) User-convenience: Ability to recover user account in case of forgetting any one of the parameters. An interesting future work is to formally establish the security of the BP-MAP scheme by using state-of-the-art model checkers/theorem provers.

References

1. Credential stuffing. https://owasp.org/www-community/attacks/Credential_stuffing. Accessed 22 July 2024
2. Dictionary attacks. https://owasp.org/www-community/attacks/Brute_force_attack. Accessed 22 July 2024
3. Password spraying. https://owasp.org/www-community/attacks/Password_Spraying_Attack. Accessed 22 July 2024
4. Sim swapping attack. https://www.verizon.com/about/account-security/sim-swapping. Accessed 30 Sept 2010
5. Amin, R., Biswas, G.: Design and analysis of bilinear pairing based mutual authentication and key agreement protocol usable in multi-server environment. Wireless Pers. Commun. **84**(1), 439–462 (2015)
6. Amin, R., Islam, S., Vijayakumar, P., Khan, K., Chang, V.: A robust and efficient bilinear pairing based mutual authentication and session key verification over insecure communication. Multimedia Tools Appl. **77** (2018). https://doi.org/10.1007/s11042-017-4996-z
7. Boneh, D., Franklin, M.: Identity-based encryption from the weil pairing. In: Annual International Cryptology Conference, pp. 213–229. Springer (2001)
8. Campbell, B., Bradley, J., Sakimura, N., Lodderstedt, T.: OAuth 2.0 mutual-TLS client authentication and certificate-bound access tokens. RFC 8705 (2020). https://doi.org/10.17487/RFC8705. https://www.rfc-editor.org/info/rfc8705
9. Chowhan, R., Tanwar, R.: Password-less authentication: methods for user verification and identification to login securely over remote sites, pp. 190–212 (2019). https://doi.org/10.4018/978-1-5225-8100-0.ch008

10. Federal Financial Institutions Examination Council: Authentication in an internet banking environment (2005). Accessed 28 June 2006
11. Diffie, W., Hellman, M.E.: New directions in cryptography. In: Democratizing Cryptography: The Work of Whitfield Diffie and Martin Hellman, pp. 365–390 (2022)
12. Dolev, D., Yao, A.: On the security of public key protocols. IEEE Trans. Inf. Theory **29**(2), 198–208 (1983)
13. Elgamal, T.: A public key cryptosystem and a signature scheme based on discrete logarithms. IEEE Trans. Inf. Theory **31**(4), 469–472 (1985). https://doi.org/10.1109/TIT.1985.1057074
14. Galbraith, S.D., Paterson, K.G., Smart, N.P.: Pairings for cryptographers. Discrete Appl. Math. **156**(16), 3113–3121 (2008). https://doi.org/10.1016/j.dam.2007.12.010. https://www.sciencedirect.com/science/article/pii/S0166218X08000449. Applications of Algebra to Cryptography
15. Groth, J., Sahai, A.: Efficient non-interactive proof systems for bilinear groups. In: Advances in Cryptology–EUROCRYPT 2008: 27th Annual International Conference on the Theory and Applications of Cryptographic Techniques, Istanbul, Turkey, 13–17 April 2008. Proceedings 27, pp. 415–432. Springer (2008)
16. Kara, M., Karampidis, K., Sayah, Z., Laouid, A., Papadourakis, G., Abid, M.N.: A password-based mutual authentication protocol via zero-knowledge proof solution. In: Zantout, H., Ragab Hassen, H. (eds.) Proceedings of the International Conference on Applied Cybersecurity (ACS 2023), pp. 31–40. Springer, Cham (2023)
17. Knudsen, L.R., Robshaw, M.J.B.: Brute force attacks, pp. 95–108. Springer, Heidelberg (2011)
18. Koblitz, N.: Elliptic curve cryptosystems. Math. Comput. **48**(177), 203–209 (1987)
19. Kunke, J., Wiefling, S., Ullmann, M., Iacono, L.L.: Evaluation of account recovery strategies with fido2-based passwordless authentication. arXiv preprint arXiv:2105.12477 (2021)
20. Li, N., Liu, D., Nepal, S.: Lightweight mutual authentication for IoT and its applications. IEEE Trans. Sustain. Comput. **2**(4), 359–370 (2017). https://doi.org/10.1109/TSUSC.2017.2716953
21. Lu, L., Han, J., Hu, L., Huai, J., Liu, Y., Ni, L.M.: Pseudo trust: zero-knowledge based authentication in anonymous peer-to-peer protocols. In: 2007 IEEE International Parallel and Distributed Processing Symposium, pp. 1–10 (2007). https://api.semanticscholar.org/CorpusID:6112726
22. Miller, V.S.: Use of elliptic curves in cryptography. In: Conference on the Theory and Application of Cryptographic Techniques, pp. 417–426. Springer (1985)
23. Nikravan, M., Reza, A.: A multi-factor user authentication and key agreement protocol based on bilinear pairing for the internet of things. Wireless Pers. Commun. **111** (2020). https://doi.org/10.1007/s11277-019-06869-y
24. Otway, D., Rees, O.: Efficient and timely mutual authentication **21**(1), 8–10 (1987). https://doi.org/10.1145/24592.24594
25. Sahai, A., Waters, B.: Fuzzy identity-based encryption. In: Advances in Cryptology–EUROCRYPT 2005: 24th Annual International Conference on the Theory and Applications of Cryptographic Techniques, Aarhus, Denmark, 22–26 May 2005, Proceedings 24, pp. 457–473. Springer (2005)
26. Tseng, Y.M., Wu, T.Y., Wu, J.D.: A mutual authentication and key exchange scheme from bilinear pairings for low power computing devices. In: 31st Annual International Computer Software and Applications Conference (COMPSAC 2007), pp. 700–710 (2007). https://doi.org/10.1109/COMPSAC.2007.32

Effects of Soft-Domain Transfer and Named Entity Information on Deception Detection

Steven Triplett[1]($\boxtimes$), Simon Minami[2], and Rakesh M. Verma[1]

[1] University of Houston, Houston, TX, USA
smtriple@CougarNet.UH.EDU, rmverma2@Central.UH.EDU
[2] Tufts University, Boston, MA, USA

Abstract. In online communication it is difficult to know when something written is genuine or deceitful. There exist many reasons for someone to act less-than-truthful online (i.e., monetary gain, political gain) and detecting this behavior without any physical interaction is a difficult task. Additionally, deception occurs in several text-only domains and it is unclear if these various sources can be leveraged to improve detection. To address this, eight datasets were utilized from various domains to evaluate their effect on classifier performance when combined with transfer learning via intermediate layer concatenation of fine-tuned BERT models. We find improvements in accuracy over the baseline. Furthermore, we evaluate multiple distance measurements between datasets and find that Jensen-Shannon distance correlates moderately with transfer learning performance. Finally, the impact was evaluated of multiple methods, which produce additional information in a dataset's text via named entities, on BERT performance and we find notable improvement in accuracy of up to 11.2%.

Keywords: Deception · BERT · Fake News · Transfer learning

1 Introduction

Online communication can have a huge impact through the posting of reviews or through social media networks. As more commerce is conducted online, the incentive to deceive others by misconstruing the quality of a product is growing. One study found that 80% of consumers changed their original decision to purchase a commodity due to the presence of many negative reviews for that commodity, and 87% of consumers will decide to purchase a commodity based upon positive reviews [20]. Another medium for deception is through news and journalism. The rise of fake and deceptive news reporting has created definitive impacts on society and led to a tumultuous political ecosystem [14]. Deception has been defined as a deliberate attempt to misconstrue or create a false impression [4] and deception detection is known to be challenging [21]. Experimental psychologists have conducted studies over nearly a century to investigate different cues that supposedly reveal deception, but despite these efforts, the results show that humans are simply not good at determining truth from lies [12]. Machine learning (ML) approaches utilizing techniques from Natural Language Processing (NLP) have proven successful, but the success is predominantly in areas such as online reviews [15] and phishing emails [8]. Certain feature spaces that prove successful in one deceptive domain may not necessarily guarantee success in another. Therefore, an open question is to develop an automated ML-based classification framework for deception detection of text that can utilize data from other similar deceptive domains to improve performance. To address the above goal, we utilized eight quality datasets to evaluate their effect on classifier performance when transfer learning is leveraged. We select a balanced deception dataset as the target dataset and experiment with multiple transfer learning methods including boosting-based methods and a deep learning based soft-domain transfer method. Additionally, we alter these datasets using multiple methods of manipulating information based on named entities in the text and examine the impact this has on classification. We also study whether distance functions can explain the performance of transfer learning methods and whether the size of the source dataset versus the target dataset size can have an impact on performance. In sum, our contributions are:

1. We show that for deception detection, a deep-learning based transfer learning method outperforms boosting-based transfer learning methods using classical methods.
2. We find that the source versus target relative dataset size is a significant factor in transfer learning performance for deception detection.
3. We find that significant increases in accuracy of deception detection, when compared to baseline BERT performance, when replacing named entities (NE) with explanations, named entities with the respective part-of-speech (POS) tag, and attaching an explanation to the named entity. The cumulative effect of transfer learning and named-entity processing is substantially higher than the base model directly trained on the target NE-unprocessed dataset.
4. We show that the Jensen-Shannon Divergence and KL-divergence between the source and target datasets have moderate correlations (Spearman rho) with the performance of transfer-learning methods.

2 Related Work on Deception Detection

Related work can be organized into machine learning approaches, deep learning approaches, and transfer learning approaches to deception detection.

Machine Learning Approaches to Deception Detection. An early work on detecting opinion spam in online reviews utilized several hand-crafted features to achieve a 98.7% AUC value on their data using a logistic regression (LR) classifier [13]. Others leverage lexical and syntactic elements [19] or part-of-speech

(POS) tags [9] to classify online reviews and others proposed markers of deception tailored towards Twitter to identify "troll" behavior around the 2016 U.S. election [1]. The last study achieved an average F1 score of 0.82 based on linguistic cues alone. Studies certainly exist that leverage non-text-based features for deception detection. For example, Banerjee et al. [3] utilized keystroke information in combination with term frequency-inverse document frequency (TFIDF) values of unigrams and achieved an accuracy of 94.3% on a dataset of deceptive and truthful essays using an SVM classifier. Additionally, Crockett et al. [5] use non-verbal head and facial features to identify deceptive or truthful behavior with an accuracy of 99% using Random Forests.

Deep Learning Approaches to Deception Detection. In recent years, deep learning models have been employed in various domains of deception detection with varying success [26]. Transformer models such as BERT [7] have been employed for deception detection in [10] and have been shown to outperform previous state-of-the-art models. However, some research shows that, although successful at capturing semantic information, BERT alone cannot capture the implicit knowledge of deception cues [10].

Transfer Learning Approaches to Deception Detection. Commonly, traditional ML relies on large amounts of training data to be available and assumes that the training and testing data are drawn from the same distribution. This assumption does not always hold for many real-world problems, but transfer-learning (TL) strategies attempt to deal with this issue. The primary goal of TL is to solve the target task by leveraging the available data from a source task in a different domain (or domains) [16]. TL has been applied to the task of deception detection in a few instances, [18] and others have attempted similar work by attempting to develop domain-independent classifiers by evaluating performance on a variety of deceptive domains (i.e., news, Twitter, and phishing) [17]. During our review of existing literature, we found few examples of TL methods being applied to the task of deception detection, and we seek to address this dearth by exploring the effects of a formal TL method used with a variety of classification models and deceptive datasets.

3 Datasets

The primary dataset for this study is from [3] and will be referred to as the Stony Brook University (SBU) deception dataset. To evaluate the effect of transfer learning, we consider the following datasets as well: PHEME [27], Politifact3 [24] (we group statements labeled as True and Mostly-True as truthful and the remaining statements as deceptive following similar work [22]), the SMS Spam Collection dataset [2], and Product Reviews (PR), Job Scams, Phishing, Political Statements (PS), and Fake News datasets as preprocessed in [25]. Descriptive statistics for all source datasets can be found in the full version of this paper [21].

4 Experimental Methods

Preprocessing consisted of removing any spurious symbols, e.g., newlines & tabs.

4.1 Boosting-Based Transfer Learning Methods

The SBU dataset was evaluated using three boosting-based algorithms. Boosting-based algorithms combine multiple weak learners into a strong classifier through an iterative process where each training sample is assigned a weight. After each iteration, the sample weights are updated to assign greater importance to certain samples. AdaBoost [11] was used as the baseline, trained only on the target dataset. TrAdaBoost [6] and gapBoost [23] were trained on both the source and target datasets. LR is used as the base learner for all methods, the number of boosting iterations is 10, and we use a 90/10 train/test split.

4.2 Deep Learning Transfer Method

A separate BERT model was fine-tuned for each dataset using bert-base-uncased from HuggingFace[1]. The following hyperparameters were used for all fine-tuning: learning rate of 0.00002, weight decay of 0.01, and 5 training epochs. For all experiments in this section, we use a 90/10 train/test split and retain the class ratio from the respective dataset during training. Those models trained on datasets that were not the SBU dataset are referred to as source models from this point forward, and the model trained on the SBU dataset will be referred to as the target model. After training, each source model was used to supplement the target model by performing the intermediate layer concatenation (ILC) as described in [18] using the hidden layer embeddings. However, a logistic regression (LR) was used as the final classifier instead of a fully connected network due to the model being the top performer of previous baseline experiments. The logistic regression is trained on the resulting ILC embeddings. A description of the process is found in Fig. 1 where dashed lines represent the input of a target instance for classification. Additionally, four variants of all datasets were created in which information was altered or added based on named entities (NEs). This was accomplished using the pipeline available in the Stanza[2] package in Python. The following four methods were used which added or replaced text in the dataset: **Method 1**: Replace NE with an explanation; **Method 2**: Replace NE with part of speech (POS) tag; **Method 3**: Attach explanation to NE; and, **Method 4**: Attach POS tag to NE.

4.3 Distance Measurements

The Kullback-Leibler (KL) divergence and Jensen-Shannon (JS) distance were calculated between each source dataset and the target dataset (SBU dataset) to

---
[1] https://huggingface.co/google-bert/bert-base-uncased.
[2] https://stanfordnlp.github.io/stanza/.

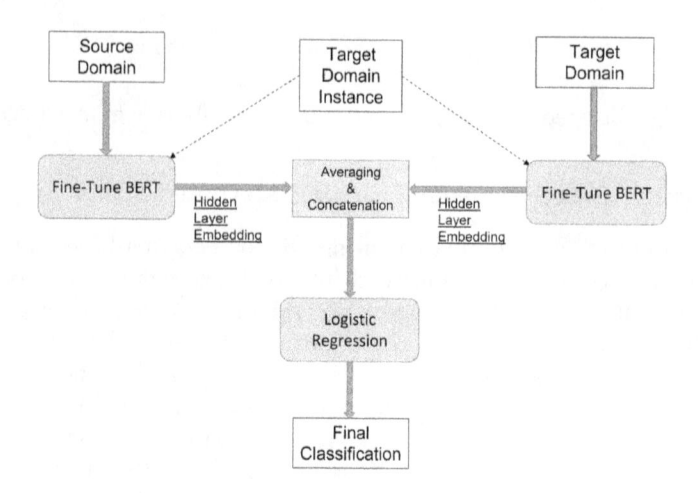

Fig. 1. Intermediate Layer Concatenation Process

evaluate the similarities. Probability distributions are calculated from smoothed inverse-document frequency (IDF) values for each dataset's vocabulary. Finally, a cosine-based similarity measurement was evaluated as well which was initially proposed by Panda and Levitan [17] and is defined in Eq. 1 where D_S and D_T are the source and target datasets, and SD_S and SD_T are the average sentence embeddings for all sentences in the source and target datasets respectively. Sentence embeddings were obtained using the sentence-transformer model all-distilroberta-v1.

$$D_{cos}(D_S, D_T) = (1 - cos(SD_S, SD_T))/2 \tag{1}$$

5 Results and Discussion

5.1 Boosting-Based Methods

The results of the boosting-based transfer learning methods can be seen in Fig. 2 with AdaBoost serving as the baseline accuracy. There is only one instance of improvement over the baseline, with TrAdaBoost improving over the baseline by 1.46% with PHEME as the source dataset. Overall, the persistence of negative transfer across most source domains indicates that boosting-based algorithms may not be best suited for text-based deception detection with the SBU dataset as the target dataset.

5.2 Intermediate Layer Concatenation and Named Entity Alteration

The effect of transfer learning via ILC is shown in Fig. 4. The baseline accuracy is a BERT model that is fine-tuned on the SBU dataset alone. Each source

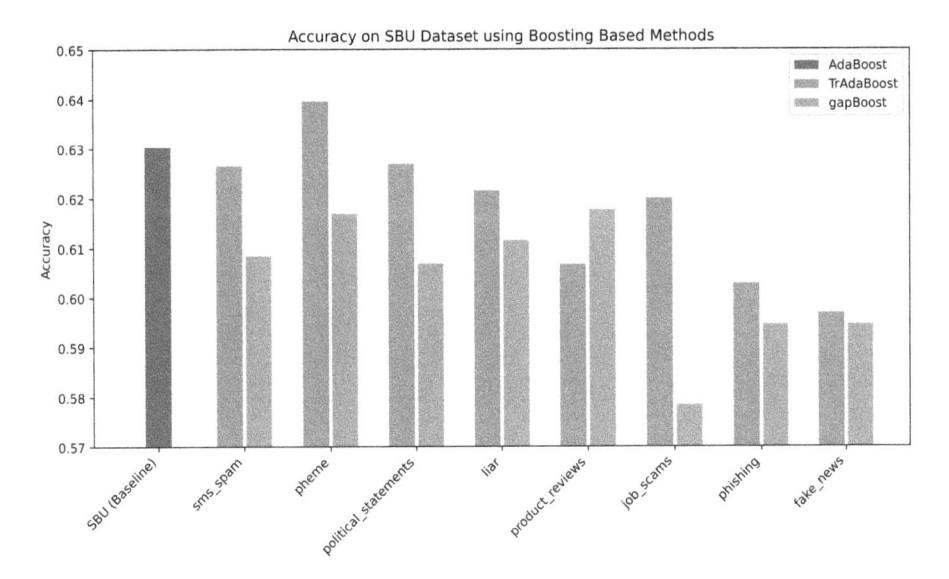

Fig. 2. Effect of boosting-based transfer learning on deception detection accuracy of SBU dataset compared to baseline performance

dataset indicates the use of that source model in the ILC process. Four datasets showed improvement over baseline BERT accuracy of 65% (Fake News, Phishing, Political Statements, Job Scams). The effect of the four NE methods on the SBU dataset are in Fig. 3 and establish a baseline effect of including NE information on a target dataset. Method three yielded the smallest improvement of 6.46%. Method one yielded an improvement of 9.38% and method two resulted in the largest improvement of 11.2% over baseline BERT performance. The ILC experiment was performed for each variant of all source datasets and the results can be found in the full paper [21].

5.3 Distance Measurements

The results for distance measurements are in Table 1 and show varying levels of similarity. The Pearson correlation coefficient (r) and the Spearman rank correlation coefficient (ρ) were calculated between each set of distance measurements and the change in accuracy that resulted from the ILC experiments performed in Fig. 4. These results are in Table 2 and show that KL Divergence ($D_{KL}(P||Q)$) and JS distance show moderate correlation for both the Pearson and Spearman coefficients. The largest correlation is a Spearman value of 0.527 for both KL Divergence ($D_{KL}(P||Q)$) and JS distance with identical values resulting from all source datasets receiving the same rank regardless of the two distance measurements. Distance measurements were ranked in ascending order for a change in accuracy from ILC and descending order for distance measurement to measure the correlation between the increase in performance and decrease in distance (i.e., increase in similarity).

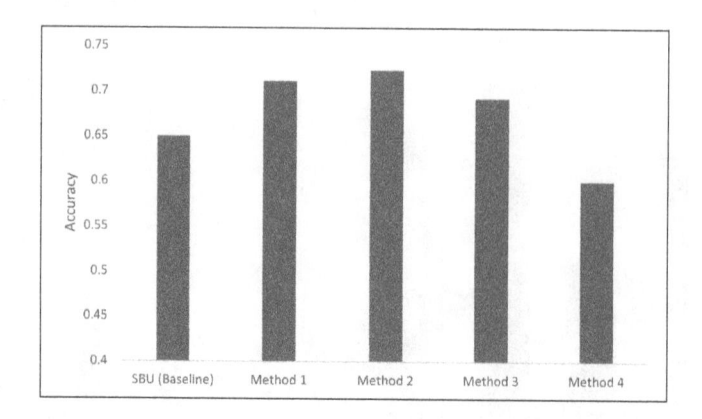

Fig. 3. Effect of altering NE information on BERT performance compared to baseline

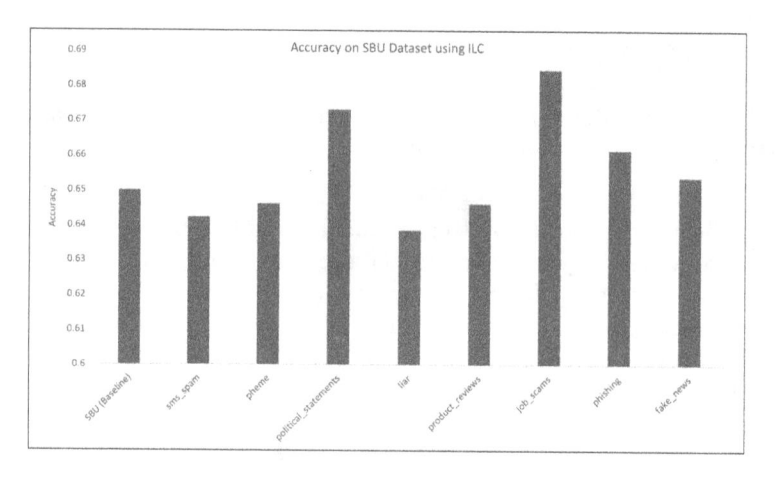

Fig. 4. Effect of ILC transfer learning on deception detection accuracy of SBU dataset compared to baseline performance

5.4 Boosting with Reduced Source Datasets

Given the relatively small size of the SBU dataset, we hypothesized that an overabundance of source dataset samples could overshadow the target samples and contribute to negative transfer. To investigate this idea, we ran the same boosting experiments on a reduced version of each source dataset composed of 100 randomly selected samples, with 50 from each class. Preliminary results are promising with TrAdaBoost exhibiting improvement over the baseline in all eight source datasets in Fig. 5. Specifically, the reduced Product Reviews dataset shows the largest improvement over the baseline of 8.56%. The largest increase over a full source dataset is observed with Fake News, where the reduced dataset improves by 9.54% over the full dataset. Although gapBoost still does

Table 1. Distance values between target dataset Q and all source datasets P.

Source Dataset	$D_{KL}(Q||P)$	$D_{KL}(P||Q)$	D_{JS}	D_{cos}
Political Statements	1.140	1.062	0.228	0.287
Fake News	0.703	0.392	0.114	0.307
Product Reviews	1.096	0.809	0.199	0.356
Job Scams	1.217	0.929	0.224	0.423
Phishing	0.689	0.353	0.105	0.356
PHEME	1.106	1.208	0.243	0.315
LIAR	1.132	1.082	0.230	0.281
SMS Spam	1.226	1.327	0.267	0.446

Table 2. Correlations between distances and change in accuracy for ILC.

Correlation	$D_{KL}(Q||P)$	$D_{KL}(P||Q)$	D_{JS}	D_{cos}
r	0.214	0.369	0.328	−0.219
ρ	0.060	0.527	0.527	−0.120

not outperform the baseline, there are significant increases in accuracy compared to the full source dataset results. The largest increase of 8.05% is seen with the Job Scams dataset. See the full paper for the results from gapBoost [21].

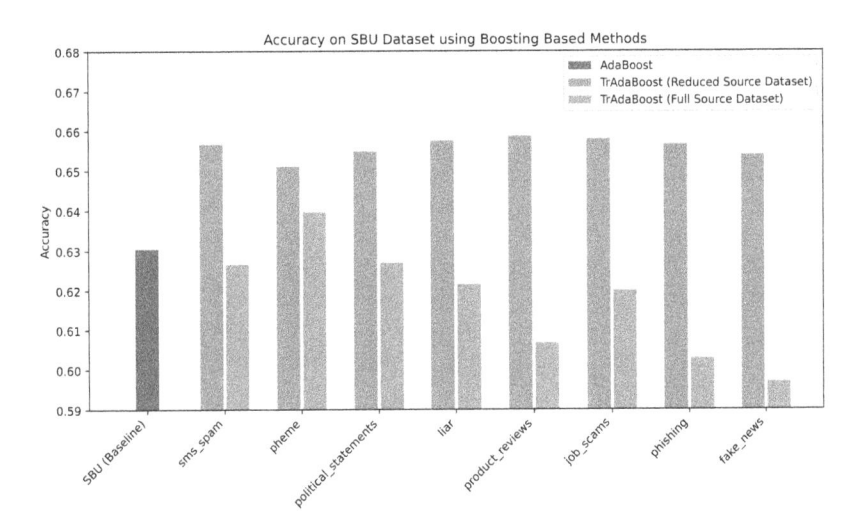

Fig. 5. Effect of Reduced Source Dataset Size on TrAdaBoost accuracy on SBU dataset

6 Conclusion

In this work, we evaluated the effect of two boosting-based transfer learning methods for deception detection and found that, except the PHEME source dataset, performance decreased, however, reducing the size of the source dataset improved performance for both methods. Additionally, we evaluated how effective BERT is for classification on the SBU dataset to establish a baseline for deep-learning based deception detection. Furthermore, we showed that the ILC approach can outperform baseline BERT performance for multiple source datasets and boosting-based transfer learning methods with the Job Scams dataset being the most useful. We calculated KL divergence, JS distance, and a cosine-based distance between all source datasets and the SBU dataset to function as similarity measurements and determined that KL divergence and JS distance have a moderate correlation with the ILC transfer learning method. Finally, we determined that NE variants of the target dataset can improve baseline BERT performance and NE variants of source datasets can improve upon ILC performance with most source datasets showing an increase in performance when compared to the ILC baseline.

Acknowledgement. Research partly supported by NSF grants 2210198 and 2244279, ARO grants W911NF-20-1-0254 and W911NF-23-1-0191, and a USDOT Cyber transportation center grant.

Disclosure of Interests. Verma is the founder of Everest Cyber Security and Analytics, Inc.

References

1. Addawood, A., Badawy, A., Lerman, K., Ferrara, E.: Linguistic cues to deception: identifying political trolls on social media. In: Proceedings of the International AAAI Conference on Web and Social Media, vol. 13, pp. 15–25 (2019)
2. Almeida, T.A., Hidalgo, J.M.G., Yamakami, A.: Contributions to the study of SMS spam filtering: new collection and results. In: Proceedings of the 11th ACM Symposium on Document Engineering, pp. 259–262 (2011)
3. Banerjee, R., Feng, S., Kang, J.S., Choi, Y.: Keystroke patterns as prosody in digital writings: a case study with deceptive reviews and essays. In: Proceedings of the 2014 Conference on Empirical Methods in Natural Language Processing (EMNLP), pp. 1469–1473 (2014)
4. Burgoon, J.K., Buller, D.B.: Interpersonal deception: III. Effects of deceit on perceived communication and nonverbal behavior dynamics. J. Nonverbal Behav. **18**, 155–184 (1994)
5. Crockett, K., O'Shea, J., Khan, W.: Automated deception detection of males and females from non-verbal facial micro-gestures. In: 2020 International Joint Conference on Neural Networks (IJCNN), pp. 1–7. IEEE (2020)
6. Dai, W., Yang, Q., Xue, G.R., Yu, Y.: Boosting for transfer learning. In: Proceedings of the 24th ICML, pp. 193–200 (2007)
7. Devlin, J., Chang, M.W., Lee, K., Toutanova, K.: BERT: pre-training of deep bidirectional transformers for language understanding. arXiv preprint arXiv:1810.04805 (2018)

8. Egozi, G., Verma, R.: Phishing email detection using robust NLP techniques. In: 2018 IEEE International Conference on Data Mining Workshops (ICDMW), pp. 7–12. IEEE (2018)
9. Feng, S., Banerjee, R., Choi, Y.: Syntactic stylometry for deception detection. In: Proceedings of the 50th Annual Meeting of the Association for Computational Linguistics (Volume 2: Short Papers), pp. 171–175 (2012)
10. Fornaciari, T., Bianchi, F., Poesio, M., Hovy, D., et al.: Bertective: language models and contextual information for deception detection. In: Proceedings of the 16th Conference of the European Chapter of the Association for Computational Linguistics: Main Volume. Association for Computational Linguistics (2021)
11. Freund, Y., Schapire, R.E.: A desicion-theoretic generalization of on-line learning and an application to boosting. In: Vitányi, P. (ed.) Computational Learning Theory, pp. 23–37. Springer, Heidelberg (1995)
12. Hauch, V., Blandón-Gitlin, I., Masip, J., Sporer, S.L.: Are computers effective lie detectors? A meta-analysis of linguistic cues to deception. Pers. Soc. Psychol. Rev. **19**(4), 307–342 (2015)
13. Jindal, N., Liu, B.: Opinion spam and analysis. In: Proceedings of the 2008 International Conference on Web Search and Data Mining, pp. 219–230 (2008)
14. Lazer, D.M., et al.: The science of fake news. Science **359**(6380), 1094–1096 (2018)
15. Li, J., Lv, P., Xiao, W., Yang, L., Zhang, P.: Exploring groups of opinion spam using sentiment analysis guided by nominated topics. Expert Syst. Appl. **171**, 114585 (2021)
16. Niu, S., Liu, Y., Wang, J., Song, H.: A decade survey of transfer learning (2010–2020). IEEE Trans. Artif. Intell. **1**(2), 151–166 (2020)
17. Panda, S., Levitan, S.: Deception detection within and across domains: identifying and understanding the performance gap. ACM J. Data Inf. Qual. **15**(1), 1–27 (2022)
18. Shahriar, S., Mukherjee, A., Gnawali, O.: Deception detection with feature-augmentation by soft domain transfer. In: International Conference on Social Informatics, pp. 373–380 (2022)
19. Shojaee, S., Murad, M.A.A., Azman, A.B., Sharef, N.M., Nadali, S.: Detecting deceptive reviews using lexical and syntactic features. In: 2013 13th International Conference on Intelligent Systems Design and Applications, pp. 53–58. IEEE (2013)
20. Tang, H., Cao, H.: A review of research on detection of fake commodity reviews. In: Journal of Physics: Conference Series, vol. 1651, p. 012055 (2020)
21. Triplett, S., Minami, S., Verma, R.M.: Effects of soft-domain transfer and named entity information on deception detection. arXiV preprint (2024)
22. Upadhayay, B., Behzadan, V.: Sentimental liar: extended corpus and deep learning models for fake claim classification. In: 2020 IEEE ISI Conference, pp. 1–6 (2020)
23. Wang, B., Mendez, J., Cai, M., Eaton, E.: Transfer learning via minimizing the performance gap between domains. In: NIPS, vol. 32 (2019)
24. Wang, W.: "Liar, liar pants on fire": a new benchmark dataset for fake news detection. arXiv preprint arXiv:1705.00648 (2017)
25. Zeng, V., Liu, X., Verma, R.M.: Does deception leave a content independent stylistic trace? In: Proceedings of ACM CODSAPY, pp. 349–351 (2022)
26. Zhao, S., Xu, Z., Liu, L., Guo, M., Yun, J.: Towards accurate deceptive opinions detection based on word order-preserving CNN. Math. Probl. Eng. **2018** (2018)
27. Zubiaga, A., Liakata, M., Procter, R.: Learning reporting dynamics during breaking news for rumour detection in social media. arXiv preprint arXiv:1610.07363 (2016)

Attack

Paving the Way: Advancing V2X Safety Through Innovative Attack Generation and Analysis Framework (V2X-SAF)

Shubham Tomar[✉] and Meenakshi Tripathi

Malaviya National Institute of Technology, Jaipur, India
tomars124@gmail.com

Abstract. Vehicle-to-Everything (V2X) communication is crucial for the advancement of modern transportation systems, enabling real-time, dependable, and actionable data exchange. This technology facilitates the dissemination of Basic Safety Messages (BSMs) between vehicles and infrastructure, thereby enhancing safety, mobility, and environmental applications. Ensuring the integrity and accuracy of V2X data is vital for effective decision-making. This paper leverages the VEINS simulation framework to introduce 25 new sophisticated attacks aimed at four newly developed safety applications. These applications have been meticulously developed from scratch. Moreover, we introduce a multi-label attack generation technique, enabling multiple simultaneous attacks within a single data packet. For instance, coordinated attacks where speed adjustments are synchronized with changes in acceleration, increasing their complexity and detection difficulty. Central to our work are the advanced detection mechanisms designed to operate on Roadside Units (RSUs). These mechanisms employ trained algorithms to identify and neutralize malicious packets in real-time simulations, significantly bolstering the security of V2X systems. This comprehensive framework not only aims to reinforce the security infrastructure of V2X networks but also to guide standardization efforts and inform deployment strategies. Additionally, the implementation of digital certificates for digital signatures serves as a primary defense against malicious entities, ensuring the authenticity and integrity of V2X communications. Our objective is to provide the security community with an effective tool for developing a resilient and secure V2X ecosystem.

Keywords: Vehicle-to-Everything (V2X) · Safety Applications · Detection Mechanisms

1 Introduction

Vehicle-to-Everything (V2X) communication plays a pivotal role in modern Intelligent Transportation Systems (ITS), enabling seamless data exchange among vehicles, pedestrians, and infrastructure. Basic Safety Messages (BSMs)

form the foundation of V2X communication, conveying critical information such as location, speed, and braking status, essential for applications like the Emergency Electronic Brake Light (EEBL) to enhance road safety [1,2].

To uphold the integrity of the V2X network, authentication mechanisms, including digital signing, are employed to thwart unauthorized data injection [14, 15]. Furthermore, local misbehavior detection systems (MBDS) analyze incoming V2X messages for anomalies, serving as a secondary defense measure [3].

As ITS applications advance with features like signal phase and timing (SPaT) messages and sensor sharing, understanding potential attack vectors becomes crucial. While previous research has focused on BSM attacks, their impact on consuming applications remains underexplored [4].

1.1 Contributions

This paper makes the following key contributions:

- **Novel Attack Introduction:** Introducing 25 new sophisticated attacks targeting four newly developed V2X safety applications: Control Loss Warning (CLW), Forward Collision Warning (FCW), Lane Change Warning (LCW), and Left Turn Assist (LTA). These applications were developed from scratch to enhance the understanding of potential threats.
- **Multi-label Attack Generation:** Presenting a methodology for generating multiclass attacks, where a single data packet can contain multiple simultaneous attacks. For example, coordinated alterations in speed and acceleration, increasing attack complexity and detection challenges.
- **Generated Attack Dataset:** Creating a comprehensive multi-class and multi-label attack dataset targeting the four V2X safety applications (Control Loss Warning, Forward Collision Warning, Lane Change Warning, and Left Turn Assist).
- **Detection Mechanisms:** Integrating deep neural network-based multi-class detection mechanisms that operate on Roadside Units (RSUs) to identify malicious packets in real-time simulations.
- **Digital Signatures:** Implementing digital certificates for digital signatures to ensure the integrity and authenticity of V2X communications.

The enhanced V2X framework aims to fortify the security posture of V2X systems, guide standardization efforts, and inform deployment strategies. The framework, available on GitHub, provides accessibility for further research and development in V2X security.

The paper is structured as follows: Sect. 2 reviews attacks and intrusion detection in V2X communications. Section 3 describes the system model, architecture, and framework. Section 4 outlines the experimental network scenario. Section 5 categorizes attack types and methodologies. Section 6 details the attack generation classes. Section 7 discusses attack policies and selection strategies. Section 8 analyzes attack scenarios targeting four safety applications. Section 9 presents the attack detection mechanism and experimental results. Finally, Sect. 10 concludes the study, summarizing findings and future research directions.

2 Literature Survey

In the domain of public attack datasets and V2X misbehavior detection research [4], VeReMi [18] and F^2MD [9] stand out as significant platforms. These resources are extensively utilized by researchers for the design, comparison, and validation of misbehavior detection systems [5,7]. VeReMi provides a labeled simulated dataset and platform, encompassing a diverse range of traffic behaviors and attacker scenarios [18]. Evaluations are conducted using the VEINS simulator within the LuST scenario, offering comprehensive testing environments [17]. The next version of VeReMi has integrated insights from F^2MD [9].

On the other hand, F^2MD is a simulation framework dedicated to generating malfunctioning V2X nodes that disseminate incorrect information, such as erroneous vehicle position, velocity, and acceleration. It also incorporates misbehavior detection algorithms based on local plausibility checks [2].

Despite the utility of VeReMi and F^2MD in developing V2X misbehavior detectors, they do not directly evaluate the impact of attacks on V2X applications [6,8]. Our framework addresses this gap by targeting two specific V2X applications: Emergency Electronic Brake Light (EEBL) and Intersection Movement Assist (IMA) [19], as discussed in Section III-B. Additionally, we introduce 25 novel attacks on critical V2X safety applications, including Control Loss Warning (CLW), Forward Collision Warning (FCW), Lane Change Warning (LCW), and Left Turn Assist (LTA), as detailed in Section V. This focused approach enhances the understanding of potential threats to safety-critical V2X applications and supports the development of robust countermeasures within the V2X ecosystem.

However, the V2X Application Spoofing Platform (VASP) [2] has several limitations. VASP does not include communication with Roadside Units (RSUs), which are crucial for infrastructure-to-vehicle (I2V) communication in real-world scenarios. Furthermore, it lacks specific V2X safety applications like EEBL, IMA, CLW, FCW, LCW, and LTA [19], which are essential for evaluating comprehensive safety scenarios. Additionally, VASP does not support digital signatures, which are vital for ensuring message authenticity and integrity in secure V2X communication environments.

3 System Model

3.1 Basic Safety Message

The Basic Safety Message (BSM) is an essential V2X transmission sent by a vehicle to nearby ITS devices. Table 1 details the information contained within a BSM. When a vehicle receives a BSM, it can determine the sending vehicle's location, kinematic state, and dimensions. V2X applications use this information to take necessary actions, such as slowing down in response to a nearby car accident.

Table 1. Description of fields in Basic Safety Message (BSM)

Field	Description
MsgCount	Counter incremented with each BSM sent
TemporaryID	ITS device identifier
Dsecond	Time since ignition start
Positions	Vehicle's latitude, longitude, and altitude (WGS84)
PositionAccuracy	Positioning accuracy parameters for each axis
TransmissionAndSpeed	Vehicle speed
Heading	Direction in units of 0.0125°
SteeringWheelAngle	Current steering wheel angle
Accelerations	Longitudinal, lateral, and vertical acceleration
Yaw rate	Vehicle yaw rate
BrakeSystemStatus	Braking control states
VehicleSize	Length and width of the vehicle

3.2 V2X Safety Applications

V2X Safety applications play a critical role in enhancing road safety by leveraging Vehicle-to-Everything (V2X) communication to analyze and respond to potential hazards on the road. This paper focuses on four key V2X applications: Control Loss Warning (CLW), Forward Collision Warning (FCW), Lane Change Warning (LCW), and Left Turn Assist (LTA) [19].

1. **Control Loss Warning (CLW):**
   The CLW safety application alerts the driver of the host vehicle (HV) in case of an emergency control loss event, defined as the activation of the antilock brake system, traction control system, or stability control system by a remote vehicle (RV) traveling in the same or opposite direction. The RV broadcasts control loss event information within the Basic Safety Message (BSM). Upon receiving this event information, the HV assesses its relevance and issues a warning to the driver.
   CLW scenarios are as follows:
   - **RV Same Direction of Travel:** In this scenario, as shown in Fig. 1, the host vehicle (HV) follows the remote vehicle (RV) in the same direction. The HV receives Basic Safety Messages (BSMs) from the RV, indicating a control loss event such as the activation of the antilock brake system, traction control system, or stability control system.
   - **RV Traveling in Opposite Direction:** In this scenario, as shown in Fig. 2, the remote vehicle (RV) approaches the host vehicle (HV) from the opposite direction. The HV receives Basic Safety Messages (BSMs) from the oncoming RV, indicating a control loss event such as the activation of the antilock brake system, traction control system, or stability control system.

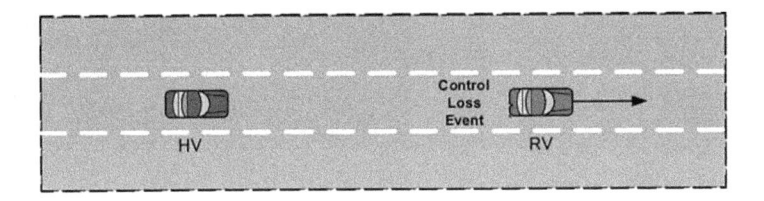

Fig. 1. Control Loss Warning(CLW)

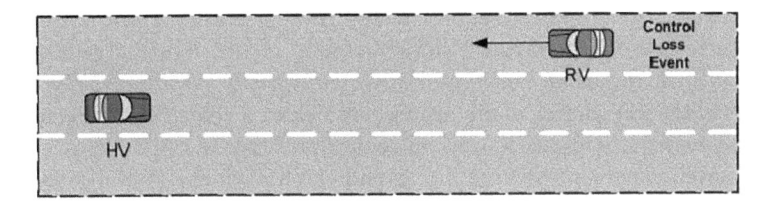

Fig. 2. Control Loss Warning(CLW)

2. **Forward Collision Warning (FCW):**
   The Forward Collision Warning (FCW) safety application alerts the driver of the host vehicle (HV) when there is an imminent risk of a rear-end collision with a remote vehicle (RV) directly ahead in the same lane and direction of travel. FCW aims to assist drivers in avoiding or reducing the severity of rear-end collisions occurring in the forward path of travel.
   FCW scenarios are as follows:
   – **Stopped RV in Same Lane:** As the host vehicle (HV) approaches a stopped remote vehicle (RV-1) in the same lane, the Forward Collision Warning (FCW) feature alerts the HV driver of the imminent risk of a rear-end collision (Fig. 3). The warning timing is crucial, aiming to enable the HV driver to take evasive action and prevent a rear-end crash with the stopped RV-1.

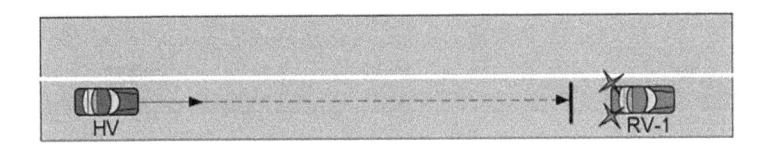

   Fig. 3. FCW Same Lane

   – **Stopped RV in Adjacent Lane:** As the host vehicle (HV) approaches a stopped remote vehicle (RV-1) in the adjacent lane, the Forward Collision Warning (FCW) feature does not issue a warning to the HV driver (Fig. 4). This is because there is no imminent risk of a rear-end collision in this scenario.

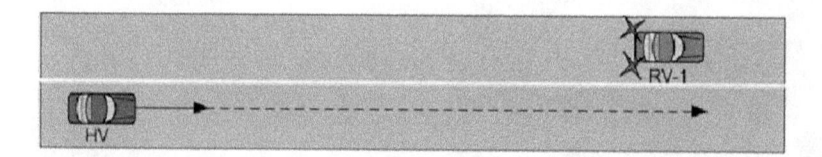

Fig. 4. FCW adjacent lane

- **Slower-Moving or Decelerating RV in Same Lane:** As the host vehicle (HV) approaches a slower-moving or decelerating remote vehicle (RV-1) in the same lane, the Forward Collision Warning (FCW) feature alerts the HV driver of the imminent risk of a rear-end collision (Fig. 5). The warning timing is critical, ensuring that the HV driver can take evasive action and prevent a rear-end crash with the slow-moving RV-1.

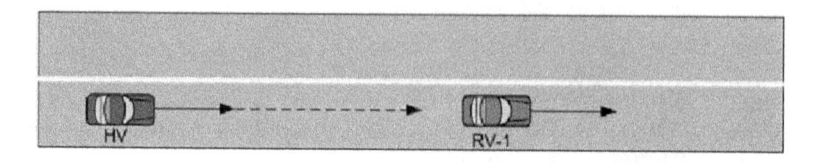

Fig. 5. FCW deaccelarating

- **Stopped and Obstructed RV :**In this scenario, the host vehicle (HV) follows a moving remote vehicle (RV-2), which maneuvers to avoid a stopped RV-1 in the same lane. The FCW feature alerts the HV driver of the impending risk of a rear-end collision with the stationary RV-1 (Fig. 6). The warning timing is adjusted to facilitate the HV driver's ability to avoid a rear-end crash with the stopped vehicle RV-1.

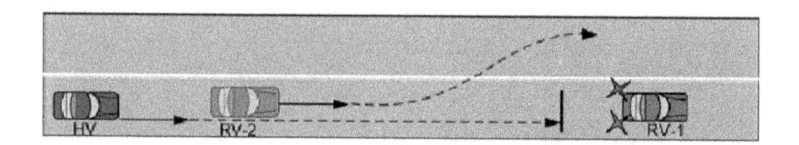

Fig. 6. FCW Stopped and Obstructed

3. **Lane Change Warning (LCW):** The Lane Change Warning (LCW) safety application alerts the driver of the host vehicle (HV) when attempting a lane change if the intended blind-spot zone is occupied or will soon be occupied by another vehicle traveling in the same direction. Additionally, the application may offer advisory information to inform the HV driver when a vehicle in an

adjacent lane is positioned in the HV's blind spot, even when a lane change is not being attempted.

LCW Scenarios are as follows:
- **RV in Blind-Spot Zone:** In this scenario, the host vehicle (HV) travels in its lane alongside a remote vehicle (RV-1) positioned within its blind-spot zone. The LCW feature may issue an advisory warning to the HV driver about RV-1's presence in the blind-spot zone (Fig. 7). Additionally, if the HV driver signals an intent to change lanes into the occupied lane, a warning is issued to prevent a potential collision with RV-1.

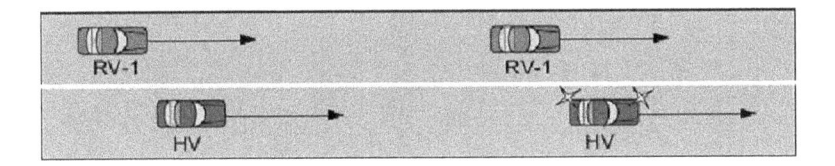

Fig. 7. BSW/LCW RV in Blind-Spot Zone

- **RV approaching in Adjacent Lane:** In this scenario, as the host vehicle (HV) maintains its lane, a faster-moving remote vehicle (RV-1) in an adjacent lane approaches, soon entering the HV's blind-spot zone. The LCW feature may provide an advisory warning to the HV driver, anticipating RV-1's presence in the blind-spot zone (Fig. 8). If the HV detects the driver's intention to change lanes into the path of RV-1, a warning is promptly issued.

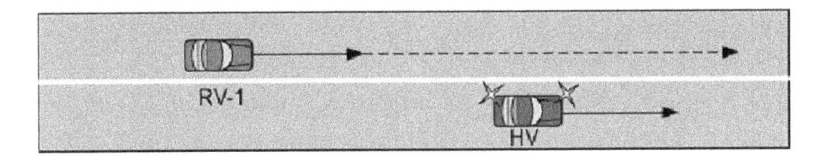

Fig. 8. BSW/LCW RV in adjacent lane

4. **Left Turn Assist (LTA):** The Left Turn Assist (LTA) safety application alerts the driver of a host vehicle (HV) when it may not be safe to proceed with a left turn due to oncoming traffic.
   LTA scenario are follow:
   - **Left Turn Across Path:** In this scenario, the host vehicle (HV) approaches an intersection to make a left turn, where visibility may be limited or obstructed by a remote vehicle (RV-2). RV-2 may or may not

have V2V communications, but another vehicle, RV-1, is equipped with V2V capability. RV-1 approaches the intersection from the opposite direction. The HV driver receives a warning from the Left Turn Assist (LTA) feature when attempting a left turn to avoid a collision with the approaching vehicle, RV-1 (Fig. 9).

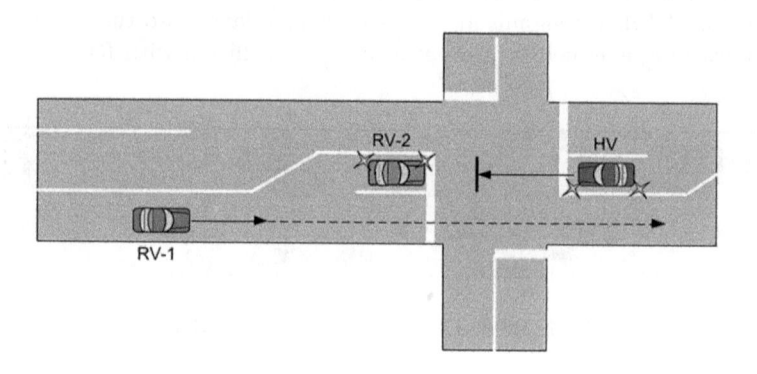

Fig. 9. LTA Left Turn Across Path

For further clarification on the above safety applications, we recommend the reader to read SAE standard J2945/1 [19].

4 Network Model

In this section, we explore the network scenario that forms the foundation of this paper.

Proposed VANET Model: In the VANET scenario described in this paper, mobile vehicles continuously broadcast information as they travel along roads, as depicted in Fig. 10. The data transmitted by the on-board units (OBUs) of these vehicles is received by roadside units (RSUs) and other vehicles' OBUs, enabling them to take appropriate action. The fundamental components of the proposed VANET model include:

- **On-Board Units (OBUs):** Each vehicle is equipped with an OBU, which is responsible for gathering data from various sensors within the vehicle and broadcasting it to nearby vehicles and RSUs. The data includes critical information such as the vehicle's current speed, location, heading, brake status, and other pertinent parameters that are encapsulated in Basic Safety Messages (BSMs).

- **Roadside Units (RSUs):** RSUs serve as communication hubs within the VANET. They receive data from passing vehicles' OBUs and can also broadcast information to vehicles. RSUs play a crucial role in disseminating traffic-related information, such as signal phase and timing (SPaT) messages, road hazards, and emergency vehicle alerts. Additionally, RSUs are equipped with detection mechanisms that analyze incoming V2X messages for anomalies, employing trained algorithms to identify malicious packets in real-time simulations, thus enhancing the resilience of V2X systems against diverse attack scenarios.
- **Communication Protocols:** V2X communication leverages standardized protocols to ensure reliable and secure data exchange. In our simulation, we use Dedicated Short-Range Communications (DSRC) exclusively. DSRC facilitates low-latency, high-throughput communication essential for real-time safety applications.
- **Basic Safety Messages (BSMs):** BSMs are the cornerstone of V2X communication, conveying essential information between vehicles and infrastructure. Each BSM contains data fields such as vehicle position, speed, acceleration, brake status, and heading. This information is crucial for enabling safety applications like Forward Collision Warning (FCW) and Lane Change Warning (LCW).
- **Safety Applications:** The network model supports a variety of safety applications designed to enhance road safety and traffic efficiency. These include, but are not limited to:
    - Control Loss Warning (CLW)
    - Forward Collision Warning (FCW)
    - Lane Change Warning (LCW)
    - Left Turn Assist (LTA)
- **Certificate Authority (CA):** A crucial component of the security infrastructure, the Certificate Authority is responsible for issuing digital certificates to OBUs and RSUs. These certificates enable secure and authenticated communication by ensuring that each message can be traced back to a legitimate and trusted source.
- **Simulation Environment:** The V2X communication simulator VEINS [17], integrated with SUMO (Simulation of Urban Mobility) [20], is used to model and simulate the VANET scenario. VEINS and SUMO together provide a detailed and realistic simulation environment, allowing researchers to test and evaluate the performance and security of V2X applications and communication protocols.

5 Attack Model

In the context of modeling attacks on connected vehicles [10,16], attackers can be categorized in several ways. First, they can be internal or external. Internal attackers possess network authentication and can communicate with other

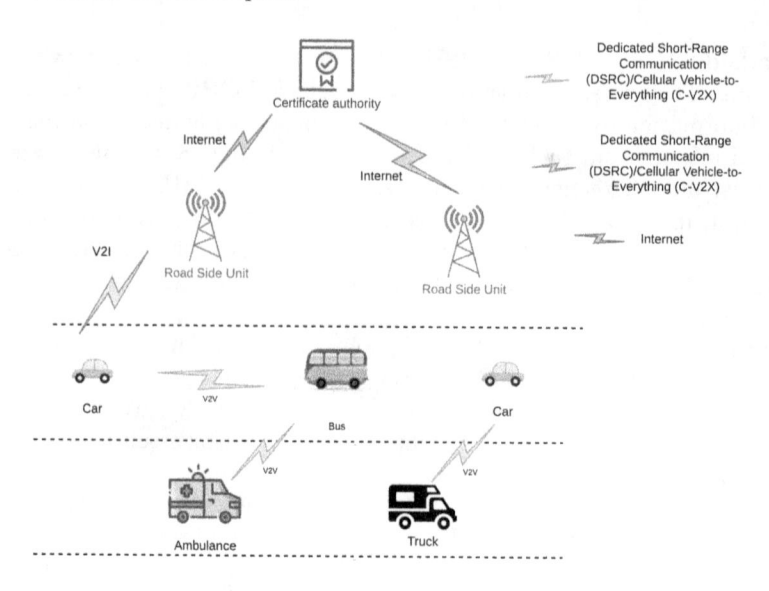

Fig. 10. Standard VANET Model

network members, while external attackers lack proper message-signing capabilities but can eavesdrop on V2X broadcast communication, complicating network security. Second, attackers can be malicious or rational. Malicious attackers aim to harm network members or functionality, often disregarding costs and consequences, whereas rational attackers seek personal gain, making their methods and targets more predictable [11,13].

Attackers can also be active or passive. Active attackers generate malicious packets or signals, while passive attackers are limited to eavesdropping on communication channels.

The scope of an attacker's influence can be localized or extended. Localized attackers operate within specific areas, even if controlling multiple entities. Extended attackers have control over entities spread throughout the network, broadening their influence.

Finally, attackers can use direct or indirect approaches. Direct attackers target primary objectives directly, while indirect attackers reach primary targets via secondary targets.

In our research, as shown in Fig. 11, we focus on internal attackers with both malicious and rational intentions. These attackers are active, localized, and primarily engage in injecting forged data to compromise the V2X communication network.

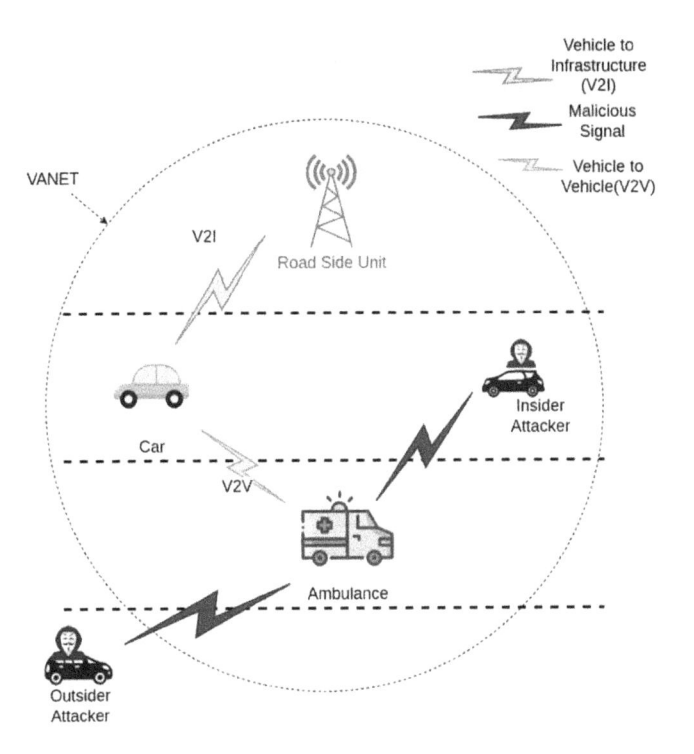

Fig. 11. Attacker Model

6 Attack Generation Classes

Attacks on V2X communication can be categorized based on the nature and scope of the manipulations involved. This classification helps in systematically analyzing and understanding different attack scenarios, thereby aiding in the development of robust countermeasures.

- **Single-Element Attacks:** These attacks involve altering or injecting a deceptive value into V2X messages, targeting specific elements within the Basic Safety Message (BSM) or other V2X data packets. For example, an attacker might manipulate the reported speed or position of a vehicle to deceive neighboring vehicles or infrastructure elements. Single-element attacks aim to disrupt the integrity and reliability of V2X communication by introducing subtle but impactful alterations to critical data elements.
- **Multi-Element Attacks:** In contrast, multi-element attacks involve the simultaneous manipulation or injection of multiple deceptive values into V2X messages. These attacks are more sophisticated, coordinating alterations across various data elements within the BSM or other V2X data packets. By targeting multiple aspects of V2X communication, multi-element attacks create more complex and challenging scenarios for misbehavior detection systems

to identify and mitigate, posing a greater threat to the security and reliability of V2X communication systems.
- **Independent Attacks:** These attacks modify only one value independently, without adjusting related values. For example, altering the speed without changing the acceleration accordingly. Independent attacks are relatively easier to detect since the inconsistency can be observed by comparing other dependent values.
- **Dependent Attacks:** In these attacks, multiple dependent values are modified simultaneously. For instance, an attacker might alter the speed and adjust the acceleration accordingly, or change the yaw rate and update the heading. Dependent attacks are more sophisticated and challenging to detect due to their coordinated manipulation of interconnected values.

In this research, we categorized attack generation into single-element, multi-element, independent, and dependent classes to systematically analyze various threats to V2X safety applications. This comprehensive framework enhances our understanding of attack characteristics and their implications, enabling the development of robust countermeasures. By considering these categories, we can better identify vulnerabilities in V2X communication and devise effective strategies to mitigate potential risks.

7 Attack Policies and Selection Strategies

Attack policies refer to the strategies adopted by attackers for transmitting attack messages. In VASP framework [2], there are two distinct attack policies: Persistent and Sporadic.

- **Persistent Policy:** Under the Persistent policy, attackers consistently transmit attack messages. This approach increases the attacker's visibility but decreases the precision of their targeting.
- **Sporadic Policy:** In contrast, the Sporadic policy involves attackers transmitting attack messages randomly, based on a probability distribution. Attackers using this policy intersperse genuine messages with attack messages, making their activities more covert.

In addition to these attack policies, there are two primary attack selection strategies:

- **Randomly Select Attack per Node:** In this approach, each attacker in the V2X network selects a single attack type at random from the complete set of possible attacks and continues to use this attack type consistently. This means that each node is associated with one type of attack, chosen randomly at the beginning of its engagement with the network.
- **Randomly Select Attack per Node per Message:** In this approach, the attacker selects a different attack type randomly for each message it transmits. This means that with each message sent, the attack type can change, introducing a high level of variability and making it more challenging for detection systems to identify a pattern or predict the attacker's next move.

8 Attacks on V2X Applications

- **Attacks on CLW:** To test the robustness and effectiveness of the Control Loss Warning (CLW) application, two attack scenarios were implemented (see Fig. 12):
    - **Attack Scenario 1 - Same Direction:** An attacker vehicle (RV-1) creates a ghost vehicle (GV-1) that appears to be moving in the same direction and lane as the host vehicle (HV). The attacker sends false position, speed, and Control Loss flag data through its Basic Safety Messages (BSMs). This causes the CLW application in HV to issue a false warning based on the fake Control Loss flag in the received BSM.
    - **Attack Scenario 2 - Opposite Direction:** An attacker vehicle (RV-2) creates a ghost vehicle (GV-2) that appears to be moving in the opposite direction of the host vehicle (HV). The attacker sends false position, speed, and Control Loss flag data through its BSMs. This causes the CLW application in HV to issue a false warning based on the fake Control Loss flag in the received BSM.

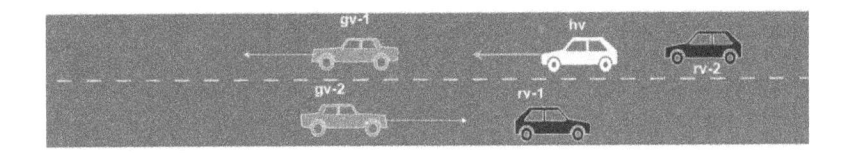

Fig. 12. Attack Scenarios on CLW

- **Attacks on FCW:** To test the robustness and effectiveness of the Forward Collision Warning (FCW) application, two attack scenarios were implemented (see Fig. 13):
    - **Stopped Vehicle Attack:** In this scenario, an attacker vehicle (RV-2) creates a stopped ghost vehicle (GV-2) in front of the host vehicle (HV) by sending false position and speed data through its Basic Safety Messages (BSMs). This causes the FCW application in HV to issue a warning for the non-existent stopped vehicle.
    - **Slow Moving Vehicle Attack:** In this scenario, an attacker vehicle (RV-1) creates a slow-moving ghost vehicle (GV-1) in front of the host vehicle (HV) by sending false position and speed data through its BSMs. This causes the FCW application in HV to predict a collision with GV-1 and issue a warning to the driver.

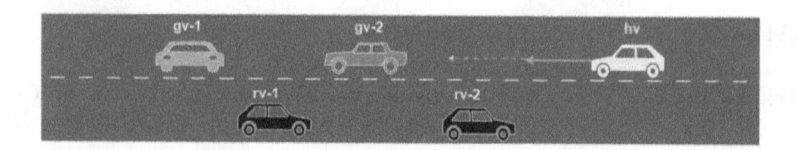

Fig. 13. Attack Scenarios on FCW

- **Attacks on LCW:** To test the robustness and effectiveness of the Lane Change Warning (LCW) application, two attack scenarios were implemented (see Fig. 14):
  - **Attack Scenario 1 - Just Attack:** In this scenario, an attacker vehicle (RV-1) introduces a ghost vehicle (GV-1) in the host vehicle's (HV) blind spot. The attacker modifies the position value in the BSM it sends to the HV to make sure the LCW application detects the ghost vehicle in the HV's blind spot and generates an LCW warning.
  - **Attack Scenario 2 - High Acceleration:** In this scenario, an attacker vehicle (RV-2) introduces an accelerating ghost vehicle (GV-2) behind the host vehicle (HV) such that it enters the HV's blind spot over time. The attacker modifies the position value and speed in the BSM it sends to the HV to ensure the LCW application detects a potential danger in a lane change maneuver and generates an LCW warning.

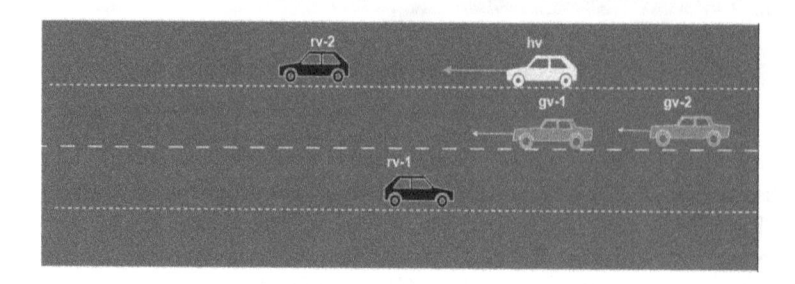

Fig. 14. Attack Scenarios on LCW

- **Attacks on LTA:** To test the robustness and effectiveness of the Left Turn Assist (LTA) application, three attack scenarios were implemented (see Fig. 15):
  - **Attack Scenario 1 - High Acceleration:** In the High Acceleration attack, a ghost vehicle (GV-3) is simulated to accelerate rapidly from the opposite direction towards the intersection. The attacker vehicle (RV-1) manipulates the Basic Safety Message (BSM) to indicate a very high acceleration value, significantly greater than the vehicle's real acceleration value. The attacker aims to trick the LTA application into predicting a collision at the intersection with the ghost vehicle and issuing a false warning.

- **Attack Scenario 2 - High Speed from Behind:** In the High-Speed Behind attack scenario, the attacker vehicle (RV-2) introduces a speeding ghost vehicle (GV-2) from behind the host vehicle (HV) towards the intersection. The BSM is altered to indicate that the ghost vehicle is moving at a very high speed toward the intersection such that it can collide with the HV before making the left turn.
- **Attack Scenario 3 - Stationary Vehicle at Junction:** In this attack scenario, an attacker vehicle (RV-1) simulates a stationary ghost vehicle (GV-1) at the junction by manipulating the speed and position of the BSM it sends to the host vehicle (HV). This scenario is again aimed at fooling the LTA application into giving a false warning.

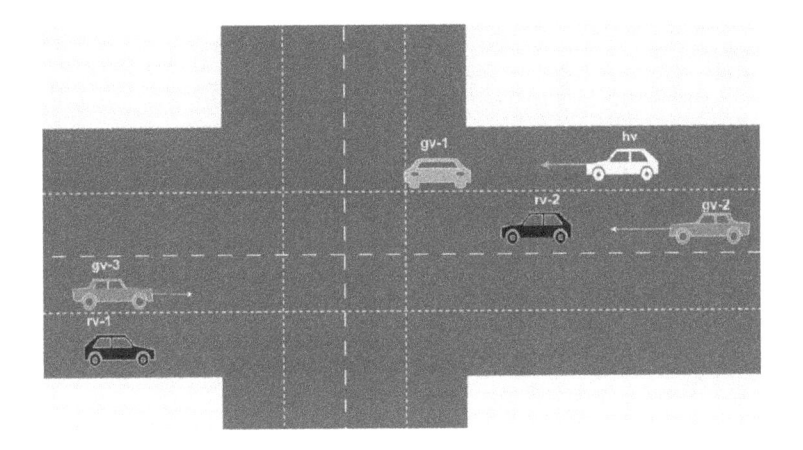

Fig. 15. Attack Scenarios on LTA

Based on the above-mentioned four applications and their attack scenario combinations, we have implemented 25 new attacks. This comprehensive implementation aims to rigorously test the resilience and effectiveness of the connected vehicle systems under various attack conditions.

9 Attack Detection

In our research, we have enhanced the Roadside Units (RSUs) in the V2X Application Spoofing Platform (VASP). These upgraded RSUs can now pass received packets through a model trained on datasets that simulate various types of network attacks. The primary function of this model is to detect and classify incoming packets as either harmless or malicious, significantly improving the security and reliability of the V2X communication network.

9.1 Proposed Deep Learning Based Attack Detection Framework

Utilizing the multiclass dataset introduced in Sect. 6, we have developed a robust Deep Neural Network-based multiclass classifier framework. These classifiers are designed to efficiently detect the attacks discussed in Sect. 8 and will operate directly on Roadside Units (RSUs). The architectural details of our models are illustrated in Fig. 16.

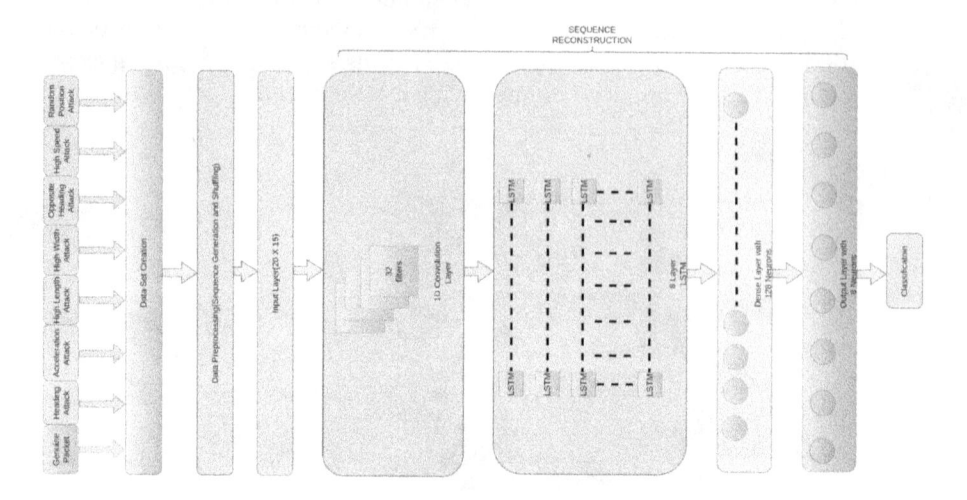

Fig. 16. Proposed Attack Detection Framework

- **Architecture:** Our model is constructed using a deep neural network that begins with a 1D Convolutional Neural Network (CNN) followed by multiple Long Short-Term Memory (LSTM) layers. This combination is selected to capture both spatial and temporal features from the V2X data.
- **Input Shape:** The input to the model consists of sequences with a shape of (20, 15), representing 20 time steps with 15 features each. This design allows the model to learn temporal patterns and relationships within the data.
- **Convolutional Layer:** The initial 1D convolutional layer applies 32 filters with a kernel size of 3, activated by the ReLU function. This layer is crucial for extracting local spatial features from the input sequences.
- **LSTM Layers:** Following the convolutional layer, the model includes eight stacked LSTM layers, each with 64 units configured to return sequences. The LSTM layers are pivotal for modeling long-term dependencies and sequential dynamics in the V2X data, which are essential for accurately detecting sophisticated attacks.
- **Pooling and Dense Layers:** After processing through the LSTM layers, global max-pooling is applied to distill the most significant features from the sequence data. This is followed by a dense layer with 128 units and ReLU activation to further refine the feature representation.

- **Output Layer:** The final output layer is designed for multiclass classification, utilizing the softmax activation function. This layer outputs the probability distribution over the different attack classes, enabling precise identification of the type of attack.
- **Compilation:** The model is compiled using the Adam optimizer, chosen for its efficient handling of large datasets and adaptability to different learning rates. The loss function is categorical cross-entropy, suitable for multiclass classification tasks, and accuracy is used as the primary evaluation metric to gauge model performance.

Training and Evaluation. To train the proposed model, we utilized a comprehensive dataset that includes multiple types of V2X attacks, ensuring a diverse training set. The training process involves the following steps:

- **Data Preprocessing:** The raw data is preprocessed to normalize feature values, handle missing data, and create time-series sequences suitable for input into the neural network.
- **Training Setup:** We employed a training-validation split to monitor model performance and prevent overfitting. Early stopping and model checkpointing techniques were used to optimize the training process.
- **Hyperparameter Tuning:** Various hyperparameters, including learning rate, batch size, and number of epochs, were tuned using grid search and random search techniques to achieve the best performance.
- **Evaluation Metrics:** The model's performance was evaluated using metrics such as precision, recall, F1-score, and confusion matrix analysis to ensure a comprehensive assessment of its detection capabilities.

Deployment on RSUs. The trained model is designed to be deployed on RSUs for real-time attack detection. Key considerations for deployment include:

- **Resource Efficiency:** The model is optimized for resource-constrained environments typical of RSUs, ensuring it runs efficiently without compromising detection accuracy.
- **Real-Time Processing:** The detection mechanism is capable of processing incoming V2X messages in real-time, providing immediate alerts and responses to detected attacks.
- **Integration with Existing Infrastructure:** The deployment process involves integrating the detection framework with existing V2X communication infrastructure, ensuring seamless operation within the ITS ecosystem.

Running the Model on RSUs: To execute the prediction function within our VEINS V2X framework, it's essential to ensure that TensorFlow, the underlying machine learning framework, is properly installed on the system. We utilize cppflow, a C++ interface for TensorFlow, to seamlessly integrate TensorFlow functionalities within our RSU module.

- TensorFlow Installation: Follow the instructions provided by the TensorFlow documentation for proper installation.
- cppflow Installation: Follow the instructions for installing cppflow to enable the integration of TensorFlow models within C++ code.

This integration allows us to harness TensorFlow's power for real-time prediction and detection of cyber attacks within VEINS. By leveraging TensorFlow through cppflow, we can deploy machine learning models directly within RSUs, enhancing the V2X system's security.

Within the RSU module, we utilize the TraCIDemoRSU11p class to predict potential attacks based on incoming Basic Safety Messages (BSMs) received from vehicles. The pre-trained machine learning model analyzes attributes extracted from the BSMs to make predictions regarding potential attacks. These attributes include information such as sender address, message generation time, sender position, speed, acceleration, and others. By processing this information through our model, we obtain predictions indicating the probability of an attack. We then select the highest probable attack. These predictions can trigger appropriate actions within the VEINS framework to prevent or mitigate potential threats.

RSU Module Overview: The diagram in Fig. 17 illustrates the RSU module's structure and how different components interact for real-time attack detection:

- **TraCIDemoRSU11p:** This class utilizes cppflow for prediction purposes.
- **cppflow:** A C++ interface for TensorFlow, enabling the deployment of TensorFlow models within the RSU module.
- **TensorFlow:** The underlying machine learning framework providing the computational power for model predictions.

The RSU module leverages these components to perform real-time attack detection, thereby enhancing the security and reliability of V2X communications. The robust defense mechanisms implemented in this architecture aim to safeguard against sophisticated cyber threats, ensuring a resilient V2X ecosystem.

9.2 Results

Our deep learning models, trained on a comprehensive multiclass dataset, achieved an average detection accuracy of over 95% across all attack categories in V2X communication networks, with minimal false positives. Deploying these models on RSUs within the VASP framework proved effective, ensuring rapid and reliable threat detection with minimal computational overhead. These results highlight the robustness of deep learning in enhancing V2X system security and resilience against cyber threats.

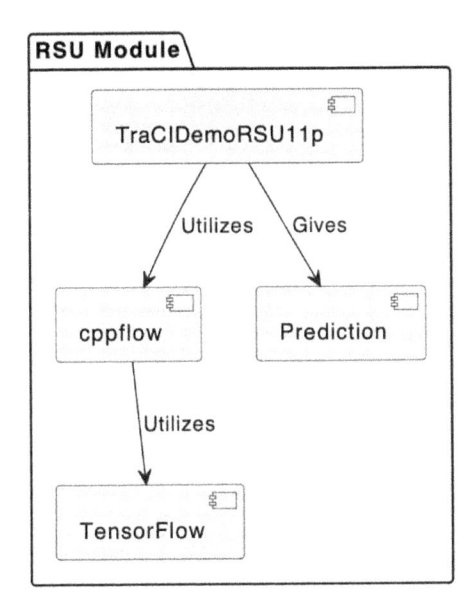

Fig. 17. RSU Module for Real-Time Attack Detection

10 Conclusion and Future Work

This study has enhanced V2X communication security by analyzing various attack scenarios and deploying deep learning classifiers on RSUs. We evaluated four safety applications against 25 attacks, highlighting vulnerabilities and potential mitigations. The integration of digital signatures has further secured V2X communications. Future work will focus on expanding detection mechanisms to counter sophisticated attacks. Incorporating anomaly detection and adaptive learning models that continuously update from real-time data will improve threat detection. These advancements aim to enhance the resilience and reliability of V2X systems for safe and efficient transportation.

References

1. Valentini, E.P., Filho, G.P.R., De Grande, R.E., Ranieri, C.M., Júnior, L.A.P., Meneguette, R.I.: A novel mechanism for misbehavior detection in vehicular networks. IEEE Access **11**, 68113–68126 (2023). https://doi.org/10.1109/ACCESS.2023.3292055
2. Ansari, M.R., Petit, J., Monteuuis, J.P., Chen, C.: VASP: V2X application spoofing platform. In: Proceedings Inaugural International Symposium on Vehicle Security & Privacy, NDSS-symposium (2023)

3. Shanmuganathan, V., Suresh, A.: LSTM-Markov based efficient anomaly detection algorithm for IoT environment. Appl. Soft Comput. **136**, 110054 (2023). https://doi.org/10.1016/j.asoc.2023.110054. ISSN 1568-4946
4. Sun, F., Brooks, R., Comert, G., Tusing, N.: Side-channel security analysis of connected vehicle communications using hidden Markov models. IEEE Trans. Intell. Transp. Syst. **23**, 1–13 (2022). https://doi.org/10.1109/TITS.2022.3164779
5. Sultan, D., Javaid, Q., Malik, A., Al-Turjman, F., Khan, M.: Collaborative-trust approach towards malicious node detection in vehicular ad-hoc networks. Environ. Dev. Sustain. **24**, 1–19 (2022). https://doi.org/10.1007/s10668-021-01632-5
6. Gonçalves, F., Macedo, J., Santos, A.: Evaluation of VANET datasets in context of an intrusion detection system. In: 2021 International Conference on Software, Telecommunications and Computer Networks (SoftCOM), Split, Hvar, Croatia, pp. 1–6 (2021). https://doi.org/10.23919/SoftCOM52868.2021.9559058
7. Alladi, T., Gera, B., Agrawal, A., Chamola, V., Yu, F.R.: DeepADV: a deep neural network framework for anomaly detection in VANETs. IEEE Trans. Veh. Technol. **70**(11), 12013–12023 (2021). https://doi.org/10.1109/TVT.2021.3113807
8. Gonçalves, F., et al.: Synthesizing datasets with security threats for vehicular ad-hoc networks. In: GLOBECOM 2020 - 2020 IEEE Global Communications Conference, Taipei, Taiwan, pp. 1–6 (2020). https://doi.org/10.1109/GLOBECOM42002.2020.9348149
9. Kamel, J., Ansari, M.R., Petit, J., Kaiser, A., Jemaa, I.B., Urien, P.: Simulation framework for misbehavior detection in vehicular networks. IEEE Trans. Veh. Technol. **69**(6), 6631–6643 (2020). https://doi.org/10.1109/TVT.2020.2984878
10. Alladi, T., Chamola, V., Sikdar, B., Choo, K.-K.R.: Consumer IoT: security vulnerability case studies and solutions. IEEE Cons. Electron. Maga. **9**(2), 17–25 (2020). https://doi.org/10.1109/MCE.2019.2953740
11. Li, Y., Luo, Q., Liu, J., Guo, H., Kato, N.: TSP security in intelligent and connected vehicles: challenges and solutions. IEEE Wirel. Commun. **26**(3), 125–131 (2019). https://doi.org/10.1109/MWC.2019.1800289
12. Lu, Z., Qu, G., Liu, Z.: A survey on recent advances in vehicular network security, trust, and privacy. IEEE Trans. Intell. Transp. Syst. **20**(2), 760–776 (2019). https://doi.org/10.1109/TITS.2018.2818888
13. Lu, R., Zhang, L., Ni, J., Fang, Y.: 5G vehicle-to-everything services: gearing up for security and privacy. Proc. IEEE **108**(2), 373–389 (2020). https://doi.org/10.1109/JPROC.2019.2948302
14. Bansal, G., Naren, N., Chamola, V., Sikdar, B., Kumar, N., Guizani, M.: Lightweight mutual authentication protocol for V2G using physical unclonable function. IEEE Trans. Veh. Technol. **69**(7), 7234–7246 (2020). https://doi.org/10.1109/TVT.2020.2976960
15. Alladi, T., Chakravarty, S., Chamola, V., Guizani, M.: A lightweight authentication and attestation scheme for in-transit vehicles in IoV scenario. IEEE Trans. Veh. Technol. **69**(12), 14188–14197 (2020). https://doi.org/10.1109/TVT.2020.3038834
16. Monteuuis, J.-P., Zhang, J., Mafrica, S., Servel, A., Petit, J.: Attacker model for connected and automated vehicles (2018). https://doi.org/10.1145/3273946.3273951
17. https://veins.car2x.org/

18. Kamel, J., Wolf, M., van der Hei, R.W., Kaiser, A., Urien, P., Kargl, F.: VeReMi extension: a dataset for comparable evaluation of misbehavior detection in VANETs. In: ICC 2020 - 2020 IEEE International Conference on Communications (ICC), Dublin, Ireland, pp. 1–6 (2020). https://doi.org/10.1109/ICC40277.2020.9149132
19. https://www.sae.org/standards/content/j2945/1_201603
20. Lopez, P.A., et al.: Microscopic traffic simulation using SUMO. In: 2018 21st International Conference on Intelligent Transportation Systems (ITSC), Maui, HI, USA, pp. 2575–2582 (2018). https://doi.org/10.1109/ITSC.2018.8569938

From Traits to Threats: Learning Risk Indicators of Malicious Insider Using Psychometric Data

N'Famoussa Kounon Nanamou[1,2]([✉])[iD], Christopher Neal[1,2][iD], Nora Boulahia-Cuppens[1][iD], Frédéric Cuppens[1][iD], and Anis Bkakria[1][iD]

[1] Polytechnique Montreal, Montreal, Canada
{nfamoussa-kounon.nanamou,christopher.neal,nora.boulahia-cuppens,
frederic.cuppens}@polymtl.ca
[2] IRT SystemX, Palaiseau, France
anis.bkakria@irt-systemx.fr

Abstract. While organizations are facing increased pressure from external cyberthreats, they must also consider attacks that can originate from within the organization. Insider threat attacks are executed by employees who utilize the access they are provided by an organization to perform malicious actions, such as data exfiltration. Previous works have proposed methods for detecting insiders based on analyzing the actions users perform in a work environment. In this work we propose to identify "at-risk" employees using solely "Big-Five" personality factors, known as OCEAN or CANOE, as an indicator of risk. We perform experiments using the CMU-CERT r4.2, CMU-CERT r5.2, TWOS, and a custom dataset, where we compare clustering results of 4 methods and detection results of 40 classification methods, with 25 sampling techniques. This work demonstrates the effectiveness, feasibility and limitations of using the psychometric profile as a method to identify potential insider threats. We suggest future work to explore the temporality of an employee's psychometric profile and consider how its evolution over time can be used in dynamic risk assessment.

Keywords: Indicator of Risk · Insider Threat · Personality Profiling · Dynamic Risk Assessment · Machine Learning · Cybersecurity

1 Introduction

In an age where cybersecurity breaches pose substantial risks to organizations worldwide, the threat landscape continues to evolve, encompassing not only external actors but also insiders with legitimate access to sensitive information and systems. Among the myriad challenges faced by cybersecurity professionals, insider threats stand out as a formidable concern, often exploiting their legitimate access privileges to perpetrate malicious activities. It is estimated that 20–30% of all cyberincidents are perpetuated by malicious insiders [29]. These numbers vary between industries, as shown by the Verizon Data Breach Investigations Report 2024, notably in the healthcare sector where 70% of threat actors were internal [54].

As organizations strive to bolster their defensive posture against insider threats, understanding the intricacies of these threats becomes paramount. There is an urgent need to develop robust mechanisms to anticipate, detect and mitigate insider threats effectively.

Central to this endeavor is the utilization of comprehensive datasets that simulate real-world environments and encompass various insider threat scenarios. The CERT-CMU dataset, provided by Carnegie Mellon University, stands out as a valuable resource in this regard [19]. Comprising of simulated logs from a typical office environment, the CERT dataset offers researchers a rich repository of data to develop insider threat detection approaches across several scenarios. Another notable dataset is The Wolf of SUTD (TWOS) dataset which contains malicious insider threat behavior gathered from a gamified competition using human participants [6].

Previous works generally look at the actions taken by users in the environment to identify when malicious insider activities are performed. In this work we analyze to what extent an individual's psychometric profile can be used to predict whether they are at risk of being an insider threat. Of particular interest within the CMU-CERT and TWOS dataset are psychometric values, specifically OCEAN values commonly referred to as the Big-Five personality traits. These values encapsulate key personality traits, namely Openness, Conscientiousness, Extraversion, Agreeableness, and Neuroticism [44].

In this paper we perform a comprehensive analysis of the CMU-CERT and TWOS datasets to understand how the OCEAN values are distributed amongst normal and malicious individuals. We then compare the effectiveness of 40 detection methods and 20 sampling methods for identifying malicious individuals. We provide insights into the extent to which the OCEAN values can be used to accurately predict malicious insiders in these dataset. The contributions of this work are summarized in the following:

- We evaluate the factors of the Big-Five model as insider threat indicators for the CMU-CERT and TWOS datasets.
- We analyze the correlation between the Big-Five factors and the insider threat scenarios defined in the CMU-CERT and TWOS datasets.
- We identify which factor(s) of the Big-Five model are relevant for predicting insider threat behaviors in the CMU-CERT and TWOS datasets.
- We determine which employee profiles are most likely to turn into insider threats according to the Big-Five model.

The remainder of this work has the following structure. Section 2 provides an overview of related work. The datasets are described in Sect. 3. We present the methodology in Sect. 4. Section 5 provides the results of the dataset analysis and insider threat classification. In Sect. 6 we provide an analysis and discussion of the results. Lastly, Sect. 7 provides a conclusion to this work.

2 Related Work

The dynamic nature of insider threats within an organization complicates the a priori identification of insider risk indicators. The analysis of these risks is based on the availability and quality of the data collected. This challenge is addressed within various approaches as discussed in the literature below.

Insider Threat. Information systems at the country-wide or organization-wide level face numerous threats: those coming from the outside (outsider threats), those coming from the inside (insider threats), or a combination of both (hybrid threats). For the latter two, it is both a cyber and a human problem. Several models for preventing and detecting insider threats have been proposed in the literature. Some are based on technological approaches [48], while others rely on human sciences such as sociology [12] or psychology [39]. Recent works tend to combine approaches from technology, social, and social technology domains [33].

Big-Five. [20] and [21] were one of the earlier works to propose the Big-Five model as we know it today. Based on these works, various measurement instruments have been developed such as the Big Five Inventory (BFI) [32], the NEO Personality Inventory-Revised (NEO-PI-R) [11], and the International Personality Item Pool (IPIP) [22]. Personality behaviour are typically assessed during the employee recruitment process, and their values remain relatively stable over time unless they interact with situational/environmental variables such as life events, self-improvement efforts [36], or security scenarios (self-efficacy, sanction severity, sanction certainty, and response cost) [55].

Big-Five and Cybersecurity. In the last decade, the integration of human aspects into cybersecurity has attracted the interest of researchers and practitioners. [9] highlights the link between user intention and action. [50] examines personality traits as predictors of cybersecurity behaviors, [37] analyzes computer skills, [16] developed SeBIS to measure users' security behavior intentions, and [51] addresses personality-attitudes-intentions. [23] extends [16]'s work by examining how individual differences (e.g., risk-taking preferences, decision-making styles, demographics, and personality traits) influence security behavior intentions in device security, password generation, proactive awareness, and updating.

Big-Five and Machine Learning. Various approaches to identifying insider threats adopt machine learning and deep learning techniques. Very few of them use psychological factors for identifying malicious users. [59] uncovers hidden patterns in crime data using various machine learning techniques. [57] uses a one-class Support Vector Machine (SVM) for classification, drawing on the Big-Five and Dark Triad personality traits. [28] uses the k-means algorithm to analyze variations within different clusters and their correlation with types of hackers: white, gray, or black hat, based on OCEAN values.

Big-Five and Insider Threat. [46] present a systematic review of the literature on the psychology (such as personality traits and psychological states of a person) of insider threats. The works of [8,17,24–26] developed the Psyber-Sleuth prototype, which integrates a predictive model of insider threats from incoming data processed to deduce observations; observations are processed to deduce indicators; indicators are evaluated to measure the insider threats. They identify 12 psychosocial indicators of an at-risk employee (e.g., not accepting feedback, self-centered, absenteeism, disgruntled, and more).

Big-Five Most Relevant Factors. Several previous studies have examined all the Big-Five factors to identify the most important factor in predicting cyber threats. [43] find that high Openness and Extraversion reduce susceptibility to phishing. [40] find that the most relevant personality traits are Agreeableness for white hat, Openness for black hat, and Neuroticism for gray hat. [42] shows that high Extraversion is correlated with reduced perception of security risk during online shopping. [50] find that Conscientiousness, Agreeableness, and Openness traits are significantly associated with risky insider threat behaviors. [34] show that the combination of personality variables (i.e. self-reported knowledge about strong/weak passwords, personality traits, and risk-taking) predicts 34% of the variance in risky behaviors. [28] confirms some results from [40], adding that Openness closely relates to Conscientiousness, Agreeableness closely relates to Extraversion, and Neuroticism does not directly depend on any other trait.

Summary. The literature shows that internal threats are complex and varied, as are the methods for their detection, prevention, and mitigation. These threats arise from few malicious activities hidden in normal data. Our work demonstrates a link between Big Five personality factors to cybersecurity attitudes and behaviors. However, there is no consensus on the most relevant factors for predicting malicious insider threats. To our knowledge, no research has deeply analyzed the use of machine learning with Big-Five traits to identify such threats.

3 Datasets

Many research studies report on various datasets that enable the development of effective machine learning models for the prevention, detection, and mitigation to insider threats [3,30]. Our research relies on two public datasets: the CMU-CERT Dataset, which is synthetic, and the TWOS Dataset, which contains real data. These datasets include measurements related to the Big Five Personality Traits, which are useful for establishing psychometric profiles of employees within an organization. The following six different Red Team scenarios related to insider threats are explored.

- **Scenario 1**: A user starts logging in after hours, using a removable drive, and uploading data to wikileaks.org. They soon leave the organization.
- **Scenario 2**: A user surfs job sites and contacts a competitor. Before leaving, they use a thumb drive to steal data.
- **Scenario 3**: A disgruntled system admin downloads a keylogger, transfers it to his supervisor's machine, and uses the keylogs to send a mass email, causing panic before leaving.

- **Scenario 4**: A user logs into another's machine, emails files to their home email, and increases this activity over 3 months.
- **Scenario 5**: A user affected by layoffs uploads documents to Dropbox for personal gain.
- **Scenario 6**: A finance executive meets with competitors and uses encryption to transmit strategic documents during off-peak hours.

CMU-CERT Dataset [19] is a synthetic dataset developed by the CERT division of the Software Engineering Institute at Carnegie Mellon University (CERT-CMU), in partnership with ExactData LLC. This dataset models the five most common insider threat scenarios: data exfiltration (Scenario 1), intellectual property theft (Scenarios 2, 4, 5), and IT sabotage (Scenario 3). The generated data includes login logs, browsing histories, file accesses, emails, device usage, psychometric information, and LDAP data. It covers 18 months of activities, both normal and malicious, from December 1, 2009, to May 31, 2011. The data is organized according to the version of the generator used, reflecting several major revisions. This work focuses on version r4.2 and r5.2.

Custom r_extended Dataset is constituted from a weighted random sampling of 1,500 observations from the CMU-CERT Dataset according to three criteria: (i) the merging of heterogeneous datasets retains the initial statistical properties [1,27,56], (ii) the Big-Five factors (O, C, E, A, N) are independently and identically distributed random variables, initially unaffected by the scenarios defined in the datasets, and (iii) the sample size corresponds to the number of employees at our institute. Section 4.1 provides more details on our data merging methodology for the CMU-CERT Dataset.

TWOS Dataset [6] is a dataset derived from interactions of 24 real users, 12 of whom are malicious[1]. It is collected during a competition organized by the Singapore University of Technology and Design (SUTD) in March 2017. This collection took place over a period of five working days. The collected data includes keystrokes, mouse movements, host monitor surveillances, network traffic, SMTP logs, system logins, and psychometric information following scenario 6.

Table 1 presents the Red Team insider threat scenarios contained in the CMU-CERT r4.2, CMU-CERT r5.2, r_extended, and TWOS datasets.

4 Methodology

This section provides details on the experimental methodology adopted in this work (Fig. 1). Here we describe the pre-processing steps performed on the datasets, our approach for training detection models, and the evaluation metrics.

---

[1] In their work, the authors indicate a total of 17 insiders, but in the dataset we find there are 12, consisting of 5 traitors and 7 masqueraders.

Table 1. Red Team Scenario explored in each dataset

Scenario	TWOS	r4.2	r5.2	r_extedend
Scenario 1	✗	✓	✓	✓
Scenario 2	✗	✓	✓	✓
Scenario 3	✗	✓	✓	✓
Scenario 4	✗	✗	✓	✓
Scenario 5	✗	✗	✗	✓
Scenario 6	✓	✗	✗	✗

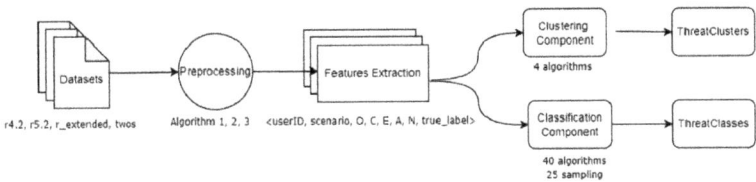

Fig. 1. Methodology scheme: Algorithm 1, 2, and 3 take the appropriate datasets (r4.2, r5.2, r_extended, twos) as input and output data matrices. These n classification and clustering tasks to distinguish between at-risk and non-at-risk employees (ThreatClusters, ThreatClasses)

4.1 Pre-processing

File Description. We utilize the *psychometric.csv* and *insiders.csv* files from the CMU-CERT Dataset and the $User\{i\}_{i=1,...,24}.xlsx$ and *ImportantInfo.xlsx* files from the TWOS Dataset. These are tabular datasets, described in Table 2 and 3, respectively. The *psychometric.csv* and $User\{i\}_{i=1,...,24}.xlsx$ files record the values of features OCEAN, while the *insiders.csv* and *ImportantInfo.xlsx* files contain the labels (true positives).

Table 2. Description of CMU-CERT Dataset Files Used in Pre-processing

pyschometric.csv		insiders.csv	
Field	Description	Field	Description
employee_name	Primary key	**dataset**	Dataset release used
user_id	User ID	**scenario**	Five Red Team scenario 1–5
O	Openness	details	Details of user activities
C	Conscientiousness	user	Primary key
E	Extraversion	start	Start time in the organization
A	Agreeableness	end	End time in the organization
N	Neuroticism		

Table 3. Description of TWOS Dataset Files Used in Pre-processing

User{i}.xlsx		ImportantInfo.xlsx	
Field	Description	Field	Description
personality_question	Big Five Related Question	Name	User's name User1-24
Disagree	Score scale: 1 or 2	E-mail	User's Email
Neutral	Score scale: 3	Leader	Leader of Team
Agree	Score scale: 4 or 5	**Team1**	User's Team 1
		Team2	User's Team 2
		IP1	User's IP
		Name1	User's Machine Name
		IP2	Team's IP
		Name2	Team's Machine Name
		Attack Period	Attack Detection Period
		Victim	Victim's Name

Data Manipulation. Python 3.11.7 is used to preprocess the datasets and generate the data matrices used in our experiments, following Algorithm 1, 2, and 3 presented in Appendix A. Binary encoding 0 (non-insider) and 1 (insider) is applied to the output features. After the pre-treatment phase, the features selected are <user_ID, scenario, O, C, E, A, N, true_label>. This matrix encapsulates the essential attributes for subsequent phases. Despite the presence of some outliers, with no missing or duplicated values, we opt to use the RobustScaler. RobustScaler is an effective feature scaling method for data with outliers [2]. The data is split into a trainset (80%) and a testset (20%) with stratification that maintains the proportions of observations from the initial dataset.

Data Visualization. We first demonstrate the distribution of the normal and insider instances for the CMU-CERT datasets (version r2 to r6.2), the r_extended dataset, and the TWOS dataset, in Table 4. The datasets are very imbalanced since they contain considerably fewer insider threats instances and more normal employees, as expected for typical organizations.

During the initial exploration phase, we conduct univariate analysis with histograms and box plots, bivariate analyses with pair plots, and dimensionality reduction using PCA[2], t-SNE[3], and MDS[4] [4,35,52]. For the sake of space limitations, we demonstrate only the results from the pair plots in Fig. 2. We find these results the most meaningful since they display significant overlap between normal and abnormal data points across all of the OCEAN features, making it difficult to differentiate them without prior knowledge of the ground truth.

---
[2] Principal Component Analysis (PCA).
[3] t-Distributed Stochastic Neighbor Embedding (t-SNE).
[4] Multidimensional Scaling (MDS).

Table 4. Distribution of insiders across CERT versions, r_extended, and TWOS

	r2	r3.1	r3.2	r4.1	r4.2	r5.1	r5.2	r6.1	r6.2	TWOS	r_extended
# insiders	1	2	2	3	70	4	99	5	5	12	191
# employees	1 000	1 000	1 000	1 000	1 000	2 000	2 000	4 000	4 000	24	1 500
% insiders	0.1	0.2	0.2	0.3	7	0.2	4.95	0.125	0.125	50	12.73

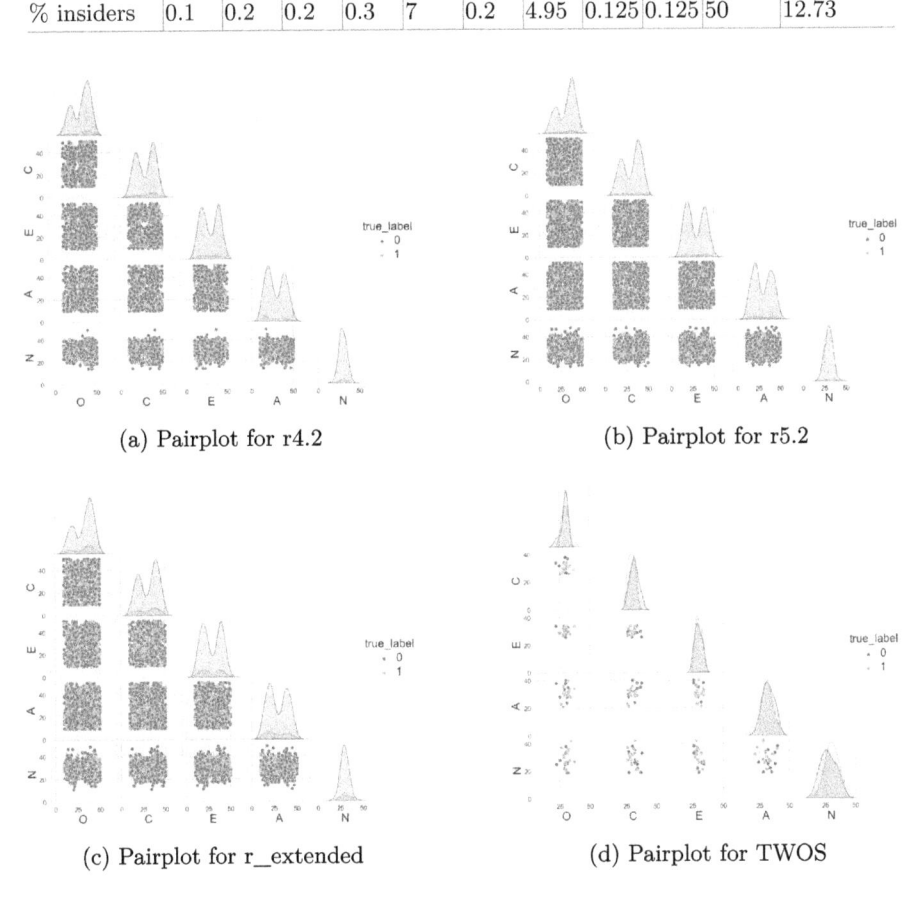

(a) Pairplot for r4.2

(b) Pairplot for r5.2

(c) Pairplot for r_extended

(d) Pairplot for TWOS

Fig. 2. Pairplots comparing OCEAN feature distributions.

4.2 Detection Models and Sampling Methods

Choosing algorithms in machine learning is not trivial, as it depends on several criteria: the type of problem, types of variables, the nature, internal structure, and the quantity of data. We therefore perform experiments with several clustering methods and classification algorithms.

Clustering Algorithms. We evaluate the performance of the 4 clustering algorithms most suitable for the data distribution across different datasets, namely K-Means, Hierarchical Agglomerative Clustering (HAC), Gaussian

Mixture Modelling (GMM), and Density-Based Spatial Clustering (DBSCAN). The optimal number of clusters is determined using the *Elbow method* [47] and *Silhouette score* [49].

Classification Algorithms. Additionally, internal threats are relatively rare events, therefore there is a need for sampling techniques to aid the classification process. Therefore we experiment with a large set of combinations of classification methods and sampling techniques. We provide the complete list of the 40 classification algorithms and the 25 sampling techniques used in Table 5. We optimize the parameters of selected models using the RandomSearch technique [7, 58]. The obtained hyperparameters are used to train the evaluated models.

Table 5. Enumeration of all classification algorithms and sampling techniques

Classification Algorithms
Linear Algorithms: LogisticRegression, LinearSVC, RidgeClassifier, SGDClassifier, Perceptron, PassiveAggressiveClassifier, LogisticRegressionCV, RidgeClassifierCV
Neighbor-Based Algorithms: KNeighborsClassifier, NearestCentroid, RadiusNeighborsClassifier
Bayesian Algorithms: GaussianNB, MultinomialNB, BernoulliNB, ComplementNB, CategoricalNB
Tree-Based Algorithms: DecisionTreeClassifier, RandomForestClassifier, ExtraTreesClassifier, ExtraTreeClassifier
SVM Algorithms: SVC, NuSVC
Boosting Algorithms: AdaBoostClassifier, XGClassifier, GradientBoostingClassifier, HistGradientBoostingClassifier
Neural Network Algorithms: MLPClassifier
Semi-supervised Algorithms: LabelPropagation, LabelSpreading
Other Algorithms: BaggingClassifier, CalibratedClassifierCV, DummyClassifier, GaussianProcessClassifier, LinearDiscriminantAnalysis, MultiOutputClassifier, OneVsOneClassifier, OneVsRestClassifier, OutputCode, StackingClassifier, VotingClassifier
Sampling Techniques
Oversampling Techniques: ADASYN, BorderlineSMOTE, KMeansSMOTE, RandomOverSampler, SMOTE, SMOTEN, SMOTENC, SVMSMOTE
Undersampling Techniques: AllKNN, ClusterCentroids, CondensedNearestNeighbour, EditedNearestNeighbours, InstanceHardnessThreshold, NearMiss, NeighbourhoodCleaningRule, OneSidedSelection, RandomUnderSampler, RepeatedEditedNearestNeighbours, TomekLinks
Combined Techniques: SMOTEENN, SMOTETomek
Ensemble Techniques: BalancedBaggingClassifier, BalancedRandomForestClassifier, EasyEnsembleClassifier, RUSBoostClassifier

4.3 Evaluation Metrics

Clustering Metrics. We use the *Davies-Bouldin Index* [45] and *Silhouette Score* [49] to evaluate the performance of clustering models. The *Davies-Bouldin Index* (DBI) measures the average ratio of intra-cluster distances to inter-cluster distances for each cluster. The *Silhouette Score* (Silh) assesses how similar points are to their own cluster compared to other clusters.

Classification Metrics. We use the metrics of *Precision*, *Recall*, *F1-score*, and Area Under the ROC Curve (*AUC*) to evaluate the performance of classification models [41]. *Precision* is the ratio of true positives to positive predictions. *Recall* is the ratio of positive predictions to correct predictions. The *F1-score* provides a single value: the harmonic mean of *Precision* and *Recall*. *AUC* measures the true positive rate against the false positive rate for different classification thresholds. [10] highlights the limitations of the *Accuracy* metric in situations where one class is significantly underrepresented; therefore, we do not use it as a metric in this work.

5 Experimental Results

In this section, we describe our computation environment, demonstrate the results of our clustering process, and show the results from the classification task.

5.1 Setup

The experimental environment consists of an 11th generation Intel Core i7-1165G7 processor, x64 architecture, running on the Microsoft Windows 11 Home operating system at 2.80 GHz. It has 4 cores, 8 logical processors, 16 GB of RAM, and a 1 TB hard drive. The tests are conducted using Anaconda[5] and data science libraries such as Pandas[6], Numpy[7], Matplotlib[8], and Scikit-Learn[9] within the Jupyter Notebook web platform[10].

5.2 Clustering Results (ThreatClusters)

Clustering Performance. In Table 6, it can be observed that the clustering models studied have DBI values greater than 1 and Silhouette scores close to 0, indicating overlapping clusters and high dispersion within clusters. K-Means stands out with low DBI values (1.777, 1.809, 1.824, 1.317) and high Silhouette scores (.184, .177, .177, .214) for the r4.2, r5.2, r_extended, and TWOS datasets. GMM and HAC have comparable but slightly lower performance. DBSCAN shows promising results for the r_extended dataset but performs less well on the TWOS dataset.

---

[5] https://www.anaconda.com/.
[6] https://pandas.pydata.org/.
[7] https://numpy.org/.
[8] https://matplotlib.org/.
[9] https://scikit-learn.org/.
[10] https://jupyter.org/.

Table 6. Performance of the clustering models across different datasets

Model	r4.2 DBI	r4.2 Silh	r5.2 DBI	r5.2 Silh	r_ext DBI	r_ext Silh	TWOS DBI	TWOS Silh
k-means	1.777	.184	1.809	.1777	1.824	.177	1.317	.214
HAC	1.935	.168	1.919	.161	1.904	.153	1.345	.196
GMM	1.935	.178	1.869	.159	1.851	.163	1.386	.178
DBSCAN	1.944	.166	1.948	.160	0.512	.333	1.448	.135

Clustering Separation. Figure 3 shows that the clustering models studied do not perfectly separate the data points of the r4.2, r5.2, r_extended, and TWOS datasets based on true labels, even when using 2 or 3 clusters. Despite some classification errors, K-Means presents a better detection rate across all datasets, in contrast to DBSCAN, which over-clustered by grouping the points into one main cluster.

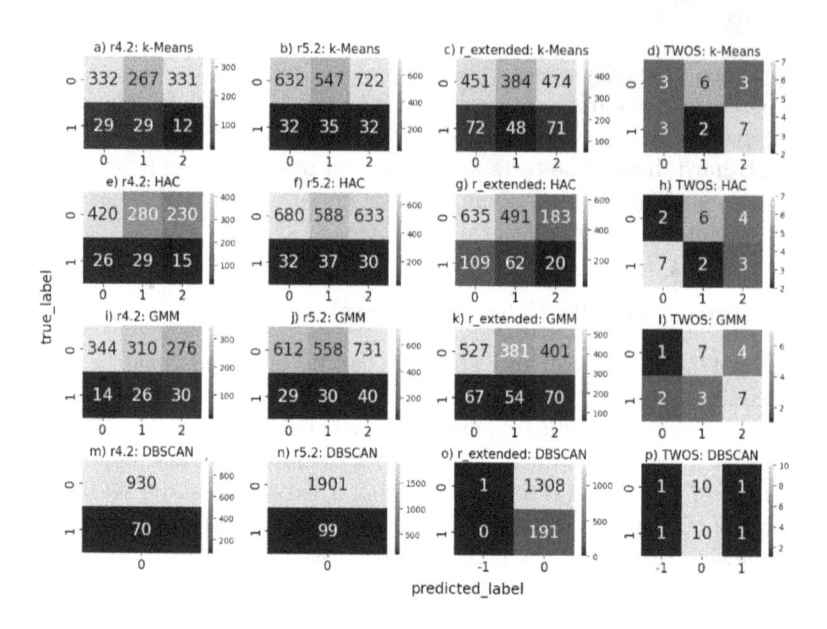

Fig. 3. Confusion matrices for clustering techniques across different datasets

Clustering Feature Analysis. Table 7 shows the average personality trait values for each cluster identified by the different clustering models. For example, in the r4.2 dataset, individuals grouped as "insiders" by the K-Means model are characterized by the scores O = 33, C = 30, E = 29, A = 29, and N = 29. In contrast, the "non-insiders" in the same dataset display scores O = 33, C = 29, E = 27, A = 27, and N = 28. This table illustrates that the personality traits O, C,

E, A, N differ only slightly between "insiders" and "non-insiders", suggesting a similarity in psychometric profiles within the clusters.

Table 7. Scores from clustering across different datasets: −1 and 0 for biased cases, 1 for insiders, and 2 for non-insiders. NA (Not Appicable) due to the non-existence of the cluster

Method	Cluster	r4.2 O	C	E	A	N	r5.2 O	C	E	A	N	r_extended O	C	E	A	N	TWOS O	C	E	A	N
Kmeans	0	33	30	28	27	29	32	31	27	28	29	32	31	28	28	29	29	30	30	33	29
	1	32	30	29	29	29	33	31	28	29	29	33	31	28	28	29	31	31	30	31	29
	2	33	29	27	27	28	33	31	29	28	29	32	31	28	29	29	29	29	30	29	28
HAC	0	33	30	29	28	29	33	31	29	29	29	32	31	29	28	29	31	31	30	31	29
	1	32	30	28	29	29	32	31	28	29	29	33	31	28	29	29	29	29	30	29	28
	2	32	31	29	28	29	33	31	27	28	29	33	31	29	28	29	29	31	29	33	30
GMM	0	33	31	29	29	29	32	31	28	29	29	33	31	28	29	29	29	31	29	35	32
	1	33	30	29	27	29	32	31	27	28	29	33	31	28	29	29	28	29	30	29	27
	2	32	30	28	29	29	33	31	28	28	29	32	31	29	28	29	31	32	30	32	30
DBSCAN	−1	NA	NA	NA	NA	NA	NA	NA	NA	NA	NA	30	18	22	14	32	31	30	28	40	37
	0	33	30	29	28	29	33	31	28	28	29	33	31	28	28	29	30	30	30	30	30
	1	NA	NA	NA	NA	NA	NA	NA	NA	NA	NA	NA	NA	NA	NA	NA	30	30	30	30	28

5.3 Classification Results (ThreatClasses)

Classification Performance. We perform an exhaustive comparison between the classification models with the sampling methods. We train each of the 40 detection models with each of the 25 sampling methods, for a total of 1000 training and testing experiments per dataset. We present the best 5 of 1000 results on each dataset in Table 8. To rank the 1000 methods, we first sort them by Precision, then Recall, then AUC, then F1-Score. We make the following observations about results from each of the datasets:

- **CMU-CERT r4.2**: Models display similar scores with a precision of 0.967, a recall of 0.535, and an F1-Score of 0.549. AUC variations show that Extra Trees with SMOTEN achieves the best score (AUC = 0.611), followed by Bagging with SMOTEN (AUC = 0.608). Other combinations have lower AUC scores, indicating better overall performance for models using SMOTEN.
- **CMU-CERT r5.2**: Extra Trees model with SMOTETomek obtains the best scores for recall (0.564), AUC (0.624), and F1-Score (0.580), although precision is slightly lower for this model (0.614). Other models such as Extra Trees with SMOTE and Random Forest with SMOTE exhibit similar but slightly lower performances in terms of F1-Score and AUC.
- **r_extended**: The performance of models is relatively uniform with a precision of 0.938 and a recall of 0.513 for all evaluated models. The Radius Neighbors model with CNN achieves the highest AUC (0.550), suggesting

better discrimination capability for this model. Other sampler combinations show slightly lower AUCs.
- **TWOS**: The XGBoost model without sampling stands out with a precision of 0.750, a recall of 0.666, and an F1-Score of 0.583. This model also displays an AUC of 0.666, which is higher than that of other evaluated models. Other models, such as Radius Neighbors and Bernoulli NB, show lower performances in terms of F1-Score and AUC.

Classification Feature Analysis. We use the top-performing classification models to identify the most relevant variables from the Big-Five model for each dataset, following the conditional permutation importance approach proposed in [5,13,15]. It can be observed in Table 9 that the variable weights are similar to one decimal place, although subtle variations are noted between different datasets. Table 10 presents the three relevant factors identified in each scenario.

Table 8. Performance of the classification models across different datasets

Models	Sampler	Precision	Recall	AUC	F1-Score
Dataset: r4.2					
Extra Trees	SMOTEN	.967	.535	.611	.549
Bagging	SMOTEN	.967	.535	.608	.549
Random Forest	ROS	.967	.535	.597	.549
Random Forest	ENN	.967	.535	.577	.549
Random Forest	OSS	.967	.535	.569	.549
Dataset: r5.2					
Extra Trees	SVMSMOTE	.643	.544	.543	.562
Extra Trees	SMOTETomek	.614	.564	.624	.580
Extra Trees	SMOTE	.593	.561	.647	.573
Extra Trees	SMOTE	.593	.561	.647	.573
Random Forest	SMOTE	.593	.561	.618	.573
Dataset: r_extended					
Radius Neighbors	CNN	.938	.513	.550	.492
Bagging	ADASYN	.938	.513	.537	.492
Radius Neighbors	SVMSMOTE	.938	.513	.525	.492
Radius Neighbors	TomekLinks	.938	.513	.521	.492
Bagging	SMOTETomek	.938	.513	.513	.492
Dataset: TWOS					
XGBoost	None	.750	.666	.666	.583
Radius Neighbors	None	.700	.500	.500	.285
Bernoulli NB	None	.700	.500	.833	.285
Random Forest	None	.700	.500	.333	.285
Hist Gradient Boosting	None	.700	.500	.500	.285

Table 9. Permutation importance of Big-Five factors

Variable/Weight	r4.2	r5.2	r_extended	TWOS
O	0.1597	0.121	0.183	0.172
C	0.134	0.157	0.142	0.110
E	0.123	0.132	0.145	0.118
A	0.176	0.112	0.169	0.151
N	0.141	0.174	0.108	0.136

Table 10. Initial correlation between insider threat scenarios and Big Five factors

Scenario	Scenario 1	Scenario 2	Scenario 3	Scenario 4	Scenario 5	Scenario 6
Factor	N, C, O	O, C, A	C, N, A	E, O, C	A, C, N	O, C, E

6 Discussion

In this section we describe the insights we draw from these findings. Here we discuss the clustering and classification results, compare these results with other works, and provide avenues for future work.

6.1 ThreatClusters and ThreatClasses

Big-Five Factors as Indicators of Threat. This study explores the use of psychometric data as early indicators to identify at-risk employees, assuming that certain trait configurations could correspond to higher risk profiles. Our findings indicate that Big-Five factors alone do not provide a sufficient distinction between at-risk employees and non-at-risk employees. Variations in the OCEAN scores between individuals labeled as "insiders" and "non-insiders" are often subtle and do not demonstrate significant divergences that could be reliably exploited for automatic detection. This observation underscores the necessity of integrating psychometric measures over time with other forms of data to enhance the effectiveness of insider threat prevention and detection systems.

Most Relevant Features. Table 9 reveals that each of the five factors of the Big-Five model plays a significant role in predicting insider threats. Table 10 shows the most dominant factors of the Big-Five model initially characterizing each of the scenarios studied. Minor variations observed between different datasets suggest that these personality traits are dynamic factors, influenced by individual characteristics, environmental and situational contexts, and developments over time. These results contrast with previous works [28,34,40,50] that rely on different methodologies and datasets, suggesting a reconsideration of all five factors of the Big-Five model in the analysis of insider threats.

Dataset Impact on Models. Insider threat scenarios and the underrepresentation of the target class significantly affect classification models.

- **Sampling Techniques Impacts.** The ratio of insider threats present in the datasets plays a crucial role in the calibration and performance of detection models. A low ratio of insider threats leads to ineffective detection, where the model may overlook real threats in favor of the majority of normal behaviors. Conversely, artificially increasing the number of threats in the datasets through sampling techniques improves the model's ability to correctly identify malicious behaviors. However, integrating these techniques into operational detection systems raises challenges, such as computational complexity and the management of false positives. [3] recommends enriching future public datasets with a greater amount of malicious data to enhance research and the development of more robust detection models.
- **Scenarios Impacts.** Insider threat scenarios and personality traits measured by questionnaires are not directly linked in the traditional sense where a specific insider threat scenario could be directly predicted by particular personality traits. However, there are conceptual and contextual links between them that can be explored and utilized to enhance the understanding and prevention of insider threats. For instance, a high score in neuroticism could coincide with unpredictable or stressed behaviors which, under certain circumstances, could lead to malicious actions in response to professional or personal stresses. Table 10 illustrates these correlations, showing the initial scenarios influenced by the Big Five personality traits could evolve over time due to varying circumstances.

6.2 Comparison With Other Works

Although there are no similar works in the literature for a direct comparison of the results, Table 11 summarizes results from related works for a general comparison, helping contextualize our findings. Our study, based solely on psychometric data, achieves results that are comparable or even superior to those previous works.

Table 11. Results of Other Works using Technological Features: Precision (P), Recall (R), Accuracy (A), and F1-Score (F1)

Paper	Dataset	Method	P	R	A	F1
[38]	r4.2	Hyperparameter tuning of the Random Forest algorithm on a balanced dataset.	.959	.959	.959	.959
[14]	r4.2	Random Forest algorithm applied with 66% of the data for training and 34% for testing.	NA	NA	.895	NA
[53]	r5.2	Application of ASW-GAN based on attribute similarity for insider threat detection.	.857	1.00	.996	.923
[18]	r5.2	Evaluation of a hybrid model combining MLP and 1DCNN on BNN with SPCAGAN augmentation.	.895	.749	NA	.738
[31]	TWOS	Semi-supervised Learning combined k-means and Decision Tree to identify malicious activities.	NA	.998	.996	NA

6.3 Limitations and Future Work

Our research utilizes the CMU-CERT and TWOS datasets, each with its intrinsic limitations. The users in CMU-CERT are simulated, whereas those in TWOS are real, but the responses to the questionnaire could be biased by the financial incentives of the competition.

Another element, is the static nature of the OCEAN scores, which do not evolve over time, despite potential triggering events. We find that it is difficult to detect insiders with a static OCEAN value since the insiders and non-insiders have similar feature distributions. It would likely be more beneficial to monitor an employee's OCEAN values, or similar psychometric values, over time. This way one can detect swings in employee mood and identify when they might perform a malicious action against the organization. We identify three directions for future work:

1. **Enrichment of datasets.** Developing scalable datasets that track changes in employees' risk profiles over the long term could prove crucial. The inclusion of temporal data and continuous monitoring of psychometric traits could enable a better understanding of risk dynamics and improve the effectiveness of predictive models. Engaging in the sharing of real data over time with time series.
2. **Automatic model retraining.** Evaluating the impact of regularly updating predictive models based on the evolution of Big-Five factors. Techniques such as federed learning, transfer learning and collaborative data-sharing can be considered to adapt models to new data without starting from scratch.
3. **Mitigation of adversarial attacks.** Examining strategies to counter adversarial attacks within internal threat risks, by studying the resilience of systems against such threats.

7 Conclusion

To combat the prevalence of insider threats, this work offers a comprehensive analysis of the applicability of machine learning-based detection approaches at identifying insiders solely using psychometric profile values. We provide a substantial comparison of clustering methods and classification methods with sampling techniques. Our work is conducted using the OCEAN values of normal and insider employees from the CMU-CERT r4.2, the CMU-CERT r4.5, our custom r_extended, and the TWOS datasets. We find moderate success identifying the insiders using OCEAN values and state that is cause the OCEAN values between the classes are very similar. This basic psychometric profiling could not be used as a definitive method to identify a true-insider, but it could potentially be used to flag "at-risk" individuals that require more scrutiny. We suggest for future work to analyze how the temporal change in employee psychometric values can indicate whether an individual is an insider threat.

A Preprocessing Algorithms

Algorithm 1. Preprocessing for r4.2 and r5.2

1: insiders ← LoadData("insiders.csv")
2: psychometrics ← LoadData("r4.2/psychometric.csv", "r5.2/psychometric.csv")
3: **function** PROCESS_PSYCHOMETRIC_DATA(insiders, psychometrics)
4:     **for** psychometric in psychometrics **do**
5:         **if** psychometric["user_id"] in insiders["user"] **then**
6:             psychometric["true_label"] ← 1
7:         **else**
8:             psychometric["true_label"] ← 0
9:         **end if**
10:     **end for**
11:     **return** psychometrics
12: **end function**
13: r42_data, r52_data ← PROCESS_PSYCHOMETRIC_DATA(insiders, psychometrics)

Algorithm 2. Preprocessing for r_extended

1: insiders_list ← []
2: benigns_list ← []
3: total_insiders ← 191
4: total_employees ← 1500
5: total_benigns ← total_employees - total_insiders
6: insiders ← LoadData("insiders.csv")
7: psychometrics ← LoadData(
8:     "r2/psychometric.csv", "r3.1/psychometric.csv", "r3.2/psychometric.csv",
9:     "r4.1/psychometric.csv", "r4.2/psychometric.csv", "r5.1/psychometric.csv",
10:     "r5.2/psychometric.csv", "r6.1/psychometric.csv", "r6.2/psychometric.csv")
11: psychometrics ← PROCESS_PSYCHOMETRIC_DATA(insiders, psychometrics)
12: **for** psychometric in psychometrics **do**
13:     insiders ← psychometric[psychometric["true_label"]==1]
14:     benigns ← psychometric[psychometric["true_label"]==0]
15:     benigns_count ← Round((Length(insiders) / total_insiders) * total_benigns)
16:     sampled_benigns ← Sample(benigns, benigns_count)
17:     insiders_list ← Concatenate(insiders_list, insiders)
18:     benigns_list ← Concatenate(benigns_list, sampled_benigns)
19: **end for**
20: r_extended_data ← Concatenate(insiders_list, benign_list)
21: Shuffle(r_extended_data)

Algorithm 3. Preprocessing for twos

```
1: users ← LoadData("User1.xlsx", ..., "User24.xlsx")
2: true_label ← ["User3", "User5", "User8", "User10", "User11", "User15",
3:                "User16", "User18", "User19", "User22", "User23", "User24"]
4: personality_questions ← [[O1, ..., O10], [C1, ..., C10], [E1, ..., E10],
5:                          [A1, ..., A10], [N1, ..., N10]]
6: for user in users do
7:     head ← user.iloc[0]
8:     for column in user.columns[1:-1] do
9:         for index in user.columns[1:-1] do
10:            if user[index, column] == "X" then
11:                user[index, _sum] ← head[column]
12:            else
13:                user[index, _sum] ← 0
14:            end if
15:        end for
16:    end for
17:    data[user] ← data[user] + user["_sum"].groupby[personality_question].sum()
18: end for
19: for row in data do
20:    if row["user_id"] in true_label then
21:        row["true_label"] ← 1
22:    else
23:        row["true_label"] ← 0
24:    end if
25: end for
26: twos_data ← data
```

References

1. Abbiati, G., Ranise, S., Schizzerotto, A., Siena, A.: Merging datasets of CyberSecurity incidents for fun and insight. Frontiers in Big Data (2021)
2. Ahsan, M.M., Mahmud, M.A.P., Saha, P.K., Gupta, K.D., Siddique, Z.: Effect of data scaling methods on machine learning algorithms and model performance (2021)
3. Al-Mhiqani, M.N., Ahmad, R., Zainal Abidin, Z., Yassin, W., Hassan, A., Abdulkareem, K.H., Ali, N.S., Yunos, Z.: A review of insider threat detection: Classification, machine learning techniques, datasets, open challenges, and recommendations. Applied Sciences (2020)
4. Ali, I., Wassif, K., Bayomi, H.: Dimensionality reduction for images of iot using machine learning. Scientific Reports (2024)
5. Altmann, A., Toloşi, L., Sander, O., Lengauer, T.: Permutation importance: a corrected feature importance measure. Bioinformatics (2010)
6. Athul Harilal, Flavio Toffalini, Ivan Homoliak, John Castellanos, Juan Guarnizo, Soumik Mondal, Martín Ochoa: The wolf of SUTD (TWOS): A dataset of malicious insider threat behavior based on a gamified competition. J. Wirel. Mob. Netw. Ubiquitous Comput. Dependable Appl. (2018)

7. Bergstra, J., Bengio, Y.: Random search for hyper-parameter optimization. Journal of machine learning research (2012)
8. Bishop, M., Gates, C., Frincke, D., Greitzer, F.L.: Azalia: an a to z assessment of the likelihood of insider attack. In: 2009 IEEE Conference on Technologies for Homeland Security (2009)
9. Caputo, D., Maloof, M., Stephens, G.: Detecting insider theft of trade secrets. IEEE Security & Privacy (2009)
10. Chawla, N.V., Bowyer, K.W., Hall, L.O., Kegelmeyer, W.P.: Smote: synthetic minority over-sampling technique. Journal of artificial intelligence research (2002)
11. Costa, P.T., McCrae, R.R.: Neo personality inventory-revised (NEO PI-R). Psychological Assessment Resources Odessa, FL (1992)
12. Dando, C.J., Taylor, P.J., Menacere, T., Ormerod, T.C., Ball, L.J., Sandham, A.L.: Sorting insiders from co-workers: remote synchronous computer-mediated triage for investigating insider attacks. Human Factors (2024)
13. Debeer, D., Strobl, C.: Conditional permutation importance revisited. BMC bioinformatics (2020)
14. Dosh, M.: Detecting insider threat within institutions using cert dataset and different ml techniques. Periodicals of Engineering and Natural Sciences (2021)
15. Duffy, D.E., Quiroz, a.J.: A permutation-based algorithm for block clustering. Journal of Classification (1991)
16. Egelman, S., Peer, E.: Scaling the security wall: Developing a security behavior intentions scale (sebis) (2015)
17. Frank, L., Hohimer, R.E.: Modeling human behavior to anticipate insider attacks. Journal of Strategic Security (2011)
18. Gayathri, R., Sajjanhar, A., Xiang, Y.: Hybrid deep learning model using spcagan augmentation for insider threat analysis. Expert Systems with Applications (2024)
19. Glasser, J., Lindauer, B.: Bridging the gap: A pragmatic approach to generating insider threat data. In: 2013 IEEE Security and Privacy Workshops (2013)
20. Goldberg, L.R.: An alternative "description of personality": The big-five factor structure. Journal of Personality and Social Psychology (1990)
21. Goldberg, L.R.: The development of markers for the big-five factor structure. Psychological Assessment (1992)
22. Goldberg, L.R., Johnson, J.A., Eber, H.W., Hogan, R., Ashton, M.C., Cloninger, C.R., Gough, H.G.: The international personality item pool and the future of public-domain personality measures. Journal of Research in personality (2006)
23. Gratian, M., Bandi, S., Cukier, M., Dykstra, J., Ginther, A.: Correlating human traits and cyber security behavior intentions. Computers & Security
24. Greitzer, F.L., Franklin, L.R., Edgar, T.W., Frincke, D.A.: Predictive modeling for insider threat mitigation (2009)
25. Greitzer, F.L., Frincke, D.A.: Combining traditional cyber security audit data with psychosocial data: towards predictive modeling for insider threat mitigation. Springer (2010)
26. Greitzer, F.L., Kangas, L.J., Noonan, C.F., Dalton, A.C.: Identifying at-risk employees: A behavioral model for predicting potential insider threats. Tech. rep. (2010)
27. Halevy, A.: Why your data won't mix: New tools and techniques can help ease the pain of reconciling schemas. Queue (2005)
28. Hani, U., Sohaib, O., Khan, K., Aleidi, A., Islam, N.: Psychological profiling of hackers via machine learning toward sustainable cybersecurity. Frontiers in Computer Science (2024)

29. Homoliak, I., Toffalini, F., Guarnizo, J., Elovici, Y., Ochoa, M.: Insight into insiders and it: A survey of insider threat taxonomies, analysis, modeling, and countermeasures. ACM Comput, Surv (2019)
30. Homoliak, I., Toffalini, F., Guarnizo, J., Elovici, Y., Ochoa, M.: Insight into insiders and it: A survey of insider threat taxonomies, analysis, modeling, and countermeasures (2019)
31. Janjua, F., Masood, A., Abbas, H., Rashid, I., Khan, M.M.Z.M.: Textual analysis of traitor-based dataset through semi supervised machine learning. Future Generation Computer Systems (2021)
32. John, O.P., Naumann, L.P., Soto, C.J.: Paradigm shift to the integrative big-five trait taxonomy: History, measurement, and conceptual issues. Guilford Press (2008)
33. Kandias, M., Mylonas, A., Virvilis, N., Theoharidou, M., Gritzalis, D.: An insider threat prediction model. Springer
34. Kennison, S.M., Chan-Tin, E.: Taking risks with cybersecurity: Using knowledge and personal characteristics to predict self-reported cybersecurity behaviors. Frontiers in Psychology (2020)
35. Lause, J., Berens, P., Kobak, D.: The art of seeing the elephant in the room: 2d embeddings of single-cell data do make sense. bioRxiv (2024)
36. MacCrae, R.R., Costa Jr, P.T., Costa, P.T.: Personality in adulthood. guilford Press (1990)
37. Magklaras, G.B., Furnell, S.M.: A preliminary model of end user sophistication for insider threat prediction in it systems. Computers & Security (2005)
38. Manoharan, P., Yin, J., Wang, H., Zhang, Y., Ye, W.: Insider threat detection using supervised machine learning algorithms. Telecommunication Systems (2023)
39. Marbut, A., Harms, P.: Fiends and fools: a narrative review and neo-socioanalytic perspective on personality and insider threats. Journal of Business and Psychology (2024)
40. Matulessy, A., Humaira, N.H.: Hacker personality profiles reviewed in terms of the big five personality traits. Psychology and Behavioral Sciences (2016)
41. Naidu, G., Zuva, T., Sibanda, E.M.: A review of evaluation metrics in machine learning algorithms. In: Computer Science On-line Conference. Springer (2023)
42. P. Riquelme, I., Román, S.: Is the influence of privacy and security on online trust the same for all type of consumers? Electronic Markets (2014)
43. Pattinson, M., Jerram, C., Parsons, K., McCormac, A.: Why do some people manage phishing e-mails better than others? Information Management & Computer Security (2012)
44. Roccas, S., Sagiv, L., Schwartz, S.H., Knafo, A.: The big five personality factors and personal values. Personality and social psychology bulletin (2002)
45. Ros, F., Riad, R., Guillaume, S.: Pdbi: A partitioning davies-bouldin index for clustering evaluation. Neurocomputing (2023)
46. Ruohonen, J., Saddiqa, M.: What do we know about the psychology of insider threats? (2024)
47. Schubert, E.: Stop using the elbow criterion for k-means and how to choose the number of clusters instead. ACM SIGKDD Explorations Newsletter (2023)
48. Schultz, E.E.: A framework for understanding and predicting insider attacks. Computers & security (2002)
49. Shahapure, K.R., Nicholas, C.: Cluster quality analysis using silhouette score. In: IEEE international conference on data science and advanced analytics. IEEE (2020)

50. Shappie, A.T., Dawson, C.A., Debb, S.M.: Personality as a predictor of cybersecurity behavior. Psychology of Popular Media (2020)
51. Shropshire, J., Warkentin, M., Sharma, S.: Personality, attitudes, and intentions: Predicting initial adoption of information security behavior. computers & security (2015)
52. Sorzano, C.O.S., Vargas, J., Montano, A.P.: A survey of dimensionality reduction techniques. arXiv preprint arXiv:1403.2877 (2014)
53. Tao, X., Lu, S., Zhao, F., Lan, R., Chen, L., Fu, L., Jia, R.: User behavior threat detection based on adaptive sliding window gan. IEEE Transactions on Network and Service Management (2024)
54. Verizon : 2024 Data Breach Investigations Report. https://www.verizon.com/business/resources/reports/dbir/ (2024), accessed: June 2024
55. Warkentin, M., McBride, M., Carter, L., Johnston, A.: The role of individual characteristics on insider abuse intentions (2012)
56. Wheatley, S., Maillart, T., Sornette, D.: The extreme risk of personal data breaches & the erosion of privacy. The European Physical Journal B (2015)
57. Yang, G., Cai, L., Yu, A., Ma, J., Meng, D., Wu, Y.: Potential malicious insiders detection based on a comprehensive security psychological model. IEEE (2018)
58. Yu, T., Zhu, H.: Hyper-parameter optimization: A review of algorithms and applications (2020)
59. Zheng, R., Qin, Y., Huang, Z., Chen, H.: Authorship analysis in cybercrime investigation. Springer (2003)

Identifying Insecure Network Configurations Through Attack Modeling and Explainable AI

Blessy Thomas, Sabu M. Thampi, and Preetam Mukherjee

Digital University Kerala, Thiruvananthapuram, Kerala, India
{blessy.res21,sabu.thampi,preetam.mukherjee}@duk.ac.in

Abstract. Every day, a multitude of IoT devices connect to the internet, enhancing functionality and user experience. However, this increased connectivity exposes these devices to external threats. Securing the network requires effective modeling of potential attack scenarios. The dynamic nature of IoT networks often alters these scenarios, making attack modeling challenging. In this context, identifying inappropriate network configurations that lead to insecure conditions becomes a practical alternative. Avoiding such configurations helps protect the infrastructure from threat actors. In this paper, an Explainable AI (XAI) approach using the Local Interpretable Model-Agnostic Explanations (LIME) algorithm is employed to assess the impact of various network configurations on security. The framework's effectiveness is demonstrated through a realistic IoT network example. The experiment explains how network characteristics influence insecurity, offering valuable insights into potential vulnerabilities.

Keywords: IoT Network · Attack Modeling · Explainable AI · Machine Learning

1 Introduction

The adoption of the Internet of Things (IoT) has gained a lot of traction recently due to its affordability and practical usefulness [2]. Despite numerous benefits, IoT networks are also prone to security risks and vulnerabilities, as strong security controls are often not implemented during the development of these systems [11]. Figuring out all possible attack scenarios for the IoT infrastructure is a crucial step before employing suitable defensive measures. Attack models are generated to represent attack scenarios in the network infrastructure. Analysing the attack model will help find scenarios of immediate concerns [4,7].

Attack model generation and maintenance require a lot of resources. On the other hand, IoT networks are dynamic in nature, with connectivity and vulnerability status changing frequently. It is not practical to regenerate the attack models for all the small changes in the network. In such cases, it will be helpful to know how the network configuration features, like connectivity, open ports, firewall configuration, etc., impact security.

Predicting the security status of the infrastructure directly from the network configuration features is possible without generating the attack model. In this paper, we use explainable AI (XAI) [6] to identify the improper network configurations that may lead to scenarios of security concerns. The integration of the XAI LIME (Local Interpretable Model-Agnostic Explanations) algorithm provides transparency and interpretability [9] in explaining the security critical aspects of the network.

The major contributions of the paper are as follows:

- A framework to determine the influence of various network characteristics on the security of the network.
- The XAI LIME algorithm is utilized to provide the necessary explanations for the obtained results.
- The framework is tested with the attack models generated for various network configurations of a realistic IoT network.

The rest of the paper is organized as follows: Sect. 2 puts forward a brief survey of the related literature. Network characteristics leading to the insecure scenarios are explained in Sect. 3. The proposed framework using XAI LIME algorithm is detailed in Sect. 4. Section 5 discusses the results obtained. The conclusion and future works are presented in Sect. 6.

2 Related Works

Attack graph generation and analysis to strengthen the security of any network infrastructure is a well-studied problem. The authors in [4], propose risk mitigation strategies to improve network security by generating attack graphs and removing high-risk, low-hop count paths and highly connected nodes. Cost and budget-aware network hardening solution called COBANOT, is introduced in [15], the technique iteratively removes exploits and initial conditions based on their cost until the network is secure or the budget is exhausted, thereby reducing the attack paths.

A methodology for building attack circuits using NLP-generated input/output pairs and conventional security score metrics, assessing attack circuits with optimization methods is introduced by authors in [8]. The autonomous security analysis and penetration testing framework (ASAP) in [3], uses attack graphs and a reinforcement learning algorithm to identify security threats and attack paths, generating autonomous attack plans validated against real-world networks. The work [12] offers a heuristic method for selecting optimal countermeasure deployment under budget constraints, using an upgraded attack graph model considering software and network vulnerabilities.

Meta Attack Language (MAL) is used to model the network infrastructure and generate probabilistic attack graphs in [14]. The work presents an algorithm for selecting countermeasures under various budgetary constraints by repeated analysis of optimal attack paths. Risk-based methodology for identifying and assessing attack paths for IoT-enabled critical cyber-physical systems is presented in [13]. The methodology prioritizes identified attack paths based on risk, integrating Common Vulnerabilities and Exposures (CVE) and the Common Vulnerability Scoring System (CVSS) for a structured threat modeling process. The paper [1] presents a method for creating attack graphs, focusing on locating and analyzing attack paths in complex networks, and computing risk levels for targeted mitigation strategies.

As discussed above, a significant amount of existing research addresses methods to analyze attack graphs to find insecure scenarios and prepare suitable mitigation strategies. However, there is a lack of research on finding the network configurations, which leads to potential insecurities.

3 Network Configuration Features Leading to Insecurity

Vulnerability refers to system weaknesses that attackers exploit to access critical network infrastructure. In multi-stage attacks, the attacker moves through several intermediate devices before reaching the target, exploiting each device's vulnerabilities along the way [4,7]. This movement of the attacker creates attack paths, forming a sequential chain of exploits that finally lead to accessing critical resources. Attack modeling techniques, like attack graphs or attack trees, can be used to proactively represent all potential attack paths in the network, helping to identify and mitigate these risks.

Shorter attack paths make the task easier for an attacker with relatively fewer obstacles. The increasing number of attack paths provides multiple opportunities for attackers, thereby improving the likelihood of a successful compromise. Consequently, an attack model with an increasing number of relatively shorter paths shows high security concern and requires immediate attention. Network configurations have a substantial impact on the number and length of attack paths. As an initial layer of protection, a robust firewall can stop an attacker from exploiting the existing vulnerabilities. Strongly configured and well-managed firewalls significantly decrease the number of attack paths by preventing unauthorized access and forcing attackers to choose longer and more difficult routes to reach target. On the other hand, network segmentation breaks up the network into smaller, more manageable segments, which reduces the spread of attacks and limits the number of attack paths in the network. Network segmentation strengthens security by adding more protection layers that attackers must bypass to reach valuable assets.

There are several network factors contributing to the increase in the number of shorter attack paths. Each port left open by the services running on the host/server provides an opportunity for attackers. The firewall, by allowing access to these open ports, further increases the risk by providing exposure to the internet or the potential for lateral movements. As the number of open ports increases, an attacker can choose from multiple entry points to compromise systems. It also increases the possibility of reaching critical systems through shorter attack paths, making network defense more difficult. Whereas network protocols with weak authentication and encryption mechanisms are also vulnerable to exploitation, further increasing the potential for compromise. Attackers can easily exploit outdated or insecure protocols to access the target assets. Again, the number of attack paths increases with high network density, indicating a large number of linked devices and nodes. When the connectivity among the devices is sparse, potential attack paths become longer and difficult to traverse.

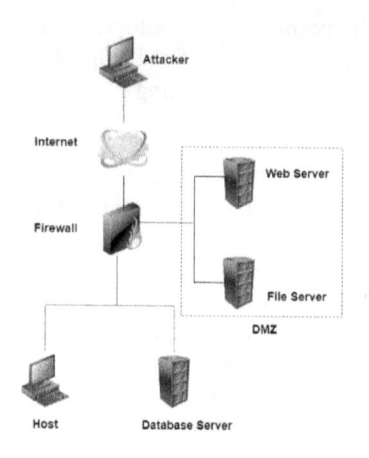

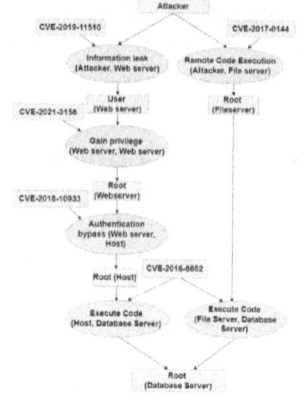

Fig. 1. Example network

Fig. 2. Attack Graph

Figure 1 presents an example of a vulnerable network. In the DMZ, a Web server and a File server are running. Port 80 (HTTP) of the Web server and port 445 (SMB) of the File server are accessible from the Internet through the firewall. In the internal network zone, a host machine and a database server are installed. While these machines are not exposed to the Internet, port 22 (SSH) of the host machine and port 3306 (MySQL) of the database server are accessible from the DMZ servers.

Figure 2 illustrates two attack paths. In the first path, the attacker may gain user access to the web server by exploiting an HTTP vulnerability. Following the initial attack, the attacker can escalate privileges by exploiting a buffer overflow vulnerability. After acquiring root access to the web server, the attacker may compromise the host machine within the internal network zone by bypassing SSH authentication. The final step in this path is made possible by the lack of network segmentation, with the host machine and the database server residing in the same network. A second, shorter attack path is also shown in the figure, where the attacker may exploit vulnerabilities in the file server and subsequently the database server. This example demonstrates that having more open ports or running unnecessary and vulnerable services creates multiple entry points for attackers. Additionally, improperly managed firewalls, flat networks without segmentation, and the use of insecure protocols further contribute to network insecurity.

4 Identification of Insecure Network Configurations

Machine learning (ML) has become essential in network security, offering advanced methods for detecting and predicting cyber threats. ML can assist in predicting the characteristics of attack paths by analyzing various network configurations. However, the complexity of ML models often leads to a "blackbox" issue, where the decision-making process remains opaque. Explainable AI (XAI) addresses this issue by interpreting and explaining the decisions made by ML models [6]. This helps the security administrators to identify the network configurations leading to an increasing number of short attack paths.

In this section, we discuss the proposed ML-XAI based framework designed to predict the characteristics of attack paths, including its quantity and length, as presented in Fig. 3.

The XAI LIME algorithm is integrated to provide the explanation for the model prediction.

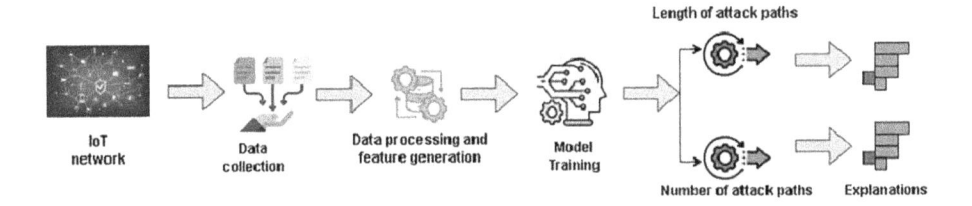

Fig. 3. Proposed framework

The data is collected through the lab-developed attack graph generation tool by adjusting the network parameters to identify the characteristics of the attack path in each network scenario. The extracted data are pre-processed, enhanced through feature generation and labeled. Binary discretization is performed to convert certain features into binary to easily find their relevance while measuring security. Binary discretization also helps in enhanced model performance. The target variables i.e. "Length of attack paths" and "Number of attack paths," are also converted into binary using suitable threshold values.

The resulting data was then employed for the training and testing of the machine learning model that is designed to predict the number and length of attack paths. We utilised K-Nearest Neighbors (KNN) algorithm as it is well suited for our multi-output classification problem. KNN effectively captures the relationship between features and target variables by evaluating the proximity of data points. The LIME algorithm explains the importance of features contributing to the prediction in each network scenario. Algorithm 1 describes the process of identifying feature importance contributing insecure network configurations.

Algorithm 1 Identify Insecure Network Configurations

Input Features F, Target Variables C, Number of Neighbors K
Output Predicted Labels Y, Explanations $\epsilon_1(x_i)$, $\epsilon_2(x_i)$
function FEATUREENGINEERING(F, C)
    for each feature that needs to be converted into binary where $f_i \in F$ **do**
        Apply binary discretization:
        if f_i is present **then**
            $f_i^{bin} \leftarrow 1$
        else
            $f_i^{bin} \leftarrow 0$
        end if
    end for
    for each target variable where $c_i \in C$ **do**
        Apply binary discretization:
        if $c_i >$ threshold **then**
            $c_i^{bin} \leftarrow 1$
        else
            $c_i^{bin} \leftarrow 0$
        end if
    end for
    Compute correlation for each feature $f_i^{bin} \cup F$ and target c_i
    return Preprocessed Features F_P and target variables C_P
end function
function TRAINKNN(D, K)
    for each data point d_i in D **do**
        Compute distances between d_i and all other data points in D
        Sort distances and select K nearest neighbors for each d_i
        for each c_i in $C_p \in D$ **do**
            Perform majority vote on class labels of K neighbors to determine y_i
        end for
    end for
    return Predicted Labels Y
end function
function GENERATEEXPLANATIONS(D, K, Y)
    for each input sample $x_i \in D$ **do**
        Generate perturbed instances $\{x_i'\}$ around x_i
        Predict labels $f(x_i')$ for $\{x_i'\}$ using the KNN model
        Assign weights π_{x_i} to $\{x_i'\}$ based on their proximity to x_i
        for each target variable c_i in $C_p \in D$ **do**
            Train an interpretable model g on $\{x_i'\}$ and their predictions $f(x_i')$
            Feature importance scores $\beta_j =$ coefficients from g
            $\epsilon_1(x_i) \leftarrow \{\beta_{j,1}, \beta_{j,2}, \ldots, \beta_{j,m}\}$
            $\epsilon_2(x_i) \leftarrow \{\beta_{j,1}, \beta_{j,2}, \ldots, \beta_{j,m}\}$
        end for
    end for
    return Explanations $\epsilon_1(x_i)$, $\epsilon_2(x_i)$
end function
function MAIN(F, C, K)
    $F_P, C_P \leftarrow$ featureEngineering(F, C)
    Process dataset $D \leftarrow F_P, C_P$
    $Y \leftarrow$ TrainKNN(D, K)
    $\epsilon_1(x_i), \epsilon_2(x_i) \leftarrow$ GenerateExplanations(D, K, Y)
    return Predicted Labels Y, Explanations $\epsilon_1(x_i)$, $\epsilon_2(x_i)$
end function

The dataset in a KNN model is defined as $D = \{d_1, d_2, \ldots, d_n\}$, where each d_i represents a data point in the dataset. Each data point is described by multiple dimensions (features) such as the number of open ports, firewall strength, and other characteristics. This dataset D is associated with a set of target variables, $C = \{C_1, C_2\}$, where C_1 and C_2 denote the two target variables of the classification task.

An input sample for classification is represented by $X = \{x_1, x_2, \ldots, x_n\}$, and the corresponding output labels for the classification are given as $Y = \{y_1, y_2\}$, with y_1 and y_2 pertaining to the respective target variables.

In KNN, the Euclidean distance is used to find the K nearest neighbors - that is, the K most similar network configurations to the input data point X, based on their feature similarities. This distance is computed as:

$$\text{Dist}(X, d_i) = \sqrt{\sum_{k=1}^{m}(X_k - d_{ik})^2} \tag{1}$$

where X is the input vector (representing a data point), d_i representing another data point in D, m is the number of features in each vector, X_k is the k-th feature of vector X, and d_{ik} is the k-th feature of data point d_i [5].

A distance matrix is constructed to capture the Euclidean distances between the vector X and the data set D within n data points. The algorithm then sorts these distances and selects the K smallest, identifying the nearest neighbors. Each neighbor d_i comes with associated class labels for each target variable, typically represented as $\{c_{i1}, c_{i2}\}$ for multi-output classification. The final label for each target variable is determined by a majority vote among the labels of these K nearest neighbors, independently for each target.

Local Interpretable Model-agnostic Explanations (LIME) significantly enhance the interpretability of KNN's predictions by explaining the algorithm's outcomes across diverse network scenarios. Specifically, LIME clarifies the reasoning behind the KNN's predictions concerning the increase or decrease of attack paths, as well as variations in their lengths. Network administrators can thus obtain a deeper understanding of the security dynamics within their networks. The insights delivered will enable organizations to make more informed decisions and optimize strategic planning to strengthen network defenses.

The following equation of LIME [10] aims to minimize the loss L and assess how well the explanation matches the original model. The term $\epsilon(x)$ represents the explanation for the instance x of the model g.

$$\epsilon_j(x) = \arg\min_{g_j} \left(L(f_j, g_j, \pi_x) + \Omega(g_j) \right) \tag{2}$$

For each target variable c_j in C, the interpretable model g_j is trained to minimize the weighted loss function:

- $L(f_j, g_j, \pi_x)$ is the loss function that measures how well the interpretable model g_j approximates the complex model f_j on the perturbed instances, weighted by π_x.

- $\Omega(g_j)$ is a regularization term that ensures the complexity of the interpretable model g_j is kept in check.
- π_x is the weighting function that assigns higher weights to perturbed instances closer to the original instance x.

The integration of LIME along with KNN model in the framework helps in understanding the security status of the network and efficient decision making.

5 Experimental Results

5.1 Experimental Setup

In this section, the proposed framework is evaluated on different machine learning models that predict the number and length of attack paths with multi-output classification using the data gathered from the attack graph generation tool. For the number of attack paths, the predicted classes are *More Paths* or *Few Paths*, and for the length of attack paths, the classes are *Longer Paths* or *Shorter Paths*.

We have investigated and analyzed the security flaws of an IoT network in a smart city use case. The models that were evaluated are K-Nearest Neighbour (KNN), Support Vector Machine (SVM), Naive Bayes (NB), Random Forest (RF) and Logistic Regression (LR). The LIME algorithm is incorporated with the best-performing model KNN to provide an interpretation of model prediction.

Dataset. Data is collected by systematically altering the characteristics of the input IoT network to generate characteristic attack graphs. Network features such as the number of open ports (`no_of_ports`), firewall strength (`firewall_strength`), network segmentation (`network_seg`), insecure protocol (`insecure_protocol`), and network density (`network_density`) are considered as independent variables, with the length and number of attack paths as target variables. Binary discretization transforms continuous data into binary variables indicating the presence or absence of features (except for the number of open ports) to enhance model performance. The dataset is split into training (70%) and testing (30%) subsets for the KNN model using five neighbors. The model used a MultiOutputClassifier to predict multiple target variables simultaneously. The LIME approach is integrated to improve model interpretability by explaining how specific features affect prediction outcomes.

5.2 Results and Discussion

The KNN model's performance is evaluated using key metrics for each output variable: "number of attack paths" and "length of attack paths." Confusion matrices for both outputs are shown in Table 1 and Table 2, respectively, and ROC curves are presented in Fig. 4. Additionally, accuracy, precision, recall, and F1 scores for different models are detailed in Table 3 and Table 4. KNN performs well by classifying based on the distance from the closest data points. This ability is consistent with KNN's use of the nearest neighbor majority voting technique, effectively predicting classes from overlapping data points in well-defined target variable groups. The predictions of the KNN multi-output classifier are explained using the LIME algorithm as shown in Fig. 5. The model accurately predicted the number of attack paths as *"More Paths"* and the length of attack paths as *"Shorter Paths"* for the particular instance. For *"More Attack Paths"*, the most influential feature is `no_of_ports` with a value greater than 50, contributing a weight of 0.38. The absence of `firewall_strength` and `network_seg`, both with values of 0.00, have weights of 0.19 and 0.18, respectively. Features like `insecure_protocol` and `network_density` with values of 1.00 also impact the prediction slightly. For predicting *"Shorter Paths"*, `no_of_ports` is a significant factor with a weight of 0.20. The absence of `network_seg` and `firewall_strength`, both with values of 0.00, contribute equally with weights of 0.12 each. The presence of `network_density` with a value of 1.00 supports longer paths but is outweighed by other features, leading to a confident prediction of shorter attack paths. The key features influencing these predictions include the number of open ports, with higher values increasing both the number and length of potential attack paths. This highlights the importance of robust network configuration, reducing unnecessary open ports, and improving firewall and network segmentation to mitigate security risks.

Figure 6 shows attack paths generated from the attack graph generator reflecting the network feature values discussed. The figure reflects a number of short paths, highlighting the need for more secure network settings to protect against potential vulnerabilities. This indicates that all paths in the network are critical, necessitating enhanced security measures.

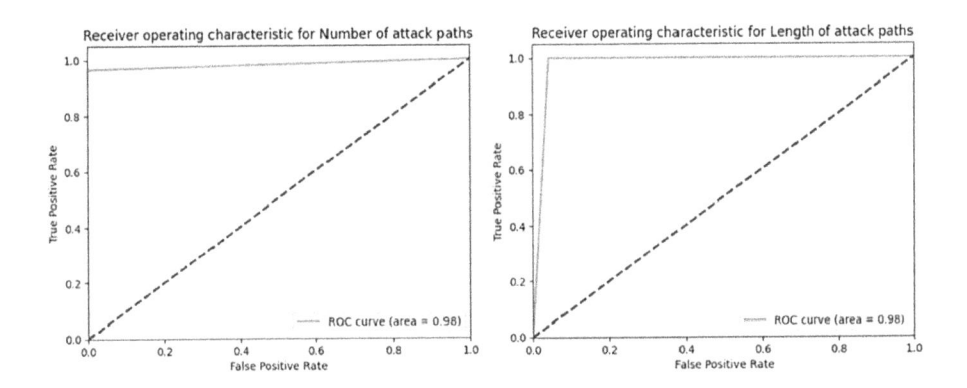

Fig. 4. ROC curve for KNN model

Table 1. Confusion Matrix for KNN Model - Length of Attack Paths

Prediction/Actual	Positive	Negative
Positive	292	5
Negative	6	283

Table 2. Confusion Matrix for KNN Model - Number of Attack Paths

Prediction/Actual	Positive	Negative
Positive	292	5
Negative	6	283

Table 3. Performance Metrics for Length of Attack Paths Across Different Models

Model	Accuracy	Precision	Recall	F1 Score
SVC	0.9683	0.9664	0.9698	0.9679
Naive Bayes	0.9761	0.9750	0.9768	0.9758
Random Forest	0.9762	0.9741	0.9789	0.9759
Decision Tree	0.9762	0.9741	0.9789	0.9759
KNN	0.9812	0.9832	0.9798	0.9815

Table 4. Performance Metrics for Number of Attack Paths Across Different Models

Model	Accuracy	Precision	Recall	F1 Score
SVC	0.4524	0.2262	0.5000	0.3115
Naive Bayes	0.9662	0.9668	0.9652	0.9659
Random Forest	0.9683	0.9698	0.9664	0.9679
Decision Tree	0.9683	0.9698	0.9664	0.9679
KNN	0.9752	0.9731	0.9798	0.9764

Explanation for Number of Attack Paths

Prediction probabilities — Fewer Paths / More Paths

0: 0.00
1: 1.00

- 50.00 < no_of_ports <... 0.38
- firewall_strength <= 0.00 : 0.19
- network_seg <= 0.00 : 0.18
- 0.00 < insecure_proto... : 0.02
- 0.00 < network_densit... : 0.01

Feature	Value
no_of_ports	52.00
firewall_strength	0.00
network_seg	0.00
insecure_protocol	1.00
network_density	1.00

Explanation for length of Attack Paths

Prediction probabilities — Longer Paths / Shorter Paths

0: 0.00
1: 1.00

- 50.00 < no_of_ports <... 0.20
- network_seg <= 0.00 : 0.12
- firewall_strength <= 0.00 : 0.12
- 0.00 < network_densit... : 0.02
- 0.00 < insecure_proto... : 0.01

Feature	Value
no_of_ports	52.00
network_seg	0.00
firewall_strength	0.00
network_density	1.00
insecure_protocol	1.00

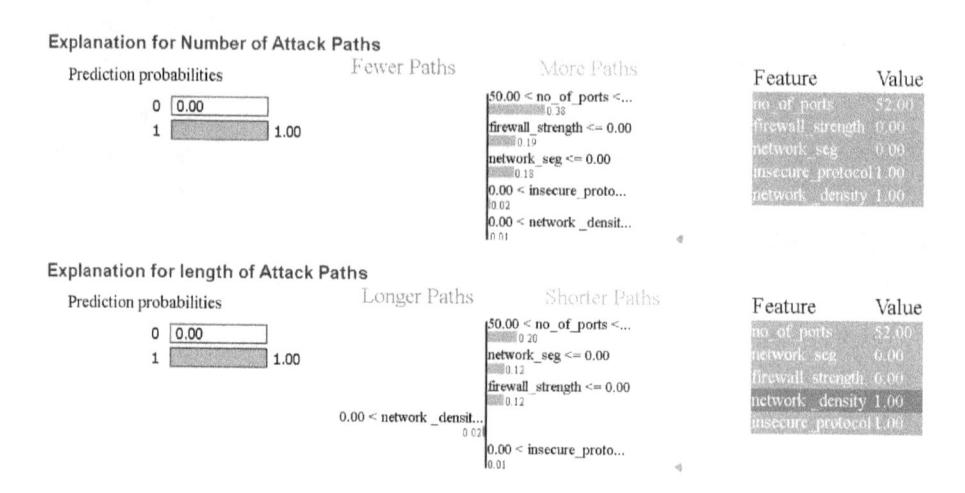

Fig. 5. Explanations for attack paths

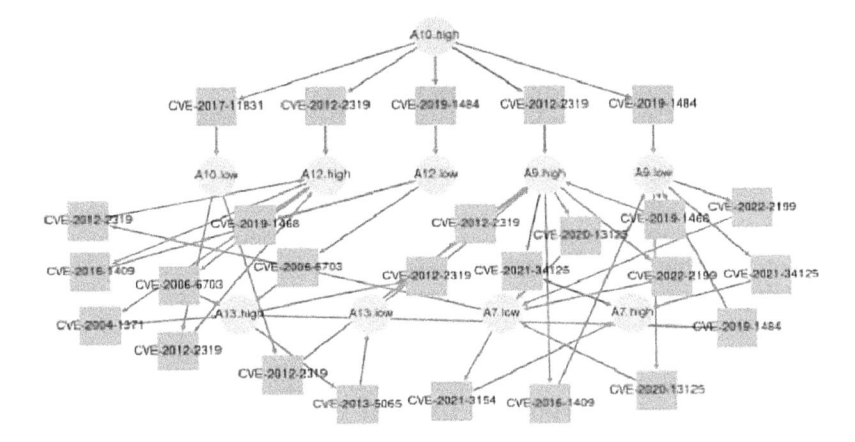

Fig. 6. Attack paths generated by the attack graph generator tool

6 Conclusion and Future Work

This paper has shown a novel way to determine the IoT network characteristics that lead to security concerns. Attack modeling is used to represent the insecure scenarios. The Explainable AI algorithm LIME is integrated into the framework to improve the interpretability of model decisions by explaining the network features that contribute to insecure network scenarios. These insights will secure IoT environments against potential cyber threats by facilitating the development of more efficient and focused measures to avoid insecure network configurations. In the future, we intend to test the framework in real-world IoT networks to check its performance in proactively identifying different insecure network configurations. The framework will also be extended to include finer network characteristics in the decision making process.

References

1. Arat, F., Akleylek, S.: A new method for vulnerability and risk assessment of IoT. Comput. Netw. **237**, 110046 (2023)
2. Brous, P., Janssen, M., Herder, P.: The dual effects of the internet of things (IoT): a systematic review of the benefits and risks of IoT adoption by organizations. Int. J. Inf. Manage. **51**, 101952 (2020)
3. Chowdhary, A., Huang, D., Mahendran, J.S., Romo, D., Deng, Y., Sabur, A.: Autonomous security analysis and penetration testing. In: 2020 16th International Conference on Mobility. Sensing and Networking (MSN), pp. 508–515. IEEE, Tokyo, Japan (2020)
4. George, G., Thampi, S.M.: A graph-based security framework for securing industrial IoT networks from vulnerability exploitations. IEEE Access **6**, 43586–43601 (2018)

5. Lakshminarayana, S.K., Basarkod, P.I.: Unification of K-nearest neighbor (KNN) with distance aware algorithm for intrusion detection in evolving networks like IoT. Wireless Pers. Commun. **132**(3), 2255–2281 (2023)
6. Linardatos, P., Papastefanopoulos, V., Kotsiantis, S.: Explainable AI: a review of machine learning interpretability methods. Entropy **23**(1), 18 (2020)
7. Mukherjee, P., Mazumdar, C.: Attack difficulty metric for assessment of network security. In: Proceedings of the 13th International Conference on Availability, Reliability and Security, pp. 1–10. ACM, Hamburg, Germany (2018)
8. Payne, J., Budhraja, K., Kundu, A.: How secure is your IoT network? In: 2019 IEEE International Congress on Internet of Things (ICIOT), pp. 181–188. IEEE, Milan, Italy (2019)
9. Ribeiro, M.T., Singh, S., Guestrin, C.: "Why should I trust you?" explaining the predictions of any classifier. In: Proceedings of the 22nd ACM SIGKDD International Conference on Knowledge Discovery and Data Mining, pp. 1135–1144. ACM, San Francisco, California (2016)
10. Sharma, B., Sharma, L., Lal, C., Roy, S.: Explainable artificial intelligence for intrusion detection in IoT networks: a deep learning based approach. Expert Syst. Appl. **(238)**, 121751 (2024)
11. Srivastava, A., Gupta, S., Quamara, M., Chaudhary, P., Aski, V.J.: Future IoT-enabled threats and vulnerabilities: state of the art, challenges, and future prospects. Int. J. Commun Syst **33**(12), e4443 (2020)
12. Stan, O., et al.: Heuristic approach for countermeasure selection using attack graphs. In: 2021 IEEE 34th Computer Security Foundations Symposium (CSF), pp. 1–16. IEEE, Virtual Conference (2021)
13. Stellios, I., Kotzanikolaou, P., Grigoriadis, C.: Assessing IoT enabled cyber-physical attack paths against critical systems. Comput. Secur. **107**, 102316 (2021)
14. Widel, W., Mukherjee, P., Ekstedt, M.: Security countermeasures selection using the meta attack language and probabilistic attack graphs. IEEE Access **10**, 89645–89662 (2022)
15. Yigit, B., Gür, G., Alagöz, F., Tellenbach, B.: Cost-aware securing of IoT systems using attack graphs. Ad Hoc Netw. **86**, 23–35 (2019)

QIris: Quantum Implementation of Rainbow Table Attacks

Lee Jun Quan, Tan Jia Ye, Goh Geok Ling, and Vivek Balachandran[(✉)]

Singapore Institute of Technology, Singapore, Singapore
{2201509,2201862,2202614}@sit.singaporetech.edu.sg,
vivek.b@singaporetech.edu.sg

Abstract. This paper explores the use of Grover's Algorithm in the classical rainbow table, uncovering the potential of integrating quantum computing techniques with conventional cryptographic methods to develop a Quantum Rainbow Table. It leverages on quantum concepts and algorithms, including the principles of qubit superposition, entanglement, and teleportation, coupled with Grover's Algorithm, to enable a more efficient search through the rainbow table. The paper also details the current hardware constraints and a workaround to produce better results in the implementation stages. Through this work, we develop a working prototype of the quantum rainbow table and demonstrate how quantum computing could significantly improve the speed of cyber tools such as password crackers and thus impacting the cybersecurity landscape.

Keywords: Rainbow Table · Hashing · Grover's Algorithm · Quantum Security

1 Introduction

In this paper, we explore the potential of using quantum computing to improve the speed of cracking hashes in legacy systems, which opens to new possibilities, highlighting the need for quantum-resilient cryptographic techniques. This research aims to create a Quantum Rainbow Table, merging and applying principles of quantum mechanics together with Grover's Algorithm [1]. This exhibits the abilities of quantum-assisted search techniques, placing emphasis on the impact quantum computing has on cryptographic analysis. The goal is to explore potential implications of quantum computing on cryptography, with the aim of contributing to advancements in cybersecurity practices.

1.1 Background

Safeguarding of password data is critical in the cybersecurity landscape. In most systems, passwords are stored as cryptographic hash values and not in plaintext, in order to prevent attackers from accessing such confidential information. However, if the attackers manage to obtain this information, they would then be able to devise methods to compare the hashes using a precomputed table, known as a Rainbow Table. These tables store the output of values put through a hash function, which then enables attackers to conduct rapid searching of said hashes in order to decipher encrypted passwords [2] in an efficient and effective manner [3]. Our work explores the potential of using the prowess of quantum computing in order to expand on this efficiency in a manner greater than that of classical search algorithms.

1.2 Motivations

Classical rainbow tables typically involve a linear search through the table, resulting in a worst-case time complexity of $O(N)$, where N is defined as the number of entries in the table. On the other hand, by leveraging Grover's Algorithm, a quantum algorithm designed for searching unsorted tables, the time complexity for the searches can be significantly reduced. In comparison to classical methods [4], Grover's Algorithm runs with a time complexity of $O(\sqrt{N})$ iterations, which is a quadratic improvement in the time taken for the search process. However, searching using Grover's Algorithm will indicate if the target entry exists within the database but it does not return the target's position or identity. Hence, in order to determine the exact position and identity of the target entry, additional steps are needed [1].

To the best of our knowledge, no practical quantum solutions have been explored for rainbow table searches with MD5 hashes. However, a study identifying the quantum resources required for applying Grover's Algorithm to extract keys from a small number of AES plaintext-ciphertext pairs is discussed in [5].

In recent years, quantum properties have been increasingly leveraged to enhance classical cybersecurity implementations, including works in opaque quantum predicate used in hybrid quantum-classical systems with a high level of accuracy [6], development of a quantum key distribution protocol [7], and a quantum implementation of AES [8]. However, in the domain of rainbow tables, the closest work that we could find was a theoretical work on Hellman's time-memory trade-off on the Rainbow Table variant [9]. These are the motivations for this work to develop a working prototype of the quantum rainbow table, providing a practical implementation to validate theoretical works in this space.

1.3 Proposed Approach

In QIris, MD5 hashing was selected to showcase the prototype's feasibility. The implementation is flexible and can be adapted to work with other hashing algorithms with minor code modification, which will be explained and indicated in the subsection on Rainbow Table Generation. This hybrid quantum-classical approach combines Grover's Algorithm with classical pre-processing checks on buckets for matches. Grover's Algorithm helps narrow down the search space by identifying the bucket, followed by performing a classical check on the bucket to determine the specific match. This hybrid approach exhibits the quantum speedup for search as compared to linear search with a worst-case time complexity of $O(N)$, ensuring that QIris can find and identify the correct plaintext in a quantum-efficient manner. QIris was developed using Python, utilizing various packages and libraries. These include Qiskit (version 1.1.0) with modules such as quantum_info, transpiler, and circuit, Qiskit Aer (version 0.14.2) for simulation with the Aer library, along with numpy (version 1.26.4) and tweedledum (version 1.1.1) to support the necessary computations and quantum operations.

Limitations and Assumptions. Throughout the development of QIris, we faced substantial hardware and processing constraints, resulting in a 4-qubit implementation of the Quantum Rainbow Table. To adhere to the constraints of quantum circuits, it is necessary to employ a simplified alternative hashing method [10], which leads to a higher hash collision. In an ideal situation without hardware constraints, the number of qubits would have no limitations, there would not be a need to implement any further hashing, and the plaintext can be represented in their ASCII binary representation. However, this would require a large number of qubits; for instance, a single character would need 8 qubits to be represented in a quantum circuit. To circumvent this limitation, keywords were mapped into 4 bit qubits representation using a simplified hash.

In addition to hardware limitations, we worked on quantum simulators for this paper instead of real quantum computers. The quantum simulator provided an idealized version of a quantum computer on classical machines to test our work and bypasses the limitations of not having access to quantum hardware. However, this approach also means that potential quantum errors and the nuanced realities of physical quantum operations were not accounted for, as the simulators operated under the assumption of ideal quantum behavior. This assumption provided a controlled environment for algorithm development and testing, but may not fully represent the challenges encountered on actual quantum hardware.

Our implementation of the Grover's Algorithm outputs a boolean value indicating the presence of a target in a search space (bucket). In order to obtain the position of the value in the bucket, the use of classical linear search is needed following the application of Grover's Algorithm.

2 Methodology

QIris aims to leverage on the speed advantages of quantum computing to enhance the classical rainbow table approach. As described in Sect. 1, Grover's Algorithm, with a time complexity of $O(\sqrt{N})$, can significantly improve search efficiency. By using Grover's Algorithm to replace parts of the linear search process, QIris achieves a faster overall time complexity. The creation of the rainbow tables and the buckets used in QIris is a one-time process as they remain static, hence, this will not be factored in the time complexity. Meanwhile, the search for a specific hash within these tables is a dynamic process that occurs at runtime, hence, this will be factored into the time complexity, where Grover's Algorithm is employed to accelerate the search. Figure 1 shows the flow of QIris during runtime.

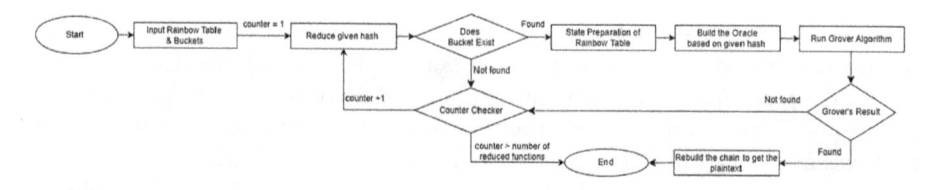

Fig. 1. Methodology of QIris.

2.1 Rainbow Table Generation And Buckets Creation

Rainbow Table Generation. The rainbow table utilized in QIris is generated by pre-computing and storing both the initial chain plaintext and the final reduction plaintext into a text file format (.txt) file. To increase the table's efficacy and diversity, four distinct reduction functions (R1, R2, R3, and R4) were used in its construction. Each reduction function converts the hash value into a plaintext of different lengths, which increases the plaintext's diversity and raises the likelihood of a successful match. The input to the reduction function is the MD5-hashed value of the plaintext starting from the initial list in the rainbow table chain.

In our implementation of the reduction function, the first 8 characters of the hash are mapped to an integer. Each reduction function adds a unique nonce, N, to this integer (N = 2 for R1, N = 3 for R2, N = 4 for R3 and N = 1 for R4). This integer is then converted to a plaintext by extracting numbers through modulus operation and mapping them to the base62 encoded character set ([0–9, a-z, A-Z]). This process is repeated X number of times (X = 6 for R1, X = 4 for R2, X = 5 for R3 and X = 3 for R4). The plaintext generated from R1 is hashed and acts as the input for R2. Similarly, the hashed plaintext from R2 is given as input to R3 and so on. In our implementation, the chain length is four. However, longer chain lengths can improve the performance of the rainbow table. The python code for the reduction function is shown in Listing 1.1.

```
def reduction_function(md5_hash):
    hash_int = int(md5_hash[:8], 16) + N
    plaintext = ""
    for _ in range(X):
        plaintext += base62_characters[hash_int % 62]
        hash_int //= 62
    return plaintext
```

Listing 1.1. Reduction Function

Bucket Creation. QIris employs a bucket strategy to streamline the search process by organizing hashes into predefined groups, termed "buckets". This strategy reduces the search space that Grover's Algorithm needs to process, thereby improving the efficiency of search through the rainbow table. This method optimizes the overall performance by ensuring that Grover's Algorithm operates on a smaller search space, thereby accelerating the post-search process.

The final reduced plaintext is hashed using Pearson's simplified alternative hashing method [10], transforming it into a 16-bit integer. These integers are then stored in buckets of size 16. Specifically, integers in the range 0–15 are placed in bucket 0, those from 16–31 in bucket 1, and so forth. Once the bucket key is derived from the plaintext, the integer is inserted into the corresponding bucket using a modulo-16 operation. If a bucket corresponding to the computed bucket key does not already exist, a new bucket is created to accommodate the value. The code for the simplified alternative hashing method is shown in Listing 1.2 and the creation of buckets in Listing 1.3.

```
random.seed(44)
permutation_16bit = list(range(65535))
random.shuffle(permutation_16bit)
def hash16bit(txt):
    h = len(txt) % 65535
    for i in txt:
        h = permuation_16bit[(h + ord(i)) % 65535]
    return h
```

Listing 1.2. Simplified Hashing

```
end_hashed = hash16bit(end)
bucket_key = end_hashed // 16
if bucket_key not in buckets:
    buckets[bucket_key] = []
buckets[bucket_key].append(end_hashed % 16)
```

Listing 1.3. Bucket Creation

2.2 Iterative Implementation

In a classical rainbow table the MD5 hash is reduced to plaintext and a linear search is conducted on a list of plaintexts at the end of rainbow table chains. In QIris, we reduce the hash to a plaintext target, T_1, using our reduction functions and then proceed to search it in the buckets. A classical linear search is performed to verify that the bucket key of T_1 exists. Grover's algorithm is then used to search for the specific target T_1 in the bucket. If the bucket key does not exist in the bucket list, QIris skips the Grover's search and subsequent linear search, moving directly to the previous chain, thus saving time. After Grover's search, if the result is found, a linear search is performed to locate for the given hash and rebuild the chain to retrieve the plaintext. If the result is not found, QIris will move on to the previous chain. This process continues until QIris has examined all four chains. If the hash is not found in any of the chains, QIris concludes with the hash being deemed not present in the rainbow table. The code for this implementation is presented in Listing 1.4.

```
funcs = get_reduction_function()
    for i in range(len(funcs)):
        i += 1
        funcs_to_use = funcs[-i:]
        remaining_funcs = funcs[:-i]
        current_hash = search_hash
        for j in range(len(funcs_to_use)):
            current_text = funcs_to_use[j](current_hash)
            if j != len(funcs_to_use) - 1:
                current_hash = md5_hash(current_text)
        current_map = hash16bit(current_text)
        bucket_key = current_map // 16
        if bucket_key not in buckets:
            continue
        good_states = buckets[bucket_key]
        lookup = current_map % 16
        if len(good_states) <= 2:
            if lookup in good_states:
                grover_result = True
            else:
                grover_result = False
        Else:
            Grover Search Codes
            if Grover Search Counts > 512:
                grover_result = True
            else:
                grover_result = False
        if grover_result is True:
            index = rainbow_table_end_hashed.index(
                current_map)
            if current_text != rainbow_table_end[index]:
                continue
            current_text = rainbow_table_start[index]
            current_hash = md5_hash(current_text)
            for k in range(len(remaining_funcs)):
                current_text = remaining_funcs[k](
                    current_hash)
                current_hash = md5_hash(current_text)
            if current_hash == search_hash:
                return current_text
    return None
```

Listing 1.4. Interative Implementation

2.3 Quantum Implementation

State Preparation. State preparation is an essential process in quantum computing that involves setting up the quantum system to the desired state before performing any quantum operations. When a quantum circuit is initialized, all qubits are set to the state |0. In a typical state preparation step, qubits are changed to be in the desired state, which generally is a superposition of states. In QIris, the state preparation involves setting the search space in which Grover's Algorithm is applied.

Assume that in a 4-qubit quantum circuit, the potential measurement outcomes range from binary 0000 to 1111, which correspond to integers 0 to 15. If there are only 7 items (1, 2, 8, 9, 10, 12, 15) in the search space (array elements), the probability of measuring the other 8 items will be 0. Therefore, in this case, the state preparation will be configured to ensure that the measurement outcomes are limited to these 7 items only.

To set the state preparation for the above example, an array [0, 1, 1, 0, 0, 0, 0, 0, 1, 1, 1, 0, 1, 0, 0, 1] with the positions 1, 2, 8, 9, 10, 12, 15 marked to be part of the superposition representation. The Frobenius norm [11] of the array is then calculated. Subsequently, the elements in the array are converted to probability amplitude values through the division of each element with the calculated Frobenius norm. The superposition of for the above array can be expressed as:

$$\frac{1}{\sqrt{7}}|1\rangle + \frac{1}{\sqrt{7}}|2\rangle + \frac{1}{\sqrt{7}}|8\rangle + \frac{1}{\sqrt{7}}|9\rangle + \frac{1}{\sqrt{7}}|10\rangle + \frac{1}{\sqrt{7}}|12\rangle + \frac{1}{\sqrt{7}}|15\rangle$$

To derive $\frac{1}{\sqrt{7}}$ as the probability amplitude, the Frobenius norm for the array is calculated to be $\sqrt{7}$. Therefore, each element that has a non-zero value in the array is divided by the Frobenius norm to create the final array:

$$[0, \frac{1}{\sqrt{7}}, \frac{1}{\sqrt{7}}, 0, 0, 0, 0, 0, \frac{1}{\sqrt{7}}, \frac{1}{\sqrt{7}}, \frac{1}{\sqrt{7}}, 0, \frac{1}{\sqrt{7}}, 0, 0, \frac{1}{\sqrt{7}}]$$

This array is then passed to the Statevector function to generate the state preparation circuit. The concept above is utilized in QIris during the state preparation process. The code used to generate the state preparation is shown in Listing 1.5.

```
norm = np.linalg.norm(data)
data = data / norm
state = Statevector(data)
```

Listing 1.5. State Preparation

Grover's Algorithm. Grover's Algorithm comprises two main components: the oracle and the amplitude amplification. The oracle marks the computational basis state as the state that it is interested in finding, while the amplitude amplification increases the amplitude of the marked state [12].

The oracle generate function is implemented to generate the oracle for the Grover's Algorithm based on the target hash lookup value. The input is first converted to binary representation in little endian format before being transformed into a boolean expression. The boolean expression is then passed into the Phase-Oracle function from qiskit.circuit.library, which will generate the oracle circuit. The code for the oracle circuit is shown in Listing 1.6.

```
def oracle_generate(target_state):
    binary_string = format(target_state, '04b')[::-1]
    boolean_expression = ""
    for x in range(len(binary_string)):
        if binary_string[x] == "0":
            boolean_expression += f"~x{x} & "
        else:
            boolean_expression += f"x{x} & "
    boolean_string = boolean_expression[:-3]
    return PhaseOracle(boolean_string)
```

Listing 1.6. Oracle Generation

The algorithm then uses an amplification circuit, also known as the diffusion operator, which amplifies the probability of measuring the correct state. The process involves repeatedly applying the oracle and the amplifier a certain number of times, which is determined by the formula:

$$\left\lfloor \frac{\pi}{4} \times \sqrt{N} \right\rfloor \tag{1}$$

where N equals the number of elements in the search space

The GroverAlgo function is implemented to generate the complete Grover's algorithm circuit and run the circuit through the simulator. Firstly, the Grover operation circuit is generated by passing through the oracle and state preparation circuit to the GroverOperator function. This Grover circuit is then appended to the end of the state preparation, with the number of iterations determined based on the formula (1) for the optimal number of iterations. At the end of the circuit, all qubits are marked for measurement. The final Grover's algorithm circuit is then transpiled and send to the simulator.

```
def GroverAlgo(init_state, oracle, iter, bits):
    grover = GroverOperator(oracle, state_preparation=
        init_state)
    for _ in range(iter):
        init_state.append(grover, range(bits))
    init_state.measure_all()
    backend = Aer.get_backend('qasm_simulator')
    compiled_circuit = transpile(init_state, backend)
    job = backend.run(compiled_circuit)
    counts = job.result().get_counts()
    return counts
```

Listing 1.7. Grover's Algorithm Function

To determine whether the Grover's Algorithm has successfully found the target state, we evaluate the result based on the measurement counts. Specifically, the state with the highest count must represent more than 50% of the total shots. In QIris, the total number of shots is set to 1024, so the maximum count for a state must exceed 512 for the algorithm to be considered successful.

3 Future Works

With this Quantum Rainbow Table, QIris demonstrates a hybrid approach that integrates classical linear search with quantum computing techniques. Moving forward, several avenues for future work are envisioned. Firstly, exploring and implementing the use of other hash functions, such as SHA-1 and SHA-2, to evaluate the versatility and performance associated with different hashing algorithms. The main focus will be on the speed of quantum computers as well as the hashing process, emphasizing the time efficiency of classical and quantum hashing. Furthermore, this project opens the possibility of exploring concepts like quantum salt, where the salt value is placed in a superposition state, which could potentially lead to significant improvements in the security and efficiency of hashing processes. Lastly, more studies will be required to investigate the feasibility of these innovations and assess various ways to optimize both classical and quantum hashing techniques. This research direction could pave the way for more advanced cryptographic methods and applications, leveraging the full potential of quantum computing.

4 Conclusion

Our work explores the forefront of integrating quantum computing with classical techniques to enhance the rainbow table, culminating in the development of QIris, a Quantum Rainbow Table. By utilizing Grover's algorithm, QIris operates with a search time complexity of $O(\sqrt{N})$, as opposed to the classical rainbow table's $O(N)$, thereby demonstrating the computational advantages of quantum computing. This hybrid approach effectively combines classical and quantum methods, overcoming hardware limitations. We anticipate that our implementation of the quantum rainbow table will serve as a valuable tool for researchers to further investigate quantum-based hash attacks. In addition, our research underscores the potential of quantum computing in cybersecurity, encompassing a variety of projects outlined in future works. QIris represents a novel application of quantum computing to cryptographic analysis, with the expectation that it will open new avenues for more secure systems as quantum hardware continues to evolve.

References

1. Younes, A.: Strength and weakness in grover's quantum search algorithm. arXiv preprint arXiv:0811.4481 (2008)

2. Oechslin, P.: Making a faster cryptanalytic time-memory trade-off. In: Boneh, D. (ed.) CRYPTO 2003. LNCS, vol. 2729, pp. 617–630. Springer, Heidelberg (2003). https://doi.org/10.1007/978-3-540-45146-4_36
3. Kumar, H., Kumar, S., Joseph, R., et al.: Rainbow table to crack password using md5 hashing algorithm. In: 2013 IEEE Conference on Information & Communication Technologies, pp. 433–439. IEEE (2013)
4. Khurana, S., Nene, M.J.: Implementation of database search with quantum computing: Grover's algorithm vs linear search. In: 2023 International Conference on Ambient Intelligence, Knowledge Informatics and Industrial Electronics (AIKIIE), pp. 1–6. IEEE (2023)
5. Grassl, M., Langenberg, B., Roetteler, M., Steinwandt, R.: Applying Grover's algorithm to AES: quantum resource estimates. In: Takagi, T. (ed.) PQCrypto 2016. LNCS, vol. 9606, pp. 29–43. Springer, Cham (2016). https://doi.org/10.1007/978-3-319-29360-8_3
6. Balachandran, V.: Quantum obfuscation: quantum predicates with entangled qubits. In: Proceedings of the Eleventh ACM Conference on Data and Application Security and Privacy, pp. 293–295 (2021)
7. Bennett, C.H., Brassard, G., Ekert, A.K.: Quantum cryptography. Sci. Am. **267**(4), 50–57 (1992)
8. Ko, K.-K., Jung, E.-S.: Development of cybersecurity technology and algorithm based on quantum computing. Appl. Sci. **11**(19) (2021). ISSN: 2076-3417. https://doi.org/10.3390/app11199085. https://www.mdpi.com/2076-3417/11/19/9085
9. Dunkelman, O., Keller, N., Ronen, E., Shamir, A.: Quantum time/memory/data tradeoff attacks. Des. Codes Crypt. **92**(1), 159–177 (2024)
10. Pearson, P.K.: Fast hashing of variable-length text strings. Commun. ACM **33**(6), 677–680 (1990)
11. Frobenius norm - mathematics - sciencedirect. Accessed 24 Mar 2023. https://www.sciencedirect.com/topics/mathematics/frobenius-norm
12. Mandviwalla, A., Ohshiro, K., Ji, B.: Implementing grovers algorithm on the ibm quantum computers. In. IEEE International Conference on Big Data (Big Data) 2018, pp. 2531–2537 (2018). https://doi.org/10.1109/BigData.2018.8622457

Malware and Vulnerability Detection

Insights from Running 24 Static Analysis Tools on Open Source Software Repositories

Fabiha Hashmat[✉], Zeyad Alwaleed Aljaali, Mingjie Shen, and Aravind Machiry

Purdue University, West Lafayette, IN, USA
{fhashmat,zaljaali,shen497,amachiry}@purdue.edu

Abstract. OSS is important and useful. We want to ensure that it is of high quality and has no security issues. Static analysis tools provide easy-to-use and application-independent mechanisms to assess various aspects of a given code. Many effective open-source static analysis tools exist. In this paper, we perform the first comprehensive analysis using 24 open-source static analysis tools (through OMEGA ANALYZER) on 4,947 repositories. Our study identified several interesting findings, such as the distribution of errors in relation to the criticality score of repositories shows that repositories with a criticality score have the highest percentage of errors. We envision that our findings provide insights into the effectiveness of static analysis tools on OSS and future research directions in securing OSS repositories.

Keywords: Program Analysis · OMEGA ANALYZER · GITHUB Network Projects · Static Analysis · OSSF critical repositories

1 Introduction

Open Source Software (OSS) plays and an important role in the software ecosystem [18,70]. Many important and high-impact software products, such as Linux kernel [69] and nodejs [8], are all open source. It is also well-known that many organizations use OSS as part of their software products [36]. Given the prevalence, it is important to ensure that OSS follows good engineering practices to avoid security vulnerabilities. Furthermore, WhiteHouse recently released an official report [7] emphasizing the importance of securing OSS and the use of secure software engineering practices.

Static Application Security Testing (SAST) [28,31] is a well- vulnerabilities. However, previous studies [66] have shown that 40% of organizations do not use any SAST tools as part of their engineering practices. Furthermore, our analysis (in Sect. 2), also shows that only 19% of the critical OSS use any SAST tools. There are various Free SAST Tools (FSTs), such as CODEQL [2], to detect common security vulnerabilities and can be used without cost or licensing issues. However, the effectiveness of FSTs on OSS is unknown. Although prior works (discussed in Sect. 8.2) try to explore the same aspect, they mainly focus on

SAST tools that find software vulnerabilities. Furthermore, their study is often limited to a small number of OSS projects.

In this paper, we perform the first large-scale study of the effectiveness of FSTs on OSS. Specifically, we investigate the following three research questions:

- **RQ 1: Execution.** *Executing FSTs on OSS Repositories.* How easy/hard is it to run static analysis tools on OSS repositories? How robust are the tools in analyzing these repositories?
- **RQ 2: Effectiveness.** *Effectiveness of FSTs on OSS Repositories.* What types of issues are found by FSTs? What types of issues are prevalent in OSS repositories?
- **RQ 3: Quality.** *Quality of Issues Found by FSTs.* What is the quality (true/-false positive rate) of the issues found FSTs?

For our dataset, we collected a suite of 24 FSTs from Open Source Security Foundation (OpenSSF)'s [3] ALPHAOMEGA [1] project. The project contains a list of stable and recommended SAST tools for OSS projects. We also identified a set of 4,947 critical OSS projects by contacting OpenSSF team. We created a GITHUB workflow [4] (i.e., a Continuous Integration (CI) pipeline) called FST-WORKFLOW, that can execute all 24 FSTs on a given repository. We also created an automated mechanism to categorize the tool's results in a common format. We investigated our research questions by executing FSTs (through FSTWORK-FLOW) on all of our repositories and analyzed the results through automated and manual analysis. In summary, the following are our contributions:

- **(FSTs Collection).** We collected a dataset of 4,947 repositories across various programming languages to evaluate OMEGA ANALYZER's performance.
- **(Study).** We performed the first extensive analysis of OMEGA ANALYZER, identifying resource constraints, failure modes, and language distribution.
- **(Findings).** We found a 98.3% success rate for OMEGA ANALYZER, with Python, JSON, and JavaScript being the most common languages. The The Source Code Scanning (SCS) tool detected more errors and warnings than the Misconfigurations (MC) tool.
- **(Open-source availability).** We made our analysis workflow, dataset, and results open-source to enable future research.

2 Motivation

OSS is important and used directly or indirectly in many software products [22]. The design and code patterns used in OSS also inspire other software products [53]. It is important to ensure that OSS does not contain any obvious security vulnerabilities in general insecure (or risky) practices, e.g., unsanitized use of `strcpy`, hardcoded private keys, etc.

SAST is a recommended practice to easily detect previously known vulnerabilities and reasonably assess the quality of a software project. Furthermore, there exist several easy-to-use (plug-and-play) free SAST tools (FSTs) to detect common classes of vulnerabilities and insecure practices. One of the well-known

FSTs is CODEQL [32]. A recent study [64] shows that just running CODEQL (with its default configuration) found more than 300 security vulnerabilities in open-source embedded software repositories. Also, the authors identified that only 4% use any sort of SAST in their repository. Our preliminary analysis also found that only 10% of critical OSS projects use CODEQL.

Many prior studies [14,26,35,54] focus mainly on software security vulnerabilities and try to investigate their effectiveness. Furthermore, most of these studies were performed on a small scale, raising concerns regarding the generalizability of their observations. OSS can contain other classes (e.g., improper configuration) of defects. *However, no existing work tries to understand the effectiveness of all categories of SAST tools at a large scale.* We argue that such a work will serve as guidance for tool developers and can potentially expose problems in the applicability of SAST tools on OSS.

3 Background

In this section, we provide the necessary background related to our methodology.

3.1 OpenSSF and Criticality Score

OpenSSF. Open Source Security Foundation (OpenSSF) [3] is a community of software developers, security engineers, and more who are working together to secure open-source software. ALPHAOMEGA [1] is an associated project of the OpenSSF , funded by Microsoft, Google, and Amazon, with a mission to protect society by catalyzing sustainable security improvements in the most critical open-source software projects and ecosystems.

Measuring Project Importance as Criticality Score. OpenSSF created a mechanism to compute a criticality score [15] for GITHUB repositories. Security analysts use this score to triage the security vulnerabilities by scanning large datasets. We use the *criticality score* to measure the importance of an open-source project. A project's criticality score is a number between 0 and 1. It is computed based on attributes, including its popularity, dependents, and level of activity. Ranges correspond to qualitative labels: 0.0–0.2 is considered low criticality, 0.2–0.4 is medium, 0.4–0.6 is high, 0.6–0.9 is critical, and above 0.9 is extremely critical. The Swift language frontend (with 2.4K stars) [6] has criticality scores of 0.51, indicating a high severity project. The Linux kernel (with 157K stars) [68] has a criticality score of 0.88, indicating a critical project. The Node.js runtime (with 97.6K stars) [5] has a score of 0.99, indicating an extremely critical project.

3.2 Static Application Security Testing (SAST)

SAST represents a class of techniques to find security issues in a given software. These techniques are *static*, i.e., they do not execute the target software. On the contrary, dynamic techniques (e.g., random testing) execute the target and need an appropriate execution environment. A well-known category of SAST tools is code scanning tools, e.g., CODEQL, which find security vulnerabilities (e.g., buffer overflow) in source code. As these vulnerabilities are often severe, most of the SAST research focused on the code scanning tools. Consequently, the security community uses SAST synonymous with code scanning. However, there are also other classes of SAST tools (e.g., identifying misconfigurations), which also try to find import security issues but are not well-studied. For our study, we classify SAST tools into the following categories as shown in Table 3.

- **Source Code Scanning (SCS):** These are classic code scanning tools; they use pattern-matching (e.g.,) or flow-based static program analysis techniques (e.g., CODEQL) to find security vulnerabilities in programs' source code. For instance, CODEQL finds use-after-free vulnerabilities by performing a flow-sensitive analysis [33].
- **Mis-configurations (MC):** These tools focus on detecting sub-optimal or insecure configurations (e.g., hardcoding a private key) at both the source level and the project level. These are similar to SCS tools but also focus on non-code entities. Similarly, Binwalk [37] can be used for the detection of private hard-coded keys in the projects.
- **Quality and Best Practices (QS):** As the name suggests, this category of tools checks for quality issues at both the source code and project levels. For instance, Lizard [74] detects code with high complexity, a well-known proxy for potential bugs.
- **Software Statistics (SS):** These tools report interesting statistics that can serve as a proxy for anomalies or potential vulnerabilities. For instance, the SCC [19] tool computes the number of people required to maintain a given repository, i.e., "Estimated People Required", based on various software-driven metrics. The increase in this number indicates potential anomaly and refactoring opportunities.

These SAST tools often report the severity level of alerts to indicate the potential risk added to the codebase; for example, CODEQL alerts classify issues as "Error," "Warning," or "Note".

4 Study Design and Research Questions

Based on our motivation and background stated before, we have devised a study design as shown in Fig. 1. The execution of GITHUB open source repositories is done on the OMEGA ANALYZER. Based on the functionality of each static analysis tool of OMEGA ANALYZER, its categorization is done. Based on running those static analysis tools on open source repositories, we have divided our study into three research questions as shown below. Research Question 1 (RQ1) focuses on the deployment of the OMEGA ANALYZER to evaluate an extensive dataset of open source repositories. Research Question 2 (RQ2) is centered on a quantitative evaluation to interpret the errors and warnings distribution that occur across different repositories while analyzing through OMEGA ANALYZER. Research Question 3 (RQ3) explores the accuracy of SCS tools by analyzing their false positive rates in our repository dataset.

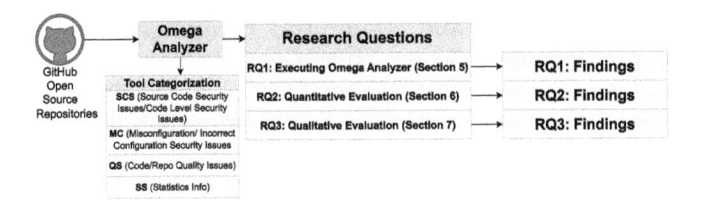

Fig. 1. Research Methodology

5 RQ1—Executing OMEGA ANALYZER

Research Question 1 (RQ1) explores the deployment of OMEGA ANALYZER on the dataset of open source software repositories, particularly focusing on the major programming languages used, the categorization of repositories and their primary languages, and the classification and language support of the OMEGA ANALYZER underlying tools.

5.1 RQ1: Methods and Results

We developed an automated workflow for running OMEGA ANALYZER on repositories. It takes the input of the GITHUB repository for running the latest OMEGA ANALYZER docker image on it and stores the results for review in SARIF format. We established self-hosted runners on eight machines, each utilizing an AWS EC2 m7a.2xlarge instance with 8 CPU cores, 32 GB of memory, and 100GB of disk space, operating on Ubuntu 22.04. The workflow timeout was configured to three hours. The execution of OmegaAnalyzer across all repositories in our dataset took approximately eight days. We succeeded to run OMEGA ANALYZER on 4,865 repositories. Failure factors include workflow timeouts (60), out-of-memory (2), and others (20), e.g. insufficient disk space. The details of our analysis are presented in the following sub-sections.

Open Source Software Dataset. For this study, we analyzed a dataset of 4,947 high-criticality projects from the Open Source Security Foundation (OSSF). These projects were chosen for their significant impact on the open-source ecosystem. They span diverse applications and sectors, including infrastructure, web development, security, and data analysis.

- **Major Programming Languages and SLOC of repositories:** Table 1 lists the major programming languages used in these repositories, along with their Source Lines of Code (SLOC) statistics. It shows the number of repositories for each language and the maximum, mean, median, and minimum SLOC values. Python is the most used language with 383 repositories, followed by JSON (369) and JavaScript (322), highlighting their roles in data interchange and web development. JSON leads in SLOC with a maximum of 30 million lines, closely followed by Java and Go, reflecting their use in large-scale projects.

- **Repository Categories and Their Top Languages:** Table 2 shows the distribution of repositories across categories and the predominant programming languages used. Python and JavaScript are most frequent, especially in hacktoberfest, python, and react categories. C is prevalent in kubernetes, android, and linux, highlighting its system-level programming relevance. Go's presence in kubernetes and docker categories indicates its growing importance in cloud technologies. This data illustrates the diverse application of programming languages across domains.

Table 1. Major programming languages and SLOC of repositories

Lang.ID	Language/Encoding Format	Num of Repo	SLOC Max	Mean	Med	Min
L1	Python	383	6M	100K	40K	40
L2	JSON	369	30M	300K	60K	200
L3	JavaScript	322	3M	100K	60K	200
L4	Java	317	9M	400K	200K	2K
L5	PHP	284	2M	100K	40K	100
L6	Go	258	10M	500K	100K	2K
L7	C	250	20M	1M	100K	7K
L8	C++	228	4M	400K	200K	3K
L9	TypeScript	216	4M	200K	60K	700
L10	Markdown	166	6M	200K	20K	4
L11	Ruby	161	5M	100K	20K	1K
L12	C#	124	10M	400K	100K	5K
L13	POFile	109	9M	700K	200K	8K
L14	XML	88	10M	700K	200K	1K
L15	YAML	83	9M	300K	70K	40
L16	C/C++Header	76	5M	400K	100K	3K
L17	Rust	60	1M	100K	50K	3K
L18	Text	60	20M	1M	200K	3K
L19	HTML	57	5M	500K	100K	1K
L20	Scala	42	900K	100K	50K	6K
L21	QtLinguist	33	6M	800K	400K	10K
L22	Kotlin	30	2M	100K	60K	6K
L23	Haskell	26	600K	70K	20K	2K
L24	diff	25	4M	300K	200K	8K
L25	BourneShell	24	70K	20K	7K	100
L26	Swift	22	500K	100K	70K	7K
L27	SVG	19	2M	300K	100K	900
L28	CSV	19	3M	500K	200K	20K
L29	CSS	17	1M	200K	40K	3K
L30	Objective-C	12	300K	70K	20K	2K
–	Others	1067				

Results of OMEGA ANALYZER Tools Under Each Category. Each tool within the OMEGA ANALYZER plays a specific role, from static code analysis to detecting vulnerabilities, ensuring code quality, and safeguarding against security threats.

Table 2. Repository Categories and Their Top Languages

Category	# Repos	Top Language
hacktoberfest	807	Python
python	371	Python
javascript	264	JavaScript
java	211	Java
php	181	PHP
kubernetes	113	C
ruby	97	Ruby
react	93	JavaScript
c	91	C
go	80	Go
c-plus-plus	68	C++
rust	59	Rust
android	51	C
typescript	50	TypeScript
dotnet	43	C
linux	39	C
security	35	C
machine learning	30	Python
nodejs	29	JavaScript
docker	28	Go

– OMEGA ANALYZER **Tools Categorization:** In our study, we have categorized the tools integrated into the OMEGA ANALYZER based on the specific types of security and code quality issues they address. These categories are defined in Sect. 3. According to those categories we have assigned an ID number to each tool in OMEGA ANALYZER. The ID number of each tool along with its description is shown in Table 3. Some interesting results of running these tools on repositories are shown below.
  • **Source Code Scanning (SCS)** The DevSkim tool found an error in the Platform Helpers repository [56] involving a weak hash algorithm. This vulnerability compromises data integrity and security, making the system susceptible to attacks. The error is shown in Listing

1.1, where the line `checksum = sha1(hashlib_encode_data(__version__))` directly uses the version string for checksum calculation. If an attacker knows the version, they can manipulate or predict the checksum.

```
import re
from hashlib import sha1

def compute_project_checksum(config):
    # rebuild when PIO Core version changes
    checksum = sha1(hashlib_encode_data(__version__))
```

Listing 1.1. Hardcoding Version Information

- **Mis-configuration (MC)** The Semgrep tool detected common misconfiguration issues in the Microsoft Terminal Workflow repository [50]. Specifically, the line `uses: craigloewen-msft/GitGudSimilarIssues@main` in Listing 1.2 sources an action from a third-party repository without pinning it to a full-length commit SHA. Pinning to a full-length commit SHA is crucial as it ensures the action remains immutable, mitigating the risk of a backdoor being added to the action's repository.

```
steps:
  - id: getBody
    uses: craigloewen-msft/GitGudSimilarIssues@main
    with:
      issueTitle: ${{ github.event.issue.title }}
      issueBody: ${{ github.event.issue.body }}
      repo: ${{ github.repository }}
      similaritytolerance: "0.8"
```

Listing 1.2. GitHub Actions workflow step.

Another error is detected under this category in Yoast SEO WordPress plugin's components directory [75]. The Yoast SEO WordPress plugin's components directory, analyzed by Binwalk, contains exposed private keys and certificates. The RSA private key is exposed in the repository. See Listing 1.3. This oversight could compromise the security of the application by allowing unauthorized access or decryption of sensitive data.

```
-----BEGIN RSA PRIVATE KEY-----
MIIEpAIBAAKCAQEAn+5QIkyjSaeAt8o+htOoVaa9/rxU95ROYbpezlofm...
-----END RSA PRIVATE KEY-----
```

Listing 1.3. RSA Private Key exposed in repository.

- **Quality and Best Practices (QS):** The issue identified in this category is in the Facebook Hermes [27] repository relates to high code complexity, as detected by the tool Lizard. High code complexity can lead to difficulties in understanding, maintaining, and modifying the code, potentially increasing the risk of errors and reducing efficiency in development processes.
- **Software Statistics (SS)** The error reported in the SageMath repository [63] by the SCC tool falls under Statistics Info (SS). SCC estimated that maintaining SageMath would require about 120 people, reflecting the project's complexity and scale. Key metrics include an estimated development cost of $111,404,644, a scheduled effort of 82.46 months, and 120 people required. These insights are vital for planning and resource allocation in software development.

Table 3. Overview of Tools Integrated in OMEGA ANALYZER and Their Categorization

ID	Tool	Description
SCS Errors		
T1	DevSkim [47]	Identifies and fixes security issues in source code
T2	NodeJsScan [9]	SAST tool for Node.js applications
T3	CppCheck [45]	Static analysis for C and C++ code
T4	CodeQL [32]	Automated code review and security analysis
T5	SecretScanner [23]	Scans for secrets in code and file systems
T6	Detect-Secrets [73]	Prevents secrets in code
T7	Brakeman [21]	Security vulnerabilities detection in Ruby on Rails
T8	Graudit [71]	Scans source code for security flaws
T9	ILSpy [38]	.NET assembly browser and decompiler
T10	npm audit [52]	Reviews npm projects for vulnerabilities in dependencies
T11	Snyk Code [66]	Finds and fixes vulnerabilities in open-source dependencies
T12	Bandit [59]	Finds common security issues in Python code
T13	Semgrep [60]	Fast tool for bug detection and code standard enforcement
MC Errors		
T14	ClamAV [67]	Antivirus engine for detecting malware
T15	Yara [13]	Helps in malware identification and classification
T16	Manalyze [41]	Static analyzer for PE files, malware detection
MC Warnings		
T17	strace [43]	Monitors interactions between processes and the Linux kernel
T18	OSS Gadget [49]	Tools for open-source intelligence
T19	binwalk [37]	Searches binary images for embedded files and hidden data
T20	ShhGit [58]	Scans GITHUB for sensitive information
T21	TBV [42]	Package verification for npm
T22	Radare2 [12]	Binary analysis and reverse-engineering tool
SS Statistics Info		
T23	Application Inspector [48]	Identifies and reports software features
T24	SCC [19]	Code counter with complexity calculations
QS Warnings		
T25	Lizard [74]	Analyzes code complexity and generates metrics

- **Supported languages for Tools of** OMEGA ANALYZER**:** The Table 4 maps the applicability of OMEGA ANALYZER tools (T1, T2, T3) across various programming languages (L1 to L30). The supported languages for the tools of OmegaAnalyzer illustrate the breadth of compatibility across different programming environments. For example, tools such as T1 and T3 support a wide range of languages, including Python (L1) and JavaScript (L3), which are commonly used in various applications. In contrast, other tools like T14 and T18 are compatible with fewer languages.

Table 4. Supported languages for Tools of OMEGA ANALYZER

	T1	T2	T3	T4	T5	T6	T12	T13	T14	T17	T18	T19	T20	T23	T24	T25
L1	✓	✓	✓	✓	✓	✓	✓	✓	✓		✓		✓	✓		✓
L2	✓	✓		✓		✓			✓					✓		
L3	✓	✓	✓	✓	✓	✓	✓	✓	✓			✓		✓	✓	
L4	✓	✓	✓	✓	✓	✓	✓	✓	✓			✓		✓	✓	
L5	✓	✓	✓	✓	✓	✓	✓	✓	✓			✓		✓	✓	
L6	✓	✓	✓	✓	✓	✓	✓	✓	✓			✓		✓	✓	
L7	✓	✓	✓	✓	✓	✓	✓	✓	✓			✓		✓	✓	
L8	✓	✓	✓	✓	✓	✓	✓	✓	✓			✓		✓	✓	
L9	✓	✓	✓	✓	✓	✓	✓	✓	✓			✓		✓	✓	
L10	✓			✓	✓	✓	✓			✓		✓				✓
L11	✓	✓	✓	✓	✓	✓	✓	✓	✓			✓		✓	✓	
L12	✓	✓	✓	✓	✓	✓	✓	✓	✓			✓		✓	✓	
L17	✓	✓	✓	✓	✓	✓	✓	✓	✓			✓		✓	✓	
L19	✓	✓	✓	✓	✓	✓	✓	✓	✓			✓		✓	✓	
L20	✓	✓	✓	✓	✓	✓	✓	✓	✓			✓		✓	✓	
L22	✓	✓	✓	✓	✓	✓	✓	✓	✓			✓		✓	✓	
L23	✓	✓	✓	✓	✓	✓	✓		✓		✓				✓	
L26	✓	✓	✓	✓	✓	✓	✓	✓	✓		✓		✓		✓	
L29	✓	✓		✓	✓	✓	✓	✓		✓		✓			✓	
L30	✓	✓	✓	✓	✓	✓	✓	✓		✓		✓			✓	

5.2 RQ1: Findings

- **Finding 1:** The execution of OMEGA ANALYZER across 4,947 repositories revealed 60 workflow timeouts, 2 out-of-memory errors, and 20 disk space failures, resulting in a 98.3% success rate out of 4,947 repositories, indicating effective processing despite some resource constraints.

- **Finding 2:** In our dataset, the major programming language is Python with 383 repositories (Table 1), followed by JSON and JavaScript with 369 and 322 repositories respectively; JSON leads in Source Lines of Code (SLOC) with 30 million lines, followed by Java and Go, indicating their use in large-scale applications.
- **Finding 3:** The distribution of repositories across various categories, as detailed in Table 2, indicates a dominant use of Python and JavaScript, especially in hacktoberfest, python, and react categories. Conversely, C is prevalent in system-oriented categories such as kubernetes, android, and linux, while Go's significant presence in kubernetes and docker categories shows its increasing importance in cloud technologies. Overall, the data illustrates the diverse application of programming languages across different domains.
- **Finding 4:** Table 4 indicates the versatility of certain tools and suggests the need for specific tools tailored to handle the unique requirements of different programming languages, considering their varied usage and complexity levels.

6 RQ2—Quantitative Evaluation

Research Question 2 (RQ2) is centered on a quantitative evaluation to interpret the distribution of errors and warnings that occur across different repositories while being analyzed through the OMEGA ANALYZER, focusing on the relationship between error distribution and criticality score, comparative error distribution across repositories by the OMEGA ANALYZER tool, and warning distribution across repositories by analytical tools.

6.1 RQ2: Methods and Results

Following is a detailed analysis of our quantitative analysis.

Errors Distribution in Relation to Criticality Score. Figure 2 shows the distribution of errors in relation to the 'Criticality Score' of repositories. The x-axis represents the criticality score from 0–0.1 to 0.9–1.0, with higher scores indicating greater importance. The y-axis represents the percentage, ranging from 0% to 80%. Blue bars indicate the percentage of repositories within each score range, while red bars show the percentage of errors. Most repositories have a criticality score of 0.5–0.6, but the highest error percentage is in the 0.4–0.5 range. This suggests that certain criticality scores are more prone to errors regardless of the number of repositories.

Distribution of Alerts in Repositories by OMEGA ANALYZER. Figure 3 presents a comprehensive visualization of the distribution of alerts generated by the OMEGA ANALYZER across a series of repositories. The x-axis represents the cumulative percentage of analyzed repositories, offering a progressive insight into the coverage of the dataset. The y-axis quantifies the number of alerts, distinguishing between errors (blue line) and warnings (red line). Notably, the graph serves as a diagnostic tool, highlighting the OMEGA ANALYZER's capability in identifying and categorizing potential issues, thereby aiding in the prioritization of repository maintenance and code quality assurance.

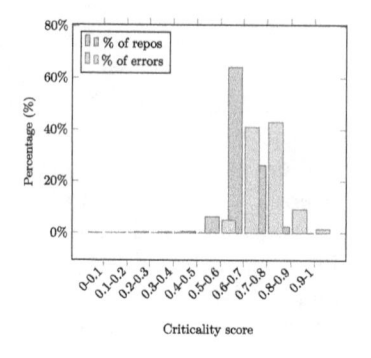

Fig. 2. Errors Distribution in relation to Criticality Score

Fig. 3. Distribution of Alerts in Repositories by OMEGA ANALYZER

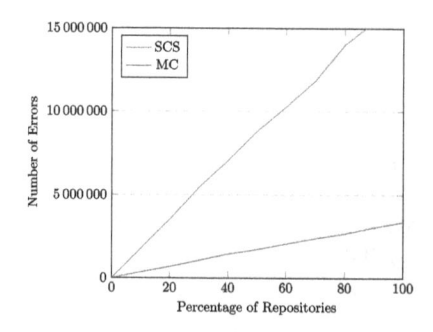

Comparative Error Distribution Across Repositories by OMEGA ANALYZER. Figure 4 shows the cumulative percentage of errors detected by different analytical tools across repositories. The x-axis represents the percentage of repositories analyzed, and the y-axis indicates the percentage of errors detected. The varied trajectories highlight each tool's unique error detection patterns and sensitivities. The graph is essential for understanding error distribution and magnitude across repositories, with the y-axis reaching up to 15 million errors.

Fig. 4. Comparative Error Distribution Across Repositories by OMEGA ANALYZER

Warning Distribution Across Repositories by Analytical Tools. Figure 5 illustrates the distribution of warnings across repositories as analyzed by three tools: QS, SCS, and MC. The SCS tool, focusing on source code security issues, shows a sharp increase in warnings past the 50% mark of analyzed repositories. The MC tool, identifying misconfigurations, exhibits consistent but moderate growth in warnings, suggesting widespread but stable configuration issues. The QS tool, targeting code and repository quality, displays a gradual increase in warnings, indicating a baseline level of quality issues. These trends reveal the diverse challenges in maintaining code quality and security across repositories.

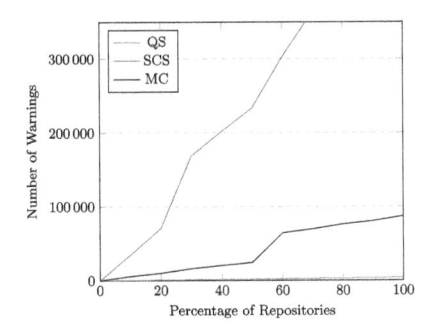

Fig. 5. Warning Distribution Across Repositories by Analytical Tools

6.2 RQ2: Findings

- **Finding 1:** The distribution of errors in relation to the criticality score of repositories shows that repositories with a criticality score of 0.4–0.5 have the highest percentage of errors, despite the majority of repositories having a criticality score in the 0.5–0.6 range (Fig. 2).
- **Finding 2:** The OMEGA ANALYZER identifies a significant number of errors and warnings across repositories, with a sharp increase in errors detected after analyzing 50% of the repositories. This suggests that errors are more prevalent in the latter half of the analyzed repositories.
- **Finding 3:** Different analytical tools, such as SCS and MC, exhibit unique error detection patterns, with SCS detecting a higher number of errors compared to MC. This difference reflects the distinct focuses and strengths of each tool, rather than a direct comparison of their effectiveness, as they are designed to address different aspects of code analysis (Fig. 4).
- **Finding 4:** The distribution of warnings across repositories by analytical tools reveals that the SCS tool identifies a significantly higher number of warnings, especially after the 50% mark of analyzed repositories. This suggests that security-related issues become more pronounced in the latter half of the repository analysis (Fig. 5).
- **Finding 5:** The QS tool, focused on detecting code and repository quality issues, shows a gradual increase in warnings, indicating a baseline level of code quality is maintained across repositories, but still highlighting prevalent quality issues (Fig. 5).

– **Finding 6:** The moderate but consistent growth in warnings identified by the MC tool across analyzed repositories implies that configuration errors are widespread but do not vary dramatically, emphasizing the need for consistent configuration management (Fig. 5).

7 RQ3—Qualitative Evaluation

In this section, we assess the quality of SCS tools. Specifically, we want to study the false positive rates of these tools on our dataset of repositories. SCS tools are pivotal in modern software development, providing automated means to detect potential vulnerabilities early in the development lifecycle. However, the efficacy of these tools is often diminished by false positives – instances where a tool reports a security issue that is not actually present in the codebase. High false positive rates can lead to wasted time and resources as developers must spend considerable time verifying and dismissing false alarms, which hinders their productivity and delays the development process.

In the rest of this section, we will first present our methodology, followed by the results.

7.1 RQ3: Methods and Results

Methods. Categorizing alerts into true and false positives requires significant manual effort. Given the large number of repositories and alerts, it is infeasible to analyze them all. To address this, we implement a random sampling approach to maintain manageability while ensuring a representative evaluation. For each SCS tool, we randomly sample 10 repositories that each has fewer than 20 errors or warnings reported.

Each reported issue is manually reviewed to determine its accuracy. This involves examining the code in question to ascertain whether the reported issue is a true positive (a genuine security vulnerability) or a false positive (an incorrectly identified issue).

Results. We managed to obtain the false positive rate for five SCS tools. Unfortunately, we did not have enough data to evaluate other tools due to the following reasons: 1) No results in the dataset: Some tools did not yield any results in any of the repositories within our dataset; 2) Lack of source line Information: Some tools failed to report the source line number for the issues detected, making it challenging for us to verify and categorize the results accurately.

The false positive rates for the evaluated tools are summarized in Table 5. These results indicate significant variability in the accuracy of the evaluated SCS tools. Tool T4 demonstrated the highest accuracy with a false positive rate of only 9%, making it the most reliable among the tools tested. In contrast, Tools T1 and T2 had the highest false positive rates, each exceeding 60%, which suggests a need for improvement in their detection algorithms.

Table 5. Number of true positives, false positives, and false positive rate for the five evaluated SCS tools.

	#TP	#FP	FP%
T1	28	50	64%
T2	9	17	65%
T4	51	5	9%
T12	53	28	35%
T13	45	35	44%

To illustrate the nature of false positives encountered during our evaluation, Listing 1.4 shows an example of a false positive reported by T1. The tool flagged a piece of code as a potential security vulnerability, but upon manual review, it was determined to be a false positive. Specifically, this tool incorrectly identified the use of the SHA-512 hash algorithm as weak or broken.

Overall, our findings highlight the importance of evaluating and selecting SCS tools carefully, as the effectiveness of these tools can vary greatly. Accurate tools can significantly aid in identifying genuine security vulnerabilities, while those with high false positive rates can burden developers with unnecessary reviews and potentially lead to overlooked issues.

```
1  "node_modules/normalize-package-data": {
2    "version": "5.0.0",
3    "resolved": "https://registry.npmjs.org/normalize-package-data/-/normalize-package-data-5.0.0.tgz",
4    "integrity": "sha512-h9iPVIfrVZ9wVYQnxFgtw1ugSvGEMO1yPWWtm8BMJhnwyEL/FLbYbTY3V3PpjI/BUK67n9PEWDu6eHzu1fB15Q==",
5    ...
6  },
```

Listing 1.4. An example of a false positive reported by T1. T1 flagged the hash algorithm used for integrity checking of the package as weak or broken. However, the integrity field uses SHA-512, which is considered secure.

7.2 RQ3: Findings

- **Finding 1:** There is significant variability in the accuracy of the evaluated tools. Tool T4 had the lowest false positive rate at 9%, indicating high reliability, while Tools T1 and T2 had the highest false positive rates, each exceeding 60%.
- **Finding 2:** High false positive rates can mislead developers. For example, one tool incorrectly flagged the secure SHA-512 hash algorithm as weak, illustrating the need for refinement in detection algorithms to reduce unnecessary reviews and potential oversight of genuine issues.

8 Related Work

This literature review examines three main areas: firstly, it looks into studies that explore the security vulnerabilities in open-source repositories, identifying the key risks and challenges involved. Secondly, it evaluates the effectiveness of existing Static Application Security Testing (SAST) tools. Finally, it reviews efforts that apply these SAST tools to open-source software.

8.1 Security Vulnerabilities in Open Source Repositories

Recent studies have significantly advanced our understanding of security vulnerabilities in open-source software repositories. Research has included case studies on major projects like Apache HTTP Server and Apache Tomcat, revealing specific security fixes and preventive measures [55]. The reliability of data in vulnerability repositories has been critically evaluated, highlighting inconsistencies and gaps in current databases [40]. Tools like CVEfixes and VCCFinder have been developed to automate the collection of vulnerabilities and assist in code audits by mining software repositories [17,76]. Empirical analyses have shed light on the nature and frequency of security issues reported in open-source projects, with some focusing on mining threat intelligence from issues and bug reports [76]. Efforts to generate datasets from vulnerable source code have enhanced the resources available for understanding and mitigating these risks [34,57,61]. Studies have also proposed models to estimate and predict security risks associated with open-source packages, contributing to more informed decision-making in software development [65,72]. Moreover, assessments of the impact of vulnerabilities in software libraries have been complemented by investigations into the release practices and secret integration channels of open-source packages [39,62].

8.2 Evaluating the Effectiveness of SAST Tools

Research has extensively evaluated the effectiveness of Static Application Security Testing (SAST) tools in diverse programming environments. Key studies have benchmarked SAST tools for C, revealing strengths and limitations [29,30]. Innovative uses, such as employing AI models like ChatGPT for static security testing, have been examined for their practicality [16]. Empirical work has shed light on the performance and reliability of these tools, particularly through security warnings [11]. Additionally, comparative analyses have highlighted SAST tools' capabilities in Java and distributed applications, contrasting them with dynamic methods to evaluate thoroughness [24,44]. The integration of SAST with reverse engineering for binary executables also illustrates a comprehensive approach to security [25].

8.3 Application of SAST Tools in Open-Source Software Environments

Mingjie Shen et al. [64] studied 258 popular EMBOSS projects using GitHub's CodeQL, finding 540 defects, 74% of which were probable security vulnerabilities, highlighting SAST tools' effectiveness and low false positive rate (23%). Feras Al Kassar et al. [10] examined the impact of code patterns on security testing in web applications, identifying over 270 patterns that hinder static analysis and discovering 440 new vulnerabilities across 48 projects. A. Nguyen-Duc et al. [51] found that combining SAST tools enhances performance in an open-source e-government project. MM Casanova Páez et al. [20] reviewed various application security testing tools, emphasizing automation, ease of use, and accuracy, and found no direct correlation between commercial tools and higher effectiveness.

Additionally, C. Gentsch et al. [29] evaluated multiple open-source Static Analysis Security Testing (SAST) tools for C, including AdLint, Clang-Tidy, and others. Using a methodology involving file-by-file analysis and a comprehensive database to track outputs, the study confirmed the tools' efficacy by comparing findings against the Juliet Test Suite. This rigorous approach assessed overall tool accuracy, overlap, and usability in various real-world and synthetic environments. Further, F. Mateo Tudela and J.R. Bermejo Higuera [46] analyzed the effectiveness of combining SAST, DAST, and IAST tools against the OWASP Top Ten vulnerabilities. Using combinations like Fortify+Arachni+CCE, they achieved notable success across various security levels in web applications.

9 Discussion and Future Work

We will responsibly disclose all critical vulnerabilities found, such as exposed private keys, to the respective maintainers. In Sect. 7, we limited our analysis to repositories with fewer than 20 errors or warnings, which may bias results by excluding projects with more issues. Future work will expand the scope to include repositories with a broader range of issues and develop a semi-automated system to classify false positives, enhancing the scalability and accuracy of our analysis.

10 Conclusion

In conclusion, this paper provides a detailed examination of the quality and security of open-source software (OSS) using 24 open-source static analysis tools through OMEGA ANALYZER. By analyzing 4,865 significant OSS projects, we have uncovered numerous insights that underscore the effectiveness of these tools in identifying security vulnerabilities and enhancing code quality. The findings from our comprehensive study not only highlight the pivotal role of static analysis tools in securing OSS repositories but also suggest future research directions aimed at refining these tools and strategies.

Acknowledgements. This research was partly supported by the National Science Foundation (NSF) under Grant CNS-2340548. Any opinions, findings, conclusions, or recommendations expressed in this material are those of the author(s) and do not necessarily reflect the views of the NSF.

References

1. Alpha Omega – Linux Foundation Project. https://alpha-omega.dev/
2. CodeQL. https://codeql.github.com/
3. Open Source Security Foundation – Linux Foundation Projects. https://openssf.org/
4. Understanding GitHub Actions. https://docs.github.com/_next/data/0DKyBPMqZhPYD1Lsg3qKt/en/free-pro-team@latest/actions/learn-github-actions/understanding-github-actions.json?versionId=free-pro-team%40latest&productId=actions&restPage=learn-github-actions&restPage=understanding-github-actions
5. Node.js (2023). https://github.com/nodejs/node. Original-date 26 Nov 2014
6. SwiftSyntax (2023). https://github.com/apple/swift-syntax. Original-date 31 July 2018
7. Fact Sheet: Biden-Harris Administration Releases End of Year Report on Open-Source Software Security Initiative - ONCD (2024). https://www.whitehouse.gov/oncd/briefing-room/2024/01/30/fact-sheet-biden-harris-administration-releases-end-of-year-report-on-open-source-software-security-initiative/
8. nodejs/node (2024). https://github.com/nodejs/node. Original-date 26 Nov 2014
9. Abraham, A.: Nodejsscan (2023). https://github.com/ajinabraham/NodeJsScan. Accessed 18 May 2024
10. Al Kassar, F., Clerici, G., Compagna, L., Balzarotti, D., Yamaguchi, F.: Testability tarpits: the impact of code patterns on the security testing of web applications. In: NDSS Symposium 2022. Internet Society, San Diego (2022)
11. Aloraini, B., Nagappan, M., German, D.M., Hayashi, S., Higo, Y.: An empirical study of security warnings from static application security testing tools. J. Syst. Softw. **158**, 110427 (2019)
12. Alvarez, S.: Radare2 (2006). https://www.radare.org/. Accessed 18 May 2024
13. Alvarez, V.: Yara (2024). https://virustotal.github.io/yara/. Accessed 18 May 2024
14. Arusoaie, A., Ciobâca, S., Craciun, V., Gavrilut, D., Lucanu, D.: A comparison of open-source static analysis tools for vulnerability detection in C/C++ code. In: 2017 19th International Symposium on Symbolic and Numeric Algorithms for Scientific Computing (SYNASC), pp. 161–168 (2017). https://doi.org/10.1109/SYNASC.2017.00035
15. Arya, A., Brown, C., Pike, R., The open source security foundation: open source project criticality score (2023). https://github.com/ossf/criticality_score. Original-date 17 Nov 2020
16. Bakhshandeh, A., Keramatfar, A., Norouzi, A., Chekidehkhoun, M.M.: Using ChatGPT as a static application security testing tool. arXiv preprint arXiv:2308.14434 (2023)
17. Bhandari, G., Naseer, A., Moonen, L.: CVEfixes: automated collection of vulnerabilities and their fixes from open-source software. In: Proceedings of the 17th International Conference on Predictive Models and Data Analytics in Software Engineering, pp. 30–39. Association for Computing Machinery, Athens, Greece (2021)
18. Bonaccorsi, A., Rossi, C.: Why open source software can succeed. Res. Policy **32**(7), 1243–1258 (2003)
19. Boyter, B.: SCC (2018). https://github.com/boyter/scc. Accessed 18 May 2024
20. Casanova Páez, M.M.: Application security testing tools study and proposal (2021)
21. Collins, J.: Brakeman (2010). https://brakemanscanner.org/. Accessed 18 May 2024

22. Cybersecurity and Infrastructure Security Agency (CISA): Government and industry partners publish fact sheet for organizations using open source software (2023). https://www.cisa.gov/news-events/news/government-and-industry-partners-publish-fact-sheet-organizations-using-open-source-software. Accessed 13 June 2024
23. Deepfence: Secretscanner (2020). https://github.com/deepfence/SecretScanner. Accessed 18 May 2024
24. Dencheva, L.: Comparative analysis of Static application security testing (SAST) and Dynamic application security testing (DAST) by using open-source web application penetration testing tools. Ph.D. thesis, Dublin, National College of Ireland (2022)
25. Devine, T.R., Campbell, M., Anderson, M., Dzielski, D.: SREP+ SAST: a comparison of tools for reverse engineering machine code to detect cybersecurity vulnerabilities in binary executables. In: 2022 International Conference on Computational Science and Computational Intelligence (CSCI), pp. 862–869. IEEE, Las Vegas (2022)
26. Esposito, M., Falaschi, V., Falessi, D.: An extensive comparison of static application security testing tools (2024)
27. Facebook: Hermes JavaScript engine. https://github.com/facebook/hermes (2024). Accessed 30 Apr 2024
28. Felderer, M., Büchler, M., Johns, M., Brucker, A.D., Breu, R., Pretschner, A.: Security testing: a survey. In: Advances in Computers, vol. 101, pp. 1–51. Elsevier (2016)
29. Gentsch, C.: Evaluation of open source static analysis security testing (SAST) tools for C (2020)
30. Gentsch, C., Krishnamurthy, R., Heinze, T.S.: Benchmarking open-source static analyzers for security testing for C. In: ISoLA 2020, Part IV, pp. 182–198. Springer, Cham (2021)
31. Ghazaly, N.M.: Learning the idea behind SAST (static application security testing) and how it functions. Int. J. Manag. Eng. Res. **1**(1), 01–04 (2021)
32. GitHub: CodeQL (2019). https://securitylab.github.com/tools/codeql. Accessed 18 May 2024
33. GitHub: Potential use after free (2024). https://codeql.github.com/codeql-query-help/cpp/cpp-use-after-free/. Accessed 24 June 2024
34. Gkortzis, A., Mitropoulos, D., Spinellis, D.: VulinOSS: a dataset of security vulnerabilities in open-source systems. In: Proceedings of the 15th International conference on mining software repositories, pp. 18–21. ACM, Gothenburg (2018)
35. Goseva-Popstojanova, K., Perhinschi, A.: On the capability of static code analysis to detect security vulnerabilities. Inf. Softw. Technol. **68**, 18–33 (2015)
36. Hauge, Ø., Ayala, C., Conradi, R.: Adoption of open source software in software-intensive organizations-a systematic literature review. Inf. Softw. Technol. **52**(11), 1133–1154 (2010)
37. Heffner, C.: binwalk (2010). https://github.com/ReFirmLabs/binwalk. Accessed 18 May 2024
38. ICSharpCode: Ilspy (2011). https://github.com/icsharpcode/ILSpy. Accessed 18 May 2024
39. Imtiaz, N., Khanom, A., Williams, L.: Open or sneaky? Fast or slow? light or heavy?: investigating security releases of open source packages. IEEE Trans. Software Eng. **49**(4), 1540–1560 (2022)

40. Jiang, Y., Jeusfeld, M., Ding, J.: Evaluating the data inconsistency of open-source vulnerability repositories. In: Proceedings of the 16th International Conference on Availability, Reliability and Security, pp. 1–10. ACM, Vienna (2021)
41. JusticeRage: Manalyze (2010). https://github.com/JusticeRage/Manalyze. Accessed 18 May 2024
42. Konves, S.: TBV (2019). https://github.com/verifynpm/tbv. Accessed 18 May 2024
43. Levin, D.V.: Strace (1992). https://strace.io/. Accessed 18 May 2024
44. Li, K., et al.: Comparison and evaluation on static application security testing (SAST) tools for java. In: Proceedings of the 31st ACM Joint European Software Engineering Conference and Symposium on the Foundations of Software Engineering, pp. 921–933. ACM, San Francisco (2023)
45. Marjamäki, D.: Cppcheck (2007). http://cppcheck.sourceforge.net/. Accessed 18 May 2024
46. Mateo Tudela, F., Bermejo Higuera, J.R., Bermejo Higuera, J., Sicilia Montalvo, J.A., Argyros, M.I.: On combining static, dynamic and interactive analysis security testing tools to improve OWASP top ten security vulnerability detection in web applications. Appl. Sci. **10**(24), 9119 (2020)
47. Microsoft: Devskim (2017). https://github.com/microsoft/DevSkim. Accessed 18 May 2024
48. Microsoft: ApplicationInspector (2019). https://github.com/microsoft/ApplicationInspector. Accessed 18 May 2024
49. Microsoft: OSSGadget (2020). https://github.com/microsoft/OSSGadget. Accessed 18 May 2024
50. Microsoft: Workflow configuration for similar issues in Microsoft terminal (2024). https://github.com/microsoft/terminal/blob/main/.github/workflows/similarIssues.yml. Accessed 30 Apr 2024
51. Nguyen-Duc, A., Do, M.V., Hong, Q.L., Khac, K.N., Quang, A.N.: On the adoption of static analysis for software security assessment-a case study of an open-source e-government project. Comput. Secur. **111**, 102470 (2021)
52. npm, I.: npm audit (2018). https://docs.npmjs.com/cli/v7/commands/npm-audit. Accessed 27 May 2024
53. Onarcan, M.O., Fu, Y., et al.: A case study on design patterns and software defects in open source software. J. Softw. Eng. Appl. **11**(05), 249 (2018)
54. Oyetoyan, T.D., Milosheska, B., Grini, M., Soares Cruzes, D.: Myths and facts about static application security testing tools: an action research at Telenor digital. In: XP 2018, pp. 86–103. Springer, Cham (2018)
55. Piantadosi, V., Scalabrino, S., Oliveto, R.: Fixing of security vulnerabilities in open source projects: a case study of apache http server and apache tomcat. In: 2019 12th IEEE Conference on Software Testing, Validation and Verification (ICST), pp. 68–78. IEEE, Xi'an (2019)
56. PlatformIO: Project helpers for platformio (2024). https://github.com/platformio/platformio-core/blob/develop/platformio/project/helpers.py. Accessed 30 Apr 2024
57. Ponta, S.E., Plate, H., Sabetta, A., Bezzi, M., Dangremont, C.: A manually-curated dataset of fixes to vulnerabilities of open-source software. In: 2019 IEEE/ACM 16th International Conference on Mining Software Repositories (MSR), pp. 383–387. IEEE, Montreal (2019)
58. Price, P.: Shhgit (2018). https://github.com/eth0izzle/shhgit. Accessed 18 May 2024

59. PyCQA: Bandit (2013). https://github.com/PyCQA/bandit. Accessed 18 May 2024
60. R2C: Semgrep (2020). https://semgrep.dev/. Accessed 18 May 2024
61. Raducu, R., Esteban, G., Rodriguez Lera, F.J., Fernández, C.: Collecting vulnerable source code from open-source repositories for dataset generation. Appl. Sci. **10**(4), 1270 (2020)
62. Ramsauer, R., Bulwahn, L., Lohmann, D., Mauerer, W.: The sound of silence: mining security vulnerabilities from secret integration channels in open-source projects. In: Proceedings of the 2020 ACM SIGSAC Conference on Cloud Computing Security Workshop, pp. 147–157. ACM, Virtual Event (2020)
63. SageMath: SageMath mathematical software system (2024). https://github.com/sagemath/sage. Accessed 30 Apr 2024
64. Shen, M., Pillai, A., Yuan, B.A., Davis, J.C., Machiry, A.: An empirical study on the use of static analysis tools in open source embedded software. arXiv preprint arXiv:2310.00205, pp. 1–14 (2023)
65. Smith, L.J.: Estimating security risk in open source package repositories: an empirical analysis and predictive model of software vulnerabilities. Ph.D. thesis, Capella University (2019)
66. Snyk: Snyk code (2020). https://snyk.io/product/snyk-code/. Accessed 27 May 2024
67. Talos, C.: ClamAV (2024). https://www.clamav.net/. Accessed 18 May 2024
68. Torvalds, L.: torvalds/linux (2023). https://github.com/torvalds/linux. Original-date 04 Sept 2011
69. Torvalds, L.: torvalds/linux (2024). https://github.com/torvalds/linux. Original-date 94 Sept 2011
70. Ven, K., Verelst, J., Mannaert, H.: Should you adopt open source software? IEEE Softw. **25**(3), 54–59 (2008)
71. wireghoul: Graudit (2010). https://github.com/wireghoul/graudit. Accessed 18 May 2024
72. Xu, R., Tang, Z., Ye, G., Wang, H., Ke, X., Fang, D., Wang, Z.: Detecting code vulnerabilities by learning from large-scale open source repositories. J. Inf. Secur. Appl. **69**, 103293 (2022)
73. Yelp: Detectsecrets (2017). https://github.com/Yelp/detect-secrets. Accessed 18 May 2024
74. Yin, T.: Lizard (2014). https://github.com/terryyin/lizard. Accessed 18 May 2024
75. Yoast: Components directory of the yoast seo wordpress plugin (2024). https://github.com/Yoast/wordpress-seo/tree/trunk/apps/components. Accessed 30 Apr 2024
76. Zahedi, M., Ali Babar, M., Treude, C.: An empirical study of security issues posted in open source projects. In: Proceedings of the 51st Hawaii International Conference on System Sciences (HICSS), pp. 5504–5513. IEEE, Hawaii (2018)

REMEDII: Robust Malware Detection with Iterative and Intelligent Adversarial Training

Sanchit Gupta[1] and Vireshwar Kumar[2]

[1] Defence Research and Development Organisation Delhi, New Delhi 110054, India
sanchitgupta.sag@gov.in
[2] Indian Institute of Technology Delhi, New Delhi 110016, India
viresh@cse.iitd.ac.in

Abstract. Malware detection traditionally relies on signature-based approaches, which suffer from limited generalization. To mitigate this issue, machine learning (ML)-based detection methods have been integrated with signature-based methods in recent years. However, ML-based detectors are vulnerable to adversarial attacks, particularly those leveraging Generative Adversarial Networks (GAN) to alter the features of malware while retaining its malicious purpose and bypassing detection. In this paper, we present an innovative defense mechanism called REMEDII (Robust Malware Detection with Iterative Adversarial Training), which improves the robustness of ML-based malware detectors. REMEDII iteratively generates mini-batches of adversarial samples from newly trained instances of GANs and intelligently selects samples with maximum hamming (bit-wise) distance from benign data, ensuring more robust training and mitigating overfitting. Extensive experiments with various ML classifiers (e.g., Convolutional Neural Networks) show that REMEDII achieves over 85% adversarial robustness against GAN-based attacks while maintaining a benign accuracy drop of less than 2%. These results significantly outperform existing defense techniques, which achieve very low adversarial robustness (<2%).

Keywords: Malware Detection · Machine Learning · Adversarial Training · Generative Adversarial Network (GAN)

1 Introduction

Malware detection is critical to establishing robust cybersecurity measures. Malicious software, or malware, poses significant risks to the security and integrity of computer systems, leading to data theft, unauthorized access, and the exploitation of system vulnerabilities. The consequences of malware attacks are widespread, resulting in substantial financial losses and disruption across institutions and their IT infrastructures. Notable examples include globally disruptive incidents such as WannaCry and Petya.

Traditional antivirus solutions rely on signature-based approaches, which compare known malware signatures with system files. This reactive method is limited to the detection of known malware, making it ineffective against evolving threats. This highlights the need for a more adaptive and advanced approach to effectively detect and mitigate malware threats.

Machine learning (ML) has emerged as a promising technique for malware detection. ML-based detectors analyze patterns, behaviors, and characteristics of files and processes, allowing the detection of previously unseen malware and the adaptation to new threats. However, vulnerabilities in these ML-based detectors have been uncovered, which exposes them to adversarial attacks. In such attacks, adversaries manipulate input data to exploit weaknesses in detection algorithms, bypass detection, or cause misclassifications. These adversarial attacks pose a significant challenge to the reliability of ML-based malware detection systems.

The idea of generating negative samples in the image domain is first proposed by [20]. They introduced small imperceptible perturbations in the images, which caused their misclassification. In the malware domain, perturbations cannot be applied randomly as they can break the malware's functionality. Hence, it is incumbent to develop ways of adding perturbations without breaking the malware's functionality, like adding features, adding data to the non-functional part of the malware binary, and padding random bytes at the end of the executable.

In the field of adversarial sample generation, researchers have proposed numerous techniques that can be categorized into two main types: white-box attacks and black-box/gray-box attacks, based on the level of access the attacker has to the internals of the malware detector. In white-box attacks [3,8,10,11,17,19], the attacker has full access to the internals of the detector. On the other hand, black-box and gray-box attacks [1,4,9,12,21,23,25] consider scenarios in which the attacker has limited or no knowledge about the internal workings of the malware detector. These techniques have demonstrated the ability to generate effective adversarial samples and significantly undermine the accuracy of the classifier. Despite the effectiveness of these adversarial attacks, only a limited amount of research has been published on how to make classifiers robust against such attacks.

Developing robust defense mechanisms to counter adversarial attacks in the malware detection domain is essential. In this paper, we propose a novel defense mechanism called REMEDII (Robust Android Malware Detection with Iterative Adversarial Training using Generative Adversarial Networks). REMEDII employs an iterative and intelligent adversarial training process that generates mini-batches of adversarial samples from newly trained instances of GANs, and selects samples with maximum hamming (bit-wise) distance to ensure robust training and mitigate overfitting. GAN-based attack models use Generative Adversarial Networks (GANs) to generate adversarial malware samples designed to evade detection while retaining their malicious behavior. We evaluated REMEDII's performance using various classifiers, including Support Vector Machine (SVM), Multi-Layer Perceptron (MLP), Decision Tree (DT), Random Forest (RF), Logistic Regression (LR), Convolutional Neural Network (CNN) and Deep Neural Network (DNN), against popular GAN-based attack models such as MALGAN and LSGAN-AT [9,23].

The rest of the paper is organized as follows. We provide an overview of the latest adversarial attacks and defenses in Sect. 2. Section 3 outlines the definition of the problem in this work. The basic structure of REMEDII, along with its implementation details, is presented in Sects. 4 and 5. The results are provided in Sect. 6, highlighting significant improvements compared to published works in this area.

2 Background and Related Work

In this section, we provide a survey of the latest adversarial attacks and defense mechanisms for ML-based malware detectors. Table 1 summarizes the recent adversarial attack techniques and corresponding defenses.

Adversarial attacks on AI-based malware detectors were first documented by Grosse et al. (2017) [8]. They introduced a white-box attack using the Jacobian matrix and saliency maps to compute gradients of deep learning models, generating adversarial malware samples for specific classifiers using the DREBIN dataset [2]. Defensive distillation [13] and adversarial learning [7] were tested, but with limited success.

Hu et al. (2017) [9] introduced MALGAN, a black-box adversarial attack using GANs. MALGAN assumed prior knowledge of the features utilized by malware detectors. Using a substitute detector to replicate the black-box detector, MALGAN was able to bypass six different classifiers (random forest, linear regression, decision tree, SVM, MLP, and Voting Ensemble), reducing their precision from 92–97% to 0–2%. Although adversarial training was incorporated, it was only effective against the specific instance of MALGAN trained at that time. Retraining the GAN could easily bypass adversarially trained detectors.

Chen et al. (2017) [3] introduced EvnAttack, an evasion attack model, and SecDefender, a secure-learning paradigm. By leveraging the Max-Relevance algorithm [14], they selected relevant features and improved the robustness of DL-based malware detectors through retraining and regularization. This enhanced resilience against attacks like EvnAttack.

Kolosnjaji et al. (2018) [11] presented a gradient-based attack strategy aimed at defeating the ML-based malware detector known as Malconv [16]. This attack method required the addition of extra padding bytes at the end of the executable, which, unfortunately, could be easily detected. Additionally, the attack involved repeated modifications to the executable, making it computationally expensive. Further analysis carried out by Octavian et al. [19] revealed weaknesses in the structure of Malconv, making it susceptible to injection attacks such as Append Attacks and Slack Attacks. These attacks highlighted the vulnerability of classifiers that utilize raw memory bytes as features, underscoring the susceptibility of such classifiers to adversarial attacks.

Usama et al. (2019) [21] used GANs for launching and defending against adversarial attacks on Network Intrusion Detection Systems (NIDS). Subtle perturbations to network traffic reduced the classifier accuracy from 84–89% to 43–69%. GAN-based adversarial training improved accuracy to 81–84%, but the study lacked details on robustness against multiple GAN instances.

Li et al. (2020) [12] introduced E-MALGAN, a bi-objective GAN for generating adversarial samples aimed at Android malware detection systems. The authors demonstrated that E-MALGAN was more effective than MALGAN at generating adversarial samples that bypassed firewall-equipped systems. Khoda et al. (2020) [10] proposed two novel adversarial training techniques focusing on careful selection of adversarial samples for retraining. By considering the distance from malware cluster centers and using probability measures from kernel-based learning (KBL), they achieved a 6% improvement in detection accuracy compared to random sample selection. This emphasizes the importance of sample selection during adversarial training.

Rathore et al. (2021) [17] introduced a white-box gradient-based attack targeting twelve self-trained Android malware detection models using permissions and intent features. Their defense strategies included adversarial retraining, GAN defense, and hybrid distillation, resulting in a notable accuracy improvement of 54%. Anderson et al. (2017) [1] introduced black-box and white-box adversarial attacks targeting Windows PE files, employing reinforcement learning techniques. Interestingly, their results showed black-box attacks outperforming white-box attacks, as adversaries could manipulate non-functional features of executables to bypass detection.

The authors of [23] proposed LSGAN-AT, a technique to generate superior adversarial malware samples compared to MALGAN. Using Least Square GANs (LSGANs), they improved the transferability of adversarial samples, successfully attacking six different ML detectors. Despite their success, the details of adversarial training were not thoroughly discussed.

While a variety of adversarial defense techniques have been explored for ML-based malware detectors, most are limited in effectiveness. Common approaches, such as adversarial training, often fail when exposed to new instances of adversarial samples. Furthermore, many studies have focused more on the attacks themselves rather than on developing comprehensive and robust defense strategies. The need for more innovative solutions to mitigate adversarial attacks, such as REMEDII's iterative and intelligent adversarial training approach, remains critical to improving the security of ML-based malware detectors.

3 Problem Statement

The findings of the above survey clearly reveal that machine learning-powered malware detectors are prone to adversarial attacks. Adversaries have honed their skills in devising effective methods to create malware samples that can evade detection by these systems. In the case of feature-based classifiers, each malware instance is transformed into a binary feature vector denoted V. In this representation, ones indicate the presence of a specific feature, while zeros signify its absence. Unlike the realm of images, where adversarial examples can be randomly modified, the malware domain presents a unique challenge.

Table 1. Overview of attack and defense strategies in the malware detection domain.

Attack Technique	Target Model & Features	Datasets	Defense Strategy/Outcome
2017 [8] White-box attack using Jacobian matrix and saliency map	DL Model on Static Features	Android-DREBIN	Adversarial training & defensive distillation slightly improved robustness
2017 [9] Black-box attack using MALGAN with GANs	SVM, MLP, DT, RF on System-level APIs	malwr.com	Adversarial training improved robustness, but new MALGAN instances still bypassed the detectors
2017 [3] White-box attack using wrapper method for feature selection	DL Model on API calls	Windows: Comodo Cloud Security	SecDefender (classifier retraining with regularization) improved detection F1 from 0.7304 to 0.8830
2018 [11] White-box gradient-based attack adding bytes to malware sample	Malconv on Raw bytes	Windows: VirusShare, Citadel	Attack evaded 70% of samples with a 1% payload. Removing padding mitigated attack
2019 [21] Black-box attack using GANs	DNN, LR, SVM on Network Traffic	KDD99	GAN-based adversarial training increased accuracy from 43–69% to 81–84%
2020 [18] Black-box attack using Jacobian-based dataset augmentation	DL Model on Domain Names	Botnets: DMD-2018	Adversarial training & distillation had limited effectiveness against evasion attacks
2020 [12] Black-box attack using bi-objective GAN	SVM, AdaBoost, CNN on Permissions, APIs	Android: Virusshare, Contagio	No adversarial defense techniques proposed
2020 [10] White-box attack using Jacobian matrix	DL Model on Permissions, Intents, and System Calls	Android-DREBIN	Adversarial training using cluster center distance improved accuracy by 6%
2021 [17] White-box gradient-based adversarial attack	12 Classification Models on Permissions, Intents	Android-DREBIN	Adversarial retraining, GAN defense, and hybrid distillation improved accuracy by 55%
2021 [23] Black-box attack using LSGAN-AT	MLP, SVM, LR, DT, AB, KNN, GB on API Calls	VirusShare	FFNN-based Adversarial Training recognized more than 50% of adversarial samples from MALGAN

As malware samples are executable files, any alteration risks compromising their functionality, making it essential for attackers to preserve all original features to maintain their malicious behavior. It is possible to introduce additional non-functional features to the executable without compromising its functionality. The authors in [4] provided a framework for adding non-functional features (permissions, intents, etc.) and repackaging Android applications without changing their original functionality.

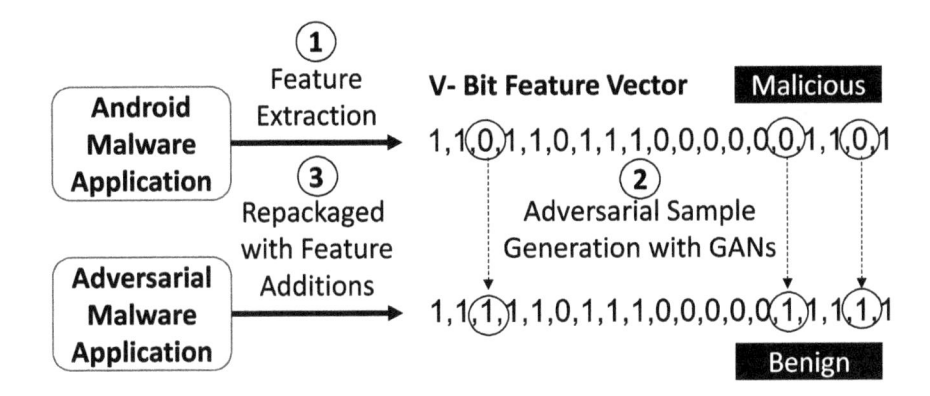

Fig. 1. Crafting adversarial Android malware which evades detection.

Figure 1 presents a typical procedure for crafting adversarial Android applications. These applications are initially flagged as malicious, but through the incorporation of additional features and repackaging, they manage to appear benign to malware detection systems while preserving their original harmful capabilities. The process of selecting features can utilize a gradient-based, optimization algorithm-based, or the most recent Generative Adversarial Network (GAN)-based method. The GAN-based procedure generates the best quality of adversarial examples [5,22,24] in the least time of these three and does not require internal access to the structure of malware detectors.

Generative Adversarial Networks (GANs), first introduced by [6], have emerged as powerful deep learning-based generative models. GANs consist of two main components: the generator and the discriminator. The generator network learns to transform random noise or input variables drawn from a Gaussian distribution into data samples that resemble the target distribution. However, the discriminator network acts as a classifier, distinguishing between real and generated samples. GANs have shown great success in the image domain and have also been applied to the malware domain to generate adversarial samples that can deceive machine learning-based malware detection systems.

Figure 2 illustrates the typical GAN-based adversarial attack techniques used to manipulate malware detectors, where the max layer is used to generate the adversarial vector between the initial input feature vector and the final adversarial feature vector. The final vector has all the original functionality features, and some non-functional features are added to make it adversarial.

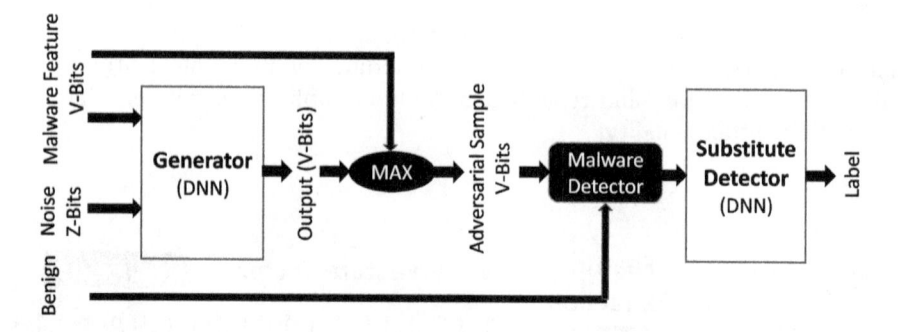

Fig. 2. GAN-based adversarial attacks on malware detectors, demonstrating max layer usage to generate vectors with original and added non-functional features.

Several notable GAN-based models have been proposed in the malware domain, including MALGAN [9], E-MALGAN [12], GAPGAN [25] and LSGAN-AT [23]. These models leverage a substitute detector that emulates the behavior of the black-box malware detection system, enabling the generation of adversarial samples without requiring white-box access to the internal workings of the detector. These techniques have demonstrated their effectiveness in generating adversarial samples efficiently and without the need for extensive knowledge about black-box malware detectors.

Our survey also highlights the existing research gap in the field of malware detection. It emphasizes that while a considerable amount of research has been conducted on developing effective adversarial attack techniques, relatively less attention has been paid to improving the robustness of classifiers against these attacks. This gap poses a significant problem, as the ability of machine learning-based malware detectors to withstand adversarial threats is crucial for their practical application and real-world effectiveness.

To address this issue, further investigation is necessary to devise defense mechanisms that can strengthen the classifier's ability to resist sophisticated adversarial attacks. By conducting research in this area and filling the void, we can reinforce the security of malware detection systems and enhance their capacity to counteract advanced adversarial exploits. This would contribute to the overall improvement of malware detection technology and its ability to protect systems against malicious software. Given the challenges presented by adversarial attacks, the next section outlines the proposed solution, REMEDII, which addresses these limitations.

4 Proposed Solution

A significant limitation of conventional adversarial training methods is that they often overfit adversarial samples generated by a specific instance of a trained Generative Adversarial Network (GAN). As a result, the detector becomes robust only for that particular GAN instance. This occurs because each trained GAN focuses on a subset of non-functional features, modifying only those to craft adversarial samples. When the GAN is retrained with random initial weights, it may target different nonfunctional features, allowing newly generated adversarial samples to evade the previously trained black-box detectors. Thus, the robustness achieved through retraining remains confined to the specific features targeted by the original GAN instance.

To overcome this limitation, REMEDII introduces an iterative adversarial training approach in which newly trained instances of GAN are used during each training round. This ensures that adversarial samples cover a broader set of non-functional features, preventing overfitting to a single GAN instance and enhancing the robustness of the malware detector against a variety of adversarial attacks.

In addition, one of the challenges in adversarial training is balancing the number of adversarial samples used. An excessive number of adversarial samples can lead to overfitting, reducing benign accuracy (the detector's original accuracy on non-adversarial samples). By selecting a small number of adversarial samples (32–64) in each round, REMEDII ensures effective training without compromising benign accuracy. This approach is in line with current research that emphasizes the need for cautious sample selection to avoid overfitting.

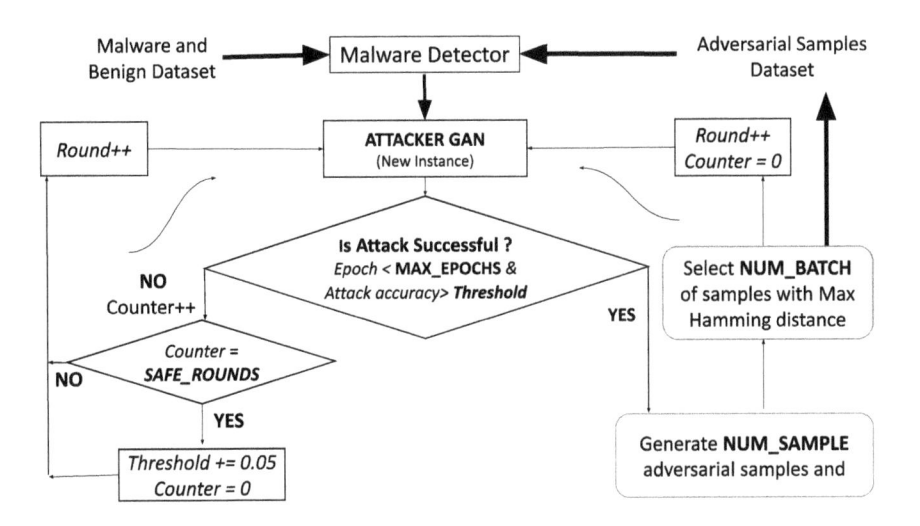

Fig. 3. Proposed REMEDII technique to enhance malware detector robustness.

Table 2. Adjustable parameters used for optimizing the REMEDII technique during adversarial training.

Parameter	Significance
`Threshold`	It refers to the minimum accuracy expected from the detector during adversarial sample detection, which is adjusted iteratively based on the detector's performance
`Rounds`	It refers to the number of rounds that can be fixed as per resources and time and also till the malware detector achieves adversarial protection equal to its original accuracy
`SAFE_ROUNDS`	We consider that the malware detector model has achieved threshold robustness if it can defend itself for rounds equal to `SAFE_ROUNDS` against GAN attacks. After this, `Threshold` is incremented step-wise
`MAX_EPOCHS`	If the attacker GAN cannot train itself in `MAX_EPOCHS` up to the threshold value, we consider the detector safe for that round. This round is considered the safe round
`NUM_SAMPLES`	It refers to the number of adversarial samples generated from attacker GAN
`NUM_BATCH`	It refers to the selected mini-batch of adversarial samples from total `NUM_SAMPLES` samples based on max hamming distance criteria

After extensive experimentation, we make two critical observations:

1. Using a small number of adversarial samples (32–64) significantly strengthens the malware detector against a specific GAN instance. Even a small number of samples can make the detector more robust, eliminating the need for large-scale sample generation.
2. Iterative training with newly trained GAN instances and mini-batches selected based on maximum hamming distance ensures that the malware detector becomes resistant to new, unknown adversarial samples. This approach helps the detector stay up-to-date with emerging threats without a significant drop in benign accuracy.

Based on these observations, we propose the REMEDII technique, which incrementally performs adversarial training in small, carefully selected batches. As shown in Fig. 3, the technique operates in multiple rounds, with adjustable parameters such as the number of rounds, thresholds, and batch sizes. Table 2 highlights the key parameters that can be adjusted to balance performance and robustness.

Furthermore, the attacker GAN can follow any GAN architecture that uses a substitute detector, as previously used in [9,23]. REMEDII continues to iterate, and if a newly trained GAN breaches the current threshold, adversarial training is performed. If not, the GAN is re-trained with random initialization, ensuring the robustness of the malware detector. The threshold is incremented once the detector demonstrates practical robustness against a specified number of attacks (`SAFE_ROUNDS`). In any round where the malware detector is breached, a specific number of adversarial samples (`NUM_SAMPLES`) are generated, from which minibatches (`NUM_BATCH`) are selected for further adversarial training.

In our study, we evaluate strategies with maximum, minimum and random hamming (bitwise) distance between adversarial samples and their original feature vectors. Through extensive experimentation, we find that adversarial samples with the maximum hamming distance from their original counterparts are the most effective for adversarial training. This intelligent sample selection helps improve robustness by ensuring that the detector is exposed to the most challenging adversarial samples.

5 Implementation Details

The dataset containing malicious files was obtained from VirusShare, an online platform available at https://www.virusshare.com. Due to intellectual property rights (IPR), there is no public repository for benign Android applications. Consequently, benign files were individually downloaded from the Google Play Store. To ensure the benign nature of these applications, they were tested using VirusTotal at https://www.virustotal.com, and only applications not flagged by any antivirus software were retained.

From the manifest files of benign and malicious applications, static features such as Actions, Services, Permissions, and Categories were extracted. In total, 9704 unique features were identified. To form the feature vector, a subset of the most significant features was selected. Specifically, 160 features were chosen as the final feature vector using the `SelectKBest` module from the `sklearn` library, which ranks features based on their K score. The selection of 160 features was made to maintain consistency with previously published work in the field. The top ten features, along with their K-scores, are:

- `ComponentDiscoveryService` (3616.40)
- `AppMeasurementJobService` (3012.69)
- `permission.BIND_JOB_SERVICE` (3002.46)
- `AppMeasurementService` (2922.80)
- `JobInfoSchedulerService` (2513.88)
- `MultiInstanceInvalidationService` (2061.386)
- `SystemJobService` (1924.918)
- `SystemAlarmService` (1921.326)
- `action.DEVICE_STORAGE_OK` (1819.314)
- `action.DEVICE_STORAGE_LOW` (1817.748)

For the malware detector, we employ seven different machine learning techniques: Support Vector Machine (SVM), Multi-Layer Perceptron (MLP), Decision Tree (DT), Random Forest (RF), Logistic Regression (LR), Convolutional Neural Network (CNN) and Deep Neural Network (DNN). These detectors were chosen based on their demonstrated success in malware detection. We utilize

Table 3. Parameters chosen for the *defence* technique in current experiments

Parameter	Value Chosen
Threshold	Initial value: 0.2 and increment value: 0.05
Rounds	Till adversarial protection is equal to benign accuracy is achieved OR maximum 1000
SAFE_ROUNDS	15 till threshold < 65; otherwise 25
MAX_EPOCHS	40
NUM_SAMPLES	1500
NUM_BATCH	48

6,000 training samples and 2,000 testing samples, divided equally between benign and malware samples for both training and testing of the malware detector. Additionally, for the GANs, we selected two attacker models, LSGAN-AT and MALGAN, due to their prominence in existing research. For each GAN, we use 4,500 training samples, equally split between benign and malware samples. If, during any round, the GAN successfully attacks the malware detector and breaches the current threshold, 1,500 adversarial samples are generated. From these, a batch of 48 adversarial samples is selected for adversarial training of the malware detector.

We conducted in-depth experimentation with different parameters of the REMEDII technique and fixed various parameters based on the results, as shown in Table 3. In our study, we started the experiment with a threshold of 0.2, which corresponds to adversarial protection 20%. Adversarial protection indicates the accuracy in detecting malicious samples specifically designed to evade the detection system. To test the resilience of the malware detector, we allowed the attacker GANs a maximum of 40 epochs (MAX_EPOCHS) to attempt to surpass the detector threshold. If the malware detector maintained its adversarial protection above the threshold, the threshold was increased by 5% (equivalent to 0.05). This iterative process continued until one of the following conditions was met:

1. The malware detector achieved satisfactory robustness, meaning adversarial protection equaled the original benign accuracy of the detector for non-adversarial samples.
2. One thousand rounds of REMEDII were completed.

The results obtained on the basis of these parameters are presented in the subsequent section.

6 Evaluation

The REMEDII technique was utilized to make seven ML-based malware detectors robust against adversarial samples. Initially, none of the seven models exhibited robustness against the two attacker GANs. The GAN models were able to

Table 4. Adversarial protection achieved with REMEDII technique for different ML-based black-box malware detectors.

Technique-GAN	Rounds	Initial Adversarial Protection (%)	Final Adversarial Protection (%)	Re-Training Rounds (T)	Total Adversarial Samples (N)	Average Adversarial Samples (N/T)
RF-LSGAN-AT	321	18.87	91.29	16	587	36.69
RF-MALGAN	357	0	91.18	19	663	34.89
CNN-LSGAN-AT	365	34.22	92.12	14	534	38.14
CNN-MALGAN	358	27.95	92.98	16	581	36.31
DT-LSGAN-AT	940	4	92.78	137	5106	37.27
DT-MALGAN	1000	13.01	87.28	190	4983	26.23
SVM-LSGAN-AT	579	22.28	92.99	48	1594	33.21
SVM-MALGAN	444	21.01	94.04	25	773	30.92
LR-LSGAN-AT	1000	16.81	91.78	173	5498	31.78
LR-MALGAN	1000	19.61	91.64	140	4176	29.83
DNN-LSGAN-AT	1000	19.94	94.04	131	4347	33.18
DNN-MALGAN	1000	0	91.01	149	4375	29.36
MLP-LSGAN-AT	1000	19.34	92.46	144	4623	32.1
MLP-MALGAN	1000	16.61	94.93	134	4206	31.39

swiftly generate adversarial samples, evading the detection capabilities of all the initially trained detectors in just a few epochs. However, after using the REMEDII technique, all models achieved significant resilience against GAN-based attackers.

Table 4 provides an overview of the final adversarial protection achieved using the REMEDII technique for various combinations of ML-based detectors and attacker GANs. Adversarial protection is measured by the recognition rate of adversarial samples, which is calculated as the ratio of detected adversarial examples to the total number of samples. The entry "Final Adversarial protection" in the table represents the average value obtained in the last 10 rounds after reaching the maximum achievable threshold.

Upon analyzing the results, several important findings emerge. Our approach consistently improves the adversarial protection of the classifiers across different combinations. Notably, certain combinations such as RF-LSGAN-AT, RF-MALGAN, CNN-LSGAN-AT, CNN-MALGAN, SVM-LSGAN-AT, and SVM-MALGAN achieve adversarial protection equal to the initial accuracy of the classifier in less than 1000 rounds. This indicates that the malware detector can now recognize adversarial samples with the same accuracy as normal malware samples. For other combinations, the REMEDII technique was stopped at 1000 rounds, although they still achieved significant protection against adversarial samples. The decision to stop at 1000 rounds was based on resource and time constraints. It is worth mentioning that completing 1000 rounds of the REMEDII technique required approximately 96 h on a machine with an 8 Core Intel Xeon CPU E5-2695 v2 @ 2.40 GHz and 8 GB RAM.

These findings highlight the effectiveness of our REMEDII technique in enhancing the robustness of malware detectors against adversarial attacks. The intelligent and iterative adversarial training process enables our approach to adapt and improve over multiple rounds, resulting in significant advances in adversarial protection.

It should be mentioned that the number of adversarial trainings (T) and the number of adversarial samples (N) used in each combination varied. This allowed us to assess the unique number of unique samples generated in each training round. The last column (N/T) value shows that one can produce more samples using certain combination in less number of training rounds.

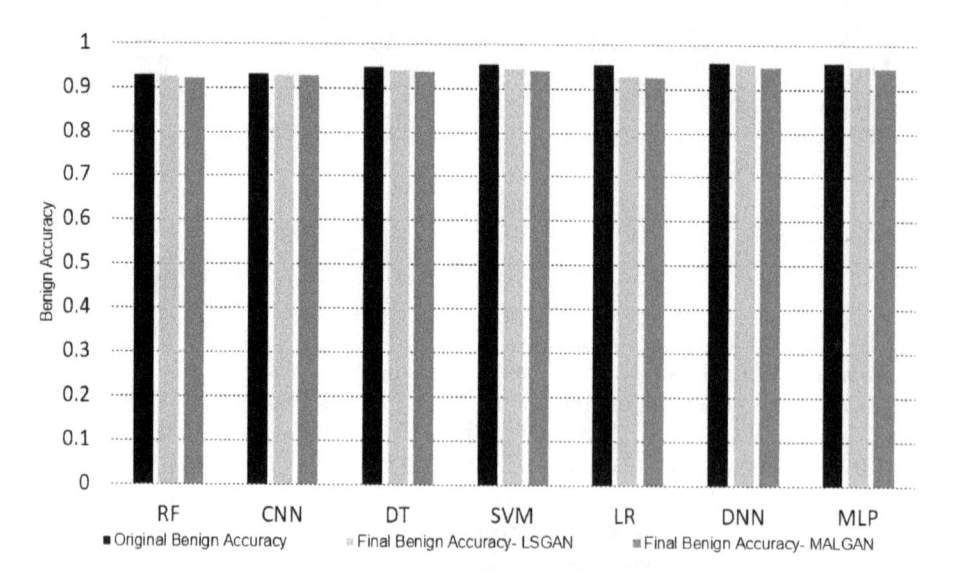

Fig. 4. Effect of REMEDII on benign accuracy with two GANs.

One potential drawback of adversarial training is the decrease in benign accuracy of the detector. However, in the case of our REMEDII technique, we ensure that only a small number of adversarial samples are used to train the classifier. This approach minimizes the impact on benign accuracy. Figure 4 illustrates the effect of applying the REMEDII technique with two attacker GANs on the benign accuracy of malware detection. The results show a modest drop in benign accuracy, ranging from 0.1% to 2.7%. This minimal decrease in benign accuracy underscores the effectiveness of our approach in maintaining the overall performance of the detector. Furthermore, it should be noted that the REMEDII technique that uses LSGAN-AT shows greater effectiveness compared to MAL-GAN. The benign accuracy drop observed with LSGAN-AT is relatively lower while achieving a similar level of robustness. This suggests that REMEDII with

LSGAN-AT strikes a better balance between benign accuracy and achievable robustness, making it a favourable choice to enhance the resilience of the malware detection system. The final adversarial protection values presented in Table 4 correspond to different instances of the same GAN attacker, with adversarial data specifically generated for a particular ML detector.

To thoroughly assess the robustness of these models, we conducted an additional experiment. In this experiment, we subjected the 14 adversarially trained models to adversarial data generated by the REMEDII technique for other GANs and ML-based detectors. This comprehensive evaluation aimed to determine the global robustness of these fourteen malware detectors as they will be subjected to unseen adversarial samples.

Table 5. Performance of the robust model (trained using MALGAN) against adversarial samples generated by MALGAN for different ML techniques.

	AMCNN	AMDNN	AMDT	AMLR	AMMLP	AMRF	AMSVM
MALCNN	0.871	0.95	0.999	0.947	0.939	0.745	0.838
MALDNN	0.945	1	0.998	0.966	0.941	0.952	0.882
MALDT	0.837	0.852	0.971	0.825	0.847	0.784	0.742
MALLR	0.876	0.942	0.999	0.906	0.919	0.79	0.829
MALMLP	0.929	0.937	1	0.956	0.926	0.881	0.865
MALRF	0.794	0.913	0.991	0.831	0.885	0.698	0.774
MALSVM	0.911	0.949	1	0.93	0.93	0.837	0.999

Table 6. Performance of the robust model (trained using LSGAN-AT) against adversarial samples generated against LSGAN-AT for different ML techniques.

	ALCNN	ALDNN	ALDT	ALLR	ALMLP	ALRF	ALSVM
LSCNN	0.951	0.87	0.941	0.909	0.835	0.898	0.76
LSDNN	0.89	0.935	0.962	0.963	0.85	0.947	0.741
LSDT	0.91	0.89	0.983	0.926	0.88	0.896	0.832
LSLR	0.931	0.845	0.919	0.848	0.814	0.92	0.745
LSMLP	0.938	0.868	0.96	0.949	0.882	0.917	0.772
LSRF	0.781	0.788	0.883	0.757	0.73	0.799	0.635
LSSVM	0.92	0.891	0.96	0.968	0.868	0.978	0.973

We provide the detailed analysis in Tables 5, 6, 7, and 8. These tables show the adversarial accuracy of fourteen malware detectors fortified using the REMEDII technique. Each table represents a specific combination of a robust model, GAN attacker, and ML detector. The first column lists robust models like MALCNN, a robust CNN model created using the MALGAN attacker with REMEDII. Subsequent columns show detection accuracy for adversarial samples generated by

Table 7. Performance of the robust model (trained using LSGAN-AT) against adversarial samples generated by MALGAN for different ML techniques.

	AMCNN	AMDNN	AMDT	AMLR	AMMLP	AMRF	AMSVM
LSCNN	0.868	0.963	1	0.962	0.949	0.768	0.881
LSDNN	0.88	0.932	0.999	0.958	0.935	0.887	0.888
LSDT	0.909	0.949	0.953	0.947	0.95	0.887	0.922
LSLR	0.892	0.95	0.999	0.918	0.938	0.754	0.851
LSMLP	0.943	0.947	0.996	0.952	0.925	0.867	0.924
LSRF	0.783	0.924	0.991	0.851	0.901	0.649	0.791
LSSVM	0.936	0.984	1	0.984	0.97	0.864	0.928

Table 8. Performance of the robust model (trained using MALGAN) against adversarial samples generated by LSGAN-AT for different ML techniques.

	ALCNN	ALDNN	ALDT	ALLR	ALMLP	ALRF	ALSVM
MALCNN	0.706	0.849	0.936	0.885	0.817	0.871	0.684
MALDNN	0.841	0.696	0.917	0.919	0.655	0.867	0.515
MALDT	0.768	0.769	0.79	0.781	0.731	0.78	0.656
MALLR	0.918	0.827	0.915	0.785	0.78	0.883	0.72
MALMLP	0.86	0.683	0.907	0.892	0.612	0.908	0.505
MALRF	0.773	0.777	0.871	0.713	0.718	0.661	0.605
MALSVM	0.876	0.765	0.899	0.833	0.718	0.881	0.464

various classifiers and GAN attackers, such as AMMLP (MLP classifier vs. MAL-GAN attacker) and ALSVM (SVM classifier vs. LSGAN-AT attacker). These tables provide a comprehensive overview of the detectors' performance against adversarial samples, helping us assess their global robustness and effectiveness in detecting adversarial threats.

The choice of GAN attacker in the REMEDII technique has a significant impact on its performance, as observed in the experiments. The average performance of malware detectors trained with adversarial attacks using MALGAN is 83.88%, whereas with LSGAN-AT, it is 89.58%. This finding supports the claim made by the authors in their work on LSGAN-AT [23], which suggests that the LSGAN-AT-based GAN architecture can generate more effective adversarial malware samples compared to the simpler MALGAN architecture.

Furthermore, the choice of ML-based technique in the REMEDII technique also has a significant effect. The combination of an SVM-based malware detector and LSGAN-AT attacker produces the most effective adversarial samples. By "effective", it means that the other 13 combinations of detectors and attacker GANs has a comparatively lower detection rate for all adversarial samples. The SVM-based malware detector trained with these adversarial samples achieves

Table 9. Comparison of REMEDII with existing adversarial defense methods.

Paper	Adversarial Defence Techniques	Why REMEDII is Better
[8,15]	Adversarial training has a limited impact on robustness, and excessive use of adversarial samples harms performance	Adversarial training with REMEDII in small batches achieved significant robustness while minimizing accuracy loss
[9]	Retraining against MALGAN defends against a specific version of MALGAN, but retrained MALGAN can still successfully attack it with a low protection level (0–2%)	REMEDII achieved robustness against repeated MALGAN attacks, with an average robustness of 90.64%
[21]	GAN-based adversarial training enhances robustness in NIDS classifiers, improving accuracy from 43–69% to 81–84%	REMEDII significantly improved accuracy against adversarial samples, raising it from 17.24% to an average of 86.74%
[18]	Adversarially trained classifiers show limited accuracy improvement (2–3%) for unknown evasion techniques. Effectiveness is limited to training-time attacks	Robust SVM trained with LSGAN-AT achieved a remarkable detection rate of 94.4% for adversarial samples generated by other ML techniques and GANs
[23]	Robust models trained with LSGAN-AT recognized 50% of MALGAN samples and 65% of LSGAN-AT samples.	On average, LSGAN-AT-trained robust models recognized 91.42% of MALGAN samples and achieved 87.77% recognition for LSGAN-AT-based adversarial malware
[17]	The highest average accuracy improvement is observed with adversarial retraining (55.86%), hybrid distillation (54.21%), and GAN retraining (36.87%) for twelve detection models	REMEDII achieved an average of 86.74% accuracy against adversarial samples

the highest average global adversarial protection of 94.4%. Similarly, DNN, DT and MLP-based malware detectors trained with the LSGAN-AT attacker show good global robustness of 91.2%, 91.7%, and 91.7%, respectively.

The experiments show that the choice of different ML-based detectors and various attacker GAN models has a considerable impact on the effectiveness of the defense technique. These results highlight the ability of the defense method to perform well against adversarial attacks from both the same GAN model used during training and against new, unseen GAN models. This demonstrates the technique's capability to generalize and maintain strong defenses against a wide range of adversarial threats.

Table 9 presents a comparison between the REMEDII technique and other published adversarial defense methods in the malware detection domain. Several key distinctions emerge from this comparison: REMEDII demonstrates significant improvements in robustness against adversarial attacks while minimizing accuracy loss. By employing adversarial training in small carefully selected batches, it addresses a common limitation of existing methods, which often overfit to specific adversarial samples. Unlike traditional defenses that are effective only against specific versions of attacks, REMEDII provides sustained robustness against repeated adversarial attempts, achieving a high average robustness rate.

Moreover, REMEDII significantly improves accuracy against adversarial samples. In contrast to other techniques showing only marginal improvements, it increases accuracy from initially low levels to a consistently higher average. When using the LSGAN-AT attacker, REMEDII achieves exceptional recognition rates for adversarial samples generated by various machine learning models and GAN-based attacks, demonstrating its effectiveness across diverse attack types.

Among the compared techniques, REMEDII is the one with the highest average accuracy improvement, underscoring its ability to improve the performance of the classifier in the face of adversarial input. Overall, REMEDII not only strengthens robustness but also achieves notable gains in accuracy and recognition rates, making it a highly effective solution for countering adversarial attacks and improving the resilience of malware detectors.

7 Conclusion and Future Work

In this study, we proposed REMEDII, a robust adversarial defense technique that addresses key limitations of existing approaches, offering significant improvements in both robustness and accuracy against adversarial samples. Our experiments and analysis demonstrate the effectiveness of REMEDII in defending against various types of adversarial attacks, including those from MALGAN and LSGAN-AT. The results indicate that adversarial training in small, carefully selected batches is crucial to achieving robustness while minimizing accuracy loss, a challenge faced by many traditional adversarial defense methods.

In particular, REMEDII consistently delivered high recognition rates for adversarial samples generated by different machine learning techniques and GAN models, showcasing its ability to combat a diverse range of attacks. Furthermore, our comparative analysis against established adversarial defense techniques highlighted that REMEDII not only outperforms them in terms of average accuracy improvement but also demonstrates superior resilience to repeated adversarial attempts. This underscores REMEDII's ability to improve classifier accuracy and overall robustness in the face of evolving adversarial inputs.

Although REMEDII has shown promising results, there are several avenues for future work to expand and refine its capabilities. First, exploring the impact of different GAN architectures on adversarial sample generation could further enhance the robustness of the technique. Furthermore, investigating the transferability of adversarial samples across various classifiers and domains will provide information on the generalizability of REMEDII. Given the dynamic nature of adversarial attacks and the emergence of new evasion techniques, continuous research and development are essential to adapt REMEDII to evolving threats. This could include incorporating advanced techniques such as model distillation to further bolster the robustness and accuracy of malware detectors.

Finally, real-world deployment and evaluation of REMEDII on large-scale datasets and production systems will be crucial for understanding its practical effectiveness and performance. This will involve testing against sophisticated adversaries, assessing computational overhead, and evaluating the scalability of the technique in operational environments.

In conclusion, REMEDII represents a promising approach to address the challenges posed by adversarial attacks in machine learning systems. With further research and development, it has the potential to contribute significantly to the advancement of robust and secure ML models across a variety of domains and applications.

References

1. Anderson, H.S., Kharkar, A., Filar, B., Roth, P.: Evading machine learning malware detection. Black Hat **2017**, 1–6 (2017)
2. Arp, D., Spreitzenbarth, M., Hubner, M., Gascon, H., Rieck, K., Siemens, C.: Drebin: Effective and explainable detection of android malware in your pocket. In: NDSS, vol. 14, pp. 23–26 (2014)
3. Chen, L., Ye, Y., Bourlai, T.: Adversarial machine learning in malware detection: arms race between evasion attack and defense. In: 2017 European Intelligence and Security Informatics Conference (EISIC), pp. 99–106. IEEE (2017)
4. Renjith, G., Laudanna, S., Aji, S., Visaggio, C.A., Vinod, P.: Gang-mam: GAN based engine for modifying android malware. SoftwareX **18**, 100977 (2022)
5. Gonog, L., Zhou, Y.: A review: generative adversarial networks. In: 2019 14th IEEE conference on industrial electronics and applications (ICIEA), pp. 505–510. IEEE (2019)
6. Goodfellow, I., et al.: Generative adversarial networks. Commun. ACM **63**(11), 139–144 (2020)
7. Goodfellow, I.J., Shlens, J., Szegedy, C.: Explaining and harnessing adversarial examples. In: 3rd International Conference on Learning Representations, ICLR 2015 - Conference Track Proceedings (2015)
8. Grosse, K., Papernot, N., Manoharan, P., Backes, M., McDaniel, P.: Adversarial examples for malware detection. In: Foley, S.N., Gollmann, D., Snekkenes, E. (eds.) Computer Security - ESORICS 2017, pp. 62–79. Springer, Cham (2017)
9. Hu, W., Tan, Y.: Generating adversarial malware examples for black-box attacks based on GAN. In: International Conference on Data Mining and Big Data, pp. 409–423. Springer (2022)
10. Khoda, M.E., Imam, T., Kamruzzaman, J., Gondal, I., Rahman, A.: Robust malware defense in industrial IoT applications using machine learning with selective adversarial samples. IEEE Trans. Ind. Appl. **56**(4), 4415–4424 (2019)
11. Kolosnjaji, B., et al.: Adversarial malware binaries: evading deep learning for malware detection in executables. In: 2018 26th European Signal Processing Conference (EUSIPCO), pp. 533–537. IEEE (2018)

12. Li, H., Zhou, S., Yuan, W., Li, J., Leung, H.: Adversarial-example attacks toward android malware detection system. IEEE Syst. J. **14**(1), 653–656 (2019)
13. Papernot, N., McDaniel, P., Wu, X., Jha, S., Swami, A.: Distillation as a defense to adversarial perturbations against deep neural networks. In: 2016 IEEE Symposium on Security and Privacy (SP), pp. 582–597. IEEE (2016)
14. Peng, H., Long, F., Ding, C.: Feature selection based on mutual information criteria of max-dependency, max-relevance, and min-redundancy. IEEE Trans. Pattern Anal. Mach. Intell. **27**(8), 1226–1238 (2005)
15. Piskozub, M., De Gaspari, F., Barr-Smith, F., Mancini, L., Martinovic, I.: MalPhase: fine-grained malware detection using network flow data. In: Proceedings of the 2021 ACM Asia Conference on Computer and Communications Security, pp. 774–786 (2021)
16. Raff, E., Barker, J., Sylvester, J., Brandon, R., Catanzaro, B., Nicholas, C.K.: Malware detection by eating a whole EXE. In: AAAI Workshops. AAAI Technical Report, vol. WS-18, pp. 268–276. AAAI Press (2018)
17. Rathore, H., Samavedhi, A., Sahay, S.K., Sewak, M.: Robust malware detection models: Learning from adversarial attacks and defenses. Forensic Sci. Int.: Digit. Invest. **37**, 301183 (2021)
18. Sidi, L., Nadler, A., Shabtai, A.: MaskDGA: an evasion attack against DGA classifiers and adversarial defenses. IEEE Access **8**, 161580–161592 (2020)
19. Suciu, O., Coull, S.E., Johns, J.: Exploring adversarial examples in malware detection. In: AAAI Fall Symposium: ALEC. CEUR Workshop Proceedings, vol. 2269, pp. 11–16. CEUR-WS.org (2018)
20. Szegedy, C., et al.: Intriguing properties of neural networks. In: 2nd International Conference on Learning Representations, ICLR 2014 - Conference Track Proceedings (2014)
21. Usama, M., Asim, M., Latif, S., Qadir, J., et al.: Generative adversarial networks for launching and thwarting adversarial attacks on network intrusion detection systems. In: 2019 15th International Wireless Communications & Mobile Computing Conference (IWCMC), pp. 78–83. IEEE (2019)
22. Wang, D., Dong, L., Wang, R., Yan, D., Wang, J.: Targeted speech adversarial example generation with generative adversarial network. IEEE Access **8**, 124503–124513 (2020)
23. Wang, J., Chang, X., Wang, Y., Rodríguez, R.J., Zhang, J.: LSGAN-AT: enhancing malware detector robustness against adversarial examples. Cybersecurity **4**, 1–15 (2021)
24. Xiao, C., Li, B., Zhu, J., He, W., Liu, M., Song, D.: Generating adversarial examples with adversarial networks. In: IJCAI, pp. 3905–3911. ijcai.org (2018)
25. Yuan, J., Zhou, S., Lin, L., Wang, F., Cui, J.: Black-box adversarial attacks against deep learning based malware binaries detection with GAN. In: ECAI 2020, pp. 2536–2542. IOS Press (2020)

Semantics-Based Static Vulnerability Detection in Solidity Using Abstract Interpretation

Maitri Kushwaha, Arnab Mukherjee, Aishwarya Pandey, and Raju Halder[✉][iD]

Indian Institute of Technology Patna, Patna, India
{maitri_2321cs03,arnab_2213cs01,aish_23ps20,halder}@iitp.ac.in

Abstract. This paper introduces a novel semantics-based static analysis approach for Solidity, leveraging the Abstract Interpretation theory to enhance Ethereum smart contract vulnerability detection. Our approach formalizes a sound approximation of Solidity semantics, balancing precision and computational efficiency through tunable abstraction levels. By integrating local and blockchain state considerations into an augmented flow graph capturing both data and control flow, we achieve effective vulnerability detection. Implemented using the APRON library's Interval and Octagon abstract domains, our approach demonstrates significant improvements over state-of-the-art tools in the case of Reentrancy and Arithmetic vulnerabilities.

Keywords: Blockchain · Smart Contract · Solidity · Vulnerability · Semantics · Static Analysis · Abstract Interpretation

1 Introduction

Among the languages used to script smart contracts for Ethereum, Solidity is by far the most popular choice for Ethereum developers. The significant surge in popularity of decentralized applications (DApps) on Ethereum has led to numerous financially motivated adversaries aiming to discover and exploit vulnerabilities within the deployed smart contracts. As a result, the Ethereum community in recent times have witnessed several disastrous attacks [8], such as the Decentralized Autonomous Organization (DAO) attack in 2016 [4] and Parity Wallet hack in 2017 [22] leading to a total loss close to $90 million.

In order to discover prevention methods and to detect the scope of possible vulnerabilities during the development of smart contracts, a number of formal analysis and verification approaches were proposed in the literature, including ZEUS [16], Oyente [19], Slither [10], Mythril [20], Maian [21]. Interestingly, the study in [5] reveals that the empirical evaluation of nine state-of-the-art automated analysis tools using SmartBugs on massive datasets shows that only 42% of the vulnerabilities were detected by all tools, with Mythril achieving the highest accuracy at 27%. This low detection rate and inadequate coverage are due to the fact that most of these proposals use off-the-shelf tools designed specifically for other languages and transpilation-based approaches. This results in a lack of theoretical foundation and consideration of Solidity semantics in the state-of-the-art.

As an alternative, this paper proposes a novel semantics-based static analysis approach for Solidity based on the Abstract Interpretation theory [2], aiming to detect vulnerabilities in smart contracts before their deployment. In essence, the use of Abstract Interpretation theory provides a systematic approach to formalizing conservative approximation of Solidity semantics, offering its tuning at different levels of abstractions so as to achieve a trade-off between precision and computation cost. To this aim, we first define the concrete semantics of Solidity, which we eventually lift to an abstract domain of interest following Galois connections. This guarantees the soundness of the analysis, eliminating the possibility of false negatives. Our initial research efforts focus on Reentrancy, Arithmetic Overflow/Underflow, and Dependency-based Vulnerabilities (e.g. Transaction Order Dependency, Block Timestamp Dependency, etc.), and we conduct an experimental evaluation on a set of benchmarks that demonstrate an improved performance in the case of Reentrancy and Arithmetic Overflow/Underflow.

To summarize, following are the contributions we impart in the paper:

- We define a sound approximation of Solidity semantics in an abstract domain of interest, considering both local and blockchain states, using the Abstract Interpretation theory.
- We present a semantics-based static analysis of Solidity programs using abstract semantics computed based on an augmented flow graph (involving both data and control dependencies), allowing one to detect possible vulnerabilities in the codes.
- We build a prototype tool in Python, based on the APRON numerical abstract domain library [14], integrating both Interval and Octagon abstract domains.
- To test the efficacy of our approach, we run experiments on *SmartBugs* [9], a curated dataset of vulnerable smart contracts, and we compare the detection rate of our approach against four popular state-of-the-art static analysis tools for Solidity. The results demonstrate significant improvements in terms of sensitivity towards detecting vulnerable contracts.

The rest of the paper is organized as follows: A brief literature survey of existing static analysis tools for Solidity is presented in Sect. 2. Section 3 provides a manifest of some of the common vulnerabilities found in Solidity. The abstract semantics of Solidity, along with our approach to identifying vulnerabilities in smart contracts, is presented in Sect. 4. Section 5 provides the implementation details of the prototype, whereas the detailed analysis of experimental outcomes is discussed in Sect. 6. Finally, we conclude our work in Sect. 7.

2 Related Work

With widespread attacks masquerading on the Ethereum ecosystem, exploiting the vulnerabilities in smart contracts, in recent years, there has been a lot of work done on smart contract vulnerability detection methods [18].

In 2016, Luu et al. [19] introduced Oyente, a smart contract detection tool that uses symbolic execution to identify potential security vulnerabilities in smart contracts. Subsequently, in 2017, Mythril [20] was developed as an official Ethereum smart contract vulnerability detection tool. Mythril employs symbolic execution to explore all possible unsafe paths, detecting 14 types of vulnerabilities, including timestamp dependency, arbitrary address writing, and Arithmetic Overflow. Further, in 2018, Nikolic et al. [21] introduced Maian, a tool for specifying and reasoning about trace properties using inter-procedural symbolic analysis and a concrete validator to demonstrate real exploits. Vandal, proposed by Brent et al. [7], utilizes Souffle logic specifications for smart contract security analysis. Another approach, EthIR [6] put forward by Albert et al. in 2018, leverages Oyente to generate control flow graphs (CFGs) and translates them into rule-based bytecode representations (RBRs) for Ethereum bytecode analysis. SmartCheck [23] introduced in 2018 follows a different strategy, converting smart contract source code into an XML-based intermediate representation and employing XPath patterns for vulnerability detection. Feist et al. introduced Slither [10] in 2019, a tool that transforms smart contracts into an intermediate representation called SlithIR. SlithIR simplifies vulnerability analysis through a static single allocation form and a streamlined instruction set, while preserving essential semantic information that might be lost during bytecode conversion. ZEUS [16], proposed by Kalra et al. in 2018, uses symbolic model checking and constraint statements to quickly test the security of smart contracts. Precisely, it uses LLVM's API to translate high-level source code into LLVM bitcode translator to accordingly insert verification state for the given specifications. In 2021, Jeon et al. [15] proposed SmartConDetect, a static analysis tool designed to detect security vulnerabilities in Solidity-based smart contracts, which identifies vulnerable code patterns using a pre-trained BERT model by extracting relevant code fragments.

3 Vulnerabilities in Solidity

In this section, we manifest the details of some of the common vulnerabilities found in Solidity.

Reentrancy Vulnerability.. Reentrancy is a common and critical type of vulnerability. A Reentrancy attack occurs when a smart contract calls another untrusted smart contract without updating its previous state. This enables the untrusted contract to enter into the original contract in the middle of execution, leading to inconsistent states or draining funds. Figure 1 demonstrates this Reentrancy attack, where the vulnerable contract allows an attacker to continuously call the withdraw function before the balance becomes zero.

Transaction Ordering Dependency Vulnerability. A Transaction-Ordering attack changes the state of a variable during the processing of a transaction due to someone else (the contract owner, miner or another user) sending a transaction that

```
1  //Vulnerable Contract
2  contract DAO {
3    mapping(address => uint) public dep;
4    function deposit() public payable {
5      dep[msg.sender] += msg.value;
6    }
7    function withdraw() public {
8      uint bal = dep[msg.sender];
9      require(bal > 0);
10     (bool sent, ) = msg.sender.call{value : bal}("");
11     require(sent, "Failed to send Ether");
12     dep[msg.sender] = 0;
13   }
14 }
15 //Attacker Contract
16 import "./DAO.sol";
17 contract AttackContract {
18   DAO public exploit;
19   constructor(address DAOAddress) {
20     exploit = DAO(DAOAddress);
21   }
22   function attack() external payable {
23     exploit.deposit{value : 1 ether}();
24     exploit.withdraw();
25   }
26   receive() external payable {
27     if (address(exploit).balance >= 1 ether) {
28       exploit.withdraw(); }}}
```

Fig. 1. Reentrancy

```
1  contract TransactionOrdering {
2    uint256 price;
3    address owner;
4    event Purchase(address _buyer, uint256 _price);
5    event PriceChange(address _owner, uint256 _price);
6    modifier ownerOnly() {
7      require(msg.sender == owner);
8      _;
9    }
10   constructor() {
11     owner = msg.sender;
12     price = 100;
13   }
14   function buy() public returns(uint256) {
15     emit Purchase(msg.sender, price);
16     return price;
17   }
18   function setPrice(uint256 _price) public ownerOnly() {
19     price = _price;
20     emit PriceChange(owner, price); }}
```

Fig. 2. Transaction Ordering Dependency

```
1  contract overflowunderflow {
2    uint8 public totalSupply;
3    function add(uint8 value) public {
4      totalSupply += value;   // potential overflow
5    }
6    function subtract(uint8 value) public {
7      totalSupply -= value;   // potential underflow
8    }
9    function multiply(uint8 value) public {
10     totalSupply* = value; }}
```

Fig. 3. Arithmetic Overflow/Underflow

```
1  contract DivByZeroVulnerable {
2    function divide(uint256 x, uint256 y) public pure
3    returns(uint256) {
4      return x / y; }}
```

Fig. 4. Division by Zero

```
1  contract OutOfBoundsVulnerable {
2    uint256[] public data;
3    function add(uint256 _value) public {
4      data[data.length] =
5        _value;   // Accessing index out of bounds
6    }}
```

Fig. 5. Array Out of Bounds

```
1  contract TimestampManp {
2    uint public pastBlockTime;
3    constructor() payable {}
4    function spin() external payable {
5      require(msg.value == 4 ether);
6      require(block.timestamp != pastBlockTime);
7      pastBlockTime = block.timestamp;
8      if (pastBlockTime % 3 == 0) {
9        (bool sent, ) =
10         msg.sender.
11         call{value : address(this).balance}("");
12       require(sent, "Failed to send Ether"); }}}
```

Fig. 6. Timestamp Dependency

```
1  contract TokenTransfer {
2    mapping(address => uint256) public balances;
3    function transfer(address _to, uint256 _amount) public {
4      require(balances[msg.sender] >= _amount,
5        "Insufficient balance");
6      for (uint256 i = 0; i < _amount; i++) {
7        balances[msg.sender]--;
8        balances[_to]++; }}}
```

Fig. 7. Gas Limit Issues

modifies the state of a variable before the previous transaction is completed. The code snippet in Fig. 2 shows how this vulnerability is orchestrated. Specifically, lines 15–18 contain the critical section where the vulnerability occurs.

Arithmetic Overflow/Underflow. In Solidity, arithmetic overflow occurs when a mathematical operation results in a value larger than the maximum value that can be stored within the given integer type. Conversely, arithmetic underflow occurs when an operation results in a value smaller than the minimum representable value. The code snippet in Fig. 3 depicts how arithmetic operations at program points 4 and 10 may lead to overflow, and at program point 7, there's a possibility of underflow.

Division by Zero Vulnerability. Division by Zero Vulnerability occurs when an expression in a smart contract tries to perform a division operation with the denominator value of the operand as zero. In such a situation, the smart contract will produce unexpected outcomes. The code snippet in Fig. 4 demonstrates this vulnerability at line 4.

Out of Bounds Array Access Vulnerability. Out-of-bound array access occurs when a smart contract tries to access any element of an array using an index that is outside the valid range of the array. The code snippet in Fig. 5 depicts how this vulnerability might exist.

Timestamp Dependency Vulnerability. A timestamp dependency vulnerability can occur when a smart contract depends on the block timestamp, which the miners can manipulate to their advantage. This vulnerability can lead to exploitation and unintended behaviour in the smart contract. The code snippet in Fig. 6 depicts how this vulnerability is exploited.

Gas Limit Issues Vulnerability. The gas-limiting vulnerability occurs when attackers exploit the gas limits by intentionally designing transactions or smart contracts that consume an excessive amount of gas. This leads to network congestion, delays in transaction processing, increased transaction fees, and a degraded user experience for legitimate users. The code snippet in Fig. 7 depicts how this vulnerability occurs. Lines 6–8 contain vulnerable code, which will cause performance issues.

4 Abstract Semantics of Solidity

This section defines the abstract syntax of the Solidity subset, followed by its semantics computation in both concrete and abstract domains.

4.1 Abstract Interpretation

Abstract Interpretation [2] is a powerful static analysis technique for gaining insights into a program's semantics without executing them. It offers a systematic approach to sound semantics approximation by substituting the concrete domain of values and semantics operations with a more manageable abstract domain and corresponding sound operations. The abstract domain focuses on specific properties of interest within the program, allowing us to reason about its behaviour at that level. This is essential for creating static analyzers to discover program properties at compile-time, ensuring no behaviours or bugs are missed, even if some spurious behaviours are reported.

Given a concrete semantics domain $\mathbb{C}$ and an abstract semantics domain $\mathbb{A}$. These domains form a complete lattices $\langle \mathbb{C}, \sqsubseteq \rangle$ and $\langle \mathbb{A}, \widetilde{\sqsubseteq} \rangle$, with elements partially ordered by $\sqsubseteq$ and $\widetilde{\sqsubseteq}$. The relation $x \sqsubseteq y$ (or $\tilde{x} \widetilde{\sqsubseteq} \tilde{y}$) signifies that x (or $\tilde{x}$) is more precise than y (or $\tilde{y}$). To relate these semantics domains, we

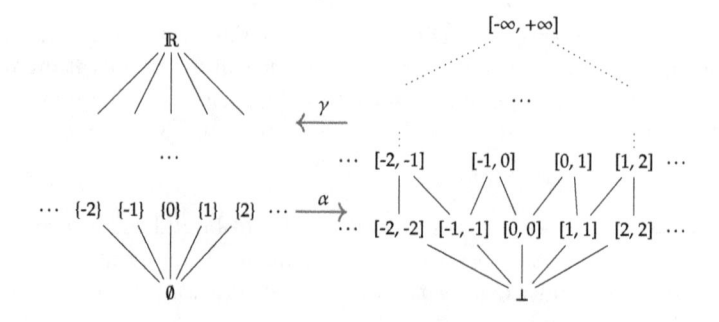

Fig. 8. Galois Connection between L_c and L_a

establish a Galois connection, $(\langle \mathbb{C}, \sqsubseteq \rangle, \alpha, \gamma, \langle \mathbb{A}, \widetilde{\sqsubseteq} \rangle)$, with $\alpha : \mathbb{C} \to \mathbb{A}$ and $\gamma : \mathbb{A} \to \mathbb{C}$ serving as the abstraction and concretization functions. This forms an adjunction such that for a program P, the concrete semantics $\mathcal{S}_c[\![P]\!] \in \mathbb{C}$ and the abstract semantics $\mathcal{S}_a[\![P]\!] \in \mathbb{A}$ satisfy $\alpha(\mathcal{S}_c[\![P]\!]) \widetilde{\sqsubseteq} \mathcal{S}_a[\![P]\!] \Leftrightarrow \mathcal{S}_c[\![P]\!] \sqsubseteq \gamma(\mathcal{S}_a[\![P]\!])$. This ensures that $\mathcal{S}_a[\![P]\!]$ is a safe approximation of $\mathcal{S}_c[\![P]\!]$.

Example 1. Let $L_c = \langle \wp(\mathbb{N}), \subseteq, \emptyset, \mathbb{N}, \cap, \cup \rangle$ be a concrete lattice of the powerset of numerical values $\mathbb{N}$. Let $\mathbb{I} = \{[l, h] \mid l \in \mathbb{N} \cup \{-\infty\}, h \in \mathbb{N} \cup \{+\infty\}, l \leq h\} \cup \bot$ be the abstract domain of intervals forming an abstract lattice $L_a = \langle \mathbb{I}, \sqsubseteq, \bot, [-\infty, +\infty], \sqcap, \sqcup \rangle$, such that:

- $[l_1, h_1] \sqsubseteq [l_2, h_2] \iff l_2 \leq l_1 \wedge h_2 \geq h_1$
- $[l_1, h_1] \sqcap [l_2, h_2] = [max(l_1\ l_2),\ min(h_1\ h_2)]$
- $[l_1, h_1] \sqcup [l_2, h_2] = [min(l_1, l_2),\ max(h_1\ h_2)]$

Then the given Galois connection between L_c and L_a is formalized as $\langle L_c, \alpha, \gamma, L_a \rangle$ where $\forall S \in \wp(\mathbb{N})$ and $\forall \tilde{v} \in \tilde{\mathbb{I}}$:

$$\alpha(S) = \begin{cases} \bot & \text{if } S = \emptyset \\ [l, h] & \text{if } min(S) = l \wedge max(S) = h \\ [-\infty, h] & \text{if } \sharp min(S) \wedge max(S) = h \\ [l, +\infty] & \text{if } min(S) = l \wedge \sharp max(S) \\ [+\infty, -\infty] & \text{if } \sharp min(S) \wedge \sharp max(S); \end{cases} \quad \gamma_{\mathbb{I}}(\tilde{v}) = \begin{cases} \emptyset & \text{if } \tilde{v} = \bot \\ \{k \in \mathbb{R} \mid l \leq k \leq h\} & \text{if } \tilde{v} = [l, h] \\ \{k \in \mathbb{R} \mid k \leq h\} & \text{if } \tilde{v} = [-\infty, h] \\ \{k \in \mathbb{R} \mid l \leq k\} & \text{if } \tilde{v} = [l, +\infty] \\ \mathbb{R} & \text{if } \tilde{v} = [+\infty, -\infty]. \end{cases}$$

A pictorial representation of the Galois connection $\langle L_c, \alpha, \gamma, L_a \rangle$ shown in Fig. 8. In order to ensure soundness, along with this value abstraction defined through the Galois connection, we also consider sound abstract versions of the concrete operations.

4.2 Solidity Syntax

Table 1 defines an abstract syntax of the Solidity subset that captures relevant constructs of the Solidity program [11]. The arithmetic expressions exp can either

Table 1. Abstract syntax of a subset of Solidity

Expressions		
exp	$\in E$	Arithmetic Expressions
exp	$::= v$	INT or UINT value
	| id	Identifier
	| exp$_1 \oplus$ exp$_2$	where $\oplus \in \{+, -, *, /\}$
bexp	$\in B$	Boolean Expressions
bexp	$::= true \mid false$	Truth/Falsity
	| exp$_1 \oslash$ exp$_2$	$\oslash \in \{\geq, \leq, <, >, ==\}$
	| bexp$_1 \otimes$ bexp$_2$	$\otimes \in \{\vee, \wedge\}$
	| ¬bexp	Negation
Commands and Smart Contracts		
type	$::= int \mid uint \mid bool$	
	| $address \mid address\ payable$	Value Types
store	$::= storage \mid memory$	Data Location
ldecl	$::=$ type store id$(:=$ exp$)?;$	Local Declaration
assgn	$::=$ id $:=$ exp;	Assignment
stmt	$::=$ ldecl | assgn	Statement
	| if bexp $then$ stmt$_1$ $else$ stmt$_2$ $endif$	
	| $while$ bexp do stmt $done$	
	| stmt$_1$ stmt$_2$	
par	$::=$ type store? id | par$_1$, par$_2$	Function Parameter
constr	$::=$ constructor(par)\{stmt\}	Constructor
func	$::= function$ id(par) $(returns$(par)$)${stmt}	Function Definition
sc	$::= \langle$SV, constr, Func$\rangle$	Smart Contract

be a numerical value v or a contract variable id or an expression obtained by applying a binary arithmetic operator $\oplus$ on two arithmetic expressions. Similarly, we define boolean expression bexp as well. We define a smart contract sc as a sequence of state variables' declarations sdecl followed by an optional constructor constr and a set of functions Func. While sdecl always refers to blockchain memory, the declaration ldecl local to a function may refer to either *storage* or *memory* as denoted by store.

4.3 Computing Concrete and Abstract Semantics of Solidity

In the rest of the paper, we denote the set of functions as $[D \mapsto R] = f \mid f$ is a function such that $\text{dom}(f) = D$ and $\text{range}(f) \subseteq R$.

Let LVar and BVar be the set of local and storage variables, respectively. Let MLoc and SLoc be the set of local memory locations and the set of blockchain storage locations, respectively. The set of local-environments LEnv : [LVar $\mapsto$

MLoc] and the set of blockchain-environment BEnv : [BVar $\mapsto$ SLoc] are defined in terms of the mapping of variables to their corresponding memory locations. Similarly, the set of local-stores LStore : MLoc $\longrightarrow$ Val and the set of blockchain stores BStore : SLoc $\longrightarrow$ Val represent mapping of respective memory locations to the domain values in Val.

Given the set of Solidity contracts $\mathbb{P}$, the semantics of Solidity is defined in terms of a state transition function, defined as $\mathcal{S} : \mathbb{P} \times \Sigma \mapsto \wp(\Sigma)$, where

- $\Sigma_l =$ LEnv $\times$ LStore and $\Sigma_b =$ BEnv $\times$ BStore represent the set of local- and blockchain-states, respectively
- $\Sigma = \Sigma_l \times \Sigma_b$ denote the set of Solidity states.

A state $\rho \in \Sigma$ is denoted by a tuple $\langle le, ls, be, bs \rangle$ where $le \in$ LEnv, $ls \in$ LStore, $be \in$ BEnv and $bs \in$ BStore.

Solidity Semantics. Below, we define the concrete semantics of various Solidity constructs.

Expressions:

$$\mathcal{S}[\![v]\!] = \{(\rho, v) \mid \rho \in \Sigma\}$$
$$\mathcal{S}[\![\text{id}]\!] = \begin{cases} \{(\rho, v) \mid \rho \in \Sigma, \ ls(le(\text{id})) = v\} \text{ if } le(\text{id}) \in \text{LEnv} \\ \{(\rho, v) \mid \rho \in \Sigma, \ bs(be(\text{id})) = v\} \text{ if } be(\text{id}) \in \text{BEnv} \end{cases}$$
$$\mathcal{S}[\![\exp_1 \oplus \exp_2]\!] = \{(\rho, v_1 \oplus v_2) \mid (\rho, v_1) \in \mathcal{S}[\![\exp_1]\!], (\rho, v_2) \in \mathcal{S}[\![\exp_2]\!]\}$$
$$\mathcal{S}[\![true]\!] = \{(\rho, true) \mid \rho \in \Sigma\}$$
$$\mathcal{S}[\![false]\!] = \{(\rho, false) \mid \rho \in \Sigma\}$$
$$\mathcal{S}[\![\exp_1 \oslash \exp_2]\!] = \{(\rho, v_1 \oslash v_2) \mid (\rho, v_1) \in \mathcal{S}[\![\exp_1]\!], (\rho, v_2) \in \mathcal{S}[\![\exp_2]\!]\}$$
$$\mathcal{S}[\![\text{bexp}_1 \otimes \text{bexp}_2]\!] = \{(\rho, b_1 \otimes b_2) \mid (\rho, b_1) \in \mathcal{S}[\![\text{bexp}_1]\!], (\rho, b_2) \in \mathcal{S}[\![\text{bexp}_2]\!]\}$$
$$\mathcal{S}[\![\neg\text{bexp}]\!] = \{(\rho, \neg b) \mid (\rho, b) \in \mathcal{S}[\![\text{bexp}]\!]\}$$

Variable Declaration: $\mathcal{S}[\![\text{type store id}]\!] \triangleq \begin{cases} \{\rho \to \rho' \mid \rho \in \Sigma\} \text{ if store is } memory \\ \{\rho \to \rho'' \mid \rho \in \Sigma\} \text{ if store is } storage \end{cases}$

where $\rho = (le, ls, be, bs)$, $\rho' = (le[\text{id} \to a_{in}^l], ls[a_{in}^l \to v_d'], be, bs)$ with $a_{in}^l \in$ MLoc as a fresh local memory location and v_d' as the default memory value, and $\rho'' = (le, ls, be[\text{id} \to a_{in}^s], bs[a_{in}^s \to v_d''])$ with $a_{in}^s \in$ SLoc as a fresh storage location and v_d'' as the default storage value.

Assignment Statement: $\mathcal{S}[\![\text{id} := \exp]\!] \triangleq \begin{cases} \{\rho \to \rho' \mid \rho \in \Sigma\} \text{ if } le(\text{id}) \in \text{LEnv} \\ \{\rho \to \rho'' \mid \rho \in \Sigma\} \text{ if } be(\text{id}) \in \text{BEnv} \end{cases}$

where $\rho = (le, ls, be, bs)$, $(\rho, v) \in \mathcal{S}[\![\exp]\!]$, $\rho' = (le, ls[le(\text{id}) \to v], be, bs)$, $\rho'' = (le, ls, be, bs[be(\text{id}) \to v])$.

Conditional: $S[\![\text{if bexp then stmt}_1 \text{ else stmt}_2 \text{ endif}]\!]$
$$\triangleq \{\rho \to \rho' \mid \rho \in \Sigma, (\rho, true) \in S[\![\text{bexp}]\!], (\rho \to \rho') \in S[\![\text{stmt}_1]\!]\}$$
$$\cup \{\rho \to \rho'' \mid \rho \in \Sigma, (\rho, false) \in S[\![\text{bexp}]\!], (\rho \to \rho'') \in S[\![\text{stmt}_2]\!]\}$$

Iteration: $S[\![\text{while bexp do stmt done}]\!] = \text{lfp}_\emptyset^\subseteq(F)$, where

$F(\psi) = \{\rho \to \rho' \mid \rho \in \Sigma, (\rho, true) \in S[\![\text{bexp}]\!], (\rho \to \rho') \in S[\![\text{stmt}]\!]\}$
$\cup \{\rho \to \rho \mid \rho \in \Sigma, (\rho, false) \in S[\![\text{bexp}]\!]\}$
$\cup \{\rho \to \rho'' \mid \rho \in \Sigma, (\rho, true) \in S[\![\text{bexp}]\!], (\rho' \to \rho'') \in \psi, (\rho \to \rho') \in S[\![\text{stmt}]\!]\}$

Constructor: Let $sc = \langle SV, constr, Func \rangle$ be a smart contract where $constr :: = constructor(par)\{stmt\}$. Let $v_{in} \in Val$ be the input values, $\rho_0 = \langle le_0, ls_0, be_0, bs_0 \rangle$ be the initial state at the time of contract deployment, and $a_{in}^l \in \text{MLoc}$ and $a_{in}^b \in \text{SLoc}$ be fresh memory addresses in the local memory and the blockchain storage respectively. The semantics of the contract constructor are defined as:

$$S[\![constr(par)\{stmt\}]\!] \triangleq \{(\rho_0, v_{in}) \to \rho' \mid \rho_0 \in \Sigma\}$$

where $\rho'' = (le_0[\text{Par} \to a_{in}^l], ls_0[a_{in}^l \to v_{in}], be_0[\text{SV} \to a_{in}^b], bs_0)$, $(\rho'' \to \rho') \in S[\![\text{stmt}]\!]$. In the case when no constructor is explicitly defined in the contract, the default constructor will be executed. The semantics of the default constructor (denoted as $constr$) is defined as: $S[\![constr]\!] \triangleq \{(\rho_0, v_{in}) \to \rho' \mid \rho_0 \in \Sigma\}$, where v_{in} represents the default values for the storage variables SV, and $\rho' = (le_0, ls_0, be_0[\text{SV} \to a_{in}^s], bs_0[a_{in}^s \to v_{in}])$ with $a_{in}^s \in \text{SLoc}$ as a fresh storage location.

Function: Let Par_{in}^{memory} and $\text{Par}_{in}^{storage}$ be the distinct set of function parameters that are located in memory and blockchain storage, respectively. Let v_{in}^{memory} and $v_{in}^{storage}$ be the input values corresponding to Par_{in}^{memory} and $\text{Par}_{in}^{storage}$ respectively, where $v_{in} = (v_{in}^{memory} \cup v_{in}^{storage}) \in Val$. The semantics of the function are defined as follows: $S[\![function\ id(par_{in})\ (returns(par_{out}))\{stmt\}]\!] \triangleq \{(\rho, v_{in}) \to (\rho', v_{out}) \mid \rho \in \Sigma\}$, where

- $\rho = (le, ls, be, bs)$,
- $\rho'' = (le[\text{Par}_{in}^{memory} \to a_{in}^l], ls[a_{in}^l \to v_{in}^{memory}], be[\text{Par}_{in}^{storage} \to a_{in}^s], bs[a_{in}^s \to v_{in}^{storage}])$, where $a_{in}^l \in \text{MLoc}$ and $a_{in}^b \in \text{SLoc}$ be fresh memory addresses in the local memory and the blockchain storage respectively.
- $(\rho'' \to \rho') \in S[\![\text{stmt}]\!]$ and $(\rho', v_{out}) \in S[\![(par_{out})]\!]$

Smart Contract Fixpoint Collecting Semantics: Given a set of states, Σ and a set of program point Label, the context vector is defined by $Context\text{-}Vector : Label \to Context$, where $Context = \wp(\Sigma)$. The context vector associated with a program P of size n is, thus, denoted by $Cv_P = \langle Cx_1, Cx_2, \ldots, Cx_n \rangle$, where Cx_i is the context associated with program point i in P.

$CS(P_0) = \langle m \mapsto \bot, a \mapsto \bot \rangle$
$CS(P_1) = \{ \rho' \mid \rho \in CS(P_0), (\rho, \rho') \in E[\![\, m = 10 \,]\!] \}$
$CS(P_2) = \{ \rho' \mid \rho \in CS(P_1), (\rho, \rho') \in E[\![\, a = 1 \,]\!] \}$
$CS(P_J) = CS(P_2) \sqcup CS(P_4)$
$CS(P_3^T) = \{ \rho \mid \rho \in CS(P_J), (\rho, \text{true}) \in B[\![\, a \le m \,]\!] \}$
$CS(P_3^F) = \{ \rho \mid \rho \in CS(P_J), (\rho, \text{false}) \in B[\![\, a \le m \,]\!] \}$
$CS(P_4) = \{ \rho' \mid \rho \in CS(P_3^T), (\rho, \rho') \in E[\![\, a = a+1 \,]\!] \}$

(a) Concrete domain

$CS^\sharp(P_0) = \langle m \mapsto \bot_{abs}, a \mapsto \bot_{abs} \rangle$
$CS^\sharp(P_1) = \{ \rho'^\sharp \mid \rho^\sharp \in CS^\sharp(P_0), (\rho^\sharp, \rho'^\sharp) \in E^\sharp[\![\, m =[10, 10] \,]\!] \}$
$CS^\sharp(P_2) = \{ \rho'^\sharp \mid \rho^\sharp \in CS^\sharp(P_1), (\rho^\sharp, \rho'^\sharp) \in E^\sharp[\![\, a =[1,1] \,]\!] \}$
$CS^\sharp(P_J) = CS^\sharp(P_2) \sqcup CS^\sharp(P_4)$
$CS^\sharp(P_3^T) = \{ \sqcup_{\rho_{atm}^\sharp}^\sharp \mid \rho^\sharp \in CS^\sharp(P_J), \rho_{atm}^\sharp \in Atom(\rho^\sharp), (\rho_{atm}^\sharp, \text{true})$
$\quad \in B^\sharp[\![\, a \le m \,]\!] \text{ or } (\rho_{atm}^\sharp, \top_b) \in B^\sharp[\![\, a \le m \,]\!] \}$
$CS^\sharp(P_3^F) = \{ \sqcup_{\rho_{atm}^\sharp}^\sharp \mid \rho^\sharp \in CS^\sharp(P_J), \rho_{atm}^\sharp \in Atom(\rho^\sharp), (\rho_{atm}^\sharp, \text{false})$
$\quad \in B^\sharp[\![\, a \le m \,]\!] \text{ or } (\rho_{atm}^\sharp, \top_b) \in B^\sharp[\![\, a \le m \,]\!] \}$
$CS^\sharp(P_4) = \{ \rho'^\sharp \mid \rho^\sharp \in CS^\sharp(P_3^T), (\rho^\sharp, \rho'^\sharp) \in E^\sharp[\![\, a = a+1 \,]\!] \}$

(b) Abstract domain

Fig. 9. Data-flow equations

Let $F_i : Context\text{-}Vector \to Context$ be a collection of monotone functions. For the program P, we therefore have

$$Cx_1 = F_1(Cx_1, \ldots, Cx_n),\ Cx_2 = F_2(Cx_1, \ldots, Cx_n),\ \ldots\ldots,\ Cx_n = F_n(Cx_1, \ldots, Cx_n)$$

Combining the above functions, we get $F : Context\text{-}Vector \to Context\text{-}Vector$. That is, $F(Cx_1, \ldots, Cx_n) = (F_1(Cx_1, \ldots, Cx_n), \ldots, F_n(Cx_1, \ldots, Cx_n))$ Each function $F_i^\sharp$ includes the transition function defined as follows:

$$Cx_i = \bigcup_{s_j \in pred(s_i)} \cup_{\epsilon_j \in Cx_j} S[\![s_j]\!](\epsilon_j) \tag{1}$$

where, $pred(s_i)$ is the set of predecessors of the statement s_i.

Starting from the initial context vector $Cv_P = \langle \bot, \ldots, \bot \rangle$ which is the bottom element of the lattice L^n where $L = (\wp(\Sigma), \sqsubseteq, \sqcap, \sqcup, \top, \bot)$, the computation of least fix-point of F results into the collecting semantics for P.

4.4 Lifting the Semantics from Concrete to Abstract Domain

In order to lift the concrete collecting semantics of Solidity to an abstract domain of interest, we follow the Galois connection for sound approximation of both values as well as operations over the lattices, as detailed in Sect. 4.1.

Accordingly, we define the set of dataflow equations in the abstract domain as follows: $F^\sharp(Cx_1^\sharp, \ldots, Cx_n^\sharp) = (F_1^\sharp(Cx_1^\sharp, \ldots, Cx_n^\sharp), \ldots, F_n^\sharp(Cx_1^\sharp, \ldots, Cx_n^\sharp))$, where $Cx_1^\sharp = F_1^\sharp(Cx_1^\sharp, \ldots, Cx_n^\sharp),\ Cx_2^\sharp = F_2^\sharp(Cx_1^\sharp, \ldots, Cx_n^\sharp),\ \ldots\ldots,\ Cx_n^\sharp = F_n^\sharp(Cx_1^\sharp, \ldots, Cx_n^\sharp)$ and

$$Cx_i^\sharp = \bigsqcup_{s_j \in pred(s_i)} \sqcup_{\epsilon_j \in Cx_j^\sharp} S[\![s_j]\!](\epsilon_j) \tag{2}$$

Similar to the concrete domain, the least fixed point solution yields the abstract collecting semantics in the abstract domain under consideration.

Example 2. Let us illustrate the computation of concrete and abstract semantics of the following code fragment $m = 10; a = 1; while\ (a <\ = m)\ \{a = a + 1;\}$. The data flow equations for computing concrete and abstract semantics of the given code are shown in Fig. 9. Given the domain of intervals as the abstract domain of interest, the fix point solutions of these dataflow equations yield concrete and abstract semantics, shown in red colour in Figs. 10 and 11, respectively.

4.5 Addressing Vulnerabilities Using Abstract Semantics

In this section, we present how the computed abstract semantics based on an augmented flow graph, exploiting both data and control dependencies, can be exploited to detect vulnerabilities in Solidity.

Reentrancy Vulnerability. Reentrancy Vulnerability occurs when a smart contract allows external calls (via call, delegatecall, send, and transfer) to untrusted contracts, enabling the untrusted contract to make recursive calls back into the original function before its previous execution is completed. This can lead to unintended behaviours like draining the contract's balance.

To detect the potential reentrancy in the smart contracts, we introduce augmented edges in the CFG representing such illicit calls by attacker smart contracts via fallback functions. This augmented CFG allows the computation of abstract semantics of the smart contracts, revealing the states that may appear along such augmented paths if an attack happens.

As repeated calls may drain out the smart contract's balance and credit them to the attacker's balance, this behaviour will be captured through abstract semantics. We follow the step below to identify the possibility of being the smart contract prone to Reentrancy through *Balance discrepancy detection*, as follows: *Scrutiny of the abstract semantics reveals a significant imbalance after each reentrant call. The attacker's balance undergoes a noticeable increase, reflected in widening intervals for its bounds. Conversely, the DAO's balance experiences a steady decrease, evidenced by narrowing intervals in its bound analysis.* Let us now illustrate this through an example.

Example 3. Given a program with a potential Reentrancy vulnerability depicted in Fig. 1 and its corresponding CFG in Fig. 12, we can augment this CFG with dotted lines representing unauthorized calls made by attacker smart contracts through fallback functions. Now, let's perform an analysis technique called abstract semantics using intervals. This analysis assigns ranges of possible values to variables throughout the program execution. Interestingly, when focusing on the abstract states associated with these attacker-initiated calls (represented by light orange squares), we observe a crucial pattern.

By analyzing these abstract semantics, we observe that after each reentrant call, a critical pattern emerges, such as the attacker's balance increases significantly. This is reflected in the intervals, where the lower and upper bounds of their balance grow progressively while the DAO's balance consistently decreases,

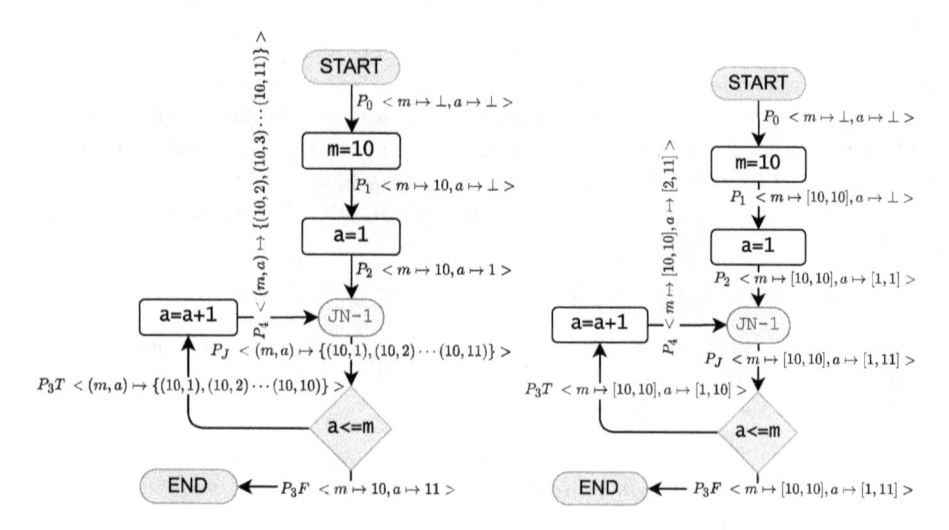

Fig. 10. Concrete Semantics

Fig. 11. Abstract Semantics

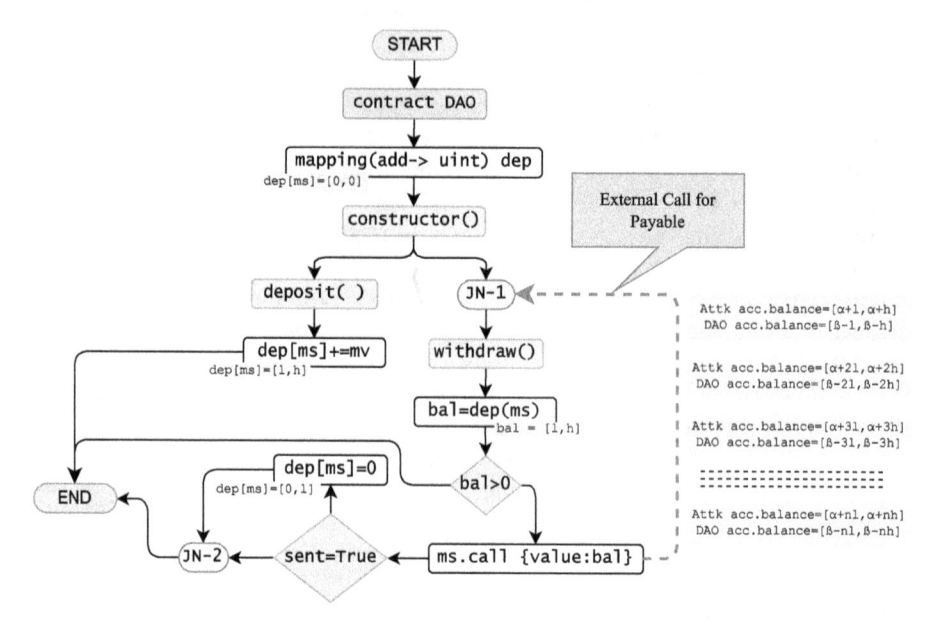

Fig. 12. Illustrating Reentrancy vulnerability detection

as shown in Table 2. This pattern continues with subsequent calls, with the attacker's advantage growing exponentially while the DAO suffers continuous losses. Additionally, we must ensure that the DAO's interval lower limit is not less than its upper limit minus the amount withdrawn by the attacker. By analyzing these changes in abstract semantics, we may conclude that there may be a possibility of a Reentrancy vulnerability in the program.

Table 2. Reentrancy Analysis in Interval Domain

Method Call	Attacker Balance	DAO Balance
1st Call	$[\alpha + l, \alpha + h]$	$[\beta - l, \beta - h]$
2nd Call	$[\alpha + 2h, \alpha + 2h]$	$[\beta - 2l, \beta - 2h]$
Thereafter	$[\alpha + nh, \alpha + nh]$	$[\beta - nl, \beta - nh]$

Interger Overflow/Underflow Vulnerability. In Solidity, integers are represented using fixed-size data types, ranging from uint8 to uint256 for unsigned integers and from int8 to int256 for signed integers, in steps of 8 bits. The range for intX is from $-2^{(X-1)}$ to $(2^{(X-1)} - 1)$, and for uintX, it is from 0 to $(2^X - 1)$. If a value outside these limits is stored in an integer variable, it leads to Arithmetic Overflow/Underflow, which attackers can exploit to fraudulently transfer funds.

The use of abstract semantics following the abstract interpretation theory can effectively identify the possibility of Arithmetic Overflow/Underflow based on the sound approximation of possible program states involving arithmetic operations. In particular, the domain of intervals is proven to be the most appropriate domain in this regard [17].

As stated earlier in Example 1, an interval is represented in the form $[l, h]$, where $l \in \mathbb{N} \cup \{-\infty\}$ and $h \in \mathbb{N} \cup \{+\infty\}$, with $l \leq h$. In case of overflow, abstract semantics in the domain of intervals experience some abstract states with $h \geqslant 2^{(X-1)} - 1$ in case of intX and $h \geqslant 2^X - 1$ in the case of uintX. Similarly, in the case of underflow, the following cases arise for some abstract states: $l \leqslant -2^{(X-1)}$ in case of intX and $l \leqslant 0$ in case of uintX.

In order to guarantee the convergence of abstract semantics computation in the domain of intervals, we apply widening and narrowing operations, defined below [1]:

Example 4 (Widening for intervals). Consider a lattice of intervals $\mathcal{D} = \{\bot\} \cup \{[l, u] \mid l \in \mathbb{Z} \cup \{-\infty\}, u \in \mathbb{Z} \cup \{+\infty\}\}$ ordered by $\forall x \in \mathcal{D}, \bot \leq x$ and $[l_0, u_0] \leq [l_1, u_1]$ if $l_1 \leq l_0$ and $u_0 \leq u_1$. Let k be a fixed positive integer constant, and I be any set of indices. The following defines a threshold widening operator defined on $\mathcal{D}$ by $\nabla^k(\{\bot\}) = \bot, \nabla^k(\{\bot\} \cup S) = \nabla^k(S), \nabla^k(\{[l_i, u_i] : i \in I\}) = [h_1, h_2]$, where $h_1 = min\{l_i : i \in I\}$ if $min\{l_i : i \in I\} > -k$ else $-\infty$, $h_2 = max\{u_i : i \in I\}$ if $max\{u_i : i \in I\} < k$ else $+\infty$

Example 5 (Narrowing for intervals). Suppose $\mathcal{D}$ be a lattice of intervals defined in Example 4. We can define Δ, a narrowing operator, on $\mathcal{D}$ as follows: $\Delta(\{\bot\}) = \bot$ and $\Delta(\{\bot\} \cup S) = \Delta(S), \Delta(\{[l_i, u_i] : i \in I\}) = [h_1, h_2]$, where $h_1 = max\{l_i : i \in I\}, h_2 = min\{u_i : i \in I\}$

Example 6. Consider the Solidity code in Fig. 3 and its corresponding CFG depicted in Fig. 13. The semantics of the code exhibiting the abstract states in

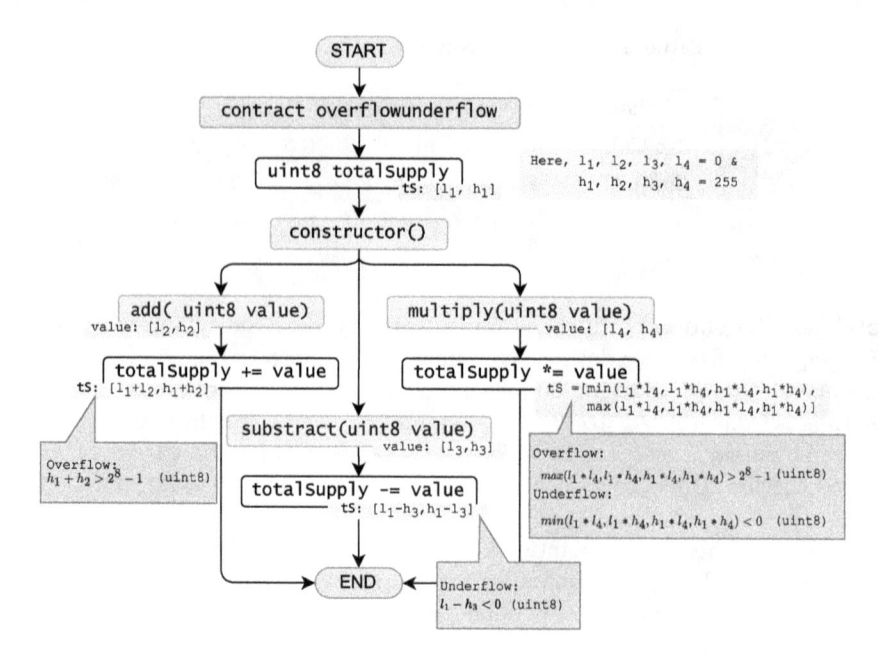

Fig. 13. Illustrating Arithmetic Overflow/Underflow vulnerability detection

the domain of intervals at each program point are shown in the yellow coloured boxes. As the datatype of the variables totalSupply is uint8, the state in the form of interval at the program points 2 is $[l_1, h_1]$, where $l_1 = 0$ and $h_1 = 2^8 - 1$. Similarly, for the parameters value in the functions add(), subtract() and multiply() at the program points 3, 7 and 12, the abstract states representing abstract value of the variable are $[l_2, h_2]$, $[l_3, h_3]$, and $[l_4, h_4]$, where $l_2 = l_3 = l_4 = 0$ and $h_2 = h_3 = h_4 = 2^8 - 1$.

During the computation of collecting semantics, if we find that at any program point where arithmetic computations are performed, the range of the state variable exceeds the maximum range of its datatype, we flag it as an arithmetic overflow. Conversely, if the value is lower than the minimum range of its datatype, we flag it as an integer underflow.

For example, at program point 5, as the range of totalSupply in interval $[h_1 + h_2]$ may exceed the maximum range of totalSupply $2^8 - 1$ for uint8, it is flagged as an Arithmetic Overflow vulnerability. Similarly, at program point 8, as value of totalSupply may become lower than interval $[l_1 - h_3] < 0$ for uint8, it is flagged as an integer underflow vulnerability. A similar applies at program point 11.

Dependency-Based Vulnerabilities. There are a number of vulnerabilities in Solidity, such as Transaction Ordering Dependency (ToD), Time-stamp dependency, which occur primarily due to dependencies among variables and hence program statements.

Recall the Solidity code in Fig. 2 and its corresponding CFG depicted in Fig. 15 where the `price` variable is accessed and modified by multiple transactions, making it a critical point for ToD vulnerabilities. For instance, the `price` variable is use by the 'buy()' function, which emits a `Purchase` event, and def by the 'setPrice()' function, which is protected by the `ownerOnly` modifier and emits a `PriceChange` event. The 'buy()' function's dependency on the `price` variable means the value returned and the `Purchase` event are based on the current price. The 'setPrice()' function def the price, creating a dependency on the sequence of transactions: the order of buy and `setPrice` affects the final price. On the other hand, the primary reason behind Timestamp dependency is the information flow along smart contracts where untrusted data (e.g. block timestamp) flows along the program code via variables' def-use in various statements and finally affects the critical computation in the code. As a result, this compromises the integrity. For example, in the code snippet in Fig. 6 under Sect. 3, the direct dependency of `block.timestamp` on the variable `pastBlockTime` via statements 7 and 8 influence the critical computation at statement 9–11.

Intuitively, the computation of variables' dependencies is the key component in identifying these vulnerabilities. Given a syntactically valid program, we can easily compute dependencies among its statements by identifying the variables defined and used by the statements, according to the following definitions [12,13].

Definition 1 (Data dependencies). *A statement s_2 is called data-dependent on another statement s_1, if there exists a variable v such that (1) v is defined by s_1, (2) v is used by s_2, and (3) there is a v-definition free path from s_1 to s_2.*

Definition 2 (Control dependencies). *Let $CFG_c = (N_c, E_c, def_c, use_c)$. Node n' post-dominates node n if $n \neq n'$ and every path from n to stop contains n'. Node n' is control dependent on node n if there is a non-trivial path p from n to n_0 such that n_0 post-dominates all nodes $n'' \notin \{n, n'\}$ on p and n' does not post-dominate n.*

Observe that the above dependency computation is completely syntax-based, hence may introduce false positive. In order to improve the analysis precision (hence to reduce false positives), we apply a refinement in the dependency analysis by leveraging the semantics approximation of the code.

```
1   uint x = block.timestamp;
2   ...
3   uint y = 4 * x mod 2;
4   ...
5   if (15 <= y && y >= 20) {
6       // Critical section
7   }
```

Fig. 14. Block Timestamp non-vulnerability

Consider the code snippet in Fig. 14. We observe a *syntactic* dependency of y on the value of 'block.timestamp' (via x). However, by critically analyzing the code in the abstract semantics domain of congruence, we can identify that y is *semantically* data independent of 'block.timestamp', as the values of y are always equal to zero. This way, semantics-based analysis of Solidity reduces false positives in detecting vulnerabilities while preserving soundness. On the other hand, considering the domain of octagons, the semantics-based analysis of the code snippet in Fig. 2 is shown in Fig. 15. Here, changing the order of the execution of the functions 'buy()' and 'setPrice()' which share the common variable 'price' yields different abstract states, as shown at the top-left corner. Hence, the code is tagged as ToD vulnerable.

Therefore, the over process is divided into two primary steps: (1) identify dependencies among the statements based on def-use variable sets, and then (2) perform semantics-based analysis of these dependencies to identify the effect of these dependencies more precisely, eliminating the redundant ones.

5 Prototype Implementation

In this section, we present the implementation details of our framework and provide experimental evaluations to compare it against state-of-the-art static analysis frameworks. Our framework is implemented in Python and leverages the APRON [14] library to handle abstract domains and their computation. Since APRON is implemented in C, we utilize the available Java wrapper and import it into our framework using JPype[1]. The overall workflow of our framework is depicted in Fig. 16. Observe that, by using APRON, our framework benefits from a robust and efficient library that has been widely adopted in the formal analysis community. Although currently the tool supports the abstract domains provided by the APRON library only, its architecture is designed in a modular way so that it can easily be extended to support additional abstract domains either by integrating other suitable libraries or by implementing custom abstract domains as needed.

Parsing and Generation of Control Flow Graph from Solidity Source Code. The process begins with the *solcx* parser consuming the source code and generating the Abstract Syntax Tree (AST). Next, the AST is then passed over to the CFG generator, which constructs the Augmented CFG from the syntactical features of the AST. This Augmented CFG enables semantic analysis of the flow of logic within the smart contracts. It is termed 'Augmented' because we augment additional nodes and edges during analysis to discover additional behaviours.

Computation of FixPoint Solution to Abstract Semantics. The core logic of our framework lies in the computation of abstract semantics from the Augmented CFGs. We utilize the APRON [14] library for this purpose. The APRON library is designed to represent properties of numeric variables in one of many numerical abstract domains, such as variable bounds or linear relations between variables, and to manipulate these properties through semantic operations, such as variable assignments, tests, conjunctions, and entailment. It is based on the theory of Abstract Interpretation [2,3] and intended for use in static program analyzers to infer invariants of numeric variables. This computation is performed iteratively to reach a fixpoint solution. The computation of the fixed-point solution is crucial for deriving accurate invariants of the numeric variables involved in a smart contract.

---

[1] https://github.com/jpype-project/jpype.

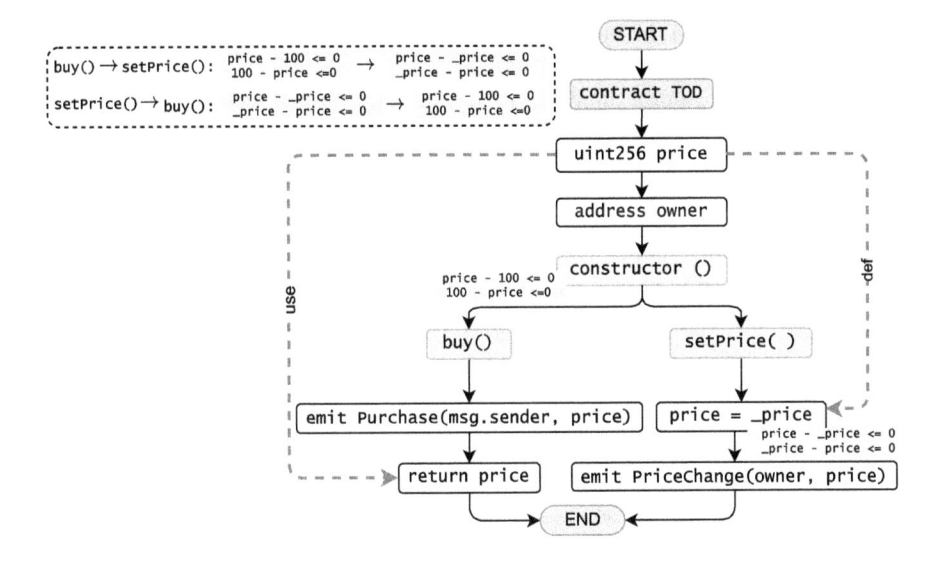

Fig. 15. Control Flow Graph illustrating ToD

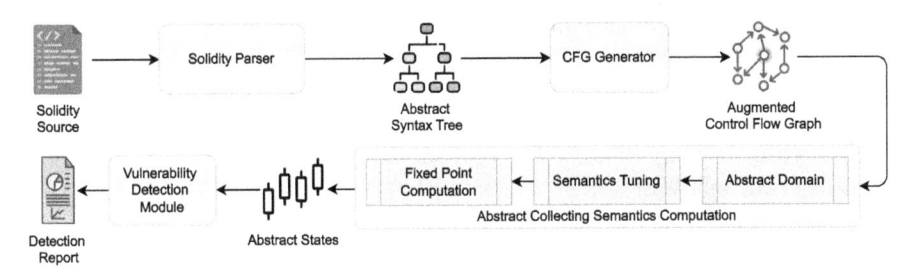

Fig. 16. Framework Workflow

Table 3. Categories of vulnerabilities

Category	Contracts	Vulnerabilities	LoC
Non-Vulnerable	18	24	933
Arithmetic	14	22	162
Reentrancy	29	29	1472
Total	**61**	**75**	**2567**

Detection of Vulnerability. Based on the computed abstract semantics, our framework's vulnerability detection logic identifies the trace of any potential vulnerabilities. The results of this analysis are compiled into a detection report, providing detailed insights into any detected issues.

6 Experimental Evaluation

In this section, we evaluate the performance of our proposal with respect to state-of-the-art tools, focusing on the following two of the most prominent vulnerabilities according to the OWASP[2]: *Reentrancy* and *Arithmetic Overflow/Underflow*. With this aim, we consider a part of the SmartBugs curated benchmark dataset [9], which is a widely recognized in the research community. We analyze (*i*) 47 smart contracts from the mentioned dataset to identify the Reentrancy vulnerability, discovering 29 vulnerable contracts, and (*ii*) 32 smart contracts from the same dataset for Arithmetic Overflow/Underflow vulnerabilities, identifying 14 vulnerable contracts. We treat additional 18 smart contracts from the dataset as non-vulnerable, which do not have any of the two vulnerabilities. Table 3 outlines the details of the contracts under each category, specifying total number of contracts, total number of vulnerabilities, and lines of code (LoC) within that category.

To perform our experiments, we select four static analysis tools, namely *Mythril, Oyente, Slither,* and *Osiris*, based on the following criteria:

- **Criterion 1:** [Public Availability] The tool must be publicly available and offer an interface for easy automation.
- **Criterion 2:** [Supports Multiple Versions of Solidity] The tool should be capable of analyzing contracts written in various Solidity versions present in the dataset.
- **Criterion 3:** [Only Source] The tool should only require the source code to perform the analysis.

Tables 4 and 5 summarize the detection performance of the four state-of-the-art analysis tools and our proposed tool for the vulnerabilities under consideration. The notations FDR, FNR, PR, SN represent False Discovery Rate, False Negative Rate, Precision, and Sensitivity respectively, and are defined below:

$$FDR = False\ Positive/(True\ Positive + False\ Positive)$$
$$FNR = False\ Negative/(False\ Negative + True\ Positive)$$
$$PR = 1 - FDR$$
$$SN = 1 - FNR$$

Table 4 depicts the evaluation results for Reentrancy vulnerability, where Slither reports 5 false positives, resulting in a False Discovery Rate (FDR) of 14.7%. This indicates that while Slither is able to detect these vulnerabilities, it also flags some safe contracts incorrectly. Our tool, on the other hand, reports only 2 false positives, yielding a lower FDR of 6.4%. Mythril, Oyente, and Osiris do not report any false positives, suggesting a more conservative approach, but this comes at the expense of potentially missing some vulnerabilities, leading to higher false negatives.

---

[2] https://owasp.org/www-project-smart-contract-top-10.

Table 4. Results of Reentrancy vulnerability analysis

Metric	Mythril	Oyente	Slither	Osiris	Our tool
True Positive	24	27	29	27	29
False Positive	0	0	5	0	2
False Negative	5	2	0	2	0
FDR	0%	0%	14.7%	0%	6.4%
FNR	17.2%	6.8%	0%	6.8%	0%
PR	100%	100%	85.3%	100%	93.6%
SN	82.8%	93.2%	100%	93.2%	100%

Table 5. Results of Arithmetic Overflow/Underflow vulnerability analysis

Metric	Mythril	Oyente	Slither	Osiris	Our tool
True Positive	8	10	0	12	14
False Positive	1	7	0	4	1
False Negative	6	4	14	2	0
FDR	11.1%	41.1%	0%	25%	6.6%
FNR	42.8%	28.5%	100%	14.2%	0%
PR	88.9%	58.9%	100%	75%	93.4%
SN	57.2%	71.5%	0%	85.8%	100%

In the evaluation of Arithmetic Overflow/Underflow vulnerability (Table 5), Oyente exhibits the highest number of false positives, leading to a False Discovery Rate (FDR) of 41.1%. This considerably impacts its overall precision. Osiris and Mythril also reports false positives, with 4 and 1 respectively, resulting in lower FDRs of 25% and 11.1%. In contrast, our tool excels in this category, recording just 1 false positive and achieving a low FDR of 6.6%. Slither, while not reporting any false positives, failed to detect any vulnerable contracts, resulting in both zero true positives and zero false positives.

These metrics clearly indicate that our proposed tool outperforms others to achieve a trade-off between precision and sensitivity in case of both Reentrancy and Arithmetic Overflow/Underflow vulnerabilities, with reduced false alarms.

7 Conclusion

In this paper, we extend the Abstract Interpretation theory to formalize the semantics approximation for Solidity at different levels of abstractions. We describe how the abstract semantics in the domain of intervals and octagons perform a sound and precise vulnerability detection for Solidity. To the best of our knowledge, this is the first attempt to leverage the most powerful formal method in this context. Our experimental evaluation using the APRON library is encouraging in the case of reentrancy and arithmetic vulnerability detection on benchmark smart contracts. This opens up a new research direction towards the analysis of smart contracts leveraging the foundations of Abstract Interpretation theory.

Acknowledgement. This research is partially supported by the Core Research Grant (CRG/2022/005794) from the Science and Engineering Research Board (SERB), Department of Science and Technology, Government of India.

References

1. Cortesi, A., Zanioli, M.: Widening and narrowing operators for abstract interpretation. Comput. Lang. Syst. Struct. **37**(1), 24–42 (2011)
2. Cousot, P., Cousot, R.: Abstract interpretation: a unified lattice model for static analysis of programs by construction or approximation of fixpoints. In: Proceedings of the 4th Symposium on Principles of Programming Languages, pp. 238–252 (1977)
3. Cousot, P., Cousot, R.: Abstract interpretation: past, present and future. In: Proceedings of the Joint Meeting of the 23rd EACSL Annual Conference on Computer Science Logic and the 29th Annual Symposium on Logic in Computer Science, pp. 1–10 (2014)
4. Daian, P.: Analysis of the DAO exploit. Hacking, Distributed, vol. 6 (2016)
5. Durieux, T., et al.: Empirical review of automated analysis tools on 47,587 ethereum smart contracts. In: Proceedings of the ACM/IEEE 42nd International Conference on Software Engineering, pp. 530–541 (2020)
6. Albert, E., et al.: EthIR: a framework for high-level analysis of ethereum bytecode. In: International Symposium on Automated Technology for Verification and Analysis, pp. 513–520. Springer (2018)
7. Brent, L., et al.: Vandal: a scalable security analysis framework for smart contracts. arXiv preprint arXiv:1809.03981 (2018)
8. Chen, H., et al.: A survey on ethereum systems security: vulnerabilities, attacks, and defenses. ACM Comput. Surv. (CSUR) **53**(3), 1–43 (2020)
9. Salzer, G., et al.: SB Curated dataset. https://github.com/smartbugs/smartbugs-curated. Accessed 24 July 2024
10. Feist, J., Grieco, G., Groce, A.: Slither: a static analysis framework for smart contracts. In: 2019 IEEE/ACM 2nd International Workshop on Emerging Trends in Software Engineering for Blockchain (WETSEB), pp. 8–15. IEEE (2019)
11. Halder, R.: State-based invariant property generation of solidity smart contracts using abstract interpretation. In: 7th IEEE International Conference on Blockchain (IEEE Blockchain 2024), Copenhagen, Denmark, pp. 235–242. IEEE Press (2024)
12. Halder, R., Cortesi, A.: Abstract program slicing on dependence condition graphs. Sci. Comput. Program. **78**(9), 1240–1263 (2013)
13. Halder, R., Zanioli, M., Cortesi, A.: Information leakage analysis of database query languages. In: Proceedings of the 29th Annual ACM Symposium on Applied Computing, pp. 813–820 (2014)
14. Jeannet, B., Miné, A.: Apron: a library of numerical abstract domains for static analysis. In: International Conference on Computer Aided Verification, pp. 661–667. Springer (2009)

15. Jeon, S., Lee, G., Kim, H., Woo, S.S.: SmartCondetect: highly accurate smart contract code vulnerability detection mechanism using BERT. In: KDD Workshop on Programming Language Processing (2021)
16. Kalra, S., Goel, S., Dhawan, M., Sharma, S.: ZEUS: analyzing safety of smart contracts. In: NDSS, pp. 1–12 (2018)
17. Küchler, A., Wenning, L., Wendland, F.: AbsIntIO: towards showing the absence of integer overflows in binaries using abstract interpretation. In: Proceedings of the 2023 ACM Asia Conference on Computer and Communications Security, pp. 247–258 (2023)
18. Liu, Y., Wang, C., Ma, Y.: DL4SC: a novel deep learning-based vulnerability detection framework for smart contracts. Autom. Softw. Eng. **31**(1), 24 (2024)
19. Luu, L., et al.: Making smart contracts smarter. In: Proceedings of the 2016 ACM SIGSAC Conference on Computer and Communications Security, pp. 254–269 (2016)
20. Mueller, B.: Smashing ethereum smart contracts for fun and actual profit. In: Proceedings of the HITB Security Conference (2018)
21. Nikolić, I., Kolluri, A., Sergey, I., Saxena, P., Hobor, A.: Finding the greedy, prodigal, and suicidal contracts at scale. In: Proceedings of the 34th Annual Computer Security Applications Conference, pp. 653–663 (2018)
22. Suiche, M.: The $280 m ethereum's parity bug. A Critical Security Vulnerability in Parity Multi-sig Wallet (2017)
23. Tikhomirov, S., et al.: SmartCheck: Static analysis of ethereum smart contracts. In: Proceedings of the 1st International Workshop on Emerging Trends in Software Engineering for Blockchain, pp. 9–16 (2018)

Privacy and Usability

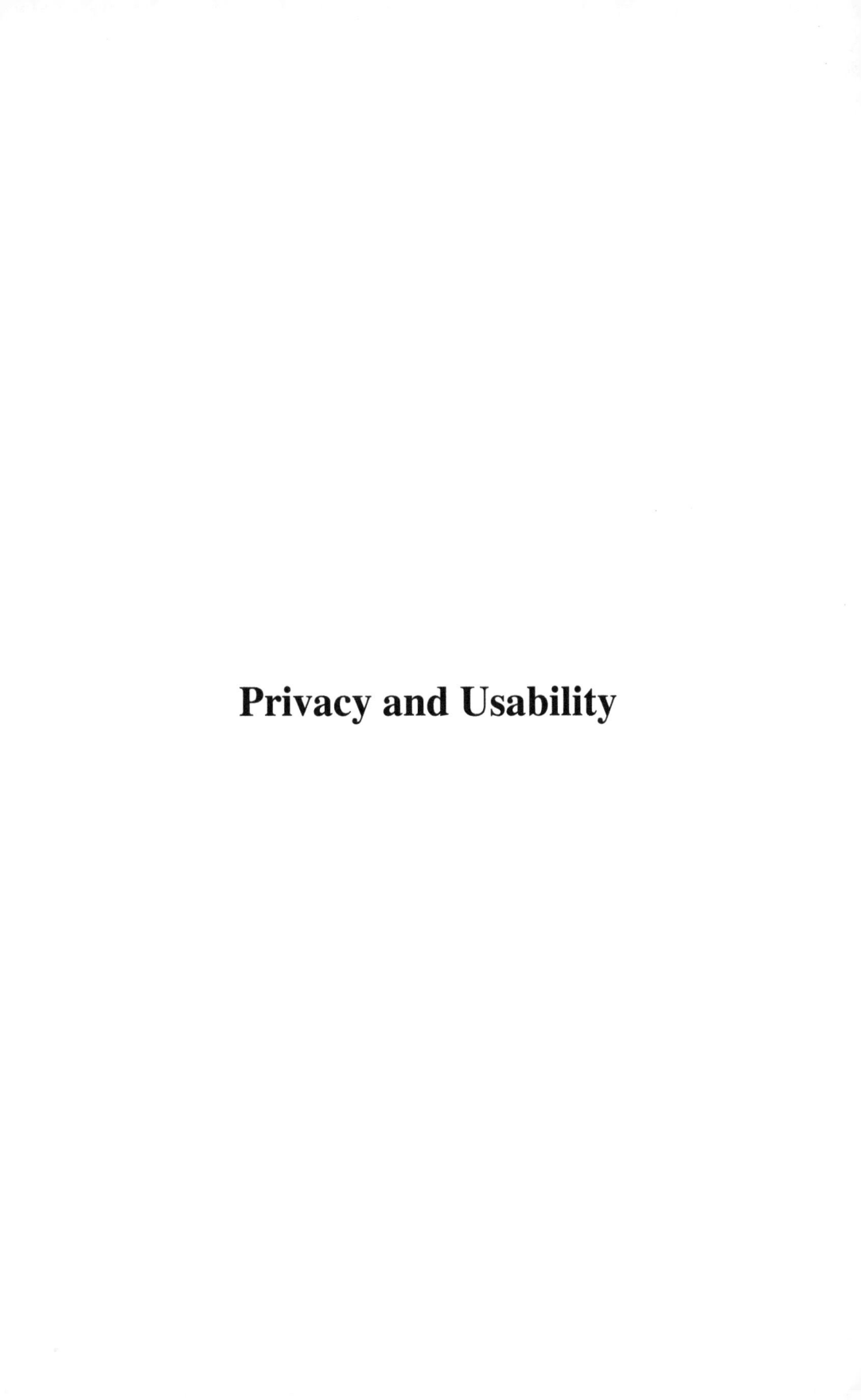

Web Privacy Perceptions Amongst Indian Users

Gayatri Priyadarsini, Anshika Saxena, Aditi Dey, Prakriti, and Abhishek Bichhawat(✉)

Indian Institute of Technology Gandhinagar, Gandhinagar, India
abhishek.b@iitgn.ac.in

Abstract. While personalized content in the digital world is necessary for a better browsing experience, users knowingly or unknowingly share a lot of data with third-party advertising networks, market analysts, and trackers. Although India is the second largest online market in the world, the privacy perceptions of Indian users is not well understood.

The focus of this work is to investigate the understanding of privacy on the web amongst Indians, and to provide a basis for making web privacy features more usable among Indian users. Through this user study, we want to understand how different attributes affect privacy choices of the users when they are accessing the web. We also investigate if the users are aware of various ways in which websites and web applications collect information, their implications, different options to handle their privacy, and if the usability of privacy settings affects their decision-making.

This study sheds light on the prevalence of various privacy violations or information leaks, if and how they target a group of people, and why they succeed. The survey also acts as an informative revision of the different aspects regarding privacy for the users from India.

Keywords: Web privacy · User perception · Indians · Regulations

1 Introduction

In recent years, the number of users having an online presence has increased dramatically [8]. These users have multiple accounts on social media, e-commerce, gaming, and video streaming applications and access and share a lot of private and sensitive information on these platforms. With the surge in the amount of private information being shared, it has become necessary to enforce data privacy and protection regulations to prevent the misuse of online data for monetary benefits. Various laws like GDPR [11], CCPA [6], and LGPD [5] have been enacted in recent years to ensure the right to privacy for online users.

According to a recent report [28], "India is the second largest online market" showing a rapid increase in the adoption of internet services in the past five years. However, India is also second globally in the number of users affected by privacy and data breach incidents [7,16,32]. For a long time, data protection rights were not well defined in the Indian law. The Indian Penal Code and Information Technology Act [17] dealt with only some aspects of the right to privacy. In 2018, the right to privacy became a fundamental right, and in 2023, the Digital Personal Data Protection Act (DPDP) [10] was established as a law. While various provisions in DPDP would allow for more control of personal data collected by the web applications, it is unclear whether Indian users are aware of these regulations and the need for the same. Moreover, prior studies based on the GDPR and CCPA [3,4,21,33] have shown that websites have failed to adopt them cleanly, often bypassing them using different approaches like dark patterns [2,14,29]. If similar patterns are adopted on Indian websites, it is unclear if the users will be able to select or navigate to their desired choices.

Our work aims to study how Indians perceive privacy on the web and the different privacy-enforcing mechanisms they are aware of; these mechanisms may include the use of consent banners, permission settings on different browsers, safe browsing options, and anonymity-providing platforms. We also want to understand if the Indian users are aware of different techniques used by websites for collecting personal (or sensitive) data, their implications, different options to handle their privacy, and if the usability of privacy settings affects their decision-making. Users may also have different preferences for privacy and sharing information based on the type of websites they are interacting with. Our study aims to report the challenges with privacy in the Indian ecosystem and suggest user-friendly mechanisms for providing better privacy. Through this study, we target the following research questions:

RQ1: Are Indians aware of the basic privacy-related features and choices provided to them? Have their behaviors led to data breaches, and are they aware of the same?

RQ2: How do Indian users manage their privacy while sharing or viewing content on different web platforms and social media? What concerns do Indian users have in managing their privacy on these platforms? Are their privacy concerns consistent across different types of web applications, i.e.,
- Do they trust certain (category of) websites more than others?
- Under what conditions are they more likely to share personal and sensitive information with the websites?

RQ3: How aware are they of the different options to manage privacy on browsers and websites in general? How frequently do they adopt these practices, and what might be the reason for non-adoption, if any?

To address the research questions above, we surveyed 155 Indian participants. Our survey focused on understanding whether Indians are well-informed about these rights and their conceptions of data privacy when interacting with different websites. In particular, we investigated their understanding of privacy concerning cookies, consent banners, advertisements, social media, and other daily-use web applications. Our analysis for RQ1 focused on the participants' basic knowledge about cookies, browser privacy preferences, information collected by websites, and the knowledge of data protection acts and regulations.

We also investigated what affected their choices when setting the preferences, e.g., whether the user interface, security, or the number of advertisements they saw affected how they set the preferences. We also discussed awareness regarding data breaches at third-party organizations and asked them to share personal incidents that compromised their privacy. For RQ2 and RQ3, we asked the participants about their standard privacy settings and data-sharing behavior when using widely-used social media applications vs. other web applications like government websites, education/research-related websites, and e-commerce websites. We also asked the participants about using browser extensions or practices like incognito mode or explicitly deleting cookies to maintain privacy.

Our main findings indicate the following: (1) Almost half the participants were not aware of the need and use of cookies, which form an important part of consent (2) 60% of the participants claimed to have heard about at least one privacy act or regulation, although 10% participants did not think that websites need to follow any privacy policy or regulations, indicating that a majority of the participants wanted websites to follow some regulations (3) Many participants were unaware if their personal information had been leaked as part of a data breach unless informed (4) The participants were comfortable sharing personally identifiable information (PII) like name and phone number but were skeptical and careful about sharing sensitive information like credit card details; they were more careful when sharing information on social-media applications than e-commerce or government websites (5) Most participants either preferred or were not concerned about being profiled on the internet and enjoyed the personalized experience but also claimed that they would prefer to keep their personal data private for tracking if given a more accessible default setting.

Overall, our survey indicated that Indians want to protect their data but only if it was deemed sensitive or confidential; they were not concerned about sharing PII or knowing if it was leaked, and would only opt for privacy if it was a default. The major contributions of our work are:

- We analyze Indian users' behavior across various web applications to ascertain their predominant usage patterns, trust levels, and privacy preferences.
- We explore awareness levels amongst Indian users regarding privacy management technologies offered by diverse web platforms and browsers.
- Additionally, we provide insights into potential reasons driving Indian users' preferences for different privacy management options available to them.

2 Related Works

User Studies in the Western Countries: Singh et al. [26] analyzed user preferences and motivations regarding cookie banners, highlighting expectations such as ease of use and regulated information. Florian et al. [12] examined whether users were aware of the extent of their data held by Google and if tools like MyActivity could raise awareness. They found that trust in Google and limited understanding of privacy risks hindered proactive changes in browsing habits, suggesting the need for stronger negative consequences to drive privacy practice changes. Our study similarly highlights scenarios where trust in certain websites impacts user behavior, echoing the significance of negative consequences in shaping privacy practices. Wei et al. [31] examined gender stereotypes in privacy behavior, finding biases suggesting women are more vulnerable to scams and less interested in computer security. While we did not directly address participant opinions on gender stereotypes, our study observed behavior across platforms. Despite lower awareness, women exhibited greater caution in managing privacy on social media.

Mayer et al. [22] surveyed reactions to real-world data breaches, finding that most participants were unaware of breaches and tended to blame themselves without feeling concerned about the impact. However, post-breach awareness and concern motivated action. Similarly, our study addressed data breaches, comparing participant awareness and compromised information with established ground truth. We compare the ground truth on our side during analysis to avoid their responses to be biased after seeing the results from the website.

Social media and other web applications in general have shown in earlier work to make privacy-oriented decision even difficult for the users using dark patterns and nudging them towards unsafe options. While majority users don't want to compromise on their user experience and are fine with advertisements, this might be due to the unawareness of the consequences and how their compromised personally identifiable information makes them vulnerable to attacks like social engineering, compromised accounts and unauthorised access to resources.

By investigating user awareness of different techniques used by websites for collecting personal data and their preferences for privacy mechanisms, our study aims to address the challenges with privacy in the Indian ecosystem and suggest user-friendly mechanisms for better privacy protection.

User Studies in Non-western Countries: Kaushik et al. [19] compared advertisement preferences across Western and non-Western countries, highlighting cultural influences. Similarly, Mustafa et al. [23] study Pakistani teens' privacy perceptions and offer personas to enhance privacy management designs, catering to diverse cultural contexts. In contrast, our study assesses general privacy perceptions beyond teenagers and explores additional online privacy aspects.

Hossain et al. [15] studied user privacy in Bangladesh, identifying social engineering vulnerabilities due to weak password practices like using phone numbers or birth dates. Their survey-based research highlighted low security awareness, urging enhanced measures and further password security studies.

Distler [9] analyzed 284 papers from top conferences (2014–2018) on usable privacy and security research, identifying common methods, risk representation challenges, and ethical implications. The review underscored a lack of research involving non-Western populations, highlighting studies on privacy practices among women in South Asian countries and smartphone locking behavior in Saudi Arabia. These findings stress the need for diverse geographical representation to enhance understanding of web security risks across different populations.

Studies in the Indian Ecosystem: Kumaraguru et al. [20] explored an empirical understanding of privacy perceptions and awareness with a sample of 10,427 participants across India and found that 50% of the participants have changed their default settings on a social network that they use. However, users rarely read the privacy policy of social media services. They also found that 46% of users interlinked social media accounts with third-party applications. Similarly, research from Bangladesh unpacked people's privacy perceptions situated in local infrastructure, social practices, and policy. While this work had similar objectives as ours, it was conducted in 2012 in India, when only a small percentage of Indians used to use social media platforms regularly. Additionally, only a few users had personal devices to use at that time. We focus on a broader range of topics covering different aspects of online privacy.

Several other studies focused on the Indian audience include works such as Sharma et al. [25], which explored perceptions of targeted ads in India and Bangladesh. Ingole et al. [18] conducted an online survey covering various privacy topics, while Srivastava [27] addressed privacy concerns on Online Social Networks (OSNs), proposing the Privacy Armor model to mitigate risks.

All the studies mentioned above are a step towards getting a non-western population's perspective on privacy. Different topics have been covered like behavioral advertising, online profiling, password strengths and social media. However, these studies focus on one or some of these topics concerning privacy and in general does not give an overall picture of the user's perspective since the users may have different behavior in different situations. Through our study, we want to cover all aspects of privacy and usability from basic knowledge to their behavior while using different web platforms and technologies.

We believe that our findings will help researchers, tool designers, and privacy advocates educate the public about privacy- and security-enhancing technologies as well as make better and specific regulations that the websites need to follow in order to make the web a usable yet safe space for the users.

3 Methodology

In order to understand the privacy perceptions of Indian users, we conducted a survey consisting of questions concerning different topics related to privacy in web applications and social media platforms.

3.1 Data Collection

Before collecting data, we got an ethical clearance from the institute's review board for conducting the survey. We reached out to potential participants online and through snowball sampling, requesting them to participate in the study. Our participants were older than 18 years of age at the time of the survey.

We also conducted a pilot study with 30 participants coming from different age groups, to ensure that the questions were comprehensible and unambiguous to the participants, and that answering them was convenient.

For people who were not fluent in English, we assisted them in understanding the questionnaire by translating certain words of the survey to their local language and by showing them the interfaces on their own devices to provide a context. We presented the participants with an informed consent form providing them the option to quit the survey at any point where they were not comfortable in continuing.

The survey instrument and the anonymized dataset is available online [13].

3.2 Survey Design

Our survey was designed to cover numerous important elements of privacy knowledge and habits among Indian consumers on various web platforms. Each portion of the questionnaire was designed to collect data on certain ideas, resulting in an in-depth understanding of the users' viewpoints and behaviors. We also added a few attention-checking questions for ensuring that the participants did not provide random responses. Below, we explain the different sections and the kind of information they targeted.

Demographic Information: We collected basic personal information such as name, email, occupation, age, gender, educational qualification, region of origin, and a payment method (for compensation). These questions help us understand the diversity of the survey respondents and allow us to compare privacy opinions across demographics. The personal information was deleted once the data was analyzed to protect anonymity.

Browsers and Cookies: The questions in this part focused on people's knowledge and preferences for web browsers and cookies. We asked the users about cookies, consent banners, the different types of cookies being used and their categorization, familiarity with privacy policies, and how they managed and interacted with cookies. We also enquired about the browsers that the users where using and their preferences for using these browsers.

Web Applications: We collected statistics on the types of applications users accessed online and their perceived safety when providing private information on these applications. Questions included customers' reactions to insecure websites, their experiences with personalised marketing, and their e-commerce platform behaviours. The purpose was to record their trust levels and privacy policies across different categories of websites.

We also analysed user behaviours and privacy procedures on social media and over-the-top (OTT) platforms. The questions addressed account creation, purposes of using social media, privacy settings, and sharing behaviours. We wanted to understand the participants' awareness of privacy issues and their actions to mitigate those risks on social media sites.

To gain insight into users' trust levels and experiences with e-commerce platforms, we asked questions about their frequency of use, preferred websites, payment methods, and practices related to storing card details.

Anonymity: Privacy settings on web browsers are critical in protecting our personal information and online activity. They provide consumers control over the information gathered by websites, advertising networks, and other third parties during their browsing sessions. We presented options such as clearing cache, updating cookie permissions, and managing other settings to the participants. Since these reduce the amount of personal data collected, awareness regarding the same is necessary and an important practice.

Data Breaches and Personal Incidents: In order to understand their awareness of data breaches, we asked them if their personal data has ever been leaked and what that data was. We further inquired if they were informed about this leak/breach by the compromised website or organization. We also asked the participants if they had experienced incidents that compromised their privacy.

3.3 Data Filtering and Processing

We received survey responses from a total of 168 participants; however, we filtered out 13 responses using attention checking questions resulting in a total of 155 valid responses. Participants spent around 40 min on the survey and were provided a compensation of 100 INR per hour of their time and effort.

Demographics: Out of the 155 valid responses that we received, 73 of them were from the age group 18–25, 38 were from the age group 26–35, 17 were from the age group 36–45, 21 from 46–55, and 6 participants were above 55 years of age. 66 of our participants had a graduate degree and 50 participants had a postgraduate degree. Majority of our participants (85) were students. 35% of our participants identified as female while the remaining identified as male.

Qualitative Analysis: We had a couple of open-ended descriptive questions as part of the survey. For the same, in the first cycle coding, we use initial or open coding, where two researchers worked on making the codes and the respective definitions to finalise the code book, with a Cohen's kappa value of 0.79. In the second cycle of coding, we perform theoretical coding and we select a central or core category that identifies the primary theme, i.e., a possible cyber attack.

One of the question was to describe a privacy compromising incident, if they had been a part of any. 24 participants responded positively; we coded their answers into 5 codes—Social Media Hacked/Impersonation, Spam Calls/Messages, Data Breach, Credit Card Fraud and Click-baiting. Rest of the participants believed that their privacy had not been compromised.

We also enquired the participants' occupation and coded them into 4 codes. Majority of the participants were from the codes "Students" (58%), "Professionals(34.9%)" and "Homemakers(5.8%)". Two participants were retired but we did not use their responses for analysis regarding this demographic, since their representation was very less in number.

Quantitative Analysis: Since majority of our questions had categorical options, we use the chi-squared test to test the correlation between a demographic (age range, gender, education, occupation) and a question. Based on the p-value and chi-squared value, we conclude if the correlational analysis is relevant.

3.4 Limitations

As platforms like Prolific [24] and mTurk [1] are unavailable in India, we reached out to potential participants online and via acquaintances. Hence, the scale of participants is not very large, and consisted majorly of students. Our study only focuses on Indians, so the findings may not apply to other non-western countries. Secondly, people might not always remember all the details about their social media use and knew that it was a privacy study, thus may have introduced social desirability bias. Lastly, because most of our participants live in cities, our findings might not accurately represent rural population using social media.

4 Results and Discussion

We report our findings from the 155 responses we collected. We start by discussing the participants' responses to questions regarding basic privacy on the web, the decisions they make when presented with an option to control their personal information. We then go on to discuss their presence and privacy on social media platforms, what worries them about sharing on social media, how they control who sees their posts, and so on. By doing this, we hope to understand their thoughts and actions when it comes to keeping their information safe online across different sites.

4.1 RQ1: General Privacy-Related Awareness

Cookies: We started the survey by asking the participants about their understanding of "cookies". We observe that among women, there is an equal distribution of people who know the correct definition vs. people who did not entirely understand how cookies work. However, among men, 64% were aware of the correct definition but complete unawareness of the term is similar in both the genders. We also observe that the older age-groups were less aware of the same as represented in Fig. 1. This might be mainly due the fact that majority of the older-generation are not well versed with the new technologies or have not been educated regarding the same when compared to younger age-groups.

We further showed a cookie banner, displaying four categories of cookies, to the participants and asked them to choose the categories they were aware of. We gave them an example of these cookies so that the heterogeneous nomenclature does not affect their response. We observed that 70% of the participants were aware of strictly necessary cookies and 65% of the participants were aware of

(a) Cookie knowledge among different age groups

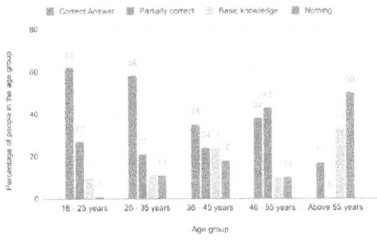

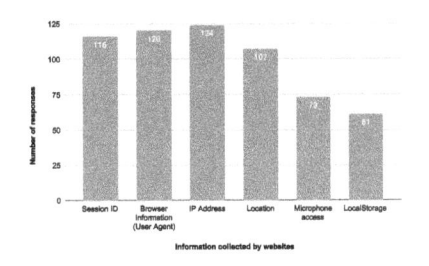

(b) Information the participants think is accessed by websites

Fig. 1. Cookies and data privacy understanding amongst users

advertisement cookies. About 50% of the participants were aware of both functionality and performance cookies. Majority of the people in the age group of 36–45 yrs knew about only one of the cookie categories. Rest of the age groups show an evenly distributed knowledge about the cookie categories. 50% of the females knew only one cookie category presented to them compared to only 7% who knew all the categories. However, around 42% of the males claimed to know all these categories while only 29% just knew one. 60% of the home makers knew only one cookie category and none of them knew all four. For all other occupations, there was an almost even distribution.

We asked the participants what cookies mean to them and gave them the following options (1) "Small pieces of data about the user's session, stored at the user side (browser) by server" (2) "Small pieces of data about the user's session, stored at the server side" (3) "Data about user sessions, I don't know who stores it and where" (4) "I don't know, just a tasty snack". We considered option (1) correct, (2) partially correct, (3) only basic knowledge and (4) as nothing as represented in Fig. 1a. While the participants may not have known the correct usage of cookies and how they are handled at the browser, they are aware of the fact that cookies are used by websites indicating that they might be able to manage their privacy on websites through banners if they choose to do so.

Browsers: We asked the participants to rank the different browsers (Chrome, Firefox, Safari, Brave, Edge and DuckDuckGo) they use. 60.5% of the participants chose Chrome as their first preference and indicated that they used it for it's "good user interface" and "more security". Other reasons mentioned in multiple responses included "Default option or available on devices", "Popular" and "Habit/using since long time". To avoid advertisements, users preferred to use Brave but otherwise the other browsers had an even distribution.

Information Collected by Websites: Figure 1b shows the number of people aware about the category of information collected. Some participants mentioned additional information like, "form details", "browsing history", "device information", "aspect ratio", "web camera access" as well. However, one participant did not know anything about the information collected. While awareness about other information is high, only 47% and 39% of participants were aware about microphone and localstorage access respectively. Since localstorage is not a popular term, this is not surprising.

Privacy Regulations: Since the DPDP had been recently passed in India, we wanted to assess the awareness about DPDP and other privacy protection laws or regulations. Figure 2 displays the participants' awareness across different age groups. More than 60% participants above 25 years of age reported that they had not heard about any privacy policy while 35% people in the 18–25 age group reported the same. The DPDP Act was the most commonly known act (42% of all the participants) followed by GDPR that is known to 37% of the participants. While the popularity of DPDP over other regulations was expected for Indian participants, it is still alarming that only 42% were aware about this act.

Data Breach Awareness: To assess the awareness concerning data breaches, we asked the participants if their information has been leaked through web application that they are aware of. We also asked if they were informed by the web application about the breach. Almost 41% of the participants did not know whether their data was leaked or not, and did not care about data leaks unless it directly affect them while 12.6% participants reported that their data was never compromised. Other participants reported that the name and phone number were the most commonly compromised data followed by location and credit card details.

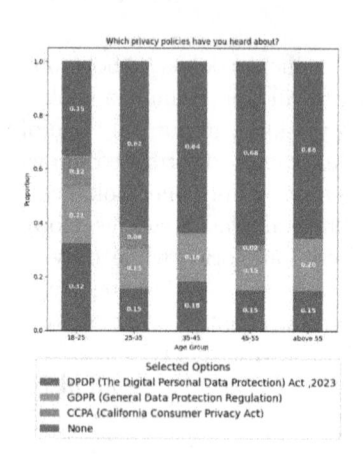

Fig. 2. Privacy regulations awareness

Given the responses by the participants about information being compromised through data breaches, we compared it with the data available online on "haveibeenpwned" [30]. The site keeps track of accounts and associated information being leaked and link them across different breaches. The site takes as input the user's email and lists all the applications which were compromised due to which the user's data was leaked. This data consisted a range of personally identifiable information like date of birth, phone numbers, addresses, etc.

75 participants consented to the use of their email-id for checking data breaches on this website. Table 1 discusses the users' awareness about the data breaches, being informed about the breach by the compromised organization and actual compromise. We can see that 31 (41%) participants were not at all aware of their data being compromised.

Privacy Compromised Incidents: 23 participants described their compromise incidents and a majority of these incidents were either social media account compromise (9) or a data breach (8). 4 participants reported getting compro-

Table 1. Data breach awareness among 75 participants

No. of participants	User knows of data breach	Informed by compromised website	Breached according to haveibeenpwned
12 (16%)	Yes	No	No
7 (9.3%)	Yes	Yes	No
18 (24%)	Yes	Yes	Yes
7 (9.3%)	Yes	No	Yes
31 (41.3%)	No	No	Yes

mised through spam calls or messages while 1 participant each were a victim of credit card fraud and clickbaiting.

Table 2. Summary of RQ-1 results

Topics	Results
Cookies	About 52% of the participants knew about cookies properly to be able to control them in their browsers or websites mindfully
Browsers	Chrome is the most popular browser. People have made their preferences mainly based on the user interface, security and the no.of advertisements they see
Information being collected by different websites platforms	Most of the participants were not aware/partially aware of the various things the browsers collect from them
Do they know that banners are shown to follow privacy policies?	All of the participants knew about atleast one policy by name surprisingly. However not all had agreed to the fact that websites need to follow some policy and regulations
Awareness about data breaches	Only 25% of the participants (out of the 75 who gave consent) were informed about a breach of their data. Almost 50% of them were breached but not informed about the same by the websites
Personal incidents	The 23 incidents shared by the participants show a prevalence of social media compromises and information leakage through data breaches

Summary of RQ1: We summarize the results for RQ1 in Table 2.

4.2 RQ2: Privacy Management on Social Media and Other Web Applications and Comparison of Behavior

Next, we discuss the different ways used by participants to protect their privacy on the web. We start with privacy settings on web applications and social media, and discuss if users trust some categories of websites more than others.

Privacy Management on the Web: We discuss which categories of websites are used, preferred and trusted by the participants. We then discuss in detail about the privacy settings that one practices while using these applications and in social media. We conclude this subsection by discussing if the behavior is different across these categories and the reasoning behind the same.

Usage of Different Web Applications: We started by assessing what type of web applications are mostly used in India. We observed that social media has been the most prevalent among people from the age group 18–35 years followed by computing education and research related platforms. People above this age bracket most use e-commerce the most, followed by social media, entertainment and news forums.

Additionally, we wanted to know how much information they share and which websites they usually trust the most. We observe that most participants felt that it was safe to share personal information on social media and on the e-commerce platforms because those platforms ask for some common information like name, phone number, and location while the most trusted websites by the people are government websites and educational websites.

Privacy Measures Followed: Websites are often blocked by the browser, if they do not seem secure, giving the user an option to not visit the site. We asked the participants what they would do in this case to explore the level of concern individuals exhibit regarding protecting their data upon discovering that a website lacks security measures, potentially leading to data leaks. Females were a little more inclined towards not choosing to proceed. We also observed that people from the older age group are more concerned and alert towards data leaks compared to younger age groups.

We also wanted to know how much people trust web applications for their important information like bank details and credit card information. All participants were equally concerned about their bank and credit card details. We also observe that elderly people are more concerned about their data privacy and data leaks compared to the younger age groups. The older age groups hesitate to make payments online in general since they do not use these services very often and do not trust on the new payment methods.

Privacy Management on Different Application Understanding Social Media Engagement: Given the profound influence of social media on communication, information consumption, and social interaction, our study delves into the diverse engagement patterns and privacy management practices across age groups and genders. We make the following observations regarding platform preferences across different age groups and occupations:

- WhatsApp is the most used platform across all age groups. This could be attributed to its widespread availability, ease of use, and the popularity of messaging services for communication among all demographics.
- LinkedIn and Twitter are the least used platforms and have very few users in higher age groups. This could be because LinkedIn is primarily a professional

Table 3. Privacy settings on social media by gender

Gender	Private in all social media apps	Different for every app	Public in all social media apps
Male	56.44%	29.70%	13.86%
Female	79.63%	12.96%	7.41%

networking platform, which may not be as appealing to older demographics who are not actively job-seeking or advancing their careers. Similarly, Twitter's focus on real-time updates and short-form content may not resonate as strongly with older users who prefer more in-depth interactions.
- The participants in the 18–25 years age group use almost all platforms, albeit to varying levels. This may be due to the varied interests and social circles within this age group, leading to engagement across multiple platforms. Additionally, younger users are often early adopters of new technologies and trends, resulting in broader usage across different social media platforms.
- Facebook is mostly used by older people. This could be because Facebook was one of the earliest and most widely adopted social media platforms, particularly among older demographics. Additionally, older users may prefer Facebook's features for connecting with friends and family, sharing updates, and joining groups related to hobbies and interests.

Despite the widespread popularity of these platforms, a substantial portion of users express doubts about the security of their personal information. According to our study, a considerable percentage of respondents expressed varying levels of unease regarding the safety of their data on popular social media platforms. The statistics reveal the following:

- Facebook: 33.55% of respondents expressed concerns about the safety of their data on this platform.
- YouTube: 25.81% of respondents indicated a lack of trust in the safety of their data on YouTube.
- Instagram: 20.00% of respondents reported feeling uneasy about the safety of their data on Instagram.
- WhatsApp: 16.13% of respondents voiced concerns about the safety of their data while using WhatsApp.
- LinkedIn: 10.32% of respondents expressed doubts about the safety of their data on LinkedIn.
- Twitter: 10.97% of respondents had reservations regarding the safety of their data on Twitter.

We then enquired the participants about their privacy settings on social media.

1. **Adjusting privacy settings:** Table 3 presents privacy settings on social media platforms categorized by gender. Each row represents a gender category

Table 4. Review privacy settings while posting content on social media by gender

Gender	Always	Never	Rarely	Sometimes
Male	43.56%	18.52%	22.77%	23.76%
Female	57.41%	9.90%	12.96%	11.11%

(male and female), and each column represents a different privacy setting. Female users tend to have higher percentages of setting their accounts to private in all social media platforms compared to male users.

2. **Location tagging and group photo sharing:** While posting, only 7% of people consistently use location tagging, and a mere 5.09% people share group photos without considering permissions, opting instead to share among close friends. Others share among close friends and also take some level of permission from everyone present in the group photo before posting.
3. **Frequency of sharing data:** Both males and females are quite selective while sharing on social media platforms, indicating a high level of awareness regarding privacy and personal boundaries. Interestingly, there were no females in the study who reported sharing everything, highlighting the diverse approaches to sharing personal information online.
4. **Review settings while posting content:** Table 4 illustrates the frequency at which individuals review their settings while posting content on social media platforms. The data is categorized by gender, with each row representing a gender category (male and female), and each column representing a different frequency of settings review. The people who opted for "Never" do not pay attention to settings while those who opted for "Sometimes" reviewed settings in case of some sensitive content. Females are more conscious than males while sharing, as they review settings for more posts.

Do they Trust Some Websites More than Others? From our observations from the above subsections, we conclude the following:

- Most of the people are concerned about their information on websites but they are fine sharing it because they need to use the websites in order to connect to the world and to get their work done.
- 20% of the participants even have public accounts and are fine with sharing their information with the world. Similarly some people are fine with sharing basic personal information like name, address and location.
- We observed that people are careful on websites that involve payments or while posting some sensitive information on social media. However, there are quite a few who do not care about what they share.

Leaking of personal information is not considered that much of a threat. This shows the need to aware people about the possibility of using this data to personalize their experience on the web and show ads and track the users. Basic user profiling is made easy using these personally identifiable information. We now proceed to evaluate if the users you other ways to protect their privacy in the web ecosystem.

Summary of RQ2: We summarize the results for RQ2 in Table 5 which discusses the behavior of the participants across various web application and the associated privacy settings and we then discuss the participants' behavior across different types of websites to see if they trust some categories more than others.

4.3 RQ3: Privacy Management and Behaviour on Browsers and Individual Websites

In the browser, users have different options to manage their privacy like using incognito modes, clearing browser cache, use of VPNs, etc. There is also an option to use extensions to manage security and privacy on particular websites. When visiting websites, the users are given an option to manage the cookies stored in the browser for different purposes through a consent banner. In this subsection, we analyse the awareness of the participants regarding these options, what they prefer/choose, and their reasoning behind the same.

Privacy Management: We start with discussing the measures that users took to protect their privacy and minimize sharing of information at that the browsing level. We observed that a majority of the participants preferred incognito modes(44%) and VPNs(48%) across all age groups. Tor browser is very unpopular among the participants, possibly because of limited availability in India. The participants also seem to look for HTTPS connections while browsing. Participants above the age of 55 years were unaware of ad and tracking blockers.

We then asked about individual settings and why one would choose that practice.

Clearing Browser Cache: Only 16% participants clean their browsing data after every single time they finish browsing. More than 50% participants (82% above the age of 55) never cleared their browsing data. Quite a few participants (43% overall) reported to clearing their data occasionally, maybe once a month. The reason behind this could be the lack of awareness about how much this data could help in tracking and profiling the user on the internet.

Incognito Mode and VPNs: We studied the level of awareness and adoption of incognito mode and VPNs among participants and identified potential knowledge and usage gaps.

– Participants in the age group of 18–25 use incognito mode the most. The proportion of users then decreases with each age group.
– The most common reason is to avoid having their search history saved (42%). Other common reasons include wanting to avoid cookies and site data being stored (22%), researching something personal or confidential (18%), and browsing websites that offer limited free content (18%).

Table 5. Summary of RQ-2 results

Topic	Results
Settings on browsers	
Which apps do they use more	Whatsapp was used across all the age groups. Instagram was mostly used by younger generation and Facebook by elder generation
Which apps do they trust more	There were concerns raised by a lot of people regarding every platform. Most of the people just share information in order to be connected to the world and for entertainment purposes
How much information do they share	They share selectively
What are the settings	Share personal information among close friends, keep account private, avoid location tagging, mostly review settings before sharing anything
Settings on other web applications	
Which websites do they trust more	Government Websites and Education/Research are most trusted by all the peoples
How much information do they share	People share information like name and phone number casually without any concern but for information like credit card they not share normally
Trust across websites	
Do they trust some websites more than others?	We observed that people though don't trust, but still use social media applications since they don't involve monetary transactions. With e-commerce websites, people are careful with the settings and while sharing and saving card details. Majority people either prefer or are not concerned about being profiled on the internet by ad agencies and like the personalized experience
	Another reason for them not being careful is the usability of the privacy settings on the websites, if given an easy clear choice, they may choose to not share their personal data to be tracked

- The results show that a significant portion of people, 33%, believe incognito mode stores browsing history, cookies and site data, and information entered in forms. In contrast, factual evidence demonstrates that incognito mode offers temporary privacy by not recording browsing history on the user's device. Additionally, cookies and site data associated with incognito browsing sessions are not stored locally. This disrupts website efforts to track user activity and tailor advertising based on browsing behavior.

- Younger generations, who have grown up alongside technology, possess a better understanding of incognito mode compared to older demographics with less exposure to the nuances of web browsing. Hence, we can see that many participants from the older age groups chose the "No Idea" option.

As discussed above, VPNs are also very popular method adopted by the participants. We made the following observations regarding the use of VPNs:

- Within the age group of 18–25, a strikingly high 78% of the participants reported using VPN, whereas only 18% of individuals aged 55 and above reported using the same. Younger users might engage in online activities that necessitate a higher level of privacy awareness, potentially driving their VPN adoption.
- There was also a substantial gender gap in VPN usage within the age group of 18–25; while 80% of male participants used a VPN, only 55% of female participants used it.

Banner Interaction: We asked the participants about how they would interact with a consent banner displayed by the websites. 45% (or less) of the participants in every age group reported that they would open the options on the consent banner and adjust their preferences. The other participants accepted the default.

Personalized Advertisement: Thirty-three participants reported seeing more advertisements without knowing the reason while 35 of them did not care about the advertisements. 43 (27%) participants preferred advertisements as they offered them a personalized experience. Only 41 participants wanted less ads and took steps towards the same.

Why Accept All Cookies - Usability of Banners: While 30% of the participants did not "Accept All" while interacting with cookie banners, the rest may or may not choose to deny the cookies. As depicted in the plot in Fig. 3, banners are not easily usable by 51% of the participants and only 4% said they do not believe they have any important data. This indicates that even though people are concerned about their data being leaked, they are not concerned enough, given an usable or clear choice would benefit them better.

Our observations suggest that more people would make better decisions if the reject option was more accessible. Clear privacy instructions on the banner or link to privacy policy would further help them make informed decisions.

Extensions: Another option to handle cookies on websites is to use extensions. We wanted to assess if they actively delete cookies for specific websites. Among the provided options, Cookie Manager was known to 28 participants, Cookie Editor was known to 28, EditThisCookie was known to 11 and Vanilla Cookie Manager was known to 11 participants. Majority of the participants (65%) did not know any of these and did not mention using any other extension as well.

Summary Results of RQ4: In this subsection we discussed the awareness about data breaches and concluded that majority of the participants were not aware of their information being leaked. We further summarize the results in Table 6.

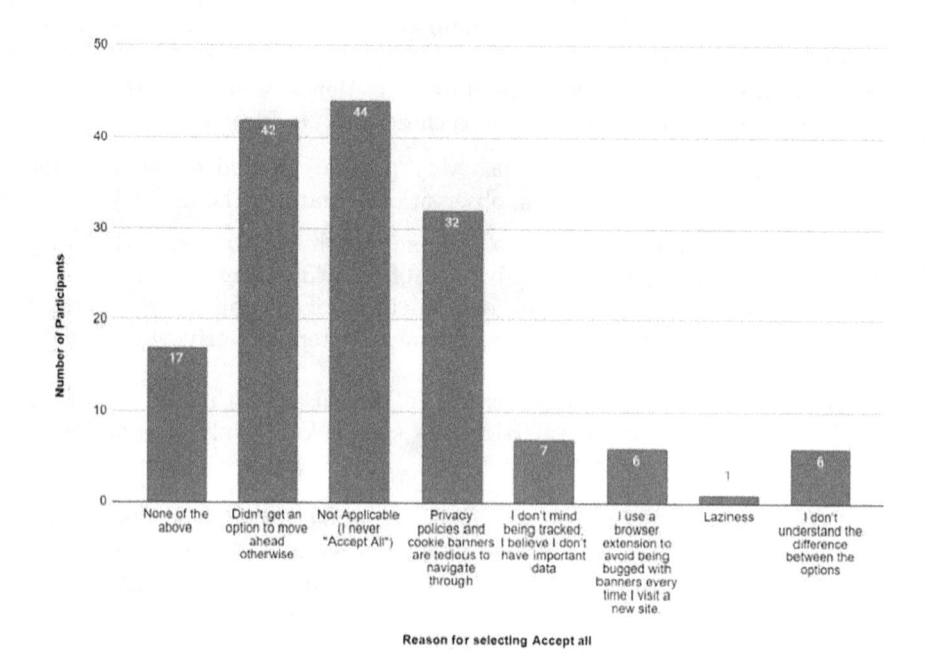

Fig. 3. Reasons for accepting all cookies in consent banners

Table 6. Summary of RQ-3 results

Topic	Results
Settings on browsers	
Privacy settings on browser	Most of the people didn't give much attention to privacy while browsing and didn't clear their browsing history.
Incognito mode	In general very less number of participants knew about incognito mode and what all information is private while using incognito mode.
VPNs	Very few number of participants were aware about VPNs VPN awareness decreased with age.
Settings on websites	
Extensions for cookies	Very less percentage of people prefer maintaining privacy using extensions and hence may not explicitly delete cookies for particular website while browsing.
Banner Interaction	People are inclined towards choosing a default or an easy option. Hence, dark patterns on banners may affect their choices.

5 Conclusion

Our work aims to study the privacy perceptions in Indian users. Our findings indicated that younger generations are mostly aware of the different technologies to manage their privacy online as compared to the older generations. While people above the age of 45 years may not have had access to the technologies initially, they might have come across them at their work place. However, awareness among people who have retired or are homemakers can be increased through sessions about online security and privacy practices as a lot of them spend significant time online.

However, the younger generation makes choices that may lead to their private information being leaked or compromised; it is either a matter of inconvenience or carelessness towards safeguarding their private data. Measures need to be taken to make these privacy management more accessible to the users. Stricter restrictions and regulations towards removal of dark patterns could be the first step to do so. If they are implemented and followed properly by web applications, it can make privacy easily accessible by everyone.

The main reason behind not choosing a privacy friendly is the lack of awareness about the consequences of being tracked and profiled on the internet. While it enhances the users' browsing experience, they fail to understand that this makes them vulnerable to various attacks like social engineering, impersonation and social media and other accounts being compromised.

Acknowledgments. We would like to thank the anonymous reviewers for their feedback on our paper. This work was supported in part by the Science and Engineering Research Board (SERB) via grant SRG/2023/000075 and in part by Department of Science and Technology via grant DST/INSPIRE/04/2020/002092.

References

1. Amazon: Amazon mechanical turk. https://www.mturk.com/
2. Bielova, N., Litvine, L., Nguyen, A., Chammat, M., Toubiana, V., Harry, E.: The effect of design patterns on (present and future) cookie consent decisions. In: USENIX Security Symposium (2024)
3. Bollinger, D., Kubicek, K., Cotrini, C., Basin, D.: Automating cookie consent and GDPR violation detection. In: 31st USENIX Security Symposium (USENIX Security 2022), Boston, pp. 2893–2910 (2022)
4. Bouhoula, A., Kubicek, K., Zac, A., Cotrini, C., Basin, D.: Automated large-scale analysis of cookie notice compliance. In: 33st USENIX Security Symposium (USENIX Security 2024). USENIX Association, Philadelphia (2024)
5. Brazilian National Data Protection Authority: Brazilian general data protection law (LGPD) (2020). https://iapp.org/resources/article/brazilian-data-protection-law-lgpd-english-translation/
6. California State Legislature: California consumer privacy act of 2018 (2018). https://oag.ca.gov/privacy/ccpa
7. Data Security Council of India: India cybersecurity domestic market 2023 report.pdf (2023). https://www.dsci.in/files/content/knowledge-centre/2023/IndiaCybersecurity_/DomesticMarket_/2023_/Report.pdf

8. DataReportal: Digital 2024: Global overview report - datareportal - global digital insights. https://datareportal.com/reports/digital-2024-global-overview-report
9. Distler, V., et al.: A systematic literature review of empirical methods and risk representation in usable privacy and security research. ACM Trans. Comput.-Hum. Interact. (TOCHI) **28**(6), 1–50 (2021)
10. Ministry of Electronics & Information Technology, G.o.I.: The digital personal data protection bill, 2022. Digital Personal Data Protection Act, 2022 (2022). https://www.meity.gov.in/content/digital-personal-data-protection-bill-2022
11. European Parliament, Council of the European Union: Regulation (EU) 2016/679 of the European Parliament and of the Council (2016). https://data.europa.eu/eli/reg/2016/679/oj
12. Farke, F.M., Balash, D.G., Golla, M., Dürmuth, M., Aviv, A.J.: Are privacy dashboards good for end users? Evaluating user perceptions and reactions to Google's my activity. In: 30th USENIX Security Symposium, pp. 483–500 (2021)
13. Gayatri-Priyadarsini: Web-privacy-perceptions-amongst-Indian-users. https://github.com/Gayatri-Priyadarsini/Web-Privacy-Perceptions-Amongst-Indian-Users
14. Gray, C.M., Santos, C., Bielova, N., Toth, M., Clifford, D.: Dark patterns and the legal requirements of consent banners: an interaction criticism perspective. In: Proceedings of the 2021 CHI Conference on Human Factors in Computing Systems, pp. 1–18 (2021)
15. Hossain, M.J.: User privacy & security in internet: a concern for Bangladesh. Ph.D. thesis, Noakhali Science and Technology University (2022)
16. IFF: IFF's cybersecurity report for the first quarter of 2024#plugthebreach (2024). https://internetfreedom.in/cybersec-report-q1-2024/
17. Indian_Parliament: it_act_2000_updated.pdf. https://www.indiacode.nic.in/bitstream/123456789/13116/1/it_act_2000_updated.pdf. Accessed 24 May 2024
18. Ingole, C.U., Bandela, M., Tanna, D., Solanki, S.K., Dhotre, P., Patil, R.: Privacy awareness and online behavior of Indian users: an analytical study (2023)
19. Kaushik, S., Sharma, T., Yu, Y., Ali, A.F., Wang, Y., Zou, Y.: Cross-country examination of people's experience with targeted advertising on social media. In: Extended Abstracts of the 2024 CHI Conference on Human Factors in Computing Systems, CHI EA 2024 (2024). https://doi.org/10.1145/3613905.3650780
20. Kumaraguru, P., Sachdeva, N.: Privacy in India: attitudes and awareness v 2.0. Available at SSRN 2188749 (2012)
21. Matte, C., Bielova, N., Santos, C.: Do cookie banners respect my choice? Measuring legal compliance of banners from IAB Europe's transparency and consent framework. In: 2020 IEEE Symposium on Security and Privacy (SP), vol. 1, pp. 791–809 (2020)
22. Mayer, P., Zou, Y., Schaub, F., Aviv, A.J.: "now i'm a bit angry:" individuals' awareness, perception, and responses to data breaches that affected them. In: 30th USENIX Security Symposium (USENIX Security 2021), pp. 393–410. USENIX Association (2021)
23. Mustafa, M., Asad, A.M., Hassan, S., Haider, U., Durrani, Z., Krombholz, K.: Pakistani teens and privacy - how gender disparities, religion and family values impact the privacy design space. In: Proceedings of the 2023 ACM SIGSAC Conference on Computer and Communications Security, CCS 2023, pp. 195–209 (2023). https://doi.org/10.1145/3576915.3623087
24. Prolific: Prolific | quickly find research participants you can trust. https://www.prolific.com/

25. Sharma, T., Kaushik, S., Yu, Y., Ahmed, S.I., Wang, Y.: User perceptions and experiences of targeted ads on social media platforms: Learning from Bangladesh and India. In: Proceedings of the 2023 CHI Conference on Human Factors in Computing Systems, CHI 2023 (2023). https://doi.org/10.1145/3544548.3581498
26. Singh, A.K., Upadhyaya, N., Seth, A., Hu, X., Sastry, N., Mondal, M.: What cookie consent notices do users prefer: a study in the wild. In: Proceedings of the 2022 European Symposium on Usable Security, EuroUSEC 2022, pp. 28–39 (2022). https://doi.org/10.1145/3549015.3555675
27. Srivastava, A., Geethakumari, G.: Measuring privacy leaks in online social networks. In: 2013 International Conference on Advances in Computing, Communications and Informatics (ICACCI), pp. 2095–2100. IEEE (2013)
28. Statsindia: Internet usage in india - statistics & facts | statista. https://www.statista.com/topics/2157/internet-usage-in-india/#topicOverview
29. Toth, M., Bielova, N., Roca, V.: On dark patterns and manipulation of website publishers by CMPs. In: PETS 2022-22nd Privacy Enhancing Technologies Symposium (2022)
30. Hunt, T., Charlotte Hunt, S.S.: Have i been pwned: check if your email has been compromised in a data breach. https://haveibeenpwned.com/
31. Wei, M., Emami-Naeini, P., Roesner, F., Kohno, T.: Skilled or gulliblef gender stereotypes related to computer security and privacy. In: 2023 IEEE Symposium on Security and Privacy (SP), pp. 2050–2067. IEEE (2023)
32. Wire, T.: The wire news India (2023). https://thewire.in/government/india-data-leak-breach-lok-sabha
33. Zhang, M., Meng, W., Zhou, Y., Ren, K.: CSChecker: revisiting GDPR and CCPA compliance of cookie banners on the web. In: Proceedings of the IEEE/ACM 46th International Conference on Software Engineering, ICSE 2024 (2024). https://doi.org/10.1145/3597503.3639159

Enabling Privacy in IT Service Operations

Rohit Gupta[✉], Rishabh Kumar, Sutapa Mondal, Mangesh Gharote, and Sachin Lodha

TCS Research, Tata Consultancy Services Ltd., Pune, India
{r.gupta25,rishabh.kumar10,sutapa.mondal,mangesh.g,sachin.lodha}@tcs.com

Abstract. IT service operations involve handling sensitive customer data, which gets logged into the system in the form of tickets describing the issues faced by customer. An authorized agent tasked with resolving a ticket may get exposed to sensitive customer information, which can lead to privacy breach, impacting the customer and potentially damaging the reputation of the organization. To address this issue, we propose a framework that minimizes sensitive data exposure to preserve privacy in IT service operations. Our framework quantifies the sensitive data misuse by an agent based on the information aggregated at their end. The sensitive data within ticket is masked and the flow of ticket is regulated to restrict the sensitive data aggregation. Additionally, we introduce a simulator, PESO (Privacy Enabled Service Operation), to study and demonstrate the implications of privacy settings on various service operation parameters.

Keywords: Privacy · Service Operations · Insider Threat · Allocation · Data Minimization · Simulation

1 Introduction

IT services are an integral part of businesses, enabling them to efficiently cater to a large customer base. However, the access to user data in such service operations ecosystems introduces the risk of breaches, which can be intentional or unintentional. Incidents where trusted and authorized personnel (agents) exploit their companies' data is prevalent throughout the service industry [15]. Also, even if the agents are crowd-sourced, they tend to engage in malicious activities by aggregating information [4]. Such threats jeopardize user data privacy and severely undermine an organization's trustworthiness, reputation, reliability, and credibility. Addressing insider threats within IT service operations remains a significant challenge [8,15].

Our work presents a comprehensive framework for service operations, grounded in the principle of data minimization. The primary objective is to reduce data exposure while maintaining efficient ticket resolution processes.

1.1 Privacy Issues in Service Operations

An IT service desk operations rely on a pool of skilled agents who collectively support the service needs of customers. These service needs are referred to as "tickets" which can be submitted through email or raised through a technical interface. These tickets are acknowledged, classified, and assigned to agents for resolution within a defined time frame, known as the Service Level Agreement (SLA). Privacy concerns arise in this process due to the sensitive nature of information contained in tickets, which contain personal information about users. During ticket resolution, agents are exposed to user data, raising the risk of both intentional and unintentional insider threats. Such misuse of data can have serious implications at both the user and organizational levels.

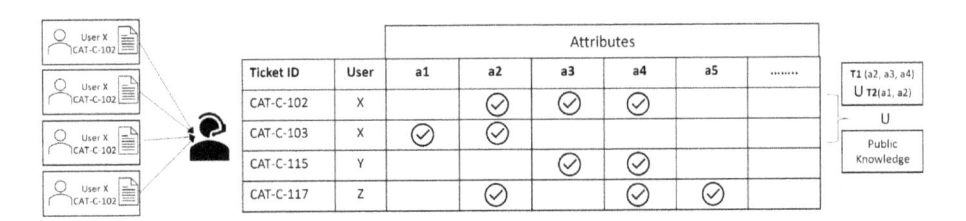

Fig. 1. Privacy Threat User and Organization Level

User-Level Privacy Threats: As illustrated in Fig. 1, privacy risks at the user level emerge when multiple tickets from the same user (e.g., user X) are assigned to the same agent. The agent's exposure to various user attributes is shown by the ticks in the respective tickets. The aggregation of information from these tickets ($T1 \cup T2$) or linking the data with publicly available information can lead to a breach of the user's privacy.

Organizational-Level Privacy Threats: At the organizational level, privacy threats can arise when an agent aggregates information from multiple users (Fig. 1). This aggregation can lead to the disclosure of more comprehensive information, allowing the agent to derive statistical inferences that could compromise organizational data privacy. For example, if several tickets related to a medical condition or treatment are assigned to the same agent, the agent can infer patterns about disease prevalence and confidential organizational policies around health insurance coverage and employee wellness programs. This aggregated information could then be exploited by the agent, leading to a privacy breach of both employee health data and the organization's confidential healthcare policies [3].

1.2 Contributions

This work makes the following contributions:

- We propose a privacy-preserving framework, referred to as Privacy-Enabled Service Operations (PESO).
- We develop a privacy-aware allocation mechanism to efficiently assign tickets to agents while minimizing sensitive data exposure.
- We investigate the impact of privacy measures on key performance indicators (KPIs) relevant to service operations.
- We design a simulation model to assist enterprises in making informed decisions regarding privacy and operational strategies.

2 Related Work

Gupta et al. [6] proposed an optimization approach to determine the best match between the tickets and the agents, introducing a heuristic algorithm that allocates tickets based on factors such as penalty for SLA breach, workload balancing, and expertise matching. Similarly, Krishnan et al. [9] developed a ranking-based strategy, utilizing agent performance metrics such as success rate and resolution time to guide allocation decisions. Bai et al. [1] and Phuke et al. [13] addressed privacy concerns in service operations using effective ticket allocation mechanisms. Bai et al. [1] have considered a task-based conflict set for managing ticket assignments, while Phuke et al. [13] defined a privacy budget for each agent. However, determining the appropriate privacy budget for each agent and conflict task-set remains a challenging task in practice. While much of the literature on ticket assignment has prioritized operational efficiency, privacy concerns in these systems have not been adequately addressed.

Current industry solutions for IT service management such as ServiceNow, SolarWinds, ServiceDesk, and Freshservice [5] provide security mechanism that include role-based access control mechanisms (RBAC) and encryption techniques. However, while RBAC can limit access based on roles, it cannot detect instances where authorized agents misuse their privileges for unintended purposes, posing a potential insider threat. Some of these platforms also track and mask identifiable information in the tickets using rule-based masking strategies. However, they do not explore how to optimally mask this information.

Techniques like Differential Privacy (DP) [12] introduce noise to mask sensitive data, but this can distort the source information, making DP less suitable for handling service requests where data integrity is critical. Traditional data anonymization techniques can be adapted for certain scenarios, but their implementation for real-time ticket masking remains challenging, as it risks reducing data utility. In this work, we propose a system that addresses the limitations of these existing methods.

3 Problem Description and Methodology

In an IT service desk scenario, agents are responsible for handling user service requests, known as tickets, which are submitted through various channels, such as online portals or email. The primary objective is privacy-aware ticket allocation such that the data exposure to agents is minimal. This approach is essential for reducing the risk of insider threats while ensuring that tickets are resolved within the defined SLAs (Fig. 2).

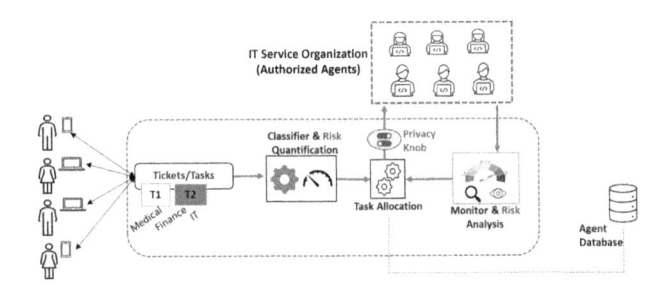

Fig. 2. PESO System Workflow

Each service request has multiple attributes, each with varying degrees of importance and sensitivity. Determining how much information should be disclosed to agents during ticket resolution is a complex task, as it requires contextual understanding of privacy risks. To address this, authors [10] proposed an optimization model for generating auto-masking plans based on vulnerability ratings and privacy factors. However, it lacks concrete guidance for implementing the masking in practice. To bridge this gap, we developed a simulator to analyze the impact of masking on KPIs. Masking sensitive information alone, however, is insufficient to ensure privacy; controlling the allocation of tickets is equally critical in mitigating privacy risks.

Each agent has a queue of service requests. If an agent is assigned multiple tickets from the same user, they may accumulate a large portion of user's information, which can lead to potential misuse. Additionally, if an agent handles tickets from multiple users, they may be able to draw statistical inferences that could reveal confidential organizational policies, which they are not authorized to access.

Thus, the proper assignment of sensitive tickets is crucial. However, given limited resources, it is challenging to optimally allocate tickets in a way that minimizes data exposure to agents while also preventing SLA breaches. Achieving this balance between privacy preservation and operational efficiency is a key focus of our proposed framework.

3.1 PESO System Architecture

The PESO system processes incoming tickets, which can be either structured or unstructured, often containing PIIs and other sensitive attributes. The system first leverages existing NLP models [14] to identify sensitive information and categorizes the ticket into different domains. The PESO architecture comprises the Sensitive Data Risk Estimator and the Ticket Regulator. The Sensitive Data

Risk Estimator is adapted from [10], and we extend this work to propose the Ticket Regulator. Our key contribution is focused on the Ticket Regulator. Each module is described in detail below.

Sensitive Data Risk Estimator: The attributes necessary for resolving a ticket can be derived from historical logs. Each attribute carries a different level of privacy risk if disclosed, which is quantified by a Vulnerability Rating (v) [10]. The vulnerability rating reflects the potential damage to user privacy caused by disclosing a particular attribute, ranging from high (e.g., risk of identity theft) to low (e.g., minimal privacy impact). The Data Privacy Officer establishes these ratings using privacy setting module. For instance, attributes can be classified in three vulnerability categories: high (directly identifiable attributes), medium (quasi-identifiers), and low (non-sensitive attributes) [2,7,11]. The number of vulnerability categories can be adjusted based on the application's needs.

To ensure privacy and limit data disclosure, a Privacy Factor (γ) is defined [10], ranging from 0 to 1. A higher γ value signifies stricter control over information disclosure. The value of γ affects both the extent of attribute disclosure and KPIs related to service operations. The proposed optimization model computes attribute disclosure based on their vulnerability rating (v) and a Sensitivity Score, which is the product of the vulnerability rating (v) and the disclosure proportion (ρ). Further, the sensitivity of an application is computed as z_m and z_{no-m}, where z_m denotes the sensitivity of the application when the attributes have some level of masking that is the disclosure proportion is not 1, and z_{no-m} denotes the sensitivity of the application when the disclosure proportion of attributes is 1, that is there is no masking. The objective is to maximizes attribute disclosure while keeping z_m within $(1-\gamma) \times z_{no-m}$. The privacy factor ($\gamma$) can be adjusted based on regulatory requirements, making it a key metric for ensuring data privacy compliance.

Ticket Regulator: The assignment of ticket to agents in a privacy-aware manner is done by Ticket Regulator. To achieve this, we define Agent Mis-usability Score and Overall Mis-usability Score as discussed below.

Agent Mis-Usability Score (M_u): The Agent Mis-usability Score quantifies the potential misuse of information by an agent, especially when the agent handles multiple tickets from the same user. This score is computed as follows:

$$M_u = \sum_{s \in S_u}(s_\rho \times s_v) + \sum_{q \in Q_u}(q_\rho \times q_v) \times (|Q_u|)^{\log_{10}^{e/2}} + \sum_{r \in R_u}(r_\rho \times r_v) \quad (1)$$

Here, S_u, Q_u, and R_u represent the sets of PII and sensitive, quasi, and non-sensitive attributes of user u, respectively. The terms (s_ρ, s_v), (q_ρ, q_v), and (r_ρ, r_v) denote the disclosure proportion and vulnerability rating for the respective attribute types. It is derived as the sum of three components: The first component computes the sensitivity of PII and sensitive attributes (s) aggregated over the tickets for user u. The second component captures the sensitivity of quasi-attributes (q), scaled by factor $(|Q_u|)^{\log_{10}^{e/2}}$ to account for the higher sensitivity when these attributes are linked. Finally, the third component addresses the information disclosed through non-sensitive attributes (r).

Overall Mis-Usability Score: The Overall Mis-usability Score (M_o) represents the aggregated risk of information misuse across multiple users handled by an agent:

$$M_o = \sum_{u=1}^{n} M_u \qquad (2)$$

The system monitors these mis-usability scores for each agent, classifying agents into low, medium, or high threat categories based on their M_o.

Privacy Aware Ticket Allocation: While allocating tickets to agents, operational as well as privacy criteria are taken into consideration. Operational factors include agent expertise (AE), average resolution time (ART), and agent workload (AW), while privacy factors are represented by the User Mis-usability (UM) score and the Overall Mis-usability (OM) score. The allocation mechanism avoids allocating tickets from the same user to a particular agent if it discloses or aggregates more sensitive information. Additionally, the allocation mechanism must avoid allocating tickets to the agents with a high over-all mis-usability (OM) score. The next task is estimating the weightages that must be given to these allocation criteria. The weightage selection depends on the choice of privacy factor.

In privacy settings, a higher privacy factor means that more severe sensitive attributes are significantly masked, while a lower privacy factor discloses more data to agents. When the privacy factor is high, the allocation mechanism prioritizes operational criteria, and when it's low, privacy criteria takes precedence. The weight for privacy (W_{priv}) and operational (W_{opn}) criteria is derived based on the value of γ and an adjustable deciding factor ($k \geq \gamma$), which balances the privacy-utility trade-off. The operational weight is derived from the privacy weight, and both are used to compute the weights for various criteria.

The weights for each criterion are calculated as follows: the relative importance of attributes such as ART, AW, AE, UM, and OM is multiplied by either the operational or privacy weight, depending on their type. These relative importance values must sum to 1 for each category and are predefined based on system or application requirements. Once these weights are determined, they guide the privacy-aware allocation mechanism. The Algorithm 1 first identifies available agents by checking their workloads. For each incoming ticket, it estimates resolution time, expertise matching, workload, and data exposure. Lower values for ART, AW, UM, and OM are preferred, while a higher AE value is desirable. After normalizing these values, agents are ranked using a weighted method, and the agent with the optimal score is chosen for ticket assignment.

Algorithm 1: Privacy-aware allocation algorithm
Data: $AA_{list}, w_{ART}, w_{AE}, w_{AW}, w_{UM}, w_{OM}$
Result: $allocated_{agent}$
1 Initialize: $ART_{list}, AE_{list}, AW_{list}, UM_{list}, OM_{list}, agent\_score_{list}, i = 0$;
2 **for** $agent \in AA_{list}$ **do**
3   Compute the values: ART, AE, AW, UM, OM with respect to ticket (t)
4 Normalize($ART_{list}, AW_{list}, UM_{list}, OM_{list}, AE_{list}$)
5 **while** $i \leq len(AA_{list})$ **do**
6   $agent\_score_{list}[i] = ART_{list}[i] \times w_{ART} + (\frac{1}{AE_{list}[i]}) \times w_{AE} + AW_{list}[i] \times w_{AW} + UM_{list}[i] \times w_{UM} + OM_{list}[i] \times w_{OM}$
7   $i+=1$
8 Update agents ART, AW, UM, OM
9 $allocated_{agent} = AA_{list}[argmin(agent\_score_{list})]$
---

4 PESO Simulation Model

We designed a Python-based simulator to model the PESO system under various privacy and operational conditions. The simulator is configurable through parameters such as arrival rate, number of agents, simulation duration (in shifts), and the percentage of sensitive tickets. The inter-arrival time of tickets follows an exponential distribution, governed by parameter λ [6]. A synthetic dataset of unstructured tickets is generated, containing both PII and sensitive and non-sensitive information. Additionally, agent data is generated, with each agent characterized by their expertise level in handling different categories of tickets. For each category, an average resolution time is synthetically generated from a normal distribution. The assignment of the ticket is handled by privacy-aware allocation mechanism and it happens in a continuous manner. We demonstrate the simulation results for three operating modes:

1. Case 1 - No Privacy Control, where privacy settings are disabled, and ticket allocation considers only operational criteria
2. Case 2 - Privacy Control in Allocation with Full Data Disclosure, where privacy is controlled through ticket allocation but without data masking, meaning agents have full access to sensitive attributes. In this case privacy criteria (W_{priv}) receive higher weight in allocation.
3. Case 3 - Privacy Control in Allocation with Partial Data Disclosure, where privacy-aware allocation is combined with a masking plan to regulate information exposure, thus achieving better privacy control and minimizing the risk of data exposure.

4.1 Simulation Results

The results are presented for a scenario involving 1000 tickets in a session with an arrival rate of $\lambda = 0.35$, 20 agents in the system, and 60% sensitive tickets. The privacy factor ($\gamma = 0.6$) and deciding factor ($k = 1.5$) are applied.

Overall Mis-usability Score Analysis. The distribution of sensitive information among agents is illustrated in Fig. 3. In Case 1, several agents have extremely high overall mis-usability scores, with uneven distribution of sensitive data. In Case 2, privacy control results in more even distribution, significantly reducing the standard deviation of mis-usability scores. Case 3 further decreases data exposure, though this stricter privacy control leads to some SLA breaches, showing a trade-off between privacy and operational efficiency.

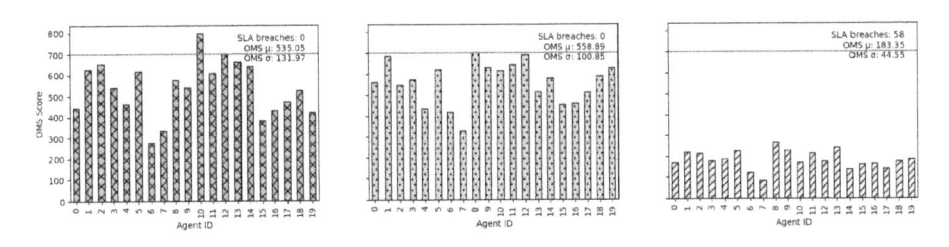

Fig. 3. Over-all Mis-usability Score across Agent

User Mis-usability Analysis. A heatmap (Fig. 4) visualizes the accumulation of sensitive user data by agents. The x-axis represents the IDs of 30 users who submitted multiple sensitive tickets, and the y-axis represents agent IDs. Darker squares indicate higher aggregation of sensitive information for specific user-agent pairs. In Case 1, where privacy settings are ignored, some agents accumulate large amounts of sensitive data from users. Cases 2 and 3 show significant reductions in data aggregation as privacy controls are applied, with Case 3 providing the greatest protection.

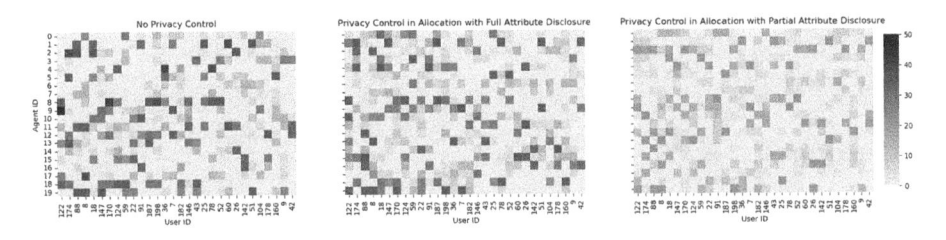

Fig. 4. Mis-usability Score distribution for 30 Users with maximum Sensitive Tickets.

Privacy Factor Analysis. Figure 5 demonstrates how the privacy factor (γ) affects SLA breaches and the overall mis-usability score. As the privacy factor increases, ticket resolution becomes more difficult due to the masking of required information, leading to more SLA breaches. However, the overall mis-usability score decreases, indicating better control over data exposure. This result highlights the importance of selecting an optimal privacy factor to balance privacy and operational utility. A higher privacy factor offers greater data protection but may lead to operational inefficiencies, while a lower privacy factor prioritizes resolution time at the cost of increased data exposure.

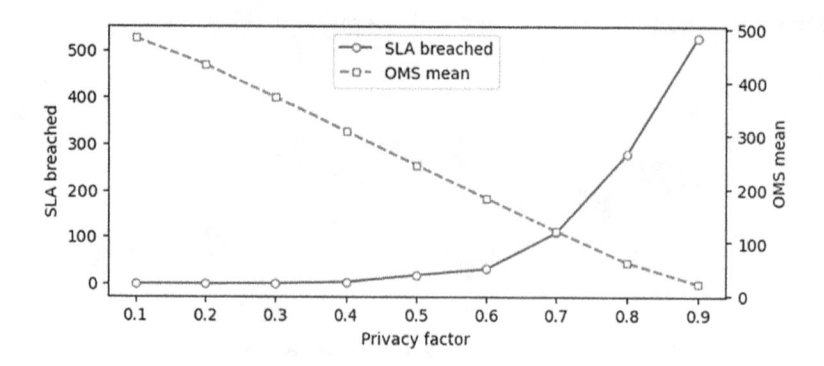

Fig. 5. Impact of privacy factor on SLA and Overall Mis-usability

5 Conclusion

Proactively minimizing data exposure to agents is critical in mitigating insider threat risks in organizations. This work introduces a privacy-aware ticket allocation mechanism that reduces both unintentional and intentional insider threats. We developed a simulator to replicate service desk operations, demonstrating the effectiveness of this approach. Future extensions of this work will explore several challenges, including task distribution across multiple geographies in line with data localization regulations, the allocation of tasks to remote or external agents based on risk, and the privacy-aware distribution of tasks between human agents and bots.

References

1. Bai, X., Gopal, R., Nunez, M., Zhdanov, D.: A decision methodology for managing operational efficiency and information disclosure risk in healthcare processes. Decis. Support Syst. **57**, 406–416 (2014). https://doi.org/10.1016/j.dss.2012.10.046
2. Benitez, K., Malin, B.: Evaluating re-identification risks with respect to the HIPAA privacy rule. J. Am. Med. Inform. Assoc. **17**(2), 169–177 (2010). https://doi.org/10.1136/jamia.2009.000026
3. De Capitani di Vimercati, S., Genovese, A., Livraga, G., Piuri, V., Scotti, F.: Chapter 57 - privacy and security in environmental monitoring systems: issues and solutions. In: Vacca, J.R. (ed.) Computer and Information Security Handbook (Third Edition), 3rd edn., pp. 823–841. Morgan Kaufmann, Boston (2013). https://doi.org/10.1016/B978-0-12-803843-7.00057-0

4. Fang, M., Sun, M., Li, Q., Gong, N.Z., Tian, J., Liu, J.: Data poisoning attacks and defenses to crowdsourcing systems. In: Proceedings of the Web Conference 2021, WWW 2021, pp. 969–980. Association for Computing Machinery, New York (2021) https://doi.org/10.1145/3442381.3450066
5. Gartner: IT service management platforms reviews and ratings (2024). https://www.gartner.com/reviews/market/it-service-management-platforms. Accessed 01 May 2024
6. Gupta, H.S., Sengupta, B.: Scheduling service tickets in shared delivery. In: Liu, C., Ludwig, H., Toumani, F., Yu, Q. (eds.) Service-Oriented Computing, pp. 79–95. Springer, Heidelberg (2012)
7. Harel, A., Shabtai, A., Rokach, L., Elovici, Y.: M-score: a misuseability weight measure. IEEE Trans. Dependable Secure Comput. **9**(3), 414–428 (2012). https://doi.org/10.1109/TDSC.2012.17
8. Koo, M.: Technology won't protect your data-humans must come first (2023). https://www.forbes.com/sites/forbestechcouncil/2023/03/30/technology-wont-protect-your-data-humans-must-come-first. Accessed 01 May 2024
9. Krishnan, M., Srinivasan, M.K., Mathews, C.A.: Agent score-based intelligent incident allocation engine. In: Fong, S., Dey, N., Joshi, A. (eds.) ICT Analysis and Applications, pp. 289–307. Springer, Singapore (2021)
10. Kumar, R., Gupta, R., Mondal, S., Gharote, M., Gauravaram, P., Lodha, S.: Privacy preservation in service operations by minimizing sensitive data exposure. In: 2024 21st Annual International Conference on Privacy, Security and Trust (PST) (2024). (in press)
11. Mansour, H.O., Siraj, M.M., Ghaleb, F.A., Saeed, F., Alkhammash, E.H., Maarof, M.A.: Quasi-identifier recognition algorithm for privacy preservation of cloud data based on risk reidentification. Wirel. Commun. Mob. Comput. **2021**, 1–13 (2021)
12. Mondal, S., Gharote, M.S., Lodha, S.P.: Privacy of personal information: going incog in a goldfish bowl. Queue **20**(3), 41–87 (2022). https://doi.org/10.1145/3546934
13. Phuke, N., Saurabh, S., Gharote, M., Lodha, S.: PETA: privacy enabled task allocation. In: 2020 IEEE International Conference on Services Computing (SCC), pp. 226–233 (2020). https://doi.org/10.1109/SCC49832.2020.00037
14. Silva, P., Gonçalves, C., Godinho, C., Antunes, N., Curado, M.: Using NLP and machine learning to detect data privacy violations. In: IEEE INFOCOM 2020 - IEEE Conference on Computer Communications Workshops (INFOCOM WKSHPS), pp. 972–977 (2020). https://doi.org/10.1109/INFOCOMWKSHPS50562.2020.9162683
15. Storchak, Y.: Insider threat statistics for 2024: reports, facts, actors, and costs (2024). https://www.ekransystem.com/en/blog/insider-threat-statistics-facts-and-figures. Accessed 01 May 2024

Privacy-Preserving Photo Sharing: An SSI Use Case

Ashley Fraser[2], Abubakar-Sadiq Shehu[1]([✉]), Nick Frymann[1], Paul Haynes[1], and Steve Schneider[1]

[1] Surrey Centre for Cyber Security, University of Surrey, Guildford, UK
{s.muhammad,n.frymann,s.schneider}@surrey.ac.uk, p.haynes@ieee.org
[2] School of Computing and Communications, Lancaster University, Lancaster, UK
a.fraser5@lancaster.ac.uk

Abstract. Sharing content, including photos, has become effortless thanks to social media and enterprise services. However, these platforms often overlook protecting content owners' rights, such as proof of ownership, usage rights, and privacy. In this paper, we present a novel SSI application that enables photographers to collect credentials for their photos and assert ownership to third parties in a privacy-preserving manner. We describe a proof-of-concept implementation using the Hyperledger Aries SSI library, which can be extended for real-world deployment. We also discuss the potential for scaling this implementation.

Keywords: Privacy-Preserving · Photo Sharing · Self-Sovereign Identity · Anonymity · Digital Identity Privacy · Zero-knowledge · Hyperledger Aries

1 Introduction

Copyright protection automatically grants owners exclusive rights over their photos upon creation, allowing them to assert ownership and control usage. While registration is not mandatory, it helps photographers manage their rights more effectively. Registration authorities, e.g, [1,2], issue ownership certificates. However, this process requires extensive personal data, compromising privacy. To assert ownership, photographers must present their certificate containing their entire data, potentially exposing personal information. This can be particularly risky for activists, whistle-blowers or others who need to protect their identity. Thus, current systems lack a privacy-preserving way for photographers to register photos or prove ownership. Therefore, to ensure that content owners can prove their ownership and control their privacy, there is a need to decentralise the control and sharing process of documents, empowering owners to manage this themselves.

Self-sovereign identity (SSI) is an emerging digital identity management model that allows users to control their identity. With SSI, users collect identity credentials from issuers and use these to prove aspects of their identity to third parties without involving the issuer [3]. Users can also derive personalised credentials, enabling more flexible and private identity data management. Researchers, governments, and businesses have explored various approaches centered on empowering data owners, including decentralised storage systems, user-managed access (UMA), and OpenID Connect (OIDC) for verifiable credentials (VCs) [4]. UMA, built on OAuth 2.0, allows digital identities to manage resources through an authorisation server.

We leverage SSI technologies to construct a privacy-preserving photo registration platform, enabling a registration body to issue credentials that photographers can use to assert photo ownership. SSI supports privacy-preserving identity proving by returning control of digital data to the owner [3]. Users can generate identity proofs revealing only relevant credential parts without the issuer's knowledge or permission. Our application of SSI is novel, allowing photographers to generate identity proofs concerning facts within credentials and photos existing independently of credentials. This differs from popular SSI applications like travel passes, health credentials [5], and user authentication. We present a use case of a photographer anonymously registering their photo with a registration authority and asserting ownership rights privately. Our proof-of-concept implementation builds upon the Aries Cloud Agent—Python (ACA-Py) Framework [6], based on the Hyperledger Aries SSI library [7].

2 Background

The digitisation of media content has transformed daily communication and information sharing [8]. Whilst dedicated photo-sharing services like Flickr, Google Photos, and Instagram enable easy content sharing and connection, they also introduce significant privacy risks and complicate personal information protection in shared media. Despite long-standing regulations protecting intellectual property, such as the UK's Copyright, Designs, and Patents Act 1988 (CDPA) [1], these platforms predate widespread internet photo sharing. Current social networks employ user-centric protocols like OpenID, SAML and FIDO [9]. However, these centralised protocols lack emphasis on content protection and fine-grained privacy controls for content owners. To address these limitations, SSI emerged, ensuring legitimate owners maintain control over their online content. As shown in Fig. 1, an SSI system involves three key roles: holders, issuers, and verifiers. Issuers provide credentials to holders, who store them in SSI-enabled wallets. These credentials contain attribute-value pairs (e.g., "Name: Ruth"), which holders can use to construct identity proofs for verifiers. SSI systems utilise a verifiable data registry for storing issuers' identifiers and cryptographic keys. W3C Decentralised Identifiers (DIDs) [10], supported by DIDComm Messaging [11], serve as common identifiers. Any actor can create DIDs for unique identification, with issuers registering public DIDs on the registry. A governance framework underpins this system, establishing issuer compliance rules and ledger writing permissions. Credentials typically take the form of standardised W3C Verifiable Credentials (VCs) [10], enabling third-party verification whilst supporting privacy-preserving identity proofs. Holders can selectively reveal credential attributes or prove facts without disclosing specific values—for instance, proving age eligibility without revealing actual birth date.

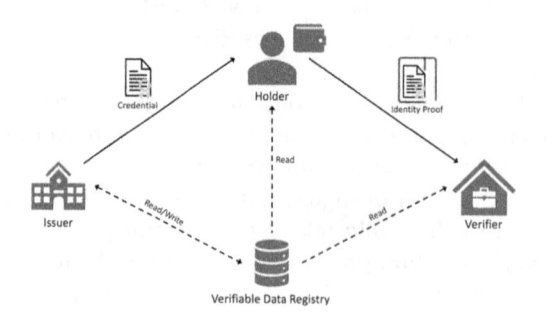

Fig. 1. SSI architecture.

3 The ACA-Py Agent Framework

ACA-Py builds on Hyperledger Aries and supports both Hyperledger anonymous credentials (Anon-Creds) and the W3C standard data model for issuing, verifying, and holding verifiable credentials. It uses JSON-LD with LD-Signatures and BBS+ Signatures, cryptographic schemes that provide integrity and verifiable authorship in various protocols. The ACA-Py architecture (shown in Fig. 2a), each actor is represented by an ACA-Py instance that runs on a server. The ACA-Py instance provides all the core capabilities and protocols required for an SSI system. This includes support for DIDComm and VCs, and the protocols required to connect with other agents, issue credentials, and present identity proofs. We elaborate on these protocols below. Developers create Controllers that connect to and control an ACA-Py instance. Controllers send HTTP requests to ACA-Py agents and receive webhook notifications. The ACA-Py Agent Framework allows developers to write the controller(s) in any language that can make and receive HTTP requests. ACA-Py agents also connect to an instance of an Indy ledger. The VON network [12] is a deployment-ready Indy ledger that is typically used in Aries deployments, and that we use in our platform.

Aries Protocols

The DID Exchange protocol facilitates the exchange of DIDs, cryptographic keys, and associated data (e.g., endpoints for agents, public websites, etc.) between an inviter and an invitee. Any actor can take the role of inviter or invitee, but in our platform, the role of inviter is taken by issuers and verifiers, and the holder plays the role of the invitee. The process involves four key messages: an

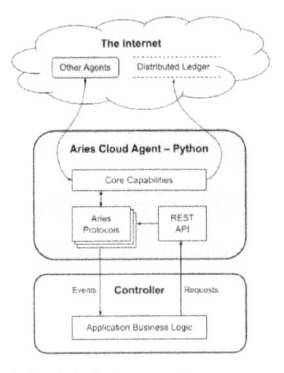

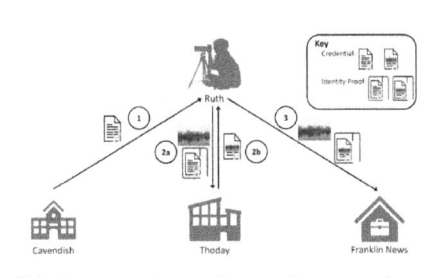

(a) ACA-Py architecture from [6]

(b) An overview of our photographer case study.

Fig. 2. ACA-Py architecture and overview of photographer case study

Invitation from the inviter containing a public DID, a *Connection Request* from the invitee, a *Connection Response* from the inviter, and a *Connection Complete* message to finalise the exchange. All messages other than the invitation are encrypted using the cryptographic keys communicated in previous messages, ensuring that only the intended recipient learns the content of the message. Following completion of the DID exchange protocol, the two parties can exchange authenticated and encrypted messages, including those in the *Issue Credentials* and *Present protocols*. The *Issue Credentials* protocol is initiated by a holder who requests a credential by sending a *Credential Proposal* to an issuer. The issuer responds with a *Credential Offer* message that communicates the format of a credential that the issuer is willing to offer. The holder includes their attribute values in a *Credential Request* message and the issuer sends the credential in a *Credential Issuance* message. The *Present protocol* is similar. A holder sends a *Presentation Proposal* and a verifier responds with a *Presentation Request*, which outlines the data required by the verifier. The holder generates an identity proof, which is transmitted in a *Presentation Proof*, and the verifier responds with an *Acknowledgement* if the proof verifies.

4 Photographer Credentials: A Case Study

Our proof-of-concept implementation, illustrated in Fig. 2b, enables photographers to securely register their work while maintaining anonymity when proving ownership. This solution is crucial for individuals in high-risk environments such as investigative journalists, whistleblowers, or freelancers covering sensitive topics. The platform involves four key actors: **Ruth** (a photographer), **Cavendish** (a photographer membership organisation), **Thoday** (a photo registration service), and **Franklin News** (a news agency). The scenario unfolds in three main steps, as depicted in the diagram: In step 1, Ruth obtains a photographer credential from Cavendish using Aries DID Exchange and Issue Credentials protocols.

Step 2 is twofold: 2a, shows Ruth proving her Cavendish membership to Thoday without revealing personal data, followed by 2b where Thoday issues a photo credential containing the photo's hash and metadata. In step 3, Ruth shares her photo with Franklin News by constructing an identity proof using her Thoday credential, revealing only the photo's hash. This allows Franklin News to verify the photo's registration and hash match without learning Ruth's identity. By facilitating anonymous yet verifiable photo registration and ownership proof, our platform protects both the work and identities of photographers operating in sensitive or dangerous contexts, giving verifiable ownership with ID protection.

4.1 Our Demonstrator

We used the open-source ACA-Py agent framework, and each of our four actors are represented by an ACA-Py agent (described in [6]) running in a local Docker container. This acts as a remote server that can be accessed by a controller application via a REST API. Additionally, each ACA-Py agent accessed a local VON network Indy ledger. We developed controllers for our four actors that listen to network changes via web sockets connected to the Docker instances. For each controller, we developed a single-page application using the React JS framework. Each application was built and tested as a web application running on local ports and in desktop Electron containers.

(a) Cavendish photographer credential application form

(b) Thoday photograph credential application form.

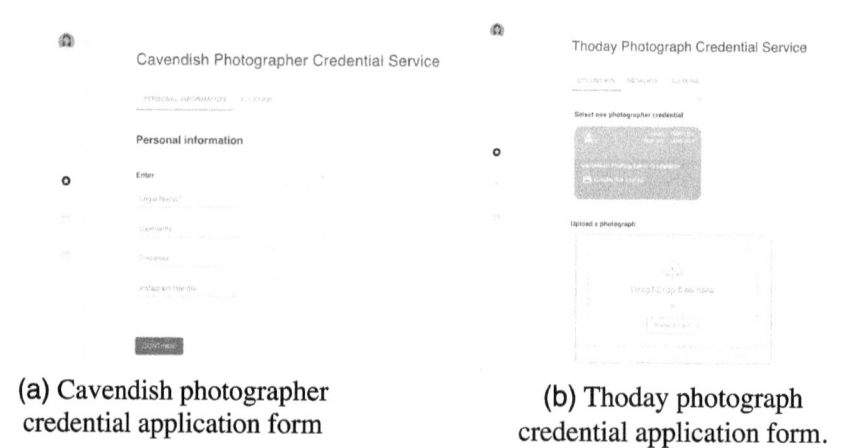

Fig. 3. Credential application forms.

Step 0: Setup. The platform initialises individual web applications for each actor, along with a VON network ledger. Ruth's application features a credential management wallet, whilst Thoday, Cavendish, and Franklin News have both public websites and private portals. These portals display credential applications and identity proof presentations, enabling actors to manage credential issuance and proof verification. The public websites display QR codes that Ruth can scan with her wallet to initiate the Aries DID Exchange protocol. Each QR code encodes an invitation containing the actor's public DID and cryptographic keys. The DID Exchange protocol operates automatically, with web applications generating and transmitting protocol messages independently after the initial invitation. All parties register their public DIDs and keys, allowing Ruth to verify their authenticity by matching invitation DIDs with ledger entries.

Step 1: Photographer Registration. After scanning Cavendish's QR code, Ruth's wallet displays a credential application form (Fig. 3a), initiating the Issue Credential protocol. Ruth enters her information, which forms the credential attributes. The Credential Proposal includes this completed form, and Ruth's wallet displays a credential card for accepting and storing the Cavendish credential (Fig. 4). Cavendish's private portal shows the credential application details, enabling a response to the Credential Proposal. Upon clicking 'Send Offer', a Credential Offer message is transmitted. Ruth can then select 'Accept' on her credential card, triggering her wallet to generate and send a Credential Request message. Cavendish completes the process by clicking 'Send Credential'. Once Ruth receives the credential, Cavendish's portal confirms issuance, and Ruth's wallet displays the credential card, confirming her as a registered photographer.

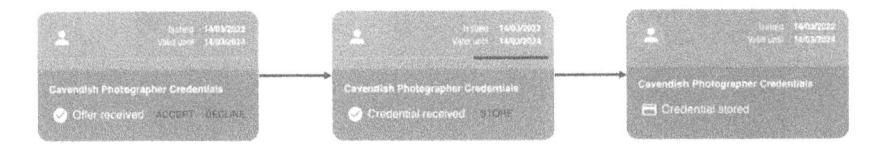

Fig. 4. Ruth receives a photographer credential from Cavendish.

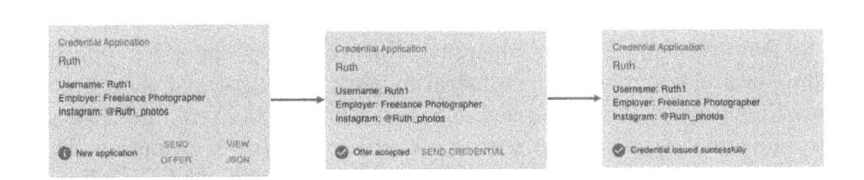

Fig. 5. Cavendish issues a photographer credential to Ruth.

Step 2: Photo Registration. Ruth uses her Cavendish credential to register photos with Thoday. Following the DID Exchange protocol, Ruth's wallet displays a Thoday application form (Fig. 3b), where she selects her Cavendish credential for identity proof generation and the photo for registration. The completed form initiates the Present protocol via a Presentation Proposal, generating a proof card in Ruth's wallet (Fig. 6) and displaying presentation details in Thoday's private portal (Fig. 7). When Thoday clicks 'Send Request', Ruth's wallet automatically generates and sends an identity proof revealing only her Cavendish photographer status. Upon verification, Thoday initiates the Issue Credentials protocol by sending a Credential Offer message. The subsequent process mirrors the Cavendish credential issuance (Fig. 4 and 5), concluding with Thoday's portal confirming issuance and Ruth storing the credential in her wallet.

Fig. 6. Ruth proves that she is a Cavendish photographer and receives a photo credential from Thoday.

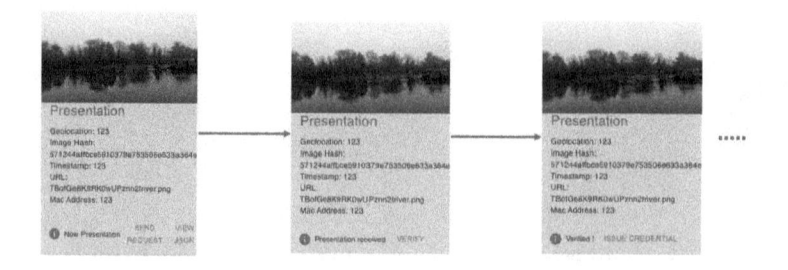

Fig. 7. Thoday verifies Ruth's identity proof and issues a photo credential to Ruth.

Step 3: Anonymous Photo Sharing. Ruth can now share her photo with Franklin News, anonymously demonstrating that she registered the photo with Thoday. This process is summarised in Fig. 8. Ruth visits Franklin News' public website and uploads her photo with some accompanying information. Ruth is directed to copy a QR code in her wallet, which executes the DID Exchange protocol. Ruth's wallet requests that Ruth choose a photo credential, which is used to create a privacy-preserving identity proof that reveals only the hash of the photo from the photo credential. Ruth's wallet then submits a Presentation Proposal. The Present protocol is automated, and Ruth can re-navigate to Franklin News' website to see that her proof verified. Ruth has now successfully shared her photo with Franklin News and, crucially, her proof only reveals the hash of her photo, therefore maintaining her anonymity.

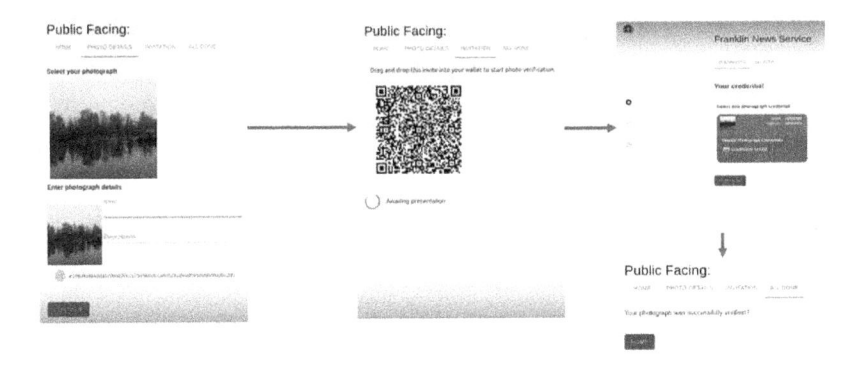

Fig. 8. Ruth anonymously shares her photo with Franklin News.

5 Security and Privacy

We discuss the desired security and privacy properties for our solution. We consider whether our solution achieves the required goals, highlighting that the security and privacy guarantees of our solution are assured due to the security of the cryptographic building blocks included in Hyperledger Ursa.

5.1 Security

Our platform's security is framed by an adversary model where the adversary aims to forge credentials, impersonate users, or compromise credential holders' privacy, with standard Dolev-Yao capabilities [13]. To counter these threats, we implement a multi-layered security approach. Credentials and identity proofs are made unforgeable through digital signatures from both issuers and holders, leveraging the security of the signature scheme to ensure only those with secret keys can produce valid signatures. For example, when Ruth constructs a presentation, she uses the secret keys in her wallet to sign it. These secret keys are associated with a public key that is shared with verifiers, such as Thoday or Franklin News, allowing them to verify the presentation. For photo integrity, we utilise hash cryptography, can also supports digital forensic tools to detect alterations. The platform leverages AnonCreds, with RSA based ZKPs. It utilises the Layer 3 VC Trust Triangle of the Trust over IP Model, which encompasses issuing, requesting, generating, and verifying presentations of verifiable claims. The data models for credentials, presentation requests, and presentations are thoroughly defined, including their applications of cryptographic primitives. Our platform ensures that presentations are sound and complete, allowing users like Ruth to prove specific claims stored in a wallet (e.g., Cavendish membership to Thoday or photo ownership to Franklin News) without revealing unnecessary information. Additionally, the security of the ZKPs implemented in the ACA-Py framework ensures that Ruth can only prove facts supported by her credentials (minimal disclosure); otherwise, the verification will fail. AnonCreds enables Ruth to prove that she is known to Cavendish and has secured a certificate that is verifiable on the decentralised registry. When Ruth proves her status as a Cavendish member to Thoday, Thoday can be assured that Ruth has a Cavendish credential in her wallet. Similarly, Franklin News can be convinced that Ruth's wallet contains a Thoday credential for her photograph. We also require that Ruth's identity proof presented to Franklin News matches a photograph submitted.

5.2 Privacy

The ACA-Py framework implements the Blind Signature scheme and DIDComm messaging such that any message transmitted between any two actors is secret to all but the sender and intended recipient of the message. Also, it ensures that both Cavendish and Thoday never sees the final credential signature or message values, preventing data correlation. As such, our solution ensures the confidentiality of messages. This holds if the intended recipient does not reveal their secret decryption keys to anyone. Our solution ensures that Ruth maintains anonymity throughout her interactions. Indeed, Ruth reveals her name only to Cavendish and does not share her real-world identity with any other actor. Furthermore, actors cannot collude to reveal Ruth's real-world identity. Accordingly, our solution supports the unlinkability of Ruth's identity using the AnonCreds linked secret. This means that credentials and identity proofs associated with a single wallet but distinct issuers/verifiers cannot be linked. Specifically, Ruth's real-world identity is associated with a unique DID that Ruth chooses for her connection with Cavendish, and the ACA-Py framework requires Ruth to create a unique DID for her connection with every other actor. Only Cavendish can associate the DID chosen by Ruth and the name 'Ruth', and Ruth's DIDs for her other connections cannot be linked. Conversely, if Ruth used the same DID for Cavendish and Thoday, and Cavendish and Thoday colluded, Cavendish could learn of each photograph that Ruth registers, and Thoday could learn the real-world identity of the Cavendish photographer who registered several photographs. Therefore, the use of unique DIDs for each connection, and the use of ZKPs to prevent the reveal of Ruth's name contained in her Cavendish credential, support Ruth to maintain anonymity throughout her interactions. Though our solution supports the unlinkability of Ruth's identity, the uniqueness of photographs submitted to Thoday and Franklin News may allow data linkage. Ruth reveals only the hash of her photo to Franklin News but, if Franklin News and Thoday collude, Franklin News learns all other attributes contained within the Thoday credential. Additionally, they learn of all photographs registered by Ruth. Thoday learns that Ruth submitted a photograph to Franklin News. This demonstrates how difficult it is to achieve unlinkability in SSI systems in the face of possible collusion. Ruth must carefully manage her connections and applications for credentials to ensure unlinkability. If Ruth wants to submit a photograph to Franklin News that cannot be linked to any other actions, including other photographs registered with Thoday, Ruth can establish a second connection with Thoday and register the photo with a new DID. In this way, Thoday cannot link this photograph with any other photographs registered by Ruth.

6 Conclusion and Future Research

This paper presents an SSI-based platform that enables photographers to assert anonymous photo ownership. Our implementation demonstrates a reliable and secure approach to ownership verification that could be readily extended to real-world deployment. Future enhancements could include photo provenance verification, allowing photographers to collect credentials that prove their photos remain untampered. Whilst we have focused on photography, this approach is applicable to any digital assets requiring privacy-preserving control. A further potential direction for future research is the creation of a formal security model for SSI systems that will enable rigorous security analysis of our SSI platform and SSI systems more generally. These extensions are interesting directions for future research.

Acknowledgement. This work was funded by the DECaDE project under UK EPSRC grant EP/T022485.

References

1. UKCS. UK copyright service. https://copyrightservice.co.uk/
2. USCO. U.S. copyright office. https://www.copyright.gov/
3. Fraser, A., Schneider, S.: On the role of blockchain for self-sovereign identity. In: CADE: Competitive Advantage in the Digital Economy (2022)
4. Abubakar-Sadiq, M.S.: Establishing secure and privacy preserving digital identity with self-sovereign identity. Ph.D. thesis, University of Porto (2023)
5. Soltani, R., Nguyen, U., An, A.: A survey of self-sovereign identity ecosystem. Secur. Commun. Netw. **1–26**(07), 2021 (2021). https://doi.org/10.1155/2021/8873429
6. Open Wallet Foundation. Hyperledger aries cloud agent—python. https://github.com/openwallet-foundation/acapy. Accessed 18 Oct 2024
7. Hyperledger Foundation. Hyperledger aries. https://www.hyperledger.org/use/aries
8. Liu, C., Zhu, T., Zhang, J., Zhou, W.: Privacy intelligence: a survey on image privacy in online social networks. ACM Comput. Surv. **55**(8), 1–35 (2022)
9. Preukschat, A., Reed, D.: Self-sovereign identity: decentralized digital identity and verifiable credentials. Manning (2021)
10. Sporny, M., et al. (eds.): textitW3C Recommendation decentralized identifiers (dids) v1.0. https://www.w3.org/TR/did-core/
11. Curren, S., Looker, T., Terbu, O. (eds.) Decentralised Identity Foundation didcomm messaging v2. https://identity.foundation/didcomm-messaging/spec/
12. Von. BC Government von network. https://github.com/bcgov/von-network. Accessed 18 Oct 2024
13. Dolev, D., Yao, A.: On the security of public key protocols. IEEE Trans. Inf. Theory **29**(2), 198–208 (1983)

Zone Recovery Attack on a Secure Privacy-Preserving Ride-Matching Protocol

Shyam Murthy[1], Santosh Kumar Upadhyaya[2(✉)], and Srinivas Vivek[2]

[1] IISc Bangalore, Bengaluru, India
[2] IIIT Bangalore, Bengaluru, India
santosh.upadhyaya@iiitb.ac.in

Abstract. The popularity of ride-hailing services (RHS) has increased all over the world as well as awareness of privacy preservation of (PP) end-users. A number of PP-RHS solutions have been proposed in the literature. Some involve a service provider (SP), while others provide a decentralized mechanism. A decentralized RHS protocol by Shen et al. was published in IEEE Systems Journal (2023) that aims to provide secure ride-matching without involving any trusted third party. Their protocol makes use of a public-key encryption scheme with an equality test and a blockchain with smart contracts. They provide a theoretical analysis of their protocol and experimental results to show that their implementation is efficient and practical. In their protocol, to provide an efficient matching scheme, the area of operation, like a city, is partitioned into zones. In the first step of their protocol, the authorized, public blockchain takes the encrypted zone ID information of the driver and rider as input to an oblivious rider-driver match protocol to provide ride matching, without revealing anything about the zone ID. In this paper, we show that an eavesdropper will be able to learn the zone IDs of all the participating users, thus negating one of the main security claims of the aforementioned RHS protocol.

Keywords: Cryptanalysis · Blockchain · Smart Contract · Location privacy preservation · online taxi-hailing service

1 Introduction

As per a recent report by Statista [15], the projected revenue for the ride-hailing services (RHS) market for the United States is estimated to reach US$ 55 billion by the year 2028 with the expected number of users to be about 98 million, while the worldwide market is expected to reach about US$ 215 billion by 2028. Together with this huge growth, there is also an increase in privacy and security concerns. An RHS system primarily consists of three entities, a service provider (SP), like Uber, OLA, Lyft, a rider or passenger subscribed with the SP, and a driver associated with the SP. A passenger would share his/her location information with the SP at the time of ride request. Similarly, a driver would also share such information with the SP. Thus, SP has access to a lot of private data that potentially can lead to privacy concerns from individuals as well as regulatory authorities. There have been many reports [12,16] where SP entities have been subjected to financial and other penalties due to data privacy breaches. Hence, there is a definite need for protocols that preserve the location privacy of drivers and riders during ride matching.

Several protocols have been presented in the literature that propose privacy-preserving RHS/ride-sharing services (PP-RHS/PP-RSS). They can broadly be categorized as those that involve an SP for ride matching and others that are decentralized [2–4,7,10,11,13,19,21,23–25], just to cite a few. There have also been works in the literature that look at privacy leakages or security issues in the PP-RHS/PP-RSS protocols [5,6,8,9,17,18,26].

A recent work in the decentralized category is the work by Shen et al. [14], published in IEEE Systems Journal and described further in Sect. 2, which makes use of blockchain technology and aims to provide a PP-RHS solution without involving any third party trusted server. At a high level, the paper aims to get the rider and driver to interact directly without the need for any central party, thus reducing travel costs, and more importantly, achieving improved privacy.

In more detail, the authors of [14] propose a privacy-preserving matching algorithm (PPMA) using a smart contract based on blockchain. In the first step of the protocol, the drivers and riders encrypt their cloaking region, or zone, and save them in the public blockchain. These are used by the PPMA to perform an oblivious comparison that gives a boolean result. Based on this result, the selected driver and rider continue with ride-matching. The paper claims (Sec. § VI(B), pp. 8) that even if an adversary obtains the ciphertexts, it cannot know the precise zone ID of drivers and riders. Further, they also claim that even if the secret key of their encryption scheme is compromised, the adversary will not be able to obtain the specific zone ID where the driver or user is located. In this work, we show that any efficient adversary just having access to the encrypted data on the blockchain can mount an attack to reveal the exact zone ID. Thus, we disprove an important privacy claim in [14].

1.1 Our Contribution

The main contribution of this paper is cryptanalysis of the protocol suggested by Shen et al. [14], focusing on the structure of *Ride_Request*, *Ride_Offer*, and their matching algorithm. Our results reveal that an interceptor can mount a passive attack to reveal all users' (drivers and passengers) zone IDs, thereby undermining the RHS protocol's key privacy claim. Specifically, combining *Ride_Request* or *Ride_Offer* data with trapdoor information (available as per the protocol) on the blockchain allows an eavesdropper to learn the zone ID. The experimental results are described in Sect. ??.

1.2 Organization of the Paper

In Sect. 2, we present a recap of the protocol by Shen et al. [14]. Section 3 presents the details of our attack. In Sect. 3.2, we present the algorithm and analysis of our attack. Section 4 concludes the paper.

2 Recap of the Protocol by Shen et al.

This section provides a broad outline of the PP-RHS protocol proposed by Shen et al. [14] that operates without a trusted third-party server while safeguarding the location privacy of both passengers and drivers.

The scheme put forth by Shen et al. [14] uses the public key encryption with an equality test (PKEET) by Yang et al. [22]. For ease of operation and efficiency, the SP divides its area of operation (e.g., a city) into zones of appropriate size and assigns an unique zone id Z_i to each of the zones, where $Z_i \in \mathbb{Z}^+$. The zone size is adjusted dynamically based on the average and peak periods of ride requests. This space generalization technique, as described in [1], also helps in disguising precise location coordinates into broader geographic areas. Zone sizes are not fixed and can be adjusted by the service provider to strike a balance between the communication bandwidth demands and the required ride-anonymity set sizes within these zones.

The SP chooses a security parameter λ and produces the system parameters $pp = (p, G, g)$ during initialization, where p is a suitably large prime, G is a multiplicative cyclic group of order p, and g is a generator of G.

In the subsequent sections, we will summarize the Ride Request (RR), Ride Offer (RO), and Ride Matching (RM) components of the scheme from Shen et al. [14]. We omit details that do not directly pertain to the current work. Recognizing that the blockchain platform does not protect privacy of users where the smart contract is visible by everyone, the paper lists and focuses on a number of possible adversarial attacks, and claims that their protocol is safe against them (Sec. § IV (B) and Sec. § VI (B), pps. 5 and 8 of [14]), one of them is listed below:

- A potential attacker may attempt to read transactions recorded on the blockchain and make use of the trapdoor information to obtain specific zone IDs of drivers or passengers.

Their claim is that the security of their protocol against the above attack reduces to the one-way security, against chosen ciphertext attacks, of their underlying encryption scheme. However, in this work we prove the said claim to be false by showing that a semi-honest adversary, by just observing the blockchain transactions, can completely recover the zone IDs of all users of their protocol.

2.1 Ride Request (RR)

When the passenger wants to request a ride, the following steps are followed before the ride request is raised.

- $KeyGen(pp)$ algorithm outputs the passenger's private key $sk_{Enc}^P := (\alpha_1, \beta_1)$. and public key $pk_{Enc}^P := (g^{\alpha_1}, g^{\beta_1})$.
- Two random integers r_1 and r_2 are chosen from a suitable range.
- Loc_p is the binary representation of the zone ID of the passenger. Loc_p is encrypted using the public key. The ride request is computed as below, with H_1, H_2, H_3 being suitable collision resistant hash functions. $Ride\_Request = Enc(pk_{Enc}, Loc_p) = (C_1, C_2, C_3, C_4, C_5)$ where

$$C_1 = g^{r_1} \tag{1}$$

$$C_2 = g^{r_2} \tag{2}$$

$$C_3 = H_1(g^{r_1\alpha_1}) \oplus Loc_p \parallel r_1 \tag{3}$$

$$C_4 = g^{H_2(g^{r_2\beta_1}) + Loc_p} \tag{4}$$

$$C_5 = H_3(C_1 \parallel C_2 \parallel C_3 \parallel C_4 \parallel Loc_p \parallel r_1). \tag{5}$$

- The $Ride\_Request$ and the passenger's trapdoor information β_1 are sent to the blockchain.

2.2 Ride Offer (RO)

When the driver wants to pick up a passenger, the steps similar to $Ride\_Request$ Sect. 2.1 are followed. A new set of private and public keys are generated, a new set of random numbers are chosen and the driver's zone information Loc_d is encrypted with driver's public key. Finally, the $Ride\_Offer$ along with the driver's trapdoor information are sent to the blockchain.

2.3 Ride Matching (RM)

The smart contract is activated by both the passenger and the driver through the initiation of a transaction, which automatically runs a algorithm to identify a compatible pairing of passenger and driver. The smart contract then proceeds to verify whether

$$C_4 \cdot g^{-H_2((C_2)^{td_p})} \stackrel{?}{=} C_4' \cdot g^{-H_2((C_2')^{td_d})} \tag{6}$$

The ride is assigned to the first driver for whom the above equality holds.

3 Attack on the Scheme of Shen et al.

We consider a semi-honest adversarial model in our attack. The adversary follows the protocol as mentioned in [14] but tries to glean more information than is available per the protocol, and note that it has access to the (public) blockchain.

The main idea of our attack is based on the following points.

- The adversary has access to the blockchain transaction that includes the *Ride_Request* or *Ride_Offer* along with the respective trapdoor information.
- When Eq. 6 is further simplified with the trapdoor information, it turns out to be

$$g^{Loc_p} \stackrel{?}{=} g^{Loc_d}. \tag{7}$$

- The number of zones is limited; in the sense that it will be possible to do brute force search over the number of zones.

Zone Size Consideration: In a densely populated urban area like New York City, which has a population density of 11,084 people per square kilometer [5], smaller zones can suffice to maintain the necessary anonymity due to the high usage of ride-hailing services. In contrast, in cities with lower population densities, such as Dallas, with 1,590 individuals per square kilometer, it becomes necessary to have larger zones to offer comparable levels of anonymity to riders due to the less frequent use of ride-hailing services. To enhance anonymity, it may be necessary to increase the size of zones, consequently reducing the total number of zones.

3.1 Description of Our Attack

Our proposed attack does a brute force over the number of zones to extract the zone ID Loc from g^{Loc}, which in turn is available from the *Ride_Request* or *Ride_Offer* transactions computed as per Sect. 2.1 or 2.2. As to why this strategy works is described below.

Recall here that a transaction consists of *Ride_Request* or *Ride_Offer* along with the trapdoor information. The *Ride_Request* and *Ride_Offer* consists of $(C_1, C_2, C_3, C_4, C_5)$ computed as per Sect. 2.1.

Upon receipt of the transaction, the adversary proceeds to compute

$$M = C_4 \cdot g^{-H_2(C_2^{td_x})}, \tag{8}$$

where td_x could be either td_p or td_d for *Ride_Request* or *Ride_Offer*, respectively.

The total number of zones in a given geographic region is denoted as n, and each zone with its unique ID. We can represent these zones as

$$Z = (Z_1, ..., Z_n). \tag{9}$$

Considering a large city like New York City with an area of about $1250\,\text{km}^2$ [20] and (hypothetically) setting the size of each zone to be as small as $0.25\,\text{km}^2$, we get $n = 20000$. For each of these zones, the adversary computes g^{Z_i} and then compares this value with the previously computed M. Upon finding a match, the algorithm identifies and returns the corresponding zone Z_i. The entire execution time for the attack is completed within a few seconds. Our attack method is given in Algorithm 1.

Algorithm 1. Brute-force attack: Find Zone

Require: $RideTransact \in \{Ride\_Request, Ride\_Offer\}$, trapdoor $td_x \in \{td_p, td_d\}$
1: $Z = (Z_1, \ldots, Z_n)$ {Global variable}
2: $T = RideTransact$
3: $M = C_4 \cdot g^{-H_2(C_2^{td_x})}$ $\{C_4, C_2, td_x)$ are available in $T\}$
4: **for** $i = 1$ to n **do**
5:    **if** M equals to g^{Z_i} **then**
6:       **return** Z_i
7:    **end if**
8: **end for**
9: **return** 0

3.2 Attack Algorithm and Analysis

The attack algorithm mentioned in this section has a time complexity of $O(n)$ in the number of zones. The precision of the attack reaches an optimal level, achieving an accuracy of 100%. It is conceivable to enhance the time complexity to $O(1)$ through the prior computation of g^{Loc} values cached in a hashtable, which would necessitate updates whenever there are modifications to the zone sizes made by the SP. Our code is available at https://github.com/Santosh-Upadhyaya/ICISS-2024.

4 Conclusion

The primary aim of this work was to develop an attack that reveals users' zone ID to counter one of the privacy claims of [14]. The feasibility of the attack stemmed from the accessibility of trapdoor information within the blockchain, coupled with a small (rather not very large) number of zones, which enabled the adversary to execute a brute-force discrete logarithm recovery attack. The proposed attack revealed that the adversary can retrieve the zone information with an accuracy of 100% and, hence, invalidates a claim made in [14]. However, the specific individual information remains undisclosed. The size of the zone is dynamically adjusted based on the average and peak periods of ride requests. Nevertheless, during the time of an attack on a given request, the zone information remains fixed. As mentioned in Sect. 3.1, for a zone count of 200,000, our attack algorithm will execute within a few seconds. This study underscores the imperative for exhaustive security evaluations in cryptographic protocol development. Subsequent studies may aim to modify the protocol of [14] to withstand the attack described in this paper. Any enhancements introduced must be rigorously validated through an extensive security analysis.

Acknowledgment. This work was partly supported by the Infosys Foundation Career Development Chair Professorship grant for the third author (Srinivas Vivek).

References

1. Aïvodji, U.M., Huguenin, K., Huguet, M.J., Killijian, M.O.: Sride: a privacy-preserving ridesharing system. In: WiSec 2018, pp. 40–50. Association for Computing Machinery, New York (2018). https://doi.org/10.1145/3212480.3212483
2. Huang, J., Luo, Y., Fu, S., Xu, M., Hu, B.: pRide: privacy-preserving online ride hailing matching system with prediction. IEEE Trans. Veh. Technol. **70**(8), 7413–7425 (2021). https://doi.org/10.1109/TVT.2021.3090042
3. Kanza, Y., Safra, E.: Cryptotransport: blockchain-powered ride hailing while preserving privacy, pseudonymity and trust. In: Kashani, F.B., Hoel, E.G., Güting, R.H., Tamassia, R., Xiong, L. (eds.) Proceedings of the 26th ACM SIGSPATIAL International Conference on Advances in Geographic Information Systems, SIGSPATIAL 2018, Seattle, WA, USA, 06–09 November 2018, pp. 540–543. ACM (2018)
4. Khazbak, Y., Fan, J., Zhu, S., Cao, G.: Preserving location privacy in ride-hailing service. In: 2018 IEEE Conference on Communications and Network Security, CNS 2018, Beijing, China, 30 May–1 June 2018, pp. 1–9. IEEE (2018)
5. Kumaraswamy, D., Murthy, S., Vivek, S.: Revisiting driver anonymity in ORide. In: AlTawy, R., Hülsing, A. (eds.) SAC 2021. LNCS, vol. 13203, pp. 25–46. Springer, Cham (2022). https://doi.org/10.1007/978-3-030-99277-4_2
6. Kumaraswamy, D., Vivek, S.: Cryptanalysis of the privacy-preserving ride-hailing service TRACE. In: Adhikari, A., Küsters, R., Preneel, B. (eds.) INDOCRYPT 2021. LNCS, vol. 13143, pp. 462–484. Springer, Cham (2021). https://doi.org/10.1007/978-3-030-92518-5_21
7. Luo, Y., Jia, X., Fu, S., Xu, M.: pRide: privacy-preserving ride matching over road networks for online ride-hailing service. IEEE Trans. Inf. Forensics Secur. **14**(7), 1791–1802 (2019). https://doi.org/10.1109/TIFS.2018.2885282
8. Murthy, S., Vivek, S.: Driver locations harvesting attack on pRide. In: Yuan, X., Bai, G., Alcaraz, C., Majumdar, S. (eds.) NSS 2022. LNCS, vol. 13787, pp. 633–648. Springer, Cham (2022). https://doi.org/10.1007/978-3-031-23020-2_36
9. Murthy, S., Vivek, S.: Passive triangulation attack on ORide. In: Beresford, A.R., Patra, A., Bellini, E. (eds.) CANS 2022. LNCS, vol. 13641, pp. 167–187. Springer, Cham (2022). https://doi.org/10.1007/978-3-031-20974-1_8
10. Pham, A., Dacosta, I., Endignoux, G., Troncoso-Pastoriza, J.R., Huguenin, K., Hubaux, J.: ORide: a privacy-preserving yet accountable ride-hailing service. In: Kirda, E., Ristenpart, T. (eds.) 26th USENIX Security Symposium, USENIX Security 2017, Vancouver, BC, Canada, 16–18 August 2017, pp. 1235–1252. USENIX Association (2017). https://www.usenix.org/conference/usenixsecurity17/technical-sessions/presentation/pham
11. Pham, A., et al.: PrivateRide: a privacy-enhanced ride-hailing service. PoPETs **2017**(2), 38–56 (2017). https://doi.org/10.1515/popets-2017-0015
12. SC Media Report: Uber data targeted in breach of third-party law firm (2023). https://www.scmagazine.com/news/uber-data-targeted-breach-third-party-law-firm. Accessed 20 Mar 2024
13. Semenko, Y., Saucez, D.: Distributed privacy preserving platform for ridesharing services. In: Wang, G., Feng, J., Bhuiyan, M.Z.A., Lu, R. (eds.) SpaCCS 2019. LNCS, vol. 11611, pp. 1–14. Springer, Cham (2019). https://doi.org/10.1007/978-3-030-24907-6_1
14. Shen, X., Wang, Z., Wang, B., Wang, L., Pei, Q.: A privacy-preserving ride-matching scheme without a trusted third-party server. IEEE Syst. J. **17**(4), 6413–6424 (2023). https://doi.org/10.1109/JSYST.2023.3289833

15. Statista Market Insights Mobility Shared Mobility: Ride-hailing - United States (2024). https://www.statista.com/outlook/mmo/shared-mobility/ride-hailing/united-states/. Accessed 18 Mar 2024
16. UpGuard Blog: What Caused the Uber Data breach in 2022? (2023). https://www.upguard.com/blog/what-caused-the-uber-data-breach. Accessed 20 Mar 2024
17. Vivek, S.: Attacks on a privacy-preserving publish-subscribe system and a ride-hailing service. In: Paterson, M.B. (ed.) IMACC 2021. LNCS, vol. 13129, pp. 59–71. Springer, Cham (2021). https://doi.org/10.1007/978-3-030-92641-0_4
18. Vivek, S.: Attack on "a privacy-preserving online ride-hailing system without involving a third trusted server". In: Proceedings of the 18th International Conference on Availability, Reliability and Security, ARES 2023, Benevento, Italy, 29 August 2023–1 September 2023, pp. 59:1–59:3. ACM (2023). https://doi.org/10.1145/3600160.3605040
19. Wang, F., et al.: Efficient and privacy-preserving dynamic spatial query scheme for ride-hailing services. IEEE Trans. Veh. Technol. **67**(11), 11084–11097 (2018)
20. Wikipedia: New York City (2024). https://en.wikipedia.org/wiki/New_York_City. Accessed 26 Mar 2024
21. Xie, H., Guo, Y., Jia, X.: A privacy-preserving online ride-hailing system without involving a third trusted server. IEEE Trans. Inf. Forensics Secur. **16**, 3068–3081 (2021). https://doi.org/10.1109/TIFS.2021.3065832
22. Yang, G., Tan, C.H., Huang, Q., Wong, D.S.: Probabilistic public key encryption with equality test. In: Pieprzyk, J. (ed.) CT-RSA 2010. LNCS, vol. 5985, pp. 119–131. Springer, Heidelberg (2010). https://doi.org/10.1007/978-3-642-11925-5_9
23. Yu, H., Jia, X., Zhang, H., Yu, X., Shu, J.: PSRide: privacy-preserving shared ride matching for online ride hailing systems. IEEE Trans. Dependable Secure Comput. **18**, 1425–1440 (2019)
24. Yu, H., Shu, J., Jia, X., Zhang, H., Yu, X.: lpRide: lightweight and privacy-preserving ride matching over road networks in online ride hailing systems. IEEE Trans. Veh. Technol. **68**(11), 10418–10428 (2019)
25. Zhang, N., Zhong, S., Tian, L.: Using blockchain to protect personal privacy in the scenario of online taxi-hailing. Int. J. Comput. Commun. Control **12**, 886 (2017)
26. Zhao, Q., Zuo, C., Pellegrino, G., Lin, Z.: Geo-locating drivers: a study of sensitive data leakage in ride-hailing services. In: 26th Annual Network and Distributed System Security Symposium, NDSS 2019, San Diego, California, USA, 24–27 February 2019. The Internet Society (2019). https://www.ndss-symposium.org/ndss-paper/geo-locating-drivers-a-study-of-sensitive-data-leakage-in-ride-hailing-services/

Making EULA Great Again: A Novel Nudge Mechanism to Improve Readability, User Attention and Awareness

Shamim Bin Zahid[1], Aishwarya Ghosh Bristy[1], Md. Musfikur Hasan Oli[1], Md. Fahim[1], Sarker Tanveer Ahmed Rumee[1,2(✉)], and Moinul Islam Zaber[1,2]

[1] Department of Computer Science and Engineering, University of Dhaka, Dhaka 1000, Bangladesh
shamimbinzahid@gmail.com, aishwaryaghoshbristy@gmail.com, musfikuroli@gmail.com, mdfahim6376@gmail.com
[2] Data and Design Lab, University of Dhaka, Dhaka 1000, Bangladesh
rumee@cse.du.ac.bd, zaber@du.ac.bd

Abstract. Software End User License Agreements (EULAs) are notoriously dense legal documents that users often skim over without fully understanding their implications, including privacy-related clauses. This research proposes a novel approach to improve the readability and privacy awareness of EULAs by implementing a nudge tool to improve user attention and comprehension of EULA contents. Through natural language processing technique, privacy-sensitive keywords within EULAs are identified and visually emphasized for users. By drawing attention to EULA clauses related to data collection, sharing, and security, users can make more informed decisions about their privacy when agreeing to software terms. Detailed user experiments involving 173 participants are performed to evaluate the effectiveness of the proposed approach demonstrating significant improvements in comprehension and awareness of privacy implications compared to traditional EULAs. The developed nudge tool is released and made freely available for the interesting readers (https://github.com/Data-and-Design-Lab/EULA-plugin).

Keywords: EULA · Privacy · Feedback · Education · Nudge

1 Introduction

End-User License Agreements (EULAs) serve as legal contracts between the provider and users, delineating the terms and conditions under which the software or service can be used. EULAs have become a ubiquitous part of the digital landscape, serving as the legal backbone for software, applications, and online services.

Despite their significance, EULAs are often dismissed by users as overly complex, lengthy, and difficult to understand [12,18]. This widespread neglect has serious implications, ranging from uninformed consent to potential legal vulnerabilities for both users and providers [18]. The need for a more user-friendly approach to EULAs has never been more pressing [22,24,44].

Historically, efforts to improve EULA readability and comprehension have met with limited success. Traditional methods, such as simplifying language or reducing length, have proven inadequate in capturing user attention and ensuring thorough engagement. Users continue to skim or entirely skip reading these critical documents, undermining the core purpose of EULAs: to inform and protect.

In response to this persistent challenge, our paper proposes a novel nudge mechanism [3] aimed at enhancing the readability of EULAs and boosting user attention and awareness. Drawing from principles of behavioral economics and cognitive psychology, we explore how subtle changes in presentation and interaction design can significantly impact user behavior. By strategically incorporating nudges, we aim to transform the EULA experience from a tedious formality into an engaging and informative process. In the proposed nudged setting, EULA is presented to the user by introducing an additional layer of information either by visualization of privacy-sensitive words or through oral briefing to aware of the data privacy leakage possibility.

We also developed a browser plugin to nudge users with a color-coded summary of the potential risks. The user studies performed in this research demonstrate the effectiveness of the proposed nudge tool in making users grasp appropriate information from EULAs with ease. The major contributions of this work are listed below:

1. A unique data set of security-related keywords that appear commonly in EULAs. This list can be used to extract parts of EULA that specifically indicate the application behavior regarding data privacy.
2. Developed a nudge tool to summarize and highlight privacy-sensitive areas in EULA to attract user attention, and comprehension and improve readability.
3. Extensive user studies are performed on 173 participants to see their behavior in dealing with an EULA with the presence or absence of the proposed nudge. User experiments showed significant improvement in fostering user privacy awareness with the help of the color-coded and categorized representation of the EULA data access disclaimers.
4. The nudge tool is released as a free-to-use browser plugin. User experiments showed a significant reduction in time to read and understand EULAs of some popular applications while using the proposed tool.

This paper begins by examining the existing landscape of EULAs, identifying key barriers to user engagement and comprehension. We then introduce our proposed nudge mechanism, detailing its theoretical underpinnings and practical implementation. Through a series of experimental studies, we evaluate the effectiveness of our approach in real-world settings. Through these analyses, we aim to demonstrate the potential of nudges in transforming EULAs from a legal formality into a user-centric tool for informed decision-making. Finally, we discuss the broader implications of our findings for software developers, legal professionals, and policymakers, offering actionable recommendations for making EULAs more accessible and meaningful for users.

2 Background and Related Work

2.1 EULA and Privacy Policies

Generally, Software end-user license agreements (EULAs) are given to the users at application start-up for the first time. EULAs often include details about warranties, disclaimers, and limitations of liability, helping to mitigate legal risks for the software provider. By explicitly defining data access terms and responsibilities, EULAs aim to mitigate potential misuse or unauthorized access to sensitive information, thereby safeguarding user privacy and protecting the interests of both the software provider and the end user [25].

Privacy policies in EULAs play a crucial role in fostering transparency and trust between software service providers and their users, ensuring that user data is handled responsibly and by legal and ethical standards [33].

2.2 Current State of EULAs

Several studies have highlighted the prevalent issues associated with EULAs. Research indicates that the majority of users do not read EULAs in their entirety; many users skip reading them altogether or merely skim through the text without grasping the critical details. This phenomenon is often attributed to several factors:

- **Complex Language:** EULAs typically employ legalese which is difficult for the average user to understand. The use of technical terms and convoluted sentence structures further exacerbates this issue, making the document inaccessible to non-experts.
- **Length and Density:** EULAs are often lengthy documents filled with exhaustive lists of clauses and stipulations. The sheer volume of information can be daunting, leading users to avoid reading the document comprehensively.
- **Presentation:** The way EULAs are presented, usually as a lengthy block of text, contributes to their unpopularity. The lack of visual aids, highlights, or interactive elements discourages user engagement.
- **Time Constraints:** Users are often prompted to agree to EULAs during software installation or account creation processes. The urgency to proceed with these actions results in users hastily agreeing to the terms without proper review.

2.3 Why People Skip Reading EULAs Without Intervention

People tend to skip reading software EULAs while they are presented, which often is dictated by several psychological factors.

- EULAs are generally long and it is difficult for users to determine how much of their data may be collected and how it might be used; a phenomenon known as *"incomplete and asymmetric information"* [37].
- Secondly, security and privacy are rarely end-users primary tasks, and users only focus on the intended tasks and ignore others such as security - a phenomenon known as "bounded rationality" [41].
- Anchoring effect [23,43] also biases users to read only the application title and decide whether it serves the intended goal without paying attention to EULA.
- Apart from these, Nowadays people share a lot of private information with cyberspace [14,17] and thus avoid reading policy documents even after being aware of the vulnerabilities.

2.4 Enhancing EULA Readability and Comprehension: The Potential of Nudges

Given the persistent challenges associated with EULAs, there is a clear need for innovative solutions that go beyond traditional methods. Our research aims to bridge this gap by introducing a novel nudge mechanism specifically tailored for EULAs. By integrating insights from behavioral economics and cognitive psychology, we seek to create a more engaging and informative EULA experience. Our approach is grounded in empirical research and aims to provide actionable recommendations for improving EULA design, thereby fostering greater user awareness and compliance.

Nudges, as defined by behavioral economics, are subtle design elements that influence user behavior without restricting their choices. Nudges leverage cognitive biases and heuristics to guide users toward desired behaviors. The Nudge technique, popularized by Thaler and Sunstein [3], has attracted the attention of educators in recent times, especially when combined with feedback. Several studies indicate that nudges as feedback can enhance motivation and learning effects. For example, Caraban et al. [10] analyzed how real-time feedback nudges on learning platforms help inform learners about altering their behavior in response to performance measures and, by extension, improve engagement and retention. Feedback nudges are slight, supportive prods that help shift students toward desired learning behaviors with no compulsion.

Nudges harnessed from educational interventions have also proved effective in influencing learners' choices. A randomized control trial by Castleman and Page [11] found that text message nudges providing personalized information and reminders increased college enrollment and persistence among high school students. Moreover, educational nudges have been found to increase public engagement with policy-related information. A study [20] explored how sending reminders and providing simplified educational explanations of government policies led to greater public participation and understanding. These nudges, in the form of brief, structured educational interventions, ensure that individuals give more attention to relevant sections of policy documents.

In the context of EULAs, nudges can be employed to enhance readability and engagement by making the document more approachable and highlighting key information.

2.5 Related Work

Here, we mention a few related research which focus on the readability of privacy policy documents and user awareness of their contents.

The introduction of the Platform for Privacy Preferences (P3P) in the early 2000s marked a milestone in the development of privacy policy explanation techniques [13]. However, adoption was limited, and privacy policies continued to vary significantly [5,39].

Several studies have focused on improving the readability and user awareness of privacy policy documents and EULAs. Privacy policies are critical communication tools that inform users about how organizations collect, use, and protect personal data, as well as policies on third-party data sharing and cookie usage [26,31,42]. Ignoring these documents can result in a loss of privacy or the unintentional sharing of sensitive information [16].

One trend in enhancing EULA usability is the movement towards simplified language. Efforts have been made to rewrite these documents in plain language, using simpler terms and sentence structures [29,45]. The researchers found that a majority of these agreements had readability levels well above the average reading ability, highlighting the need for improved accessibility.

Recently, there has been a shift towards more interactive and visual representations of privacy policies. Reinhardt et al. proposed a visual interactive privacy policy system, transforming static text into a more engaging format through clickable elements and visual cues, allowing users to explore the document more intuitively [35]. Similarly, Alabduljabbar et al.'s TLDR project introduced deep learning models to automatically extract and annotate key privacy policy highlights, allowing users to quickly grasp critical terms without reading the full document [2,6]. While these systems significantly streamline user interaction with privacy documents, there is room for a simpler and more lightweight intervention by highlighting crucial terms in a color-coded manner [15], making it easy for users to grasp key points without being overwhelmed by excessive interactivity.

A notable project in this space is the "Terms of Service, Didn't Read" (ToS; DR) initiative, which processes terms of service (ToS) and EULA documents to provide users with simplified summaries and key information [31]. ToS; DR uses a community-driven approach to rate and summarize terms, enabling users to understand these often complex legal documents better. While effective in providing detailed and thorough analyses, ToS; DR is effort-driven and heavily reliant on manual contributions [4], making it a time-consuming and labor-intensive process.

In this evolving landscape, there is an opportunity to explore methodologies that improve user understanding of privacy policies. While previous studies have focused on interactive formats and automated summarization, integrating these approaches with nudging strategies [32] could enhance user awareness.

The European Commission's General Data Protection Regulation (GDPR) introduced "layered" privacy notices, a method where key information is presented upfront, with the option to delve into more detailed explanations if needed. Although this layered approach offers greater transparency and user control, it is less frequently applied to EULA summarization and visualization [34,38,40].

However, such measures are rarely applied to EULA privacy policy summarization and visualization [34] and do not give feedback at the time of use. Our work aims to build on these advancements by proposing that the automated extraction of key parts of privacy policies, combined with nudging techniques, can effectively direct user attention. Highlighting important sections through color-coded summaries allows for clearer insights while keeping cognitive load manageable. Additionally, introducing pre-awareness sessions may further enhance user understanding before they engage with EULA content, providing a foundation for future research on these strategies in improving privacy literacy.

3 Methodology

In this section, we present the nudge tool to aware users about the privacy-sensitive contents in the software EULAs. The detailed working principle of the nudging mechanism along with the user experiments performed to validate it is also described.

3.1 Approach Overview

Figure 1 shows a high-level overview of the user experiments done to explore the effect of the presence or absence of the proposed nudge.

At first, we collect the texts from EULAs of 134 popular web applications. These texts are then forwarded to the keyword extraction module (step 1).

The keyword extraction module (step 2) finds frequently occurring words and phrases in the EULA text data set. From that list, we isolate the keywords (step 3) related to privacy, security, and sensitive data access, and disclosure-related ones to form an updated word list. This mechanism to identify which words are related to privacy and security is done with the help of a list we built as part of this work. It serves as the baseline knowledge base for the proposed system which gives users a modified EULA with the security-critical words highlighted (step 4).

Next, to evaluate the effect of nudges on users we perform three user experiments (steps 5 and 6). This experiment consisted of a test environment where participants had to physically attend a session. They were shown a sample EULA document and asked a few questions on how they perceived the read EULA from

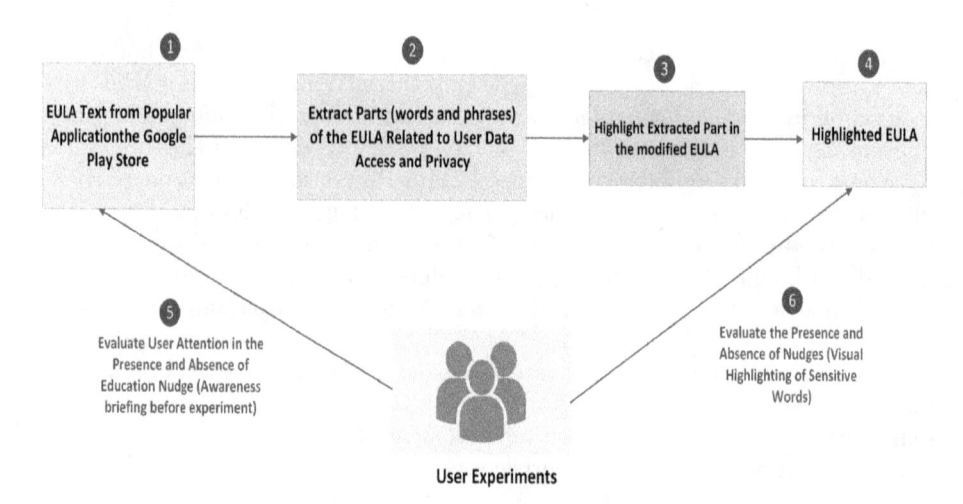

Fig. 1. User experiment setup for evaluating nudge tool in making EULAs more readable and understandable

the aspect of potential privacy exposure. Then we score the participants' answers to evaluate their level of attention and comprehension.

For experiments, participants were divided into two groups: Group 1 having 108 participants, and Group 2 containing the remaining 65. In the first experiment, one group was given the EULA text as it is (no nudge), and the second group where tested with privacy-sensitive keywords highlighted (feedback nudge).

Next (second experiment), we repeat the same test with the first group of users now receiving an oral briefing about the privacy issues of EULAs (education nudge) and the second group with prior warning but sensitive keywords highlighted (feedback nudge).

Finally, in the third experiment, we evaluate the nudge tool (browser plugin with highlighted keywords in EULA) on all the users (173 participants) to see its effectiveness in creating a positive impact on users in terms of privacy awareness and behavior.

Our experiment shows that the proposed nudge indeed makes the security-specific contents in EULA easier to understand and aid users with their decision-making. The following discussions describe these steps in more detail.

3.2 Data Collection and Extraction of Privacy Sensitive Keywords

We collected EULA texts from 134 most popular applications in the Google Play Store which fall under the following categories: Travel, Finance, Entertainment, Consumer Products, Social Media, E-commerce, Edu-tech, Medical, News, House & Home, Food, Productivity and Streaming Content.

These EULAs are scraped from their respective websites and stored in a text-only form using the Python package beautifulsoup4 [36].

Privacy policies and data usage declarations in EULA can be lengthy and complex, making it difficult for users to understand and engage. A crucial first step in this process is identifying and extracting the privacy-sensitive information contained within these policies. This includes finding the keywords and phrases that are most likely to indicate the collection, use, and sharing of personal data. This involves the following steps:

The raw text files were then stemmed and lemmatized using the NLTK library [21]. We used the keyword model from KeyBERT [19] to extract keywords and then YAKE (Yet another keyword extractor) [8] was used which found a slightly different set of words. We combined the two sets of keywords and then read through real privacy policies to find the occurrence of words and also identify even less occurring but privacy-intensive sentences.

Our findings reveal that certain keywords, such as "data," "information," and "privacy," were present at a high frequency, indicating their importance in privacy policies. Other keywords, such as "location" and "camera," were found to have a higher frequency in specific categories, such as "Travel" and "Photography."

We found that individual EULA analyses yielded a large number of trademark words [7] that were not particularly useful for our analysis. However, when we combined the frequency of words across all EULAs in each category along with a list of security and privacy-specific keywords [9,28,30], we were able to identify a *privacy sensitive keyword dictionary (PSK)*, which form the basis of our privacy analysis model of EULA documents.

Finally, by combining the results of our manual intervention with those of our automated keyword extraction algorithms, we were able to create a final keyword list of 130 words. These were deemed to be the most important and privacy-sensitive, which were used as the basis for further analysis and visualization. The complete list is included in the Appendix A.

Figure 2 shows the top 50 keywords from this list in terms of their frequency of occurrences in our EULA text extraction phase.

3.3 Proposed Nudge Mechanism and Tool Design

With the help of the list of privacy-sensitive words, we alert the user either by briefing sessions before they are evaluated on test EULA or highlight the sensitive keywords for better attention.

However, in no way, do we impede the user from its intended tasks regardless of their behavior. So, the proposed nudge follows the principle of Soft Parental Intervention [1].

We distinguish two general approaches for providing information (nudge): *Education* and *Feedback*. Education provides information before the user engages with the system or a specific feature. Thus, education primarily supports future decisions.

In our design, education comes in the form of a pre-awareness briefing before users are evaluated against an EULA (not highlighted).

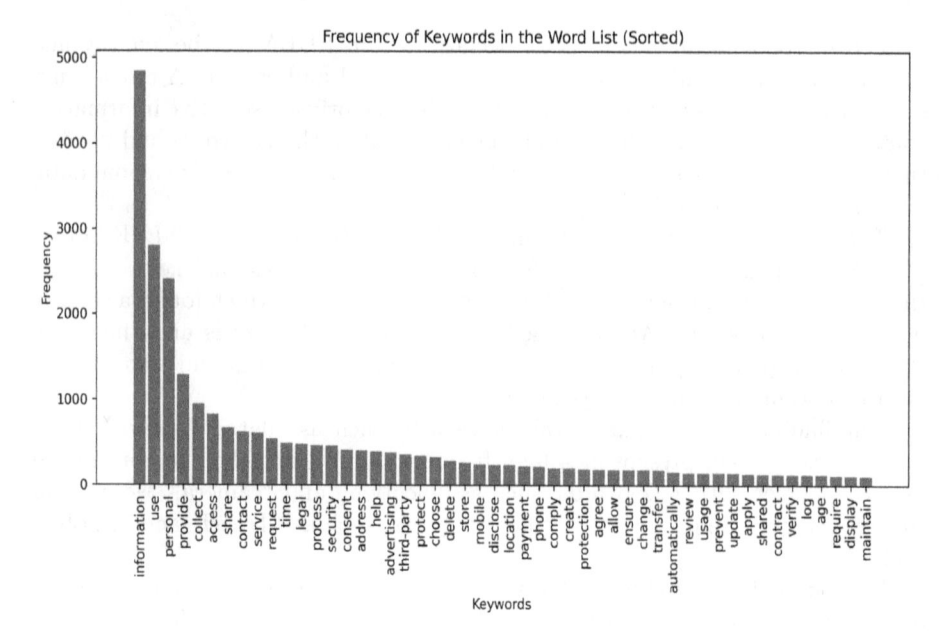

[Figure: Bar chart titled "Frequency of Keywords in the Word List (Sorted)" showing frequency (0-5000) on y-axis and keywords on x-axis. Keywords from highest to lowest: information, use, personal, provide, collect, access, share, contact, service, request, time, legal, process, security, consent, address, help, advertising, third-party, protect, choose, delete, store, mobile, disclose, location, payment, phone, comply, create, agree, protection, allow, ensure, change, transfer, automatically, review, usage, prevent, update, apply, shared, contract, verify, log, age, require, display, maintain.]

Fig. 2. Most frequently occurring (top 50) privacy critical words in the extracted EULAs

On the other hand, Feedback is commonly provided alongside system usage. Feedback can make users aware of the consequences of their actions and assist them in making better decisions over time. Well-designed nudges may allow users to revise their decisions if the outcome does not meet their expectations.

In this work, we highlight the privacy-sensitive words in an EULA sample on the fly as users are evaluated. The highlighting provides feedback on users' prior education of security concerns regarding EULAs. To test the further usability of the highlighting, we developed a browser extension that analyzes the privacy policy document loaded in a browser tab and shows a summarized output. Appendix B shows a snapshot of the proposed tool in highlighting critical areas of an EULA and categorizing threats based on their severity level.

Here, the privacy issues are categorized and further color-coded to indicate their potential effect on users' privacy (red = most severe, green = no privacy issue but needs attention, yellow = privacy policy is not clear about data usage). Visual icons are also added to grab further user attention. To describe the individual warnings in the EULA being analyzed, A description of the parameter in the EULA that is being analyzed is generated by the GPT-3.5-turbo model.

3.4 Experiment Setup and Questionnaire Design

Figure 3 shows a high-level overview of the workflow followed to design the user experiments for the nudge tool design and validation.

At first, we conducted semi-structured interviews with a select group of participants from the pool of users who participated in this study. They were asked about the various aspects of their usage, comprehension, security awareness, and behavior while presented with an EULA.

Fig. 3. Steps Followed in Questionnaire Design for User Experiment

Next, all the recorded interviews were transcribed resulting in an anonymized text version of the responses. After that, we thoroughly analyzed the transcripts and mined the key terms and factors that repeatedly came up during the interviews. These frequently occurring themes laid the foundation of the questionnaire used in our experiment.

Apart from that, to effectively gather data on participants' perception and understanding of privacy policies in EULA, we at first, manually identify privacy-sensitive words and sentences in the data set. Then, we put these sentences into groups based on OPP-115 Corpus [27], an online repository of 115 privacy policy documents. We identified the top 10 key themes/categories from this privacy parameter list and further updated the questionnaire based on that. Apart from the basic information like name, email, age, and area of study, participants were evaluated against the following two sets of questions.

- **Participants' perception of privacy:** to assess user's comprehension of personal privacy protection in cyberspace.
  - **Q1:** How often do you read EULAs when hopping into a new platform?
  - **Q2:** Do you have a good idea of how to protect privacy information online?
  - **Q3:** Are you aware of the potential consequences of sharing personal information online?
- **Participants' perception and behavior about EULA:** to measure attention and comprehension about the potential issues stated in EULA (with or without nudges)
  - **Q1:** Can the application be used by users younger than 15 years old?
  - **Q2:** Is the User's personal information shared with law enforcement agencies?
  - **Q3:** Are User's interests analyzed to show personalized ads?
  - **Q4:** Does the application inform any events of account credential breaches?
  - **Q5:** Is the User's communication encrypted in transit?
  - **Q6:** Does the application have access to contacts?

- **Q7:** Does the host platform keep user information even after deletion?
- **Q8:** Are User activities in other applications or browsers tracked?
- **Q9:** Does the application track the user's geolocation?
- **Q10:** Are users allowed to delete all of their information from the device?

A feedback section was also included to gather additional insights and suggestions from participants.

3.5 User Experiment Workflow

Participant Demographics. We recruited 173 undergraduate students to participate in the proposed user experiments. Figure 4 shows demographic differences in terms of gender and major areas of study.

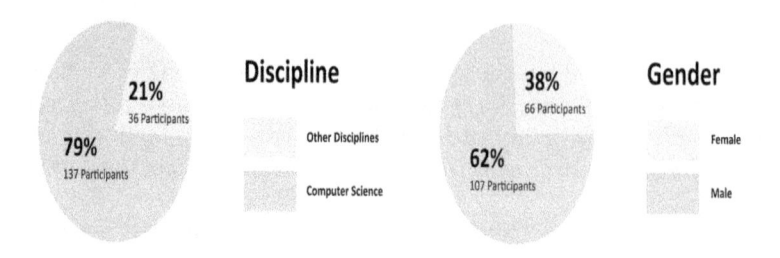

Fig. 4. User Experiment Participants' Demographic

Most of the participants came from the Computer Science discipline (79%) and the rest (21%) had undergraduate majors in different disciplines. Among them, 62% are male and 38% female.

Experiment Setup, Evaluation Metrics, and Workflow. Among the 173 participants, 108 participated in Experiment 1, and Experiment 2 was conducted on the rest of 65 users. In each experiment, the participants were further divided into two groups, where one group received the nudge and the other did not. Additionally, we also evaluated two groups with different kinds of nudges to see their effectiveness.

User groups were gathered in a facility where they were individually given an EULA document on a computer. Everyone in particular experiment settings was given the same EULA. After the users are evaluated on the test EULA, their responses to questions are annotated and mapped to numerical scores. The responses to EULA-specific questions (*YES, NO and Not Sure*) are mapped to numerical scores of 1 and 0 depending on the correctness. If user responses match with EULA contents the score of 1 is recorded, otherwise 0 is stored. However, if the EULA does not mention an issue correctly and is difficult to grasp even after careful reading, then the *Not Sure* is given a score of 1.

Using these, we calculate various statistical measures (mean, standard deviation). Then, a two-tailed t-test is performed to evaluate whether differences in outcome between the two groups are statistically significant.

4 Evaluation and Findings

This section describes our user studies and findings in detail. We perform three user experiments. The first one evaluates whether nudging can improve user attention and awareness about EULA. The second one tests whether the nudge works both with an oral pre-awareness briefing and visually highlighting areas of interest in an EULA document. Finally, we test the effectiveness of the proposed nudge tool (browser plugin) to see if it can indeed grab user attention by popping up a color-coded categorized summary of the EULA.

4.1 Findings of User Experiment 1: Nudging (Feedback) has a Significant Impact on User Awareness Compared to the Absence of Nudge

Here, a total of 108 participants were divided into two groups (G1 and G2), with 63 in G1 and 44 in G2. They were evaluated on the two sets of questions as mentioned in the previous section (perception on personal privacy, EULA specific).

For the first set, both groups received the same questions related to the perception of personal privacy. Here, we observed that most people tend to skip reading EULAs. Only 7% said they read often, 23% sometimes, and the rest of the 60% very rarely or never. Similarly, we found that most users have an elevated sense of personal privacy protection in cyberspace (Fig. 5), which is concerning.

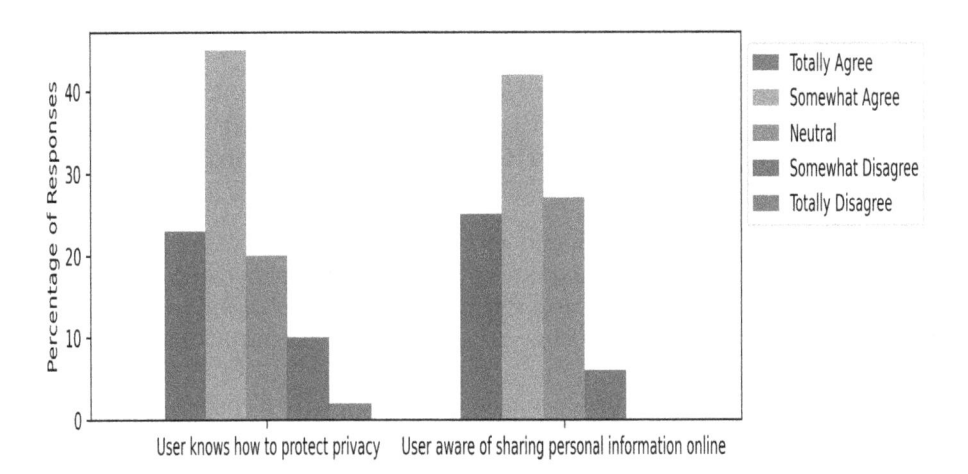

Fig. 5. Users claimed to have control over personal privacy

For EULA-specific questions, G1 receives the EULA without any nudges or intervention (as it is done now in practice). However, participants in G2 received a nudged (privacy-sensitive keywords highlighted) EULA. For this study, we have two hypotheses:

Null Hypothesis (H0): There is no difference in test performance between the highlighted text group (feedback nudge) and the non-highlighted text group.

Alternative Hypothesis (H1): There is a significant difference in test performance between the two groups.

Table 1. Scores of users with the presence or absence of nudges (privacy keywords highlighted in EULA)

User Group	Test EULA	Sample Size	Mean	Std. Deviation
G1	Non-highlighted	63	5.4	1.75
G2	Highlighted	45	6.09	1.29

Findings are shown in Table 1. For a 5% confidence level we find that, $t-statistic = 2.24196$ and $p-value = 0.027067 \ll 0.05$. Thus we can reject our null hypothesis and conclude that we are 95% sure that there is a significant difference between the two groups.

The results indicate that the use of highlighting privacy-sensitive keywords in EULAs leads to an increase in user awareness of privacy issues. Specifically, the t-test, show a significant difference in mean scores between the group who had the EULA with highlighted keywords (feedback nudges) and the group who had the EULA without highlighted keywords.

4.2 Findings of User Experiment 2: Nudging (Prior Awareness Building (Education) or Visual Assistance (Feedback)) has a Positive Impact on User Comprehension Regardless of Its Type

This time we nudged the participants by explaining what we were doing. Before answering the questions, participants were briefed in-person on the importance of privacy policies, why we should read them, why people don't seem to read them, and how we can better protect online privacy through gaining comprehension of privacy policies in EULA.

The experiment was conducted among another group of 65 people. They were divided into two groups of 32 and 33 people respectively labeled as G3 and G4. G3 were given a non-highlighted EULA and participants of G4 were given the highlighted one (feedback nudge). But, unlike the first survey, here G3 members received the nudge in the form of a pre-awareness briefing on EULA contents (education nudge). Here also, we perform our evaluations on the two following hypotheses:

Null Hypothesis (H0): There is no difference in test performance between the highlighted text group (feedback nudge received) and the non-highlighted text group (education nudge received).

Alternative Hypothesis (H1): There is a significant difference in test performance between the two groups.

Table 2. Scores of users in the presence of different nudges (oral and graphical) while reading EULA

User Group	Test EULA	Sample Size	Mean	Std. Deviation
G3	Non-highlighted	32	4.72	1.87
G4	Highlighted	33	4.64	1.93

The findings are listed in Table 2. For a 5% confidence level, we find that we find $t-statistic = 0.17452$ and $p-value = .86202 > 0.05$. Thus we can not reject our null hypothesis. This implies that there is not a significant difference between the two groups this time. Therefore it demonstrates that pre-awareness briefing (education nudge) has almost the same effect on users' perception buildup as the explicit highlight of keywords in EULA (feedback nudge).

However, we repeat the above-mentioned test to validate that the observed result did not occur due to any bias introduced while choosing the members of G3 and G4. For that, now we only consider the participants from G3 and evaluate them with a new sample EULA document. Now, in both settings (highlighted and non-highlighted) the same participants are surveyed and we use the same hypotheses as used before. The result of this experiment is shown in Table 3.

Table 3. Scores of G3 participants only in the presence of different nudges (oral and graphical) while reading EULA

Test EULA	Mean	Std. Deviation
Non-highlighted	4.72	1.87
Highlighted	4.64	1.93

For a 5% confidence level we find that, $t-statistic = -0.44441$ and $p-value = .658291 >> 0.05$. The result is yet again not significant. It further backs up the fact that triggering a pre-awareness (education nudge) does really affect the way users view and perceive their privacy through privacy policies while they are highlighted (feedback nudge) almost in the same way.

4.3 User Experiment 3: Usability Test of the Nudge Tool

To evaluate the effectiveness of the proposed privacy warning nudge tool (implemented as a browser plugin), we conducted another experiment with the combined group of participants taken from G3 and G4 (a total of 65 participants). However, G3 had only the EULA with the plugin popping up with a privacy summary, whereas participants in G4 also received a highlighted EULA along with the plugin. Figure 6 shows the summary of this user experiment.

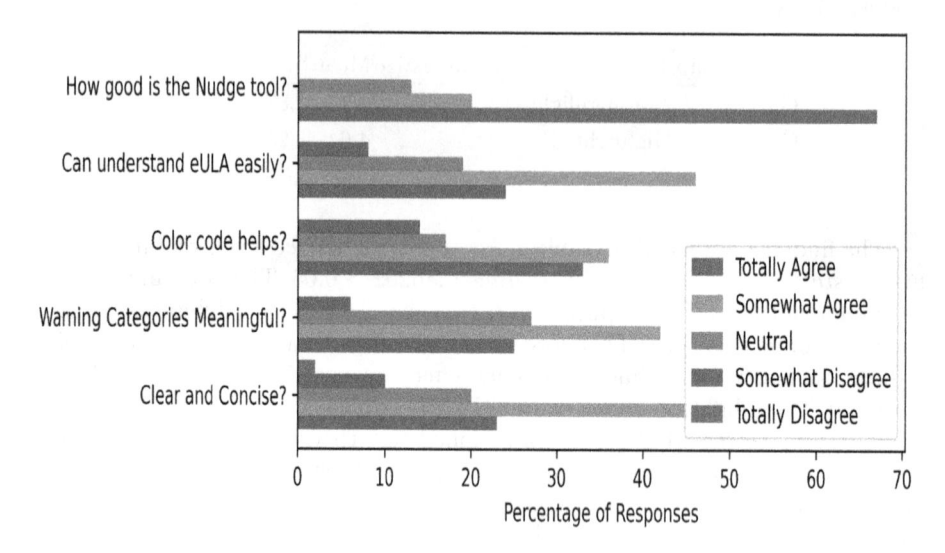

Fig. 6. Users responses towards the effectiveness study of proposed nudge tool

Around 40–60% of participants in each group said that the browser plugin we developed as the nudge tool helped them to better understand the EULA. While only around 5–15% expressed disagreement. This distribution suggests a predominant positive sentiment among respondents.

It is also to be noted that, the color-coded categorization also helped users in getting a quick summary of potential issues in the EULA and their severity level (more than 65% users strongly agreed).

We further evaluated the performance of this nudge tool (named EULA Analyzer) on applications in terms of the time needed to read and answer a few questions for the respective EULAs. The results are shown in Fig. 7. It further demonstrates the effectiveness of the proposed tool.

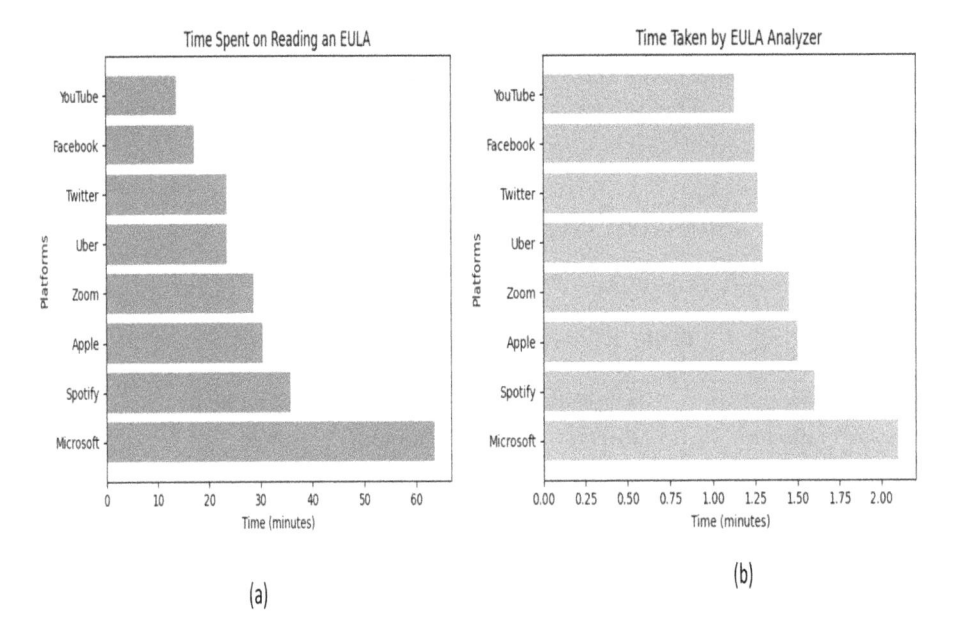

Fig. 7. Time required to read EULAs of popular applications (a) Regular EULAs (b) Assisted EULAs with the proposed tool - EULA Analyzer

5 Conclusion

This study demonstrates the efficacy of nudging users about privacy-sensitive content as a means to enhance the readability and comprehension of End-User License Agreements (EULAs). By drawing attention to critical terms about data privacy and security, users are better equipped to make informed decisions about their digital interactions. The results of your survey showed that participants scored higher and took less time to answer questions after reading a highlighted EULA than a non-highlighted EULA.

However, the nudge tool also has some limitations which we plan to address in the future. The core of the system is the security-sensitive keyword list, which currently contains only 130 words. For a more comprehensive warning generation, this list is not sufficient and will be augmented with more privacy-related words in later versions. Also, our knowledge base is built on 134 mobile applications, which may not be representative of all the different kinds of EULAs we encounter in desktop and web-based applications.

In the future, we plan to expand more on the nudge tool by making it work for various kinds of mobile, web-based, and desktop applications. Further user studies involving a diverse pool of participants of diverse is also needed to make the proposed tool more effective and user-friendly, which we plan to do next.

Ethics and Safety. For the user studies described in this paper, we received an Institutional Review Board (IRB) certificate for human subjects research, approved study questionnaire, and ensured no personally identifiable data was collected from the participants.

A Privacy Sensitive Keywords in EULA

Table 4. Privacy Sensitive Keyword List

access	aggregate	connect	consolidate
disclose	display	maintain	mare
investigate	post	reserve	review
allow	contact	enforce	maximize
prevent	share	apply	contract
ensure	minimize	prohibit	specify
avoid	customize	exchange	monitor
protect	store	block	deny
help	notify	provide	update
change	destroy	honor	obligate
recommend	urge	choose	disallow
imply	opt-in	request	use
collect	comply	discipline	disclaim
inform	limit	opt-out	require
verify	personal	ip address	third-party
publish	consent	process	create
delete	retention	registration	mobile
phone	speech recognition	cloud	service
jurisdictions	password	protection	information
location	real-time	upload	download
shared	first-party	automatically	usage
trend	log	mapping	advertising
track	payment	chat	history
record	anonymous	biometric	cookie
GDPR	correction	child	age
legal	erasure	deletion	withdraw
retention period	security	sell	monetization
transfer	under-age	accountability	agree
disagree			

B Snapshot of Proposed Nudge Tool in Alerting Users on EULA Contents

Fig. 8. Nudge tool (Browser extension) to generate categorized and color-coded warnings of privacy issues in EULA (Color figure online)

References

1. Acquisti, A., et al.: Nudges for privacy and security: understanding and assisting users' choices online. ACM Comput. Surv. (CSUR) **50**(3), 1–41 (2017)
2. Alabduljabbar, A., Abusnaina, A., Meteriz-Yildiran, Ü., Mohaisen, D.: TLDR: deep learning-based automated privacy policy annotation with key policy highlights. In: Proceedings of the 20th Workshop on Workshop on Privacy in the Electronic Society, pp. 103–118 (2021)

3. Anderson, J.: Nudge: improving decisions about health, wealth, and happiness, Richard H. Thaler and Cass R. Sunstein. Yale University Press, 2008. x+ 293 pages. [paperback edition, penguin, 2009, 320 pages.]. Econ. Philos. **26**(3), 369–376 (2010)
4. Binns, R., Matthews, D.: Community structure for efficient information flow in 'tos; dr', a social machine for parsing legalese. In: Proceedings of the 23rd International Conference on World Wide Web, pp. 881–884 (2014)
5. Brunotte, W., Chazette, L., Kohler, L., Klunder, J., Schneider, K.: What about my privacy? Helping users understand online privacy policies. In: Proceedings of the International Conference on Software and System Processes and International Conference on Global Software Engineering, pp. 56–65 (2022)
6. Bui, D., Shin, K.G., Choi, J.-M., Shin, J.: Automated extraction and presentation of data practices in privacy policies. In: Proceedings on Privacy Enhancing Technologies (2021)
7. Butters, R.R.: Trademark linguistics: trademarks: language that one owns. In: The Routledge Handbook of Forensic Linguistics, pp. 364–381. Routledge (2020)
8. Campos, R., Mangaravite, V., Pasquali, A., Jorge, A., Nunes, C., Jatowt, A.: Yake! keyword extraction from single documents using multiple local features. Inf. Sci. **509**, 257–289 (2020)
9. Cao, N., Wang, C., Li, M., Ren, K., Lou, W.: Privacy-preserving multi-keyword ranked search over encrypted cloud data. IEEE Trans. Parallel Distrib. Syst. **25**(1), 222–233 (2013)
10. Caraban, A., Karapanos, E., Gonçalves, D., Campos, P.: 23 ways to nudge: a review of technology-mediated nudging in human-computer interaction. In: Proceedings of the 2019 CHI Conference on Human Factors in Computing Systems, pp. 1–15 (2019)
11. Castleman, B.L., Page, L.C.: Summer nudging: can personalized text messages and peer mentor outreach increase college going among low-income high school graduates? J. Econ. Behav. Organ. **115**, 144–160 (2015)
12. Cherry, M.A.: A eulogy for the Eula. Duq. L. Rev. **52**, 335 (2014)
13. Cranor, L.F.: P3P: making privacy policies more useful. IEEE Secur. Privacy **1**(6), 50–55 (2003)
14. Cranor, L.F., Reagle, J., Ackerman, M.S.: Beyond concern: understanding net users' attitudes about online privacy (2000)
15. Cutler, A., Rivest, J., Cavanagh, P.: The role of memory color in visual attention. Attention Perception Psychophysics **86**(1), 28–35 (2024)
16. Desautels, E.: Software license agreements: ignore at your own risk
17. Dowthwaite, L., et al.: "It's your private information. it's your life". Young people's views of personal data use by online technologies. In: Proceedings of the Interaction Design and Children Conference, pp. 121–134 (2020)
18. Ericson, J.D., Albert, W.S., Bernard, B.P., Brown, E.: End-user license agreements (eulas) investigating the impact of human-centered design on perceived usability, attitudes, and anticipated behavior. Inf. Des. J. **26**(3), 193–215 (2021)
19. Grootendorst, M.: Keyword extraction with BERT. Towards Data Science (2021)
20. Halpern, D., Sanders, M.: Nudging by government: progress, impact, & lessons learned. Behav. Sci. Policy **2**(2), 53–65 (2016)
21. Hardeniya, N., Perkins, J., Chopra, D., Joshi, N., Mathur, I.: Natural Language Processing: Python and NLTK. Packt Publishing Ltd. (2016)
22. Hsieh, P.-H., Hsu, P.-I.: Displaying software installation agreements to motivate users' reading. Int. J. Hum.-Comput. Interact. 1–18 (2022)

23. Jacowitz, K.E., Kahneman, D.: Measures of anchoring in estimation tasks. Pers. Soc. Psychol. Bull. **21**(11), 1161–1166 (1995)
24. Khan, B., Syed, T., Khan, Z., Rafi, M.: Textual analysis of end user license agreement for red-flagging potentially malicious software. In: 2020 International Conference on Electrical, Communication, and Computer Engineering (ICECCE), pp. 1–5. IEEE (2020)
25. Kortum, P.T., Bangor, A.: Usability ratings for everyday products measured with the system usability scale. Int. J. Hum.-Comput. Interact. **29**(2), 67–76 (2013)
26. Kretschmer, M., Pennekamp, J., Wehrle, K.: Cookie banners and privacy policies: measuring the impact of the GDPR on the web. ACM Trans. Web (TWEB) **15**(4), 1–42 (2021)
27. Liu, F., Wilson, S., Story, P., Zimmeck, S., Sadeh, N.: Towards automatic classification of privacy policy text. School of Computer Science Carnegie Mellon University (2018)
28. Manandhar, S., Singh, K., Nadkarni, A.: Towards automated regulation analysis for effective privacy compliance. In: ISOC Network and Distributed System Security Symposium (2024)
29. McDonald, A.M., Reeder, R.W., Kelley, P.G., Cranor, L.F.: A comparative study of online privacy policies and formats. In: Goldberg, I., Atallah, M.J. (eds.) PETS 2009. LNCS, vol. 5672, pp. 37–55. Springer, Heidelberg (2009). https://doi.org/10.1007/978-3-642-03168-7_3
30. Nowrozy, R., Ahmed, K., Kayes, A.S.M., Wang, H., McIntosh, T.R.: Privacy preservation of electronic health records in the modern era: a systematic survey. ACM Comput. Surv. (2024)
31. Obar, J.A., Oeldorf-Hirsch, A.: The biggest lie on the internet: ignoring the privacy policies and terms of service policies of social networking services. Inf. Commun. Soc. **23**(1), 128–147 (2020)
32. Ortloff, A.-M., Zimmerman, S., Elsweiler, D., Henze, N.: The effect of nudges and boosts on browsing privacy in a naturalistic environment. In: Proceedings of the 2021 Conference on Human Information Interaction and Retrieval, pp. 63–73 (2021)
33. Pollach, I.: What's wrong with online privacy policies? Commun. ACM **50**(9), 103–108 (2007)
34. Regulwar, G.B., Majji, R., Kottu, S.K., Kachi, A., Sureddy, R.R.: Content analysis and visualization of privacy policy using privacy management. In: AIP Conference Proceedings, vol. 2942. AIP Publishing (2024)
35. Reinhardt, D., Borchard, J., Hurtienne, J.: Visual interactive privacy policy: the better choice? In: Proceedings of the 2021 CHI Conference on Human Factors in Computing Systems, pp. 1–12 (2021)
36. Richardson, L.: Beautiful soup documentation (2007)
37. Stiglitz, J., Barkley Rosser, J., et al.: A Nobel prize for asymmetric information: the economic contributions of George Akerlof, Michael Spence and Joseph Stiglitz. In: Leading Contemporary Economists, pp. 162–181. Routledge (2008)
38. Rossi, A., Palmirani, M.: A visualization approach for adaptive consent in the European data protection framework. In: 2017 Conference for E-Democracy and Open Government (CeDEM), pp. 159–170. IEEE (2017)
39. Schellekens, M.: Is an icon worth a thousand words? Grounded legal strategies for standardised icons under the GDPR (2023)
40. Schufrin, M., Reynolds, S.L., Kuijper, A., Kohlhammer, J.: A visualization interface to improve the transparency of collected personal data on the Internet. IEEE Trans. Vis. Comput. Graph. **27**(2), 1840–1849 (2020)

41. Simon, H.A.: Models of Bounded Rationality: Empirically Grounded Economic Reason, vol. 3. MIT Press, Cambridge (1997)
42. Solove, D.J.: The myth of the privacy paradox. Geo. Wash. L. Rev. **89**(1) (2021)
43. Tversky, A., Kahneman, D.: Judgment under uncertainty: heuristics and biases: biases in judgments reveal some heuristics of thinking under uncertainty. Science **185**(4157), 1124–1131 (1974)
44. Waddell, T.F., Auriemma, J.R., Sundar, S.S.: Make it simple, or force users to read? paraphrased design improves comprehension of end user license agreements. In: Proceedings of the 2016 CHI Conference on Human Factors in Computing Systems, pp. 5252–5256 (2016)
45. Zhang, S., Sadeh, N.: Do privacy labels answer users' privacy questions? In: Workshop on Usable Security and Privacy (2023)

A Decoupling Mechanism for Transaction Privacy

Vishwas Patil[✉][iD] and R. K. Shyamasundar[iD]

Department of Computer Science and Engineering, Indian Institute of Technology Bombay, Mumbai 400076, India
ivishwas@gmail.com

Abstract. Unlike traditional monolithic approaches to web-service composition, modern web services are built by integrating various external sub-services, such as OpenID authentication, cloud-based IaaS for compute and storage, payment gateways, and more. Additionally, application-specific sub-services, like JavaScript libraries and web-analytics, are often incorporated-particularly in e-commerce platforms. This modern modular approach offers clear advantages, including faster deployment, enhanced user convenience, and lower service delivery costs. However, it also raises significant privacy concerns, as users' interactions with these services are exposed to third-party sub-services, allowing for observation and inference. In the early days of online banking, David Chaum proposed eCash, a system that allowed banks to authenticate payments without monitoring their customers' transaction details. Beyond payments, however, the issue of linking users to their online actions—by both the primary service provider and its associated sub-services—has made it difficult to identify and prevent privacy violations. Schneier and Raghavan introduced strategies to enhance privacy in online services through the *decoupling principle*, which focuses on separating user actions from their identity to prevent linkability. The foundation of privacy breaches in online transactions is the ability to observe and connect an authenticated user's identity with their actions. SPKI (Simple Public Key Infrastructure) offers a way to define, use, and manage identity and authorizations independently. In this paper, we propose an SPKI-based framework that can be integrated into online transaction processes to decouple identity from actions. Through illustrative examples, we demonstrate the framework's utility and argue that it provides greater expressiveness and flexibility compared to existing privacy frameworks.

Keywords: Identity · Authentication · Authorization · Linkability · SPKI · Privacy

1 Introduction

Online services have become ubiquitous and transcend across all of our interactions with the world around us; may it be use of financial services, online shopping portals, or just staying in touch with our acquaintances on social media platforms. Identity plays a crucial role in these interactions. Identity serves two purposes: i) *authorization* – to determine whether an identified user is allowed to access a service, and ii) *accountability* – to identify a user when things go wrong. This implies that a record-keeping of identity to her actions is necessary; true. But who can access or infer these identity-to-actions records has enormous repercussions on user privacy. In a monolithic service, such records stay within a well-defined administrative boundary where verifiable techno-legal protection mechanisms can be implemented. Whereas, in a non-monolithic service, a copy of these sensitive records is also stored with external service provider to enforce accountability. As the number of underlying service providers increase in a service composition, the copies of sensitive records multiply; each one of them logging identity-to-action records. Probability of privacy violation increases when the external service providers provide authentication services. This is because the identifiers maybe pertaining to users' PII (Personally Identifiable Information). There are non-PII type of identity-to-action records that get logged in an online transaction; for example, a DNS server logs requester IP to queried domain name. There is a multitude of logs that get generated when an online service is accessed. In this paper, we limit ourselves to the PII type of identity-to-action based scenarios of privacy violation.

Depending on the complexity in service composition, different types of IAM frameworks come into picture to provide the authentication (identity) and authorization operations. In some types of IAM, authorization is implied upon successful authentication, For example, a login-password based mechanism, which authenticates users and provides access to all operations available in the online service. If the service wants to restrict certain operations to a set of users then the IAM may facilitate that by employing one more layer of authentication. IAMs come with multiple types of authentication mechanisms and can also coordinate with other IAM platforms.

In today's world of agile business process composition (i.e., non-monolithic service composition), the users and resources belong to independently controlled administrative domains. To cater the evolving needs of authentication and authorization in such process composition across organisations, several new frameworks for authentication and authorization are proposed [13]. Frameworks like SSO (Single-Sign-On [17]) allow organisations to hook-in their in-house authentication layer on to an authentication service layer which can be extended to users across the Internet. Such IAM service layers for authentication and authorization are deployed and maintained by entities who may not be directly part of the service and just act as facilitators – getting partial visibility of the user transactions. This brings us to the question of privacy, which usually emanates by the presence of an *observer* who is not part of a transaction but capable of inferring about the identity-to-action records. Most of the transaction facilitating trusted third parties are observers of transactions who may not have access to the details of the transaction but do have a view of the metadata of those transactions, which is sufficient to emanate the scope for *inverse privacy* [9,16,22,23].

In this paper, we shall briefly give preliminaries for privacy through decoupling principle. We will show how some of the authentication mechanisms are inherently unsuitable for this principle. Furthermore, among the mechanisms that are conducive to implement decoupling principle why we chose one over the other to demonstrate our framework. We will also briefly discuss the expressiveness of our framework over the alternatives.

2   Background and Preliminaries

In an online service a user needs to present credentials to the service provider in order to access the service. These credentials could be of various types; ranging from simple alphanumeric strings like login and password to cryptographic tokens. Depending on the environment in which the service is deployed a choice of mechanism for authentication followed by authorization is made. For example, in a service deployed in a small organization with users from the same organization accessing the service internally, the login password mechanism will suffice. A moderately large organization offering services across its departments may use the LDAP type of authentication to classify users into groups/roles so simple authorization policies can be used in service delivery/access. In an environment where several independent organizations collaborate (e.g., a workflow or a supply-chain), the users authentication in foreign domain can be done with the help of SSO framework, which is, in a simplified way, a protocol to extend LDAP beyond the host organization environment. However, all these deployment scenarios are from organizational/enterprise setup, which we can term as trusted environments. But, similar user authentication mechanisms in setups like social media, e-commerce, cloud services, mobile apps do not evoke similar trust due to user privacy violations, either due to perceived or factual experiences. Despite the governing privacy laws on these services from untrusted environments, privacy violations occur. The key reason behind such privacy violations is the ability of the entities involved in these service compositions – they can collect metadata of service interactions and infer user choices for various objectives like targeted advertisement. Let us list out entities involved in a typical online transaction and their relationship with each other (See Fig. 1).

- **Subject (Identity Holder).** A user/principal capable of being identified. A subject gets associated with an identifier that distinguishes her from others.
- **Issuer.** An entity that vouches for identity of a subject in an environment (organization/jurisdiction). Issuer may bind an identity with a permission to create a credential.
- **Verifier.** An entity capable of asserting the validity of a credential, at times with a help from the Issuer who has issued the credential. An entity called Resolver may facilitate the interaction between the Verifier and Issuer.
- **Observer.** An entity that facilitates online transaction by means of supporting the communication, storage, and processing needs of the transaction.

(a) Triangle of Trust

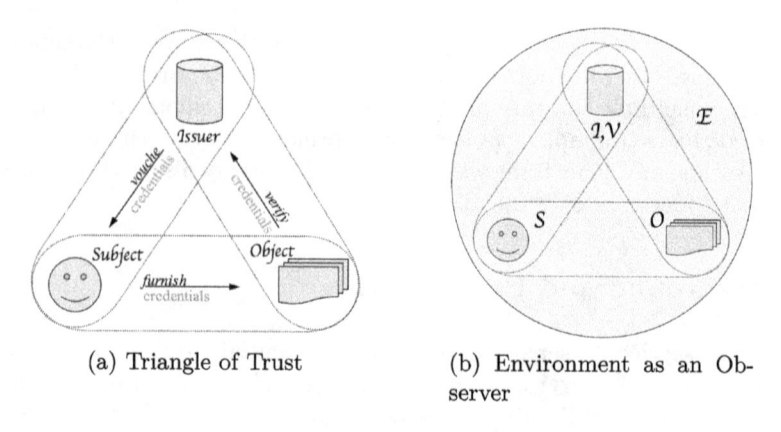

(b) Environment as an Observer

Fig. 1. User Authentication with the help of TTP to access an Object

Avenues of Privacy Violation; Where does it Start? *In an online service, a service requesting subject trusts the service provider and the verifier implicitly. The service provider and the credential verifier are part of the "trust-triangle". However, the "Observer" and "Resolver" are the unavoidable trusted-third-parties to the service, at times unknown to the "Subject" and out of purview of the agreed privacy policy of the triangle. Observer, being the witness to all the interactions among the triangle, has ability to undermine privacy of a "Subject". In the following sections we will continue to discuss the role of an Observer trespassing on the roles of an Issuer and Verifier; demarcating the source of privacy leaks. We need new design strategies that decouple all potential observers from online transactions by limiting the observers to their role of facilitating a transaction without deriving insights from transaction metadata.*

The data from online transactions traverses through three phases: i) at rest (storage), ii) in transit (communication), and iii) in process (compute) [28]. In today's deployment of online services, cloud infrastructure touches upon all these three phases, while end-users being oblivious to such an entity who is not covered by the privacy policy[1] agreement between the end-user and the online service that is deployed on the cloud. The cloud is a service facilitator and has capability to observe the interactions (metadata) between the deployed service and its users. The observer may link metadata of users from one service to another service deployed on the same cloud infrastructure! In [30], to address this linkability problem, the authors present *decoupling principle* which states that: to ensure privacy, information should be divided architecturally and institutionally such that each entity has only the information they need to perform their role. However, in practice, privacy is used as a currency to deliver online services. There are three-fold reasons for user privacy being used as a currency to deliver online services: i) services require security, which is dependent on user authentication, which in turn leaves a trace of user actions on the platform; ii) it is financially

---

[1] Users seldom read/understand privacy policies [36].

lucrative to collect and monetize user profiles despite privacy regulations; and iii) lack of a generic framework that supports the decoupling principle in practice.

In this paper, we will be presenting a practical framework to achieve the decoupling principle. Before doing so, let us briefly revisit the preliminaries on decoupling principle as compiled in [30]. A sensitive user identity known by some entity is depicted by ▲ and a non-sensitive user identity as △, sensitive data as ●, and non-sensitive data as ⊙. A system is *decoupled*, if *only* the user is (▲, ●) and other entities participating in the transaction may have at most one of ▲ or ●, with all other tuple entries as △ or ⊙. Out of these applications, e-commerce payments, privacy pass, and cellular phone location privacy are the ones where users' PII is linked to their actions and have direct privacy implications. And, out of these three applications, only privacy pass is deployed practically (with variants like SSO, OAuth, DID), the other two still continue to operate in classical way. In the following section we discuss how SPKI based IAM is far more expressive, independent, and truly distributed in terms of control and deployment (Fig. 2).

APPLICATION	APPROACH	DECOUPLING			
e-commerce payments	Blind Signatures	Buyer (▲, ●)	Signer (Bank) (▲, ⊙)	Verifier (Bank) (△, ⊙/●)	Seller (△, ●)
Anonymous access (un-authenticated services)	Mix-Net	Sender (▲, ●)	Mix 1 (▲, ⊙) ...	Mix N (△, ⊙)	Receiver (△, ●)
Privacy Pass Authentication	Tokenization		Client (▲, ●)	Issuer (▲, ⊙)	Origin (△, ●)
Oblivious DNS	Mix-Net	Client (▲, ●)	Resolver (▲, ⊙)	Oblivious Resolver (△, ⊙/●)	Origin (△, ●)
Cellular Phone Location Privacy	TTP Gateway (PGPP-GW)		User (▲$_H$, ▲$_N$, ●)	PGPP-GW (▲$_H$, △$_N$, ⊙)	NGC (△$_H$, △$_N$, ●)
Apple Do-Not-Track Browser	Mix-Net	User (▲, ●)	Relay 1 (▲, ⊙)	Relay 2 (△, ⊙/●)	Origin (△, ●)
Private Aggregate Statistics	TTP Gateway		Client (▲, ●)	Aggregator (▲, ⊙)	Collector (△, ⊙)

Fig. 2. Applications using Decoupling Principle

3 Coarse-Grain Privacy Analysis of an Online Transaction

Protected online services require user authentication. Different types of authentication mechanisms are available and service composer may choose one. IAMs provide a suit of such authentication mechanisms.

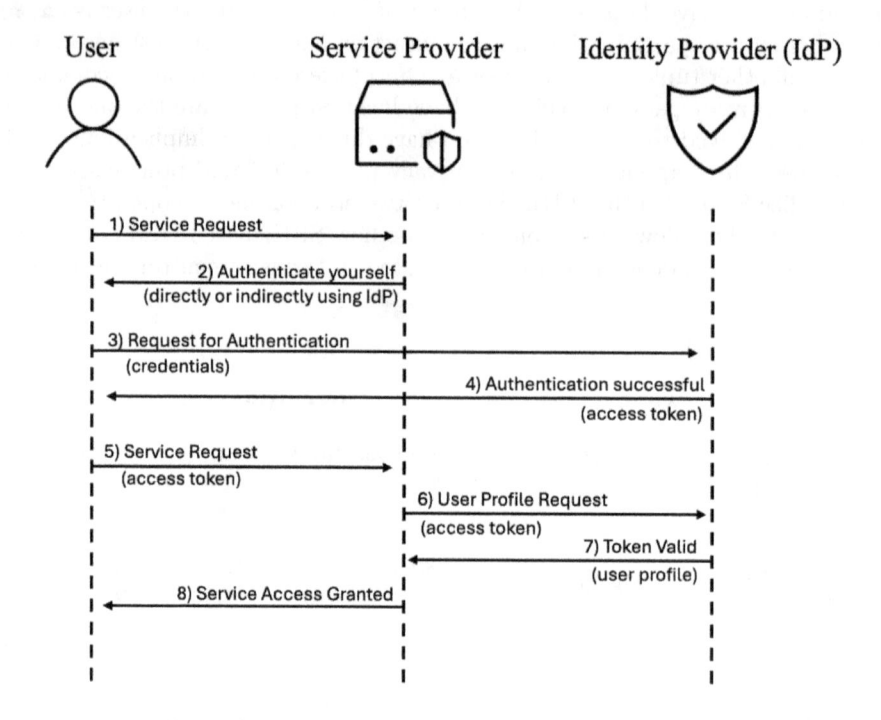

Fig. 3. An abstract view of a typical online transaction

Figure 3 depicts an abstract view of a typical online transaction where a user U requests a service SP upon successful authentication from the identity provider IdP. If a SP composes its services on top of other services, the user's interaction with those other sub-services also occur. Similarly, if the IdP uses MFA (multi-factor authentication) then the user's interaction with those verifiers will also occur. We ignore such recursions for the sake of simplicity.

We can denote the abstract view of an online transaction shown in Fig. 3 by following ways:

– Tightly composed (monolithic service): In this type of services, all the three entities are deployed within a single administrative domain, which is a trusted space. All plausible observations (logs) in this space are collected, processed, and discarded by the administrator of the domain. Since this is a trusted space, users do not have expectation of privacy.

$$[U \cdot SP \cdot IdP] \qquad (1)$$

– Loosely composed (non-monolithic service): In this type of services, the IdP (identity provider) belongs to a different administrative domain than the domain of SP (service provider). For example, the online LaTeX writing service Overleaf allows users to either authenticate directly with it or indirectly via IdP like Google, Facebook, Apple.

$$[U \bullet (SP||IdP)] \equiv [(U \bullet SP)||(U \bullet IdP)] \qquad (2)$$

When the user registers directly with Overleaf and transacts by providing the login-password credentials; the SP assumes the role of an IdP, therefore;

$$[U \bullet (SP||IdP)] \equiv [U \bullet SP] \qquad (3)$$

The privacy exposure for the service depicted in Eq. 2 is denoted as;

$$[U \bullet (SP||IdP)] \implies \{IdP_{u:sp}, SP_{u:idp}\} \qquad (4)$$

where, $u : sp$ indicates the identity-to-action records available to IdP and $u : idp$ indicates the identity-to-action records available to SP. Since SP is the counter-party to the transactions created by the user, the user is aware of her actions are known to the service provider and are typically governed by an agreed privacy policy. However, the identity provider is a facilitator of transactions between the user and the service and still is able to observe/infer meta-data about the transactions between the user and the service. An IdP observing a user across services allows the IdP to build a behavioural profile of the user – potential privacy violation avenue.

To achieve transaction privacy, while designing a service, one should avoid such potential avenues for privacy violation. For example, consider a digital certificate based IdP in the above setup. Digital certificates are self-contained authentication proofs and therefore a user can present it and the service provider can verify it without communicating with the IdP; except for revocation status, which again can be checked without the help of IdP through services like Certificate Transparency [12,18,19].

Of course, there are certain advantages and disadvantages of using a particular type of IdP. Typical IAM (Identity and Access Management – IdP) frameworks support a variety of authentication and authorization methods. In the following we analyze three important classes of IAM frameworks for their inherent characteristics and their suitability for transaction privacy preservation. The first two classes (LDAP and X.509 PKI) are prevalent methods that are widely used in IAM frameworks. The third class is a very flexible and expressive method but not widely used. We find it a natural fit to realize transaction privacy. In the following section we present a detailed primer on it and present our framework based on it.

3.1 Coarse-Grain Analysis of Prominent IAM Methods

A well-known method to authenticate and then authorize users in a large enterprise setup is through LDAP (Active Directory) – the login/password method. In a setup of single administrative domain but physically separated or a setup of multiple administrative domain who explicitly trust each other and act in cohesion, uses Kerberos type of mechanism. As the level of trust comes under stress, the administrative domain controllers may rely on a mechanism like digital certificates issued by a trusted third party called certificate authority. Here, we would like to classify the authentication mechanisms into two categories:

1. *Privately verifiable*: These are the authentication mechanisms where the credentials required for user authentication require a private communication with the credential issuer or a designated verifier who has access to the list of all valid credentials. LDAP and Kerberos methods fall in this category. From the communication perspective, this category can be termed as *online* verification method.
2. *Publicly verifiable*: These are the authentication mechanisms where the credentials do not require involvement of the issuer, the credentials are self-verifiable. Digital certificates fall in this category. From the communication perspective, this category can be termed as *offline* verification method.

Thus, the centralized frameworks can be classified into two categories:

1. *Online* (Credential Issuer + Credential Verifier): in this type of administrative setup the credential verifier operates in sync with the credential issuers. If a previously vouched for user is revoked, the verifier will not grant the requester the permission to access the protected object. User/permission revocation is immediately reflected in the *state* of such setups.
2. *Offline* (Credential Issuer | Credential Verifier): in this type of administrative setup the verifier of the credentials need not contact the credential issuer for its authenticity because the authentication mechanism used has inherent property to verify itself – for example, digital certificates. However, if a previously vouched for user is revoked, the verification process will find it out from the revocation list, which either the issuer maintains or outsources to a separate entity called CRLs (Certificate Revocation Lists). Similar, approach is used while using cryptographic tokens instead of certificates.

Public Key Infrastructures (PKIs) provide a set of procedures to issue, distribute, and revoke digital certificates. X.509 is a type of PKI that is widely deployed. It facilitates authentication of two previously unknown subjects via a trusted third party called certificate authority (CA). Equation 5 and 6 denote the digital certificates issued by a CA to Alice and Bob, respectively.

$$K_{CA}\ Alice \rightarrow K_A\ \text{(digital certificate of Alice)} \qquad (5)$$

$$K_{CA}\ Bob \rightarrow K_B\ \text{(digital certificate of Bob)} \qquad (6)$$

Since both Alice and Bob have obtained their respective certificates from the same CA, they both can verify the authenticity of each other's certificates as both of them are digitally signed by the same public key, which they trust. When the digital certificates are issued by different CAs, the end users can take help of a trusted set of CA certificates to determine the authenticity of a certificate in question by verifying whether that certificate is signed by a CA from the trusted set – *trust anchor*. The proof of such a verification is a chain of certificates that starts with the certificate of the subject to be verified and ends with a certificate in the trust anchor – called certificate chain or *trust chain*. The length of a certificate chain is at least 2 when Alice and Bob have their respective digital certificates issued by two different CAs from a common trust anchor set. The key distinction of this PKI-based verification, in contrast to LDAP-based verification, is that it is done without the participation of certificate (credential) issuer. Therefore, this type of authentication is privacy preserving since the credential issuer cannot track how/when the credential is being used. Figure 4 highlights the position of "verifier" in each type of setup.

(a) Type: LDAP (online verification)

(b) Type: X.509 (offline verification)

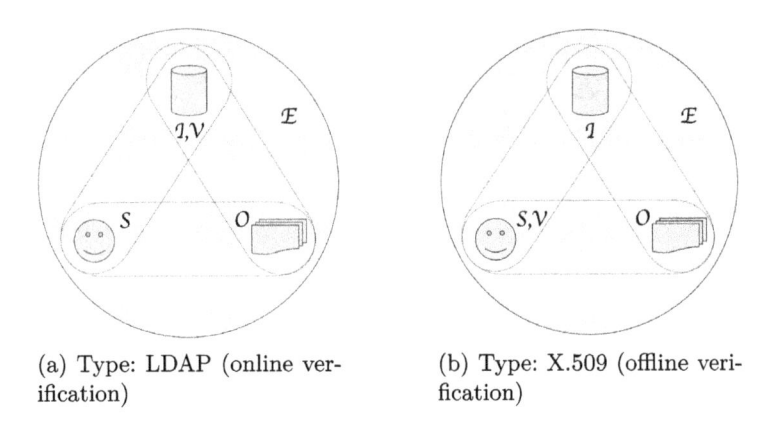

Fig. 4. Online vs. Offline Credential Verification: Impact on User Privacy

Unlike in X.509 PKI, in SPKI type of PKI, each user is allowed to issue certificates. This allows each user to express their relations with other users without relying on the designated "root CAs"; building a web-of-trust among users. Any user willing to access a resource controlled by another user builds a chain of certificates starting with self and ending at the resource controller; and there could be multiple such chains that allow the requester to choose a chain that suits her privacy preferences. SPKI and X.509 both have advantage over LDAP type of online authentication mechanisms due to the self-verifiable credential type – the digital certificate. SPKI has further advantage over X.509

because it allows separate name certificate and authorization certificates. The advantage comes at a cost (see Table 1) of computing chain of certificates as a proof to access a protected resource, which is proportional to the number of certificates involved in building the proof and the distance between the protected resource and its requester on the web-of-trust graph (see Fig. 5).

To summarize:

1. authentication mechanisms that support offline verification of credentials helps in preserving user privacy by depriving the credential issuer from tracking credential usage,
2. PKIs (Public Key Infrastructures [27]) support offline authentication mechanism based on digital certificates,
3. Decentralized PKIs are best suited for designing authentication frameworks. This motivates our choice of SPKI as the underlying framework.

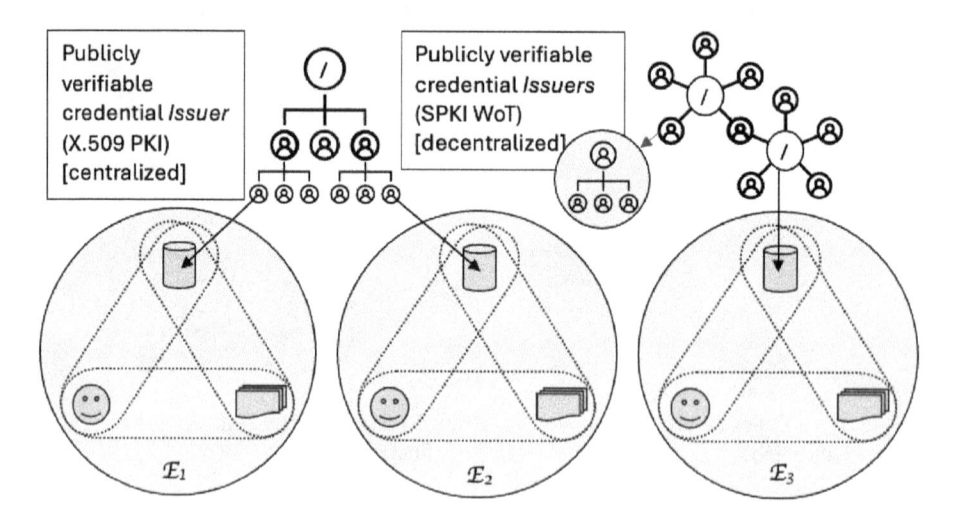

Fig. 5. Decentralization of Trust Using Publicly Verifiable Certificates (PKIs)

3.2 A Broad Comparison of Authentication Frameworks

Table 1. Comparison of Authentication Mechanisms in Different Architectural Setups

Framework Type → ↓ Features	Centralized (e.g., LDAP)	Centralized (e.g., X.509)	Distributed (e.g., SPKI)
Namespace	local: acceptability of identity is within the administrative domain	local: acceptability of identity is within the domains that cross-certify each other	local + extended: each user is a CA and therefore a user can issue identity mappings beyond her administrative domain
Resolution by	the Credential Issuer: the issuer acts as verifier thus tracking the user	the Verifier (i.e., the resource controller): since the digital certificate allows self-verification without a need to contact the Credential Issuer; privacy preserving	the Verifier (the resource controller with the help of intermediate principals who have delegated their resource access permissions further): there could be multiple certificate chains that prove requester's authorization, requester chooses which proof to present; privacy preserving
Delegation	NA (not available)	through sub-CA (restricted)	unrestricted: each user is free to delegate the authorizations it has
Revocation check	not required: online	through revocation registry: CRL database	using namespaces: each access request requires certificate closure computation on namespaces
Trust anchor	the LDAP Server	the set of root CAs	user-defined: web-of-trust allows each node to act as a root CA
Trust chain	of length 1: since the requester and verifier trust a central authority	predictable: proof chain starts with one of the root CAs and ends with the certificate of the requester	user-controlled: proof chain starts with the certificate that is specified by the resource controller as its access policy
Deniability	NA	NA	available
Resolution cost	$O(1)$	$O(n)$: where n is number of certificates in the certificate chain	$O(n^2 l)$: where l is the length of the certificate chain [31]
Decoupling support	NA	limited	inherent

4 Transaction Privacy Using SPKI-Based Decoupling

Transaction privacy can be enhanced by decoupling a transaction's actuating authorization from that transaction's subject's identity. SPKI/SDSI (Simple PKI/Simple Distributed Security Infrastructure) [6,31] has inherent mechanisms to handle identity and authorization assertions independently from each other. It allows a principal to choose an identity (with least privilege) out of many to actuate an authorization, thus minimising the inadvertent exposure of other identity attributes that are not necessary to actuate a particular authorization. For example, if an authorization requires just a proof of being adult, then SPKI allows to hide attributes like gender, actual DoB and the address of the principal. Therefore, SPKI is a natural fit for implementing the decoupling principle. In this section before presenting two examples of decoupling principle's implementation, we present a primer on SPKI.

4.1 SPKI Primer

SPKI was a clean slate approach to rethink PKIs for distributed systems where key management is done in bottom-up approach; unlike the top-down approach in the prevalent X.509 PKI. In SPKI *all keys are equal*, i.e., each key can be a CA and is allowed to issue certificates, thus giving the freedom to manage their respective namespaces without depending on the global CA. Let us provide the terms and their definitions used in SPKI.

Names. In SPKI, subjects (alternatively we use the term principals) are represented by their public keys. A *principal* is either an individual or a process or an active entity. Let $\mathcal{K}$ be the set of all public keys in a deployment environment. An *identifier* is a word over some alphabet Σ. Let $\mathcal{A}$ be the set of all identifiers in the environment. A *term* is a key followed by 0 or more identifiers. Let $\mathcal{T}$ denote the set of all the possible terms.

- Local name: it is a term of the form K, A
  where $K \in \mathcal{K}$ and $A \in \mathcal{A}$ and $|A| = 1$
- Extended name: it is always a term of length greater than 1
  The utility of extended namespace is that a key is not required to be generated before referring to it, unlike in X.509. Access policies can be written for subjects who are not known a priori. An extended name certificate referring to a name owned by another subject remains valid even if the key of the referred subject changes.

Certificates. SPKI isolates name bindings from authorization bindings by providing two types of digital certificates.

- Name certificate: represented as a 4-tuple string $\langle K,A,S,V \rangle$
- Authorization certificate: represented as a 5-tuple string $\langle K,S,D,T,V \rangle$ where,
  - K – public key of the principal who is issuing the certificate
  - A – is an identifier from $\mathcal{A}$

- S – is a subject from T
- T – tag specifying a set of permissions provided to the subject
- D – binary flag; if set, permissions can be delegated
- V – certificate's time validity interval

Re-write Rules (Name Reduction Rules). Having provided the ability to issue two types of certificates to organize keys and their authorizations, it is necessary to evaluate the set of principals and their authorizations at the time of access control decision; because, from the time of issuance to the time of access new definitions/bindings could be added/revoked. Let us provide the re-write examples for name and authorization certificates.

- Name re-write: Given a name $KA_1A_2\ldots A_n$ & certificate $\langle K,A_1,K_1,V\rangle$, the name can be re-written as: $K_1A_2\ldots A_n$. Thus, if:
$C_1 = \langle K,A,K_1A_1A_2\ldots A_n,V_1\rangle$
$C_2 = \langle K_1,A_1,K_2B_1\ldots B_m,V_2\rangle$, then $C_1 \circ C_2$ re-write gives C_3 as below
$C_3 = \langle K,A,K_2B_1\ldots B_mA_2\ldots A_n,V_3\rangle$, where $V_3 = V_1 \cap V_2$
- Auth certificate re-write: If
$C_1 = \langle K,K_1A_1A_2\ldots A_n,D,T_1,V_1\rangle$
$C_2 = \langle K_1,A_1,K_2B_1\ldots B_m,V_2\rangle$, then $C_1 \circ C_2$ re-write gives C_3 as below
$C_3 = \langle K,K_2B_1\ldots B_mA_2\ldots A_n,D,T_1,V_3\rangle$, where $V_3 = V_1 \cap V_2$
Similarly, if;
$C_1 = \langle K_1,K_2,1,T_1,V_1\rangle$
$C_2 = \langle K_2,S_2,0,T_2,V_2\rangle$, then $C_1 \circ C_2$ re-write gives C_3 as below
$C_3 = \langle K_1,S_2,0,T_3,V_3\rangle$, where $T_3 = T_1 \cap T_2$; provided it is well-defined.

Certificate-Chain Discovery (Closure Computation). SPKI/SDSI provides a closure algorithm [31] to derive a certificate-chain as a proof by a principal requesting a resource protected by an ACL, which is typically an authrorization certificate. Given a resource/object with a set of permissions $\mathcal{P}$: let $T_1 \subseteq T$, and let $K_{resource}$ be the owner of that given resource; then, $\langle K_{resource},S,D,T_1,V\rangle$ acts as an ACL (access control policy). Any principal who can provide a proof of membership to S, can access this resource with T_1 permissions, provided that the requesting principal constructs a sequence of name-reducing certificates (certificate-chain), which starts with the ACL certificate and ends with a certificate whose subject is the requester. It is the responsibility of the requester to gather all the intermediate certificates necessary in deducing the transitive sequence (closure) of namespace re-writes.

Authorization Tags. In an authorization certificate, the tag field allows a resource administrator to specify a subset of the resource permissions under a label called tag; the label could be an explicit permission itself or a label defined in the namespace of the resource owner. Tags allow the resource owner to functionally arrange the resource permissions; for example, labels could be created to arrange permission sets as roles (similar to RBAC). It is possible for a principal to access the protected resource by submitting more than one certificate-chains, each chain allowing the principal to operate under a different role as organised by the resource owner through tag labels and delegation. A principal may submit more than one chains to obtain elevated privileges on the resource. This shows the expressive power of SPKI/SDSI framework. Let us consider two authorization certificates $\langle K_{resource}, S, 1, T_1, V \rangle$ and $\langle K_{resource}, S, 0, T_1, V \rangle$ which can be denoted using arrows (see Eq. 7) to indicate flow of authorization (and indicates an extension of name space, in the case of name certificates):

$$\begin{aligned} K_{resource}\ T_1 &\to S\ \square & \text{(delegation bit set to 1)} \\ K_{resource}\ T_2 &\to S\ \blacksquare & \text{(delegation bit set to 0)} \end{aligned} \quad (7)$$

when the delegation bit is set to 1, all principals associated with the name S are authorized by the principal $K_{resource}$ for accessing the resource with the scope specified in T_1 and delegate the inherited authority further; whereas T_2 cannot be delegated but only used.

Summary of SPKI/SDSI Features that Complement Decoupling

- Local name space certificate allows a principal to organize her identities under natural labels, which help in writing and managing understandable access control policies over names rather than actual identities thus isolating revocation of subjects from access policy specification.
- Extended name space certificate allows a principal to point to other principals or their name spaces thus not only isolating revocation of subjects from access policy specifications but also providing a decentralization where principals manage their respective name spaces independently. In non-certificate types of identity assertions as in LDAP, the issuer needs to be contacted (*online*) for each authentication. Note that digital certificates are publicly verifiable *offline* assertions, thus eliminating TTP's role in authentication.
- Authorization certificate with delegation bit enabled has a special significance: the resource owner who issues authorization certificate (source of authority) allows its subjects to further delegate the tagged permissions. This has two utilities to the subjects of the certificate: i) straight forward delegation of inherited authority to other subjects, ii) delegate the inherited authority to own keys, which can be discarded after each access. Identity of such keys is indistinguishable from the keys of other subjects.
- Authorization tags allow the resource owner (the access policy specification entity) to structure the permissions in subsets (as distinct tags) in such a way that the resource requester gets freedom to choose how to identify itself by choosing a particular certificate-chain, thus giving the requester a choice.

4.2 Scenario 1: Eduroam WiFi Access

eduroam[2] provides a simple, easy, secure connectivity from thousands of hotspots across more than 100 countries and major universities have it deployed across

---

[2] https://eduroam.org/how/.

their campuses. A principal affiliated to one of the member institutes will get a seamless wifi access in any other partner institute. In current practice, this service employs a mix of LDAP/RADIUS and X.509 authentication. A guest user's credentials are sent to guest's organization for verification before granting access. In our hypothetical scenario, unlike the current practice, let us assume a SPKI based authentication-cum-authorization framework with following ACL for access is deployed on eduroam access points.

$$\begin{aligned}
K_{eduroam}\ \text{WIFI} &\rightarrow K_{eduroam}\ users\ \square \\
K_{eduroam}\ users &\rightarrow K_{eduroam}\ partner\ users \\
K_{eduroam}\ partner &\rightarrow K_{IITB}\ users \\
K_{eduroam}\ partner &\rightarrow K_{IITD}\ users
\end{aligned} \quad (8)$$

The administrators of partner institutes issue the following certificates.

$$\begin{aligned}
K_{IITB}\ users &\rightarrow K_{IITB}\ current\_users \\
K_{IITB}\ current\_users &\rightarrow K_A \quad\text{(key of Alice)} \\
K_{IITD}\ users &\rightarrow K_{IITD}\ current\_users \\
K_{IITD}\ current\_users &\rightarrow K_B \quad\text{(key of Bob)}
\end{aligned} \quad (9)$$

Alice issues the following as she is a recipient of *wifi* permission.

$$\begin{aligned}
K_A\ \text{WIFI} &\rightarrow K_A\ devices\ \blacksquare \\
K_A\ devices &\rightarrow K_A\ Laptop \\
K_A\ devices &\rightarrow K_A\ Mobile \\
K_A\ Laptop &\rightarrow \{K_{L1}, K_{L2}, K_{L3}, ...\}\ \text{(set of keys)} \\
K_A\ Mobile &\rightarrow K_M
\end{aligned} \quad (10)$$

From Eq. 8, 9 and 10, Alice's Laptop presents the following chain to eduroam.

$$\begin{aligned}
K_{eduroam}\ \text{WIFI} &\rightarrow K_{eduroam}\ users\ \square \\
K_{eduroam}\ users &\rightarrow K_{eduroam}\ partner\ users \\
K_{eduroam}\ partner &\rightarrow K_{IITB} \\
K_{IITB}\ users &\rightarrow K_{IITB}\ current\_users \\
K_{IITB}\ current\_users &\rightarrow K_A \\
K_A\ \text{WIFI} &\rightarrow K_A\ devices\ \blacksquare \\
K_A\ devices &\rightarrow K_A\ Laptop \\
K_A\ Laptop &\rightarrow K_{L1}
\end{aligned} \quad (11)$$

In the above certificate-chain, Alice may choose to use K_{L2}, K_{L3}, K_{Ln} for successive accesses so that identity-based user-profiling gets difficult.

Privacy Analysis. SPKI based implementation clearly reduces the need for RADIUS communication between the guest & the host institutes' LDAP servers.

In current practice of LDAP/RADIUS based eduroam deployment, the LDAP server of a roaming user will know where the user is visiting because the host RADIUS server will reach out to guest's LDAP for authentication. Now, let us explore the avenues to further minimize the observations or inferences from access requests. Let us assume that Bob also has a set of certificates similar to Alice's as shown in Eq. 10. Now consider the following certificate in which Alice adds Bob's devices to her list (maybe they both know each other and trust each other). Note that Alice and Bob belong to different institutes.

$$K_A \text{ devices } \rightarrow K_B \text{ devices} \tag{12}$$

Because of the certificate shown in Eq. 12, Bob gets an option to build a certificate-chain involving wifi authority delegation given to Alice's institute. In other words, Alice is acting as a proxy for Bob's devices and the access point cannot distinguish the requesting device's owner. We can extend this identity masking approach to certificates at institute level as shown below:

$$\begin{aligned} K_{IITB} \text{ users } &\rightarrow K_{IITD} \text{ users} \\ K_{IITD} \text{ users } &\rightarrow K_{IITB} \text{ users} \end{aligned} \tag{13}$$

These two certificates shown in Eq. 13 allow the users from the institute IITB to present themselves as users of institute IITD and vice versa; providing organisational level proxy mechanism.

Let us consider another scenario where transactions have to compulsorily pass through a trusted third party: e-commerce transactions where banks as a TTP facilitate payment.

4.3 Scenario 2: E-Commerce Transactions

In a typical e-commerce transaction a buyer makes the payment through a bank. The role of the bank is to facilitate the payment from a buyer to the seller, however the bank observes the transaction metadata and potentially knows the purchase history of the buyer, which is unnecessary and has a potential (inverse privacy) to violate the buyer's privacy. The challenge in enforcing decoupling principle in this scenario is that the bank/s is/are strongly coupled on either side of the transaction due to a legal requirement called KYC. Therefore, one must introduce a new entity (TTP-Escrow or TTPE) where decoupling can be enforced. K_{TTPE} is also a type of bank which is tightly coupled with the seller K_{seller}, whereas K_{bank} is tightly coupled with the buyer K_{buyer}. Given these constraints, let us work out a typical e-commerce transaction using our SPKI/SDSI approach.

Let us assume that the seller is an online movie/content distributor. The seller accepts payments via TTPE and upon receiving a payment proof (i.e., a valid certificate-chain), releases the movie. The SPKI ACL for releasing a movie MOVIE1 to a buyer is:

$$K_{seller} \text{ MOVIE1 } \rightarrow K_{TTPE} \text{ m1 } \blacksquare \tag{14}$$

Equation 14 states that any principal who can prove membership to the name space K_{TTPE} m1 will get access to the resource MOVIE1. Alice, a potential buyer, interested in MOVIE1, initiates a payment with her bank K_{bank} for a specified price of the movie. The bank debits the specified amount from Alice's account and credits it to the account of K_{TTPE}. If the payment from K_{bank} to K_{TTPE} goes through, the bank issues the following certificate to the buyer:

$$K_{bank} \ payment\_id \rightarrow K_A \ payment\_id \qquad (15)$$

Equation 15 acts as a payment proof and the bank is decoupled from the action intended by this payment. The escrow entity K_{TTPE} has the knowledge of $payment\_id$ but not its source nor for the item for which it is been paid. K_A approaches K_{TTPE} with proof of payment as shown in Eq. 15 and makes a signed request to K_{TTPE} to mark the payment (identified by $payment\_id$) against the service MOVIE1. Upon verifying the validity of the request from K_A, the escrow entity issues the following:

$$K_{TTPE} \ m1 \rightarrow K_A \ payment\_id \qquad (16)$$

By issuing the certificate in Eq. 16, the escrow entity has moved the payment to its final destination K_{seller}. Alice issues a certificate to one of her keys K_{A1}

$$K_A \ payment\_id \rightarrow K_{A1} \qquad (17)$$

To watch the movie MOVIE1, Alice compiles the following certificate-chain built using Eq. 14, 16 and 17

$$\begin{aligned} K_{seller} \ \text{MOVIE1} &\rightarrow K_{TTPE} \ m1 \ \blacksquare \\ K_{TTPE} \ m1 &\rightarrow K_A \ payment\_id \\ K_A \ payment\_id &\rightarrow K_{A1} \end{aligned} \qquad (18)$$

For successive access requests, Alice may opt to use different keys.

Privacy Analysis. Through the above example, we have seen how a user's identity can be decoupled from her actions from her bank's observations. The bank's role is limited to just make payment without knowing the reason. In this setup the bank is tightly coupled with the buyer and the escrow entity is tightly coupled with the seller and the communication between the bank and the escrow (Eq. 15) is through a quasi-identifier, which is unlinkable to the seller unless the escrow entity collaborates with the bank.

5 Discussion and Related Work

In the previous section we have seen decoupling mechanisms for two of the most commonly occurring online transactions: i) identity-based, and ii) capability-based. In the eduroam scenario we modified the identity-based resource access, which is typically an atomic authentication-cum-authorization method, into authorization due to an offline authentication proof with least-privilege. In the e-commerce scenario we modified the capability-based resource access by stripping the capability proof (again offline) from PII-linkable identifiers like email/phone to quasi-identifiers like payment-id. SPKI-based mechanism has two distinct features that helps in decoupling: i) separate name and authorization certificates, and ii) digital certificates are offline verifiable, which minimises the communication with their issuers. A mechanism based on X.509 digital certificates with a limited flexibility because: i) a single certificate asserts about identity and authorization (though a limited variety of authorization types are supported), and ii) not all principals can issue certificates. However, in [24] the authors have shown how SPKI name & authorization assertions can be incorporated into X.509 v3 type of certificates; thus addressing the deployment concerns of SPKI vis a vis X.509 PKI.

The concerns of linkability of identity to its actions over the Internet was highlighted long ago by David Chaum in his work [4] on blind signatures for digital payments. It (anonymous digital payments) did not realize in practice because of double-spending problem. Like in Scenario 2 of this paper, David Chaum's objective was to constrain the bank to the role of making payments and not collecting the transaction metadata. In our example, we have allowed linkability using quasi-identifier for practical reasons, whereas a completely decoupled payment mechanism will lead to a bitcoin type of payment, which is legally not acceptable. It would be worth investigating to replace service payment by a CBDC (which claims to imitate cash-like untraceability property) in the e-commerce scenario. However, CBDC are yet to address cross-border payments and not widely used.

A family of privacy-preserving authentication and authorization mechanisms based on blockchain framework exist and are typically known as DID (Decentralized ID) frameworks [13–15,29,32] also deal with concept of decoupling by defining the authentication and authorization assertions on a blockchain and providing appropriate assertions for a transaction processing – giving the end user control on how to manage her identity. These mechanisms are characterised by their underlying blockchain framework's properties [3,20]. One of the practical drawbacks of public blockchain based DID mechanism would be the size of ledger the verifiers have to hold while performing the lookups. Also the revoked assertions stay on the ledger giving a different type of metadata, which is not the case with our SPKI based approach, the certificates are collected on need basis and leaves no public trail.

To implement the decoupling principle in online transactions one would require a clear analysis of the architectural and semantic flow of the transaction and apply decoupling principle wherever transaction handover happens between the entities handling the transaction. As shown in e-commerce scenario, there could be hard coupling between entities as a legal requirement; one would require to redesign the transaction flow. Several examples of implementation of decoupling principle exist in practice. For example, mix-nets [5] and Tor [8] provide identity decoupling for online communication, usually these are one-way communications. For two-way anonymous communication decoupling mechanisms like Privacy Pass [7] could be employed. Token-based approaches like Single-Sign-On [17] could be useful if the observability of the platform can be decoupled. Tokens are useful quasi-identifiers. Passkey [2] are an effort to login-password authentication method (online) to a public key based authentication mechanism (offline). However, it is only for authentication purpose. In [25, 26], the authors have shown how SPKI can be realised as an over-arching framework to encapsulate various disparate mechanisms under the `tag` construct provided in SPKI.

6 Conclusion

Privacy violations remain a significant and lucrative issue. Safeguarding privacy has become increasingly difficult, especially with the growing complexity of modern service compositions. Today, numerous external entities play a role in delivering services, and the trend of leveraging meta-services—such as cloud infrastructure, payment systems, SSO authentication, DNS, and ISPs—has exacerbated the privacy challenge. These external service providers become observers of user transactions, allowing them to harvest metadata that is often sufficient to profile users. There is an urgent need for *privacy-by-design* mechanisms to prevent user profiling. One effective approach is decoupling users' identities from their actions, which reduces the ability to link an identity to specific actions and thereby limits privacy violations. This paper addresses this objective by leveraging SPKI (Simple Public Key Infrastructure), a distributed PKI. We demonstrate, through two working examples, how decoupling identity from authorization can be achieved in online transactions under observation. Our approach can be seamlessly integrated into existing applications as a trusted third-party interface, providing a drop-in solution to separate a user's identity from their actions.

Acknowledgments. This work is carried out as a part of the project RD/0120-NCSC001-001 "AI Powered Security Operation Product Suite for National Critical Information Infrastructure", funded by the NSCS, Government of India.

References

1. Abdelaziz, Y., Napoli, D., Chiasson, S.: End-users and service providers: Trust and distributed responsibility for account security. In: 2019 17th International Conference on Privacy, Security and Trust (PST), pp. 1–6. IEEE Computer Society (2019). https://doi.org/10.1109/PST47121.2019.8949041
2. Alliance, F.: Passkeys (2022). https://fidoalliance.org/passkeys/
3. Brunner, C., Gallersdörfer, U., Knirsch, F., Engel, D., Matthes, F.: Did and VC: untangling decentralized identifiers and verifiable credentials for the web of trust. In: Proceedings of the 3rd International Conference on Blockchain Technology and Applications, pp. 61–66. ACM (2021). https://doi.org/10.1145/3446983.3446992
4. Chaum, D.: Blind signatures for untraceable payments. In: Chaum, D., Rivest, R.L., Sherman, A.T. (eds.) Advances in Cryptology, pp. 199–203. Springer, Boston, MA (1983). https://doi.org/10.1007/978-1-4757-0602-4_18

5. Chaum, D.: Untraceable electronic mail, return addresses and digital pseudonyms. In: Gritzalis, D.A. (ed.) Secure Electronic Voting. AIS, vol. 7, pp. 211–219. Springer, Boston (2003). https://doi.org/10.1007/978-1-4615-0239-5_14
6. Clarke, D.E.: SPKI/SDSI HTTP server/certificate chain discovery in SPKI/SDSI. Ph.D. thesis, Massachusetts Institute of Technology (2001)
7. Davidson, A., Goldberg, I., Sullivan, N., Tankersley, G., Valsorda, F.: Privacy pass: bypassing internet challenges anonymously. Proc. Priv. Enhancing Technol. **2018**(3), 164–180 (2018). https://doi.org/10.1515/POPETS-2018-0026
8. Dingledine, R., Mathewson, N., Syverson, P.: Tor: the second-generation onion router. In: 13th USENIX Security Symposium. USENIX Association (2004)
9. Dwork, C.: A firm foundation for private data analysis. Commun. ACM **54**(1), 86–95 (2011). https://doi.org/10.1145/1866739.1866758
10. Ellison, C.: Establishing identity without certification authorities. In: 6th USENIX Security Symposium, p. 7. USENIX Association (1996)
11. Ellison, C.: SPKI Requirements. RFC 2692 (1999). https://www.rfc-editor.org/info/rfc2692
12. Eskandarian, S., Messeri, E., Bonneau, J., Boneh, D.: Certificate Transparency with Privacy. CoRR abs/1703.02209 (2017)
13. Ferdous, M.S., Chowdhury, F., Alassafi, M.O.: In search of self-sovereign identity leveraging blockchain technology. IEEE Access **7**, 103059–103079 (2019). https://doi.org/10.1109/ACCESS.2019.2931173
14. Foundation, H.: Hyperledger indy (2024). https://www.hyperledger.org/projects/hyperledger-indy
15. Foundation, T.S.: Sovrin basics (2024). https://sovrin.org/library/
16. Gurevich, Y., Hudis, E., Wing, J.M.: Inverse privacy. Commun. ACM **59**(7), 38–42 (2016). https://doi.org/10.1145/2838730
17. Hardt, D.: The OAuth 2.0 Authorization Framework. RFC 6749 (2012). https://doi.org/10.17487/RFC6749
18. Kales, D., Omolola, O., Ramacher, S.: Revisiting user privacy for certificate transparency. In: 2019 IEEE European Symposium on Security and Privacy (EuroS&P), pp. 432–447 (2019). https://doi.org/10.1109/EuroSP.2019.00039
19. Khan, S., et al.: Accountable and transparent TLS certificate management: an alternate public-key infrastructure with verifiable trusted parties. Sec. Comm. Netw. (2018)
20. Korir, M., Parkin, S., Dunphy, P.: An empirical study of a decentralized identity wallet: usability, security, and perspectives on user control. In: Eighteenth Symposium on Usable Privacy and Security (SOUPS 2022), pp. 195–211. USENIX Association (2022)
21. Mayrhofer, A., Klesev, D., Sabadello, M.: The Decentralized Identifier (DID) in the DNS. Internet-Draft draft-mayrhofer-did-dns-05, Internet Engineering Task Force (2021). https://datatracker.ietf.org/doc/draft-mayrhofer-did-dns/05/, work in Progress
22. Narayanan, A., Shmatikov, V.: Myths and fallacies of "personally identifiable information". Commun. ACM **53**(6), 24–26 (2010). https://doi.org/10.1145/1743546.1743558
23. Narayanan, A., Toubiana, V., Barocas, S., Nissenbaum, H., Boneh, D.: A critical look at decentralized personal data architectures. CoRR abs/1202.4503 (2012)
24. Patil, V., Gasti, P., Mancini, L., Chiola, G.: Resource management with X.509 inter-domain authorization certificates (InterAC). In: Martinelli, F., Preneel, B. (eds.) EuroPKI 2009. LNCS, vol. 6391, pp. 34–50. Springer, Heidelberg (2010). https://doi.org/10.1007/978-3-642-16441-5_3

25. Patil, V., Shyamasundar, R.K.: Trust management for e-transactions. Sadhana **30**(2), 141–158 (2005). https://doi.org/10.1007/BF02706242
26. Patil, V., Shyamasundar, R.: ROADS: role-based authorization and delegation system. In: International Conference on Computational & Experimental Engineering and Sciences (2003)
27. Patil, V., Shyamasundar, R.: Evolving role of PKI in facilitating trust. In: 2022 IEEE International Conference on Public Key Infrastructure and its Applications (PKIA), pp. 1–7. IEEE, USA (2022). https://doi.org/10.1109/PKIA56009.2022.9952249
28. Raghavan, B., Schneier, B.: A bold new plan for preserving online privacy and security: Decoupling our identities from our data and actions could safeguard our secrets in the cloud. IEEE Spectr. **60**(12), 22–29 (2023)
29. Reed, D., Law, J., Hardman, D.: The technical foundations of Sovrin. The Technical Foundations of Sovrin (2016)
30. Schmitt, P., Iyengar, J., Wood, C., Raghavan, B.: The decoupling principle: a practical privacy framework. HotNets, Association for Computing Machinery (2022)
31. Schwoon, S., Wang, H., Jha, S., Reps, T.: Distributed certificate-chain discovery in SPKI/SDSI. Technical report. University of Wisconsin-Madison Department of Computer Sciences (2005)
32. Sporny, M., Longley, D., Sabadello, M., Reed, D., Steele, O., Allen, C.: Decentralized Identifiers (DIDs) v1.0 (2022). https://www.w3.org/TR/did-core/
33. Wouters, P.: DNS-Based Authentication of Named Entities (DANE) Bindings for OpenPGP. RFC 7929 (2016). https://doi.org/10.17487/RFC7929
34. Ylonen, T., Thomas, B., Lampson, B., Ellison, C., Rivest, R.L., Frantz, W.S.: SPKI Certificate Theory. RFC 2693 (1999)
35. Zhang, L., et al.: Identity confusion in WebView-based mobile app-in-app ecosystems. In: 31st USENIX Security Symposium, pp. 1597–1613. USENIX Association (2022)
36. Zhou, L., et al.: Policycomp: counterpart comparison of privacy policies uncovers overbroad personal data collection practices. In: Proceedings of the 32nd USENIX Conference on Security Symposium, SEC 2023. USENIX Association, USA (2023)

AI Security

Protecting Ownership of Trained DNN Models with Zero-Knowledge Proofs

Shungo Sato[✉] and Hidema Tanaka

National Defense Academy of Japan, Yokosuka, Japan
{em62041,hidema}@nda.ac.jp

Abstract. Neural Networks are used in various fields such as research and development. Because it takes much time and cost to make high-performance models, we tune a trained model in order to make the model for our purpose more efficiently. Hence, it is important to share high-performance trained models for the development of AI technologies. In such cases, it is important to protect its ownership. In this paper, we propose a method of protecting ownership of trained DNN models by using zero-knowledge proofs. Our scope is protecting white box models whose algorithms and parameters are completely open. Our proposal does not impair the performance of the models because no additional training and parameters are required. By our proposal, adversaries who know our proposal can not forge ownership and the owners can claim ownership multiple times. In the security analysis, we show the successful probability that adversaries can spoof as the owners for two attack scenarios. We also show the false positive rate for the unrelated model when the owners verify ownership of the unrelated model.

Keywords: AI · Machine Learning · DNN · ownership · ZKP · STARK

1 Introduction

Since AI technologies have rapidly spread and developed in recent years, Machine Learning including Neural Networks is used in various fields and recognized as general technologies. In particular, AlexNet [1] and so on have high-performance in various fields. The frameworks such as TensorFlow [2] make it easier for us to use Machine Learning for research and development. However, it needs an enormous amount of time and training data to make high-performance models. We tune a trained model that has high-performance for our purpose in order to efficiently use Machin Learning. Hence, sharing the high-performance models is important for the development of Machine Learning. We should respect that the high-performance models are important property for the owners. There are two methods to protect the models. The first method is providing the models as an online service so that the details of the models are not open. The second method is making a contract or authentication about the use of the models in order not to let the users abuse the models beyond the owners' permission. In the second method, the users know the details of the owners' models because the owners distribute or sell the model to the users. In this case, the adversaries can sell the forged model to the others without the owners' permission.

1.1 Protecting Black Box Models

As the first method, there is MLaaS (Machine Learning as a Service) that provides the models as cloud-based services without opening the details of the models. The clients can not ensure that the MLaaS has the expected performance because they can not access the details. This problem can be solved by using zero-knowledge proofs [3,4]. In MLaaS, preserving the client's sensitive information is another problem. This problem can be solved by using Privacy-Preserving Machine Learning [5,6]. We show the intuitive description of the first method in Fig. 1. The research of combining black box models with preserving clients' sensitive data is out of our scope.

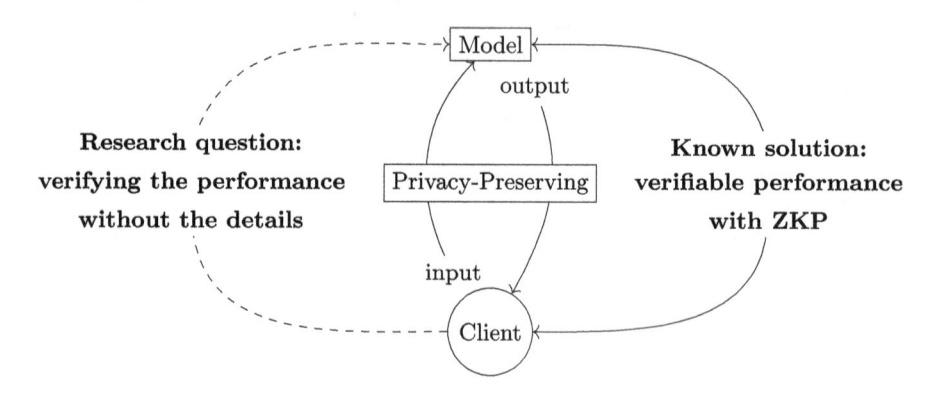

Fig. 1. Privacy-Preserving Verifiable Machine Learning

1.2 Protecting White Box Models

As the second method, digital watermark algorithms [7–9] are the known solutions to detect abusing the models by users. This framework can be applied to the models whose details are open. We can identify ownership of the models by embedding a digital watermark into the models. We show the intuitive description of the second method in Fig. 2. This framework has the following two problems. The first problem is that adversaries who know this algorithm are able to steal ownership. The second problem is that the owners are able to claim ownership only once. The reasons why these problems are considered are mentioned in Sect. 2.3. The research [10] of a robust watermark focusing on API, and other related research on a model whose parameters are not open to users are out of our scope. Our scope is the case of white box models such as the owners distributing or selling the models to others. The digital signature is also a known solution for protecting ownership of white box models. The reason why we do not use a digital signature is shown in Sect. 5.

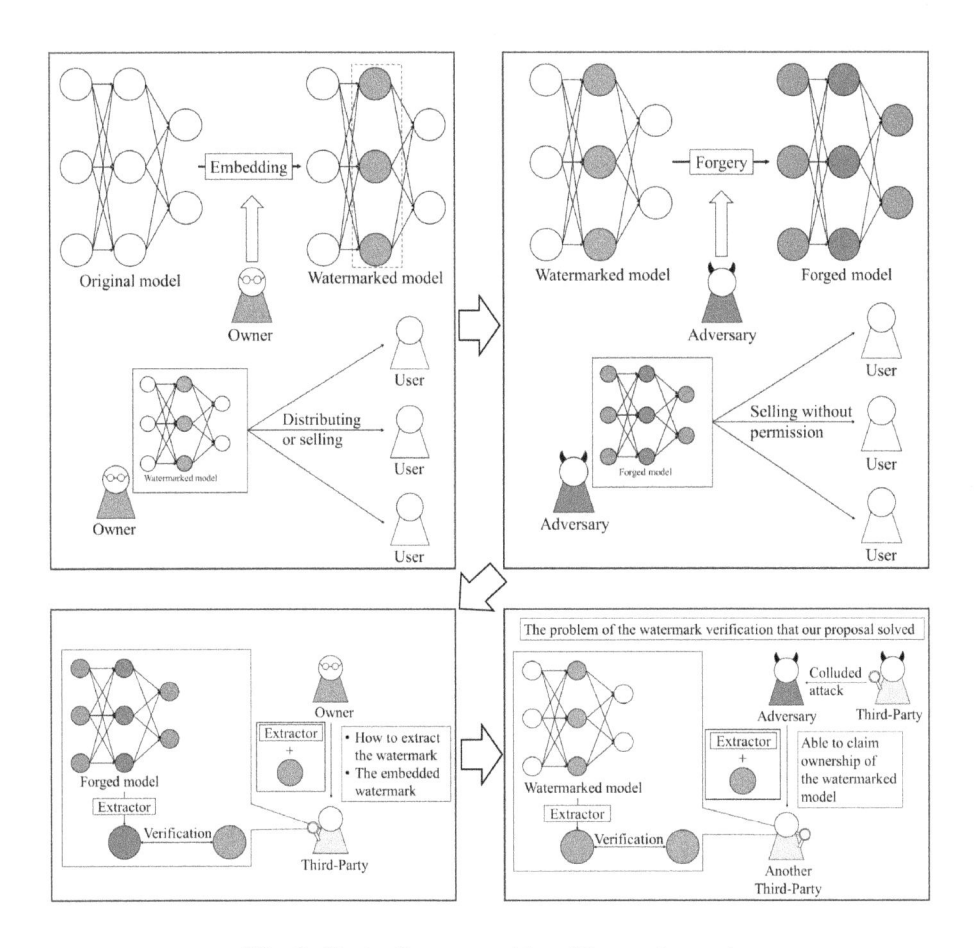

Fig. 2. Protecting ownership with a watermark

1.3 Our Contribution

In this paper, we propose a method to protect ownership of the trained DNN (Deep Neural Network) models by using zero-knowledge proofs in the case that the details of the models are open. Zero-knowledge proof is a method by which the prover can prove to the verifier that the statement is true without opening any information except the fact that the statement is true. Our proposal can solve the problems of a digital watermark for DNNs. By applying our proposal, adversaries can not spoof as owners, and owners can claim ownership multiple times. We show the detailed security analysis of our proposal. In this analysis, we show the successful probability that adversaries can spoof as the owners for two attack scenarios. We also show the threshold in order to ensure the computational security and the relation between how many times the owners can claim ownership and the computational security. Our proposal does not impair the performance of the models at all, unlike a digital watermark for DNNs. Additionally, by applying our proposal, we can identify whether an AI application is made based on the model that we provide. This means that our proposal can contribute to the topic of traceability in AI ethics [11].

2 Related Work

Many digital watermark algorithms for DNN such as [7–9] have been proposed. Some of them extract the watermark from the parameters of the models using the secret information. Others extract the output as the watermark using the secret input. We show one of the examples of digital watermark algorithms for DNN in order to show what the problems are.

2.1 Digital Watermarking for Deep Neural Networks [7]

Nagai et al. [7] propose embedding a digital watermark into DNNs in order to identify ownership of DNNs. They formulate embedding a digital watermark for DNNs based on its parameters. They train DNNs using a regularizer for its cost function after selecting the secret information which is an embedding binary vector and extracting parameters. We show the outline of their proposed algorithm in the following sections.

2.2 Embedding and Extracting a Digital Watermark

Let (S, S), D, and L be the size of the convolution filter, the depth of input to the convolutional layer, and the number of filters in the convolutional layer respectively. The parameters of this convolutional layer are characterized by $\boldsymbol{W} \in \mathbb{R}^{S \times S \times D \times L}$. The parameter $b \in \{0,1\}^T$ denotes a T [bit] embedding vector into $\boldsymbol{W}$. The order of filters does not affect the output of the network if the parameters of the subsequent layers are appropriately reordered. Therefore, we calculate the mean of $\boldsymbol{W}$ over L filters as

$$\overline{\boldsymbol{W}}_{ijk} = \frac{1}{L} \sum_l W_{ijkl}. \tag{1}$$

The value $w \in \mathbb{R}^M$ ($M = S \times S \times D$) denotes a vector of flattened $\overline{\boldsymbol{W}}_{ijk}$. Our objective is to embed a vector b into w.

The cost function $E(w)$ with regularizer is defined as

$$E(w) = E_0(w) + \lambda E_R(w), \tag{2}$$

where $E_0(\cdot)$ denotes an original cost function, $E_R(\cdot)$ denotes an embedding function which is defined in Eq. (5), and λ denotes an adjustable parameter.

We select the secret information $X \in \mathbb{R}^{T \times M}$ to extract a digital watermark from w. We calculate as the following in order to extract $b = (b_0, \ldots, b_j, \ldots, b_{T-1})$.

$$b_j = s(\sum_i X_{ji} w_i), \tag{3}$$

where

$$s(x) = \begin{cases} 1 & x \geq 0 \\ 0 & \text{else} \end{cases}. \tag{4}$$

In order to execute the above procedure, we define $E_R(w)$ as the following:

$$E_R(w) = -\sum_{j=1}^{T} (b_j \log(y_j) + (1 - b_j) \log(1 - y_j)), \tag{5}$$

where

$$y_j = \sigma(\sum_i X_{ji} w_i), \quad \sigma(x) = \frac{1}{1 + \exp(-x)}. \tag{6}$$

2.3 The Problems of Previous Work

The owners need to open b and X for ownership authentication. This results in the owners being able to claim ownership only once. In another case, if adversaries know that this watermark algorithm is adopted for the target DNN model, adversaries will be able to embed another chosen b' and X' into the DNN. As a result, they will be able to claim ownership by their digital watermark regardless of whether the owners open the secret information.

Generally speaking of digital watermark algorithms, the owners can check whether the suspicious models are based on the owners' model by themself. However, in the case that the owners want to convince the verifier such as a judge that the suspicious models are based on the owners' model, the owners need to send the secret information to the verifier. As a result, the secret information becomes leaked to the verifier. This means that the verifier has to be trusted as a TTP (Trusted Third Party). The description of this problem is shown in Fig. 2.

Hence, our purpose in this paper is to solve the following two problems.

Problem 1. Adversaries who know this algorithm are able to steal ownership.
Problem 2. The owners are able to claim ownership only once.

3 Our Proposal

We focus on the parameter $\boldsymbol{W}$ as the characteristic parameter of DNN in the same way as [7]. The watermark algorithms cause performance degradation in some cases. In fact, [7] shows, based on computer simulations, how to set parameters such that performance degradation does not occur. However, our method does not impair the performance of the model. We construct the statement from the parameter $\boldsymbol{W}$ and improve to claim ownership more than once without opening secret information by applying zero-knowledge proofs. The purpose of the statement is that the prover convinces the verifier that the prover is the owner who knows the secret information of the model. Table 1 shows the symbols.

Table 1. Notation

Symbol	Detail
$\mathbb{R}$	Set of real numbers
$\mathbb{F}$	Finite field
$\mathbb{F}^*$	$\mathbb{F}\setminus\{0\}$
$\mathbb{K}$	Finite field extension of $\mathbb{F}$
G	Cyclic subgroup of $\mathbb{F}^*$
H	Coset of a cyclic subgroup of $\mathbb{F}^*$
$|A|$	Size of a set A
$\deg\{f(x)\}$	Degree of a polynomial $f(x)$
$MTR(\cdot)$	Root of Merkle Tree
$MTP(\cdot)$	Set of nodes to calculate $MTR(\cdot)$

3.1 Treatment of the Parameter w

In the same way as [7], w is a vector of flattened $\overline{\boldsymbol{W}}_{ijk}$. We select M' significant parameters of w based on the weight pruning [12–14]. For example, we set the threshold T in order to select the top 10% parameters based on the magnitude of the parameters. Let $\{w_{i_1}, \ldots, w_{i_{M'}}\}$ be the selected parameters. We arbitrarily set ε_1 and $\varepsilon_2 \in \mathbb{F}$ ($\varepsilon_1 \neq \varepsilon_2$) to define w'_m as

$$w'_m = \begin{cases} \varepsilon_1 & w_{i_m} \geq 0 \\ \varepsilon_2 & \text{else} \end{cases} \quad (m = 1, \ldots, M'). \tag{7}$$

This definition results in the owners becoming able to claim ownership of tuned models which are slightly changed values of w such as Fine-tuning.

3.2 Setup Procedure

We propose a construction of a statement and a method of proof in order to claim ownership of DNNs by applying STARK (Scalable Transparent ARgument of Knowledge) [15–17]. STARK has the following characteristics.

Scalability. The prover runs in time $O(n \log n)$ and the verifier runs in time $O(\log n)$, where n is the computation size of the statement.
Transparency. It does not need any trusted setup.
Argument. It assumes that the prover has at most polynomial computational resources.
Of Knowledge. It can prove the prover owns a witness for the statement, not only its existence.

Because of these characteristics, our proposal does not need a verifier assumed as a TTP.

The symbol G denotes the cyclic subgroup of $\mathbb{F}^*$ and $|G| = n + 1$. The elements of G are denoted by $x_i \in G$ for $i \in \{0, \ldots, n\}$. We determine $f_1(x), f_2(x), \ldots, f_{M'}(x)$ which are the polynomials of degrees at most n with coefficients over $\mathbb{F}$. Combining $f_1(x), f_2(x), \ldots, f_{M'}(x)$ with w', we define $b = \{b_i\}_{i=0}^n$ as

$$w'_1 f_1(x_i) + w'_2 f_2(x_i) + \cdots + w'_{M'} f_{M'}(x_i) = b_i. \tag{8}$$

The statement that the prover wants to prove to the verifier is that "the prover knows $f_1(x), f_2(x), \ldots, f_{M'}(x)$ satisfying Eq. (8)".

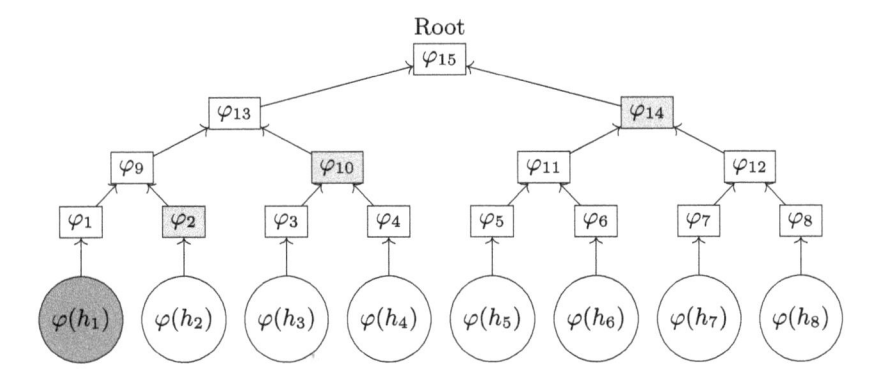

Fig. 3. A Merkle Tree of $\varphi(x)$ over H

We define $C(\cdot)$ which is a polynomial with coefficients over $\mathbb{F}$ as

$$C(x) = C(f_1(x), f_2(x), \ldots, f_{M'}(x))$$
$$= \prod_{i=0}^{n}(w'_1 f_1(x) + w'_2 f_2(x) + \cdots + w'_{M'} f_{M'}(x) - b_i). \tag{9}$$

Obviously, Eq. (9) has a factor $x - x_i$ for all x_i because $C(x_i) = 0$ holds for all x_i. Hence, the original statement is converted into the new statement which is "$C(x)$ has a factor $x - x_i$ for all x_i". By using $Z(x) = \prod_{i=0}^{n}(x - x_i) = x^{n+1} - 1$, the statement can be formulated as

$$C(x) = Z(x)Q(x), \tag{10}$$

where $Q(x)$ is a polynomial of degree at most $n^2 - 1 (= \deg\{C(x)\} - |G|)$ with coefficients over $\mathbb{F}$. By using $S = n \ (= \lceil \frac{\deg\{Q(x)\}}{n} \rceil)$, we split $Q(x)$ as the following in order to express $Q(x)$ with polynomials of degrees at most n.

$$Q(x) = \sum_{i=1}^{S} x^{i-1} Q_i(x^S). \tag{11}$$

The symbol H denotes a coset such that $G \cap H = \emptyset$ and $|G| < |H|$. We discuss the secure size of H in Sect. 4. We calculate Merkle Tree [18] of $f_1(x), \ldots, f_{M'}(x)$ and $Q_1(x), \ldots, Q_S(x)$ over H respectively. Merkle Tree is a complete binary Hash Tree whose each node is a calculated hash value from its left and right child node. Figure 3 shows an example of $\varphi(x)$ over $|H| = 8$. MTR (Merkle Tree Root) is the value of a root node in a Merkle Tree. In Fig. 3, $MTR(\varphi(x))$ is φ_{15}. MTP (Merkle Tree Path) is a set of nodes to calculate $MTR(\varphi(x))$ from $\varphi(h)$. In Fig. 3, $MTP(\varphi(h_1)) = \{\varphi_2, \varphi_{10}, \varphi_{14}\}$.

As a result, we set the following public and secret information.

Public information: $w, w', \mathbb{F}, \mathbb{K}, G, H, C(\cdot), Z(\cdot), Q(\cdot), b$, and all $MTR(\cdot)$
Secret information: $f_1(\cdot), \ldots, f_{M'}(\cdot), Q_1(\cdot), \ldots, Q_S(\cdot)$, and all $MTP(\cdot)$

Note that the total number of $MTR(\cdot)$ is $M' + S$. Therefore, the total number of $MTP(\cdot)$ becomes $(M' + S)|H|$.

3.3 Proof-Verification Procedure

Note that "the prover knows $f_1(x), f_2(x), \ldots, f_{M'}(x)$ satisfying Eq. (8)" is converted into "the prover knows $C(x)$ and $Q(x)$ such that $C(x) = Z(x)Q(x)$".

Figure 4 shows Proof-Verification procedure. Let $\overline{H} = \{x \mid x^S \in H\}$, the verifier sends $z \in \mathbb{K} \backslash (G \cup \overline{H})$ to the prover. The prover calculates $f_1(z), \ldots, f_{M'}(z)$ and $Q_1(z^S), \ldots, Q_S(z^S)$, then the prover sends back these values to the verifier.

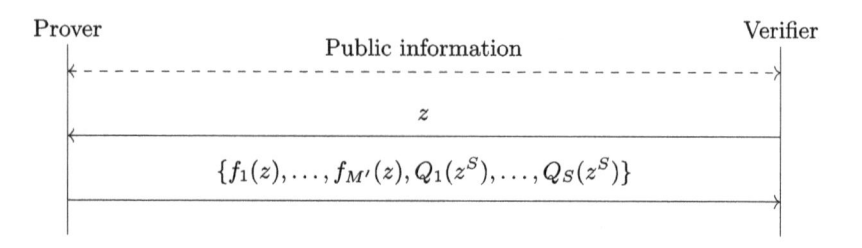

Fig. 4. Verification procedure

The verifier verifies $C(z) \stackrel{?}{=} Z(z)Q(z)$. At the same time, the verifier additionally needs to confirm the following two points.

Point 1. $f_1(x), \ldots, f_{M'}(x), Q_1(x), \ldots, Q_S(x)$ are the polynomials of degrees at most n.

Point 2. $f_1(z), \ldots, f_{M'}(z)$ are the calculated values from substituting $x = z$ for $f_1(x), \ldots, f_{M'}(x)$, and $Q_1(z^S), \ldots, Q_S(z^S)$ are the calculated values from substituting $x = z^S$ for $Q_1(x), \ldots, Q_S(x)$.

FRI (Fast Reed-Solomon Interactive Oracle Proofs of Proximity) [19] can solve **Point 1** and FRI as a Polynomial Commitment Scheme [20] can solve **Point 2**. Since the method [20] can also solve **Point 1**, we adopt it combined with Batched FRI [21] which can process all polynomials at once.

The prover receives $\alpha_1, \ldots, \alpha_{M'}, \beta_1, \ldots, \beta_S \in \mathbb{K}$ from the verifier and proves that the following $F(x)$ is the polynomial of degree lower than n.

$$F(x) = \sum_{i=1}^{M'} \alpha_i \frac{f_i(x) - f_i(z)}{x - z} + \sum_{i=1}^{S} \beta_i \frac{Q_i(x) - Q_i(z^S)}{x - z^S}. \tag{12}$$

To prove the above $F(x)$ of degree lower than n, the prover uses FRI. In FRI protocol, the verifier sends $r \in H$ and receives $f_1(r), f_1(-r), \ldots, f_{M'}(r), f_{M'}(-r), Q_1(r), Q_1(-r), \ldots, Q_S(r), Q_S(-r)$, and these $MTP(\cdot)$. All polynomials and all $MTR(\cdot)$ are verified simultaneously in FRI protocol.

As a result of FRI, the verifier can accept that "the prover knows $C(x)$ and $Q(x)$ such that $C(x) = Z(x)Q(x)$" is true. This is converted into the verifier can accept the original statement which is "the prover knows $f_1(x), f_2(x), \ldots, f_{M'}(x)$ satisfying Eq. (8)".

3.4 Verification for Suspicious Models

We assume a suspicious model in order to verify the problem distinguishing the forged model based on the owner's model from an independent original model. We consider the case that the owner as the prover wants to convince the verifier that the suspicious model is based on the owner's. Let a vector v be the parameters of the suspicious model. We extract the parameters from v whose positions are the same as the selected parameters from w. We calculate the vector v' in the same way as Eq. (7). Therefore, we calculate $\{v'_1, \ldots, v'_{M'}\}$ as

$$v'_m = \begin{cases} \varepsilon_1 & v_{i_m} \geq 0 \\ \varepsilon_2 & \text{else} \end{cases} \quad (m = 1, \ldots, M'). \tag{13}$$

Note that we only check whether $v_{i_m} \geq 0$, not the threshold at all. The verifier selects μ values out of v'. In Proof-Verification procedure, the verifier uses these μ values and the rest $M' - \mu$ values from the original w' in order to calculate $C(x)$. Concretely, let $\{i_1, \ldots, i_\mu\}$ be the indexes of the chosen values of v'. The indexes of the used values of w' can be represented as $\{1, \ldots, M'\} \setminus \{i_1, \ldots, i_\mu\}$. In the same way as Sect. 3.3, the prover convinces the verifier that the prover knows the polynomials satisfying the following.

$$\sum_{j \in \{i_1,\ldots,i_\mu\}} v'_j f_j(x_i) + \sum_{j \in \{1,\ldots,M'\} \setminus \{i_1,\ldots,i_\mu\}} w'_j f_j(x_i) = b_i. \tag{14}$$

4 Security Analysis

In this section, we show that the two problems which we mentioned in Sect. 2.3 can be solved by our proposal. We also show the analysis of Sect. 3.4.

We suppose that adversaries already know all the parameters of the owner's model and the public information that is shown in Sect. 3.2, while adversaries do not know the secret information that is shown in Sect. 3.2. We also suppose that adversaries have polynomial computational resources and that all exchanges between the prover and the verifier are open to everyone including adversaries.

The attempt that we assume adversaries make is that the adversaries convince the verifier as if the adversaries are the owners of the model. To achieve this attempt, the adversaries need to respond correctly to all of the verifier's challenges by obtaining the secret information in some ways and using it. In the following, we analyze the cases in which adversaries presume or know some of the secret information.

4.1 The Probability that Adversaries Who Know This Algorithm Are Able to Steal Ownership (Problem1)

Adversaries can take the following two attack scenarios.

Scenario A: Forgery of polynomials $f_1(x), \ldots, f_{M'}(x)$

Scenario B: Forgery by using public information

Scenario A: In this scenario, we consider the probability of success in the verification by adversaries using the forged polynomials $f'_1(x), \ldots, f'_{M'}(x)$. There are two cases; (i) All of the polynomials forged by adversaries are the same as the polynomials generated by the owner, and (ii) Part of the polynomials forged by adversaries are the same as the polynomials generated by the owner.

(i) All of the polynomials forged by adversaries are the same as the polynomials generated by the owner

Because the probability that $f'_i(x) = f_i(x)$ is $\frac{1}{|\mathbb{F}|^{n+1}}$ for $i = 1, \ldots, M'$, the probability of **Case (i)** becomes $(\frac{1}{|\mathbb{F}|^{n+1}})^{M'}$. This probability is negligibly lower. However, there is a possibility that the polynomials are leaked to adversaries. Hence, we consider such attack cases. Obviously, $Q'_j(x)$ which is calculated from $f'_i(x)$ based on Sect. 3.2 satisfies $Q'_j(x) = Q_j(x)$ for $j = 1, \ldots, S$. The adversaries need to satisfy $MTR(f_i(x)) = MTR(f'_i(x))$ for $i = 1, \ldots, M'$ and $MTR(Q_j(x)) = MTR(Q'_j(x))$ for $j = 1, \ldots, S$ in order to pass the verification.

For instance, in Fig. 3, the true order is $(h_1, h_2, h_3, h_4, h_5, h_6, h_7, h_8)$, and, on the other hand, supposing the forged order is $(h_1, h_3, h_5, h_4, h_8, h_2, h_7, h_6)$. In this case, the root value calculated by adversaries is different from the true root value with high probability even though the forged polynomial is the same as the true polynomial. However, in some cases, the adversaries' root value matches the true root value because of a hash collision.

We focus on one Merkle Tree of $f'_i(x)$. We label each node in each Merkle Tree. The root is labeled as 1. Let a_l be the probability that the l-th node in the Merkle Tree of $f'_i(x)$ matches the l-th node in the Merkle Tree of $f_i(x)$. By using this definition, we have

$$\text{Prob}\{MTR(f_i(x)) = MTR(f'_i(x))\} = a_1.$$

Let ρ be the collision probability of the hash function and A_d be the maximum value among the probabilities $\{a_{2^d}, \ldots, a_{2^{d+1}-1}\}$. The following evaluation holds for a_l in d-th depth of this Merkle Tree.

$$\begin{aligned} a_l &= a_{2l} a_{2l+1} + (1 - a_{2l} a_{2l+1})\rho \\ &\leq (\max(a_{2l}, a_{2l+1}))^2 + (1 - (\max(a_{2l}, a_{2l+1}))^2)\rho \\ &\leq A_{d+1}^2 + (1 - A_{d+1}^2)\rho \\ &< A_{d+1} + \rho. \end{aligned} \quad (15)$$

Now, we evaluate the probability of one of the adversaries' leaves matching the true leaf. Supposing that just t leaves in the adversaries' Merkle Tree differ from the true leaves, we consider the probability of one of the adversaries' leaves matching the true leaf. This probability is evaluated as

$$\begin{aligned} &\left(\frac{1}{(|H|-t)!} \sum_{k=0}^{t} \frac{(-1)^k}{k!}\right)\left(\rho + (1-\rho)\frac{|H|-t}{|H|}\right) \\ &< \left(\frac{1}{(|H|-t)!} \cdot \frac{1}{2}\right)\left(\rho + (1-\rho)\frac{|H|-t}{|H|}\right). \end{aligned} \quad (16)$$

In the left-hand side of Eq. (16), the first term denotes the probability of just t leaves out of $|H|$ becoming a "derangement". A derangement means the permutation of a set in which no element appears in its original position. The second denotes the probability of a leaf matching the true leaf.

Note that Eq. (16) is independent for each t, the total probability is calculated by the sum of Eq. (16) from $t = 1$ to $|H|$. Since $e^x = \sum_{k=0}^{\infty} \frac{x^k}{k!}$, the sum is evaluated as

$$\begin{aligned} &\sum_{t=0}^{|H|} \left(\left(\frac{1}{(|H|-t)!} \cdot \frac{1}{2}\right)\left(\rho + (1-\rho)\frac{|H|-t}{|H|}\right)\right) \\ &= \frac{\rho}{2}\left(\sum_{t=0}^{|H|} \frac{1}{(|H|-t)!}\right) + \frac{1-\rho}{2|H|}\left(\sum_{t=0}^{|H|-1} \frac{1}{(|H|-t-1)!}\right) \\ &< \rho\frac{e}{2} + (1-\rho)\frac{e}{2}\frac{1}{|H|}. \end{aligned} \quad (17)$$

Since the Merkle Tree has $|H|$ leaves, the depth of the Merkle Tree becomes $\log_2 |H|$. Therefore, from Eq. (15), a_1 is evaluated as

$$\begin{aligned}a_1 &< \rho + A_1 \\ &< \rho + (\rho + A_2) \\ &\quad\vdots \\ &< \rho \log_2 |H| + \rho \frac{e}{2} + (1-\rho)\frac{e}{2}\frac{1}{|H|} \\ &< \rho(2 + \log_2 |H|) + (1-\rho)\frac{2}{|H|}.\end{aligned} \qquad (18)$$

The above evaluation suggests that even if the probability is overestimated, it is lower than $\rho(2 + \log_2 |H|) + (1-\rho)\frac{2}{|H|}$. The above Eq. (18) also holds for $f'_1(x), \ldots, f'_{M'}(x)$, and $Q'_1(x), \ldots, Q'_S(x)$. As a result, the successful probability of **Case (i)** is lower than

$$\left(\frac{1}{|\mathbb{F}|^{n+1}}\right)^{M'} \left(\rho(2 + \log_2 |H|) + (1-\rho)\frac{2}{|H|}\right)^{M'+S}. \qquad (19)$$

Note that the first term is the probability that

$$f_1(x) = f'_1(x), f_2(x) = f'_2(x), \ldots, \text{ and } f_{M'}(x) = f'_{M'}(x).$$

Since the degree of the polynomial is n, the number of the coefficients over $\mathbb{F}$ becomes $n+1$. The second term denotes the evaluated probability that

$$MTR(f_1(x)) = MTR(f'_1(x)), \ldots, MTR(f_{M'}(x)) = MTR(f'_{M'}(x)), \text{ and }$$
$$MTR(Q_1(x)) = MTR(Q'_1(x)), \ldots, MTR(Q_S(x)) = MTR(Q'_S(x)).$$

(ii) Part of the polynomials forged by adversaries are the same as the polynomials generated by the owner

Let m' $(1 \leq m' \leq M')$ be the number of the forged polynomials which are not the same as the true polynomials. This means the case that

$$f_j(x) \neq f'_j(x) \text{ for } j \in \{i_1, \ldots, i_{m'}\} \subset \{1, \ldots, M'\},$$
$$\text{and } f_j(x) = f'_j(x) \text{ for } j \in \{1, \ldots, M'\} \setminus \{i_1, \ldots, i_{m'}\}.$$

The probability of **Case (ii)** becomes

$$\binom{M'}{m'} \left(\frac{1}{|\mathbb{F}|^{n+1}}\right)^{M'-m'} \left(1 - \frac{1}{|\mathbb{F}|^{n+1}}\right)^{m'}. \qquad (20)$$

Similar to **Case (i)**, $f'_i(x)$ which are the same as $f_i(x)$ are evaluated as Eq. (18). For $f'_i(x) \neq f_i(x)$, $h \in H$ such that $f'_i(h) = f_i(h)$ are at most n different points because $f'_i(x)$ and $f_i(x)$ are the polynomials of degrees at most n. According to Schwartz-Zippel lemma [22], the probability of $f'_i(h) = f_i(h)$ is at most $\frac{n}{|H|}$. Therefore, for $f'_i(x) \neq f_i(x)$, the probability of one of the adversaries' leaves matching the true leaf is lower than

$$\frac{n}{|H|} + \left(1 - \frac{n}{|H|}\right)\rho. \tag{21}$$

From the above Eq. (21) and **Case (i)**, the successful probability for $f'_i(x) \neq f_i(x)$ is evaluated as

$$a_1 < \rho \log_2 |H| + \frac{n}{|H|} + \left(1 - \frac{n}{|H|}\right)\rho \tag{22}$$
$$= \rho(1 + \log_2 |H|) + (1 - \rho)\frac{n}{|H|}.$$

From Eq. (9) and Eq. (10), adversaries calculate $C'(x)$ and $Q'(x)$ such that $C'(x) = Z(x)Q'(x)$ for $f'_1(x), \ldots, f'_M(x)$. In this $C'(x)$, $C'(x) = C(x)$ holds if

$$w'_1 f_1(x) + w'_2 f_2(x) + \cdots + w'_{M'} f_{M'}(x) = w'_1 f'_1(x) + w'_2 f'_2(x) + \cdots + w'_{M'} f'_{M'}(x).$$

Since $f'_i(x)$ and $f_i(x)$ are the polynomials of degrees at most n, the probability of the above holding is $\frac{1}{|\mathbb{F}|^{n+1}}$. We consider the two cases; (a) The case of $C'(x) = C(x)$, and (b) The case of $C'(x) \neq C(x)$.

(a) The case of $C'(x) = C(x)$
The probability a_1 of $Q'_j(x)$ is evaluated as Eq. (18) because $Q'(x) = Q(x)$ obviously holds. From Eq. (18) and Eq. (22), the successful probability for **Case (a)** is lower than

$$\frac{1}{|\mathbb{F}|^{n+1}} \left(\rho(2 + \log_2 |H|) + (1 - \rho)\frac{2}{|H|}\right)^{M'+S-m'} \tag{23}$$
$$\left(\rho(1 + \log_2 |H|) + (1 - \rho)\frac{n}{|H|}\right)^{m'}.$$

(b) The case of $C'(x) \neq C(x)$
Obviously, $Q'_j(x) \neq Q_j(x)$ holds for some of $Q'_j(x)$ because $Q'(x) \neq Q(x)$ holds. Let m be the number of $Q'_j(x)$ which are not the same as $Q_j(x)$. The probability a_1 of these $Q'_j(x)$ is evaluated as Eq. (22). Hence, from Eq. (18) and Eq. (22), the successful probability for **Case (b)** is lower than

$$\left(1 - \frac{1}{|\mathbb{F}|^{n+1}}\right)\left(\rho(2 + \log_2 |H|) + (1 - \rho)\frac{2}{|H|}\right)^{M'+S-m'-s} \tag{24}$$
$$\left(\rho(1 + \log_2 |H|) + (1 - \rho)\frac{n}{|H|}\right)^{m'+s}.$$

From Eq. (20), Eq. (23) and Eq. (24), supposing $n \geq 2$, the successful probability for **Case (ii)** is lower than

$$\binom{M'}{m'}\left(\frac{1}{|\mathbb{F}|^{n+1}}\right)^{M'-m'}\left(1-\frac{1}{|\mathbb{F}|^{n+1}}\right)^{m'}\left(\rho(2+\log_2|H|)+(1-\rho)\frac{n}{|H|}\right)^{M'+S}. \quad (25)$$

The three terms on the left denote the probability that just m' forged polynomials are not the same as the true polynomials. The rightmost term denotes the evaluated probability that

$$MTR(f_1(x)) = MTR(f'_1(x)), \ldots, MTR(f_{M'}(x)) = MTR(f'_{M'}(x)), \text{ and}$$
$$MTR(Q_1(x)) = MTR(Q'_1(x)), \ldots, MTR(Q_S(x)) = MTR(Q'_S(x)).$$

We sum the above probabilities from $m' = 1$ to M'. By using $(x+y)^n = \sum_{k=0}^{n} \binom{n}{k} x^{n-k} y^k$, the sum is evaluated as

$$\left(1-\left(\frac{1}{|\mathbb{F}|^{n+1}}\right)^{M'}\right)\left(\rho(2+\log_2|H|)+(1-\rho)\frac{n}{|H|}\right)^{M'+S}. \quad (26)$$

In the case that at least one forged polynomial is not the same as the true polynomial, the probability that adversaries succeed in the Merkle Tree verifications is lower than the above evaluation.

Hence, from **Case (i)** and **Case (ii)**, the probability of success in **Scenario A** by adversaries is less than the following with $n \geq 2$.

$$\left(\rho(2+\log_2|H|)+(1-\rho)\frac{n}{|H|}\right)^{M'+S}. \quad (27)$$

Supposing that the successful probability is up to 2^{-128}, we should satisfy the following conditions.

$$\begin{cases} \rho(2+\log_2|H|) < 2^{-\frac{128}{M'+S}-1}, \\ \frac{n}{|H|} < 2^{-\frac{128}{M'+S}-1}. \end{cases} \quad (28)$$

Therefore, the size of H is determined within the following range.

$$n \cdot 2^{\frac{128}{M'+S}+1} < |H| < 2^{(\rho^{-1} \cdot 2^{-\frac{128}{M'+S}-1}-2)}. \quad (29)$$

Note that, as shown in Sect. 3.2, we set $S = n$. For example, if we set $n = 100, M' = 1, \rho = 2^{-256}$, then we have $482 \leq |H| < 2^{(2^{(253+\frac{74}{101})}-2)}$, and if we set $n = 100, M' = 1, \rho = 2^{-128}$, then we have $482 \leq |H| < 2^{(2^{(125+\frac{74}{101})}-2)}$. The size of H is freely determined within the above range. However, the larger we set the size of H, the more complicated the calculation for Merkle Tree is required. To be less computational complexity, we should set the size of H as small as possible.

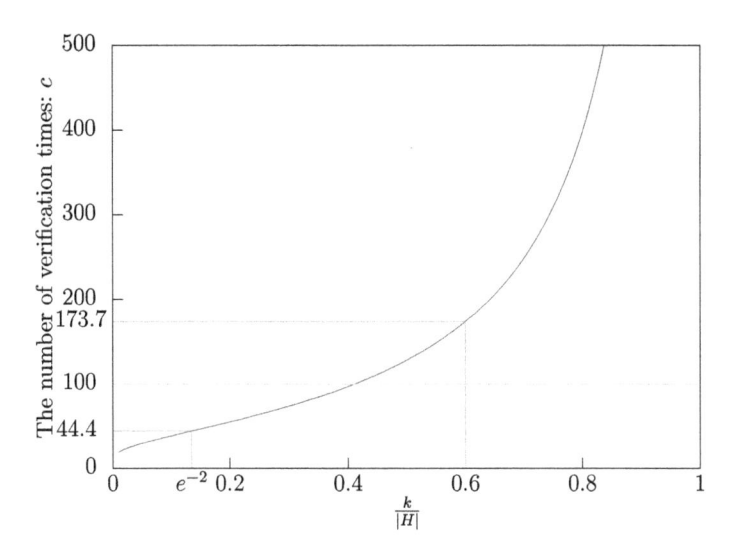

Fig. 5. The relation between the leaked information rate into adversaries $\frac{k}{|H|}$ and the number of verification times c so that the successful probability becomes less than 2^{-128}.

Scenario B: Decoding the public information $MTR(\cdot)$ into $MTP(\cdot)$ can be prevented because of the preimage resistance of the hash function. In this scenario, we consider the successful probability in the case that adversaries already know k out of $|H|$ about $MTP(\cdot)$ by eavesdropping all the exchanges between the prover and the verifier. The prover and the verifier repeat our proposed verification multiple times until the statement is accepted. Therefore, adversaries can spoof easily using these exchanges. We consider the relation between the decrement of the security and the number of the leaked exchanges. Let c be the number of repeated times of the verification. According to [23], the successful probability in all c times of the verification by adversaries is evaluated as

$$\left(\frac{k-c+1}{|H|-c+1}\right)^c \leq \frac{k}{|H|} \cdot \frac{k-1}{|H|-1} \cdots \frac{k-c+1}{|H|-c+1} \leq \left(\frac{k}{|H|}\right)^c. \tag{30}$$

We evaluate c as the following so that the successful probability is less than 2^{-128}.

$$c \geq -\frac{128}{\log_2 \frac{k}{|H|}}. \tag{31}$$

Figure 5 shows the graph of Eq. (31). Note that the value of $\frac{k}{|H|}$ denotes the rate of the leaked exchanges to adversaries. For example, where $\frac{k}{|H|} = 0.6$, we need to set the repeated times of verification to at least 174 for one verifier in order to keep the successful probability less than 2^{-128}. Conversely, in the case that the repeated times is less than 174, the successful probability becomes more than 2^{-128}.

As shown in Fig. 5, the repeated times of the verification rapidly blow up over the inflection point $\frac{k}{|H|} = \frac{1}{e^2}$ (≈ 0.135) on the right side of Eq. (31). At this point, the repeated times of the verification is 45. Given the computational complexity of the verification and the amount of data traffic, we assume that the repeated times of the verification per one verifier should be restricted up to 100. From Fig. 5, adversaries who already know approximately 41% of response values can respond to at most 100 challenge values with a probability over 2^{-128}. In other words, adversaries who already know approximately 41% of response values can spoof as the prover with a probability over 2^{-128} in this restricted situation. Therefore, we need to recalculate Merkle Tree and renew the public information in this case. The prover who keeps claiming the statement even though the leaked rate is over the threshold should be considered as adversaries.

Another problem is that adversaries may be able to restore some of $f_i(x)$ by eavesdropping the information that the prover and the verifier exchange. However, the problem that adversaries' attempts cause in this case is the same as **Case (i)** in **Scenario A**.

4.2 The Analysis that the Owners Are Able to Claim Ownership Multiple Times (Problem2)

In the previous section, we concluded the condition that 100 verifications are required for one verifier where the leaked rate is approximately 41% in order to make the successful probability less than 2^{-128}. Therefore, we consider how many verifiers we can claim ownership against until that percentage is reached in this section. In the case of claiming ownership against the l-th verifier, the number of repeated times of the verification between the prover and the verifier is denoted as c_l. From Eq. (31), the following holds.

$$\begin{cases} c_1 = 1, \\ c_l = \left\lceil \dfrac{128}{\log_2 |H| - \log_2 \sum_{i=1}^{l-1} c_i} \right\rceil & (l \geq 2). \end{cases} \quad (32)$$

We need to consider the possibility that adversaries who spoof as the verifier verify the statement multiple times. This is because adversaries attempt to collect the pairs of the challenges and the responses to spoof as the prover. We also consider the possibility that adversaries get the prover to run out of resources and to recalculate Merkle Tree.

To have a tolerance against the above attacks, the size of $|H|$ should be determined depending on the computational security. For example, we show c_l where $|H| = 2^{32}$ in Fig. 6. We set $c_l \leq 100$, then we have $l \leq 37,120,430$ where $|H| = 2^{32}$. According to [24], there are 150,000 Machine Learning engineers and 29,000,000 software engineers. Considering these number of engineers, we conclude that the above size of H is enough to ensure the security.

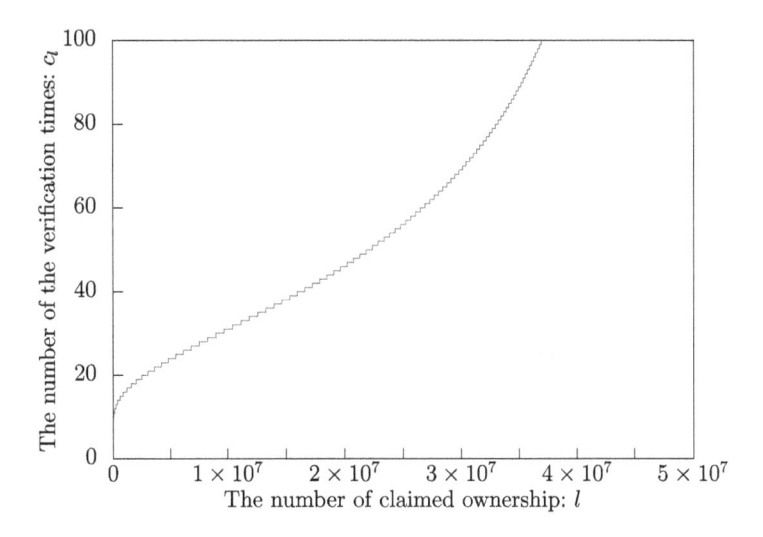

Fig. 6. The relation between the number of claimed ownership l and the number of the verification times c_l where $|H| = 2^{32}$.

4.3 The Analysis of the Verification for Suspicious Models and the False Positive for Unrelated Models

We suppose that adversaries attempt to make the owner fail to claim the ownership of suspicious models. To achieve this attempt, adversaries need to change some values of the selected parameters of the owner's model. Let ν be the number of changed values. This attack scenario is always successful if $M' - \nu < \mu$ because at least one of the changed values is used for the verification. However, this attack scenario causes a significant degradation of the model's performance.

Supposing $M' - \nu \geq \mu$, the probability of success in this attack scenario is equal to the probability that at least one of the changed values is used in the verification. Supposing $\nu = qM'$ ($0 < q \leq 1 - \frac{\mu}{M'}$), this probability is

$$1 - \frac{\binom{M'-\nu}{\mu}}{\binom{M'}{\mu}} = 1 - \prod_{i=0}^{\nu-1}\left(1 - \frac{\mu}{M' - i}\right)$$

$$\leq 1 - \left(1 - \frac{\mu}{M' - \nu + 1}\right)^{\nu} \quad (33)$$

$$= 1 - \left(1 - \frac{\mu}{(1-q)M' + 1}\right)^{qM'}.$$

Let c be the number of repeated times of the verification in the same way as **Scenario B**, and suppose M' is sufficiently large. Then, Eq. (33) is evaluated as

$$1 - e^{-\frac{qc\mu}{1-q}}. \quad (34)$$

Supposing that the distribution of the parameters of the unrelated model is a normal distribution whose mean is 0, the probability of the false positive for the unrelated model in the verification is

$$\left(\frac{1}{2}\right)^{c\mu}. \tag{35}$$

From Eq. (34) and Eq. (35), there is a trade-off between the successful probability by adversaries and the probability of the false positive for the unrelated model. However, changing the parameters impairs the model's performance because the parameters are significant for the performance. Hence, adversaries should select q as small as possible in order to get Eq. (34) lower.

As a result, adversaries need to take the degradation of the performance or the risk that adversaries are sued for infringing ownership of the model. In other words, adversaries can not steal the high-performance model.

5 Discussion

In this section, we discuss the following three points which our proposal achieved.

First, considering the development of quantum computers and quantum algorithms, we need to use a quantum-resistant method. The security of our proposal depends on the security of a hash function which is supposed to be quantum-resistant. If the owner does not care about the quantum resistance, other efficient zero-knowledge proofs based on the hardness of the Discrete Logarithm (DL) assumption can be applied for low-cost computation.

Second, we have intended to ensure that the theoretical security is only based on the algorithm. As we mentioned in Sect. 1.2, a digital signature can be applied in order to claim ownership of the model in some ways. However, even if an applied digital signature is quantum-resistant, its disadvantage is that it depends on the security of organizations such as PKI (public key infrastructure) and Time Stamp Authentication. In other words, since we can not confirm that organizations are inherently reliable, the security of the ownership authentication of a digital signature is nothing less than supposing the reliability of such organizations. On the other hand, our proposal does not.

Finally, any additional training should be avoided for the model's performance and for applying a method to the existing models. Most of the digital watermark algorithms require changing the parameters of the model during a training phase or after training in order to embed a digital watermark. In order to minimize the degradation of the model's performance, we need to consider the optimal settings for each model. By using our proposal, we do not have to consider this issue of optimization.

6 Conclusion

In this paper, we show the method of protecting ownership of trained DNN models by using zero-knowledge proofs. Our proposal is an interactive scheme. However, it can be improved into a non-interactive scheme using Fiat-Shamir transformation [25]. Such improvement will be shown in our forthcoming paper.

We solved the two problems of the previous work shown in Sect. 2.3. In the security analysis, we show how to determine H so that the successful probability is at most 2^{-128}. Moreover, we show the relation between the number of claimed ownership, the repeated times of the verification, and the size of H. In the case of using our proposal, the security depends on the preimage resistance of a hash function. In the case that we use a larger size of a secure hash function, the data traffic of the exchanges increases, however, the computational complexity is not much affected. On the other hand, in the case that the larger degree of $C(\cdot)$ is chosen to become more secure, the computational complexity becomes larger. The analysis of how the hash function and the degree of $C(\cdot)$ affect the performance of the implementation is our future work.

The calculated w' from the parameter w of the model whose ownership is claimed ownership has the features that owners can claim ownership of the model whose w is fine-tuned. This conversion can solve the problem of dealing with DNN with millions or billions of parameters in practical settings.

However, there are the following two problems. The first problem is the possibility of stealing the model by abusing the conversion from w to w' if the adversaries do not care about the degradation of the performance and the risk that is shown in Sect. 4.3. The second problem is that our proposal can not be applied to the model such that the number of w is changed by transforming to compressed models. The countermeasure for such problems is our future work. However, we expect the second problem can be solved by applying IPGuard [26].

Our proposal has the possibility that claiming ownership becomes excessive. This means that our proposal causes a negative impact that owners can claim ownership of a significantly improved model. Reducing this negative impact is our future work.

References

1. Krizhevsky, A., Sutskever, I., Hinton, G.E.: ImageNet classification with deep convolutional neural networks. Commun. ACM **60**, 84–90 (2017)
2. Abadi, M., et al.: TensorFlow: large-scale machine learning on heterogeneous systems. Software available from tensorflow.org
3. Liu, T., Xie, X., Zhang, Y.: zkCNN: zero knowledge proofs for convolutional neural network predictions and accuracy. In: Proceedings of the 2021 ACM SIGSAC Conference on Computer and Communications Security (CCS 2021), pp. 2968–2985 (2021)
4. Lee, S., Ko, H., Kim, J., Oh, H.: vCNN: verifiable convolutional neural network based on zk-SNARKs. IEEE Trans. Dependable Secure Comput. (01), 1–17 (2024)

5. Weng, J., Tang, G., Yang, A., Li, M., Liu, J.-N.: pvCNN: privacy-preserving and verifiable convolutional neural network testing. IEEE Trans. Inf. Forensics Secur. **18**, 2218–2233 (2023)
6. Nuttapong, A., et al.: Privacy-preserving verifiable CNNs. In: Applied Cryptography and Network Security: 22nd International Conference, ACNS 2024, 5–8 March 2024, Proceedings, Part II (2024)
7. Nagai, Y., Uchida, Y., Sakazawa, S., Satoh, S.: Digital watermarking for deep neural networks. Int. J. Multimed. Inf. Retrieval **7**, 3–16 (2018)
8. Lv, P., et al.: MEA-defender: a robust watermark against model extraction attack. In: 2024 IEEE Symposium on Security and Privacy (SP), p. 98 (2024)
9. Yasui, T., Tanaka, T., Malik, A., Kuribayashi, M.: Robustness against pruning models using constant weight code. J. Imaging **8**(6), 152 (2022)
10. Szyller, S., Atli, B.G., Marchal, S., Asokan, N.: DAWN: dynamic adversarial watermarking of neural networks. In: Proceedings of the 29th ACM International Conference on Multimedia (MM 2021), pp. 4417–4425 (2021)
11. DIB. AI principles: Recommendations on the ethical use of artificial intelligence by the Department of Defense - Supporting document. Defence Innovation Board (DIB) (2020). https://media.defense.gov/2019/Oct/31/2002204459/-1/-1/0/DIB_AI_PRINCIPLES_SUPPORTING_DOCUMENT.PDF
12. Tran, C., Fioretto, F., Kim, J.-E., Naidu, R.: Running has a disparate impact on model accuracy. In: 36th Conference on Neural Information Processing Systems (NeurIPS 2022) (2022)
13. Hooker, S., Courville, A., Clark, G., Dauphin, Y., Frome, A.: What do compressed deep neural networks forget? arXiv preprint arXiv:1911.05248 (2019)
14. Gale, T., Elsen, E., Hooker, S.: The state of sparsity in deep neural networks. arXiv preprint arXiv:1902.09574 (2019)
15. StarkWare. ethSTARK documentation. Cryptology ePrint Archive, Paper 2021/582. https://ia.cr/2021/582
16. Ben-Sasson, E., Bentov, I., Horesh, Y., Riabzev, M.: Scalable, transparent, and post-quantum secure computational integrity. Cryptology ePrint Archive, Paper 2018/046. https://ia.cr/2018/046
17. Masip-Ardevol, H., Guzmán-Albiol, M., Baylina-Melé, J., Muñoz-Tapia, J.L.: eSTARK: extending STARKs with arguments. Cryptology ePrint Archive, Paper 2023/474. https://ia.cr/2023/474
18. Merkle, R.C.: A digital signature based on a conventional encryption function. In: Pomerance, C. (ed.) CRYPTO 1987. LNCS, vol. 293, pp. 369–378. Springer, Heidelberg (1988). https://doi.org/10.1007/3-540-48184-2_32
19. Ben-Sasson, E., Bentov, I., Horesh, Y., Riabzev, M.: Fast Reed-Solomon interactive oracle proofs of proximity. In: Proceedings of the 45th International Colloquium on Automata, Languages, and Programming (ICALP 2018). LIPIcs, vol. 107, pp. 14:1–14:17 (2018)
20. Vlasov, A., Panarin, K.: Transparent polynomial commitment scheme with polylogarithmic communication complexity. Cryptology ePrint Archive, Paper 2019/1020. https://ia.cr/2019/1020
21. Ben-Sasson, E., Carmon, D., Ishai, Y., Kopparty, S., Saraf, S.: Proximity gaps for Reed-Solomon codes. Cryptology ePrint Archive, Report 2020/654. https://ia.cr/2020/654
22. Schwartz, J.T.: Fast probabilistic algorithms for verification of polynomial identities. J. ACM **27**, 701–717 (1980)

23. Ateniese, G., et al.: Provable data possession at untrusted stores. In: Proceedings of the 14th ACM Conference on Computer and Communications Security, pp. 598–609 (2007)
24. Riggins, J.: Tech works: how to fill the 27 million AI engineer gap. The New Stack. https://thenewstack.io/tech-works-how-to-fill-the-27-million-ai-engineer-gap/
25. Fiat, A., Shamir, A.: How to prove yourself: practical solutions to identification and signature problems. In: Odlyzko, A.M. (ed.) CRYPTO 1986. LNCS, vol. 263, pp. 186–194. Springer, Heidelberg (1987). https://doi.org/10.1007/3-540-47721-7_12
26. Cao, X., Jia, J., Gong, N.Z.: IPGuard: protecting intellectual property of deep neural networks via fingerprinting the classification boundary. In: Proceedings of the 2021 ACM Asia Conference on Computer and Communications Security (ASIA CCS 2021), pp. 14–25 (2021)

MALAI: ML-Based Attack on Learning with Error Problem

Mandru Suma Sri[1]([✉]), Chakka Srikanth Yadav[1], Tikaram Sanyashi[2], and Virendra Singh[1]

[1] Department of Computer Science and Engineering, IIT Bombay, Mumbai, India
{22d0381,23m0794,singhv}@iitb.ac.in
[2] Department of Information Security and Communication Technology, NTNU, Trondheim, Norway
tikaram.sanyashi@ntnu.no

Abstract. With the advent of quantum computers, traditional public key cryptosystems will no longer be safe to use for the exchange of private information over the web. This shift necessitates the development of quantum-safe cryptosystems to ensure secure online communication. Out of the different hard problems secure against quantum computers, lattice-based encryption schemes, viz., the LWE problem, are well understood from a security perspective; furthermore, they are versatile and provide reasonable performance characteristics. The hardness of the LWE problem is based on learning noisy data in the presence of modulo operation.

Over time, machine learning models have become better and are known to learn patterns even from noisy data samples. Recently, machine learning models have been employed to challenge the hardness of the LWE problem. However, the models used are resource-intensive transformer models, requiring significant computational power and time. In this work, we demonstrate that we can replace these expensive transformer models with simpler models while achieving the same success rate. Our approach uses only one-fourth of the computational resources for data preprocessing and reduces the time for secret key recovery to 1.5 min, compared to 2 h with transformer models.

Keywords: LWE problem · Lattice reduction · Linear Regression · Elastic Net · Orthogonal Matching Pursuit

1 Introduction

The construction of large-scale quantum computers offers unprecedented computational power, enabling them to solve complex problems that are presently beyond the capabilities of classical computers. However, the faster computation power of quantum computers carries some challenges in the field of cryptography. The traditional cryptosystem, which is based on integer factorization [35] and/or the discrete logarithm problem [24] in an abelian group, will no longer be safe anymore due to polynomial time quantum attacks using Shor's Algorithm

[38]. Therefore, the race is to find a new Post-Quantum Cryptosystem (PQC) built using quantum-safe, hard problems.

To ensure data protection and secure communication in the presence of quantum computers, NIST launched the PQC standardization challenge [30] in 2016. This challenge concluded in July 2022, selecting several lattice-based schemes, notably those based on the Learning With Errors (LWE) problem. The hardness of which is backed by the hardness of the Shortest Vector Problem (SVP) [31] requiring to find shortest vectors in high dimensional lattices. The known techniques to solve the SVP problem are largely based on the lattice-basis reduction algorithms with an aim to find the short vectors via algebraic techniques. The well-known lattice reduction algorithm viz., LLL (Lenstra-Lenstra-Lovász) algorithm [19] was the original template for lattice reduction. Though the algorithm runs in polynomial time (in lattice dimension), it returns an exponentially bad approximation to the SVP problem. The best-known classical attacks on the PQC candidates run in exponential time in the dimension of the lattice.

Fundamentally, the hardness of the LWE problem comprises learning noisy data in the presence of modulus operation. Machine Learning (ML) techniques are good at learning noisy, unstructured data. Furthermore, LWE data samples are highly structured data; thus, in the literature, ML has been explored as an alternative way to attack the LWE problem [20,21,39,41] using costly model architectures viz., transformer models requiring high computational resources and time. Thus in this work, we aim to investigate whether high computational models can be replaced by simple ML models and obtain similar results as that of the high computational models present in the literature.

Contribution: In this work, we have investigated the hardness of the LWE problem using simple ML-based models viz., Linear Regression, Elastic Net, and Orthogonal Matching Pursuit(OMP) in place of the high computational models used in the literature [20,21,39,41]. Our experimental results show that even using simpler models we can achieve similar results as that of the high computational models, with reduced computational resources. To be precise, we have noted that by using simpler models, we can recover the secret key by using only 1 million samples, which in the literature required 4 million samples [20]. Reduction in the number of samples has a significant decrease in the computational resources required for preprocessing, viz., we need 2048 cores in comparison to 8192 cores [20] for lattice reduction, which is 4 times fewer cores for the same work to perform. Additionally, by using the simpler model for secret key recovery, we can recover the secret key in around 1.5 minutes which is roughly 2 hours in the case of the transformer models used in the literature [20].

Furthermore, we have also divided the pre-processed data samples (obtained after lattice reduction) into two categories viz., noMod data and Mod data as specified in [20], and carried out a thorough investigation to check the number of noMod data samples required to recover the secret. Experiments suggest that an increase in noMod data requires fewer samples and vice-versa to recover the secret key, which was expected. We have observed that OMP performs well for secrets with lower Hamming weights, whereas Linear Regression and Elastic Net performed well for secrets with higher Hamming weights, because of their respective strengths. As OMP is a greedy algorithm it performs well for low Hamming weights because its design focuses on identifying and leveraging the few non-zero elements in the secret vector, as sparsity is its strength. In contrast, Linear Regression treats all features equally, so it performs well for high dimensions without considering the density and Elastic Net balances between sparsity while dealing with multicollinearity, making it more versatile for various higher Hamming weights.

Additionally, we have observed that as the Hamming weight hwt increases, samples required to recover the secret key decrease. This is because, in higher Hamming weights, the secret has more non-zero entries, providing more information that can be leveraged to distinguish signal from noise, making it easier to recover the secret even with a low noMod percentage. Conversely, as an additional finding, we have observed that for very low Hamming weights, a high noMod percentage (greater than 80%) is required to recover the secret. This is because, in a low-Hamming weight secret, we have fewer non-zero entries. This makes it hard for the model to go in the correct direction in the presence of noise, as the data samples come from the same distribution, and hence, they have an equal probability of getting selected, making it hard for the model to converge towards the direction of the secret key. Hence requires a high percentage of noMod samples, which helps the error distribution become clearer, and the sparse non-zero entries of the secret become more apparent, facilitating recovery of the secret key.

Notations: In this paper $[a, \cdots, z]$ represents constants, $[\mathbf{a}, \cdots, \mathbf{z}]$ represents vectors and $[\mathbf{A}, \cdots, \mathbf{Z}]$ represents matrices. A set with numbers $[1, \cdots, N]$ is represented by $[N]$. $e \leftarrow \$\mathbb{Z}_q$ represents sampling e uniformly at random from $\mathbb{Z}_q$. Term Mod data is used to represent all samples where the mod operation gets applied viz. if $b = \mathbf{a} \cdot \mathbf{s} + e > q$ while the noMod data samples represent all samples where the Mod does not get applied viz., $q > b = \mathbf{a} \cdot \mathbf{s} + e$ after lattice reduction operation is carried out in the data samples.

Roadmap: In Sect. 2, we have defined the LWE problem and existing attacks to break the LWE problem and recover the secret key. In Sect. 3, we have covered the ML-based attacks from the literature. In Sect. 4, we have covered simple ML-based models used to attack and recover the secret key of the LWE problem. Section 5 covers the result and analysis, and Sect. 6 covers the discussion and future research directions. Finally, Sect. 7 ends the paper with a conclusion.

2 Background

Introduced by Oded Regev in 2005, the Learning With Error (LWE) problem [33,34] is a generalization of learning with parity problem [6]. The problem is to solve a polynomial number of linear equations with noise in the presence of a mod operation. Several reductions and hardness proofs underpin the hardness of the LWE problem to the worst-case lattice problem, such as the SVP [25,31] and the GapSVP [18,32] problem. These reductions provide a solid theoretical foundation for the security of the LWE problem.

The LWE problem is believed to be safe against classical and quantum adversaries [34]. Due to its hardness assumption against quantum computers, recently, it has been increasingly adopted to build secure cryptosystems as the traditional crypt-systems that are based on integer factorization [35] and the discrete logarithm problem [24], that are vulnerable against the growing threat posed by quantum computers [38].

The LWE problem has significant implications in cryptography due to its presumed hardness and versatility. It finds application in various cryptographic primitive constructions not limited to public-key encryption [7], digital signatures [15], fully homomorphic encryption [9,12,14,17], etc. In short, the mathematical rigor and presumed security of the LWE problem have made it a cornerstone of modern cryptographic research, especially in the quest for quantum-resistant cryptographic system design. Formally, the LWE problem is defined as

Definition 1 (Learning With Errors (LWE) [33]). *For given integer $n \geq 1$ and q representing respectively dimension and modulus, the LWE function is defined as: Sample fixed secret vector $\mathbf{s} \leftarrow \$\chi$ over integers $\mathbb{Z}_q$ of dimension n and error elements $e \leftarrow \$\chi$ and $\mathbf{a}$ uniformly at random $\mathbf{a} \leftarrow \$\mathbb{Z}_q^n$ and output*

$$(\mathbf{a}, \mathbf{a} \cdot \mathbf{s} + e) \in \mathbb{Z}_q^{n+1}.$$

The decision-$\text{LWE}_{n,k,q}$ problem is to distinguish k samples sampled using LWE function from same number of uniform random samples sampled from $\mathbb{Z}_q^{n+1}$. The search-$\text{LWE}_{n,k,q}$ problem is to recover secret $\mathbf{s}$ and or $\mathbf{e}$ from k independent LWE samples.

Over the years, several attacks have been proposed to challenge the hardness of the LWE problem [5,6,33,34]. These attacks can be broadly categorized into three categories:

1. Combinatorial attacks [6]
2. Algebraic attacks [5] and
3. Lattice-based attacks [22]

Combinatorial Attacks: These are some of the earliest attack techniques proposed to attack the LWE problem. Examples of these categories of attack techniques include the BKW (Blum, Kalai, Wasserman) algorithm [6]. The BKW algorithm works by reducing the dimension of the LWE problem by combining several equations, which helps to find the secret vector $\mathbf{s}$. While effective against small instances, the BKW algorithm becomes infeasible for larger instances due to its exponential time complexity and high memory requirements. Variants and improvements on the BKW algorithm have been proposed [2–4,23], but they generally face similar limitations.

Algebraic Attacks: These categories of attack leverage the algebraic structure of the LWE problem to find solutions. One notable approach is the Arora-Ge attack [5], which transforms the LWE problem into a system of polynomial equations. Solving these polynomial equations can theoretically recover the secret vector **s**. However, this approach is generally not practical for large instances of LWE due to the difficulty of efficiently solving high-degree polynomial systems. A few attacks of these categories include [10,16] that are focused on structured LWE, i.e., mostly on ring LWE.

Lattice-Based Attacks: These are the most powerful and widely studied attacks against the LWE problem. Attacks of this category viz., primal and dual lattice reduction methods, exploit the relationship between LWE and hard lattice problems viz., Shortest Vector Problem (SVP) and Closest Vector Problem (CVP) [26,27]. These methods leverage sophisticated lattice reduction techniques to approximate the secret vector by solving these underlying hard lattice problems, compromising LWE-based cryptographic schemes' security assumptions.

In the primal lattice reduction method, the attacker constructs a lattice from the LWE instance and then applies lattice reduction techniques, viz., the LLL (Lenstra-Lenstra-Lovász) [19] or BKZ (Block Korkine-Zolotarev) [11] algorithms, to find short vectors in the lattice, which correspond to the secret vector **s**, we tend to recover. Alternatively, the dual lattice reduction method focuses on finding a short vector in the dual lattice and hopes that the recovered short vector is the secret vector we tend to recover. These attacks are highly effective, particularly for small noise levels, but their complexity grows significantly with the problem size and increase in the noise level. However, continuous advancement in lattice reduction algorithms and their implementations has made lattice-based attacks an active area of research. Furthermore, constant evaluation of attacks is of utmost importance as it helps in proper parameterization for using the LWE problem for practical application, restricting and/or avoiding any possible attacks.

In addition to the different categories of attacks presented above, recently machine learning-based attacks have also been used to exploit the possible vulnerabilities of the LWE problem. As our main focus is to optimize the machine-learning-based attacks, we will cover it in more detail in Sect. 3.

3 Related Work

In recent years, Machine Learning (ML) techniques have been explored as potential methods for attacking the LWE problem. The idea is to leverage the power of data-driven algorithms to find patterns and make predictions about the secret vector **s**. Several machine learning-based attacks on LWE have been proposed, showcasing varying degrees of success.

One of the pioneering works in this area was presented by Albrecht, Player, and Scott in 2015 [4]. They used a binary classifier to distinguish LWE samples from that of random samples. It involved training a classifier on a set of labeled LWE samples and random samples to learn a decision boundary. While providing some insights, this was limited by the complexity of accurately classifying high-dimensional LWE instances.

Recently, SALSA [41] acronym for Secret-recovery Attacks on LWE via Sequence to sequence models with Attention, introduced transformers to learn the modular arithmetic, one of the reasons behind the hardness of the LWE Problem. The idea was to leverage the transformer's powerful sequence modeling capabilities to learn the modular arithmetic and use it to break the LWE problem. The idea is to train the SALSA framework using standard transformer models on a large dataset of 4 million LWE samples of data dimensions 30 and 128 consistent with typical LWE instances.

On successful training, the trained model successfully recovered the binary secrets corresponding to a Hamming weight (number of non-zero elements present in the secret vector) of 3 for dimension 128 and a Hamming weight of 4 for dimension < 70. The aim was to capture the complex dependencies present in the LWE samples, leveraging the self-attention mechanism of transformers to model the complex relationships between different components of the data effectively. However, the model failed to learn the modular arithmetic and also could not predict the binary secrets with higher Hamming weight. Furthermore, obtaining 4 Million samples in real-world scenarios may not be feasible.

SALSA is superseded by SALSA PICANTE [21] with enhancements in the data pre-processing techniques and the transformer architecture, such as modified attention mechanisms and deeper layers, to capture the nuances of the LWE samples better. It uses a TinyLWE to sample ($\frac{2^{21}}{n}$), $n \times n$-matrices from initial $4n$ samples with reputation and pre-processes them to obtain 4 million samples (lattice reduction increases size by multiple of 2) using lattice reduction techniques like BKZ and LLL [19]. Using the combination of the modified training model and the use of the lattice reduction step for data pre-processing enhanced SALSA PICANTE to recover the secrets for larger dimensions than that of the SALSA. It could recover binary secrets of Hamming weight up to 31 for $(n,q) = (256, 2^{23})$ and Hamming weight up to 60 for $(n,q) = (350, 2^{32})$. Though PICANTE showed a significant improvement over SALSA, it has several limitations that include the use of larger modulus for smaller dimensions viz., $(n,q) = (256, 2^{23})$ and $(n,q) = (350, 2^{32})$, but in the practical scenarios, LIZARD [13] recommends using $(n,q) = (608, 2^{10})$ for sparse binary and HE standard [1] recommends using $(n,q) = (1024, 2^{25})$ for ternary and Gaussian secrets, which are more common in practical applications, including homomorphic encryption [9,12,14,17] and KEM [8]. Furthermore, the key recovery techniques of PICANTE can also be improved to recover the non-binary secret, which is done in its successive version viz., SALSA VERDE [20].

SALSA VERDE [20], an optimized version of SALSA PICANTE, uses the optimized training process by introducing advanced hyperparameter tuning and incorporating techniques like dropout and layer normalization that made pre-processing 40 times faster and 20% more effective for recovering sparse binary, ternary, and narrow Gaussian secrets for $(n, q) = (512, 2^{41})$ with sparsity $h <= 63$. It is claimed that VERDE can recover secrets for a smaller modulus that is $(n, q) = (256, 2^{12})$ with sparsity $h = 8, 9, 5$ for binary, ternary, and Gaussian. Thus, VERDE showed significant improvements in the accuracy and robustness of the model, particularly while dealing with larger noise levels in the LWE samples compared to [21]. Though SALSA VERDE recovered secret for $(n, q) = (512, 2^{41})$ with $h = 63$, it has taken 36 days, and if we scale it to higher dimensions then the space in which the secret resides increases exponentially, which makes it harder for the model architecture of Verde to recover due to its complex geometry, and Verde can recover only secrets for smaller q, with smaller h though it has outperformed PICANTE. It has also claimed that Verde can recover the secret for $(n, q) = (256, 2^{20})$ only if the noMod data percentage is $> 67\%$, which states that the model architecture of Verde has to be improved to perform modular arithmetic better.

SALSA FRESCA [39] is the recent paper after VERDE [20]. It uses a different pre-processing step for lattice reduction; for angular embedding to enhance the modular structure in the embedding space, it encodes the integers with a single token, whereas the previous models [20, 21] took $2n$ tokens long, which eventually slowed them down as n grows. FRESCA also uses the FLATTER [36], a lattice reduction technique recently introduced in [36] to decrease the lattice reduction time. FLATTER promises a similar quality on a reduced basis as that of LLL but in much less time. Thus, using FLATTER, an improvement of almost 25X in preprocessing and the use of angular embedding coupled with an encoder-only transformer helped in reducing the model's logical and computational complexity by reducing the input sequence length to half, which made the model attain sample efficiency and also reduced the preprocessing cost by 10X.

Using SALSA FRESCA, secrets with Hamming weight $h = 13$ for an LWE sample $(n, q) = (1024, 2^{50})$ can be recovered within 73.4 hours. FRESCA has also reduced the secret recovery time for a secret having Hamming weight $h = 44$ and $(n, q) = (512, 2^{41})$, to 50 hours from 36 days in [20]. Introducing a new lattice reduction technique and using an angular embedding technique resulted in significant improvement in the pre-processing time and increased the model's performance by reducing the logical and computational complexity of the model. With these improvements, FRESCA has attained higher dimensions from that of [20, 21, 41] with and without angular embedding. It has recovered the secret for up to $h = 13$ for the dimensions $n = 768$ and $n = 1024$.

Though over the years, the SALSA series of work made a significant improvement in attacking the LWE problem with large Hamming weights by using stronger and stronger lattice reduction techniques still, the core techniques used for secret recovery is a powerful model, viz. a transformer model requiring a hefty amount of training data and computationally very expensive. Our work focuses and lies in the core model part viz., recovery of the secret key using the reduced LWE samples. We have experimentally seen that even using fewer LWE samples and using simpler and less expensive models we can recover the LWE secrets in significantly less time, more detail about the same is covered in Sect. 5.

4 Proposed Techniques to Attack LWE Problem

In this section, we will briefly cover different techniques from literature mapped to solve the LWE problem. The different techniques used to exploit the vulnerabilities of the LWE problem include

1. Linear Regression
2. Elastic Net and
3. Orthogonal Matching Pursuit

Below, we briefly review and explain how these techniques are adopted in our model to solve the LWE problem.

4.1 Linear Regression

It is a statistical method to model the relationship between a dependent variable and one or more independent variables by fitting a linear equation to the observed data [28]. Here, we can consider the LWE problem as a Linear Regression task and leverage techniques like Ordinary Least Squares (OLS) to estimate the secret vector **s** that minimizes the residual sum of squares:

$$\mathbf{s} = \arg\min_{\mathbf{s}} \|\mathbf{b} - \mathbf{A}\mathbf{s}\|_2^2$$

The solution to this minimization problem assuming **A** as a full rank matrix is given by

$$\mathbf{s} = (\mathbf{A}^T\mathbf{A})^{-1}\mathbf{A}^T\mathbf{b}$$

This approach can be adapted to solve the LWE problem given a specific percentage of noMod data (cf. Sect. 5). Despite the noise, Linear Regression can provide a close approximation to the secret, particularly when the noise level is not excessively high and a specific percentage of noMod data is fed to the system.

However, the effectiveness of Linear Regression in solving and recovering the secret vector can be limited by the noise inherent in the LWE problem. The presence of significant noise can lead to inaccurate estimates, necessitating more robust techniques or regularization methods to improve the accuracy of the secret recovery.

4.2 Elastic Net

It is a regularized regression method that has the properties of both L1 (Lasso) and L2 (Ridge) regularization [29]. It is particularly effective in scenarios where the predictor variables are highly correlated or when there are more predictors than observations. In the context of the LWE problem, the Elastic Net [43] can be employed to recover the secret vector by balancing the sparsity-inducing effects of L1 regularization [37] with the stability provided by L2 regularization [29].

This dual regularization approach helps in handling the noisy and ill-conditioned systems identical to that of the LWE problems by solving the following equation.

$$\mathbf{s} = \arg\min_{\mathbf{s}} \left(\|(\mathbf{b} - \mathbf{A}\mathbf{s}) \pmod{q}\|_2^2 + \lambda_1 \|\mathbf{s}\|_1 + \lambda_2 \|\mathbf{s}\|_2^2 \right)$$

To solve this problem, we use coordinate descent [42] with modular arithmetic data incorporated in each update step as shown by Algorithm 1 presented below.

Algorithm 1. Elastic Net with Modular Arithmetic

1: Initialize with an initial guess for the secret **s**
2: **while** stopping criterion not met **do**
3:   **for** each secret coordinate s_j **do**
4:     Update considering modular arithmetic:
      $s_j = \arg\min_{s_j} \left(\|(\mathbf{b} - \mathbf{A}_{\neg j}\mathbf{s}_{\neg j} - \mathbf{a}_j s_j) \pmod{q}\|_2^2 + \lambda_1 \|s_j\| + \lambda_2 \|s_j\|^2 \right)$
5:     Reduce the updated modulo q:
      $s_j \equiv s_j \pmod{q}$
6:   **end for**
7: **end while**

By tuning the regularization parameters, one can control the trade-off between sparsity and smoothness in the estimated secret vector. This flexibility is particularly valuable in the LWE scenarios where the noise level and the structure of the secret vector may vary, allowing for a tailored recovery strategy.

Elastic Net's ability to handle multicollinearity among the predictors is another significant advantage in the LWE context. If the columns of the public matrix in the LWE problems exhibit any correlations among its columns, it can complicate the secret recovery process. In such situations, this model addresses this issue by combining the strengths of Lasso and Ridge regression, effectively managing the correlations and leading to more stable and reliable estimates of the secret vector. Additionally, the algorithm can be efficiently implemented using the coordinate descent methods, making it suitable for large-scale LWE problems. Furthermore, the versatility and robustness of Elastic Net make it a powerful tool for secret recovery in a noisy environment such as that of the LWE problem.

4.3 Orthogonal Matching Pursuit

It is a greedy algorithm widely used for sparse signal recovery and approximations [40]. In the context of the LWE problem, orthogonal matching pursuit (OMP) can be instrumental in the recovery of the secret vector by exploiting its potential sparsity. The algorithm iteratively selects the columns of the public matrix that are most correlated with the residual error, thereby building an approximation of the secret vector step-by-step. This iterative process continues until a stopping criterion, such as a predefined number of iterations or a residual error threshold, is met. The working process of the OMP can be illustrated by Algorithm 2 given below.

Algorithm 2. OMP with Modular Arithmetic

1: Initialize residual $\mathbf{r} = \mathbf{b}$, set of selected indices $\Lambda = \emptyset$, and approximation $\hat{\mathbf{s}} = \mathbf{0}$
2: **while** stopping criterion not met **do**
3:     Select the index j that maximizes the correlation with the residual modulo q:
    $j = \arg\max_i \left|(\mathbf{a}_i^T \mathbf{r}) \pmod{q}\right|$
4:     Update the set of selected indices:
    $\Lambda = \Lambda \cup \{j\}$
5:     Solve the least squares problem for the selected indices modulo q:
    $\hat{\mathbf{s}}_\Lambda = \arg\min_{\mathbf{s}_\Lambda} \|(\mathbf{b} - \mathbf{A}_\Lambda \mathbf{s}_\Lambda) \pmod{q}\|_2^2$
6:     Update the residual modulo q:
    $\mathbf{r} = (\mathbf{b} - \mathbf{A}_\Lambda \hat{\mathbf{s}}_\Lambda) \pmod{q}$
7: **end while**

By incorporating the modular reduction at each step, OMP can effectively account for the modular nature of LWE and iteratively build an accurate approximation of the secret vector. In the case of the LWE problem, when there is a moderate level of noise, the OMP model can effectively isolate and recover the sparse secret components, yielding a high-quality approximation.

Moreover, OMP's flexibility and adaptability make it suitable for various extensions and enhancements. For instance, it can be combined with thresholding techniques to improve the robustness against noise or integrated into hybrid methods that leverage both greedy and optimization-based approaches. The application of OMP to the LWE problem also benefits from its compatibility with parallel and distributed computing environments, enabling the handling of large-scale problems. Overall, OMP's ability to efficiently recover sparse signals makes it a powerful tool in the arsenal of techniques for solving the LWE problem.

5 Result and Analysis

This section covers the experimental setup, methodology, and results. In brief, the technique used in this work to solve the LWE problem works by sampling LWE data samples using TinyLWE sampler as that of SALSA PICANTE [21]. The sampled LWE data samples are later pre-processed using the standard lattice reduction algorithms from the literature. The pre-processed data samples are later fed to different algorithms discussed in Sect. 4 for secret recovery. Below, we have covered each of these steps in detail. Using our implementation code, results can be verified using publicly available code shared and is available in GitHub link[1].

---
[1] https://github.com/srikanthyadav007/MALAI.

5.1 Data Preprocessing

The attack proceeds by fixing security parameters viz., the lattice dimension (n), modulus (q), secret distribution (χ), and Hamming weight (hwt). Once the security parameters are fixed, $4n$ LWE samples are generated. Using sampled matrices basis matrices are constructed and are pre-processed using the standard lattice reduction algorithms. However, suppose we construct a lattice basis using these $4n$ samples. In that case, the reduced sample size will be only $8n$ (Lattice constitution increases the total sample size by a multiple of 2), and to use a machine learning algorithm to work, we need more samples. Thus, we used the TinyLWE sampler from [21] to sample n samples with repetition a total of 2048 times to get a total of 2048 matrices. Once we sample a total of 2048 matrices of size $n \times n$, we reduce these matrices using standard lattice reduction algorithms to get a total of 2^{20}, i.e., 1 million (2048 × n × 2, n = 256) reduced LWE samples. Since [20,21] used transformer models for recovering the secret, they required a large set of 4 million data samples, whereas our method uses simple linear models like Linear Regression, OMP, and Elastic Net; hence we do not require a large number of samples set for training, cutting down the data pre-processing costs almost by 4 times in terms of number of cores.

For the experiment, we have considered the binary secret vector **s** with Hamming weight (hwt) up to 40, with a modulus $q = 842779$, and the noise vector **e** is sampled from a discrete Gaussian distribution with standard deviation 3.2. The data includes 10 different secrets for every Hamming weight (hwt) ranging from [3, 40]. In short, for 38 different Hamming weights, we have 380 different secrets to calculate, which are calculated using different techniques mentioned in Sect. 4 and are discussed below.

5.2 Results

In our experiments, we have applied Linear Regression, Elastic Net, and Orthogonal Matching Pursuit (OMP) to the pre-processed data samples obtained using techniques mentioned in Sect. 5.1. Our dataset comprises 1 million LWE samples of $(n, q) = (256, 842779)$. We trained three models on approximately 1 million LWE samples (**A, b**), ensuring all elements of **A** and **b** are within the range $(\frac{-q}{2}, \frac{q}{2})$.

Given that our models are regression-based, the model coefficients represent the secret of the given instance, adhering to the LWE samples, which are non-binary, viz., real values. To convert these real values representing coefficients of the secret vector, we used a threshold to determine whether to round it to 0 or 1. The threshold is calculated by computing $\frac{(\min+\max)}{2}$ based on the smallest and greatest values in the recovered real-valued secret vector. The coefficients greater than or equal to this threshold are converted to 1, while others are set to 0. This method allowed us to convert the recovered real-valued secret vector into a binary secret vector.

Out of the 380 secrets, some secrets are successfully recovered by all three models using the thresholding technique mentioned above, whereas in a few cases, only one model among the three recovered the secret. Experimentally, we have observed that OMP performs well for secrets with lower Hamming weights, whereas Linear Regression performs well for secrets with higher Hamming weights. Elastic Net showed behavior similar to that of Linear Regression. This variation among the models has been seen because of their respective strengths. As OMP is a greedy algorithm it performs well for low Hamming weights because its design focuses on identifying and leveraging the few non-zero elements in the secret vector, as sparsity is its strength. In contrast, Linear Regression treats all features equally, so it performs well for high dimensions without considering the density and Elastic Net balances between sparsity while dealing with multicollinearity, making it more versatile for various higher Hamming weights.

For experiments, we have divided the data samples into two categories viz., Mod data samples and noMod data samples. As it is clear from the name itself, noMod data samples **a** are the ones that do not require mod applied in the calculation of b after pre-processing. Mathematically, noMod data samples **a** consist of all data samples where the calculated value b is less than q viz., $b = \mathbf{a} \cdot \mathbf{s} + e < q$, whereas Mod data samples are the one where the mod gets applied in the calculation of b viz., $b = \mathbf{a} \cdot \mathbf{s} + e > q$. Hence, the mod operation gets applied in the pre-processed data samples for the calculation of b in the Mod data samples. After pre-processing, each element of the obtained data samples is in the range $(0, q]$ which are converted in the range $[\frac{-q}{2}, \frac{q}{2}]$ by performing a simple calculation as follows: if $x > \frac{q}{2}$, then replace it by $x = q - x$, to each element of **a** and b. Now, using these modified data samples, we have calculated the percentage of noMod and Mod data samples and plotted a figure, which is shown by the Fig. 1 below.

From Fig. 1, it is clear that an increase in Hamming weight results in a decrease in the percentage of noMod data samples viz., from 91% for Hamming weight 3 to 45% for Hamming weight 40. We have experimentally seen that the percentage of noMod data has a strong correlation with secret key recovery. An increase in noMod data samples results in easy secret key recovery, while below a certain threshold number of noMod data samples may not lead to secret key recovery at all. In Verde, using the transformer model, they could recover the secret key for the LWE samples having noMod data samples no less than 67%. In our experiments, we have obtained similar results using the different models covered in Sect. 4.

To further investigate the relationship between noMod data and that of the number of samples, we have performed experiments by varying noMod data percentage and data sample sizes. To be precise, we have performed experiments with noMod data percentages of 60%, 65%, 70%, 75%, and 80%, with varying numbers of samples for secret key recovery. Experiments revealed that an increase in the percentage of noMod data requires a lesser number of data samples for the secret key recovery and vice-versa, which was expected. This is because a high percentage of noMod data means more data to send the secret in the correct direction. Hence, it eventually requires fewer data samples, while a

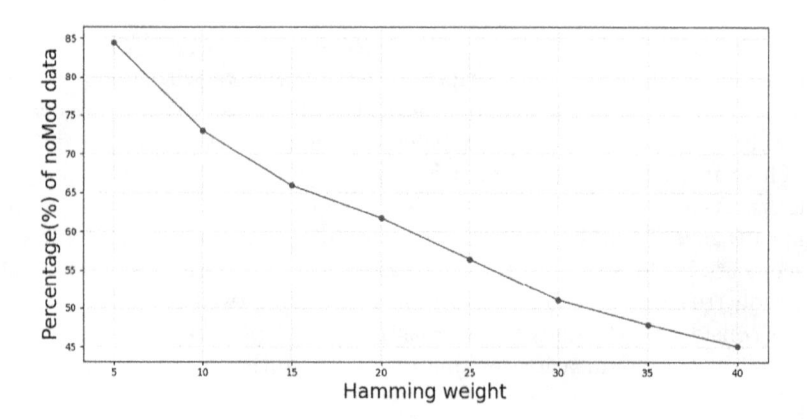

Fig. 1. Figure showing the percentage of noMod data for varying Hamming weight (hwt). A high value of noMod data means the instance can be solved, while a low value of noMod data makes the instance hard to solve.

decrease in the percentage of noMod data requires more samples. This is because more number of Mod data samples means more random data samples, which the model is not able to learn; thus, it eventually requires more number of data samples. Experiments performed with varying percentages of noMod data and the required number of data samples for successful secret key recovery have been shown in Table 1 below.

Table 1. Table showing minimum # of total samples required for different percentages of noMod data for each secret key recovery with a given Hamming weight. No of samples are in a multiple of 10, 000.

Hamming weight		16	18	20	22	24	26	28	30	32	34	36	38	40
100% Recovery	noMod %	80	70	80	75	75	70	65	70	70	65	65	60	60
	# of samples	10	50	50	20	20	50	75	50	50	50	50	50	75
90% Recovery	noMod %	70	70	75	70	70	70	65	65	65	65	60	60	60
	# of samples	75	50	75	50	50	50	50	75	50	50	100	100	75
80% Recovery	noMod %	65	70	75	70	65	70	65	65	65	60	60	60	60
	# of samples	75	50	20	50	75	50	50	75	50	100	100	50	75

Table 1 below shows the minimum number of samples required for secret key recovery in multiples of 10, 000. The required number of samples of type noMod and Mod for secret key recovery for each Hamming weight can be calculated by computing

$$\text{noMod samples} = \text{\# of samples} \times \left(\frac{\text{noMod \%}}{100}\right)$$
$$\text{Mod samples} = \text{\# of samples} - \text{noMod samples}$$

Furthermore, experiments also resulted in an interesting finding: the models exhibited different recovery capabilities based on the Hamming weights. For lower Hamming weights, only OMP was effective in recovering certain columns, whereas for higher Hamming weights, Linear Regression and Elastic Net were more effective, with OMP failing to recover secrets.

The experiment also revealed that the secret key can be recovered with a lower noMod percentage as the Hamming weight increases. Conversely, for very low Hamming weights, a high noMod percentage (greater than 80%) is required to recover the secret. This is because for higher Hamming weights, the secret has more non-zero entries, providing more information that can be leveraged to distinguish signal from noise, making it easier to recover the secret even with a lower noMod percentage. The larger number of non-zero entries helps in identifying patterns and correlations that can be exploited by machine learning models or other recovery techniques. Conversely, for very low Hamming weights, there are fewer non-zero entries in the secret. This scarcity of information makes it more challenging to distinguish the secret from the noise, requiring a higher noMod percentage to provide sufficient information for recovery. With more noMod samples, the error distribution becomes clearer, and the sparse non-zero entries of the secret become more apparent, facilitating the secret key recovery.

Figure 2 shows the percentage of time the secret key got recovered (number of times the secret key recovered from 10 different secrets) with a varying number of samples for different noMod data percentages. From the figure, it is clear that for 80% noMod data, 50K samples are sufficient to recover the secret, for 75% noMod data, 100K samples are sufficient to recover the secret, and so forth.

6 Discussions and Future Research Direction

In this work, we have shown that costly models used for LWE secret key recovery can be replaced by simpler models requiring less computational resources and time. The obtained results are similar to those of the results obtained using the transformer models used in the literature. However, the current work is unable to answer a few questions in its current form.

In the work presented in this paper and even in the literature, we are not aware of any methods to identify data samples of similar type, viz., an algorithm to identify noMod and/or Mod data samples from a chunk of data samples without having access to the secret key. If we can find any method to classify data samples into noMod and Mod data types without having access to the secret

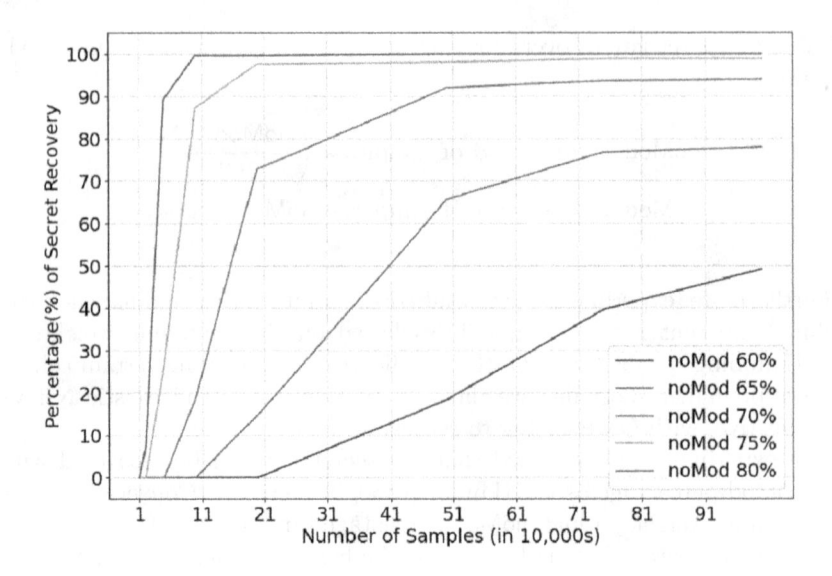

Fig. 2. Figure showing Percentage of Secret Recovery vs noMod data

key then the secret key with a much higher Hamming weight can be recovered. Thus, one of our goals for the future is to find techniques/algorithms to classify data samples into two categories without having access to the secret key.

Additionally, in the present work, we have only focused on recovering binary secret keys, while in most of the practical cases, secrets with ternary distribution and/or Gaussian distribution are used. Thus, in the future, we will try to generalize our secret key recovery techniques to more general cases, including ternary and Gaussian secrets.

7 Conclusion

This paper investigates the application of linear models, viz., Linear Regression, Orthogonal Matching Pursuit (OMP), and Elastic Net, to recover the binary secret vector in the LWE problem. Our experimental results show that these linear models can effectively recover the secret vector with high success rates similar to the transformer models given pre-processed data samples. The key findings of our experiments include:

- Linear models, particularly Linear Regression and Elastic Net, showed strong performance across various Hamming weights, while OMP excelled at lower Hamming weights and Linear Regression at higher Hamming weights.
- The noMod percentage is critical for the secret key recovery, with higher percentages correlating with successful secret recovery using fewer samples and vice versa.

- Comparing our results with the transformer-based approach highlights the efficiency and computational advantages of our linear models, achieving comparable recovery rates with fewer samples and reduced computational time.

In conclusion, our study suggests that attacking the LWE problem using pre-processed LWE samples does not require high-cost computation models, viz., transformers, as used in the literature. These models can be replaced by the simpler linear models saving both computational time and resources. Experiments suggest that by using simpler models, we can cut down the number of cores required to pre-process the LWE samples by almost an order of four to that of the earlier models and the secret key recovery process by an order of 80.

References

1. Albrecht, M., et al.: Homomorphic encryption standard. Protecting privacy through homomorphic encryption, pp. 31–62 (2021)
2. Albrecht, M.R., Cid, C., Faugere, J.C., Fitzpatrick, R., Perret, L.: On the complexity of the BKW algorithm on LWE. Des. Codes Crypt. **74**, 325–354 (2015)
3. Albrecht, M.R., Fitzpatrick, R., Göpfert, F.: On the efficacy of solving LWE by reduction to unique-SVP. In: Lee, H.-S., Han, D.-G. (eds.) ICISC 2013. LNCS, vol. 8565, pp. 293–310. Springer, Cham (2014). https://doi.org/10.1007/978-3-319-12160-4_18
4. Albrecht, M.R., Player, R., Scott, S.: On the concrete hardness of learning with errors. J. Math. Cryptol. **9**(3), 169–203 (2015)
5. Arora, S., Ge, R.: New algorithms for learning in presence of errors. In: Aceto, L., Henzinger, M., Sgall, J. (eds.) ICALP 2011. LNCS, vol. 6755, pp. 403–415. Springer, Heidelberg (2011). https://doi.org/10.1007/978-3-642-22006-7_34
6. Blum, A., Kalai, A., Wasserman, H.: Noise-tolerant learning, the parity problem, and the statistical query model. J. ACM (JACM) **50**(4), 506–519 (2003)
7. Boneh, D., Di Crescenzo, G., Ostrovsky, R., Persiano, G.: Public key encryption with keyword search. In: Cachin, C., Camenisch, J.L. (eds.) EUROCRYPT 2004. LNCS, vol. 3027, pp. 506–522. Springer, Heidelberg (2004). https://doi.org/10.1007/978-3-540-24676-3_30
8. Bos, J., et al.: Crystals-kyber: a CCA-secure module-lattice-based KEM. In: 2018 IEEE European Symposium on Security and Privacy (EuroS&P), pp. 353–367. IEEE (2018)
9. Brakerski, Z., Vaikuntanathan, V.: Efficient fully homomorphic encryption from (standard) LWE. SIAM J. Comput. **43**(2), 831–871 (2014)
10. Chen, H., Lauter, K., Stange, K.E.: Attacks on the search RLWE problem with small errors. SIAM J. Appl. Algebra Geom. **1**(1), 665–682 (2017)
11. Chen, Y., Nguyen, P.Q.: BKZ 2.0: better lattice security estimates. In: Lee, D.H., Wang, X. (eds.) ASIACRYPT 2011. LNCS, vol. 7073, pp. 1–20. Springer, Heidelberg (2011). https://doi.org/10.1007/978-3-642-25385-0_1
12. Cheon, J.H., Kim, A., Kim, M., Song, Y.: Homomorphic encryption for arithmetic of approximate numbers. In: Takagi, T., Peyrin, T. (eds.) ASIACRYPT 2017. LNCS, vol. 10624, pp. 409–437. Springer, Cham (2017). https://doi.org/10.1007/978-3-319-70694-8_15

13. Cheon, J.H., Kim, D., Lee, J., Song, Y.: Lizard: cut off the tail! a practical post-quantum public-key encryption from LWE and LWR. In: Catalano, D., De Prisco, R. (eds.) SCN 2018. LNCS, vol. 11035, pp. 160–177. Springer, Cham (2018). https://doi.org/10.1007/978-3-319-98113-0_9
14. Chillotti, I., Gama, N., Georgieva, M., Izabachène, M.: TFHE: fast fully homomorphic encryption over the torus. J. Cryptol. **33**(1), 34–91 (2020)
15. Ducas, L., et al.: Crystals-dilithium: a lattice-based digital signature scheme. IACR Transactions on Cryptographic Hardware and Embedded Systems, pp. 238–268 (2018)
16. Elias, Y., Lauter, K.E., Ozman, E., Stange, K.E.: Provably weak instances of ring-LWE. In: Gennaro, R., Robshaw, M. (eds.) CRYPTO 2015. LNCS, vol. 9215, pp. 63–92. Springer, Heidelberg (2015). https://doi.org/10.1007/978-3-662-47989-6_4
17. Fan, J., Vercauteren, F.: Somewhat practical fully homomorphic encryption. Cryptology ePrint Archive (2012)
18. Khot, S.: Hardness of approximating the shortest vector problem in lattices. J. ACM (JACM) **52**(5), 789–808 (2005)
19. Lenstra, A.K., Lenstra, H.W., Lovász, L.: Factoring polynomials with rational coefficients. Math. Ann. **261**, 515–534 (1982)
20. Li, C., Wenger, E., Allen-Zhu, Z., Charton, F., Lauter, K.E.: Salsa Verde: a machine learning attack on LWE with sparse small secrets. In: Advances in Neural Information Processing Systems, vol. 36, pp. 53343–53361 (2023)
21. Li, C.Y., et al.: Salsapicante: a machine learning attack on LWE with binary secrets. In: Proceedings of the 2023 ACM SIGSAC Conference on Computer and Communications Security, pp. 2606–2620 (2023)
22. Lyubashevsky, V.: Lattice-based identification schemes secure under active attacks. In: Cramer, R. (ed.) PKC 2008. LNCS, vol. 4939, pp. 162–179. Springer, Heidelberg (2008). https://doi.org/10.1007/978-3-540-78440-1_10
23. May, A., Ozerov, I.: On computing nearest neighbors with applications to decoding of binary linear codes. In: Oswald, E., Fischlin, M. (eds.) EUROCRYPT 2015. LNCS, vol. 9056, pp. 203–228. Springer, Heidelberg (2015). https://doi.org/10.1007/978-3-662-46800-5_9
24. McCurley, K.S.: The discrete logarithm problem. In: Proceedings of Symposium in Applied Mathematics, vol. 42, pp. 49–74. USA (1990)
25. Micciancio, D.: On the hardness of the shortest vector problem. Ph.D. thesis, Massachusetts Institute of Technology (1998)
26. Micciancio, D., Goldwasser, S.: Complexity of Lattice Problems: A Cryptographic Perspective, vol. 671. Springer, Cham (2002)
27. Micciancio, D., Regev, O.: Lattice-based cryptography. In: Bernstein, D.J., Buchmann, J., Dahmen, E. (eds.) Post-Quantum Cryptography, pp. 147–191. Springer, Heidelberg (2009). https://doi.org/10.1007/978-3-540-88702-7_5
28. Montgomery, D.C., Peck, E.A., Vining, G.G.: Introduction to Linear Regression Analysis. Wiley, Hoboken (2021)
29. Ng, A.Y.: Feature selection, l 1 vs. l 2 regularization, and rotational invariance. In: Proceedings of the Twenty-First International Conference on Machine Learning, p. 78 (2004)
30. NIST: Post-quantum cryptography (PQC) standardization, 03 January 2017. https://csrc.nist.gov/Projects/post-quantum-cryptography/post-quantum-cryptography-standardization. Accessed 31 July 2024
31. Peikert, C.: Public-key cryptosystems from the worst-case shortest vector problem. In: Proceedings of the Forty-First Annual ACM Symposium on Theory of Computing, pp. 333–342 (2009)

32. Peikert, C., et al.: A decade of lattice cryptography. Found. Trends® Theor. Comput. Sci. **10**(4), 283–424 (2016)
33. Regev, O.: On lattices, learning with errors, random linear codes, and cryptography. In: STOC 2005. Association for Computing Machinery, New York (2005). https://doi.org/10.1145/1060590.1060603
34. Regev, O.: On lattices, learning with errors, random linear codes, and cryptography. J. ACM (JACM) **56**(6), 1–40 (2009)
35. Rivest, R.L., Shamir, A., Adleman, L.: A method for obtaining digital signatures and public-key cryptosystems. Commun. ACM **21**(2), 120–126 (1978)
36. Ryan, K., Heninger, N.: Fast practical lattice reduction through iterated compression. In: Handschuh, H., Lysyanskaya, A. (eds.) CRYPTO 2023. LNCS, vol. 14083, pp. 3–33. Springer, Cham (2023). https://doi.org/10.1007/978-3-031-38548-3_1
37. Schmidt, M., Fung, G., Rosales, R.: Fast optimization methods for L1 regularization: a comparative study and two new approaches. In: Kok, J.N., Koronacki, J., Mantaras, R.L., Matwin, S., Mladenič, D., Skowron, A. (eds.) ECML 2007. LNCS (LNAI), vol. 4701, pp. 286–297. Springer, Heidelberg (2007). https://doi.org/10.1007/978-3-540-74958-5_28
38. Shor, P.W.: Algorithms for quantum computation: discrete logarithms and factoring. In: Proceedings 35th Annual Symposium on Foundations of Computer Science, pp. 124–134. IEEE (1994)
39. Stevens, S., et al.: SALSA FRESCA: angular embeddings and pre-training for ML attacks on learning with errors. arXiv preprint arXiv:2402.01082 (2024)
40. Tropp, J.A., Gilbert, A.C.: Signal recovery from random measurements via orthogonal matching pursuit. IEEE Trans. Inf. Theory **53**(12), 4655–4666 (2007)
41. Wenger, E., Chen, M., Charton, F., Lauter, K.E.: Salsa: attacking lattice cryptography with transformers. In: Advances in Neural Information Processing Systems, vol. 35, pp. 34981–34994 (2022)
42. Wright, S.J.: Coordinate descent algorithms. Math. Program. **151**(1), 3–34 (2015)
43. Zou, H., Hastie, T.: Regularization and variable selection via the elastic net. J. R. Stat. Soc. Ser. B Stat. Methodol. **67**(2), 301–320 (2005)

Patch Based Backdoor Attack on Deep Neural Networks

Debasmita Manna and Somanath Tripathy[✉]

Department of Computer Science and Engineering, Indian Institute of Technology Patna, Patna, India
{debasmita_2121cs18,som}@iitp.ac.in

Abstract. Deep neural networks *(DNNs)* have become prevalent and being used across various fields. Meanwhile, their extensive use has been raising some major security concerns. *DNNs* can be fooled by an adversary as a small intelligent change in input would cause change of output label. Existing methodologies require model retraining on a poisoned dataset or inserting additional multilayer perceptron *(MLPs)*, which involves additional computation and time constraints. This work presents a backdoor attack, which generates a small patch to misclassify the prediction, if added to the image. Interestingly, the patch does not affect the physical appearance of the image. The patch is generated by determining influential features through sensitivity analysis. Subsequently, negative-contributing features are generated as the intended patch using Intersection over union *(IoU)*. The most interesting part of our proposed technique is that it does not require the model re-training or any alterations to the model. Experiments on three different types of datasets (*MNIST*, *CIFAR-10*, and *GTSRB*) demonstrate the effectiveness of the attack. It is observed that our proposed method achieves a higher attack success rate around 50–70%, without compromising the test accuracy for clean input samples.

Keywords: Data poisoning · model security · patch generation

1 Introduction

Deep Neural Networks *(DNNs)* are now accepted as the most promising technology, being widely used across different sectors [1,14–17,20]. *DNNs* include several layers, each composed of interconnected neurons, that process and extract features from data [27]. Through iterative training *DNNs* learn complex patterns, enabling them to make accurate prediction. Numerous emerging markets Berkeley's Caffe model zoo[1], BigML[2], and ModelDepot model market[3] etc. have surfaced for the trading of pre-trained *DNNs* models.

---
[1] https://modelzoo.co/.
[2] https://bigml.com/.
[3] https://modeldepot.io/.

Meanwhile, an attacker may intentionally target *DNNs* to misclassify a target instance as any other instance. For instance, the presence of four small rectangles attached to the surface of the sign misled the car, to misinterpret the signal *stop* as *speed limit 120* [6].

Such deliberate attacks are more severe, because these are crafted insidiously against particular models. Some earlier studies on deliberate attacks introduce trojaned behaviors by training the target model again using a contaminated dataset [5,12,21,23]. The patch is utilized in the form of a trojan trigger that is independent of input data, enabling universal attacks where triggers are effective across all inputs. An adversarial attack can lead to misclassification in *DNNs* by introducing a specific trigger [4,9]. Adversarial triggers, typically irregular and noisy patterns, are crafted post-model training. Adversarial attacks are input-specific, necessitating the generation of perturbations for each input. On the other hand, in [26], the attacker inserts an *MLP* into the target model to manipulate predictions, altering the model's structure in the process and in [22] the attacker drops out some target neurons and subsequently re-trains the model too, which leads to the alteration of the target model.

In [10], the attacker uses a pre-trained autoencoder to generate adversarial examples, which can be thought of as the original images with minor perturbations. The adversarial samples are then used to train the object detector, and after that, they create two optimization paths for the loss function with the goals of minimizing the probability of the ground truth class and maximizing the probability of the background class, thus leading to the incorrect prediction of any label as background class. In [24], the attacker generates the hash code of the target category, concatenates it to the benign image, re-trains the encoder-decoder to generate the final poisoned image, and re-trains the model to predict the label incorrectly.

In [13], the attacker subtly poisons the training data. The attack operates in two main phases including gradient ascent and gradient descent. During the gradient ascent phase, the attacker identifies and modifies a small subset of the training data to maximize the loss on a validation set, effectively degrading the model's performance. Concurrently, gradient descent is applied to optimize the model's parameters for the combined original and poisoned datasets, ensuring that the model still appears to perform well during training. This dual-step process, which utilizes conjugate gradient methods to efficiently compute gradients, allows for the introduction of poisoned data points without needing extensive computational resources.

Recent works [5,11,12,21,23,26], has emerged in implanting trojans into target models. The basic intuition behind these attack methods involves preparing a dataset that contains the poisoned data and then fine-tuning the target model with corrupted samples. This process compels the model to understand how trojan triggers are correlated to specific behaviors, such as incorrectly categorizing inputs into a predetermined label. During testing, compromised *DNNs* would demonstrate the predetermined responses when the trigger is introduced into input. Despite progress in trojan attacks, several technical challenges persist. To begin with, the process of retraining a target model with a contaminated dataset tends to be resource-intensive and time-consuming owing to the intricate nature of widely employed *DNNs*. Secondly, this additional retraining may potentially decrease model functionality when incorporating trojans into multiple labels.

In this paper, we address the critical gap by proposing an attack with several key advantages. This method eliminates the need to retrain the target model on a poisoned dataset by employing stealthy trigger patterns as influential patches. By being model agnostic, our attack can be easily applied to various deep neural networks with minimal effort. The patch is generated by determining influential features through gradient calculation, where only negative features are considered. Subsequently, the patch is generated by taking the maximum of a few highly negative-contributing features utilized by Intersection over union (*IoU*). For instance, when aiming to misclassify the target label 9, we identify the patches with negative contributions. When these generated patches are inserted into target label 9, it results in misclassification as any other label with a misclassification rate of 70.86% and attack success rate of 68.4%. Lastly, trojan injection does not impact the *DNN's* performance on original tasks, ensuring the attack remains imperceptible. Additionally, it only requires access to target samples and the addition of a small patch on that. Thus, it significantly broadens the scope of potential attack scenarios.

The key contributions of this work are as below.

- We propose a patch-based backdoor attack, to misclassify a label to the desired label without re-training the model.
- The patch is generated by identifying influential features through sensitivity analysis, considering the maximum of only highly negatively contributing features. Patches associated with negative contributions are generated using IoU.
- The attack is performed on digit recognition (*MNIST*), object recognition (*CIFAR-10*), and traffic sign classification (*GTSRB*). It is demonstrated that the attack success rate is higher around 50–70%, without creating any impact on the regular inputs.
- The effectiveness of attack is analyzed analytically through *Chi-square* test and *Bayes theorem*. It is observed that there is a strong co-relation between the insertion of the patch and the misclassification.

The remaining sections are arranged as follows: Sect. 2 gives a comprehensive review of existing literature. Section 3 discusses the threat model. Section 4 details the methodology of the proposed work. Section 5 discusses the experimental results followed by analytical results in Sect. 6. Section 7 concludes this proposed work.

2 Background and Related Work

This section briefs the basic concepts used in the proposed attack, and the related work in similar direction.

2.1 Sensitivity Analysis

Sensitivity analysis is an explanation technique of post-hoc interpretability. It determines the impact of individual input features on model predictions in the context of *DNNs* [7,18,19,25]. To determine the relevance of each feature x_i for explaining $f(x)$, a relevance score R_i is computed for each sample image x. Relevance score indicates the contribution of that feature in the prediction of the model. The relevance score of a pixel (x_i) in image x may be defined as:

$$R_i(\boldsymbol{x}) = \left(\frac{\partial f(x)}{\partial x_i}\right) \quad (1)$$

2.2 Chi-Square Test

The Chi-square test is performed to estimate the relationship between categorical variables. This statistical method evaluates the significance of the association by quantifying the difference between observed frequencies (O) and expected frequencies (E) within a contingency table. The Chi-square statistic derived from this comparison is then evaluated against a critical value. The test is performed using the following formula:

$$\chi^2 = \sum (O-E)^2/E \quad (2)$$

2.3 Bayes Theorem

Bayes' theorem provides a mathematical framework to estimate the probability of an event based on prior knowledge of conditions related to the event. Mathematically, it is represented as:

$$\begin{aligned} P(A \mid B) &= \frac{P(A \cap B)}{P(B)} \\ &= \frac{P(B \mid A) \cdot P(A)}{P(B)} \end{aligned} \quad (3)$$

where, P(A): Probability of event A; P(B): Probability of event B; $P(A \mid B)$: Probability of event A, given B; $P(B \mid A)$: Probability of event B, given A.

2.4 Related Work

DNNs pose challenges for interpretation due to their complex structure, with several neurons representing uninterpretable features in the input space. Current trojan attacks seek to embed malicious behaviors within a model. These behaviors are activated by specific input patterns known as trojan triggers. When a trigger-laden input is presented, the model misclassifies it to the attacker desired label, while functioning normally otherwise. Typically, trojan triggers manifest as patches, such as small squares overlaid on regular input images, not much affecting the appearance of the image.

Authors in [5] proposed injecting a trigger in the randomly selected inputs. The label of the triggered input is set by the attacker to re-train the model, such that the model classifies the clean input accurately and triggered input as the attacker's target. They used yellow square, bomb, and flower as triggers. Liu et al. [12] proposed a technique to generate the trojan trigger and training data. The attacker initializes a trojan and some selected neurons. The trojan is generated in such a way that, by changing the values in the trojan the values of the selected neurons can be easily manipulated. Similarly, to generate the training data, the attacker uses the reverse engineering technique. This technique tunes the pixel values in the image until the selected nodes (final output) receive the highest values compared to the remaining nodes. The generated trojan includes the square, apple logo, and watermark. After generating the trojan and poisoned data, they re-train the model to misclassify the label.

Lin et al. [11] proposed a backdoor attack, where the attacker generates poisoned samples by mixing up two labels and re-training the model. The trigger includes two images and pastes one image on the other. In the presence of the triggers, an input is misclassified as the attacker's desire. Tang et al. [26] proposed a method where the attacker inserts 4 layers of trained *MLP* containing 32 neurons within the target model. The target model is not re-trained by the attacker, while they infect the target model by inserting *MLP* into it. A QR code is used as a trigger, containing zero and one. The *MLP* is trained based on the triggers and then the attacker merges the prediction of the *MLP* and the target model prediction. The prediction of the *MLP* dominated the output of the target model.

Saha et al. [21] proposed a technique, where the attacker inserts a patch on the clean source and optimizes between the patched source and the clean target to generate the poisoned targets using optimization technique *L2 norm*. Then the poisoned data is injected into the training data by the attacker and re-trains the model based on the modified training dataset. At the testing time, the attacker inserts the trigger to the source images and the model mispredicts the source image as the target images. A random matrix of colors is used as a trigger.

In [2] a specially designed patch is utilized to mislead image classifiers. Instead of subtly modifying the entire image, the patch can be transformed and placed at various locations. They train the patch using a variety of images so it can be effective regardless of what's in the background. In [8] instead of simply adding noise to the entire image, the attacker replaces a specific area of the image by using a mask, which controls where the noise is applied. Rather than just maximizing the probability of the target class or minimizing the probability of the source class, they use a combined approach. Loss function encourages the model to increase the likelihood of predicting target class while simultaneously reducing the likelihood of predicting the actual class. They achieve this by working with the network's activations before the final classification layer, which allows us to better separate the outputs for different classes and improves the speed of optimization. In [3] the process of creating an adversarial patch that resembles a QR code involves several steps. First, they generate a QR code from a text or URL, which consists of black and white areas represented as 0 s and 1 s. Then create a blank mask matching the original image size and randomly rotate and place the QR patch on this mask. The black areas of the patch are set to 0 initially, meaning they won't be trained. During the training phase, the masked patch is applied to various training images, with the goal of maximizing the classifier's confidence in recognizing the QR patch as a target class. This involves using backpropagation to adjust the patch based on its performance and updating it accordingly. Once the patch is trained, they enhance the black areas to create a transparent zone around the QR code, ensuring it remains effective for classification while still being scannable by QR code scanners.

Shafahi et al. [23] introduced an attack strategy wherein the attacker aims to misclassify the target instance as the base instance. Using the L_2 norm optimization technique, poisoned images closely resembling the target instance in the feature space are generated and labeled similarly to the base instance. Upon retraining the model with these poisoned instances, the target instance is misclassified as the base instance. Additionally, Salem et al. [22] proposed a method to misclassify any label as label 0 using dropout technique. Here, the attacker re-trains the target model with the target label instead of the ground truth label while dropping out the target neurons, although the concept of target neurons remains unclear.

The existing works [5,11,12,21–23,26] require either re-training the target model on the poisoned data or inserting a trained *MLP* to the target model or dropping some neurons from the target model to re-train it. They utilize some external patches including *squares, watermarks, logos, flowers, bombs, and QR codes*. In [2,8] the attacker modifies the model, because in [8] the method applies noise to specific parts of the image while balancing the goal of promoting the new class and reducing the old one by using model's internal output and in [2] the attacker trains the patch. In our proposed work, the attacker includes an intended patch to misclassify the model's prediction, without the requirement of re-training the model. Also, the intended patch is not external. It is the combination of the negative contributed features of the target label. It is also assumed that the attacker have no knowledge about the actual training dataset.

3 Threat Model

Let $\mathcal{D}_{train} = \{(x_1, y_1), ..., (x_n, y_n)\}$ and $\mathcal{D}_{test} = \{(x_1, y_1), ..., (x_m, y_m)\}$ represent the training and testing data, where x_i, y_i denote the input sample and corresponding label (probability vector) and n, m is the total number of samples present in the $\mathcal{D}_{train}$ and $\mathcal{D}_{test}$ respectively. The target model trained on $\mathcal{D}_{train}$ is denoted as f. For an attacker ($\mathcal{A}$) the challenge is to discover a way to impel the target model to misclassify the prediction, without re-train the target model. It is assumed that the attacker can access both the model's architecture and its weights, so the attacker possesses full white-box access to the target model. The attack is considered successful if the model f misclassifies an input x_i as a different instance during testing, without requiring re-training of the target model.

4 The Proposed Attack

4.1 Overview

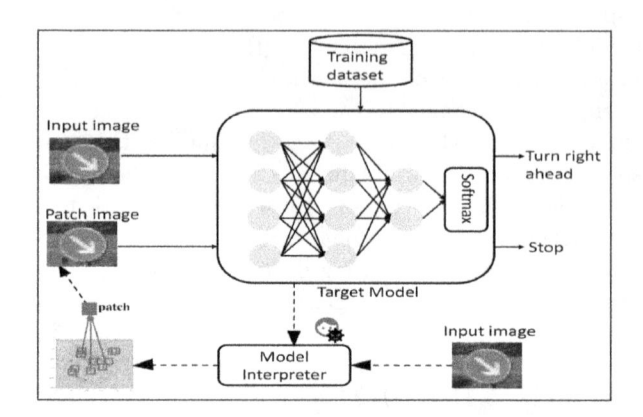

Fig. 1. Attack overview

The schematic representation of our proposed approach is as demonstrated in Fig. 1. The proposed methodology focuses on creating a patch that has a significant impact. When this patch is added to an image, that image can be misclassified to another (desired) label. To achieve this objective, the attacker executes three steps: initially, the attacker employs sensitivity analysis to identify the influential features of the target label. Following that, the attacker focuses solely on the negatively impact features (identified earlier) and employs Intersection over Union *(IoU)* to pinpoint them. In the final stage, the attacker aggregates all the considering bounding boxes to create the final patch, which is given in detail, subsequently in Sect. 4.2. After generation of the intended patch, the attacker inserts it into that target sample to misclassify it to the desired label. For instance, in Fig. 1, *Turn right ahead* is misclassified as *Stop* after injecting the intended patch. Note that here, the model is neither re-trained nor parameters have been changed.

4.2 Patch Generation

Positively influential features enhance the likelihood of correct classification. Conversely, negatively influential features have a detrimental effect on the classifier's decision, leading to misclassification or errors in prediction. The attacker determines the negatively influential features through sensitivity analysis. Relevance score for each pixel represents its impact on the model's output. Pixels with lower relevance scores are marked as negative features and are often depicted in blue.

Several bounding boxes are created around regions of lower relevance using sliding window. By centering on that pixel (x, y) whose relevance score is less than the threshold, a bounding box is created. The two main points define each bounding box: the bottom-left corner $(x - \frac{s_{min}}{2}, y - \frac{s_{min}}{2})$ and the top-right corner $(x + \frac{s_{min}}{2}, y + \frac{s_{min}}{2})$. The size of the box is defined by s_{min}. The co-ordinates of the bounding boxe is defined as follows:

$$\text{bounding box} = \left(x - \frac{s_{min}}{2}, y - \frac{s_{min}}{2}, x + \frac{s_{min}}{2}, y + \frac{s_{min}}{2}\right)$$

IoU is a metric used to quantify the overlap between two bounding boxes. If the IoU between that newly created box and any existing box exceeds a certain threshold, the new box may be discarded to prevent redundancy and ensure that the final set of box represents distinct regions of interest. The intersection of two boxes is defined by the overlapping region. The coordinates of the intersection of two boxes are denoted as follows:

$$x_{intersect}^{min} = \max(x_1^{new}, x_1^{existing})$$
$$y_{intersect}^{min} = \max(y_1^{new}, y_1^{existing})$$
$$x_{intersect}^{max} = \min(x_2^{new}, x_2^{existing})$$
$$y_{intersect}^{max} = \min(y_2^{new}, y_2^{existing})$$

where intersection bottom-left corner are $(x_{intersect}^{min}, y_{intersect}^{min})$, and the intersection top-right corner are $(x_{intersect}^{max}, y_{intersect}^{max})$.

The width and height of the intersection region defined as follows:

$$\text{width}_{intersect} = \max(0, x_{intersect}^{max} - x_{intersect}^{min})$$
$$\text{height}_{intersect} = \max(0, y_{intersect}^{max} - y_{intersect}^{min})$$

Subsequently, the area of the intersection region is determined as follows:

$$\text{Area}_{intersection} = \text{width}_{intersect} \times \text{height}_{intersect}$$

The area of the new bounding box $Area_{new}$, and the existing bounding box $Area_{existing}$ are as follows:

$$\text{Area}_{new} = (x_2^{new} - x_1^{new}) \times (y_2^{new} - y_1^{new})$$
$$\text{Area}_{existing} = (x_2^{existing} - x_1^{existing}) \times (y_2^{existing} - y_1^{existing})$$

The area covered by the union of two bounding boxes is the union of two bounding boxes is the total area covered by both boxes combined, without counting the overlapping area twice is given below:

$$\text{Area}_{union} = \text{Area}_{new} + \text{Area}_{existing} - \text{Area}_{intersection}$$

To assess the degree of overlap between two bounding boxes, we use the *IoU* metric, which is defined as follows.

$$\text{IoU} = \frac{\text{Area}_{\text{intersection}}}{\text{Area}_{\text{union}}}$$

This value provides a measure of the overlap between the bounding boxes.

After calculating *IoU*, compare the *IoU* value with a predefined threshold. This threshold determines the maximum acceptable overlap between boxes:

- If the *IoU* with any existing box is greater than or equal to this threshold, the newly created box is considered overlapping significantly and is discarded.
- If the *IoU* is below the threshold, the created box is added to the list of bounding boxes and labeled accordingly. Subsequently, the attacker extracts the intended patch, by aggregating the created bounding boxes.

5 Evaluation Results

Table 1.

Dataset	Number of Labels	Input size	Training size	Testing size	Model	Accuracy
MNIST	10	$28 \times 28 \times 1$	60000	10000	CNN	98.9%
CIFAR-10	10	$32 \times 32 \times 3$	50000	10000	VGG-19	91.29%
GTSRB	43	$32 \times 32 \times 3$	35209	12603	VGG-19	98.26%

Experiments were carried out across three distinct applications: digit recognition, object classification, and traffic sign recognition.

The experiments are carried out on *MNIST*, *CIFAR-10*, and *GTSRB* datasets. Table 1 specifics the models and datasets utilized for this experiment. The accuracy of models are 98.9%, 91.29%, and 98.26% on *MNIST*, *CIFAR-10*, and *GTSRB* datasets respectively. The size of the generated patch is 6X6.

Setup: Following model architectures have been used for training the model.

- *CNN Model:* There are two convolutional layers in the model architecture, where the first layer takes a $1 \times 28 \times 28$ input and employs 16 filters of size $1 \times 5 \times 5$ with a stride of 1, using the *ReLU* activation function. Subsequently, a max-pooling layer reduces the dimensions to $16 \times 24 \times 24$ with 2×2 filters and a stride of 2. The second convolutional layer operates on this output, transforming it into a $32 \times 12 \times 12$ feature map, utilizing 32 filters of size $16 \times 5 \times 5$ and the *ReLU* activation function. Another *max-pooling* layer is applied with 2×2 filters, reducing the dimensions to $32 \times 8 \times 8$. The subsequent fully connected layer *FC1*, has $32 \times 4 \times 4$ input neurons and 256×512 filters with *ReLU* activation. Finally, *FC2* takes 512 input neurons and applies 512×10 filters with the *softmax* activation function to produce the model's output probabilities across ten classes.

Algorithm 1. Patch Generation
───
1: **Input:** R, $s_{\min}$, iou_{thresh} ▷ Relevance map, minimum box size, IoU threshold
2: **Output:** $\mathcal{P}$ ▷ Final patch
3: Initialize an empty list B
4: **for** each pixel (x, y) in relevance map R **do**
5:    **if** relevance score at (x, y) ¡ threshold **then**
6:       Bounding box $= (x - \frac{s_{\min}}{2}, y - \frac{s_{\min}}{2}, x + \frac{s_{\min}}{2}, y + \frac{s_{\min}}{2})$ ▷ create a bounding box by centering (x, y)
7:       Add bounding box to B
8:    **end if**
9: **end for**
10: Initialize an empty list B_{final} to store final bounding boxes
11: **for** each bounding box B_{new} in B **do**
12:    OverlapDetected = False
13:    **for** each bounding box B_{existing} in B_{final} **do**
14:       **if** IoU $\geq iou_{\text{thresh}}$ **then**
15:          OverlapDetected = True
16:          **break**
17:       **end if**
18:    **end for**
19:    **if** not OverlapDetected **then**
20:       Add B_{new} to B_{final}
21:    **end if**
22: **end for**
23: **for** each bounding box in B_{final} **do**
24:    Aggregate the selected bounding boxes to generate the final patch
25: **end for**
26: **return** $\mathcal{P}$
───

- *VGG19*: VGG-19 model used for traffic sign detection *(GTSRB)* and object detection *(CIFAR-10)*. Specifically, it is shown that the output layer contains 43 for *GTSRB* dataset and will contain 10 for *CIFAR-10* dataset. There are 19 layers in *VGG19*, consisting of 3 fully connected layers and 16 convolutional layers. It adheres to a consistent architectural pattern, employing 3 × 3 convolutional filters with a stride of 1, coupled with 2 × 2 max-pooling layers with a stride of 2 for downsampling. *VGG19* is renowned for its versatility, often initialized with pre-trained weights on extensive datasets and then fine-tuned for specific tasks. The rectified linear unit *(ReLU)* serves as the activation function throughout the network, fostering nonlinear transformations that capture complex image features. The output layer employs *softmax* activation making *VGG19* particularly well-suited for multi-class classification tasks. Its ability to learn intricate hierarchical features from images, coupled with batch normalization layers for training stability, renders *VGG19* an invaluable tool in the deep learning landscape. When applied to datasets such as *GTSRB*, and *CIFAR-10* adaptation of input dimensions and the output layer allows for efficient training and robust classification performance.

Evaluation Metrics: The efficacy of the proposed attack is measured by considering three metrics as follows:

- *Misclassification rate*: The rate at which patched input is misclassified as desired label.
- *Attack success rate*: The difference between the misclassification of a label before and after the attack happens.
- *Accuracy*: The accuracy rate of the model while classifying inputs, including those with applied patches, on the test set.

5.1 Result

Attack on Digit Recognition. In Fig. 2a, the misclassification rate prior to conducting the attack is observed to fall within the range of 0.5% to 1.9%. Subsequently, in Fig. 2b, following the execution of the attack, the misclassification rate expands significantly, ranging from 63% to 70.5%. Additionally, Fig. 2c depicts the attack success rate, which fluctuates within the range of 62% to 68%. In Fig. 6a, the misclassification rates for individual labels, indicating how often one label is misclassified as another, range from 0% to 0.89% before the attack. After the attack, as shown in Fig. 6b, these rates experience a substantial increase, ranging from 0.1% to 28.97%. In Fig. 5a, the accuracy ranges from 91.34% to 92.98% after the attack is executed. From these experiments, it becomes apparent that when the attacker refrains from injecting a patch into the input data, the misclassification rate remains relatively low. However, when they introduce an influential generated patch, the misclassification rate significantly escalates across a broad spectrum. Moreover, the Fig. 9a indicate that after inserting a random patch, the misclassification range hovers between 5% to 9%. This observation suggests that the attack performs notably better when a specific patch is inserted, as evidenced by the considerable expansion in the misclassification range.

Attack on Object Detection. Figure 3a illustrates that prior to the attack, the misclassification rate ranges from 7.5% to 9.8%. However, in Fig. 3b, after the attack, this rate significantly increases, ranging from 65% to 73%. Additionally, Fig. 3c presents the attack success rate, fluctuating between 57% and 64%. Examining individual label misclassification rates in Fig. 7a, we observe a range of 0% to 3.7% before the attack, which notably expands to 1% to 25.9% after the attack, as depicted in Fig. 7b. Figure 5b indicates post-attack accuracy ranging from 84% to 85%. These findings suggest that abstaining from patch injection results in relatively low misclassification rates while introducing an influential patch leads to a significant rise in misclassification across various labels. Moreover, Fig. 9b reveals a misclassification range of 7% to 9% after inserting a random patch, emphasizing the effectiveness of specific patches in enhancing the attack's performance.

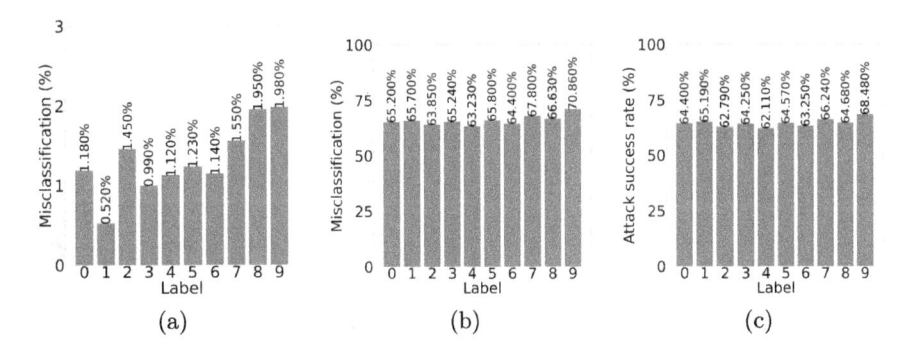

Fig. 2. Misclassification rate (a) before, (b) after attack, and (c) attack success rate over *MNIST* dataset

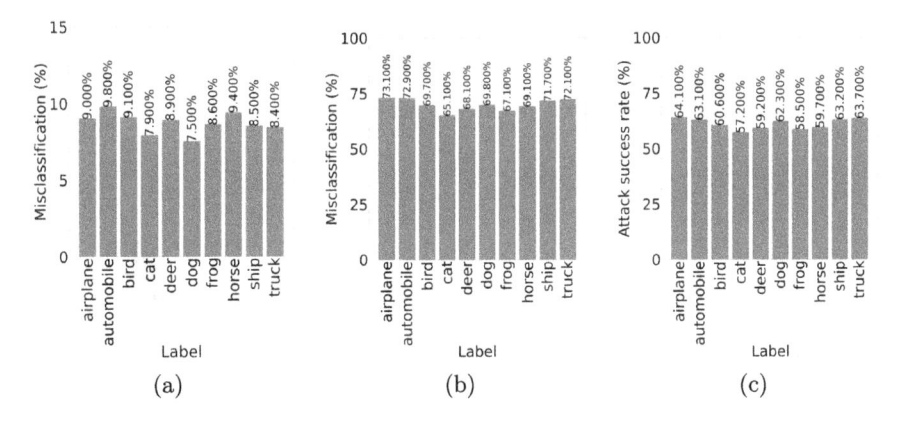

Fig. 3. Misclassification rate (a) before, (b) after attack, and (c) attack success rate of *CIFAR-10* dataset

Attack on Traffic Sign Classification. Figure 4a displays a pre-attack misclassification rate ranging from 0.2% to 2.5%. After executing the attack, as shown in Fig. 4b, the misclassification rate significantly rises to between 60% and 71%. Figure 4c illustrates the fluctuation of the attack success rate, ranging from 59% to 70%. Prior to the attack, misclassification rates for individual labels in Fig. 8a range from 0% to 0.8%, whereas after the attack, depicted in Fig. 8b, rates expand notably, ranging from 0% to 28.97%. Figure 5c indicates post-attack accuracy ranging from 96% to 97%. These results indicate that refraining from patch injection keeps misclassification rates relatively low, but introducing influential patches leads to significant escalation across various labels. Additionally, in Fig. 9c, inserting a random patch results in a misclassification range of 5% to 9%, underscoring the effectiveness of specific patches in enhancing the attack's impact.

The experimental results of the proposed attack on *MNIST*, *Cifar-10*, and *GTSRB* datasets are compared with that of [2,5], and [13] in Table 2. In [11] the overall accuracy degradation is 0.5% while the attack success rate is 76.5%. In [5], BadNet misclassifies more than 99% of the backdoored image for *MNIST* dataset.

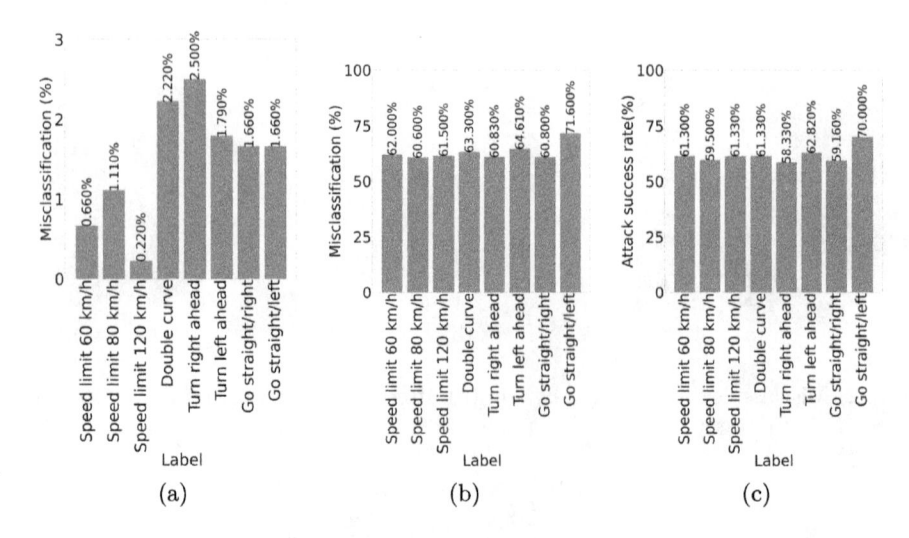

Fig. 4. Misclassification rate of (a) before, (b) after attack, and (c) attack success rate of *GTSRB* dataset

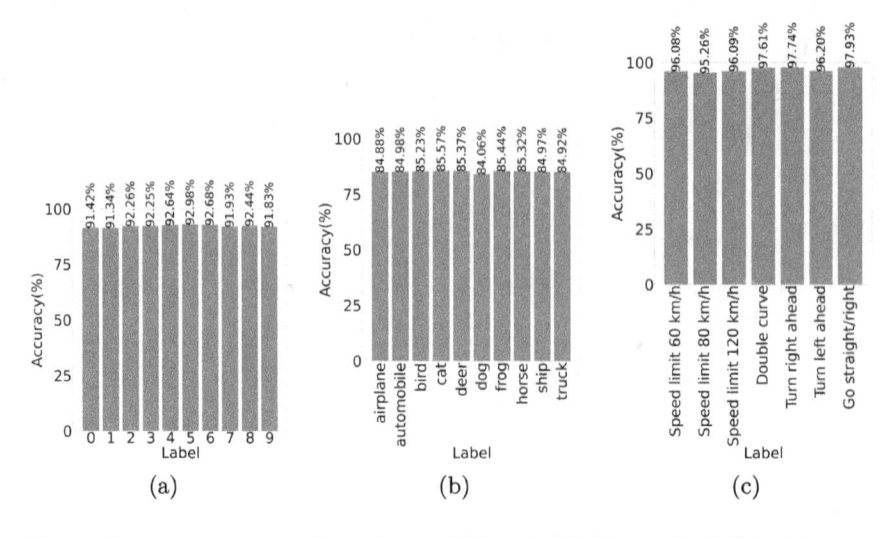

Fig. 5. Accuracy after attack on (a) *MNIST*, (b) *CIFAR-10*, (c) *GTSRB* dataset

Along with it, BadNet misclassifies more than 98% of backdoored images to random target classes and also with a drop in accuracy of 25% on the traffic sign dataset. The misclassification rate is 99% for MNIST and 98% for Traffic sign dataset. In [2] the misclassification rate for CIFAR-10 is 89%. In [13] the range of accuracy degardation falls between 65.15%, and 89.41%. The misclassification rate is 98% and 96% for MNIST and CIFAR-10 dataset. Our proposed attack accuracy after performing the attack is 91%, 84%, and 96% for MNIST, CIFAR-10, and GTSRB respectively.

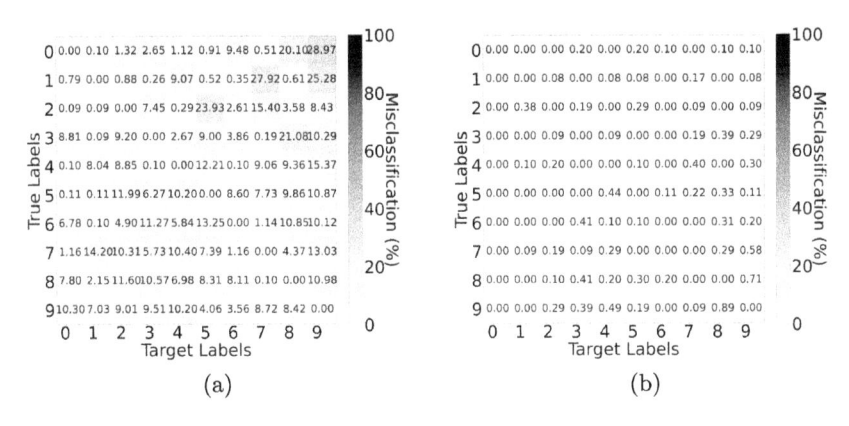

Fig. 6. Misclassification rate label-wise of (a) before attack, (b) after attack of *MNIST* dataset

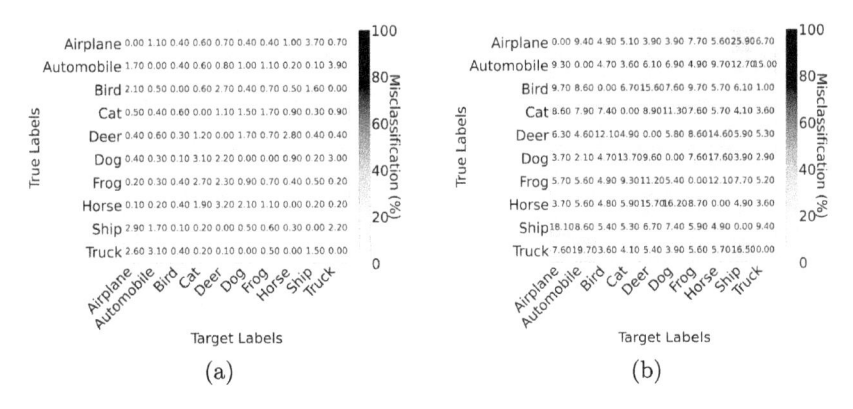

Fig. 7. Misclassification rate label-wise of (a) before attack, (b) after attack of *CIFAR-10* dataset

Table 2. Comparison of performance

Dataset	Existing			Proposed		
	MNIST	CIFAR-10	GTSRB	MNIST	CIFAR-10	GTSRB
Reference	[5]	[5]	[5]			
Accuracy	99.91%	-	61.6%	92%	85%	97%
Misclassification	99%	-	98%	70%	73%	71%
Reference	[13]	[13]	[13]			
Accuracy	96.54%	65.15%	-	92%	85%	97%
Misclassification	98%	96%	-	70%	73%	71%
Reference	[2]	[2]	[2]			
Accuracy	-	-	-	92%	85%	97%
Misclassification	-	89%	-	70%	73%	71%

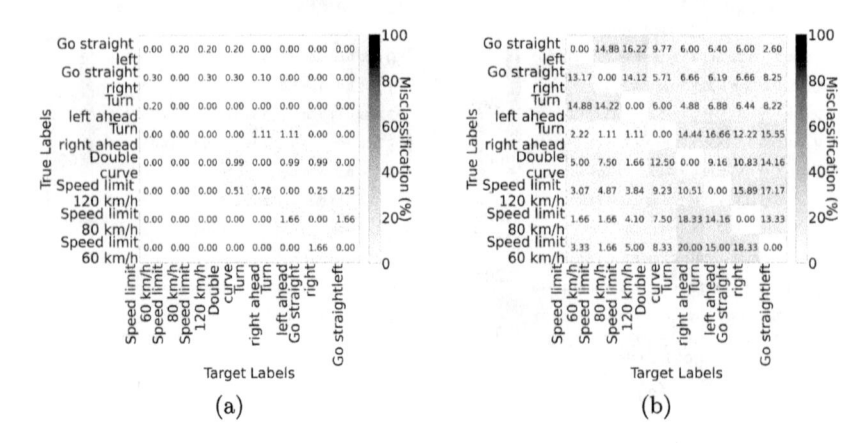

Fig. 8. Misclassification rate label-wise of (a) before attack, (b) after attack of *GTSRB* dataset

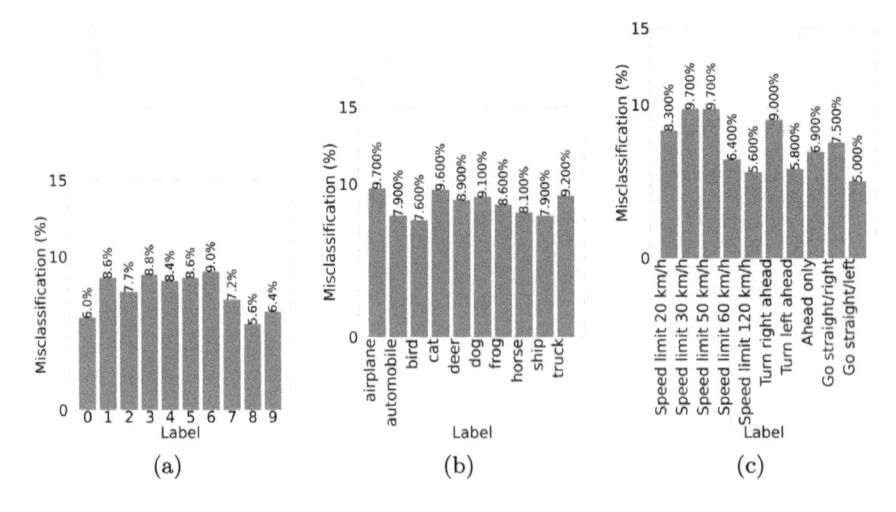

Fig. 9. Misclassification after inserting random patch on (a) *MNIST*, (b) *CIFAR-10*, (c) *GTSRB* dataset

In the contemporary landscape of machine learning, where models are increasingly complex and datasets extensive, the norm has become the utilization of pre-trained models obtained from various platforms. While this practice streamlines workflows, it introduces a potential vulnerability, as users inherently trust third-party models. In response, our proposed methodology introduces an adversarial attack strategy capable of manipulating model outcomes, even without re-train it or alter it, and direct access to the model parameters. Our proposed approach misclassifies the target label at 70.86%, 73.10%, and 71.60% respectively of *digit, object, and traffic sign* classification task.

Table 3. Chi square (χ^2) Test

MNIST		CIFAR10		GTSRB	
Target	χ^2	Target	χ^2	Target	χ^2
2	42.84	Airplane	4.5	Sp. limit 60 km/h	11.6
3	45.65	Automobile	4.41	Sp. limit 80 km/h	4.01
4	34.83	Bird	4.03	Sp. limit 120 km/h	36
5	40.96	Cat	4.12	Double curve	18.6
6	39.69	Deer	4.5	Turn right ahead	10.83
7	43.56	Dog	5.4	Turn left ahead	4.64
8	42.25	Frog	4.2	Go straight/right	16.82
9	23.12	Horse	5.12	Go straight/left	24.5

Table 4. Bayes Theorem

MNIST			CIFAR10			GTSRB		
Target	P1	P2	Target	P1	P2	Target	P1	P2
1	0.014	0.005	Dog	0.014	0.039	Go straight/right	0.5	0.01
3	0.03	0.009	Cat	0.26	0.077	Sp. limit 80 km/h	0.03	0.01
6	0.03	0.01	Truck	0.45	0.11	Go straight/left	0.06	0.01
0	0.02	0.007	Automobile	0.07	0.019	Sp. limit 120 km/h	0.05	0.002

6 Analytical Result

This section discusses the analytical proof of the proposed Algorithm 1. The Chi-square test is performed to establish the co-relationship between the patch insertion and the misclassification by using Eq. 2.

It is shown that if the intended patch is inserted into the target sample, then the target label is misclassified as the desired label.

Table 3 shows that the *chi-square* value of the target label *2, 3, 4, 5, 6, 7, 8, 9* containing $\mathcal{P}$ is 42.84, 45.65, 34.83, 40.96, 39.69, 43.56, 42.25, 23.12 respectively of *MNIST* dataset. Similarly, the chi-square value of the target label *Airplane, Automobile, Bird, Cat, Deer, Dog, Frog, Horse* including the $\mathcal{P}$ is 4.5, 4.41, 4.03, 4.12, 4.5, 5.4, 4.2, and 5.12 respectively of *CIFAR10* dataset. In the same way, the *chi-square* value of the target label *Speed limit 60 km/h, Speed limit 80 km/h, Speed limit 120 km/h, Double curve, Turn right ahead, Turn left ahead, Go straight/right, and Go straight/left* is 11.6, 4.01, 36, 18.6, 10.83, 4.64, 16.82, 24.5 respectively. The calculated chi-square value of *GTSRB* is found to be between 4.01 and 18.6 (ex. speed limit 80 km/h is 4.01 because the value of (O) is 0.61 while the value of (E) is 0.01).

Considering, the p-value to be 0.05, and the degree of freedom as 1, the corresponding tabular chi-square value[4] is 3.841. As the calculated chi-square value in Table 3, is observed to be greater than the tabular chi-square value in every case, it rejects the null hypothesis. Therefore, it is assured that there is a strong co-relationship between patch insertion and misclassification.

If the intended patch is applied to the target sample, then the target label is misclassified as the desired label with significant probability.

Table 4 shows the probability of misclassification in the presence of the patch by using Eq. 3. P_1, and P_2 represent the Probability(Misclassification | Patch) and Probability(Misclassification) respectively. It is found that the P_1, and P_2 of target label 1 is 0.014 and 0.005 for *MNIST* dataset. Similarly, the P_1, and P_2 is 0.26 and 0.077 for the target label Cat of *Cifar-10* dataset respectively. Likewise, the P_1, and P_2 of the target label Truck are 0.45, and 0.11 respectively.

It is observed that in every case, the value of P_1 is greater than that of P_2. Therefore, the target label would be misclassified with the insertion of the patch.

7 Conclusion

This work proposed an effective approach to misclassify the prediction of the model without re-training the model. In this work, we introduced an attack strategy involving the addition of a small patch to the input, inducing the model to misclassify predictions without impacting physical vision. A noteworthy aspect of our proposed technique is its independence from model retraining or any modifications to the underlying model structure. The experiments on three datasets *MNIST, CIFAR-10,* and *GTSRB* confirm that this approach could misclassify an input 63%, 65% and 60% respectively for *(MNIST), (CIFAR-10), (GTSRB)*. Note that our approach does not affect the prediction on input without patch.

Acknowledgement. We acknowledge the Ministry of Education (MoE), Government of India, and Ministry of Electronics and Information technology for funding this research under the project ISEA Phase-III.

References

1. Ancona, M., Ceolini, E., Cengiz Öztireli, A., Gross, M.H.: A unified view of gradient-based attribution methods for deep neural networks. CoRR, abs/1711.06104 (2017)
2. Brown, T.B., Mané, D., Roy, A., Abadi, M., Gilmer, J.: Adversarial patch (2018)
3. Chindaudom, A., Siritanawan, P., Sumongkayothin, K., Kotani, K.: AdversarialQR: an adversarial patch in QR code format. In: 2020 Joint 9th International Conference on Informatics, Electronics & Vision (ICIEV) and 2020 4th International Conference on Imaging, Vision & Pattern Recognition (icIVPR), pp. 1–6 (2020)

---

[4] Critical values of chi-square (right tail) https://www.scribbr.com/wp-content/uploads/2022/05/Chi-square-table.pdf.

4. Goodfellow, I.J., Shlens, J., Szegedy, C.: Explaining and harnessing adversarial examples (2015)
5. Tianyu, G., Liu, K., Dolan-Gavitt, B., Garg, S.: Badnets: evaluating backdooring attacks on deep neural networks. IEEE Access **7**, 47230–47244 (2019)
6. Heaven, D.: Why deep-learning AIS are so easy to fool. Nature **574**(7777), 163–166 (2019)
7. Holzinger, A., Saranti, A., Molnar, C., Biecek, P., Samek, W.: Explainable AI Methods - A Brief Overview. Springer, Cham (2020)
8. Karmon, D., Zoran, D., Goldberg, Y.: LaVAN: localized and visible adversarial noise. In: Dy, J., Krause, A. (eds.) Proceedings of the 35th International Conference on Machine Learning. Proceedings of Machine Learning Research, vol. 80, pp. 2507–2515. PMLR (2018)
9. Kurakin, A., Goodfellow, I., Bengio, S.: Adversarial examples in the physical world (2017)
10. Li, X., Jiang, Y., Liu, C., Liu, S., Luo, H., Yin, S.: Playing against deep-neural-network-based object detectors: a novel bidirectional adversarial attack approach. IEEE Trans. Artif. Intell. **3**(1), 20–28 (2022)
11. Lin, J., Xu, L., Liu, Y., Zhang, X.: Composite backdoor attack for deep neural network by mixing existing benign features. In: Proceedings of the 2020 ACM SIGSAC Conference on Computer and Communications Security, pp. 113–131. ACM, New York (2020)
12. Liu, Y., et al.: Trojaning attack on neural networks. In: Network and Distributed System Security Symposium (2018)
13. Lu, Y., Kamath, G., Yu, Y.: Indiscriminate data poisoning attacks on neural networks (2024)
14. Melamud, O., Goldberger, J., Dagan, I.: context2vec: learning generic context embedding with bidirectional LSTM. In: Proceedings of the 20th SIGNLL Conference on Computational Natural Language Learning, Berlin, Germany, pp. 51–61. Association for Computational Linguistics (2016)
15. Mikolov, T., Sutskever, I., Chen, K., Corrado, G.S., Dean, J.: Distributed representations of words and phrases and their compositionality. In: Advances in Neural Information Processing Systems, vol. 26. Curran Associates, Inc. (2013)
16. Miotto, R., Wang, F., Wang, S., Jiang, X., Dudley, J.T.: Deep learning for healthcare: review, opportunities and challenges. Briefings Bioinform. **19**(6), 1236–1246 (2017)
17. Mishra, C., Gupta, D.: Deep machine learning and neural networks: an overview. IAES Int. J. Artif. Intell. (IJ-AI) **6**, 66 (2017)
18. Montavon, G., Samek, W., Müller, K.-R.: Methods for interpreting and understanding deep neural networks. Digit. Signal Process. **73**, 1–15 (2018)
19. Min-Hye, O., Kwon, M.-W., Park, K., Park, B.-G.: Sensitivity analysis based on neural network for optimizing device characteristics. IEEE Electron Dev. Lett. **41**(10), 1548–1551 (2020)
20. Parkhi, O.M., Vedaldi, A., Zisserman, A.: Deep face recognition. In: British Machine Vision Conference (2015)
21. Saha, A., Subramanya, A., Pirsiavash, H.: Hidden trigger backdoor attacks. In: Proceedings of the AAAI Conference on Artificial Intelligence, vol. 34, pp. 11957–11965 (2020)
22. Salem, A., Backes, M., Zhang, Y.: Don't trigger me! a triggerless backdoor attack against deep neural networks. CoRR, abs/2010.03282 (2020)
23. Shafahi, A., et al.: Poison frogs! targeted clean-label poisoning attacks on neural networks. In: Advances in Neural Information Processing Systems, vol. 31 (2018)

24. Sun, W., et al.: Invisible backdoor attack with dynamic triggers against person re-identification (2023)
25. Sung, A.H.: Ranking importance of input parameters of neural networks. Expert Syst. Appl. **15**(3), 405–411 (1998)
26. Tang, R., Du, M., Liu, N., Yang, F., Hu, X.: An embarrassingly simple approach for trojan attack in deep neural networks. In: Proceedings of the 26th ACM SIGKDD International Conference on Knowledge Discovery & Data Mining, pp. 218–228. ACM, New York (2020)
27. Wang, X., Zhao, Y., Pourpanah, F.: Recent advances in deep learning. Int. J. Mach. Learn. Cybern. (2020)

Industry Demo/Practice

Integrating Crypto-Based Payment Systems for Data Marketplaces: Enhancing Efficiency, Security, and User Autonomy

Vipul Walunj[✉], Vasanth Rajaraman, Jyotirmoy Dutta, and Abhay Sharma

Centre of Data for Public Good (CDPG), Bengaluru, India
{vipul.walunj,vasanth.rajaraman,jyotirmoy.dutta,abhay.sharma}@cdpg.org.in

Abstract. Data exchanges, as Digital Public Infrastructures are poised to significantly contribute to the data driven economies across the world. Cities worldwide have leveraged Data Exchanges to enhance efficiency, improve citizen services, reduce costs, and generate new revenue streams. Beyond serving as a public good, data exchange platforms also establish a framework where stakeholders, such as data providers and consumers, can trade and monetize data. While financial payment gateways offer significant utility, they also present several challenges, including security issues and the reliance on third-party applications. These limitations must be addressed to ensure the efficacy and trustworthiness of the system. This work explores the integration of crypto-based payment systems into Web 2.0 applications, with a specific focus on their application within Data Marketplaces, the India Urban Data Exchange (IUDX), and Agricultural Data Exchange (ADeX) platforms. The integration of crypto payments offers significant technical advantages, including enhanced security, faster settlement times, lower transaction fees, and decentralized control over funds. This work discusses the technical aspects of crypto payment integration, such as crypto payment gateways, smart contracts, and wallet integration. Additionally, it highlights the specific benefits for Data Exchanges, including seamless data discovery and purchase flows, secure transactions, and innovative business models like tokenized data access and decentralized governance. Addressing regulatory challenges, scalability, and user adoption are identified as crucial steps for realizing the full potential of crypto payments. This integration proposes to create a secure, efficient, and user-friendly ecosystem that fosters innovation and promotes the growth of the data economy.

Keywords: Blockchain · Data Marketplace · Ethereum · Metamask

1 Introduction

In an increasingly data-driven world, the efficient management and utilization of data are paramount for fostering innovation, improving services, and driving economic growth. Data Marketplaces are pivotal in this field, offering structured platforms where data can be shared, bought, and sold. These marketplaces facilitate the exchange of diverse data sets between various stakeholders, including government entities, policy makers, private companies, researchers, and developers.

The concept of a Data Marketplace is rooted in the need for a federated repository that standardises data formats, ensures data quality, and provides a seamless interface for data transactions. By aggregating data from multiple and diverse sources, these marketplaces enhance data accessibility and usability, promoting transparency, innovation and collaboration. For instance, cities like Copenhagen, Columbus, and Manchester have pioneered the creation of Data Exchanges to harness their data assets, resulting in improved efficiency, better services, reduced costs, and enhanced revenue streams.

2 Background

2.1 Introduction to IUDX (Indian Urban Data Exchange) and ADeX (Agricultural Data Exchange)

The Indian Urban Data Exchange (IUDX) and Agricultural Data eXchange (ADeX) are cutting-edge platforms designed to facilitate the exchange of urban and agricultural data respectively. These platforms aim to break down data silos and enable seamless data sharing.

IUDX is a government-backed initiative that provides a standardised, open-source framework for sharing urban data of Indian cities amongst stakeholders. It enables interoperability between different data systems and applications, fostering a collaborative ecosystem where data can be utilized to improve urban services, infrastructure, and governance. IUDX supports diverse data types, including real-time sensor data, demographic data, and infrastructure data, making it a versatile tool for smart city initiatives.

ADeX is a pioneering initiative, a first of its kind platform, designed to revolutionize the agriculture sector by providing efficient and seamless data exchange through open and standardized interfaces. ADeX aims to address the challenges of feeding a growing global population. By making agricultural data accessible and useful, ADeX empowers farmers and stakeholders to create innovative, data-driven solutions. AdeX is currently operational in Telangana, India and continues to act as a blueprint for other cities in India and other countries.

2.2 Relevance of Integrating Crypto-Based Payment Systems

Data Marketplaces are digital platforms that facilitate the buying, selling, and sharing of data. They serve as intermediaries, connecting data providers with data consumers and offering a structured and secure environment for data transactions. These marketplaces standardize data formats, ensure data quality, and provide robust mechanisms for data governance, making data more accessible and valuable. As traditional payment methods often involve higher fees, slower processing times, and increased vulnerability to fraud, there is a pressing need to transition to crypto payments.

Integrating crypto-based payment systems with platforms like IUDX and ADeX offers a transformative approach to data monetization and transactions. Crypto payments leverage blockchain technology to provide a secure, transparent, and decentralized method for conducting financial transactions. This integration is particularly relevant for Data Marketplaces, where the need for secure, efficient, and low-cost payment solutions is critical. By incorporating crypto payments, Data Marketplaces can benefit from enhanced security due to blockchain's immutable ledger, which ensures all transactions are secure and tamper-proof, significantly reducing the risk of fraud.

Crypto transactions can be processed much faster than traditional banking methods, especially for international transactions, eliminating delays caused by intermediaries. The decentralized nature of blockchain reduces the need for intermediaries, thereby lowering transaction fees and making micropayments viable. Additionally, users retain full control over their funds and private keys, promoting financial autonomy and reducing reliance on centralized institutions. Crypto payments offer superior security, speed, and cost-efficiency compared to traditional payment methods, making them a highly advantageous option for modern Data Marketplaces.

3 Data Exchanges and Data Monetization

3.1 Definition and Significance of Data Marketplaces

The significance of Data Marketplaces lies in their ability to unlock the potential of data as a critical asset. By enabling efficient data exchange, these platforms help organizations and cities derive actionable insights, drive innovation, and enhance decision-making processes. They also promote transparency and collaboration, breaking down data silos and fostering a culture of data sharing. The economic impact of Data Marketplaces is profound, as they create new revenue streams for data providers and offer cost savings for data consumers through optimized data acquisition processes.

Monetization through Data Marketplaces involves leveraging these platforms to generate revenue from data assets. By creating a centralized and standardized environment for data transactions, Data Marketplaces allow data providers to sell their data to a diverse range of consumers, including businesses, researchers, and government entities. This process transforms raw data into a valuable commodity, opening new revenue streams for data providers who can monetize their data sets based on demand. Moreover, Data Marketplaces implement quality assurance measures and standardized formats, ensuring that data is reliable and easily integrated into various applications. For data consumers, this offers cost-effective access to high-quality data, which can be used to enhance decision-making, drive innovation, and improve operational efficiency. Thus, Data Marketplaces not only facilitate the efficient exchange of data but also create economic opportunities by turning data into a tangible, marketable asset.

4 Integrating Payment Gateways

In a Data Marketplace, the Catalog server maintains a comprehensive directory of available datasets, allowing users to search and discover data offerings. The AAA (Authentication, Authorization, and Accounting) server manages user identities, permissions, and tracks usage to ensure secure and controlled access to data. The Resource server stores and provides access to the actual data assets, ensuring they are delivered efficiently and securely to authorised users.

4.1 Purchase Flows in Data Marketplaces

Once a user identifies a suitable dataset through the discovery process and authenticates themselves, the next step is the purchase flow. This flow encompasses all the actions required to acquire and gain access to the data. Efficient and secure purchase flows are critical for user satisfaction and the overall success of the data marketplace.

A key component of purchase flows is user authentication and authorization. Secure authentication mechanisms, such as multi-factor authentication (MFA), ensure that only authorized users can access and purchase datasets. Role-based access control (RBAC) can also be implemented to restrict access based on user roles and permissions. These measures are essential to protect sensitive data and maintain the integrity of the marketplace.

Payment processing is another crucial element of the purchase flow. Integrating secure and convenient payment gateways facilitates smooth financial transactions. Support for multiple payment methods, including credit cards, bank transfers, and crypto payments, enhances user flexibility. The use of smart contracts can automate payment and access provision, ensuring trust and efficiency by eliminating the need for intermediaries and reducing the risk of disputes.

Finally, data access and delivery must be handled promptly and securely. Upon successful payment, users should receive immediate access to the purchased data. This can be achieved through secure download links, API endpoints, or direct integration with the user's systems. Efficient and reliable data delivery is essential to prevent any disruptions in the user's workflow and to maintain the reputation of the data marketplace as a dependable source of valuable information.

4.2 Integrating Crypto-Based Payments into Data Marketplaces

Implementing crypto payments in data marketplaces involves several technical steps:

Crypto Payment Gateway Integration: Secure and reputable crypto payment gateways, such as Coinbase Commerce or BitPay, provide APIs for integrating crypto payments into the marketplace. These gateways handle secure user wallet connections, transaction processing, and optional fiat conversion.

Smart Contract Deployment: For complex payment scenarios, smart contracts can automate escrow services, conditional payments, and decentralized autonomous organization (DAO) functions. Smart contracts ensure that funds are released only when predefined conditions are met, enhancing trust and transparency.

Wallet Integration: Users need secure ways to connect their crypto wallets to the marketplace. This can be achieved through browser extensions like MetaMask or mobile wallet apps using deep linking protocols. Secure communication standards such as Web3.js or WalletConnect facilitate wallet interactions.

5 Technical Framework

Traditional payment systems facilitate online transactions using conventional banking methods and infrastructure. In this system, a user must enter their bank details, and the transaction can only proceed once the bank approves it. This process often involves intermediaries, multiple verification steps, and can be subject to delays due to the need for bank approval.

In contrast, a crypto wallet is a digital tool that allows users to store, send, and receive cryptocurrencies such as Bitcoin or Ethereum. Unlike a traditional wallet that holds physical money, a crypto wallet stores private keys-secure digital codes known only to the user and the wallet. These keys are essential for accessing cryptocurrency and making transactions. Crypto wallets come in various forms, including mobile apps, hardware devices, or even paper printouts. They provide a secure and convenient way to manage digital assets, enabling users to interact with blockchain networks for various operations, including payments and investments.

Metamask is a widely used crypto wallet designed as a browser extension, making it easy to interact with the Ethereum blockchain directly from a web browser. It allows users to manage their Ethereum accounts, store Ether (the currency of Ethereum), and handle various types of Ethereum-based tokens. Using Metamask, users can send and receive cryptocurrency, monitor their account balance, and securely authorize transactions—all through an intuitive interface that integrates seamlessly with their web browsing experience.

The cryptocurrency wallet interface plays a critical role in facilitating secure and efficient transactions within the data marketplace ecosystem. By providing a simple yet functional user interface for interacting with blockchain networks, it enables users to seamlessly connect their wallets and initiate cryptocurrency payments. This functionality is crucial for ensuring low-cost, high-speed transactions, particularly for micropayments, which traditional payment systems often struggle to handle effectively. The integration of blockchain technology and wallet interfaces enhances user autonomy, allowing individuals to retain control over their funds and reduce reliance on centralized intermediaries. Furthermore, the wallet's compatibility with Ethereum, a widely adopted blockchain, ensures broad accessibility and trust, encouraging adoption among diverse stakeholders in the data marketplace, including data providers, consumers, and other participants in the ecosystem.

The Ethereum blockchain is a decentralized platform that enables developers to build and deploy smart contracts and decentralized applications (dApps). Unlike Bitcoin, which primarily functions as a digital currency, Ethereum aims to create a global computer network where anyone can build apps that run exactly as programmed without downtime, censorship, or fraud. Ether (ETH) is the native cryptocurrency of the Ethereum network, used to pay for transaction fees and computational services. Ethereum serves as both a digital currency and a vast, shared computer that developers can use to create innovative applications and services.

Gas fees are transaction fees paid when performing operations on the Ethereum blockchain. These fees compensate miners, who use computational power to validate and secure transactions. For this implementation, we have used the Sepolia network, a test network (or testnet) for Ethereum, designed to allow developers to experiment and test their applications without using real Ether.

When a user initiates a transaction by clicking a payment button, a function is triggered to create a transaction object containing the recipient's address, the payment amount, and the gas fee. Upon creating the transaction object, the user is prompted by Metamask to review and confirm the transaction. Once confirmed, Metamask signs the transaction using the user's private key and broadcasts it to the Ethereum network. The transaction enters the mempool, awaiting inclusion in the next block mined by Ethereum validators. This transaction happens on the testnet Sepolia.

After the transaction is broadcasted, a unique transaction hash is generated. This hash is a cryptographic identifier that allows tracking and verification of the transaction on the blockchain. The web app captures this transaction hash and uses it to query transaction details from the blockchain. Etherscan, a popular blockchain explorer for Ethereum, enables users to look up transaction details using the transaction hash. The web app sends an API request to Etherscan, retrieving comprehensive data such as the transaction status, block number, timestamp, gas used, and more.

The objective of integrating a crypto-based payment facility is that users can easily connect their crypto wallets, initiate payments, and confirm transactions, all within the marketplace platform. This integration not only simplifies the payment process but also ensures transparency and traceability through Etherscan, allowing all parties to verify transaction details. This approach addresses traditional payment system limitations, offering a cost-effective, accessible, and secure solution for data transactions in a decentralized environment.

Imagine you have tokens on one blockchain, like Ethereum, but want to use them on another blockchain, like Binance Smart Chain, where transaction fees are lower. You can use a "bridge" that locks your tokens on Ethereum and then gives you an equivalent amount of new tokens on Binance Smart Chain. It's like

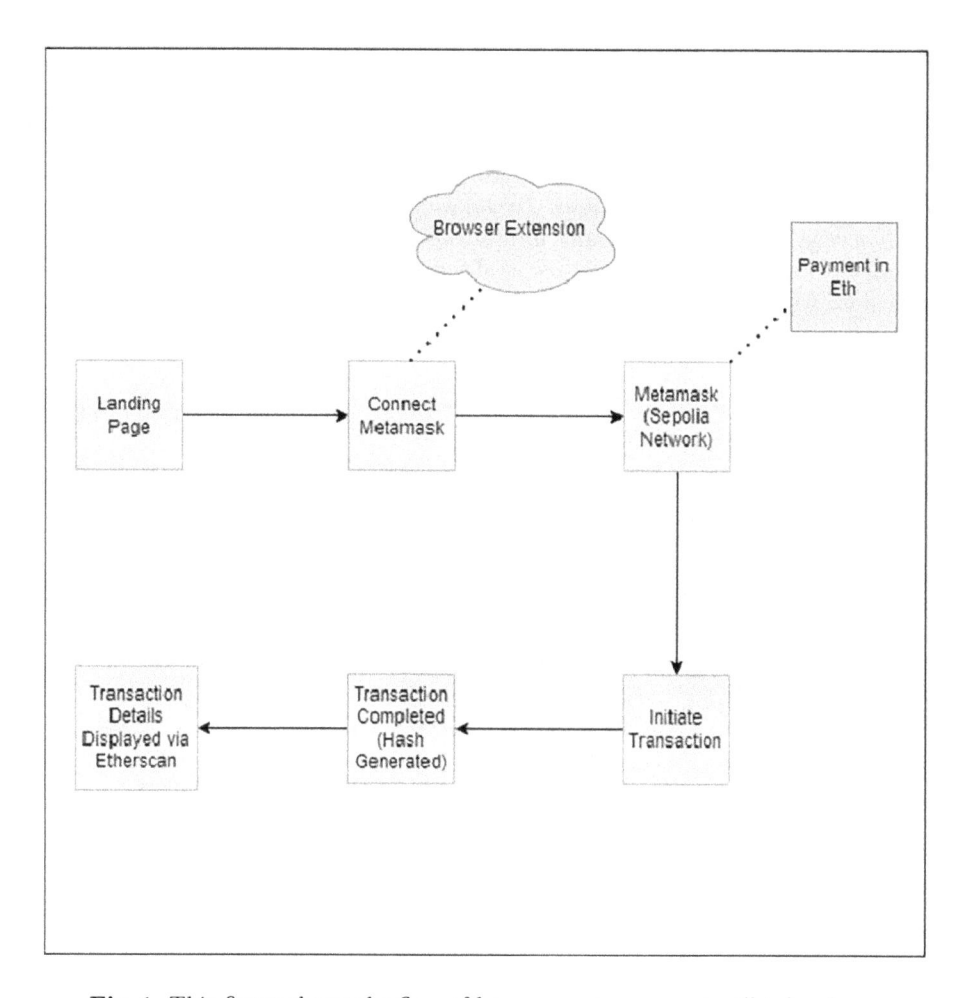

Fig. 1. This figure shows the flow of how a crypto payment will take place.

```
const transactionParameters = {
    to: 'recipient_wallet_address', // embedded in the code
    from: userAddress, // obtained from Metamask
    value: web3.utils.toHex(web3.utils.toWei('amount_in_eth', 'ether')),
    gas: 'gas_limit',
    gasPrice: web3.utils.toHex(web3.utils.toWei('gas_price_in_gwei', 'gwei'))
};
```

Fig. 2. This part of the code contains the addresses' of users and the gas fees.

exchanging your local currency at a bank before traveling to a different country so you can spend money there. Later, if you want to bring your tokens back to Ethereum, the process reverses—your tokens on Binance Smart Chain are burned, and the original ones are unlocked on Ethereum. Services like Chainlink act like referees, confirming everything is correct on both sides.

This process is crucial for cross-chain transactions, enabling flexibility and scalability for Web 2 applications. By allowing assets to move between different blockchains, we remove many limitations and open new possibilities for e-commerce, micropayments, and decentralized services. Cross-chain technology is critical for widespread adoption, as it ensures users and businesses can access the best features of different blockchains without being restricted to one platform.

```
const etherscanApiKey = 'your_etherscan_api_key';
const transactionHash = 'generated_transaction_hash';
const url = `https://api-sepolia.etherscan.io/api?module=transaction&action=gettxreceiptstatus&txhash=${transactionHash}&apikey=${etherscanApiKey}`;

fetch(url)
    .then(response => response.json())
    .then(data => {
        console.log('Transaction Details:', data.result);
        // Display transaction details on the webapp
    })
    .catch(error => console.error('Error fetching transaction details:', error));
```

Fig. 3. This part of the code fetches details of the transaction on Sepolia network from Etherscan.

For related code and implementation examples, please refer to the GitHub repository.

6 Conclusion and Future Work

The integration of crypto-based payment systems into data exchanges presents a transformative opportunity, offering numerous advantages over traditional payment methods. Key benefits include enhanced security and transparency, as blockchain technology ensures tamper-proof transactions with cryptographic security, decentralized control, and a public ledger that promotes transparency and traceability. Additionally, crypto payments provide faster settlement times by eliminating intermediaries and operating 24/7 without geographical barriers, drastically reducing settlement times. Lower transaction fees are another significant advantage, as the peer-to-peer nature of crypto transactions makes them cost-effective, particularly for micro-payments and international transfers.

Furthermore, innovations such as tokenized access, micropayments, and smart contracts enable new business models and services, enhancing flexibility and operational efficiency within data exchanges.

Integration with platforms like IUDX and ADeX amplifies these benefits, offering secure and efficient transactions through blockchain technology, smart contracts, and seamless wallet integration. These advancements contribute to a more robust and innovative data exchange ecosystem, driving growth and enhancing user experiences. However, to fully realize the potential of crypto-based payments, data exchanges need to address several key areas.

Firstly, regulatory challenges must be tackled by implementing robust compliance measures to navigate the evolving legal landscape surrounding cryptocurrency and blockchain technology. Scalability issues also need to be addressed by developing solutions to handle increased transaction volumes and ensure the system remains efficient as adoption grows. User adoption barriers can be mitigated by creating user-friendly interfaces and educational resources to facilitate wider adoption and ease of use.

Moreover, the integration of smart contracts is crucial for automating and streamlining complex transaction scenarios, such as conditional payments and escrow services. Smart contracts can enhance trust and efficiency within data exchanges by enabling automated, transparent, and trustless interactions between parties. This could also involve integrating decentralized governance mechanisms through DAOs to support community-driven decision-making processes. Enhanced tokenization is another area of focus, expanding tokenized access models, such as subscription services and micropayments, to further facilitate innovative business models and improve user flexibility.

Overall, the shift from traditional to crypto-based payments in data exchanges holds the promise of creating a more secure, efficient, and innovative ecosystem. By addressing regulatory, scalability, and user adoption challenges, and leveraging smart contracts and tokenization, data exchanges can fully harness the transformative potential of blockchain technology.

The authors are working towards exporing the integration of crypto-based payments with IUDX and ADeX which represents a significant step forward in the evolution of data exchanges. By addressing these areas, data exchanges can build a secure, efficient, and innovative ecosystem that fosters growth and promotes the widespread adoption of crypto payments.

Disclosure of Interests. The authors declare that there are no conflicts of interest regarding the publication of this paper. The research was conducted independently and without any financial support or influence from commercial entities or organizations with vested interests in the subject matter of the study. Furthermore, the authors have maintained objectivity throughout the research process and have ensured that all data, analyses, and conclusions are presented transparently and without bias. The intention of this research is to contribute to the academic and practical understanding of blockchain-based payment systems and to advance the state of knowledge in this field for the benefit of the broader community.

References

1. Zamani, M., Movahedi, M., Raykova, M.: RapidChain: Scaling blockchain via full sharding. In: Proceedings of the 2018 ACM SIGSAC Conference on Computer and Communications Security, pp. 931-948 (2018)
2. Buterin, V.: Ethereum: a next-generation smart contract and decentralized application platform (2014). https://ethereum.org/en/whitepaper/
3. Pilkington, M.: Blockchain Technology: Principles and Applications. In: Research handbook on digital transformations, Edward Elgar Publishing (2016)
4. Bonneau, J., Miller, A., Clark, J., Narayanan, A., Kroll, J. A., Felten, E.W.: SoK: research perspectives and challenges for bitcoin and cryptocurrencies. In: IEEE Symposium on Security and Privacy, pp. 104–121 (2015)
5. Zhang, R., Xue, R., Liu, L.: Security and privacy on blockchain. ACM Comput. Surv. **52**(3), Article 51 (2019)
6. Gervais, A., Karame, G.O., Wüst, K., Glykantzis, V., Ritzdorf, H., Capkun, S.: On the security and performance of proof of work blockchains. In: Proceedings of the 2016 ACM SIGSAC Conference on Computer and Communications Security, pp. 3–16 (2016)
7. Xu, X., Weber, I., Staples, M.: Architecture for Blockchain Applications. Springer (2019)
8. Wang, Y., Kogan, A.: Designing confidentiality-preserving blockchain-based transaction processing systems. Int. J. Account. Inf. Syst. **30**, 1–18 (2018)

IntelliSOAR: Intelligent Alert Enrichment Using Security Orchestration Automation and Response (SOAR)

Surabhi Dwivedi[✉], Balaji Rajendran, P. V. Akshay, Akshaya Acha, Praveen Ampatt, and Sithu D. Sudarsan

Centre for Development of Advanced Computing (C-DAC), Bengaluru 560100, India
{surabhi,balaji,akshaypv,aakshaya,apraveen,sds}@cdac.in

Abstract. A typical Security Operations Center (SOC) receives several millions of alerts everyday. An analyst in SOC needs to use sophisticated tools to drill down to the most concerning alerts. Security Orchestration Automation and Response (SOAR) provide the much needed relief to them. However, though a large number of SOAR tools are available, customising them to the specific requirements is a grand challenge. This study bridges the gap between the theoretical understanding of SOAR system and practical implementation by step wise elaborating the SOAR architecture with the help of a use case of Intelligent alert enrichment using SOAR system. The process of data ingestion, and integration with various tools, workflow and orchestration are described in detail. An use case illustrating the automation of alert enrichment is presented. Various open source tools and technologies required for SOAR system implementation are explained. Also a summary of other popular SOAR tools are provided.

Keywords: Security Orchestration Automation and Response (SOAR) · SOAR Tools · Alert enrichment · Playbooks

1 Introduction

The Cyber security threats are evolving and becoming very challenging to handle. The organizations are using various tools to protect their data, network, endpoint devices and other critical infrastructure. High volume and high speed of data of varying nature are being generated across the intrusion detection systems (IDS), Host-Based Intrusion Detection System (HIDS), Security Information and Events Management(SIEM) and firewalls etc. [8].

The organizations set up Security Operations Centers (SOCs) to protect the organization from cyber threats. These SOCs have a wide variety of sensors that generates different types of data such as audit logs from workstations and servers, network flows from switches; intelligent feeds such as vulnerability scanning reports, malware information; alerts from endpoint Anti Virus (AV) and Network Intrusion Detection Systems (NIDS) etc. Security Information and Event Management (SIEM) system are facilitated in these SOCs to aggregates the diverse data feeds into a centralized platform, provide configurable dashboards and query interfaces to monitor and find artifacts from the network. Substantial manual efforts are involved to analyse the huge data for further action [3].

SANS [1] incident response defines six steps - Preparation, Identification, Containment, Eradication, Recovery, Lessons Learned (PICERL). The traditional systems and the SIEM systems works on the Identification phase as per the SANS framework and based on the methodology of human in the loop (HITL). A security operation center (SOC) analyst is required to provide the final approval before the autonomous agents completes the tasks. It involves a huge cost and time to automate a simple task. Therefore a Human On The Loop (HOTL) solutions are required where machine autonomously perform a task whilst the SOC analyst monitors and intervenes the operations only when necessary. The Security Orchestration, Automation, and Response (SOAR) facilitates HOTL mechanism, provides an automated and orchestrated response throughout the identification, containment, eradication and recovery phases. SOAR tools attempts to automate the manual tasks with the goal to improve efficiency, consistency and security. SOAR tools provide configurable workflows and playbooks that guide analysts and automate many investigation and incident response actions, whereas a SIEM tool's primary function is widespread data collection and query [3]. SOAR aims to improve four important metrics such as mean time to detect (MTTD), mean time to respond (MTTR), time to qualify (TTQ) and time to investigate (TTI).

Alert enrichment is a technique used to improve the information contained in security alerts generated by NIDS, HIDS etc. The Proposed system will enrich more data about the Indicator of Compromise (IoC's) in alerts from different sources and allow an automatic response. An IoC can be a file, IP address, domain name, registry key, or any other evidence of malicious activity.

The study of this paper will facilitate to understand the detailed SOAR architecture and its implementation with a case study of alert enrichment. The study can be used for an extensive understanding of SOAR architecture and implementation using open source technologies. The paper also gives an overview of the most popular commercial SOAR tools available as defined by Gartner.

The proposed SOAR automation first enriches indicators of compromise (IoC) associated with a security alert with data provided by VirusTotal[1]. The enriched data is then analyzed to assign a reputation value to the IoCs. IoCs determined to be likely related to malicious activity are automatically searched from the client environment, and if any are found, SOAR suggests incident response action.

The remaining sections are organized as follows; Sect. 2 provides literature survey on SOAR; Sect. 3 gives an overview of popular SOAR tools; Sect. 4 illustrates the tools and technologies used for an end to end implementation of Open

---

[1] https://www.virustotal.com/gui/home/upload.

Source SOAR platform; Sect. 5 explains about a proposed SOAR architecture and case study of SOAR implementation for alert enrichment; Sect. 6 concludes the paper with a focus on future scope of work.

2 Literature Survey

This section explores the various research on study and usage of SOAR system.

Kinyua et al. [8] conducted a survey about leveraging AI/ML in SOAR solutions, along with a comparative analysis of SOAR and the Security Operations and Automation Platform Architecture (SOAPA). Baratwal et al. [2] utilised the SOAR systems to dynamically deploys custom honeypots inside the internal network infrastructure based on the attacker's behavior. Lee et al. [9] proposed a novel architecture of SOAR with collaborative units of blended environment (SOAR-CUBE). Kantola et al. [7] utilised Virus Total web service to automate the initial processing of information security alerts on the SOAR platform. Johnson et al. [6] suggested SOAR4DER: SOAR for Distributed Energy Resources(DER). It ingests data from multiple Intrusion Detection Systems (IDSs) to block attacks and revert DER systems to good states. Multiple SOAR playbooks then used the IDS data streams to automatically defend the system. Islam et al. [4] extensively reviewed the academic and grey (blogs, web pages, white papers) literature for SOAR systems and identified key functionalities, quality attributes and core component of a SOAR system. Nguyen et al. [10] presented a framework of multi-layer SOAR decision-making methods and orchestration tools that leverage Reinforcement Learning (RL)-based adaptation intelligence, virtual reality, avatar-human interaction and advanced Cyber Threat Intelligence (CTI) tools. Based on our previous study [12] we understood that even with the sophisticated intrusion detection systems, it is tedious for the network security engineers to identify the real intrusion attempts.

Lots of studies have been performed on usage of SOAR system for various different purposes, however, there is a lack of studies for complete end to end implementation of SOAR model with a theoretical and practical explanation of it's detailed architecture. Through this paper we would try to bridge the gap with a case based explanation of complete SOAR system architecture.

3 Popular SOAR Tools

This section explains about various popular SOAR tools as published by Gartner[2].

Phish ER manages and respond to the high volume of potentially malicious emails reported by users, developed by KnowBe4[3]. **FortiSOAR**[4] enables organizations to centralize, standardize, and automate IT/OT security operations

---

[2] https://www.gartner.com/reviews/market/security-orchestration-automation-and-response-solutions.
[3] https://www.knowbe4.com/products/phisher-plus.
[4] FortiSOAR: https://www.fortinet.com/products/fortisoar.

and critical enterprise functions. **Splunk SOAR**[5] provides automated playbooks, comprehensive case management, intelligence, event management complex workflows. **Cortex XSOAR**[6] by Palo Alto ingests aggregated alerts and indicators of compromise (IoCs) from detection sources, such as SIEM, network security tools, threat intelligence feeds and mailboxes. **Smart SOAR (D3 security)**[7] supports various use cases such as investigate, block and respond to phishing incidents, respond to ransomware, cryptojacking detection, endpoint protection, vulnerability management etc. **QRadar SOAR**[8] by IBM Security optimizes security team's decision-making processes, improve SOC efficiency, provide intelligent automation and orchestration solution for incident response. **FireEye Security Orchestrator (FSO)**[9] provides 200 python based plugins for automation. **Microsoft Sentinel SOAR**[10] provides a wide variety of playbooks and connectors for SOAR.

4 Tools and Technologies Used

This section describes various tools, technologies and methodologies used for the complete implementation of alert enrichment use case using SOAR. The tools are selected based on the popularity and availability as an open source.

Snort[11] is an Intrusion Prevention System (IPS) used for real time traffic analysis and packet logging. **Suricata**[12] is a high performance network IDS, IPS and network security monitoring engine. **Zeek**[13] is network security monitoring tool. **n8n**[14] is used for workflow automation, also acts as a playbook. **Velociraptor**[15] is being used as a digital forensic and incident response tool. **Wazuh**[16] is being used as unified extended threat detection, investigation, response (XDR) and SIEM protection. **ELK Stack**[17] consists of Elasticsearch, Kibana, Beats, and Logstash. This stack helps to securely take data from different sources, in various format, search, analyze and visualize. **Filebeat**[18] acts as log shipper for forwarding, monitoring and centralizing log. **VirusTotal**[19] is used to analyzes files and URLs to detect viruses, trojans, and other malicious content.

---

[5] Splunk: https://www.splunk.com/.
[6] XSOAR: https://www.paloaltonetworks.com/cortex/cortex-xsoar.
[7] D3 security: https://d3security.com/solutions/by-use-case/.
[8] QRadar: https://www.ibm.com/products/qradar-soar.
[9] FSO: https://fireeye.dev/docs/helix/fso/.
[10] Sentinel: https://learn.microsoft.com/en-us/azure/sentinel/automation/automation.
[11] Snort: https://www.snort.org/.
[12] Suricata: https://suricata.io/documentation/.
[13] Zeek: https://zeek.org/.
[14] n8n: https://docs.n8n.io/.
[15] Velociraptor: https://docs.velociraptor.app/.
[16] Wazuh: https://wazuh.com/.
[17] ELK: https://www.elastic.co/elastic-stack.
[18] https://www.elastic.co/guide/en/beats/filebeat/current/filebeat-overview.html.
[19] VirusTotal:https://docs.virustotal.com/reference/overview.

Webhook[20] allows to configure HTTP endpoints to receive data from external systems in near real-time.

5 SOAR Architecture and Implementation

This section illustrates how the tools and techniques described Sect. 4 are interleaved together in a form of robust IntelliSOAR system. It describes the six layer architecture of the SOAR system, evolved from the SOAR architecture proposed by Chadni Islam et al. [5]. It also explains a sample use case implementation of alert enrichment using SOAR. We are using distributed architecture, where sensor nodes will be placed at the end devices for data collection and the manager node will process those data. The sensor node contains the network intrusion detection system (NIDS), host intrusion detection system (HIDS), intrusion prevention system (IPS). We are using the tools as described in Sect. 4; Suricata, Snort, and Zeek to monitor the traffic. Velociraptor will be installed on each client machine to take the action based on the result of the pre-defined workflow. The client will be invoked by the Velociraptor server from the manager node. The subsequent section will explain the proposed SOAR architecture as shown in Fig. 1.

5.1 Data Ingestion Layer

The data ingestion layer is responsible for ingesting data from various security tools, sensor nodes placed on the gateway or end device. IntelliSOAR system integrates data from several security tools broadly HIDS, NIDS, File Scanner System. HIDS monitors individual systems for any suspicious activities or patterns based on the predefined rules or signatures. NIDS monitors network traffic for any malicious activity or potential breaches producing logs and alerts[21]. File scanning system scans the files carved from the network and issues alerts on finding malicious content. Suricata and Snort are being used to match the rules with signature and generate alerts. Zeek is used to create a log for each events in the network traffic. The logs generated by each tool will contain different set of IoC like IP address, domain name, URL etc.

We are using signature-based detection to identify patterns in network traffic. The proposed solution is utilising a rule/signature in Suricata. It consists of action, header and rule. The action, determines what happens when the signature matches. Header, defines the protocol, IP addresses, ports and direction of the rule and the rule defines the specifics of the rule.

5.2 Data Integration Layer

This layer is designed to integrate the data generated from the security tools. This tool has six major components: integration manager, tool registry, wrapper, log shipper, plugin repository and API gateway.

---

[20] https://docs.n8n.io/integrations/builtin/core-nodes/n8n-nodes-base.webhook/.
[21] https://www.neumetric.com/hids-vs-nids/.

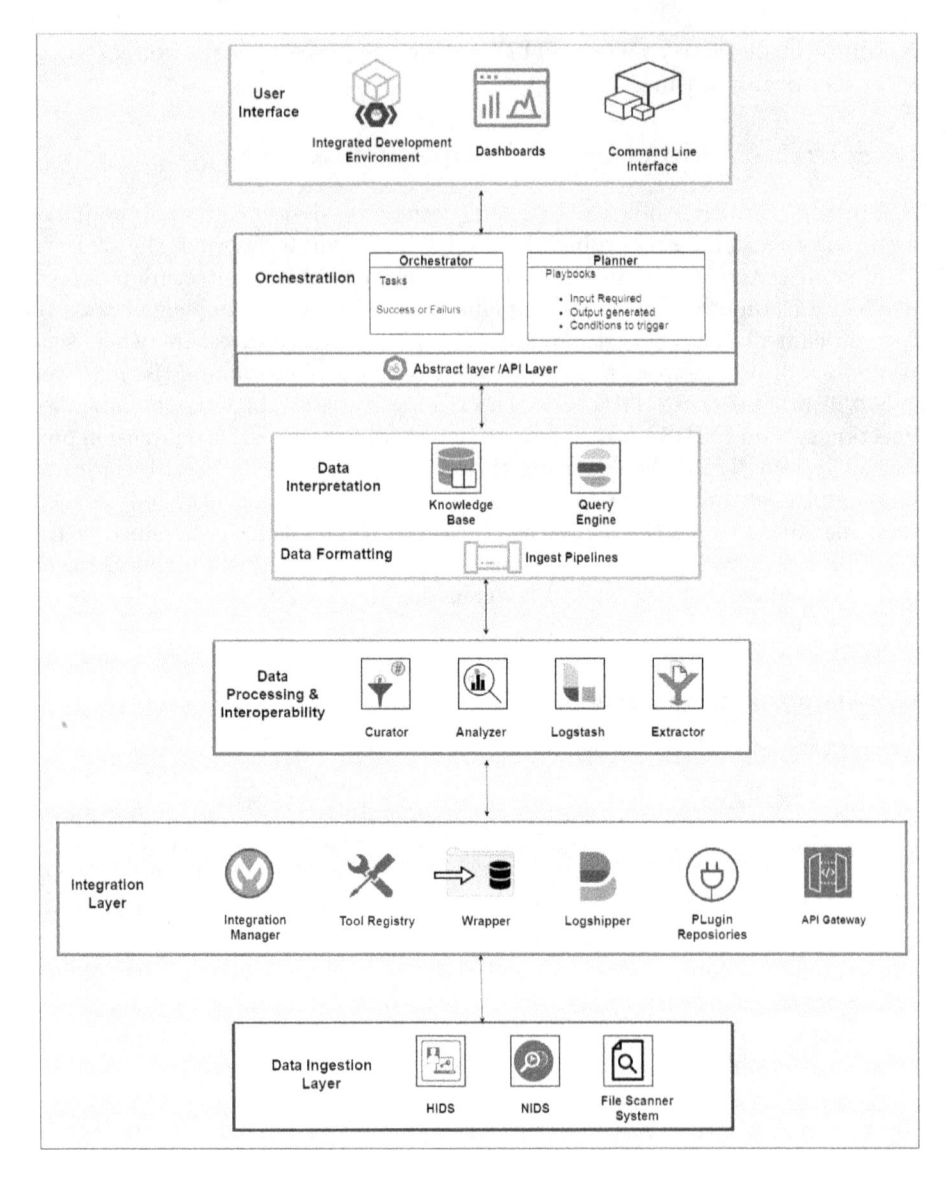

Fig. 1. SOAR Platform Architecture [5]

The integration manager provides an information about security tool being integrated and manage the interoperability among their data. A tool registry registers the available security tool in terms of their input, output and monitor their status. The API gateway provides secure communication of the API's. The wrapper and plugins provide an interface to encapsulate security tools for data translation. Log shipper transports data from sensor nodes to manager node.

Proposed system supports RESTful APIs in order to create, update and selectively remove objects from the system. REST API requests are performed over HTTPS only to authorized users and devices. User and token based authentication methods[22] are being used.

5.3 Data Processing and Interoperability

The SOAR uses systems logs, alerts logs and malicious activities that will be processed by the data processing layer. It has data curator, extractor and analyzer. This layer provides interoperability and interpretation capability to interpret heterogeneous structured and unstructured data coming from different security tools and playbooks. The data curator will gather the data produced by tools for analysis.

The logs are processed by the logstash on reaching the manager node. Logstash unifies log data then transport to elastic search for storage and analysis. It can be configured to specify the index where the logs will be stored and designate an ingest pipeline for preprocessing. The preprocessing of the logs includes renaming of fields, adding additional fields such as name, location etc. The logs will be indexed according to the predefined index templates after preprocessing.

5.4 Data Formatting and Interpretation

This layer formats the data to provide it to the manager node. It provides knowledge base and a query engine for data interpretation. In proposed solution the alerts generated from sensor node is shipped to manager node via log shipper, Filebeat. It ships logs generated by the tools to the elastic search for storage.

5.5 Orchestration Automation and Response

This layer has two components orchestrator and the planner. Orchestrator automates the execution of Incident response plan (IRPs). Planner automates the execution of an IRP with playbooks. The playbook contains the details of the input required and the output generated after the execution of the task, the conditions to trigger the execution of a specific task etc. The orchestrator monitors if the task executes successfully or not. This layer will also provide APIs through which a user govern the execution of an IRP and update the orchestration process.

Workflow automation is implemented using n8n. It executes and enriches more details about the IoC's from different sources. If IoC's are reported as malicious in any of the sources, n8n generates an incident response. This includes blocking the IP/URL from firewall or from the endpoint.

Figure 2 explains the work flow automation for alert enrichment use case. The workflow starts with the Webhook node, which is designed to receive data

---

[22] https://docs.splunk.com/Documentation/SOAR/current/PlatformAPI/Using.

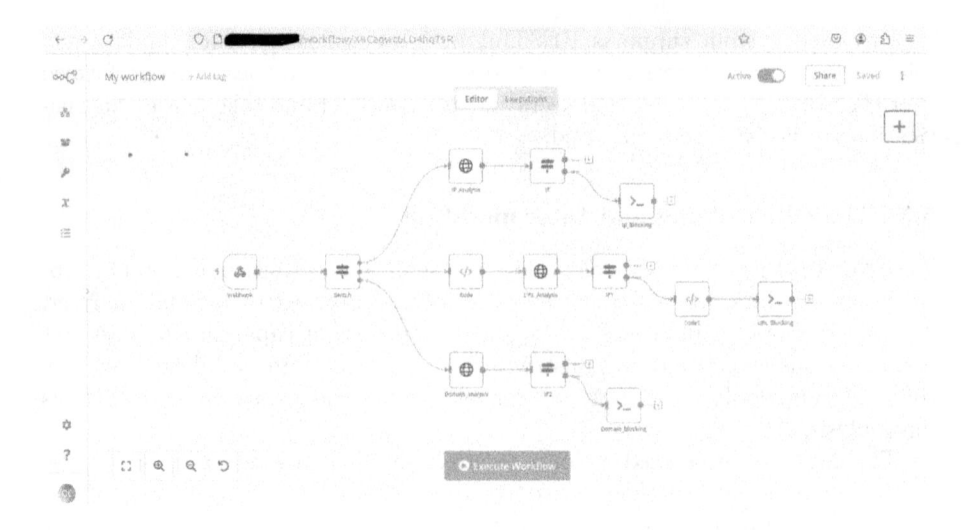

Fig. 2. Alert Enrichment using n8n

from various applications and services. The detailed explanation of each node of Fig. 2 is as following

Webhook node: It starts executing the predefined workflow on receiving the request. This node receives type of observable, its value and case_id.

Switch node: The switch node allows conditional branching within the workflows. It evaluates the incoming data against the predefined conditions and directs the workflow. Currently the workflow is being branched based on observable types like IP address, URL and domain.

If the incoming data is defined as IP address the IP Analysis branch gets triggered, URL analysis and domain in case of URL and domain, respectively. HTTP node will call Virustotal API to analyse the IP address, encoded URL or domain. Virustotal gives a comprehensive report along with a reputation score. IF node checks the condition of reputation scores and splits workflow into two branches TRUE and FALSE. In case of FALSE for IP address, it will be considered as malicious and execute command node will be utilized to run a hunt across Velociraptor clients by Velociraptor manager. Then it will add the malicious IP address to IP tables. If the condition is false (reputation less than zero) for URL and domain analysis then a code node will be used to extract domain name from the URL and an execute command will be used to run a new hunt across velociraptor clients by velociraptor manager.

5.6 User Interface

The security staff can initiate the IRPs using a user interfaces (UIs) such as interactive dashboards; integrated development environment (IDE); command line interface (CLI). An abstraction layer or API layer can be implemented as part of the UI layers to maintain and encapsulate the interaction among a SOAR's user and its components.

IntelliSOAR fecilatets a GUI for the analyst to see the IoC's. If an alert needs further investigation, cases can be created and any of the IoC's can be added as an observable. Figure 3 depicts an alert and case. The alert contains a count that signifies the number of time the alert with a particular rule name is being generated. This can be further added and assigned as a case for an analyst.

Fig. 3. Alert Generation and CASES in SOAR

6 Conclusion and Future Work

The proposed solution explains how a human intervention can be minimized by automatic execution of a trigger on detection of a malicious file. The result of this study can be used to set up SOAR system with the help of open source tools and technologies. All these tools mentioned from Sect. 3 are commercial tools and involves a huge cost of acquisition, maintenance and up gradation. There are very limited open source SOAR systems available.

Although open source tool Security Onion[23] can be customized to provide SOAR solution but it is challenging. Security onion maintains the configuration using salt stack (configuration management and orchestration tool). It is very difficult to make a permanent changes to the configuration and customise the playbooks and incident response tools.

IntelliSOAR provides Identification, containment, alert enrichment, and automatic blocking. The contextual characteristics such as attack likelihood, it's criticality and severity can be used to prioritized the alerts using machine learning (ML). ML models can also be used to analyze user entity behavior analytics (UEBA) to detect insider threats. The quantity of false positives can also be reduced by using the ML models by detecting duplicate warnings and ranking them according to their relevance and severity.

In future we are planning to integrate Artificial Intelligence (AI), Machine Learning (ML) and Deep Learning (DL) techniques to enhance the automation, orchestration, prediction of alerts, recommendation for required remedial. Based on our studies we found that end-to-end implementations of AI/ML to security

---

[23] SecurityOnion: https://securityonionsolutions.com/software.

orchestration, automation, and response are yet to be developed [8]. Deep reinforcement learning (DRL) has some state-of-the-art DRL algorithms that can be explored for SOAR empowerment to solve complex and sophisticated intrusion detection problems [11].

References

1. Incident response steps and frameworks for sans and nist (2018). https://cybersecurity.att.com/blogs/security-essentials/incident-response-steps-comparison-guide. Accessed 22 Jul 2024
2. Bartwal, U., Mukhopadhyay, S., Negi, R., Shukla, S.: Security orchestration, automation, and response engine for deployment of behavioural honeypots. In: 2022 IEEE Conference on Dependable and Secure Computing (DSC), pp. 1–8. IEEE (2022)
3. Bridges, R.A., et al.: Testing soar tools in use. Comput. Secur. **129**, 103201 (2023). https://doi.org/10.1016/j.cose.2023.103201
4. Islam, C., Babar, M.A., Nepal, S.: A multi-vocal review of security orchestration. ACM Comput. Surv. **52**(2), 1–45 (2019). https://doi.org/10.1145/3305268
5. Islam, C., Babar, M.A., Nepal, S.: Architecture-centric support for integrating security tools in a security orchestration platform. In: Software Architecture: 14th European Conference, ECSA 2020, L'Aquila, Italy, September 14–18, 2020, Proceedings 14, pp. 165–181. Springer (2020)
6. Johnson, J., Jones, C.B., Chavez, A., Hossain-McKenzie, S.: Soar4der: security orchestration, automation, and response for distributed energy resources. In: Power Systems Cybersecurity: Methods, Concepts, and Best Practices, pp. 387–411. Springer (2023)
7. Kantola, T.: Exploring virustotal for security operations alert triage automation (2022)
8. Kinyua, J., Awuah, L.: AI/ML in security orchestration, automation and response: future research directions. Intell. Autom. Soft Comput. **28**(2), 527–545 (2021)
9. Lee, M., Jang-Jaccard, J., Kwak, J.: Novel architecture of security orchestration, automation and response in internet of blended environment. Comput. Mater. Continua **73**(1), 199–223 (2022)
10. Nguyen, P., et al.: Towards smarter security orchestration and automatic response for CPS and IoT. In: 2023 IEEE International Conference on Cloud Computing Technology and Science (CloudCom), pp. 298–302. IEEE (2023)
11. Nguyen, T.T., Reddi, V.J.: Deep reinforcement learning for cyber security. IEEE Trans. Neural Networks Learn. Syst. **34**(8), 3779–3795 (2021)
12. Rajendran, B., Pawar, D.: An intelligent contextual support system for intrusion detection tasks. In: Proceedings of the Symposium on Computer Human Interaction for the Management of Information Technology. Association for Computing Machinery, New York, NY, USA (2009). https://doi.org/10.1145/1641587.1641593

InTrust: An Asset Monitoring, Analysis and Vulnerability Assessment System for Zero Trust Network

N. Muraleedharan[✉], Hrishikesh Rajendra Neve, Samar Sarkar, and Balaji Rajendran

Centre for Development of Advanced Computing (C-DAC), Bangalore, India
{murali,hrishineve,samarsarkar,balaji}@cdac.in

Abstract. In the present day, as the number of connected devices increases exponentially, an organization faces challenges in monitoring, managing and detecting vulnerable devices. Moreover, by the introduction of Bring Your Own Device (BYOD) schemes in an organization, the device management and vulnerability assessment has become one of the key security requirements. The zero trust system uses both the user and device identity to provide the access to the requested resources. Hence, it is important to understand the security posture of the device before providing the requested resource access. 'InTrust' is an asset monitoring, analysis and vulnerability assessment system for zero trust network access system. InTrust automatically keeps track of the list of assets, operating system, services & their vulnerabilities and brings out the security posture. These inputs can be used to derive the dynamic trust score for a resource access in the Zero Trust network. As InTrust uses a non-intrusive and privacy-aware approach for data collection, it can cater to all enterprise and e-governance networks where security and transparency are critical to the organization.

Keywords: Asset management · Zero Trust Network · Device security

1 Introduction

The traditional perimeter security architecture assumes that the entities inside the internal network are trustworthy. Hence, they mainly focused on addressing the threat from the external network. But once the attacker breaches the perimeter, the traditional perimeter-based network security approach may not detect and block the further movement. Due to this limitation, the traditional perimeter security architecture and solutions need modifications to adapt to the modern enterprise network. In modern networks and systems, due to the increase of security breaches using device compromise, it is inevitable to identify the security posture of the device before connecting to the organization's networks.

The Zero trust model assumes that external and internal threat exists in the network. Hence, no entities, internal or external, are trustworthy. The Zero trust approach reduces the attack surface and mitigates the effect and severity of cyber attacks, reduces the time and cost of response and recovery after a security breach [1].

The traditional security system uses the user identity to provide the resource access. But the zero trust system uses both the user and device identity to provide the access to the requested resources. Hence, it is important to understand the security posture of the device before providing the resources access requested from the device.

In the present day, as the number of devices and their categories are increased, the organization faces challenges to address the security issues due to the vulnerable devices. Moreover, by the introduction of Bring Your Own Device (BYOD) in an organization, the device management and vulnerability assessment has become one of the key security requirement [2].

The devices that are owned by the organization and are used for specific business purposes can be considered as managed devices. The managed devices are configured, maintained, and secured by the organization, and may have specific policies and procedures in place for their use. The organization can maintain a list of all managed devices in a searchable database which can be accessed to verify the device's existence. Further, the devices connected to the network can be scanned to detect the device status(up/down), open port, services, operating system etc.

The un-managed devices, on the other hand, are devices that are not under the control or management of the organization. These devices are typically owned by individual employees or contractors and may be used for personal or business purposes. The un-managed devices are not typically configured, maintained, or secured by the organization. Hence, access from these devices needs to be detected and further needs to enforce proper access policy for the organizational resource access.

2 Product Description

'InTrust' is an asset monitoring, analysis and vulnerability assessment system for zero trust network access system. InTrust automatically keeps track of the list of assets, operating system, services & their vulnerabilities and brings out the security posture of an organization. These inputs can be used to derive the dynamic trust score for a resource access in the Zero Trust network.

Based on the input collected from the host and network, InTrust detects and notifies the attacks and anomalies targeting the network. It can also detect and track the activities from new and rogue devices that are connected to the network. Communication from a host to a blacklisted IP, URL and anonymous IPs are also detected and notified by InTrust. The web-based interface provided by InTrust can be used to monitor and manage its functionalities through an intuitive dashboard. It can also generate custom reports on traffic trends, security events and anomalies.

The system is implemented using an agent-less approach where it has not used any data collected from host for deriving the trust score. The system uses active scanning to identify the devices and their security postures. It uses passive approach for monitoring and analyzing the network traffic for application, anomaly and attack detection.

As InTrust uses a non-intrusive and privacy-aware approach for data collection, it can cater to all enterprise and e-governance networks where security and transparency are critical to the organization.

2.1 Innovation and Contributions

- The InTrust asset monitoring, analysis and vulnerability assessment system has been implemented using an agent-less approach. Unlike the typical zero trust based system, the agent-less approach provides a non-intrusive and privacy aware approach for data collection. Hence, it can cater to all enterprise, e-governance, financial and government networks where security and transparency of the data are critical to the organization.
- The agent-less approach used by InTrust shall be suitable for any heterogeneous environment that has different devices, operating systems etc. Moreover, the overhead due to the installation, configuration and management of the agent in the individual devices are totally removed in the InTrust.
- The passive traffic data used by InTrust is used to monitor and analyze the network. Hence, once a new device connected to the network, it can be immediately detected and notified by InTrust. Further, the vulnerability analysis of newly detected devices can be done to detect the vulnerabilities and derive the security posture of the device. This will be useful to calculate the trust score of the device and to detect and block rouge device in the network automatically.
- The combination of device data, which includes the device vulnerability & the security posture of the device, and the network traffic used by InTrust provides unique correlation features for vulnerability-aware attack detection. The anomalies and attacks detected using the traffic data can be correlated with the vulnerability present in the target machine for accurate attack detection and remedial steps.
- The traffic trend analysis carried-out by InTrust can be used for analysing the traffic at different granularity such as per minute, hourly, daily, weekly, monthly etc. This will help to detect short-term and long-term traffic anomalies and attacks including low and slow attacks.

2.2 Components

The InTrust asset monitoring, analysis and vulnerability assessment system consists of different components. Figure 1 shows the basic components of the InTrust system.

- Asset Monitoring and Management
- Traffic Monitoring & Analysis
- Vulnerability Assessment and Security Posture Module

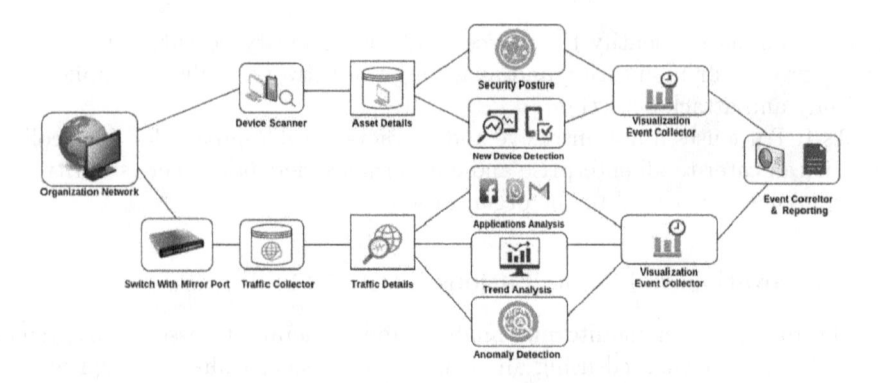

Fig. 1. Architecture components of the system

– Application Identification

As shown in the figure, the system uses device and network traffic data as the input for asset management, monitoring and analysis. The device details are collected using the network scanner components in an active manner. However, packet sniffing tool is used to collect the traffic details in a passive manner.

The active network scanner is configured to scan the network and collect data periodically. The InTrust system provides the flexibility to configure the periodicity of the scan as per the organizational requirement. The output of the scan consists of the details about available system in the network (IP, MAC address), type of the device, their operating system, open ports and service details etc. Further, the vulnerability details of the available system and services are derived using the vulnerability scanner deployed as part of the InTrust system. The vulnerability scanner provides the details related to the service, their vulnerability, criticality of the vulnerability, CVE score etc. [5]. The device and vulnerability details are maintained in the asset database [6].

The traffic collector components of InTrust collects the network traffic details from the organizational network. Typically, the mirrored traffic from the gateway network device are used to collect the network traffic details. In the InTrust system, we have configured a flow based traffic monitoring tool to derive the flow data from the sniffed network traffic. The collected flow data consists of the meta data derived from the packets grouped by the five tuples (Source IP, Source Port, Destination IP, Destination port and protocol) [4].

As part of the traffic monitoring, InTrust provides the near real-time view of the network, host and application details. Further, it carries out the data analysis to detect network, host and application anomalies. It also carryout the traffic trend analysis to detect the behavior change of the network traffic pattern [7]. The traffic trend analysis of InTrust can be carried out per minute, hour, day, week and monthly basis. In addition, the trend analysis can be customized as per the organizational requirement.

2.3 Functionalities Supported

The major functionalities supported by the InTrust system is described below.

Asset Monitoring and Management. The asset detection and monitoring has been carried out using an agent-less approach where the network scanner probe the devices connected to the network. By scanning the network, it can collect the device details such as active machines, IP address, MAC address, Operating system, open ports, service/applications running and their vulnerabilities. Monitor and analyze the assets including the status, open ports, services, applications, and their security posture. Following are the supported features of this module

- Device Identification (type of the device, operating system, services)
- Device status (up/down) and device tracking
- Device Security posture(CVE and Severity)
- New and rouge device Detection and Event Generation
- Automatic Vulnerability Identification and Reporting
- Service details (Port number, application and version)
- Vulnerability details (CVE ID, Severity, Type and description)
- Vulnerability grouping and consolidation (Severity, Service, Host and Type)
- Automatic Vulnerability reports

Traffic Monitoring and Anomaly Detection. The system collects network traffic details from the mirrored port of the switch. Near real-time traffic monitoring and analysis using mirrored traffic from the switch. The features provided by the Traffic monitoring and Anomaly detection module are

- Details of communication entities (IP, Port, Protocol, Packet, Bytes etc.,.)
- Application Details (Application wise traffic distribution, bandwidth usage)
- Traffic Profiling and Trend analysis
- Top communication (Talker/Listener, Upload/Download, Applications and Bandwidth usage)
- Network and Host Anomaly Detection and notification
- Network and Host scan detection and notification
- Attack detection (brute-force, malware and botnets)
- Denial of Service (DoS), Distributed Denial of Service (DDoS) Detection
- VPN/Anonymous Access Detection and notification

Graphical User Interface. The system provides an intuitive web based GUI to monitor and manage the key functionalities if the system. The GUI provides a role based, multi-factor based authentication to manage the functionalities of the system. The key features of the GUI are shown below

- Dashboard to provide the important information (Asset, Traffic, System Health, and events)
- Role based Access
- Reporting (PDF, HTML and CSV format)
- E-mail notification for important events

2.4 Use Case

Some of the use-cases of InTrust system is shown below.

Zero Trust Network Access. The Zero Trust Network access system uses device, user, application and network related parameters to derive the trust score and further to enforce the resource access policy. The usage of InTrust in a zero trust network is depicted in Fig. 2. As shown in the figure, the asset monitoring, analysis and vulnerability assessment output of InTrust can be used as an input for the trust score calculation of the Zero Trust network access system.

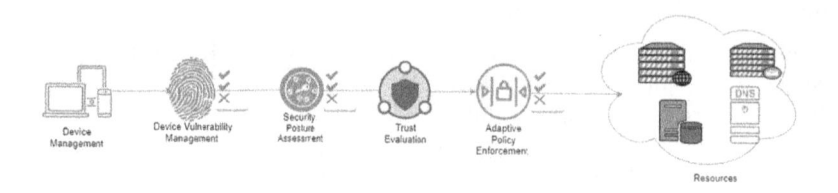

Fig. 2. Usage of InTrust in Zero trust network

Asset Monitoring and Management. The organizational assets require continuous monitoring and management to ensure the accountability, security and compliance. The InTrust system supports asset monitoring and management using a non-intrusive agent-less approach by collecting the required data from the network. The in-built network scanner available in InTrust scan the network and collect required data.

Vulnerability Aware Attack Detection. InTrust leverages the latest machine learning and statistical approaches to identify anomalies and trends in network traffic data. InTrust integrates a comprehensive knowledge base that includes CVE IDs, CVSS scores, descriptions of vulnerabilities along with organizational asset. The combination of device security posture and the network traffic used by InTrust provides an unique correlation features for vulnerability aware attack detection. Unlike the traditional anomaly detection systems, the anomalies and attacks detected using the traffic data can be correlated with the vulnerability present in the target machine for accurate attack detection and remedial steps.

Vulnerability Assessment. InTrust is also capable to identify, quantify, and prioritize the security vulnerabilities within an organization's IT infrastructure. In addition to identifying vulnerabilities, InTrust also provides detailed information, such as CVE IDs, Common Vulnerability Scoring System (CVSS) scores, and descriptions of vulnerabilities associated with specific ports. It can also provide the list of top vulnerabilities, affected services and their severity.

Table 1. Comparison of Asset Monitoring and Vulnerability Assessment Tools

Feature/ Tool	Manage Engine	OpenVAS	NfDump	Snort	Nessus	InTrust
Primary Function	Asset management & monitoring	Vulnerability assessment	Network traffic monitoring & analysis	Network intrusion detection	Vulnerability assessment	Asset Management for Zero trust network
Asset Discovery	Yes	No	No	No	Yes	Yes
Vulnerability Assessment	Yes	Yes	No	No	Yes	Yes
Network Traffic Analysis	Limited	No	Yes	Yes	Limited	Yes
Intrusion Detection	Limited (via add-ons)	No	No	Yes	No	Yes
Data Collection	Agent & agent-less	Agent-less	Agent-less	Agent-less	agent & agent-less	Agent-less
Deployment Type	On-premises, cloud	On-premises	On-premises	On-premises	On-premises, cloud	On-premises
Real-time Monitoring	Yes	No	No	Yes	Limited	Yes
Automated Threat Detection	Yes (with alerts and automation rules)	No	No	Yes (signature-based)	Yes (scans for known vulnerabilities)	Yes (continuous monitoring with alerts)

2.5 Comparison of InTrust with Other Asset Management, Traffic Monitoring and Vulnerability Assessment Tools

The popular tools for asset management, traffic monitoring and vulnerability assessment, such as 'ManageEngine' [9], 'OpenVAS' [11], 'Nfdump' [12] and 'Snort' [10] are compared in the Table 1. To accommodate diverse monitoring and security requirements, these solutions provide a range of methodologies, including agent-based, agent-less, or a combination of both. Their main roles, asset detection capabilities, vulnerability assessment, and other aspects necessary for thorough network security are all covered in the comparison. Additionally, InTrust is a comprehensive solution that integrates all these functionalities into a single product, providing a more unified approach to security.

2.6 Screenshots

The screenshot of the InTrust appliance and some of the important features of InTrust system are depicted in Figs. 3, 4, 5 and 6. The screenshot of the dashboard of InTrust system is shown in the Fig. 3. Sample device security posture and vulnerability details screenshot are shown in the Figs. 4 and 5 respectively. Figure 6 shows the image of the InTrust appliance.

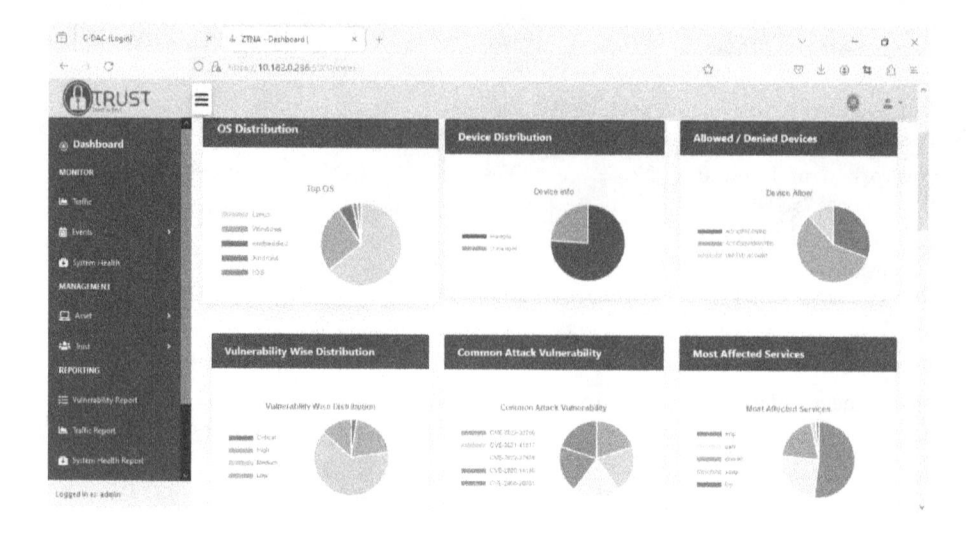

Fig. 3. Screenshot of InTrust Dashboard

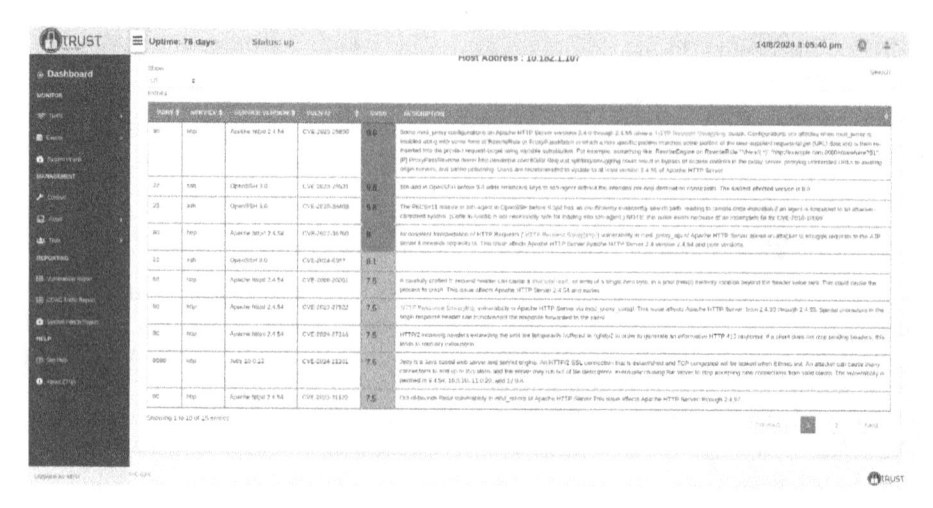

Fig. 4. Screenshot of the Vulnerability details

Fig. 5. Screenshot of the device security posture

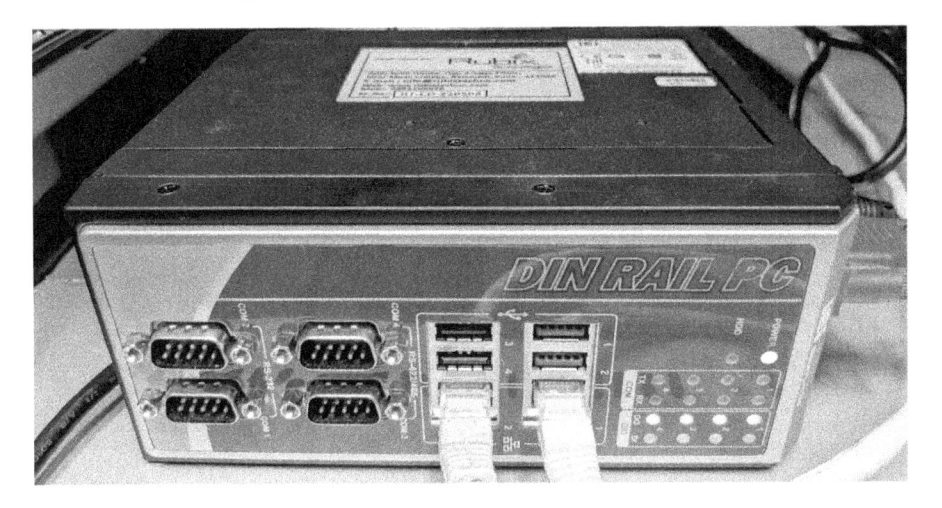

Fig. 6. InTrust Appliance

3 Conclusion

The features and functionalities of InTrust, an asset monitoring, analysis and vulnerability assessment system for provisioning zero trust network access system is described in this paper. The system architecture and their components are explained. A feature comparison with other asset management products are also carried out. Unlike other asset monitoring and management products, InTrust uses agent-less approach for data collection that provides a non-intrusive and privacy aware solution.

Acknowledgment. The authors would like to express their sincere gratitude to the Ministry of Electronics and Information Technology, Government of India, for the support.

References

1. Rose, S., Borchert, O., Mitchell, S., Connelly, S.: Zero trust architecture. Nat. Inst. Stand. Technol. **800**, 207 (2020). https://doi.org/10.6028/NIST.SP.800-207
2. Eke, C.I., Norman Anir, A.: Bring your own device (BYOD) security threats and mitigation mechanisms: systematic mapping. In: 2021 International Conference on Computer Science and Engineering (IC2SE), Padang, Indonesia, pp. 1–10 (2021). https://doi.org/10.1109/IC2SE52832.2021.9791907
3. Aleena, G., Hrishikesh, N., Muraleedharan, N.: A trust score calculation approach for zero trust access system. In: 2023 IEEE 20th India Council International Conference (INDICON), pp. 392–397 (2023)
4. NFStream: flexible network data analysis framework. https://www.nfstream.org. Accessed 10 Aug 2024
5. CVE: Common vulnerabilities and exposures. https://cve.mitre.org/. Accessed 10 Aug 2024
6. NVD: National vulnerability database. https://nvd.nist.gov/. Accessed 10 Aug 2024
7. Muraleedharan, N., Janet, B.: Slow TCP port scan detection using flow data. In: International Conference on Security, Privacy and Data Analytics, pp. 17–32 (2023)
8. Nessus. https://www.tenable.com/products/vulnerability-management. Accessed 16 Oct 2024
9. ManageEngine OpManager Plus. https://www.manageengine.com/it-operations-management/?pos=ITOM&loc=SolPage&cat=op. Accessed 16 Oct 2024
10. Snort Documents. https://www.snort.org/documents. Accessed 16 Oct 2024
11. Greenbone OpenVAS - Open vulnerability assessment scanner. https://www.openvas.org/. Accessed 16 Oct 2024
12. Nfdump - Netflow processing tools. https://github.com/phaag/nfdump. Accessed 16 Oct 2024

Author Index

A
Abdelgawad, Mahmoud 63
Acha, Akshaya 453
Akshay, P. V. 453
Aljaali, Zeyad Alwaleed 225
Ampatt, Praveen 453
Anspach, Evan 63

B
Balachandran, Vivek 213
Bichhawat, Abhishek 289
Bkakria, Anis 180
Boulahia-Cuppens, Nora 180
Bristy, Aishwarya Ghosh 338

C
Cuppens, Frédéric 180

D
Das, Sanchari 87
Dey, Aditi 289
Dutta, Jyotirmoy 443
Dwivedi, Surabhi 453

E
Eisenbarth, Thomas 3

F
Fahim, Md. 338
Falebita, Oluwatosin 63
Fraser, Ashley 320
Frymann, Nick 320

G
Gharote, Mangesh 310
Gupta, Rohit 310
Gupta, Sanchit 246

H
Halder, Raju 265
Hashmat, Fabiha 225
Haynes, Paul 320

K
Kato, Soma 25
Kishnani, Urvashi 87
Koyanagi, Yui 25
Kumar, Rishabh 310
Kumar, Vireshwar 246
Kushwaha, Maitri 265

L
Ling, Goh Geok 213
Lodha, Sachin 310

M
Machiry, Aravind 225
Maddali, Lakshmi Padmaja 127
Manna, Debasmita 422
Minami, Simon 146
Mondal, Sutapa 310
Mukherjee, Arnab 265
Mukherjee, Preetam 201
Muraleedharan, N. 463
Murthy, Shyam 330

N
Nanamou, N'Famoussa Kounon 180
Narendra Kumar, N. 127
Narumanchi, Harika 127
Neal, Christopher 180
Neve, Hrishikesh Rajendra 463

O
Oli, Md. Musfikur Hasan 338

© The Editor(s) (if applicable) and The Author(s), under exclusive license to Springer Nature Switzerland AG 2025
V. T. Patil et al. (Eds.): ICISS 2024, LNCS 15416, pp. 473–474, 2025.
https://doi.org/10.1007/978-3-031-80020-7

P

Pandey, Aishwarya 265
Parkin, Julian 107
Patil, Vishwas 359
Podder, Rakesh 42
Prakriti, 289
Priyadarsini, Gayatri 289

Q

Quan, Lee Jun 213

R

Rajaraman, Vasanth 443
Rajendran, Balaji 453, 463
Raman, Presanna 42
Ray, Indrajit 42
Ray, Indrakshi 63
Righi, Stefano 42
Rios, Tyler 42
Rumee, Sarker Tanveer Ahmed 338

S

Sanyashi, Tikaram 404
Sarkar, Samar 463
Sato, Shungo 383
Saxena, Anshika 289
Schneider, Steve 320
Sharma, Abhay 443
Shehu, Abubakar-Sadiq 320
Shen, Mingjie 225
Shyamasundar, R. K. 359
Singh, Virendra 404
Sudarsan, Sithu D. 453

Suma Sri, Mandru 404
Sunar, Berk 3

T

Tanaka, Hidema 383
Thampi, Sabu M. 201
Thomas, Blessy 201
Tiemann, Thore 3
Tomar, Shubham 159
Tripathi, Meenakshi 159
Tripathy, Somanath 422
Triplett, Steven 146
Tripunitara, Mahesh 107

U

Ukezono, Tomoaki 25
Upadhyaya, Santosh Kumar 330

V

Verma, Rakesh M. 146
Vivek, Srinivas 330

W

Walunj, Vipul 443
Weissman, Zane 3

Y

Yadav, Chakka Srikanth 404
Ye, Tan Jia 213

Z

Zaber, Moinul Islam 338
Zahid, Shamim Bin 338